Paul P. Harris in his later years, from an oil painting by Brigitte Trace. (*Reproduced by courtesy of the artist.*)

The Golden Wheel

The story of Rotary 1905 to the Present

David Shelley Nicholl

Foreword by H.R.H. The Prince Philip,
Duke of Edinburgh

MACDONALD AND EVANS

Macdonald & Evans Ltd
Estover, Plymouth PL6 7PZ

First published 1984

© David Shelley Nicholl 1984

British Cataloguing in Publication Data
Nichol, David Shelley
    The golden wheel.
    1. Rotary International — History
    I. Title
    369.5   HF5001.R78
    ISBN 0-7121-0746-0

Typeset by
Academic Typesetting Service, Gerrards Cross
and printed by
Butler & Tanner, Frome, Somerset

Contents

Foreword   vii

Preface   ix

Acknowledgments   xi

List of Illustrations   xiii

1   The Source of Rotary   1

2   The Man from Racine   14

3   Rotary One   31

4   Rotary Two — and Romance   56

5   Man into Men into Movement   71

6   Travels of a Medicine Man   92

7   Wheels across the Sea   108

8   The Wheel at War — 1   122

9   The Wheel at War — 2   138

10   Paul Harris at War   156

11   The First 21 — Edinburgh   169

12   Death of a Salesman   189

13   The Second 21 — Denver   198

14   Travels of a Boy Wonder   216

15   Travels of a Boy King — 1   239

16   Travels of a Boy King — 2   262

17   Death of the Boy   288

18 Birth of the Man   311
19 The Wheel at War — 3   343
20 The Wheel at War — 4   365
21 The Wheel at War — 5   388
22 The Wheel at War — 6   408
23 Once Every Fourteen Hours   430
24 The Dam-Busters   455

Selective Bibliography   482
Index   484

Foreword

by H.R.H. The Duke of Edinburgh

The sheer size of Rotary International in 1984 is impressive. Almost 1 million members in 158 countries are awesome statistics, but they really mean nothing at all unless the members are inspired by Rotary's challenging philosophy, expressed by its splendidly simple motto "Service Above Self". The motto would be irrelevant if there were no selfishness in the world, but the temptation to cheat, to exploit and to dominate for the sake of personal wealth and power has always been a feature of human existence and the chances are that it always will be.

The significance of Rotary is that it has become one of the most active and effective lay forces on the side of righteousness, co-operation and goodwill. It provides, therefore, a most powerful encouragement of the potential for good that is in all men and by so doing it also acts as a severe restraint on what is evil and corrupt. It is no coincidence that Rotary flourishes in the free and open societies of this world while it is ruthlessly suppressed under ideological dictatorships.

This book may not be the only history of Rotary to be written but it is probably the first to trace the course of events and to follow the development of an idea at the same time. What comes through is that while fashions and attitudes may vary between countries and over periods of time, the central principle and philosophy of Rotary runs through the whole story as if it were the track of the Golden Wheel.

Preface

It was in late June 1983, the dawn of that glorious summer, that David Shelley Nicholl honoured me, as a Past President of both Rotary International in Great Britain and Ireland and of Rotary International itself, with a first reading of this remarkable treatise, and I use this adjective and term advisedly. Now, he has honoured me further by requesting me to write an introduction to the work, which I am indeed privileged, and delighted, to have the opportunity to do.

When I agreed to read and comment on the manuscript, I had envisaged a relatively quick run-through of another "history" of Rotary of moderate length and early accomplishment. In the event I found myself absorbed for the better part of my leisure time during a period of some two months, sitting in my garden during that splendid English summer, reading in depth one of the most carefully researched and entrancing stories – subject quite apart – which has ever come my way. From the outset, bearing in mind that I was requested to give a critical assessment of the text, I had to discipline myself to avoid just reading on in sheer fascination with the story line, leaving analysis of the subject-matter to a later reading. I found, basically, a carefully observed biography of two men, totally opposed in character and approach, the one purposely chosen by the other, without both of whom, working in concert, Rotary would today be merely a word in the dictionary with a small "r". But it was far more than that. The author has given the definitive history of a phenomenon and of an epoch, of which the two men in question, Paul Harris and Chesley Perry, were the Prophets. David Shelley Nicholl has set out for all to read the *raison d'être* of the present-day Service organisation based not on religious doctrines and certainly not specifically on Christianity (as distinct, for instance, from the International Red Cross, the YMCA, the Salvation Army, *et al.*), but in man's immature and almost subconscious

ix

gropings in the realm of the spirit, ever seeking an outlet, which Rotary suddenly offered and which Paul Harris engineered for him, leaving Ches Perry to interpret the blueprint. Taking Rotary International as the prototype that it is, the author has skilfully blended its origins and history with a superb analysis of the demands of the epoch which gave it birth and of the extraordinary characters entrusted with its nurturing. They had to be extraordinary to conceive and rear such a fellowship of men in so unlikely a climate as that of what we now term the Edwardian era, a dilettante decade if ever there were one. He explains with startling clarity how an association of men united in fellowship could possibly survive two exhausting world wars, and not only survive but emerge from each the stronger. I had often posed that question and failed to find a satisfying answer. The author has furnished such an answer for all time.

Paul Harris merely wrote his reminiscences. Chesley Perry did not, so far as I am aware, write at all in the accepted sense in this context. Others have attempted a history but seem to have abandoned the attempt. Mr Nicholl with the utmost scholarship, tireless research, inspired assortment of fact and impression, boundless energy and a most readable text, has done what someone, some time, had to do, and done it quite splendidly. Here is the story of Rotary, and therefore *ipso facto* of the Service movement as a whole of the past three-quarters of a century, which must serve as the authoritative analysis and reference book well into the next century. I commend it to all Rotarians, past, present and to come in the next generation, to all members of similar organisations who may wonder as to their association's origins and motivation, and to all those, not necessarily themselves members, who are interested in the social sciences of the twentieth century; indeed to anyone who, other considerations apart, enjoys a gripping tale.

William C. Carter
Past President, RI (1973–4)
Old Windsor, January 1984

Acknowledgments

In a work of this length and ambitious scale my footsteps have trod, not where others have feared to go, but where many have gone before, not the whole way indeed but along crucial stretches of the road. The Bibliography itself will stand as tribute to my main Rotarian literary sources, and my enquiries have always met with a courteous and helpful response from all the Clubs consulted, beginning with the first two ever formed, those of Chicago — the famous Rotary One — and San Francisco.

My fellow-editors of Rotary journals all around the world have provided invaluable local and regional histories, both formal and informal, through the years of research that preceded, and accompanied, the two years of actual composition. Willmon L. White, Communications Manager of the Rotary International Secretariat, has guided me to several priceless sources, in addition to giving me constant encouragement during the long gestation of *The Golden Wheel*, and to the Associate Editor of *The Rotarian*, Mrs Jo Nugent, and all the editorial staff at Evanston, Illinois, I have never turned in vain.

The illustrations in this work, with the exception of the frontispiece, are all photographs from the archives of the Rotary International Secretariat, which owns the copyright, and all are reproduced by the generous permission of RI. The posthumous portrait in oils of Paul Harris, reproduced in the frontispiece, was painted by Brigitte Trace from several photographs and has been declared by many who knew the Founder in his later years as the most lifelike they have seen. The artist, who lives in Richmond, Surrey, has exhibited in London galleries and also painted the posthumous portrait of Earl Mountbatten of Burma which now hangs at Broadlands, the Mountbatten family home. I am much indebted to Miss Trace for her permission to present the portrait to public view for the first time in this book.

I am indebted to that great World Rotarian, Bill Carter, for his generous encouragement and assessment as "first reader" of my text. To all who read these pages, it will be evident that my full and grateful appreciation must go on record both to Herbert A. Pigman, General Secretary of Rotary International, and John H. Jackson, Secretary of Rotary International in Great Britain and Ireland, for giving me free access to the wealth of written and illustrative material, both published and unpublished, which has accumulated in the archives of their two secretariats. To the published work of Roger Levy, my predecessor as Editor of *Rotary*, and James P. Walsh, my debt will be obvious, but both have also given me priceless nuggets from the tireless mining of their own researches.

So many individuals, not all Rotarians, have contributed to my store of information indeed, that most must go unlisted, or I should require a separate chapter to include them all. But I must name the following: George R. Means, Past General Secretary of Rotary International who re-established Rotary in Japan after the Second World War; the late Wing Commander N.V. Carter, son of Vivian Carter — Secretary and Editor in RIBI and Editor also of *The Rotarian* — for vivid childhood memories of Chicago in its prohibition-gangster heyday; the Reverend Andrew Youngson Howe, nephew of Jean Harris, with his clear recollections of Paul; and Theo C. Bernsen, who provided a rare insight, owing much to personal experience, into the trials of Rotarians in Europe under the Nazi Occupation.

For cheerfully and skilfully accomplishing the monumental task of typing the final draft of this book, my lasting gratitude must be expressed to Miss Sandra Glitherow, whose ingenuity at deciphering interpolated scrawls and patchwork-quilts of manuscript possibly owes much to her endurance for nearly ten years as my Editorial Assistant on *Rotary* magazine. The encouragement of others at RIBI Headquarters has also cheered me on.

Finally, I must pay tribute to the fortitude of my family, as every author must. My son Adrian viewed my immersion in the Rotary past, and battles with the type-ribboned present, with some amazement but always enthusiastic (and sometimes refreshingly caustic) observation. My deepest appreciation of all, however, must be given to the loving patience of my wife Jill for bravely containing her dismay, verging on horror, at the gradual conversion of my study into mountain ranges of volumes of every size, shape, weight and state of cleanliness, with foothills of tumbled files and waterfalls of paper. Through the dusty miasma of all this, there emerged at intervals an equally dusty husband who at last announced "THE END" — only to wander into the fogs again to find what he had written. Without her, there would have been nothing to find.

D.S.N.

List of Illustrations

Frontispiece: Paul P. Harris in his later years

Between pages 98 and 99
1. The Founder, Paul Harris, in his early years
2. Chesley Perry, the dynamo recruited in 1908
3. Ches Perry in his prime
4 The first four Rotarians
5 The "little red schoolroom" in Wallingford, Vermont
6. Madame Galli's restaurant
7. Unity Building, Chicago, as it was in 1905 and as it is today.
8. Sherman House Chicago, in 1906.
9. Entrance to the Chicago Club today

Between pages 226 and 227
10. Stuart Morrow, the "wonder-working Irishman"
11. Harry Ruggles, initiator of the Rotary songs
12. Rotary International President Estes Snedecor greeted by Rotarian William Logie at the Edinburgh Convention in 1921
13. Arthur Sheldon, Rotary salesman supreme and inventor of the motto "He Profits Most Who Serves Best"
14. Jim Davidson, the "Marco Polo" of Rotary
15. King Albert I of the Belgians opens the Rotary International Convention at Ostend in 1927
16. Paul Harris being hosted in South Africa by Generals Smuts and Hertzog
17. One of the first television broadcasters: Paul Harris and Chesley Perry in 1940
18. Paul and Jean Harris in 1941
19. Paul and Ches at Comely Bank in 1942

Between pages 354 and 355

20. Four world-famous Rotarians
21. Pope John Paul II accepts the Paul Harris Award in 1981 from RI President Rolf J. Klarich
22. Rotary road signs in Chile
23. The "Christ of the Andes" monument
24 Rotary marker in Portugal
25. Interactor in Paysandu, Uruguay, carrying flag to an RI rally.
26. The modern Headquarters of Rotary International in Evanston, Illinois
27. The Paul P. Harris Room at RI Headquarters
28. Comely Bank, home of Paul and Jean Harris

CHAPTER ONE

The Source of Rotary

Rotary will go round and round
And round and round the world.
Rotary will go round and round
And round and round the world.
And if it should start for the stars,
It surely will go up to Mars.
Rotary will go round and round
And round and round the world.

Songs for the Rotary Club

Round and round it still goes, round the world, proving more and more the aptness of the name Rotary with each decade. But all circles start from a point and Rotary's point of reference was probably the least likely one that fate could have chosen from which to launch such shock-waves of compassion on mankind — while the cause of that launching was even more improbable, if one looks for romance.

Our century was just getting into its catastrophic stride and the city of Chicago — literally still the "mud-hole of the prairies" only a few decades before, but already one of our era's most turbulent nuclei — could boast of great museums, lavish parks, a monster phalanx of industries, a magnificent symphony orchestra, crime, corruption and vice on an heroic scale, more meat on the hoof and more railway termini than anywhere else on the continent, all overlooked by the world's first skyscrapers. If one believes Tin Pan Alley, moreover (and social historians are rash to ignore it), you could even find a man who danced with his wife — if you looked hard enough. But incredible though it may seem in our more pampered times, the town where you could throw around

1

several fortunes in a day — and many did — made it almost impossible for you to spend an urgent penny.

A man called Paul Harris changed that alarming situation, thus giving lasting honour to the man his biographer rightly calls "the First Rotarian". Chicago has not put up a statue to its very own "St Paul", but it should have. There is, however, a monument to him, and a not inconsiderable edifice either, which you can find on the corner of La Salle and Washington Streets. It doesn't have his name on a plaque, but I have always felt it should have the superscription penned by Sir Christopher Wren's son for his father in that older St Paul's, *Si monumentum requiris circumspice* (If you would seek his monument, look around you), for there still stands Chicago's first public convenience. Here then was a remarkable man who, not for the last time, managed the seemingly impossible: at a stroke, he solved the problem of what to give a town that had everything. And so Rotary began.

It wasn't easy. From the beginning, Rotary inspired powerful enemies. Paul and his small band called themselves the Conspirators, which was asking for trouble perhaps, and had ranged against them powerful vested interests, all of whom had City Hall in their wallets — or billfolds, as the Americans say. The saloon-bar owners and big store magnates wanted to convert strained bladders into customers, and if the average Chicago citizen or visitor wanted to answer the call of nature while strolling the "toddlin' town", he had to hurry into either a bar or a department store. And to get the facility demanded, Paul and his Conspirators had to face a series of planning meetings, public and private hearings and entrenched protests, which the British reserve for less pressing projects such as choosing London's third airport.

The campaign lasted two years and small wonder that Paul and his friends came to behave in the true manner of conspirators. They met in huddled groups in a succession of hotel rooms or gathered in each other's offices — all being professional or business men — to work out strategy. The venues varied in careful rotation and sooner or later it was inevitable that someone should suggest they signify this circumstance by calling themselves Rotarians. Paul Harris himself suggested the name, with his habitual diffidence. None of his friends liked it much (they probably quite enjoyed being Conspirators), but in seventy-nine years no one has come up with anything better. So their first club became a Rotary Club, on the crest of a notable, if bizarre, victory.

Paul Harris always said that Chicago's first public lavatory was the most significant thing Rotarians ever accomplished, then or later, and who can disagree with him? As they started, they meant to continue, even if the urgent needs were to diversify greatly. The pattern was set. Rotarians were to benefit communities from San Francisco to Singapore, from Paris to Pretoria, from Jersey to Jerusalem, from Turin to Tokyo, in an endless variety of ways, simple to sumptuous; but no dire need, it is safe to say, was ever satisfied, no want supplied, with more direct action or success. The local YMCA director bestowed his accolade: "The Rotary Club of Chicago has now shown reason for its existence." History has never demurred, and the same sentiment has been echoed in most of the world's tongues, and by some of this century's most powerful men. Theodore Roosevelt, an early enthusiast for the Movement, spoke prophetic words: "Contact between men such as compose Rotary International will certainly contribute towards mutual understanding"; while his most famous remark, "Speak softly and carry a big stick and you will go far", might have been addressed to Rotary, with the alteration of one word — "Speak softly and carry a Big Club".

The "First Rotarian" was then a shy but strong-minded lawyer of thirty-seven, a bachelor of transparent honesty, who possessed an almost frightening single-mindedness and had deliberately settled in what was regarded as one of the most corrupt cities on earth. But Chicago held no terrors for this strange, prowling innocent, who called its wickedness "evidence of virility", a choice of noun perhaps not without significance. What troubled him was the same fear which haunted the hero of Arthur Miller's play *Death of a Salesman*, that of not being "well liked". The initial steps he took to banish his fear we shall probably never know. For nine years he explored the city, continually changing his lodgings — and his law partners — and, in Nelson Algren's vivid phrase, "walking the wild side", a taste cultivated by a stay in Jack the Ripper's Whitechapel several years before. He emerged fascinated, untainted, still lonely. The fear of not being "well liked" remained.

When he vanquished that fear in 1905 by forming a club with three friends who were fellow-sufferers, Paul Harris brought about one of the most profound social developments of this century, destined to proliferate and be endlessly imitated all over America and then the world: the concept of the Service Club defined in the *Encyclopaedia Britannica* as "an organization, usually composed of business and professional men or women, that promoted friendliness among its members and is devoted to the principle of service to society". In our universal loneliness, we are all in his debt, even if we have never met a Kiwani, Lion or Soroptimist in our lives — or a Rotarian, to our knowledge. An exaggerated claim? Paul Harris himself would certainly have thought so, though, when pressed, he

3

would admit to being "the Architect not the Builder", an incautious remark which perhaps led many to equate Rotary with Freemasonry. This was a quite erroneous supposition; the only "secrecy" ever attached to Rotary was of the fantastic joking sort such as that imagined by the superb clerical wit Sydney Smith when he conjured up a heretic Brahmin who "ate beefsteaks in private". Yet we have quite startling testimonials to the structure of which he was architect. President Franklin D. Roosevelt was to write: "Thinking of Rotary, I visualize a series of concentric circles which, starting with the smallest and going to the largest, I denominate as the community, national and international influence. In the center, I see Rotary International as a generating force of incalculable value." Winston Churchill (himself an Honorary Rotarian) would state: "All thinking men recognise the moral and spiritual value of Rotary. There is indeed a wealth of meaning in the motto Service Above Self. Few there are who do not recognise the good work which is done by Rotary Clubs throughout the free world." And as recently as 1979, finding the Rotarians holding their Seventieth Convention in his own "parish", Pope John Paul II was to call them to a special audience when the Convention was over, to tell them: "Your presence here today indicates a great power for good. You come from many different nations and backgrounds. You bring with you vast experience in the economic, industrial, professional, cultural and scientific fields. In the solidarity of your association, you find mutual support, reciprocal encouragement and a shared commitment to work for the common good."

If it is true, as Paul's favourite philosopher, Ralph Waldo Emerson, wrote, that "An institution is the lengthened shadow of one man", then Paul Percy Harris was that man where Rotary is concerned. And what have presidents, prime ministers and popes to do with those groups of rather ordinary business men — most of whom nowadays seem to be in their fifties and sixties rather than their thirties — who meet in pubs, small hotels and village halls once a week all over the world to consume often indifferent food, ring Rotary bells in hearty mateyness, say Rotary Grace, and indulge in the little social rituals of what they call "fellowship"?

If anyone could have made the world dance to Rotary's tune, one would have put one's money on Rotarian Franz Lehár — and lost. If anyone could have established communication between members and non-members across the globe, surely it would have been Rotarian Guglielmo Marconi or Rotarian Orville Wright? Again, no.

No one seemed to notice that it was to the Rotary Club of London that Ernest Bevin first unveiled the Beveridge Plan for post-war Britain, nor that Rotary International supplied special consultants to the San Francisco Conference which bred the United Nations. And by then, of course, everyone had forgotten that Woodrow Wilson, creator of that precursor of the UN, the League of Nations, had hailed Rotary as an example of the "only cement which will hold the nations of the world together in permanent peace . . . the cement of friendship". Cement is what one sinks to make foundations; unfortunately, it often just sinks. At which moment, today's eulogy becomes tomorrow's epitaph.

Rotary of course has an enduring image, composed of standard elements which have not changed for decades. It suggests clubs composed of stolid men of comfortable means and leading complacent lives. Regularly, local papers announce that Rotarians have given money to charity, taken old people to the seaside, presented equipment to hospitals. They are known to be addressed by guest speakers, on which occasions they put on dinner-jackets if their guests are of particular renown, and they constantly make speeches to each other. They pursue these activities with irregular enthusiasm, give no trouble to anyone, and in summary are well-intentioned nonentities who are generally considered harmless. They enjoyed a brief spell of unwanted limelight when Bernard Shaw was once unwisely asked about Rotary's future and where he thought Rotary might be going. He crisply replied on a postcard, "to lunch". Shaw was wrong, as he often was, but memorably wrong, as usual, and the label stuck, the image hardened. Not that Shaw's opinion was shared by his totalitarian idols, whether of Right or Left, then or now, from Franco's 1936 banning of all Rotary Clubs, through the years of their suppression by Hitler's Germany, the war-lords of Japan and Stalin's empire, to the horrifying day in 1968 when Rotarian Jan Masaryk was hurled to his death from his office window in Prague as prelude to Russia's invasion of Czechoslovakia. Only in what we term the "free world" of today, where men are permitted to make fools or whatever of themselves at will, provided they don't make a fuss about it and frighten the politicians, do the "nonentities" flourish and multiply.

The story of Rotary, said the man who started it all, would have to be written again and again. Which is no doubt why neither he nor anyone else ever wrote it. Paul Percy Harris produced, it is true, a number of books of personal recollections, usually based upon extensive travels on his brainchild's behalf; yet his could not be impartial records and were of restricted perspective. And such was his personal standing as the Founder of the Rotary Movement, that others were intimidated from trespassing on paths he had already trodden.

After Paul's death in 1947, forty-two years after he had presided over the world's first Rotary meeting — of just four men in a Chicago office in the middle of the night — it was his intimidating Scottish widow, his "Bonnie Jean", who was to ensure that the hallowed trail remained inviolate. Jean was buried in 1963 at Edinburgh, 4,000 miles from her husband's grave in the American Midwest. That fact indeed might have spoken volumes, but they still remained unwritten. Now we do at last have a biography of Paul Harris — uncharacteristically, his fellow-Americans never quote his name in full — and during the world-wide celebrations of Rotary's Seventy-Fifth anniversary, I decided it was time the story of his extraordinary Movement itself was at last fully told, the biography of the sole offspring of Paul and Jean Harris — Rotary, the Movement of the Golden Wheel.

This is not a fanciful conceit. In his last book of memoirs and reflections, published posthumously, Paul Harris confessed disarmingly that "Having no children of our own, Jean and I have adopted Rotary International". A few pages farther on came his remark, "We Americans are hero worshippers; it would be well for us to choose our heroes wisely". The juxtaposition, I believe, was not an accidental one, though probably subconscious, for a crucial part of the story of Rotary is the matter of who adopted whom. What can be in no dispute whatever is that the Movement's adoption of its hero was a wise, indeed a brilliant one. If the opposite were true, this story will surely reveal the fact. Paul's book was called *My Road to Rotary*. The road it described was really an old man's ramble back through childhood, however, and whole sections were lifted from earlier works. For the hard fact was that Paul's walk to Rotary lasted exactly seven years. By 1912, when there were fifty Rotary Clubs in existence, three of them outside the United States, the Founder was made the Movement's first and only "President Emeritus" and spent the rest of his days "in retirement" as its beloved figurehead. In 1980, the Board of Rotary International decided not to issue any more editions of *My Road to Rotary*. After all, they could now count nearly 19,000 Clubs and 1 million Rotarians and had decided to move out of the lengthened shadow. Especially now that seven new Clubs were formed outside the United States for every one within, and new Clubs were being formed all over the world, at the rate of one every fourteen hours; all wanting to be "well-liked", too.

But why start it all in Chicago? Before Rotary evolved into the world's first Service Club, its concept as a Club where men congenial to one another met for purely social companionship and relaxed enjoyment, while partaking of a meal or refreshment — in other words, for "fellowship" — was far from an original one. The idea was clearly anticipated by the famous coffee-houses of Britain and France in the eighteenth century, and Benjamin Franklin with his Junto Club in Philadelphia even anticipated the qualifications of vocational membership — each member representing a different trade, business or profession — which were very much the first distinguishing feature Paul Harris insisted on in 1905. Franklin's Junto indeed holds the parallel that it produced mutually beneficial business for its members, also true of early Rotarians, and unashamedly so. Franklin laid down also that "to prevent warmth, all expressions of positiveness in opinions, or direct contradiction, were after some time made contraband, and prohibited under small pecuniary penalties", which anticipates uncannily the rules against Rotary taking public attitudes on political, religious or racial matters, with "fines" for contravention of these rules.

Before that time, Pepys belonged to a club called Rota, though the names have nothing common in derivation. For that matter, Cicero belonged to "symposia" in Ancient Rome, where the regulated talk and ritual of dining were governed by club officers and committees. La Société des Philanthropes in Strasbourg had ideals almost identical with Rotary. The earliest English dining club we know of goes back to the time of Henry VIII; and we know of Sir Walter Raleigh's Bread Street Club at the Mermaid Tavern and Ben Jonson's Apollo Club at the Devil's Tavern. Doubtless, all shared with Franklin's group (everyone, in whatever century, was exclusively male, as is Rotary still) the desire to be "studied in our rules which might prevent our disgusting each other. . . ."

Hence the long continuance of the "club". Yet none had a long continuance — the literary-political clubs are of a quite different category, of course — and we must try to discover why this deeply embedded need in mankind should re-emerge and flourish in Chicago when it did, supplanting all those brief shoots in London, Strasbourg, Philadelphia and Ancient Rome. We must look at the time and the place, and then at the man.

"I have struck a city — a real city — and they call it Chicago," noted Kipling in his diary. Though he probably was unaware the word was Indian for skunk, he would not have demurred, for the comment is loaded with ambiguity, and was the most polite thing he ever said about the place. Dickens had also been uncomplimentary and Oscar Wilde, though he was paid $200 a lecture — a vast sum in the 1880s — adjudged the city "positively dreary", than which no insult could have struck deeper. This was added to the injury of

his description of its famous Water Tower as a "castellated mon-
strosity" while he affected to admire its pumping machinery as
"simple, grand and natural". In return, one reporter wrote a rhymed
interview about their exotic visitor:

> Here, in the energetic West
> We have no vacant niches
> For clowns with pansies in the vest
> Or dadoes in the breeches.

All the same, Chicagoans knew quality when they saw it and
tried unsuccessfully to get from Wilde the rights to the world
première of *A Woman of No Importance* for their World's Fair of
1893, the year of Paul Harris's first visit to the city. Moreover,
Wilde's favourite restaurant in London, the Café Royal, was in time
to become the meeting-place of the first chartered Rotary Club
in the British Isles. Which is why his love-hate relationship with
Chicago seems useful to quote as symbolic of the ambivalent nature
of the Anglo-Chicago contact which prevailed then and later and
which was to be echoed within Rotary (London was then and
always Paul's second favourite city).

Burlesque began in the United States with the appearance in
Chicago of "Lydia Thompson and her British Blondes", a dubious
tribute later generously repaid when Charles Tyson Yerkes, supreme
paymaster of politicians who had built the city's transit system still
visible today, was run out of town for being "too fond of sofas"
and came to London to advise on the building of the Underground
system — also still visible today. Chicago's miles of reeking stockyards supplied meat for the whole of Kitchener's army when it
marched against Khartoum.

But all this interplay was but preliminary to the most volcanic
British visitor Chicago ever had, the crusading London journalist
W.T. Stead, another who flocked to the World's Fair of 1893,
fresh from cleaning up "Modern Babylon" (i.e. London). Looking
at the same scene as young Paul Harris (who came back later that
year for a second look), Stead noted the gambling dens within a
block of City Hall, the rampant vice of all kinds, the crooked
business men, the corrupt police, bribed politicians and the town's
fast-flowing lifeblood of crime and venality, and wrote a book
that shocked the world, *If Christ Came to Chicago.* What most
horrified him, and probably Paul Harris too, was the discovery
that neither Cyrus McCormick, founder of the giant International
Harvester Company, nor Pullman, the railway king, nor Marshall
Field, the department store tycoon, paid more property taxes on

their coach and horses than did Carrie Watson, owner of the largest
and most luxurious brothel in America. Stead, giving the devil-
woman her due, admitted she was "liberal in her gifts to the only
churches in her neighbourhood, one a Catholic just across the way
and the other a Jewish synagogue which local rumour asserts is run
rent-free owing to Carrie's pious munificence. . . . Carrie Watson can
be all things to all men". What possibly made things worse in Stead's
eyes — even more so than her tainted wealth — was Miss Watson's
sense of humour. Her twenty-room establishment was in no seamy
red-light district, nor did she allow any young ladies to flaunt their
wares on doorsteps or in windows; she had simply trained a parrot
which sat in its cage all day outside her front door, saying over and
over, "Carrie Watson. Come in, Gentlemen. Carrie Watson. Come in,
Gentlemen".

In 1905, Chicago was therefore in essence still a frontier town.
Along its muddy streets, liquor stores and brothels jostled each
other, there was a burglary every three hours, a street-mugging
every six hours and a murder a day. Literally, it was also a stinking
town, suffocating under the odours of glue, pickles, cattle and
slaughterhouses. The river took such a mass of sewage, stockyard
oils, fats, guts and blood to the already filth-choked Lake Michigan
— which alone of the Great Lakes had no outlet — that its surface
often blazed from floating remains of smouldering rubbish. This
same water was funnelled back into the "toddlin town" for its
citizens to bathe in, to drink and catch typhoid from. No wonder that in later prohibition years rotgut booze seemed like nectar!
Unemployment, homelessness, destitution, even starvation forced
hundreds daily to plan how to be gaoled for a night's lodging and a
square meal, about the only truly "square" feature in many police
stations, for here policemen owned crooks and vice versa, with
emphasis on the vice. Extortion, prostitution, gambling and casual
thuggery were so common that the *Chicago Tribune* declared "A
reign of terror is upon the city" and increased its circulation at
once. And the monarch of this reign beamed, for all the "better
elements" flocked to one of America's most famous night-clubs on
South Wabash Avenue, Colosimo's Café, named after Jim Colosimo,
the first of Chicago's many Italian–Sicilian tsars of crime who
would run the Black Hand, the Mafia, the Syndicate, right through
Chicago's halcyon years.

No wonder Paul Harris was fascinated, stunned and appalled by
the city. When, in 1898, he announced plans to settle there, a
friend suggested that more money could be made in Florida, to
which the Founder of Rotary replied, "I am not going to Chicago
for the purpose of making money, I am going for the purpose of

living a life." The life he made may be inferred by his own later admission that during fifteen years of bachelor life, up to the very day of his marriage, he "was setting new records for change of domicile" and sampled "everything from Hell's Half Kitchen up". But he also made plenty of money from an epidemic of fraud cases which followed the city's general bankruptcy in the wake of the World's Fair.

After the initial outrage at Stead's revelations, however, Paul claimed that he and other citizens took the book as a challenge to reform. "Chicago's civic consciousness and pride were considerably shaken," he later recalled. "Its implications were manifold and shocking, but the Chicago which had managed to lift itself out of the mire and rebuild itself after its devastating fire was game enough to lift itself out of the slough of bad repute." That Great Fire had almost destroyed the whole of Chicago in twenty-nine hours (the famous Water Tower excepted, which was why Wilde's scorn was so resented). Yet — be it noted, with a great deal of aid from Britain, including Queen Victoria herself, a substantial stockholder in the Pullman Company — the city had recovered enough to stage the World's Fair. It had then plummeted, it is true, almost at once into the mire again — this time, moral rather than physical — but now crusaders aplenty were on hand, inspired by the work in London of the likes of Toynbee Hall, the Salvation Army, the Working Men's Institutes, YMCA and Shaftesbury Society.

Yet the frontier analogy holds for deeper reasons than the obvious surface one of disorganised crime, rough justice and the casual brutalities which govern the survival of the fittest and fleetest, though even those surface manifestations were not far away. Dearborn Street — future home of the first Rotary Club — was named after the incompetent soldier who nearly lost America its war with the British in 1812. Fort Dearborn grew into Chicago, thanks largely to Captain John Whistler, grandfather of the waspish painter who became such a social rival to Oscar Wilde (which may help explain some of Wilde's comments on the place). Indeed, the last Indians had left, in a defiant war-dance right through Chicago streets, only seventy years before 1905, when Paul Harris founded his Movement.

But there was another frontier in America, epitomised in Chicago, which was that of the robber barons of business, exact blood brethren of the cattle barons of the Wilder West. For example, there was George Pullman of sleeping-car fame who had broken strikes with the use of 14,000 soldiers; and Samuel Insull (he had worked as a boy with Bernard Shaw on a telephone exchange), who had come from London to manage the Chicago Edison Company and ended up the "Utility Monarch", serving the city with all its gas and electricity — and one-eighth of the United States, too — and buying every politician in sight (he was part inspiration for *Citizen Kane* in his building of an opera-house for his untalented wife's performances). Charles Yerkes, before his hasty departure for London, was another unscrupulous franchise glutton, and he nearly managed to buy enough votes to have an Eternal Monopoly Bill passed by the State Legislature.

The general tone of business dealing can be graphically summed up by a group of Chicago aldermen who successfully created an imaginary Universal Gas Company with exclusive franchise to light Chicago streets and then sold the non-existent firm to its main rival. The great steel mills (the first steel railway track rolled out from Chicago), the giant Armour and Swift meat-packing industries, the McMormick Harvester Company, all were ruthlessly anti-union — as a result of strike riots at the latter firm, four men were hanged in the 1880s. In the America of the Morgans, Vanderbilts, Rockefellers and Carnegies, Chicago was of course not unique in its quota of unscrupulous business men and exploiters of immigrant labour, but it certainly attracted world attention and always went that much farther that much more brazenly. By 1905, however, the nation's business conscience was very active — Carnegie and Rockefeller started giving millions to charity. Chicago's way was less expensive but more enduring. It gave birth to the Ethics of Rotary, and just in time. That same year it also gave birth to the Industrial Workers of the World, the radical "Wobblies".

It was Paul Harris's moment and Rotary's. "It is conceivable", said the Founder, "that Rotary might have been born under sunnier skies, in a climate more equable, and in a city of mental composure; but many will contend that there could have been no more favorable birthplace for a Movement like Rotary than paradoxical Chicago, where the battle for civic righteousness was being so fiercely waged."

There were many allies for reform: the Citizens' Association, the Municipal Voters' League, the Women's Christian Temperance Union, the Society of Social Hygiene, the Law and Order League, the evangelists Dwight Moody and Billy Sunday. There was also a "mole", a black seductress who kept a most prosperous "house of ill-fame", the insider who told all to Stead so he could write his book. The journalist claimed that Miss Vina Fields ran her house as strictly as a "Sunday School", brought up her daughter "in the virginal seclusion of a convent. . . . Nor is her bounty confined to her own family. Every day, this whole winter through, she has fed a hungry, ragged regiment of the out-of-work. The day before I called, 201 men had had free dinners of her own providing". What menu she provided for Stead he did not reveal, but one can understand Shaw's outburst (Stead had been his editor on the *Pall Mall Gazette*) during an earlier Stead crusade that he should "humble your bumptious spirit with a new sense of the extreme perversity and wickedness of that uncharitable Philistine bringing-up of yours", adding mischievously: "Hoping that your mission will end in your own speedy and happy conversion."

William Thomas Stead, the inventor of the "interview", and thus modern journalism, was converted to spiritualism eventually, and his reforming works included *The Truth about Russia* and *The Americanisation of the World*, titles which make him seem very contemporary. But in 1912, the year he went down with the *Titanic*, the torch of reform in Chicago was secure and aflame in other hands, and a voice was proclaiming with evangelistic fervour:

> The United States of America has capitulated to the demands of Rotary. Not content with this, the cause is urged ever onward. The Dominion of Canada and the British Isles give way to the crusader's demands. Paris is ours and today the slogan is "On to Berlin, Vienna, then to the Antipodes" . . . . The ambitions of our conquest know no limitations save the limitations of the civilized world. Unlike the conquest of the Napoleonic forces, our conquest is, and will continue to be, in the interests of men and the principles which make for the practical idealization of trade.

Stead's prophecy had, in a way, come true. But the words were the words of Paul Harris, who was about to announce his notorious "retirement" from Rotary, only seven years after he had created the Movement in an office of the Unity Building, built in 1893, the unity referring prophetically to ethnic unity. For that matter, it was only five years after Rotary's first act of Community Service, the public convenience, that this unique combination of pragmatic do-gooding and business moral hygiene was now set to go "round and round and round the world". As Stead had foretold, a redeemer had indeed come to Chicago, but though it seemed a mouse was roaring, not a Messiah, the mouse was roaring out across the globe in the first of many "last farewells". When the very last one was heard, thirty-five years later, it was from a memorial address in St Paul's Cathedral, appropriately enough, that a phrase struck most memorably home. "Unknown, yet well known," said the Dean.

It was true of the Movement and of the man who started it, but it need be true no longer. Chicago as the unlikely home where Rotary bred has been examined, and may perhaps be likened to the man who claimed that he didn't know the true worth of his wife till he married her and by then it was too late. Let us now look at the equally unlikely man who brought the seed.

CHAPTER TWO

The Man from Racine

Let ev'ry good knight raise his helmet and glove!
To carry our message of service and love . . .
The grooming of man is a duty we claim,
Let's carry on business with fame to our name.
The man with a smile is the fellow we need,
Who loses himself in the shaming of greed.

Vive le Rotary!

Songs for the Rotary Club

As it happened, the pollen hadn't far to travel; Chicago lies only
sixty-five miles south of Racine, where Paul Percy Harris was born
on 19th April 1868. The towns and cities of the American Midwest
have largely these French and Indian names, reflecting the French
and Indian Wars of the eighteenth century, the New World's branch
of Europe's great dynastic conflicts and struggles for empire, which,
among other things, presumed to settle whether America should be
governed from London or Paris. Thirty years after the dust had
settled, it was being governed from neither, of course, while the
Indians had no say whatever — but the place-names stayed to tell
their tales, and nothing could be more contrasted with Chicago's
rather earthy nomenclature, referred to in the last chapter, than
naming the little river up the Lake Michigan shore after France's
great tragic dramatist. Paul's birthplace was duly named after the
Racine River and little therefore separated the pilgrim and his goal
than the state-line between Wisconsin and Illinois. It was still
twenty-eight years before he arrived there, his achievement taking
that old saw of the longest way round being the shortest way
home to almost ridiculous lengths.

The Paul Harris "shrine" is not to be found in Racine, however,
but in Wallingford, Vermont, for reasons which will soon be clear,

and many have come to regard him as the epitome of a tall, lean New England Yankee, when he was nothing of the kind; though it was a role he did not disdain. He was a Midwesterner and his home was never anywhere but in that dynamic heartland of America where he was born and buried, where the great railroads began, the vast farmlands sweep away to incredible horizons, enormous industries crowd the ports of the largest group of lakes in the world, the "melting-pot" of nations is most often on the boil and, beneath those French and Indian place-names, the accents are German, Swedish, Polish, Russian, Irish and Italian. Fifteen years after the Second World War, about one in five Chicagoans was still of foreign birth. Even today, your taxi-driver from O'Hare International Airport is likely as not to be barely comprehensible in English, his fares even less so, though his gestures are entirely familiar. These Midwesterners have left Europe for a variety of reasons, the urge to make a fast buck or a quick getaway not being the least of them, but all have forsaken the old country with sighs of relief. No wonder that here was the seed-bed of pre-war American "isolationism"; enormous wonder that the same seed-bed nurtured what has become the world's foremost non-political, non-religious international organisation. To Rotary's own great surprise, though not to its Founder's — excepting the rate of growth, which astonished him to the day he died.

Paul Harris's own antecedents were Irish and Scottish. The Battle of the Boyne (just as much in the news today in Northern Ireland as when it took place nearly 300 years ago) did not in itself defeat the Irish armies fighting on behalf of the exiled James II of England (the crucial battle was won and lost between French and Dutch generals trampling over County Clare, which scarcely lends itself to topical parades), but William of Orange's conquest, barely thirty years after Cromwell's, brought complete repression. In England, the Glorious Revolution that kicked out the Stuarts brought the start of parliamentary democracy, religious toleration, freedom of the press and — that bastion of modern economic enlightenment — the national debt. Across the Irish Sea it took away from Catholics the right to bear arms, teach, practise law, vote, carry on trade, even own a horse. Small wonder that many young Irishmen decamped for the New World. One of the many, named O'Brien, joined the fast-growing Irish community in Massachusetts. This was one and a half centuries before young Patrick Kennedy took the same route, and by the end of this book it may be surprisingly clear which of these immigrants had the most profound effect on world history through their children's children.

O'Brien soon contracted his name to Bryan; and Reuben Bryan,

15

his grandson, was to become one of the earliest settlers of New York State. They were a restless breed, these Bryans, a trait vividly manifested in their famous descendant and in 1850 (the year Patrick Kennedy followed the emigrant trail from County Wexford) Henry Bryan was leading a band of "Forty-Niners" in the great California gold-rush, one of 80,000 who crowded into territory ceded from Mexico barely a year before. Henry not only led his band but financed it as well, and the modest fortune he had built up through his law practice back East vanished overnight. Loss of wealth did not bring loss of influence, however, or of astuteness, and we next find him ensconced in Racine, whose fine harbour on Lake Michigan gave it a splendid opportunity to profit from a rather different and far more lasting boom — Britain had in 1846 repealed the Corn Laws, consequently agricultural exports soared and farmers poured westward from the Atlantic, needing tools, homes and supplies. This meant not only an incredibly swift mushrooming of factories making farm implements, but a complete range of industries for domestic products, lumber to build the farmers' homes, appliances to run them and garments to clothe their families. When Henry Bryan returned from California, Racine had just been made a city; he became its second Mayor.

Though Paul Harris inherited his grandfather Henry Bryan's restless yearnings and followed him into law, and indeed he was to lead a far more successful assault upon California, he affected to deprecate the side of the family he most resembled and the forbear whose qualities were most dominant, if later sublimated, in his own character. His posthumous memoirs refer to Bryan but fleetingly and are one long paean to Harris virtues from which he derived, so he claims, all the virtues he later embodied in Rotary. His biographer, by a somewhat Freudian deduction, assumes this side of his ancestry to be Scottish. Harris tweed is a dubious pointer, since the name was brought over from Normandy with the family of William the Conqueror, being derived from Henry via "Harry"; and Harrisburg, Virginia, is named after a Yorkshireman. None the less, many Yorkshire families have links with Scotland and certainly the hardworking, thrifty puritan virtues of the citizens of Wallingford, Vermont, have much in common with certain Scots traditions. The Congregational Church, of which the Harris family were staunch pillars, sent Scottish missionaries all over the world, of whom Livingstone is only the best known. Paul worshipped his mother, married late and, when he married, chose a Scottish bride — and it was Scotland which hosted the first Rotary Convention outside the North American continent. These are slender clues, but no one has ever disputed the conclusion they drew. Certainly not

Harris himself. What is quite certain is that Cornelia Bryan, eighth child of the "feckless" Irish lawyer-adventurer, somehow met and married George Harris — who had possibly fled West to escape his four sisters — and they settled in Racine to run a drugstore purchased for them by the groom's father, Henry Bryan having died leaving them penniless.

George Harris resembled Cornelia's father much more than he did his own, which was doubtless why she married him, the crucial difference being that the money he freely spent he never managed first to earn.

Harris Senior, back in Wallingford — where he spent his entire long life — met their debts for some years and the spendthrift couple had three children before the cheques stopped coming and the prodigal son went home cap in hand, taking his two sons with him and leaving the proud Irish girl behind in Wisconsin with a baby daughter. Removed from Racine as Paul was at the age of three, all his memories of growing up were naturally not of the Midwest but of village life in New England, which was narrow and straight-laced maybe, but good, kind and generous within its limited horizon. And, in spite of several periods of reconciliation which produced three more brothers, he could recall only a broken home-life, however well cushioned by grandparents, perhaps over-eager to rescue his Micawberish father, an impractical man who dreamed up many inventions, of which the most persistent was his delusion that he could make any of them work. Thus, from the beginning, Paul Harris was bequeathed, by inheritance and his environment, two warring elements: the wild, brilliant, impulsive Irish flair which knew no bounds; and the thoughtful, hard-working Scottish prudence which knew its place and stayed there. It took thirty-seven years for these elements to be reconciled in a sudden glorious fusion — the founding — and even then, the pattern of reconciliation and separation was yet to continue. When Paul was fifty-five, Racine unveiled a plaque to honour its most famous son, but the First Rotarian resolutely refused to attend the ceremony.

But whatever the slightly priggish, saintly charisma that was to be bestowed on him by some in the future, broken homes produce wild boys and Paul Harris was no exception. He was the leader of a band of youths called "the rapscallions", a quaint old-fashioned sounding word that in fact was probably another heritage of French settlement, like the name Vermont itself, meaning Green Mountains. He placed bent pins in the chapel pews for ample congregationalists to sit on, stole out of the house at midnight to take hair-raising rides with his friends on the front cowcatchers of passing loco-motives, often played truant from school, and added to his father's and grandparents' miseries by vanishing on walks through the deep, drifting snow of Bear Mountain. The worthy folk of Wallingford literally regarded Paul and his gang as holy terrors with their "not infrequent lapses into savagery". The extent and dangerous edge of their wildness can be gauged by the fact that Paul's best friend and co-leader, Fay Stafford, was soon to die in a mental asylum. Thinking of those days in old age, Paul remarked, "Rapscallions sometimes wonder why God takes the clothes off the trees in November at just the time folks put extra clothes on", a distinctly odd observation and one it was probably just as well he kept to himself when young.

To his grandmother's mind "all the sins of the universe were committed under cover of night" and she had her eye on young Paul when she said it. With reason, for he also later wrote (referring to himself, as he often did, in the third person): "Paul was supposed to be in bed by nine o'clock and in fact he always was. It did not, however, necessarily follow that he was in bed at ten o'clock." Doubtless his grandparents made many allowances because of his disturbed home life and certainly Howard Harris noted the persistent thrust and originality, however wayward, in the boy, and in Paul's quieter moments tried to encourage in him an interest in literature, fortunately unaware that their beloved old family rooster was meanwhile being trained up for cock-fights at the local blacksmith's!

Allowances were duly made for the young man at the local high schools, his quick intelligence being noted along with its indiscipline, but when he progressed to college level and the Black River Academy (where the future President Calvin Coolidge was soon to be educated) he lasted only a year before being expelled for "excess of spirits", an ambiguous verdict.

At the Vermont Military Academy an improvement in Paul showed itself — his latent powers of leadership clearly blossomed under regimentation and a sense of order which his distracted home life had lacked. But at the University of Vermont his old ways reasserted themselves and expulsion once more followed. With amazing and admirable perseverance, determined that their son's failure should not be repeated in another generation, his grandparents engaged a private tutor for the nineteen-year-old. Paul seized this last chance, took control of his strange, errant nature, and entered Princeton University with flying colours, only to have to leave after just one year on the sudden death of Howard Harris, who was never to know how his disturbing and obviously disturbed grandson was to vindicate his trust so magnificently.

After the funeral the burgeoning undergraduate discovered that, because of a canny Scottish doubt on the part of his grandfather, he had been left no provision for his further education unless, in the judgment of his grandmother, he should "prove himself". With the taste of Princeton on his lips, Paul was determined to do exactly that, and a year spent uncomplainingly at a job as office boy for a dollar a day (for which he had to get up at 5.30 a.m.) duly convinced his grandmother, Pamela, that the wild rapscallion was now tamed. He wasn't, but the shock of being untimely ripped from Princeton's cultural womb had harnessed unorthodox drives to a carefully calculated schedule. The money was forthcoming and it was agreed between him and his grandmother that he should study law at Iowa University.

So the Midwest called its own back again, and New England fell away behind his westbound train for ever. Paul did not see his grandmother again, nor did he even return for her funeral the following year. By that time the finger of destiny had touched him, he was immersed in the study of his grandfather Henry Bryan's profession, and — had he any doubts — the fact that Iowa is Indian for "this is the place" would have made him come to a firm decision. Not that Iowa City itself was "the place", but to get there one had to change trains at fabulous Chicago, where Paul felt immediately he had come home. He went on to take his law degree at Iowa State, having had his first glimpse, that September of 1889, of the city where he would lay the cornerstone of his life's work. On that first visit, he stayed seven days. He did not visit Racine.

What he did visit, guided by a college friend, now a journalist, was the scene of the Haymarket riots of three years before, which he followed by a trip to the site of a famous murder and a look-in at the town's most notorious gambling den. These sights — and presumably others unmentioned — made, he admitted long afterwards, a "profound impression" upon him. He was a few months too late to witness the country's most sensational divorce case (involving the actress Mrs Leslie Carter and many prominent citizens), in which for much of the time the bedroom evidence was so typically candid and uninhibited that no one under thirty-five was allowed in the court anyway, but he was in time to marvel at the start of the new elevated railway at Twelfth Street. Chicago had not been the first to plan such a transit system but it was the first city to run the cars by electricity. He was also in time to see the start of Hull House, which young Jane Adams, only eight years older than himself, was setting up in direct emulation of Toynbee Hall in Whitechapel. All these aspects combined made an intoxicating mixture, but "the sights which attracted me also repelled me".

Paul Harris was twenty-three when he faced the world as a fully qualified lawyer. It was a brief confrontation, for he then took to the road. There was no money from either the Bryans or Harrises, so his need to earn a living was imperative. Indeed, all of his class-mates at Iowa State had immediately dispersed to their home towns to start their professional lives. Yet Harris at once cocked a snook at convention, proving that the essential "rapscallion" was far from extinct. He now had no ties. Both his surrogate parents were dead and he seldom saw his true parents again, though George and Cornelia both lived to a good age, playing out their marital charade of separation, reunion and separation over and over, cushioned from destitution, or even a mild risk of genuine want, by old Howard Harris's final act of double betrayal of his clan. For surely we can judge it as no less. The old man (already seventy-two when Paul came to live with him at the age of three) had broken up his son's marriage and family and poured derision on George's ability to support himself; and his will — one could almost call it his "wicked will" — then guaranteed that his son would never be different, for he left him an income in the trust of George's brother-in-law. One wonders if Paul Harris ever forgave this insult to his father or, worse, whether — since he never expressed any sense of outrage — he despised his father as much as Grandfather Howard possibly hoped he would. If so, his grandfather was much to blame, quite apart from the result of encouraging ambitions in Paul and withholding the money for him to carry them out. It all added up, consciously or unconsciously, to a successful vendetta against the big-city world, epitomised by the Bryans of Racine, whose spend-thrift daughter had lured George Harris away from the frugal, God-fearing, respectable, dour world of Wallingford, Vermont, and whom Old Howard held in contempt.

But the vendetta was only a half-success. And for the moment it seemed a total failure. Paul Harris had not only returned to the Midwest and — almost — to the land of his Irish grandfather, where indeed his father George had been drawn before him; more, he was determined to practise the Bryan profession of law in a place which incorporated and magnified all the big-city characteristics abomin-ated by the good folk of Wallingford and hundreds of similar New England towns and villages. But even before that, before settling in Chicago, in an act of seemingly calculated defiance of all that his grandparents had sought to instil in him — caution, discipline, thrift, forbearance — he used up his few remaining dollars on a fishing expedition to nearby Lake Okaboja, and then embarked on a completely unplanned five years of wandering, during which he tried his hand at all the types of work his father had briefly attempted, and his grandparents loudly scorned. In succession, he took the roles of travelling salesman, journalist, labourer, factory worker, not caring whether he failed or succeeded, just earning enough to move on. He walked hundreds of miles on dusty mountain roads and hard city pavements, and worked his way all over the United States, as reporter, fruit-picker, hotel clerk, actor, cowboy and farmhand. He also made trips to England as a low-paid seaman on rat-infested cattle-boats, and later, as sales representative of a Florida firm, he travelled to Cuba, the Bahamas, and eventually all over Western Europe.

It seems an extraordinary odyssey to us, but many young people, even as they do today, took similar diversions across the world before settling down. Chicago's own poet laureate, Carl Sandburg, who bestowed "Big Shoulders" on the Midwest metropolis for ever, was to do exactly the same a few years later before settling down in the "Windy City" to write:

> Passing through huddled and ugly walls
> By doorways where women
> Looked from their hunger-deep eyes . . .
> I came sudden, at the city's edge,
> On a blue burst of lake,
> Long lake waves breaking under the sun
> On a spray-flung curve of shore.

This was its fascination. Like a fortification thrown up before its acres of squalid streets, Chicago, alone of great shipping cities, had ensured that its shoreline remained uncluttered by commerce and preserved for beautiful drives and parks. That glory remains today, even though it is no longer the world's grime capital.

Paul's vagabondage was a lone decision. In describing the elation he felt while enduring daily adventures, the exhausting journeys, the hunger, hardships and coarse brutalities of these years, he explained, "I was on my own at last". He was, he believed, exorcising the psychological strains of both the Bryans and the Harrises, which had tugged him this way and that from the age of three to twenty-three, buffeting his mind with two conflicting codes of life and morality, one a compound of feckless, gay, daring uncertainties, the other a cement-hard mix of unwavering, unforgiving, intolerant certainties. In this, he was wrong; the two strains had to be reconciled and they were, in the great Movement he founded. He caught malaria, and he may have avoided suffering a nervous breakdown. If so, it was only postponed, and in that sense, and that only, was he right to call his five-year sabbatical from facing life a "folly". To the extent — considerable, we may be sure, but unknown — that his wanderings reconciled him to his nature and his fate and clarified his future road and role for him, Rotary is indebted to his "folly", his courage in undertaking it and all those good friends he made, before and after, who helped him along his way with shelter, money and kind words. The Bryan in him was having its first and last fling. And at the end, the Harris strain saw that he struck his life-long roots as deep as ever did Grandfather Howard; though he rooted in Bryan soil. His years of "folly", which were really a quest not for the world but himself, led him to this victory.

In importance to Rotary, through its importance to the Founder, one year in the odyssey stands out. In 1893, his *annus mirabilis*, Paul Harris made his first two trips to Great Britain and then came back to the Chicago World's Fair, that "Columbian Exposition" which was to celebrate the 400th anniversary of the founding of America — albeit, one year late.

From boyhood, Paul had determined to see London and he willingly endured two hideous and degrading Atlantic crossings as a crewman on foul cattle-boats to do so. He stayed in Whitechapel, as Jane Adams had done before him to draw inspiration for Hull House in Chicago. It is no calumny to suggest that the rapscallion relished the sights around his "cheap boarding-house" quite as much as those up West on the traditional tourist slog. He himself described the neighbourhood wryly as "of exceptional interest to the embryonic sociologist from Vermont". Vice and crime were on all sides and immigrants from all over Europe dominated the native poor by the Commercial Road (the two favourite candidates for the Ripper murders were at the time a Pole and a Russian), which must have made an atmosphere very reminiscent of Chicago. He probably was unaware that exiled Communists were also all around him (they were the most well-off inhabitants of the East End) but probably knew that the Labour Party had just been created on the basis of its first Manifesto written by George Bernard Shaw. As a part-time actor, we can be sure he marvelled at, and maybe sampled, the rich offerings in this capital of great theatre, highlighted for a rapscallion by the show whose name was coined to typecast a generation of glamour, *A Gaiety Girl*. And there were shows in abundance to remind him of his peculiarly self-conscious destiny: Tennyson's *Becket*, about another young man who prefaced fate with years of "folly"; *Saving the Wind*, a convenient title to remind him that Chicago had just been dubbed the "Windy City" for its non-stop promotional success in grabbing the Columbian Exposition away from such rivals as New York, St Louis and Washington; and Wilde's play *A Woman of No Importance*, refused to the World's Fair as noted in the previous chapter, in which the Fair is wickedly

22

referred to as "an iron Exhibition at that place that has the curious name" and a dig is made at one of Paul's most precious beliefs: "... the youth of America is their oldest tradition. It has been going on now for three hundred years. To hear them talk one would imagine they were in their first childhood. As far as civilisation goes, they are in their second". And in Gilbert and Sullivan's latest production, *Utopia Limited*, there was a lyric describing Harris to perfection, as some were later to see him (it is quoted shortly), while its leading lady was, of all things, a fellow-Yankee Midwesterner of Scottish descent.

From these delights, which would have horrified Grandfather Howard, Paul's ship, most aptly named the *Michigan*, bore him back to another cornucopia of wicked big-city enticements. Paul left London for Chicago during the same sultry August that another young man, also estranged from a feckless father and beautiful mother, and likewise edging towards his destiny, at last succeeded at this third attempt in scraping into the Royal Military College, Sandhurst, only to receive a scathing put-down from his father, Lord Randolph Churchill: "I no longer attach the slightest weight to anything you may say about your own acquirements and exploits ... if you cannot prevent yourself from leading the idle, useless, unprofitable life you have had during your schooldays and later months, you will become a mere social wastrel ... and degenerate into a shabby, unhappy and futile existence." Rapscallions of destiny had a thin time of it on both sides of the Atlantic in the late Victorian days, and pleasant it is to know that these two young men, only six years apart in age, were both to live long and in old age would pay homage to each other's very different achievements in life.

Undoubtedly from that year's visit — though he would come many times again — derived Paul's determination that "London was the choice of all other cities". To win London to the Movement was Paul's admitted "grand objective" and he noted with great pride before his death that "the total number of Rotarians in that city exceeds the number of any other city in the world". But Chicago was always "Number One" to Paul (as its Rotary Club still labels itself today) and his visit to the World's Fair sealed his determination to settle there for life. The finest sculptors and architects in the United States had created a "White City" of palatial buildings there on nearly 700 acres of land and this was visited by half of the country's population during the 183 days the Fair lasted, the Mayor having had the foresight to make a deal with the crime tsar of the day that no one's pocket should be picked until its owner had entered the grounds. In addition to grand exhibition halls, such as the Palace of Fine Arts and the Transportation Building, a Bazaar of Nations one mile long contained, wrote a French visitor sardonically, "the Tunisian and Algerian café ... the Dahomey village ... a street in Cairo, a Persian harem, a German village, and an Irish market town. China has its corner and its teahouse, and Morocco its mosque. There are many Indians and Eskimos; there are two panoramas: the Hawaiian volcano and the Alps around Berne". But Chicago itself was bound to be the main exhibit and, to cope with this contingency, the Illinois Central Railroad puchased forty-one locomotives and 300 extra coaches, while a special factory was built by a gambling syndicate to produce enough roulette wheels to go round for the millions. Since these wheels turned within a block of City Hall, Mayor Carter Harrison took a personal and profitable interest in them. All the states had their pavilions, and in that of Vermont Paul Harris spotted two cousins from home before they spotted him and hastily left. It was a pity the Mayor didn't follow suit, since he was assassinated at home by a religious fanatic in the closing days of the Fair.

And all through these days of Chicago's glory, out beyond the "White City", the Chicago river went on packing the lake with its constant outpourings of sewage and oils and fats from the stockyards into the source from which the citizens drew their drinking water, along with periodic epidemics of typhoid. So thick was the scum on the polluted water that cigarette-stubs were known to float alight on the slimy surface, so what could have been more natural than that London's cynical crusader would reckon the lake was in prime shape for a Messiah to walk on!

When Stead's book came out, Harris was well into the second half of his determined five years of folly, and when he came back for good in February of 1896, Chicago was only starting to move out of its post-World's Fair depression. But he would have read the *Chicago Tribune*'s "Farewell to the Fair", in which that now-vanished White City by the lake was called wistfully "a little ideal world, a realization of Utopia . . . in which for the time all thoughts of the great world of toil, of injustice, of cruelty, and of oppression outside its gates disappeared . . . some faraway time when all the earth should be as pure, as beautiful, and as joyous as the White City itself". When Paul returned, he had not lost sight of that dream of Utopia, even though everyone else had, and in time he would see Rotary as the instrument of that dream, though — just as in the Gilbert and Sullivan opera in London — a Utopia organised on pragmatic, commonsense lines by business men with a sense of fun: "Utopia Limited", in fact, plucked from the Savoy stage and played for real. Its king would be himself and perhaps he recalled Gilbert's description:

> Of a tyrant polite,
> He's a paragon quite.
> He's as modest and mild
> In his ways as a child;
> And no one ever met
> With an autocrat, yet,
> So delightfully bland.

Always a tall, handsome fellow, Paul Harris had acquired a serious moustache and spectacles when he opened a law office in the Unity Building, one of those he had watched going up for the World's Fair (like much else in Chicago, it leaned slightly out of true, but was no less impressive for that). Elsewhere in that sixteen-storey block worked another lawyer, even then an extremely famous one, called Clarence Darrow. But apparently the two men never met, and neither of their offices became an object of pilgrimage. The office that did is on the seventh floor, right opposite the elevator doors. The number 711 is on the door and it was there that, nine years later, almost to the day, Paul Harris pulled all the strands of his life together and declared a new sort of Club.

Swivelling our eyes eastward for a last look at that other well-known Irish immigrant family, we may note that the Kennedys were running a saloon by this time, reaching a not dissimilar conclusion to Bryan's grandson that the way to win friends and influence people was through their alimentary canal or, as a later generation was to put it less elegantly but more trenchantly, their gut feeling. Even the thirty-fifth President of the United States could recall the days when "Pat the Tavern Keeper" was a name still known all over Boston. For his part, Paul Harris was to evolve what one might call a mobile tavern and with the same essential intent at first: fellowship through regular sociable gatherings for food and drink. It is no accident that the first Rotary Clubs outside North America were in Ireland. Though when Paul Harris formulated his plans he decided he needed something more stimulating than saloons, of which Chicago then had one for every twenty-six men and was rapidly boring the demon drink out of everyone. His brilliant solution was to combine worthy self-interest with hotel bedrooms and sandwiches, thus collecting many recruits who simply couldn't believe it was true. Nor could the hotel proprietors, which must have amused the Founder of Rotary no end.

The town of Racine might always be at his elbow, just over the state line, but Harris was not that liberated from New England grappling-irons that he could take the final step — indeed one bound might have set our hero free — so he had to be careful; just apprehending maturity was exhausting enough. Yet a voice might have spoken from the hovering shadow, the voice of the man from whom Racine had taken its name. Paul's literary enthusiasms had been for British authors like Dickens and Scott, Shakespeare and Robert Burns, but it was the French tragedian who had words to pierce his heart, had he known them, the words of Hippolytus, longing to turn aside his father's wrath:

> I with a fire am filled
> Banned by his hate. How changed he findeth me,
> Now, from the son he looked on formerly!
> Black bodings rise, and I would be afraid,
> But innocence hath surely naught to dread.
> I must away and ponder how I best
> May rouse the kindness in my father's breast,
> And tell him of a love which he can make
> Unhappy, but which he can never shake.

Harris really believed that innocence had naught to dread — of which his emergence unscathed from his five-year folly was proof — but he was experienced enough to believe in a belt-and-braces innocence and he armoured his solitary nature by creating his own surrounding crowd. Speaking again of himself in the third person, he recalled: "The way people lived was of great interest to him . . . but the way was not open and he lacked the determination and steadfastness of purpose to create an opening." He belonged to the Bar Association, the Press Club and the Bohemian Club, and he was a familiar, solitary figure at every ethnic restaurant in town. He strolled amidst the swarming parks and beaches near Lake Michigan. It didn't work. He took a place among the packed worshippers of not only his own religious denomination but among Quakers, Christian Scientists, Jews, Methodists, Ethical Culturalists, Theosophists, Baptists, Presbyterians, Bahites, and often basked in the vast comfort of the largest Roman Catholic diocese in the world. It still didn't work. It took him all of nine years to realise he would have to build his own temple and become his own apostle before he could, at one and the same time, be about both his grandfathers' businesses. And, for a time, find peace.

Finally, he even paid a brief summer visit back to Wallingford and sought the help of his Sunday School teacher, Miss Anna Laurie Cole. She talked to him and helped the runaway rapscallion, now well into his thirties, to "build a bridge between the pulsating present and the dreamy past", a phrase which only an innocent could write. That bridge, however, did not survive the return journey, and he set about building his own, a bridge that a million men of all nations round the world are still using.

His prospering law practice — he was not a courtroom swash-buckler like his office neighbour, Darrow, but, out of the Depression bankruptcies that uncovered many dubious corporations, he literally made his fortune in fraud — brought him increasing contracts but few relationships. Yet those few he endowed with a special aura. "There are a good many different kinds of friends" — it was a voice protesting too much — "but when we are in search of success, the friend of all the most desired is the business friend." If we are wise — and Paul was — we take care to find desirable the only thing we can get. Two favourite clients of his were Silvester Schiele, a coal-dealer, and Gustavus Loehr, a mining engineer, both of them sons of German immigrants. Gus Loehr had introduced Paul to Hiram Shorey, a merchant tailor. These four judged themselves "best friends" to each other. They were from small towns, all had their Wallingfords, and all four were desperately lonely, isolated in the huge city which had given them growing incomes but could not feed their starving hearts. On 23rd February 1905, a way was found of "realizing substantial dividends upon their investment in acquaintance". It saved three of them, but was too late for the volatile, brilliant Gus in whose office they met, No 711, the Unity Building. In a few years life got too much for Gus and he died of it, as Fay Stafford had died. When the past reached out to touch him again so cruelly, Paul must have felt that even if Emerson were right and institutions were indeed the lengthened shadow of one man, one man was nothing but the lengthened shadow of one town, if the man were himself and the town were Wallingford. What Wallingford had made, Wallingford must not be allowed to destroy, however, and history attests to Paul's triumph. Yet, before the weight of a million-strong World Movement obliterates Wallingford, it deserves our pause for tribute, who inherit where Paul was denied.

Harris had no qualms about settling in Chicago, in "the most wide open town that American had ever seen", as one historian of the time described it. In such circumstances, he knew the fly was never safer than in the web and, as a man of great self-knowledge, he made for the biggest web of all. As a Shakespearian addict, he relished the truth of Sir Toby Belch's pronouncement that because anyone was virtuous it did not mean a shortage of cakes and ale; and of cakes and ale there was an abundance in Chicago, and he wasted no time in enjoying them. When he came to form his Club he had the revolutionary idea of making his experience available to others in offering cakes and ale and virtue all in the same package. It wasn't till some years afterwards that he realised that, though the spider's web was there all the time, it was not the one into which he had ventured. To use the very apt modern parlance, Paul Harris was a very "fly" man in the best sense, but it took time for him to appreciate that he had guarded against the wrong web. Not that of wicked Chicago, but, as with all of us, the one he had woven himself, starting with the first strand back in Green Mountain State, whose official state bird is the hermit thrush. Harris's was always a hermit life, his song a lone one.

Where we love, we lie. And when our love lies in the past, as all loves do — and especially when it is first love and lies back the farthest — it is then the lies are largest and last the longest. Even to death. Paul Harris's last sight of Vermont as a home was in the autumn, when the Green Mountain State is at its loveliest, its many beautiful lakes surrounded by great masses of leaves turning all shades of red, brown and bright gold in the sharp clear air, and the neat townships punctuated by white steeples, colonial town clocks and backed by soaring peaks already tipped with snow. The trees which cover two-thirds of the state were filled with wild animals, from bear and deer to fox and bobcat, and Paul had never-fading memories of expeditions for trout and to gather huckleberries, and of watching the tapping of the maple-trees whose syrup Grandfather Harris used to buy in fifteen-gallon quantities.

Even today, Vermont symbolises sturdy backwoods America; it even boasts the oldest original log cabin in the country. Harris would remember that its simplicities were strong, its faiths rudimentary but unshaken. After 1776, when thirteen states had declared themselves independent, Vermont had held aloof as a separate republic until 1790; even though its troops had been the first with guts enough to attack an English garrison. The year before Harris had been brought there as a child, the Irish-American Fenian brotherhood had launched an "invasion" of Canada from Vermont, in case the British lapsed into complacency. Even in Harris's old age, when the beautiful people went skiing there, when the nation's most exclusive girls' finishing school was established at Bennington, and rock festivals were about to put the name Woodstock on the cinematic map, Vermont had changed so little that he took to paying regular Rotary "state visits" to Wallingford.

He had tried for five years of "folly" to escape its thrall and had failed. What makes Vermont so important to his account is that, by an astonishing effort of will, he recognised, but did not

accept, defeat, tried a different line of attack and made the thral-
dom his servant not his master. It was a victory which exacted a
fearsome cost later on in his lifetime and which could not last, and
in turn he himself was to succumb under the strain of that conflict;
by which time, however, Rotary, the sublimation of that conflict,
was safely launched. Meanwhile, it mattered not that, in Wilde's
words from *The Importance of Being Earnest*, memory "usually
chronicles the things that have never happened". Harris's memory
of Vermont, accurate or not, gave him the psychological matrix
in which Rotary was born, and it is entirely right that the univer-
sally accepted shrine for Rotary should be neither the mining
engineer's office in Chicago where the first meeting took place, nor
the site of his birthplace in Racine, but the small L-shaped building
where he first went to school — in its time also, and most apparently
a church, technical college and tea-house — and which is now
known as the Paul P. Harris Memorial Building. The harbingers
crowd in on all sides.

   The bells of Wallingford, which haunted Harris all his life, sum-
moning the inhabitants to worship, to meals, to fires and celebrations, unifying the community, because the Rotary bell which
governs every Club and is its most treasured possession. The moral
codes of upright behaviour within the home and business and of
mutual help and sharing with one's neighbours, became those of
Rotary. And central to Rotary was the belief Paul Harris expressed
in his final published memoirs of his youth, with his grandparents,
all of them at tables stuffing themselves with buckwheat cakes, that
"every well-regulated home should have one ceremonial meal a day
at which all members of the family could be expected to be present
and participate in the discussion of events and plans for the future".
In many respects the First Rotarian — though the stern old man
could never know it — was Grandfather Howard himself. The
"horseplay" of early Rotary meetings, however, which lingers in
many Clubs today, was the rapscallion's own idea.

   And that gives us the "key" to that emblem, the Golden Wheel
of Rotary. "I still see my New England Valley through the eyes of a
'boy'," Harris freely admitted. His re-creation of that vision in the
ideas of practices of the Club he formed was through those same
eyes: "The Salutation, 'Good morning, Paul!' which gladdened my
heart in boyhood days in my valley is now the greeting of my
fellow Rotarians." That first Chicago Club "was like an oasis in a
desert . . . dignified reserve was checked at the door; the members
were boys again". No reflection that the more beguiling an oasis
seems, the more likely it is to prove a mirage, ever gave pause to
that enthusiasm. The hazards of preserving boyhood capers in

grown men range from the clownish to the grotesque to the downright pathetic and dangerous — it is almost painful to comprehend
that his Club's first gesture towards the city of its birth was to offer
it toilet-training — but the successful surmounting of such hazards
only proves the enduring strength of the Wallingford inspiration and
its thrall. Vermont may be all gentle villages, fields, soft rivers and
mountains in clear air, but its valleys also contain huge granite
quarries and over half the statues and monuments of America are
fashioned in Vermont marble. And, as if to show objective evidence
that the source of Rotary was not just a feverish figment of Harris's
imagination, Kipling, settling in Brattleboro, a few miles from
Wallingford, just when Harris had left there for the Chicago Kipling
despised, wrote prescient words in his notebook: "America knows
neither liberty nor equality, only fraternity." And in truth Harris
always saw his valley through the eyes of two boys, not one. What
mystical, almost religious, power Harris, like all his countrymen,
attached to fraternity, for Kipling's observation was right on target,
was evidenced very near to Kipling's home. In Brattleboro asylum
Fay Stafford, Paul's first, and greatest "best" friend, died insane.
Thinking often of that grave in the Vermont hills, Paul Harris was
to write: "Perhaps when future generations think of Rotary and
the power of friendship, they will give passing thought to the red-
headed boy of the granite hills." That poor boy's real significance
to Harris was one of many mysteries of this strange, complex man
that we may never solve. But the meaning was lasting and unbreak-
able; it was immortal to him. Fraternity was a bond of granite and
blood. Thence rose Rotary, and thus it lured the world.

CHAPTER THREE

Rotary One

Hail! Cherished Rotary!
In purpose strong,
To thee in loyalty
We raise our song!
Loud in our chorus clear
Our tributes ring,
Hail! Cherished Rotary!
To thee we sing!

Songs for the Rotary Club

The twin slogans under which the World Rotary Movement was to
operate are "Service Above Self" and "He Profits Most Who Serves
Best". Both would make admirable chapter headings for a manual
on waiting at table and this — if we take them together with their
intentional parallels in the language of certain religious observances
— is entirely appropriate. Yet neither slogan was there at the
beginning when the food was probably better than it has ever been
since, and if the College of Heralds is ever commissioned to evolve a
coat of arms for Rotary, the most apposite motto to be enscrolled
across the bottom would surely be "Food for Thought". The
Reverend Sydney Smith once scandalised a dinner-table by announcing that his idea of heaven was eating *pâté de foie gras* to the
sound of trumpets, yet Paul Harris would have known exactly what
he meant, and this undoubtedly comes near to what every over-
earnest Rotarian conceives as the ideal of his last Great Convention
in the Sky.

Fellowship Clubs through the ages, as shown in Chapter One,
have always centred upon the pleasures of dining with friends; the
satisfaction of the inner man has always taken place on two planes

at once, the mental and alimentary processes aiding and abetting one another. While the fate of the post-Napoleonic world was once decided during late-night suppers at Holland House in London, the destiny of post-war spheres of influence is now debated over dawn breakfast at the White House in Washington. And in both eras, philosophy, art and global strategies were and are discussed at inns, bars and pubs by lesser mortals. In private homes, one waited of course till ladies had left the table; in Rotary, they weren't asked to sit down in the first place, since women belonged to the simper, the sampler and the sink.

But we are examining four lonely men, not great philosophers or political giants, and eating has always been recognised as a sublimation for uneasy spirits. "When I am in trouble," Wilde confided to those who chided him on his growing corpulence, "eating is the only thing that consoles me. Indeed, when I am in really great trouble, as anyone who knows me intimately will tell you, I refuse everything except food and drink." Paul Harris was never inclined to corpulence, so perhaps he was never similarly chided, but he lived in a city whose multinational nature ensured a wide variety of fine restaurants at all prices, and whether he was in funds or not, he became a familiar face at Italian, Greek, German, Scandinavian and Hungarian restaurants throughout Chicago. And it was not many years before he was able to afford the best. He was not the first, or the last, man to believe that being on good terms with as many head-waiters as possible is a prime requisite for contentment and status in life, but he was the first to make it a guiding principle for the Clubs of a World Movement.

His so-called five years of folly having been studiously set aside to enable him to find out how other classes and nations lived (at least, so he was later persuaded), his second odyssey seemed dedicated to discover how they ate. On 23rd February 1905, Paul's researches had brought him — as they had many times before — to Madame Galli's restaurant at 18 Illinois Street. He was in good company, for his fellow-diners often included men whose love of good food, good drink and good talk were proverbial; men like George Ade, playwright and author of *Fables in Slang* whose pronouncement that "the vague generality is a lifesaver" might have been coined especially for later generations of Rotary missionaries; like W.C. Fields, whose world fame then rested on his juggling, but whose well-known friendship with "Ed" (known to others as King Edward VII) gave a splendid example of first-name fellowship to the Club about to be formed; and like Enrico Caruso, who had become the world's first top recording star three years before, and whose frequent presence guaranteed availability of the best Italian dishes. Another famous patron, now dead, had been Eugene Field, who had combined writing the saccharine saga *Little Boy Blue* with acerbic theatre reviews — his comment "King Lear played the king as though he expected someone to play the ace" was soon to prove an uncanny description of the appearance and behaviour of the Founder of Rotary, for better or worse.

With the exception of the latter, all the above were men from poor homes, and they had no hesitation in celebrating their success in life by unblushing enjoyment of one of Chicago's finest restaurants; they had sophisticated palates. Both these traits were shared by Paul Harris and his companion that evening, Silvester Schiele, a prosperous coal-merchant, who was perhaps the closest friend Harris ever had, inside Rotary or out of it; the men were neighbours all their lives and almost so in death. One grave, however, separates them, and even as the distant resting-place of Jean Thomson Harris tells us something about Paul's relationship with his wife, so the not quite side-by-side interments of Paul and Silvester tell us something about his friendships — even at his closest with his fellow-men, the Founder of Rotary held them at one remove and the earth tells its parable to posterity.

We may also note here that the Vermont marble which has been fashioned to the likeness of so many great national figures has never yet been used for that purpose to commemorate its own greatest son. In which, one feels sure, the spirit of Rotary's Founder takes a very special wry satisfaction.

Men who are born to great wealth, sated from childhood with opulent larders, are often happiest with the most rudimentary dishes. Those who have worked their way up to worldly success usually take unabashed pleasure in the food and drink made accessible to them by their own efforts. As a result, they are on the whole much nicer company. For over forty years Madame Galli's restaurant had catered for such men, and we must remember that these were Victorians with Victorian appetites, whose grosser frontier tastes were in the process of being tempered by culinary artists from Europe. New Orleans, California and New York might boast more renowned restaurants, but none of them could flaunt so many — and, since gluttony and lust have formed self-indulgent partnerships through the ages, a city with 5,000 prostitutes in extremely full employment naturally laid on meals in proportion. The dinner menu at one establishment, for example, is recorded as follows: "Supreme of guinea-fowl, pheasant, capon, roast turkey, duck and goose, quail on toast, cauliflour au gratin, spinach cups with green peas, parmesan potatos, pear salad, asparagus, candied and plain carrots, followed by fruit, pecans and bonbons". You couldn't eat better in Chicago in 1900, and this was the Everleigh Club (not a restaurant).

The term restaurant itself for a place for regular dining had been in use only for several decades; the Paris original had sold only special soups for "restorative" (restaurant) purposes. And since over-eating had certain unpleasant side-effects, ladies were presumed to be as little aware of the preparation of menus as of the methods of catering to other male appetites. Hence, famous chefs were usually male, as were the clientele of restaurants. It is not surprising, therefore, that women were not expected to participate in the first Rotary luncheons. More so perhaps that the exclusion remains, but other reasons have buttressed the first, and those will be considered in later chapters.

So it is not hard to imagine the sort of marvellous food which Paul Harris and Silvester Schiele enjoyed in that early evening of 23rd February 1905. And they were there for another reason, which is stated with robust candour in the Chicago Rotary Club's Official History: "... it satisfied their desire for importance". Legions of Rotarians have joined the Movement since for precisely this very human, and harmless reason.

We do not need to imagine their conversation, the substance of which was often set down by Harris, and in great detail by others who were not there. The friends discussed in more concrete terms than before an idea which Paul had tried out on all his closest friends and clients over several years. This was to form a club for business and professional men which would afford its members both the regular *pleasure* of one another's company (in a social sense) and the regular *advantage* of one another's company (in a profitable sense). No two members, moreover, should have the same occupation; in this way, there would be no competition. On the other hand each member would have an obligation, wherever possible, to put business the way of a fellow-member rather than direct it to an outsider.

None of this will sound startlingly original to anyone who has become a member of any club of standing and tradition, for every club has an element of exclusivity, or there would be no point in its formation, a truth perfectly expressed by Groucho Marx in his pronouncement that he would never dream of joining any club which allowed him to be a member (it's of some significance, too, that several clubs have claimed to be the original inspiration of that remark). What Paul and his friend, buoyed up by Madame Galli's cuisine, were proclaiming was simply the *noblesse oblige* of middle-management to its own. The complete development of the idea was yet to come — it was several years away — and when it

34

did so, the true originality of Rotary would then be evident to those of its members who cared, or dared, to look. For the time being, what was happening was simply that two young men, still in their thirties (as were all the early Rotarians), having felt aliens in big-city life, were setting up a new passport barrier of their own.

We have seen that Paul Harris had been brought up in the state where you could find the oldest log cabin in America. His friend Silvester, a coal-dealer, could go one better. He had actually been born in a log cabin, and during harsh winters "home in Indiana" snow had fallen through the roof on him while he slept! Eager to prove his patriotism as the son of German immigrants, he had fought in Cuba during the summer of the Spanish-American War, as indeed had another man destined to become the main builder of Rotary though not yet on the scene.

Kind and generous, Schiele ran his coal business with true Teutonic paternalism, but assimilation into this turbulent society eluded him. He saw Paul's suggestion as a club for those who didn't "belong", and it appealed to him. So doubtless did the opportunity to decide that there were other people who did not belong. Ordering another course of Madame Galli's ample fare, both men discoursed on the lost virtues and simplicities of their humble childhoods.

Afterwards, they strolled over to the Unity Building where, by an odd prearrangement, Gus Loehr awaited them in his office with Hiram Shorey (Harris had by this time moved his own office to the Wolff Building, his business arrangements being nearly as peripatetic as his domestic ones). Here, with Gus in "the chair" behind his desk, discussion on the proposed club continued, after dutiful reference had been made by everyone to their similar beginnings in small farming communities.

Hiram Shorey came from Maine, so the meeting virtually resolved into two elements, Germany versus New England, and we can surmise that the German side predominated, since Gus Loehr was the most outgoing, volatile and extrovert character there. Harris did not refer to him in his memoirs as an engineer but as a "promoter", further describing him as "vehement, impetuous, domineering", capping his impression with the ambiguous phrase "the good in him easily outweighing the bad", without specifying the ratio. He was a wheeler-dealer, a fast talker, a man of impatient drive, and it is not hard to see why he soon removed himself from the little group and their little club. Indeed, as noted in the previous chapter, his chaotic business affairs, together with (we do not know what) personal difficulties, were soon to overwhelm him, sending him to an early grave.

What is hard to understand is the attraction between Loehr and

Harris. We may hazard three guesses about it, each in turn complimenting the other. If the tie were not closely personal, but primarily a business connection, with Harris's legal corporate know-how an essential lifeline for Gus Loehr's shifting pyramids of "deals", it would explain why Loehr was not present at the preliminary dinner at Madame Galli's. It would also suggest, however, that Harris felt Loehr's persuasive gifts were needed to draw in the first nucleus of members, his own not being sufficient. Thirdly, it would explain why, after only three meetings, when the club project was clearly gaining a footing, Gus Loehr vanished from the scene. Though Rotary's Founder never relished the front-and-centre role in life, that would not have prevented his jealousy of the possibility that the dynamic and garrulous Gus was rather putting him in the shade and that there was a danger of his being robbed of his brain-child from its cradle, especially by someone who perhaps did not conceal his belief that the idea was narrow and childish. (Harris would have taken the second adjective as a compliment.) It would also explain the presence of Hiram Shorey, who was there at the personal invitation of Loehr, not of Harris, no doubt for company while he was awaiting the arrival of Harris and Schiele from Madame Galli's table. Otherwise, it is quite incomprehensible why these four did not dine together. As it was, it represented a division of hierarchy, even at Rotary's inception, which was to bedevil the Movement time and again in later years.

Whether Clarence Darrow was at his desk elsewhere in the building late that night, we do not know. Surprisingly, he was to become for a time a formidable critic of Rotary, so perhaps he should have been invited!

Meanwhile, the four were friends, though not equally so one with another, and they made a satisfactory quorum. They had a tailor for clothing them, a coal-dealer to heat their homes, a mining engineer with fingers in many pies for nourishing diverse needs, and a legal brain to hold all the skeins together: the brain of Paul Harris.

Having served his purpose, Shorey too was to leave Rotary, though he stayed in Chicago many years longer before returning to his beloved village in Maine. No doubt he respected the Club but felt no obsessive need of it. The true nucleus was formed between Schiele and Harris. It was their true love and they stayed with it all their lives. And though Harris preferred to stay in the background, it was he who nominated the first office-holders and we find that, at only the third meeting, Silvester Schiele was named first President. He was altogether a safer, more predictable type of German than the "promoter" and it is after that meeting that we hear of Gus Loehr no more. The Club by then had quite enough recruits and propulsion was fast gaining momentum; the first-stage rockets could be dispensed with. There is a certain chill to Harris's final words on Loehr's early death soon after: "Dear Gus, you rested a while here."

Harris had a very individual idea of friendship. He always said that the germ of Rotary was formed in his mind five years before, in 1900, when he was walking (with another lawyer) one evening in a Chicago suburb, and he was impressed and envious of all the acquaintances his companion seemed to have in various shops they passed. He obviously did not hold the view that to be on close terms with tradesmen seldom reflects anything but credit. Later he was always quoting Emerson, to the effect that "He who has a thousand friends has not a friend to spare". Indeed, the words hung framed on his office wall throughout his life, though he sat with his back to them. He might well have included the complete quotation, "And he who has one enemy will meet him everywhere", for he personified the antithesis. Not that this made him exceptional. To achieve the first, one has only to live in a hall of mirrors; to accept the second is to live in front of one's own. Did Harris realise, one wonders, that Emerson was translating a verse by Muhammad's betrayed son-in-law, when later Rotary had set up its own Prophet and Mecca, with all that that implied?

Gus Loehr had brought a strident, vulgar touch to the Club, granted — a "pushy" quality from which Paul Harris recoiled but which he probably realised was indispensable to his Club's beginnings. As we shall see in the next chapter, this brash, aggressive salesmanship was needed again to launch the Movement when it started overseas and, in the same progression, though not so quickly, the "pushy" salesman there too was persuaded to leave when Rotary was well established. Though the second time it happened was in London rather than Chicago, and the circumstances were fortunately not followed by personal tragedy, the essential pattern was the same. In pioneering days, a certain ruthlessness is perhaps inevitable, an apparent callousness, and this harsh fact, combined with the protective shield of time, enabled Harris, in his last memoirs, to dismiss Loehr and Shorey briefly with the phrase "they failed to follow through".

Today, of course, reaction to a member's resignation would be diametrically opposite; it would be accepted that the failure was the Club's not the member's and an urgent, compassionate enquiry would be made into his personal difficulties to see if his fellow-members could help in any way. Back in 1905, however, in a Club where "members were boys again", the unconscious cruelties of boyhood still held sway.

While we are dwelling on Rotary's inception, its early hours, days and years — and it is important that we do so, since the seeds of all the Movement's later developments and aspects, all the harbingers of future triumphs and troubles, were implanted then — it should be noted that, in the manner of the "three" musketeers of Dumas's romance being really four, the Founding Four of the world's first Service Club were really Five and (as with Dumas) that that extra personality was a dominant one. His name was Harry Ruggles and he had been party to Paul Harris's dreams of a new sort of club long before that supper at Madame Galli's restaurant. Indeed, there exists some letter-heading of the Rotary Club of Chicago stating that the founding took place fully a year before, on 26th February 1904, and since the man who printed that paper was Ruggles, one might reasonably presume he knew what he was doing and that what he was doing was correct. Yet printers are uniquely placed to create instant history and Ruggles may merely have been staking a claim which others were tending to ignore. Fifteen years later, however, Harris was persuaded to ignore it no longer and wrote to Schiele, his dining companion at Madame Galli's, that Harry Ruggles's work "completely overshadows all others in connection with the founding of the Chicago Club".

It cannot be denied. Ruggles fitted the personal criteria of the Founding Members, in that he was raised in a small farming community and came to the big city when he was only sixteen. He had printed Paul Harris's legal stationery for some time and the two of them had often discussed (such as it was) the Rotary concept. He was a warm, gregarious man, and more than any other was responsible for the successful infusion of the "fellowship" ideal into meetings. He was a recruiter of phenomenal success. Above all, when he sensed, and sensed quite soon, that the Club was foundering under Harris's rather vague direction, since the inhibitions which had prevented members from making friends in Chicago naturally could not be made to vanish overnight by their simply calling themselves a club, he stood up and started everyone singing. The Club had been going for only eleven months and the innovation was crucial. Ruggles reminisced later that he stood on a chair, waved his arms and got everyone to sing "Let Me Call You Sweetheart". Thenceforward, at Silvester Schiele's suggestion, Ruggles proceeded to do this at every meeting, and the ploy worked marvellously. Inhibitions fell away and that sense of freedom and power which had previously been available only to warblers in the bath, became a group — later, a mass — phenomenon.

The fact that the particular song Ruggles recalled himself singing was not actually composed till five years later in no way invalidates the incident. His spontaneous action not only marked a turning-point in the Club's survival during its precarious infant days, but has ensured him an honoured place in the development of American popular music. No less an authority in the field than Dr Sigmund Spaeth credits Ruggles as a major influence in establishing community singing in the United States. No one, then or now, appears to mind that "Let Me Call You Sweetheart" was being sung by a group of men who resolutely excluded any sweethearts from their gatherings (perhaps the "sweethearts" thus being fantastically serenaded were not always the ones they should have been). The tune still appears in *Songs for the Rotary Club*, the first copies of which were printed by the obliging Ruggles. However, a far more likely song that Rotary tradition claims to have roused them in 1905 was "Hail, Hail, the Gang's All Here!", a number well calculated to rouse the "boys" of those early meetings, nervous of the city, nervous of themselves, nervous of women, nervous for their Club.

Whenever boredom or bickering threatened, Harry Ruggles united them all by conducting from a chair or table-top. Perhaps significantly, "Hail, Hail" no longer appears in the Rotary song-book, though all the famous melodies written in honour of such damsels as Sweet Adeline, Irene, Susanna, Annie Laurie, Nellie Dean — and even Queen Elizabeth II — comprise a large part of it. It may be as well, since "Hail, Hail" (to a tune from *The Pirates of Penzance*) did not come along till 1917! Neither, alas for legend, did "Smiles", also supposed to have figured in Ruggles's 1905 repertoire. All in all, it may be as well not to research too closely into exactly what they sang. The point is, community singing worked — and not only in Chicago, but all over America and wherever Rotary spread in the years to come. It did not catch on much in Europe — though Rotarian Sir Harry Lauder regularly included "In the Rotary", a song he had written himself, in his performances — but did so in surprisingly far-away places with older cultures. The most ardent Rotary community singers today, and indeed some of the most ardent Rotarians, are to be found in Japan. This was true in 1920, when the Movement reached Tokyo; it is even truer today, when Japan is increasing Rotary membership faster than anywhere else in the world, with the difference that now the songs are sung in Japanese. And it is thus interesting to observe that 1920 was the year Paul Harris paid Ruggles the belated tribute quoted. Harry Ruggles, who succeeded Harris as the Club's fourth President, was to remain its song-leader for fifty-four years.

It is tempting to wonder if the frequent sight of opera's great names like Caruso and Tito Schipa at nearby tables in Madame

Galli's restaurant might have played a part in promoting Rotary singing, so soon after the Club began. It is true that both Italians and Americans sing in the same way as they eat, but in doing so Italians demonstrate their natural propensity to exult in life, while Americans show their appetite to exceed at it. Far more likely an element was the fact that community singing in the States was a simple step away from frontier camp-fire songs and had the same purpose: to banish loneliness and keep night fears at bay in a hostile environment.

And yet . . . and yet . . . was it really true that "everyone suddenly burst out singing", as the celebrated opening of Sassoon's poem says in another context? All overdue credit given to Ruggles, we should still not overlook the significance that it was Silvester Schiele, knowing Ruggles's gifts, who urged him on. Schiele's German parentage would have made him very familiar with the Bavarian *Bierkeller* and *Biergarten* tradition of flushed and hearty patrons' bellowing out familiar choruses while banging foaming tankards on the table. Indeed, such men had brought the live and active tradition with them, as did all the other Germans who poured into the United States in the thirty years up to 1890, a period when they formed the largest national contingent amongst immigrants — at one time, a new German nation west of Lake Michigan was even envisaged — introducing not only lager itself to the New World but the idea of drinking it, plus white wine and seltzer, to the accompaniment of song and dance. One thousand Germans even armed themselves and took to the streets in Chicago's Lager Beer Riots of 1855, when their saloons were threatened with Sunday closure!

Wallingford would have frowned severely on such things, but Paul Harris, now free — at least, outwardly — of formal Wallingford restraints, would no doubt have agreed with the social historian J.C. Furnas, in his magnificent book *The Americans*, that "the genial, urban Germans had a genuinely civilizing effect on Midwestern crudities". Indeed, Herr Theodore Thomas, who started the great Chicago Symphony Orchestra, had only just died. The tradition was to meld with the romantic image of German student songs in the apotheosis of *The Student Prince* by Sigmund Romberg who, however, came from Hungary, one of two famous composers that country has given to Rotary, the other being Franz Lehár. And not just "image"; the custom of drinking champagne from a lady's slipper began in a Chicago brothel, when one of the Everleigh House girls kicked off hers during a dance on the dinner-table for the German Kaiser's brother.

We must not rush to the conclusion, however, that with the song came the wine, where Rotary was concerned. Even Paul

Harris's pragmatism drew the line at that. This could have been interpreted as a sign of the triumphant New England conscience of the Founder, or a sensible liver consciousness, or a combination of both, but consumption of alcoholic beverages did not play a part in those early meetings of Rotary, nor has it since, at least in American Clubs. As an incredulous reporter from the Chicago *Examiner* noted in 1910, the main motto of what he termed "rotarianism" was that "business and alcohol don't mix". The mobsters of the Capone era would never have agreed with this, and indeed in 1930 were master-minding a business turnover, mainly from liquor, of some $3½ million per week! However, in 1905, Rotarians were reflecting a growing opinion that was typically, if extravagantly, expressed in a pamphlet which referred to booze as *The Curse of Chicago* and raged, "Drink is powerful enough [to be] more than a match for the prudence of thousands", and another which posed the doubt *Can Chicago Live Without Saloon Revenue?* and denounced the shameful state of affairs which suggested otherwise: "The city that built the first skyscraper on earth . . . will surely build herself a better revenue system than that which is based upon the degradation of her citizens?" A forlorn hope that was in the city whose most notorious saloon-owner had the "Mickey Finn" named after him, with good reason, and in which a city alderman, "Bathhouse" John Coughlin, had as his private zoo's chief attraction in 1907 a permanently drunk elephant.

At this time, regrettably, it was not moral outrage that prompted Rotary's official abstemiousness. If such outrage may have been in the heart of the Founder, he was wise enough to conceal his true ends from his fellows — not for the last time — by promoting the phrase "business and alcohol don't mix". He could also have quoted Lord Stowell, that other eminent lawyer and Admiralty judge, a member of Samuel Johnson's club, to the effect that "a dinner lubricates business" quite sufficiently on its own. In any case, the Club remained consistent, and indeed in the 1970s Rotary International elected to office three World Presidents in succession who were teetotallers.

Human nature being what it is — and whatever it is, it doesn't come more human than in Chicago — the United States' second city to this day, however, thinks in perverse pride of itself as the town of Al Capone. Few Chicagoans have ever heard of the lawman from Racine. But the business community of the early 1900s took comfort from the most celebrated admonition ever heard in a temple: "wist ye not that I must be about my Father's business?" Nor did they quote from St Luke with any sense of irony or blas-phemy; one of the most popular books of the twenties was a life of Christ called *The Man Nobody Knows*, a fascinating prefiguring of the epitaph of 1947, pronounced in St Paul's Cathedral from the Second Epistle to the Corinthians (see page 12). Was Stead wildly wrong after all? Was "He" really there in Chicago all the time? The final impetus to examine behind the tradition of Rotary songs reinforces the suspicion!

For there was another very potent Chicago phenomenon, though it was one that was rapidly becoming national and international, which gave added strength to Harry Ruggles's conducting arm. This was the non-denominational "tabernacle" where Dwight Lyman Moody, shoe clerk turned soul-saver was nightly, if temporarily, rescuing the souls of conscience-stricken Chicagoans by thundering sermons at all the sinners who had matured in vice and corruption since he had started a 1,000-strong Sunday School thirty years before upon his arrival in the city. Every night, suitably chastised with threats of damnation, the huge congregations would erupt into the roaring, pounding beat of Ira David Sankey's swinging hymns, and since these evangelistic songfests were handsomely financed by Chicago's business men, who thus combined hedging their bets as regards the hereafter with the hope that music would soothe the savage breasts of their underpaid workers more effectively than union rabble-rousers, the odds are that not a few of the early Rotarians had bellowed their hearts out under Sankey's direction. Moody's influence on the town's rampant corruption — and he was another escapee from a New England farm at the age of seventeen — was as negligible as that of his more dubious disciple Billy Sunday (the popular song was perfectly right), but his and Sankey's demonstration of the power of uninhibited community singing had a vital effect on Paul Harris's new Club in its first wavering days and, through Harry Ruggles, undoubtedly "saved" that too.

There were no clergymen listed amongst the first Rotarians, and Paul Harris made it perfectly clear very early on that there would be no religious or political discussions at their meetings, a ban that remains. On legal discussion, there was and is no such ban, which is not surprising in view of the Founder's profession. Indeed, legal discussion, especially of the barrack-room variety, often came to seem the very life-blood of Rotary. Quite apart from the rationalisation of this rule, which was in the name of tolerance and liberty of personal belief, Paul's insistence on the point made sense in a city packed with followers of almost every religion known and refugees from most political systems. Yet while W.T. Stead titled his own grim denunciation with a threat, *If Christ Came to Chicago*, those who sang their hearts out for Moody and Sankey were convinced the Lord was probably due in on the next train. So when the printer leapt to his feet after the coffee had been poured, waving the song-sheets he himself had just run off on his presses, he was tapping in on a sure vein of response. The full-hearted singing that burst forth has never stopped.

For these lonely, unsure men, their new Club was nothing less than their salvation in the maelstrom of greed, violence, vice and corruption, that was Chicago at the beginning of the century. That atmosphere might not affect them personally, but it was in the air they breathed. Simple and naïve as most were, their practical jokes, loud laughter, shouted greetings, noisy slaps on the back, and now their tempest of song, all helped to still the voice of alarm within the incessant city clamour around them.

Apart from the zealots, of whom Paul Harris was of course the first, though destined shortly to be superseded by a more efficient and calculating breed — the ones who were needed to carry the dream into practice and administer the wildfire-spread shortly to come — apart from these, those early members did not philosophise their motives; but they vocalised them unmistakably when Harry Ruggles brought them to their feet singing. Moody and Sankey had shown the way. Business men responded at once, anxious to show their human face to the recording angel while W.T. Stead's warning still rang in their burning ears. They had welcomed with pleased surprise the new open-door policy of the collection plate. If they were not yet confident enough of full repatriation into the temple, and did not accept the tabernacle as an adequate (or exclusive enough) substitute, the money-changers were primed in 1905 at least to the half-way stage offered by Rotary. They had stockyards bursting with golden calves for feeding back their inherited guilt, and Service Above Self, when the slogan duly arrived, offered a near-divine means of expression. As has been noted above, there were no clergymen at the Rotary table in those early days — what cleric could coexist with that overwhelming lay prophet who had come crying his message out of the Vermont wilderness? The "Classification" was already filled, and the first to be filled, too. For five years, since Harris originally conceived his unique idea, it had been a classification in search of a club.

Even if that first soaring, stomping, thundering luncheon chorus, still echoing down eight decades, has lost some of its power to stir the blood today, it has lost none of its meaning, though Harry Ruggles's conducting arm finally fell back to his side for the last time in October 1959 when at the age of eighty-eight he suddenly died en route to lead some more singing at a gathering of Clubs in California. And the meaning of that chorus is a religious one, only slightly camouflaged by Ruggles's cheerful call that day (carefully noted by Schiele): "Hell, fellows, let's sing!" Hell? Perhaps it was "Hail".

It is important to establish this, for it marks a great difference in the way Rotarians perceive themselves today and the way the First Rotarians perceived their association. I use the word "perceive" because, by and large, those lonely, ambitious, lively young men of the Chicago Club — all still immigrants in their hearts, surrounded by big-city life — were not, in any profound sense, thinkers. They said what they thought, which thinkers seldom do. When Ruggles decided to introduce singing into Club meetings, to stop Rotary disintegrating as so many Chicago clubs, with roughly similar membership, had done before, his explanation was direct and incontrovertible, and he clearly thought it obvious: "It's no more than we do in church. It's the same in a Club." And when in 1913 the first Rotary magazine (printed by himself) was reporting with approval an address used to the newborn Glasgow Club, we find the phrase "the Rotary Gospel". This is elaborated into "the Gospel of Service", words with which missionaries of any Christian faith would have been content. There are those who deny such an inference, and they always quote Paul Harris's dictum that "Rotary is not a religion nor a substitute for religion". However, they omit usually to quote his following sentence, that "it is the working out of religious impulses in modern life", which at once contradicts the dictum, since if this is not the job of a Church, what is?

An early look at these Americans calling themselves Rotarians produced the following unequivocal, and far from disapproving, report back home from a visiting British journalist, S.K. Ratcliffe: "The Rotary Club is quite a momentous variant of the last century's revivalism. With perfect simplicity, a member will write that he has 'found Rotary', exactly as his father would have confessed that he had found salvation or 'got religion'." It is certainly clear in retrospect that the introduction of Club singing was an inevitable stage, for it is surely a natural progression from asserting that the devil shouldn't have all the best tunes to proposing that the crooks shouldn't have all the best business ethics.

From the depths of his own psychological needs Paul Harris had glimpsed a means of circumventing an impasse within himself. Quite correctly, instinct told him that by putting that method to the test he would satisfy a deeply felt need of his, as could many others of his age and background with similar needs. That first meeting in the Unity Building was followed a fortnight later in Harris's own office — he no longer needed Gus Loehr to make the front-running for him. Harry Ruggles was now present, and was ready with his first recruit, a real-estate dealer named William Jensen. There was also a seventh man, Albert (just call me "Al") White, a manufacturer of pianos and organs. At the second gathering the important decision was agreed that not only should members represent different and non-competitive firms, but that, in order that they should be in a position to give each other business, each member should either own or have high executive authority in his firm. After another fortnight the venue was Silvester Schiele's coal-yard, and the fact that he was the host for the evening helped Harris to get everyone to make the affable German the Club's first President. Hiram Shorey became Recording Secretary, Jensen Corresponding Secretary and Ruggles the Treasurer. Harris hung back once his great friend was elected President, intervening hesitantly just to ensure that the Club was called Rotary. It was an extraordinary achievement: he seemed to say nothing, yet all happened as he wished.

And it was happening very fast. The careful diversity of occupations was already agreed (it was soon to be called a member's "Classification" and the term remains today), and in Schiele's coal-yard it was agreed that "any members failing to attend four successive meeting would forfeit their membership". At only a Club's third meeting this was an extremely confident step to take and one for the new Secretary to minute formally as his first job.

In fact, all the Rotary basics were slotted into place before another twelve months were out. Again at that third meeting, President Silvester Schiele was giving a talk on the coal industry, to set an example which the others bravely followed. So the "My Job" talk became a regular feature, and with it the initial but positive stirring of Vocational Service.

By the following year a ban was already in place on off-colour stories, which is perhaps slightly surprising in view of the origins of so many members in robust farming communities. The Club also had appointed an "Official Greeter", Dr Will Neff, to make sure that every newcomer or casual visitor felt at home at a Club meeting. The first Ladies Night had been held at the Hyde Park Hotel, which was soon to be the locale for the most momentous — and secret — event in Rotary's history, which will be related shortly.

The first Constitution and By-Laws had already been drafted by a Committee — chaired by Paul Harris, of course. Since he was the "legal" member, one wonders how many colleagues realised that, even without holding office, he was in an impregnable position to say such-and-such a proposal would not be "correct practice" while approving those which suited him, all Founder Members still being his business clients. The other members of that Committee were another lawyer, Max Wolf, and the insurance man, Charles Newton, another veteran of that third session in the coal-yard.

Provisions already mentioned were codified and several added which hold to this day. New members could be elected at any meeting, a record of attendance would be kept, "Honorary Members" could be elected for one year, after which they would have to be submitted for re-election. And then we collide with dramatic and significant differences. Today, Honorary Members enjoy most rights of ordinary membership, except voting privileges and visiting other Rotary Clubs. In 1906, the advantage they were explicitly denied was the right to develop business deals within the Club, which was at this time the principal purpose of the Rotary Club's existence, apart from forming friendships — and these friendships were related to the deals. Another difference was the stern admonition to secrecy about what Rotary stood for, except when it was necessary to explain to potential recruits that "mutual benefit is the chief desideratum".

These were all valid lures, but as the Club grew larger and larger in those first years, appearing at different hotels all over town in the same bewildering style with which Paul Harris himself was still changing his home address (it cannot have been an accidental similarity), this secrecy was attracting some criticism, especially amongst those who could not get elected. "Business transacted at meetings shall be kept strictly secret" was now enshrined in the Constitution and By-Laws (a document which, as time went by, was to become as bulky, cumbersome and heavy-going as those stones under which Moses staggered down from Mount Sinai), and therefore Harris intended it should be there. For, like many who feel at odds with their environment — and he had felt at odds with two — Harris was a secretive man. As hinted, he intended to keep things that way until he had transacted the most secret business of all, which would transform the Movement and be a secret even from the Club, even to his fellow First Rotarians.

Before that happened, the Chicago Club had to expand and reach a certain stability, achieve a certain recognition and status in the town. Let us just pick up the trace again of those exciting early meetings through 1905, and the two years following, what we might fairly call the incubation of Rotary.

After the coal-yard, the tailor's workroom. Hiram Shorey hosted the fourth meeting on 6th April, Jensen's real-estate office the fifth. Harry Ruggles printing shop welcomed the sixth meeting and then came the turn of Al White, the organ-maker. But at that point the "rotating" between members' places of work came to a halt. White had never been an enthusiast for gatherings in offices, and was not keen to have his own put to this use. Members had been at their desks all day, he reasoned, and besides, growing numbers meant increasing discomfort, since few had lavish office space. He suggested that the next meeting be in an hotel and clinched his argument by revealing he could arrange this without charge. Since the room he had found was off a balcony of the old Palmer House, one of the most elegant hotels in town (and, from old photographs, with few balconies), no one demurred. After all, Rotary business over, they could always get their hair cut and moustaches trimmed in the only barber-shop in the world whose floor was inlaid with silver dollars!

From then on, the "rotating" went on between hotels and occasionally restaurants. Sometimes the Rotarians would take a room, or have part of the hotel dining-room screened off, or have sandwiches in one of the bedrooms. Madame Galli's, where it had all begun — indeed, which might well have claimed to have served the first Rotary meal — was not neglected, but the third hotel chosen, Sherman House, a block which contained both hotel and offices, eventually became the regular favourite and served members their first proper sit-down lunch. Thanks to the co-operation of the Sherman House, whose architect had also built the famous Water Tower (about which Oscar Wilde had been so rude), Paul Harris discovered he was creating not only the world's first Service Club but its first "Luncheon Club" as well. Located opposite City Hall, it might also claim to have inspired the Movement's first Community Service, since that public convenience was placed outside City Hall — perhaps the gesture was not an entirely disinterested one! At all events, when rotating had got a little tiresome and dizzy for everyone, the Rotary Club settled down for many decades at the Sherman House, where it maintained the Club offices as well as its meeting-place.

In spite of the first generous offer from the Palmer House, the fledgling Club had no doubt found it a bit awesome for their taste. Apart from that barber-shop, the flooring elsewhere contained 90,000 feet of marble tiling, and the manager's office was wainscoted with Italian marble, as was the reception-counter and the main staircase. These building materials may have appealed to that acc marble salesman, Paul Harris, but he may also have heard Kipling's acid opinion that its entrance hall was "a gilded and mirrored rabbit warren ... crammed with people talking about money and spitting about everything", and he would not have wished these words to go down to posterity as a description of his First Rotarians. Moreover, the remarkable real-estate genius who owned it, and whom the hotel (now in its fourth incarnation) still immortalises, had a wife who had insulted Princess Eulalia of Spain, the first female royal ever to visit the United States, by referring to her as "this bibulous representative of a degenerate monarchy" and Harris — while he could not possibly foretell that Spain would have the first Rotarians on the Continent of Europe — already had far-reaching plans for his Movement beyond America (plans his colleagues were not yet privy to, of course), in which such chauvinistic exchanges would have no part. None the less, in future years, when the Club instituted an award for distinguished community service called the Chicago Merit Award, Potter Palmer served on the first selection committee.

Another hotel which was frequently used by Rotarians in those early days — along with the Hyde Park, it was a favourite for Ladies Night — was the Metropole, and one can only bless the good fortune which drew their final choice away from *that* particular venue, since in the key decade of the twenties when the Movement was enjoying its most rapid expansion (not in numbers but in countries) and evolving its final shape and constitution, the Metropole was more or less the private fortress of Al Capone, the world's most murderous gangster. He and his cronies occupied fifty rooms on two whole floors, including a large gymnasium, and fitting-rooms where his well-tailored hoodlums were dressed to kill, and the foyer (through which some of Chicago's most prominent citizens paraded to pay court to the scar-faced monster) was block-aded by a small army of "soldiers". Capable as Paul Harris had shown himself to be of walking untouched through the town's most depraved areas in his search for diversion and diversity, one hesitates to reflect on how the Rotarians who had by then long taken over the Movement's destiny from his hands, but remained committed to "business and alcohol don't mix", would have survived the ambience. Or how Capone would have, for that matter!

As each new member was recruited through those first two years, the concept of diversity was rigidly adhered to. Following the lawyer, the coalman, the mining engineer, the tailor, the printer, the real-estate dealer and the organ-maker, had come the insurance man, the laundryman, the banker, the engraver, the undertaker, the architect, the sign-manufacturer, the ear-nose-and-throat special-ist, the street-cleaner, the decorator, the furniture-dealer and the florist. Their names, for the most part, are not important to this story; their range of occupations is. All of them joined during 1905, and several were to be instrumental in forming other Clubs through-out the United States. But what mattered, in Harris's words, was that "each represented an honorable calling differing from all others in the membership; each viewing it as a special privilege to be selected as the representative of his vocation". Nor was any time wasted in fulfilling the other purpose as outlined by Harris that February evening over Madame Galli's renowned spaghetti: putting business each other's way. Indeed, a detailed ledger of transactions between members was carefully kept. The benefits rendered to his fellows by the street-cleaner had no need of record, however, when one remembers that the streets were full of horses, pulling carts, carriages, and buses day and night! Alone of all the First Rotarians, that gentleman was undoubtedly rendering true community service. At the other end of the spectrum, the florist, genial Charlie Schneider, provided free carnations for everyone's buttonhole at each fortnightly meeting; though blossom-time at Rotary had to stop when the membership passed fifty, which was surprisingly soon.

For the most part, as the list of occupations shows, these were ordinary business and professional men. They were not tycoons, and it was three years before the attention of tycoons was drawn to this odd little Club, by the public convenience controversy recounted at the start of Chapter One. They were lonely men and simple men and they paid no membership fees. Funds came in from the imposition of "fines" (one of the earliest Rotary traditions) for lateness and other little joky transgressions, and their only expense was for the meals. By the autumn of that first year, when their numbers had reached fifteen, Sherman House was charging them 50 cents for lunch. By 1918, the charge had skyrocketed to 65 cents! Almost by definition the First Rotarians were shy men, and Harry Ruggles's songs (whatever they were) were designed partly to help them overcome their natural reserve. Yet presumably they did not burst into song in their corner of whatever hotel dining-room they were in without advance warning; if they did do so, we need seek no further for an explanation of their constant shift of premises. So was the rule that they would all call each other by their first names; even better, by nicknames. One was "Al", another "Doc", there was "Rough-house", there was "Boy Orator", even "Cupid" (he was the undertaker).

Before we leave 1905, we must consider one other major figure. Everyone called him "Monty", though his real name was Montague Bear and, fitting the prescribed pattern perfectly, he too had arrived in Chicago at the age of sixteen from a small country town. While still an apprentice in steel and copper engraving, he had made use of his beautiful handwriting by standing in a doorway at the corner of State and Madison, scripting special cards on order for passers-by, taking wise advantage of the fact that the most self-confident self-made Chicagoans were often deficient in the basic tools of communication, when bluff, bullets, booze, money and women had proved inadequate, which was not often. Twenty-five years with his own business established, he was doing the same thing on the same corner, but by that time Potter Palmer's Hotel was built on it and he was inside, drawing wheels for fellow-Rotarians. For the third requirement of Harris's ideal to alleviate loneliness in the hearts of small-town "boys" who felt they didn't "belong" in the big city, was an identity for their Club, a badge to solace their solitude, to armour them when they sallied forth again after lunch into the commercial jungle from which they had come. With Harris's suggestion of the name Rotary, a wheel symbol was unavoidable. Nor could it be abstract, since wheels were as evident as horses in the Midwest of 1905, whether attached to carts, wagons, carriages or bicycles. Monty Bear volunteered to sketch one in his engraving shop, producing at the next luncheon (by now these were held every fortnight) a plain, straightforward wagon-wheel. This may have been in deference to behind-the-scenes prompting from Harris (who was a past-master of the art), in memory of Grandfather Bryan who had gone on the trail with the Forty-Niners to California, but it didn't satisfy the others. What is certain is that neither then nor later did Monty intend the wheel to signify any literal purpose. Rather, he wished it to represent civilisation and progress (though since it had been introduced to the New World by the Conquistadors, it's just as well he didn't have the susceptibilities of any Aztec Rotarians to consider). However, the prosaic coalman, furniture-dealer and laundryman and their fellows wanted their wheel to be utilitarian. Fortunately, long arguments about key-ways and the number of spokes it should have still lay in the future, but, prompted by the streets outside, the immediate and unanimous reaction was for some dust to be added to indicate movement. Monty obliged ironically with a puff of dust on each side of the wheel and, for the moment, all were satisfied, even though this could imply only that Rotary was somehow managing to go two opposite ways at once. With the addition of the words "Rotary Club" curving above the rim, the Movement's emblem was born.

There were variations inflicted upon the wheel in the ensuing years, as not only the national but the international emblem were altered and various Clubs produced their own version. Some older Clubs indeed still stubbornly retain their own. Monty bore with the more idiotic changes patiently, as the Rotarians' stamina in arguing — sometimes with great heat — over numbers of cogs and spokes proved far superior to the medieval appetite for debating how many angels could dance on the point of a pin. Finally, in 1935 he wrote a very sensible letter suggesting the symbolic form it should take (four spokes for the four Founders, fifteen cogs for the original members), but because he designed the emblem in the first place, his views were naturally deemed completely irrelevant and of no interest to anyone. The present form of the wheel design is now under international copyright, and since any such continuing arguments would mean lawsuits and costs, they have ceased.

Having achieved its straightforward, practical purpose of encouraging friendships and new business, with its hearty songs (and an early ban on those with double entendres), its membership badge and occasional invitations to ladies to join in, the Club was well set on its way — only one man, Paul Harris, having any notions at all about turning it into a Movement, notions which for the time being he kept to himself. Though sex, we are told, is the most powerful driving force in man, the urge to sing must follow it a close second, and it was Harry Ruggles who brought in nearly two-thirds of the 200 who joined over the first three years. Even amongst that nucleus of "The First Fifteen", you had doctors to bring you into the world and check your health, a coalman to keep you warm, a tailor to dress you, a florist to help you court your girl, an insurance agent to help protect your home and family, a banker to tend your finances, men to furnish and decorate your rooms and wash your clothes, someone to keep you on the right side of the law and write your will, and an expert to bury you. On this solid foundation young Rotarian business men — and we must always remember that all were in their thirties — could build and quantify the substance of their lives. They began to realise there was no other club like it and that Chicago had the only one there was.

They did not know Paul Harris. The epitaph spoken of him in St Paul's Cathedral, "Unknown, yet well known", was as true then as later and indeed all his life. They may have been puzzled that he allowed Silvester Schiele and then Al White, the organ-maker, to become the Club's President in 1905 and 1906 respectively, but he had other and deeper things to do in those formative years and we have seen them getting done. Besides which, like the Duke of Plaza-Toro (only much more purposefully), he really did prefer to lead from behind because he "found it less exciting". It is ironic that the Movement which came to place such stress on leadership had its way charted by a man who dreaded its exercise. It shows his enormous strength of character and vision that he finally stepped forward as he had always known he must. Accepting that he would pay a fearsome toll, he was now prepared to take office, having fashioned the Club as he more or less wanted it. In February 1907 he became Rotary's third Club President.

He held firmly to the job, once he had taken it, because no one else, at that crucial moment, could lead where he wished to go, and he was elected for a second term in February 1908, taking the opportunity of his second inauguration ceremony to introduce two new members: Chesley Perry, like Schiele a veteran of the summer war in Cuba and now a librarian whose father owned a chain of stationery shops; and Arthur Sheldon, who ran an extremely success-ful school of salesmanship. Ruggles, the indefatigable and prolific recruiter, had introduced "Ches" Perry to Harris and the two, so alike and so opposite, were to strike sparks from each other. Both Perry and Sheldon, in fact, were to have an enormous influence on the Movement, but we shall come to that in the next chapter. For the present, it is sufficient to observe that they were the latest signs that, in his first presidential year, Harris had managed to turn the Rotary Club of Chicago's world upside-down and the fever of creation, innovation and, perhaps most of all, secrecy, exacted its inevitable price. He could not, even with his giant will, last out the second term and, exhausted by the strain of work and no doubt antagonism, handed over to Harry Ruggles after eight months.

Having played a part against his retiring nature, Harris had never-theless done his greatest task. We can appreciate it now as an heroic performance. That task was twofold. We followed the first at the very start of this book, the two-year fight to install Chicago's first public convenience, a project which took all his perseverance, patience and legal skill at handling people and committees. It also cost $20,000 by the time it was finished and (another typical Rotary touch) the money was not from members' pockets — they were young men, remember, with little money to spare — but dragged out of City Hall. There was a touch of Shaw's *Widowers' Houses* here, since, whether the Rotary Club knew it or not, a large share of City Hall's income was derived from pay-offs from Big Jim Colosimo and similar crime bosses and vice-lords. But Harris might have reasoned that if brothels could exist on property owned by the Church of England (which he could have learned during his stay at Whitechapel), sources of income were not always the top consideration. In any event, another clause was written into the Constitution and By-Laws in 1907, that a prime aim of Rotary was "to advance the best interests of Chicago and spread the spirit of loyalty among its citizens". It was called Rotary's Third Object, the other two being friendship with mutual business advantage and the requirement that members be "proprietor, partner or corporate officer" in their firms.

So civic service, soon to be called community service, was now the third name of the game. In the words of the mover of the new clause: "An organization that is wholly selfish cannot last long. If we, as a Rotary Club, expect to survive and grow, we must do some things to justify our existence." Well, the desired result occurred. During Harris's presidency, membership of the Club increased from 80 to 200.

But the total membership of Rotary grew even more, and in that (then) shocking apparent paradox lay the second and secret part of Paul's finest hour, though one which was to bring him into his first serious conflict with his fellows. Amongst the sudden influx of new members was Manuel Munoz, whose name announced his Spanish descent. He was another to be personally recruited by Harris in the spring of 1908, the latter's second year as Club President, and before the year was out it was clear that this recruitment had an ulterior motive behind it, about which Harris was less than frank. Not to put too fine a point on it, he was downright devious.

Munoz had a Classification relating to his job as a salesman for the Sperry and Hutchinson Group of factories, which manufactured the inventions of that remarkable genius Elmer Ambrose Sperry, inventor of the gyrocompass among many other things based on the gyroscope which revolutionised sea warfare and navigation. His name was immortalised in the Second World War by the Sperry bomb-sight (though he himself died in 1930). Munoz was also an old friend, having shared rooms with Harris at Iowa State University, just before the five "folly" years. The two men began sharing rooms again, and Munoz made a series of moves with Harris, as the latter continued his ceaseless shifting of residence that had gone on now for twelve years. And they talked of new plans, plans about which the other Founder Members knew nothing. They talked in rooms at the Hyde Park Hotel, then in a boarding-house just outside Chicago in Elmhurst, then back in town in a suite at the Del Prado Hotel — perhaps chosen by Harris as a gracious gesture to his friend's ancestry and to seal Munoz's agreement to be his special messenger.

Messenger to where? What had they talked about? Since one of Sperry's many inventions was a motor transmission machine for streetcars, it was scarcely surprising that Munoz went on frequent trips to San Francisco, then engaged on its massive reconstruction after the terrible earthquake of two years before. That autumn Munoz had an extra selling job to do, for suddenly in November — the month after Paul resigned the presidency, partly perhaps because of quarrels over what he had done — the world's second Rotary Club was announced!

Harris had triumphed where Grandfather Bryan had failed in 1849: he had gone prospecting in San Francisco, staking everything on the outcome, his prestige and popularity in the Chicago Club — and he had struck gold. The yield of the claim startled even him by its extent and flow: within a year of that mission West by Munoz, Clubs sprang up in Oakland, Seattle and Los Angeles.

Back in Chicago, Harris's fellow-members were taking their own seismic readings; they were stunned. Many felt betrayed. What had happened to "advancing the best interests of Chicago and spreading the spirit of loyalty"? Where was loyalty in this? Just when the rather aimless fun and frolic of the early meetings was crystallising into strength, purpose and a distinct identity, when membership was at its zenith and all had pride in the honour of belonging to Chicago's own very special kind of Club, they had been let down by the Founder himself. Chicago, it seemed, was not to be a special case; Harris was bent on setting up similar Clubs all over America, having used them as guinea-pigs, and clearly this had always been his purpose. Grandmother Pamela and Grandfather Howard would not have been surprised. The "rapscallion" had pulled off his biggest, most outrageous stunt yet.

But this wasn't Wallingford. He couldn't get away with it this time. Chicagoan pride was hurt, its faith in Rotary and in Harris disillusioned. There were murmurs that he was too autocratic, going his own way without reference to others. He had even set up an "Extension" Committee to monitor the spread of Rotary to other cities (and such committees are still called by that name). This Committee (to the suspicion of many who didn't believe in coincidence) was first chaired by Arthur Sheldon, then by Ches Perry, Harris's new and favoured acolytes. Their reports began to consume most of the time at Club luncheons, till one member finally exploded, "We are degrading our own meetings . . . I'm not much interested in what goes on out West."

Resentment smouldered and then quickly caught fire; it had to find an outlet. The crisis when it came was farcical, but fateful too. A meeting at the Bismarck Hotel — again an appropriate venue — erupted into a formal denunciation of the way the Founder was conducting Rotary affairs. Amidst uproar, an appalled, shattered Harris resigned, till it was hastily explained to him that the proceedings had all been an elaborate practical joke, such as those he himself was so fond of and so expert at perpetrating on others. Harris allowed himself to be persuaded, but resigned in earnest soon after anyway. And he was certainly wise to do so. The new Clubs out West were no practical joke, and they were there to stay. The "rapscallion" had been caught red-handed again, and scolded again.

His impatience had carried him on too fast. "Nothing", Harris wrote afterwards, "is more disconcerting than the blank look of friends to whom one's hopes are unintelligible." Then the admission (which at the time he naturally denied): "I soon learned that the best way to get things done was to do them myself."

But it wasn't the best way, not when your membership consisted of thrusting young executives of independent minds.

"Notwithstanding the fact that Rotary had come to mean to me something very different from what it still meant to some of them, our friendship remained unaffected." This was certainly true. All the same, between the Rotary Club of Chicago and Paul Harris it was now to be "never glad confident morning again", in the words of Browning's poem "The Lost Leader". Yet Club members swung into song again with youthful resilience, as if responding to the poem's further line, "We shall march prospering".

Rotary was never to be the same again, nor was the sometimes boisterous comradeship between Harris and the Club he had founded, but the Club determinedly retained and fostered its unique identity. No other Club, after all, could ever be the "first", and the whole onrushing World of Rotary would always see Chicago as the epi-centre. It would always remain the largest Rotary Club in the world, and its members would soon call themselves defiantly "Rotary One". They still do, and the name stays on their door. In seventy-nine years there's been no rotating of *that* honour.

CHAPTER FOUR

Rotary Two — and Romance

Hello! Hello! Hello!
What a wonderful word,
Hello! Hello! Hello!
Means a lot ev'rywhere you go.
Hello! Hello! Hello!
All Rotarians ev'rywhere,
Say, Hello!

Songs for the Rotary Club

San Francisco was an inevitable choice for Paul Harris, once he had determined to make the first extension of his revolutionary idea. First, there was the opportunity it gave him, already noted, to succeed where Grandfather Bryan had failed. This was not entirely subliminal to his self-perception; he described his new recruits thus: "Californians are hard to beat, particularly in games calling for co-operation. . . . They are true sons of the Forty-Niners, the most intrepid and indomitable of American pioneers." And by impli-cation, he saw himself as a true *grandson* of the Forty-Niners, of course, though irrevocably bound to the concept of Rotary being for the games of men-as-boys. He also knew California well, from his days of "folly" when he worked as a reporter for the *San Francisco Chronicle*, covering the hotel-beat, spending as much time as he could at the most luxurious of all, the Palace, then the grandest hotel in all America. He might have been amongst those who watched Diamond Jim Brady swallow six dozen oysters at one go. But if he did, his puritan soul was no doubt appeased by his subsequent spell of fruit-picking on several ranches, followed by a trek of some 300 miles across the High Sierras. Including his period of teaching in Los Angeles, he had spent eight months in the state, plenty of time to assess its potential for Rotary, which was in no way incommoded by the later destruction of the Palace in the earthquake. The smaller Sheraton-Palace which replaced it is where Rotary Number Two still meets today. Nor can it ever have been far from Paul's thoughts that here was a town named after a young man very like himself. A man whose relations had tried to persuade him to follow the family business, who had certainly had his years of spectacular "folly", after which he had also abruptly begun a new Movement which discarded worldly rewards. Paul, as it happened, lived about twice as long as the merchant's son of Assisi, though in Rotary terms we can observe that his active life was spent at almost the same age.

According to Paul Harris's own account, it had taken a gestation of five years for him to form his first Rotary Club. From the same starting-date, it took nine to form the second, since there is no doubt whatever (though he concealed his purpose from fellow-Founders) that he had every intention of turning Rotary into a Movement. But the second was a much more difficult proposition. As he expressed it himself, with Chicago, "the work was near at hand. To bring about the organization of a second club vicariously was another matter. The record of having organized one club in Chicago was not convincing . . . to believe that the same thing could be done elsewhere called for a measure of faith beyond that which might, with reason, have been expected". He, for one, had no such expectation, since he consulted no one else in Chicago at all about his plans, as we have seen. So what accounted for his own faith? Not only that there should be a second Rotary Club, but that it should be in San Francisco?

The immediate reaction of the Chicagoans held premonition enough to deter all but the strongest will, and they could not be flattered by the wisdom of mankind from Euripedes onward which maintained that second thoughts were invariably best. Even one's loved ones are always ready to hail first steps in life as forward; second steps can go either way. Given the intensity of Harris's conviction, which amounted to compulsion, the risk was enormous; it probably kept him sane. It was not till he saw he was right, and others saw he was right, that reason slipped. But how could he have seen that his justification would come so soon?

Looking back from the present plateau of 1 million members in 158 countries, the triumph is still hard to explain. How much more impossible must it have seemed then? Perhaps the rapid success was his greatest disappointment and the burden of his life, yet he could not deny it, even when it was staring him in the face. His courage was prodigious, all the more awesome for being mysterious to himself. Yet he drove on, though obstacles fell before him.

San Francisco was the natural Number Two. It had everything in common with Chicago; it had nothing in common with it. Amidst a brawling frontier mentality, there were outside temples of culture. Symphonic societies and great universities rose while gambling dens and brothels multiplied. Equally multinational, enclaves of French, Germans, Italians, Mexicans, Basques and Portuguese flourished. As the former city once formed the possible nucleus of a Teutonic state, so the latter soon incubated the largest oriental settlement outside the Far East. To Kipling, the town was as "mad" as he was to find Chicago "savage".

In parallel to Chicago's becoming one of the largest railway centres in the world, San Francisco had become the world's third largest port, and the topmost sail on its schooners gave Chicago a famous christening – "skyscraper." The Great Fire of one was matched by the Great Quake of the other; both cities, after virtual destruction, had rebuilt themselves in an incredibly short time, a resurrection displayed by the Columbian Exposition of Chicago (which had so fascinated Harris) and, in due time, by the Panama-Pacific Exposition of San Francisco. Before either catastrophe, the slamming down of a great golden spike had brought George Pullman's sleeping-cars out of Chicago and into San Francisco on the backs of Chinese labourers sweating east and Irish labourers sweating west. As the shores of Lake Michigan saw an Englishman (the amazing Insull) become the electricity and gas tsar of half the United States, so the Bay watched an Italian start, not another restaurant, but the Bank of America. What skyscrapers had done for the office, bungalows did for the home. Where one town put steaks on the paunch of the world, the other placed fruit salads. From one town came the Mickey Finn, from the other dry martinis. Both towns in turn were dominated by the glowering Al Capone. In Chicago, however, he glowered from a pedestal; in the Bay he glowered from a rock.

Chicago was the indispensable forcing-house of Rotary, and history must always accord that glory to it. But dearly as Paul Harris loved the vibrant, villainous city he had made his own on his own terms, he probably knew, even before he set up the meeting in Gus Loehr's office, that the flowering must take place elsewhere and had already made the choice. More, had persuaded himself that there was no other choice. Chicago would never have let Rotary escape (in a sense, it never has); only San Francisco, so ripely similar, so vitally different, could set the Founder's shy dreams free, turn a Club into a Movement, could lead the export boom.

More than one social historian has observed the "umbilical chord" which bound Chicago and San Francisco together. Together with New York, they formed the triple peaks of the American Dream, factual and Freudian. Even Boston Rotarians were soon to advocate the construction of a super-highway straight across the continent to San Francisco. The respect between Chicago and Bay City was mutual. Bret Harte, finding his journalistic feet out West, wrote dramatically on Chicago's Great Fire:

> Blackened and bleeding, panting, helpless, prone
> On the charred fragments of her shattered throne
> Lies she who stood but yesterday alone.
> Queen of the West! by some enchanter taught
> To life the glory of Aladdin's Court
> Then lose the spell that all that wonder wrought.

The "Gem of the Prairies" — or "Windy City", depending on your mood — was to regain its spell very quickly, and San Francisco learned both from Chicago's courageous energy and what it accomplished with it when the Great Earthquake came. San Francisco's new buildings that soon towered up in 1906 were closely modelled on Louis Sullivan's work.

That factor made the difference, where so much else seemed the same. Chicago absorbed everything, turned nothing away, voraciously lapped up the diversity of men. San Francisco turned none away either, welcomed rich diversity and returned it to the world even richer. Chicago was America writ large; San Francisco was the world wrought to new magic. Amadeo Pietro Giannine might have robbed banks in Chicago; in San Francisco he opened one. Johann Augustus Sutter was a Swiss bankrupt and con-man; he might have sold cuckoo clocks that didn't work, but instead built the sawmill that supplied wood for the first California ranches — and its excavations revealed the yellow gleam which began the great Gold-Rush.

There was plenty of crime and vice; here, after all, was the "Barbary Coast", and the name for the region was well earned. But it was not part of the fabric of life, just a corner of the pattern. When it got out of hand, politicians were not paid off, the business community sent the crooked judges packing, formed vigilante committees and wiped terror from its streets. The guardians of ethical behaviour sprang spontaneously from the prosaic combustible norm that held the frontier against barbarity — especially needful when there were no further frontiers before them, only the vast sea. The vigilantes were an extraordinary phenomenon; in needful when there were no further frontiers before them, only the vast sea. The vigilantes were an extraordinary phenomenon; in Chicago their brisk hangings would have provoked a vendetta through generations. On the coast, their activities were efficient and brief, voluntary and without masks. In later, more ordered times, their descendants still saw the need to maintain standards of behaviour, though without the old raw extremes. They made excellent and eager candidates for Rotary.

In contrast to Chicago's swarming immigrants, who were determined on their American destiny and yet paradoxically aimed at a transplant of the Vaterland, Auld Reekie, the Ould Sod, Little Italy, etc., the Germans started great vineyards in the valleys near the Bay, the French and Dutch the famous department stores, an Englishman invented the city's trade mark, the cable-cars, and even the Russians brought furs and settled a farming colony before leaving the legacy of Russian Hill to the artists and wealthy merchants. Whereas Chicago was an American multinational, San Francisco was an international enclave in America. Its citizens lived and thought internationally, rather than thinking American with foreign accents. Kipling termed Chinatown "A ward of the city of Canton". St Patrick's Church, often called "the most Irish" church in the States, was founded by the only priest in the city who spoke English. Kipling's reference to Chinatown could have equally applied to any of the foreign-born groups; even today, only half its citizens have native ancestry. And it was San Franciscans who built the first opera-house in America, the first one to be open all year round – Caruso calmed the panicking crowds during the Great Quake by singing to them from his hotel room.

It was therefore scarcely surprising that America's first indigenous literature emerged, not in the "cultured" Eastern states, where the great figures, from Fenimore Cooper to Henry James, modelled themselves on Europe and indeed lived over there for long periods, but from the dusty, topsy-turvy streets beside the Bay. Mark Twain learned his craft on one of San Francisco's newspapers – and there were more of them in San Francisco than in London. So did Jack London and Bret Harte and Richard Henry Dana Jr, whose *Two Years Before the Mast* was a classic bred on the Bay schooners. These were the men who first spoke to the world of America in the American idiom and did not write as expatriate Europeans. When we think of hoodlums, we think of Chicago. We shouldn't. The word is pure San Francisco, a contraction of "Huddle 'em!" which the press-gangs shouted as they grabbed another drunken victim for the fast boats to China.

In Paul Harris's mind was ever the thought of the first export goal of Rotary, a goal referred to again and again: the British Isles. No part of the Old World had been more crucial to creating San Francisco. Indeed, the area had originally been named New Albion by none other than Sir Francis Drake, Elizabeth I's rapscallion globe-trotter, who had discovered the Bay. Drake then sailed on across the Pacific, missing out on a golden horde far greater than a hundred raids on the Spanish Main could have garnered. Centuries later it was another Englishman, William Richardson, a botanist who took a fancy to the little village called Yerba Buena, "Good Herb", on the Bay shore, who reaped the harvest of discovery. Yerba Buena grew into San Francisco.

We have noted that it was an Englishman who invented the cable-cars. Edward Berwick, an English bank clerk, planted the first strawberries in Carmel Valley. Robert Louis Stevenson married in San Francisco, wrote of the area, has a monument put up there in his memory, and a bit of rock named after Treasure Island in the Bay. In Stevenson's words are the purest evocation of San Francisco: "Here in the flavoursome stream we meet. . . . May the good God see fit all over the world to bring together Italians, Spaniards, Portuguese, Englishmen, Americans, Frenchmen and Chinamen, to meet in friendship and eat in peace and happiness." Then we find Kipling, repenting his sourness, almost outdoing Stevenson when he writes: "What enchantment from the Arabian nights can equal this evocation of a roaring city . . . from the marshes and blowing sands."

The sailing-ships which, up to the end of the century, took Californian grain harvests to the world (dropping dirty laundry off in Honolulu), unloaded them at Liverpool, as fate had unloaded the Founder of Rotary. The ships that came the other way brought iron rails from Britain upon which history rode America to San Francisco's doorstep.

Irishmen (still British then, of course) planned Market Street and set the famous semaphore on top of Telegraph Hill. And the first villain to be hanged by the vigilantes was, alas, an English villain. The notorious Lola Montez, mistress of kings, danced her way into San Franciscan hearts without many being aware that the "Spanish" temptress was the daughter of a British army officer.

And many were the contributions made to the city of oddballs by the world's imperial home of eccentricity: the first of many Indian religious sects was installed there by a Londoner, Annie Besant, on the rebound from a non-requited affair of the mind with Bernard Shaw. W.T. Stead, whose comments on Christ's coming to Chicago we nave noted, said acidly of this particular San Francisco visitor: "She could not be the bride of Heaven, and therefore became the bride of Mr. Frank Besant, who was hardly an adequate substitute." The town's most extravagant and beloved nut-case was the Emperor Norton, who wore sword and uniform clanking up and down the hills, declaring himself Emperor of the United States and Mexico to anyone who would buy him a drink or several . . . but since he loudly advocated the building of the city's two famed bridges sixty years before they were built, perhaps he wasn't so much eccentric as thirsty.

San Francisco's most vivid memento of its seafaring past is the square-rigged *Balclutha*, moored near Fisherman's Wharf. She was build on the Clyde. Nob Hill, the town's most famous landmark, derives its name from a contraction of Nabob, the English name for the unscrupulous rich. Golden Gate Park, symbol of the city, was built from the sand up in 1887 by a Scotsman, who modelled it on English gardens he had known. He built there an exact replica of Kew – he was still doing it in 1943, when he suddenly died at ninety-five.

And the Bay City's – perhaps America's – greatest contribution to the Valhalla of Mythical Heroes, its King Arthur, its Roland, its Siegfried, has proved not to be the Marshall of Dodge but the Private Eye, invented by an American whose romantic code of honour and chivalry was, however, entirely imbued from his education at Dulwich College. Though, be it noted, Raymond Chandler was born in Chicago.

Looking at it with hindsight, the outcry of indignation by Chicago-ans on their discovering that a second Rotary Club had appeared on the West Coast seems extraordinary, for only ten years after its founding the Rotary Convention itself was held by the Golden Gate – and it was an International Convention at that. But a great deal happened in those ten years.

The outrage of the Chicagoans at their "betrayal" by the Founder – and one suspects that the scars have never fully healed – might have escalated to near-apoplexy had they realised that San Francisco would be, and the metaphor is sadly appropriate, but the first seismic shock whose waves would not only streak across the continent and back but would, within a few years, shoot to the surface across the Atlantic!

At the time, the local Rotary giant was certainly another lawyer named Homer Wood, the first convert made by Munoz amongst the business men on the coast. Wood not merely formed the San Francisco Club but by the end of the following year had helped form Clubs in Seattle, Los Angeles, and just across the Bay in

Oakland. In the proud words of the San Francisco members, "Manuel Munoz may have been the cap that caused the explosion, but Homer Wood was the explosion." It was natural for them to use such language, because of the earthquake which had devastated San Francisco just two years before. Yet there was a crucial distinction: whereas the havoc caused by an overlap in the great San Andreas fault was soon obliterated, Homer Wood's detonation rippled north and south of the West Coast, then east to New York and Boston, west again to Portland, Oregon, then by 1920 to the South and back to the Midwest where it had all started, until Rotary flames were burning in New Orleans, St Louis, Kansas City, St Joseph, Lincoln, Minneapolis, St Paul, Tacoma and Detroit.

Indeed, for a while there were two eruptions at once in Los Angeles, where a man with the Dickensian name of Herbert Quick leapt rapidly on to the bandwagon, appropriated the fireball and started selling memberships in an enterprise he called "The National Rotary Club of Los Angeles". Only a few decades before, California was teeming with firms which appeared overnight to sell shares to the gullible, but Quick was a man out of his time and, while Paul Harris raised his hands in pious horror, Chicago had seen far too many of that piratical ilk on its own streets, and its Club had been formed expressly to counter their efforts. If Rotary's burgeoning Constitution would have allowed it, Quick would have been lynched. Even so, Los Angeles stubbornly maintained two Rotary Clubs of that name for three years, after which they amalgamated.

Quick's example was not lost on an early member of Rotary Number Two, however, for Homer Wood's fellows soon included a member who had joined the Club in 1909, under the Classification of "Collecting Agent". An expatriate Irishman, William Stuart Morrow had arrived in California in 1885, about the time Paul Harris was expelled from the University of Vermont, in possession of a Gold Medal from Trinity College, Dublin, and experienced both in commerce and as the youngest ever Justice of the Peace in the United Kingdom. It may be that his welcome in the birthplace of the vigilantes – committees of business men dissatisfied with corrupt judges and bought juries, who periodically took law and order briskly into their own hands (which usually carried a rope) – was accelerated by an illusion about his role as a JP. Or he may simply have enjoyed the backwash of popularity left behind by another Dubliner three years before, Oscar Wilde – a contemporary of Morrow's at Trinity College – who, as in Chicago, had begun by drawing sneers and had then proceeded to outdrink, outgamble and outwhore the roughest trade in town, still of course a benchmark of manliness in many parts of America, though not in San Francisco where today the Bay vigilantes are more likely to be armed with handbags and floating on pot.

But by 1909 Morrow seems to have declined into a rather inferior Classification. He was soon to prove its accuracy, none the less, on a broader canvas and become in the process the real giant of Rotary from the West. As "Collecting Agent" for Rotary, he was to expand on Herbert Quick's example and the year that worthy consented to close down his "Rotary business" in San Francisco was the year Morrow saw his way clear to open up shop back in Dublin.

When "Rotary One in Europe" was formed, however, there was no outburst of pious rage from Paul Harris, as poor Quick had suffered. Harris didn't know about it. He was too busy spreading the gospel around the Midwestern states, igniting his own sparks at Detroit in Michigan, St Louis, Kansas City and St Joseph in Missouri, Lincoln in Nebraska, then laying his powder-trail north-west through Minnesota to Minneapolis and St Paul, threading even across the border to Winnipeg. He had Ches Perry with him all the time now, and he was in a frenzy of successful evangelism. It was as well the steady, calming influence of "the builder" was beside "the architect", for the psychological pressures were mounting within this tall, frail-looking Messiah. Within a year of the first Clubs being formed overseas, he gave in to worsening health and ceased to play any active official role in Rotary. For the remaining thirty-five years of his life, he rooted into a shrine and a figurehead. Though he spent the rest of his life denying intimations of immortality, yet, for all his late maturing, he could not deny the Wordsworthian progression. The Founder of Rotary had dwindled into a husband; shades of the prison-house had closed upon the "growing boy".

After her retirement, the great opera star, Mary Garden, wrote the following in her biography, trying to explain a personality which many intimates — if she ever permitted any such beings — had found baffling and infuriating by turn:

> Early in life I taught myself a very simple lesson — don't lean on anyone but yourself. I have always been independent in my work and in my life. I could never belong to anyone. I never needed anyone, and that was why I could give so much to my art. When I chose my career I resolved to crowd everything else out. . . .
>
> I never let people interfere with my work or influence me. I had very few close friends . . . for I wanted myself for myself and my work. Two months a year I had to be alone with nature, away from people. But that was solitude rather than loneliness. And from nature I drank in peace and health.

I believed in myself, and I never permitted anything or anybody to destroy that belief. My eye never wavered from the goal . . . I wanted liberty and I went my own way. Some called it a lonely way, but that wasn't true. I had myself and my music. . . . My help always came from myself, never from outside.

We are soon to meet Mary Garden in this narrative, when she and Rotary became briefly, and hilariously, "neighbours". She was a lovely Scottish girl and she arrived in Chicago in the same year, 1910, that Paul Harris met and married his own "bonnie lassie". But I quote her because, substituting Rotary for music, the words could have come from the Founder. They summed him up exactly — at any rate, inasmuch as he knew himself — as he frankly admitted in a long article which appeared in *The National Rotarian* the following January: "I have never felt myself under positive obligation to patronize anyone in Rotary, and yet I do patronize Rotarians. I can't help it, but I have a mortal dread of strangers."

The dread was very real; and certainly his fellow-Club members did in time suspect that they were, in the prejorative sense of the word, being patronised — and they resented it. It was his weakness and why he had to leave the active scene, or risk more damage by remaining. To himself. For to have a noble dream is splendid; to find it shared by so many a nightmare. He did remain always, of course, but as a figurehead. That, unlike Mary Garden, he did not have to remain alone was due entirely to his immense good fortune in meeting Miss Garden's compatriot, Miss Jean Thomson. He was "strolling through the park one day" when the idea of Rotary had come to him; that was Rogers Park in 1901. Now, in Morgan Park, rambling with the Prairie Club of Chicago in the spring of 1910, drinking "peace and health" from nature, the idea of love came to him.

Jean hailed from Edinburgh and was extremely attractive in looks and personality. As a very young girl, she had served as lady's maid in the household of Lord Charles Beresford, the brave and brilliant admiral who is most remembered today as having called Churchill a "Lilliput Napoleon, a man with an unbalanced mind, an egomaniac" — it was on the subject of Ireland, a subject guaranteed to produce unbalanced rhetoric — but who had in his younger days been renowned in London society for his wild practical jokes (the Prince of Wales, later Edward VII, adored his company). Jean Thomson had therefore had experience from the best circles of that boisterousness which was marked in Harris and characterised the early days of his Club meetings. She knew, in other words, exactly how to handle rapscallions.

She had come to Chicago to keep house for her brothers, who worked in Marshall Field's department store. Her sister Mary came over, too, and took a job in the First National Bank, soon to house Rotary's first official office. On Saturdays they also walked in the parks, and the two girls were with the same group as Paul in 1910 when he tore the sleeve of his jacket climbing through a fence. Noting the cloth was tweed, Jean offered to mend the tear, possibly under the delusion that he was the manufacturer! In doing so, she mended a great deal more in its owner's existence and they were married three months later, on 2nd July, just slightly over a month before Rotary's First National Convention at the Congress Hotel on Michigan Avenue (see Chapter Five). "Having no children of our own, Jean and I have adopted Rotary International," wrote Paul a long time after. This is not the place to speculate on the nature of their marriage, or on why it should have been so closely followed by his retirement from an active role in organising his great Movement. A later chapter will find room for that. Here we can simply echo Bernard Shaw's words to Frank Harris, "Do not forget that all marriages are different", and, himself a man of childless marriage who took a wife at almost the same age as Paul, his memorable passage in the Preface to his play *Getting Married*: "Healthy marriages are partnerships of companionable and affectionate friendship . . . cases of chronic lifelong love, whether sentimental or sensual, ought to be sent to the doctor if not to the executioner. . . ." Paul and Jean Harris's marriage lasted for nearly thirty-seven years.

The partnership with Jean took care of Paul, who might have died without it, and whom it contented and protected. It left no one to take care of the Founder's concept of Rotary, and we can only speculate that he thought his life's work done and that, more importantly, so did she. When he died, she flew away from it all for good. Here, another thought from Shaw will suffice: "The greatest sacrifice in marriage is the sacrifice of the adventurous attitude towards life: the being settled. Those who are born tired may crave for settlement; but to fresher and stronger spirits it is a form of suicide."

In the average man's mind, there are many mansions. In Paul Harris's, as with most of those who change the world, there was only one. And he did not wish to turn it into a doss-house. At all events, it was at this point in his life that Paul Harris and Rotary parted company. Yet his achievement was already immense and his exit unforgettable, splendidly managed. And he stayed around for another generation to see it was not forgotten. We find Ches Perry calling him (in deference to Jean?) not the Founder but *Father* of Rotary; and, when Harris came to write of those early days, he referred to the Movement which has always rigorously opposed the admission of women as his "charming daughter" and his "precocious minx". We can thank Jean for that. It must have been marvellous for the rapscallion to be able to share his past and greatest practical joke so long with such a companion. The great are seldom so lucky.

With that sense of destiny which distinguishes all great makers of history — and those even greater ones, the makers of social history — Harris, on his pinnacle of glory as both husband and National President of Rotary, was not caught unprepared. Since his resignation as Club President, we have observed his frenetic activity in forming new Clubs. Yet he was not quite finished with the groundwork; and since he could no longer count on the full trust of the Chicagoans, he concentrated his tuition on a flow of letters to San Francisco.

Throughout these months of his second term as President of the Chicago Club, which he had endured before breaking under his fellows' suspicions, Harris had kept up a flow of correspondence with Homer Wood. From October 1908, constraints were gone. Besides, the Westerners were moving much faster than their model in Chicago. Their very first meeting had been addressed by Charles Schwab, the steel magnate, and John Britton, Vice-President of the California Gas and Electric Company, and it was attended not just by a cub reporter of the *San Francisco Chronicle* — the same post Paul Harris had filled seventeen years before — but by its owner, M.H. de Young. This triumph must have been sweet indeed! And by January 1909, San Francisco already had over a hundred members, more than Harris had had when he had become Chicago's President. Soon it was deciding to meet for lunch every week, with a grand banquet every month. The same rules had been adopted as in Chicago, but with ramifications persisting on a larger scale.

Paul was ecstatic. In Chicago, he had preferred running affairs from behind the scenes; now he could run them from 2,000 miles away. He wrote Homer: "You will find that one of the readiest avenues to the hearts of prospective members will be the business advantage route." It seemed a harder, more cynical note; but of course this time the new members were not held by the common denominator of all being friends or clients of one man, a fellowship which reciprocal business deals then cemented. It was the other way round. Five members knew each other on joining, the weekly talks were given on methods of conducting deals more profitably and, at their first anniversary, members decided to admit only people who brought business in with them and to get rid of those who could not meet this criterion.

In another letter Harris warned Wood: "To mention the business advertising end of public work before mentioning the result to be expected by the public and from your work, would be to place the cart before the horse; but while your main purpose will be to accomplish something for your city, indirectly you will benefit yourselves, and men of prominence will be glad to ally themselves with you and your efforts." But he had nothing to worry about in his West Coast disciples. Indeed, the ex-reporter of the *Chronicle* got such a kick out of the large spread given in that newspaper of Homer's opening night that he had a thousand reprints done and flooded the East with them — we may be sure he kept copies out of the hands of his fellow-members in Chicago, however!

Not all of Homer Wood's activities could have pleased the Founder, all the same. Rotary Number Two set weeks aside for members actively to "boost" each other's business, the most celebrated "Boost Week" being one that urged all Rotarians' wives to besiege stores asking for a cosmetic called, rather unglamorously, Skin Jelly, a product manufactured by Founder Member Roy "Rusty" Rogers. It boosted sales astronomically. Yet Harris was pragmatic above all, and he was in a hurry. So the success of such schemes encouraged him to urge similar practices elsewhere in the other new Clubs now rapidly forming, and at the First National Convention in Chicago he even entertained a resolution that the reciprocal business requirements should be practised on a national scale. This proposal did not succeed, largely owing to Arthur Sheldon's vigorous protests over the twenty-eight others present.

Letters from Harris urging San Franciscans to follow the example of Rotary's "comfort stations" in Chicago were not successful; the ideal of service needed Sheldon's oratory. Homer Wood's Rotarians showed no great interest in public conveniences — after all, they had the Bay — but a downtown fire-alarm system was mooted and plans for a new Civic Auditorium. However, the notion did not catch on, the ideal of service became confused with public affairs in the political sense and from this arose the principle that Rotary takes no stance in politics or matters of public controversy, a stance still deep-rooted in all Rotary thinking, though one less and less tenable in a Movement nearly 1 million strong straddling the globe.

Letters from Paul were now shooting all round America to the new Club Presidents, accompanying those San Francisco newspaper reprints, and he kept juggling the two balls of business, reciprocity and community service, until he could draw the San Francisco-Chicago-New York axis together at the First Annual Convention. After Sheldon's stirring speech, Harris and Ches Perry made sure that another old classmate of Harris's from the University of Vermont, New Yorker Daniel L. Cady, made his impact there. Cady declared: "The Rotary idea includes all that is meant by the new business conscience and progressive business methods. It brings together people who desire to deal honestly, and who would not otherwise meet. It is co-operation among gentlemen."

When Paul went home and told "Bonnie Jean" all about what had happened, she must have been pleased. It made a perfect honeymoon.

While Rotary was in its first ferment of "Extension" from coast to coast of the United States, the members of Rotary One were counteracting the disturbing news from abroad (i.e. outside Chicago city limits) by stepping up their efforts to lay a firm example and foundation for Rotary practice and custom which would last. In this way, though their monopoly of this wonderful new "Club" idea, whose reputation was fast spreading through the city and attracting a lot of news coverage, was not broken, they were determined to make an ineradicable stamp upon methods of Club conduct, before San Francisco got there first — a stamp which other Clubs, no matter how many or where located, would have no option but to follow.

And they succeeded. Harry Ruggles followed Paul Harris as President, so the tradition of the Club singsong was guaranteed perpetuity. The wheel emblem was now there for the world to copy, as was the tradition of members' calling each other by their first names, and the custom of "fines" for farcical infringements of various "rules". The essential form of the original Constitution and By-Laws, as we have seen in the previous chapter, was never changed. There were some minor local variations. For example. Rotary Number Two accepted the Chicago Constitution word for word, merely amending the last Object, "To advance the best interests of Chicago", to read "the best interests of San Francisco". The other cities which fell early into the net reacted in the same way, especially out West, where the spirit of sturdy independence simply had to find outlet for expression, and we find these words occurring: ". . . and for the further purpose of encouraging the business development of the City of Tacoma and to foster a spirit of civic pride and loyalty among its citizens". But even that word "civic" was an echo from Chicago, where Rotary had been given its call of destiny by the British journalist W.T. Stead, after his investigative blockbuster *If Christ Came to Chicago* had made his name a byword (or expletive) in most Chicago homes. At a mass meeting following publication of this book, a woman in the audience had jumped up and shouted, "Give us a plan of action!" Stead didn't, having set off to fry other fish (and feed them), but a few years later Paul Harris and his three friends did when they met in the Unity Building. How that action grew and evolved, and slipped from the grasp of that founding quartet, we can illustrate by glancing ahead to 1911 and elsewhere in the Unity Building where, as previously remarked, the great trial lawyer, Clarence Darrow, was probably even at that moment burning midnight oil.

The following chapter will show how Rotary's Chicago structure and ideals were developed in 1911 at the Second National Convention in Portland, Oregon, on that so-distrusted West Coast. Here we can note ironically that 1911 was also to bring San Francisco's most morale-busting triumph over its Midwest rival, when its most controversial and colourful character, Earl Rogers (yet another lawyer and the model for Erle Stanley Gardner's Perry Mason), had to rescue "Great Defender" Darrow from a charge of bribing jurors! It is an episode usually omitted from the Darrow legend, not surprisingly, yet the Californian courtroom swashbuckler thus saved Darrow for his greatest years, peaking in Chicago's famous Leopold-Loeb murder trial — which was to turn, incidentally, on the evidence of an optician member of Rotary One.

Clarence Darrow, whether for that reason or another, was to become a waspish critic of the Movement. Yet in time, duly converted, he wrote in a *Rotarian* article: "Anyone who honestly and carefully tries to know about either natural or social phenomena, must start with a certain open attitude of mind." It was a lesson even he had needed to learn painfully when he tried to impose his Chicago style on California. Californians were indeed hard to beat, as Harris noted. And, as everyone knows, those whom you can't beat, you allow to join. So Rotary spread.

CHAPTER FIVE

Man into Men into Movement

R-O-T-A-R-Y, that spells Rotary;
R-O-T-A-R-Y is known on land and sea;
From North to South,
    From East to West,
He profits most who serves the best;
R-O-T-A-R-Y, that spells Rotary.

Songs for the Rotary Club

Whatever else one may call a public convenience, it is certainly a "civic service". With this most practical specimen before them and also perhaps now aware that their precursor, Ben Franklin's Junto, had chosen as its first project the provision of a public library (today the Philadelphia Library), Chicago Rotarians were anxious to do more and looked eagerly, almost frantically, for opportunities to perform civic service, though the more grandiose adjective seemed to prohibit lesser and individual kindnesses and the term community service superseded it.

A preacher without a horse was given a new steed, after much impassioned oratory from the ear-nose-and-throat specialist, whose speech, a listener ruefully recalled, was as fervent as if "he had been pleading for money to move the Statue of Liberty to the Chicago lakefront". His fellows agreed at length to give the preacher his horse, simply to get the doctor to sit down and shut up, a motive still frequently apparent behind many Rotary decisions, large and small. Fortunately, no one suggested the gift should be commemorated by placing a plaque somewhere on the animal. Plaque addiction was not yet a Rotary "fix". The same dedicated orator also successfully pleaded the cause of handicapped children at those early meetings.

71

The Club's next act of charity exhibits the all too human as well as humane aspects which fortunately have never successfully been expunged from the Movement.

On his way to a Rotary lunch, during 1908, a member stopped to buy a newspaper and, filled with new community spirit and civic pride, observed that the newsboy was not only crippled but had barely enough clothes to cover his shivering, frail body. The smallest sum of money on his own person, the Rotarian found to his dismay, was a $10 bill. Rather than embarrass the urchin — or tempt him — with such largesse, the Rotarian took the boy with him to lunch and borrowed a nickel to give him from another member. The lad then turned to go, his light of expectation perhaps slightly dimmed, whereupon his benefactor gave him the sweater he was wearing, after which, in silence, all members present contributed some article of clothing — shirt, hat, gloves, etc. What Paul Harris gave is not on record. What is, however, is that the newsboy left feeling much warmer than when he came in. But no less hungry, for no one thought of offering him lunch. It may be we are doing those early Rotarians an injustice — the boy's Classification might have been filled, after all — but no doubt the members fell to with appetite renewed from the warmth of their benevolence.

In a few years individual inspirations towards community service were to combine into co-ordinated activities towards helping the disabled, especially crippled children, and the setting up of Boys' Clubs and other Youth activities. This reflected their Founder's obsession with having a club where men "could be boys again", of course. Efforts, always in co-operation with other bodies (another Rotary trade mark), followed in regard to better housing, recreational facilities, Chicago's fire brigade and even the city band! Soon there were visits organised to members' places of work and, in 1911, the Club's first manufacturing exhibition which showed, amongst many wonders such as storage batteries, some of the world's first vacuum cleaners, a household necessity deemed essentially American but which had in fact been invented by an Englishman concerned with the dust on St Pancras Station.

Chicago had also been compelled to face its growing influence by a terrible gaffe in public relations, whose lesson many other Clubs have yet to learn. Its member who was classified "lumberman" chose to give a "My Job" talk at a lunch in 1909, extolling the virtues of wood over brick as a building material. Amongst many poetic metaphors about Nature's great trees, mighty oaks from acorns and so forth, he referred as a clincher to Abraham Lincoln's birth in a log cabin (Lincoln was the first of many US presidents nominated at a Chicago convention). This may have been meant to flatter co-Founder Silvester Schiele — in the home of the sky-scraper, no steelman deigned to comment — but dealers in brick rose in vociferous rage all over Chicago, via the helpful press, to ask why there was no Classification under "bricks" filled by the Club. Rotarians might have replied that in a Club so adept at dropping them, it had seemed superfluous. Instead, the next meeting passed a rule that "no resolution henceforth can be presented without having first been considered and acted upon by the Board of Directors". That rule remains and the bricks are still being dropped all over the world. Chicago had simply shown their fellows now popping up all over the country how to get themselves on to the diaries of news editors everywhere.

Indeed, it was only a few months later that the quote already referred to about "business and alcohol" not mixing appeared in the *Chicago Record-Herald*, whose reporter was chronicling the Club's first dinner under the man who had succeeded Harry Ruggles as President, A.M. Ramsay. Continuing its new-found flair for public relations, the Club had held its presidential election at the Chicago Press Club, much to the disapproval of Harris since he hadn't voted for Ramsay. His choice had been Ches Perry, head of his "Extension" Committee and already his chief confidant.

He needn't have worried. True, he hadn't got Perry on to the Club's first Board of Directors when he had persuaded members, during the last fraught months of his own period in office, that the Club should be incorporated. But Perry would make the Club Board in 1912; and, even though he wouldn't make Club President for another thirty-five years (at the age of seventy-two), he was already a proposed member, with Harris, of the six-man Chicago delegation to the "National Board of Directors of Rotary Clubs in America". *National* Board, already? This was Harris's and Perry's brainchild, for though, in 1909, there were still only six Clubs, Number Six was the key recruitment of New York and the "National" tag, they felt, was well justified.

One of Harris's original twelve Club members in 1905, it will be recalled, was a sign-maker. By name Fred Tweed, it was he, together with two of Harris's classmates from the University of Vermont days, who had now put Rotary on the East Coast, as Munoz had put it on the West. As with San Francisco, this was the outcome of much personal correspondence from Harris himself, so the Great Rotary Triangle of Chicago-San Francisco-New York was very much the Founder's personal achievement and deliberate strategy. Fred Tweed was also of course a proposed delegate for the National

73

Board, and rightly so. Rotary One might blink, but Harris's hand had always moved quicker than most members' eyes anyway, and now the four hands of Harris and Perry combined were manipulating plans and ideas so fast that Rotary One could scarcely perceive what they were up to. Clearly, they perceived enough to take small revenge by not voting Perry into their President's chair, but a far greater destiny was only twelve months away. In his inaugural address, President Ramsay declared, "Rotary is going to live for a long time." That the prediction was an understatement is entirely due to the man whom he had just narrowly defeated for office.

In 1945, two years before Paul Harris died, at which time Ches Perry had been retired for three years after his marathon stint as General Secretary, Harris, who had brought Perry into Rotary nearly forty years before, observed with typical generosity and self-knowledge, "If I can in truth be called the architect, Ches can with equal truth be called the builder of Rotary International." It was a mutual respect. For though the Founder, as we have seen, was so soon to step aside from the juggernaut behind whose steering-wheel Perry sat so confidently, the man who succeeded Harris as "Mr Rotary" never let himself or the world forget the Movement's true "onlie begettor". For as long as he wished it, Harris had his office at Rotary Headquarters, and there the pilgrims came, walking blithely past the door behind which the powerhouse really hummed. Ches Perry himself never wished for the smell of greasepaint, the roar of the crowd, any more than did Harris particularly, but he got it and occasionally enjoyed it. And thus he found himself recruited in his turn by the extraordinary man who had subtly changed places with him.

Perhaps a psychiatrist could make something of the fact that the first President of Rotary, Silvester Schiele, and the first General Secretary of Rotary International — each hand-picked by Harris — were both veterans of the Spanish–American War, in which one of Harris's brothers had been killed. Something, but perhaps not much, though nothing relating to the Founder's family can be discounted as an influence on his actions and motives. Nevertheless, there are rich psychological pickings lurking in the fact that the two prime movers and shapers of Rotary were as unlike the popular image of the Rotarian — or indeed his typical reality — as it was possible to get. It is highly doubtful if the Extension Officer of any average Rotary Club today would dream of either of them as likely candidates for membership. There were only four years between them, Perry being a native Chicagoan, born on 12th September 1872, the year after Paul Harris was removed from nearby Racine to Vermont, and the year after the Great Fire had removed great chunks of Chicago from existence. Perry's life, therefore, coincided with the rebirth of his home town and it soon became clear that the tremendous surge of construction and determination to build better than before which suffused Chicago insinuated itself into his own character. It is no chance coincidence that for a number of years he combined running the administration of Rotary with running a cement brick business.

Like Chicago and San Francisco, their Club parallels as Rotary One and Rotary Two, Paul and Chesley — whom everyone would now call simply Ches — were at once very alike and very unalike. There is no point in labouring this common enough paradox, and we have already explored the background and character of Rotary's Founder. Yet the paradox lies at the heart of the Movement's success, and must be comprehended.

Ches Perry was, if anything, more shy and introverted than Paul Harris. It was Paul the Apostle who was in time to be sent to rekindle the flame of fellowship round the world, against all his inclinations, while Ches remained sheltered behind the ramparts of the Secretariat he was building round himself. Yet Ches had a far more stable family background than had Paul, and no worries about money or career. If he had won no academic laurels, he had proved an outstanding athlete at school, from field games to hunting, shooting and riding. He had always been a manager, always a man in control. He had run the school baseball and football teams, and later had even been President of Cook County baseball and football leagues, too (Capone was Cook County's most notorious wielder of baseball bats, but tended to use them at banquets). While Paul had conformed, subduing his rebellious nature until he had earned his law degree, after which he took off on his five-year "folly", Ches hadn't moved from the Chicago streets, first working in his father's stationery stores and then getting his head down in the Chicago Public Library (established the year of his birth). Here he accumulated, through voracious reading, a wide range of knowledge. His athletic aptitudes and methods of self-education startlingly resembled those attributed to himself by the young Winston Churchill, and indeed he seems to have deliberately prepared himself for his destiny with similar care. In 1898, Ches Perry experienced battle in Cuba both as soldier and journalist (for the *Chicago Times Herald*), and coincidentally Churchill had been there only a few months before in a similar dual role (much to the simulated rage and disgust of papers he wasn't writing for).

Ches Perry came home unscathed as a lieutenant, with fluency in Spanish and a military bearing which was to intimidate others and effectively mask his insecurities for the rest of his life, one which he was to dedicate wholly to Rotary as a monk does his to the cloister. He joined Rotary at the age of thirty-six, Harris having started it when he was thirty-seven. He didn't require conversion; he grasped at once from his first moment of induction what Rotary could do, the void Rotary could fill, in his own life, in the lives of others, the dreams Paul Harris dreamed.

But we do not always thank the man who translates our dreams into reality, and Harris did not thank Ches Perry. The tall, stooping lawyer did not thank, or respond easily to, those unwavering, penetrating eyes which unnerved most people upon whom their gaze was turned and which perhaps saw deeper into Harris than Harris cared they should. Years later, the recollection would make him smile: "No one could by the widest stretch of the imagination say that Ches and I were chums. . . ." And even though they had desks near each other at Headquarters, they "seldom went to lunch together. Often I would have hailed the opportunity to spend an hour with Ches at noon time talking over the happenings of the day, but that was not to be". It is clear from these words whose choice it was that the distance was kept. And yet one is left wondering who was more afraid and who stood in greater awe of the other, until Jean stepped between them.

By the beginning of 1910 everything was happening too fast, all was far too exciting, for such thoughts to be in either of those busy brains. Through his network of associates in law, of old college chums, Harris was striking while the iron was hot with the white heat of inspiration and zeal to establish Rotary on a national scale before the Chicago Rotarians could take it all in. Perry was working out the structure, fitting in the pieces even as they sprouted from Harris's original conception, imposing a necessary order on that tumble of genius. Harris, he saw, could not keep the frenetic pace of expansion up for long and, when he paused, the constitutional framework had to be ready. And it is a measure of Harris's greatness that no thought of envy or rivalry entered his soul when Perry observed, "As Rotary grows in membership, the necessity for more definitive principles and more positive adherence to them becomes more essential, for . . . there may be a diffusion that leads to impotence."

It is greatly to the Chicago Club's President's credit (the same Ramsay by whom Perry had so recently been defeated) that when he saw the power which was being generated by these two men, Harris and Perry, who at that moment held no executive office whatever, he decided that if Chicago couldn't beat Rotary extension, it must join it and assume the lead, or risk obliteration. "There are responsibilities which we as the parent Club should assume," said Ramsay. "We must adopt standards and recommend them for the use of every Club organized . . . with a chain of Rotary Clubs from the Atlantic to the Pacific, we could wield a mighty power indeed. Therefore, let us combine in a good, strong push."

It was like pushing a runaway train, but what Ramsay said was wise and pragmatic. Brave also, since the Chicago Club was still not happy, even though the "National Board of Directors" was setting up the first Convention to be held in their city. Nor was the Club happy that Ramsay was pushing for its own Founder to be the National President — it was still wincing from the shock of San Francisco two years before.

Carried away by his passionate enthusiasm (for other things than Rotary, as we have seen), Harris grandly informed the press in June, "The National Association of Rotary Clubs will be one of the most powerful factors in the civic life of the nation", and hinted that a total of 4,000 delegates were expected. In fact, the total Rotarian membership then was no more than 1,800, but Perry left such booster tactics in public relations to Harris, and got on with organising, and that historic First National Convention began on 15th August 1910 under Perry's chairmanship, with delegates from all sixteen Clubs. Held at the Congress Hotel (now the Pick-Congress) it lasted for three days, at the end of which a National Constitution and By-Laws had been agreed, Ches Perry had been elected Secretary of what was now officially called the National Association of Rotary Clubs, and Paul — not without some last-ditch opposition from Chicago — was named Rotary's first National President. "I don't know how any person could be presented a greater gift," declared Paul, flustered but pleased, and no doubt much relieved to hear unanimous support then given a resolution proposed by (of all delegates) a West Coast Rotarian, from Los Angeles, which praised Chicago "for having started this Movement". Whether the hand of Ches Perry was behind the resolution we can only surmise, but the Convention also agreed that their unanimous gratitude be suitably engraved in permanent form and presented to the Chicago Rotarians — and the complaints on Lake Michigan were effectively stifled.

Orchestrated or not, Chicagoans could not help but be further mollified when the laudatory West Coast speech was followed, and even topped, by a speaker from the East Coast, a New York delegate who roundly declaimed, "within 101 years the Rotary Wheel, radiating from the Club in Chicago, will have a thousand supporting spokes!" Chicago men, while confident of requiring no support whatever, were the sort to appreciate that touch of adding one to the century, and rewarded the speech with applause that resounded through the Congress Hotel and perhaps caused some alarm next door in the massive Auditorium Building, one of Louis Sullivan's more monumental efforts which had experienced many foundation problems from sheer weight, being so near the lakeshore.

But the most memorable words at that first Convention were spoken by Arthur Sheldon. Again, with Ches Perry as Chairman, it was auspiciously — indeed suspiciously — well timed.

Arthur Frederick Sheldon had first met Perry, and perhaps contributed to his education, when he sold the assiduous bookworm a set of encyclopedias during Perry's spell at the Chicago Public Library, and we have seen that Paul Harris brought them into Rotary together, noting what a formidable pair they made. Sheldon's arrival signalled the second influence upon Rotary exercised by those Moody-Sankey meetings of the nineties. Harry Ruggles had borrowed their community singing. Now, as Harris himself wrote, came "an evangelist in the realm of business, as Dwight L. Moody had been in the world of religion".

I don't think Paul Harris ever doubted the magnitude of his own achievement and inspiration, first in his conception of his Service Club idea and then in its realisation as Rotary. He was aware of the misconstructions which would be put upon his aims, sometimes wilfully, and he was from the first aware that his fellow-Rotarians would have to have personal ideals and convictions about the role of his new Movement "revealed" to them in discreet rations. And, as full of courageous self-knowledge as any man could be, Harris knew that his unique gifts of romantic exposition and exuberant enthusiasms (the Bryan "Irish" inheritance) combined with no-nonsense, even ruthless, practical sense of the possible (his "New England" Harris strain), could manage alone just for so long.

The "rapscallion" could happily spur along the high spirits and horseplay of the first two years. The prosaic member of the Chicago Chamber of Commerce could pass on the news that civic alarm was growing over the lack of public conveniences and get the young business men who were his unwitting shock-troops to form a United Societies Committee for Public Comfort Stations. That was still fun; boys were still being boys. But when Harris started to implement his plan to spread, to form Rotary Clubs elsewhere, to emphasise the service aspect of his brand of what he called "clubdom" (which was manifestly unlike anyone else's in Chicago), he had taken over the presidency and enlisted the aid of Perry as the strong-man builder and Arthur Sheldon as the big-sell expert, a man who had already "captained characteristic Chicago revolts against unrighteousness", Paul noted.

Chicago's first public lavatory, as we saw at the start, was outside City Hall. Ches Perry's prompt influence on his fellows can be gauged by the fact that the Club's second project was another toilet — in Perry's Public Library. Sheldon's influence is revealed in what he said at that First National Convention, where he unveiled the aphorism which (so he always claimed) had come to him in a barber's chair. "It is our blessed privilege", said the President of the Sheldon School of Business Building (claiming 60,000 students nation-wide), "to be standing in the glow of the early morning of this 20th Century upon which the light of wisdom is beginning to shine . . . as man comes into the light of wisdom, he comes to see that only the science of right conduct towards others pays. He comes to see that the science of business is the science of human service. He comes to see that he profits most who serves his fellows best."

As Sheldon was speaking during the final banquet at the Congress Hotel, those final words did not perhaps register as strongly as he intended. He wasn't dismayed. He was to repeat them the following year at Portland, Oregon, during the Second National Convention. But there already, in August 1910, he had spoken the phrase which has appeared on Rotary headed notepaper of Clubs all over the world ever since.

As head of an institution which taught "The Science of Salesmanship" and "The Science of Business Building", Sheldon was of course conscious of the value of repetition. He was also quite conscious of his powers, which lost nothing from his formidable appearance. "An ugly, sloppy sort of man," noted the historian of the Rotary Club of Edinburgh two years later, "on the lines of Dr. Johnson or G.K. Chesterton: but what an orator!"

The effect of that oratory and that presence was soon in the process of being dramatically proved in Des Moines, Iowa, and Omaha, Nebraska, where two business clubs Sheldon had organised in those towns were about to become Rotary Clubs overnight without any apparent change of aim or rules. Armoured in successful righteousness, and standing complacently with that famous haircut of his in the glow of a good brandy and cigar, how was he to know that the light of wisdom suffusing modern man was in four years, almost exactly, to destroy a generation before the guns of another August? Yet there were guns, nearer home, destined to have a far-reaching moral effect on the world long after the idealistic warriors of the First World War had gone singing over the parapets to their doom. For 1910 also brought to Chicago one Johnny Torrio, initially to be Big Jim Colosimo's bodyguard but ultimately to bring "the science of business" into Chicago crime as history had never seen it done before (Torrio's own bodyguard was Capone and he died in bed). Moreover, on the second day of the Convention, the General Superintendent of Police had received a detailed census on brothels in the city for submission to a Vice Commission, whose eventual Report was adjudged too shocking even to be permitted through the US mails.

Did Sheldon know nothing of all this? Did none of them? If not, they did not read newspapers. Chicago at the time did indeed have a "reforming" mayor, one who helped save the spectacular lake-front. But Fred Busse was a reforming mayor only by local standards. He was a large, vulgar, foul-mouthed coal-merchant who extended the opening hours (against the law) of his own favourite bar, looked the other way when gangster friends murdered policemen and owned the major shareholding of the firm which supplied Chicago with manhole-covers. One of his opponents' principal accusations against him was, regrettably, that he was too close to "business interests". Regrettably, because the same criticism was being made of that new National Association meeting in the Congress Hotel.

Nor could that Rotary audience — though in fairness we must not forget that most of them were out-of-towners — scarcely be unaware that the Auditorium next door had foundations which were shaky from other than structural reasons. Opera was presented there and Mary Garden was scandalising the town deliciously with her bold performances in such works as *Salome*, dancing with those seven veils, and *The Love of Three Kings*, during which she enjoyed (or at least the audience did) a ten-minute kiss. Billy Sunday, evangelist successor to Moody and Sankey, was nightly consigning her to perdition for her scandalous beauty (her glorious voice did not concern him), but to no avail. After all, similar dances were being performed throughout Chicago, to far less aesthetic effect, and the passionate Italian love-making and poisonings of *L'Amore dei tre re* reflected the city's daily soap opera headlines. One reason that Chicago was a town "Billy Sunday couldn't shut down" was that all the gangster fraternity happened to adore opera as much as they adored food. Indeed, they *lived* opera. When Garden, Caruso, Tetrazzini and other stars were not dining at Madame Galli's, they were relishing the *risotto aux truffles* with imported Italian tomatoes at Colosimo's Café. And one reason why Rotary was so badly needed there was that it was more damaging to the Mayor's reputation to accuse him of being too close to business than of being too close to crime.

Turning deaf ears to the goings-on of Miss Garden next door in the Auditorium, therefore (even as Herod was singing, "Surely some terrible thing will befall. Put on the torches. I will not look at things, I will not suffer things to look at me"), the Convention listened to Prophet Sheldon's uplifting forecasts and to Ches Perry's stern admonitions: "We are here ready to do our part of the world's work, anxious to have a share in the great civic uplift of our day. . . . You have important work to do in establishing the fundamental laws of this association." And, though some of them may have slipped next door to watch Salome kiss her own Prophet's head and be crushed by shields, the majority stayed long enough to knuckle under to Perry's commanding glare and adopt a Constitution and By-Laws and to approve these five objects:

1. To extend and develop Rotary principles by the organization of Rotary Clubs throughout America.
2. To unify the work and the principles of the affiliating Rotary Clubs and to promote their common good.
3. To arouse and encourage civic pride and loyalty.
4. To promote progressive and honorable business methods.
5. To advance the business interests of the individual members of the affiliating Clubs.

Paul Harris, in a state of romantic euphoria, had informed the Chicago press that 4,000 delegates would attend Rotary's first Convention. In fact, twenty-nine came — an average of two each from fourteen of the sixteen Clubs — but future Conventions of many thousands have accomplished much less. Offices could now be taken and space was rented in the First National Bank Building at 189 La Salle Street — one room only. The Chicago Club, still smarting from "Extension", moved swiftly to ensure that Rotary Number One kept an eye on things and was not caught napping again. It rented the room adjoining, and the two Clubs shared one typist between them.

Paul Harris also moved swiftly, for the umpteenth time, and took his own law firm into the same building. He was not ready to let go yet. He and Ches Perry had every reason to be delighted with that first Convention. Harris was President, Perry was Secretary and they had a further secret with which they were soon to stun the Chicagoans — a convert from north of the border! This Canadian, named McIntyre, had come on business from Winnipeg. In Indian terminology, this had brought him unflatteringly from "Muddy Water" to "Skunk", but in fact the towns had much in common, both becoming local points for grain, slaughtering, meat-packing, mail-order houses and rail and air communications. McIntyre had a cousin who belonged to Rotary Number One and who took him on one of the Club's picnics in those interesting and pregnant Chicago parks. The sandwiches must have been good, plus the hip-flasks, since McIntyre set up the first Club outside the United States that same November of 1910. He had got on well with Ches Perry and Paul Harris, though that didn't prevent the former, getting into his stride in his new offices, from sternly and quickly asking for $1 per member as dues to the National Association. Sheldon made a rapid follow-up visit north to consolidate purpose and fire morale. Winnipeg was actually Rotary Number Seventeen, but its chartering took nearly two years, so that it is officially Number Thirty-Five, an anomaly which was shortly to cause much commotion on the other side of the Atlantic between Dublin and London.

And was Harris to be lured at all by the seductive music from next door to the Convention? Hardly. Mary Garden was a canny Scots lass from Aberdeen, but Harris had already got his own canny lass, whose parents were from Aberdeen. Is it surprising that he had announced in June that 4,000 delegates were due? In a month he was to be married, and his uncharacteristic euphoria is excusable. The rapscallion was just having a little final fling.

The following year marked the end of the beginning for Rotary, a watershed in the development of the World Movement to which one lonely and determined man had given birth, and the climax and summit of that man's life. It was the year Rotary reached across to the British Isles (see Chapter Six) and stepped upon the world scene. It was the year Ches Perry issued as editor the first number of *The National Rotarian*, soon to become simply *The Rotarian*, published as a vehicle for Paul Harris's major essay expounding his Rotary philosophy. It was also, of course, the first year of Harris's marriage, after which it took all his stamina to live happy ever after, his life ceasing to have any active significance to the Movement. As he freely admitted, Rotary was his only child and he proved to have little aptitude as a parent. Nor did the child, as with normal offspring everywhere, pay much attention to him. Yet in 1911, as he reached the apotheosis of proud fatherhood, on the excited verge of a second nervous breakdown, he stood by at the rebirth, his supreme moment.

The Second National Convention was held again in August, at Portland, Oregon, and, introducing a note of typical Western flair and extravagance, was held not in an hotel but on one of Portland's famous stern-wheeled river-boats, the events moving worthy of their extravagant setting. The main session produced two great "declarations" and voted Paul Harris in as President for the second year running, and to no other man did Rotary give that honour. The declarations came from two Committees Harris had set up at the Congress Hotel. One, chaired by Ernst Skeel of Seattle, was to formulate a statement of Rotary policy; the other, the Business Methods Committee, chaired by Arthur Sheldon, was to formulate Rotary attitudes. In the event, both Committees did their jobs superbly, though they could have swapped names with advantage, for to Skeel service was business, while to Sheldon business was service. (Skeel's declaration, called the "Portland Platform", was part-authored by one James Pinkham, who as another lumberman was doubtless aware of the public relations gaffe committed by the Chicago Club, and part by Paul Harris himself, in a splendid final creative burst.)

From the Skeel platform came the following:

> Matters of general importance affecting the common welfare may be considered at meetings of the Rotary Club for the following purposes *only*:
> 1. The information and cultivation of the members.
> 2. That the members may intelligently co-operate as individuals to exercise such influence in the community and on public sentiment as could with propriety be exercised by an individual.
> 3. To render such assistance to organized public movements when requested by the central commercial organization or the sponsor of such public movement as is within its power when such movements seem of sufficient importance and merit.

Skeel was an energetic pontificator who was to write an article of enormous length to pack the pages of the first Rotary journal published outside the United States, Great Britain's *The Rotary Wheel*, in January 1915. (His comments the more acceptable for the time being, since the First World War had entered a quiet phase with little news since the extraordinary Christmas armistice, when Germans and British had sung "Auld Lang Syne" and "Tipperary" together, just like good Rotarians!) Yet the pomposity of his style was not a reflection of Rotary self-esteem but untoward humility — Sheldon soon took care of that aberration — in regard to organisations already established in public affairs. Such groups had suspicions of Rotary and Harris was pleased to see them allayed.

The star performer at Portland in 1911, however, was again Arthur Sheldon, and he wasn't even there! Personal and business commitments had kept him away, but he didn't let Harris down and had sent a sort of personal Rotary Credo to be read out to the delegates. It had a surging eloquence and the delegates (representing twenty-four instead of sixteen Clubs now) listened spellbound to the magnificently tuned phrases which were enunciated by the stiffly formal Ches Perry, backing into the limelight:

THAT the science of business is the science of service; he profits most who serves best.

THAT the success of any institution is the sum of the successes of the people engaged in its service.

THAT in the broad sense every one is a salesman; each has something to sell, whether it be service or goods.

THAT success in life in its broad sense is a matter not of luck or chance, but is governed by laws or nature — mental, moral, physical and spiritual.

THAT to work in harmony with all of these laws would mean success of the highest order.

THAT cosmic consciousness is a development of the universal sense, and appreciation of the solidarity of the race, the all-oneness of things, the reality of the brotherhood of man, on which plane man comes to see the reality of the fact that in business or anywhere else, *he profits most who serves best.*

This time, at second hearing, the phrase broke through. It was Rotary's moment of Pentecost, when the gifts of someone else's tongue descended upon all, and there was a thunderous ovation in the hall, the cheers and applause perhaps making Harris quite pleased Sheldon was not there in person, though Ches Perry would no doubt have steered delegates away from over-reacting into drafting the Super-Salesman into the National Presidency. It was Perry, after all, who had done the reading of the Prophet's words, and he had events well under control. Indeed, spoken by the precise, unemotional General Secretary, the words may have gained an impact which had been submerged the previous year by Sheldon's more florid style of oratory.

At the heart of the ecstatic uproar, Conference Chairman Perry drew precise attention to the fact that Jim Pinkham, who had watched the Portland platform being completely upstaged, was waving his arms for attention. "Mr Chairman, I move that 'He Profits Most Who Serves Best' be made the concluding words of our platform!" Another uproar brought instant acclaim and approval, and the platform drafted by Skeel, Pinkham and Harris survived in the appropriated plumes of Sheldon's inspiration in the barber's chair.

All was not yet done. Within a few minutes Harris had the satisfaction of seeing another lawyer, Frank Collins, President of one of the first dozen Clubs formed, that of Minneapolis, ride over the swelling din with a speech rousing another ovation:

> In the organization of a Rotary Club there is only one thing to do, and that is to start right. The men who come into Rotary for what they can get out of it for themselves are in the wrong class; that is not Rotary. The principle that has been adopted by the Minneapolis Club, and has been adhered to since its inception, had been 'Service, Not Self!'

In the space of a few minutes, therefore, the Movement had found the double-motto which, slightly amended, has waved on its banners, dominated its stages, and streamed over its processions ever since: *Service Above Self: He Profits Most Who Serves Best.* Legions of committees were to do their best to mangle the two phrases out of existence through the years ahead, but their power could not be denied, though Paul Harris had been dead three years when in 1950 the double-motto was at last declared official. It was a triumph that was the supreme illustration of Rotary's genius, which has often seemed to adapt Edison's notorious definition to mean that the 1 per cent inspiration of a few has always had to survive the 99 per cent perspiration of a thousand, trying on committees to argue and debate inspiration out of existence. Forty years on, with all its authors dead and beyond due credit, the world's Rotarians took to their hearts the twin-slogans first heard that sunny August morning on a large boat sailing up the Columbia River.

The first and last Rotary Convention ever held afloat — the Movement was a pioneer in this as in much else — was thus the most significant the Movement ever organised. Those Chicagoans present who resented the fact that it wasn't taking place on the shores of Lake Michigan could draw comfort from seeing their own Paul Harris and Ches Perry still dominant on the platform, Sheldon's Credo given the status of Instant Holy Writ, and from witnessing finally that even the second motto had come from their Midwestern neighbours.

Looking back on that momentous August of 1911, we can see how Harris and Perry had brilliantly pre-empted every move, foreseen every development.

Since Arthur Sheldon had his own permanent platform, a journal he called *The Business Philosopher*, Paul had obtained his also, *The National Rotarian*, which back in January had flooded the multiplying Clubs across the land with 3,000 copies delivered post-free. The delegates to Portland, knowingly or not, had already been primed seven months before by the six-page newspaper through which the Founder could at last fulfil his journalistic ambitions, refired by the sight of that San Francisco write-up in his old employer, the *Chronicle*. "President Harris had a message which he wanted to deliver not only to every Rotary Club but to every Rotarian," Editor Perry informed his readers. The President did indeed, and the editorial introduction brooked no nonsense in its tone.

So the 3,000 copies were read (and hundreds of thousands of facsimiles of it have been read since) and there, underneath a "thinker" photograph of Paul Harris, cheek resting on pensively curled finger, to make it clear that Paul the Philosopher was speaking, a Manifesto was laid down in column after column of close-set type. It began: "If by interposition of Providence I some day were to find myself standing on a platform in some great Coliseum looking into the eyes of every living Rotarian [the dead ones presumably being spared], and were to be told that I could have one word to say, without an instant's hesitation and at the top of my voice, I would shout "Toleration!"'"

We know to whom his shout was directed: the Rotarians of Chicago. But one notes with interest the fantasy in which Paul was indulging. He had seldom, if ever, shouted; would certainly never have dreamed of doing so from a platform. If faced with a packed coliseum, he would have fled. Yet it seems an uncanny pre-vision of that Portland stern-wheeler when he goes on to write: ". . . it was in pursuit of it [Toleration] that the pilgrim fathers embarked in their frail craft upon the stormy seas".

It remained fantasy. The Columbia River was hardly stormy on that hot August morning, though the Conference in the river-steamer was — yet with only auspicious gales — and the craft was anything but frail. And though Paul Harris was harking back to his beloved, and romanticised, New England boyhood, was he not only too aware that the society established by those Pilgrim Fathers was the most intolerant ever known on the North American continent? His two natures, the Bryan and the Harris, were still fusing within him. But, knowing his Rotary time was short, he had important things to say and nothing more important has ever been said about Rotary. We shall refer to other parts of his 5,000-word article later in this book, but for now we can skip the Bunyanesque bits — involving characters like Mr Cash Discount and Mr Vigorously Definite — and quote these powerful, prophetic lines, packed as they are with disturbing insight:

> Life in Rotary should consist of a rational mixture of business with civic activities and good fellowship. . . .
>
> There should be no occasion for meeting behind closed doors. If Rotarianism cannot stand the test of trial before a jury comprised of the entire American people, then it lacks rationality and should be changed. . . .
>
> No doctrine is immune from criticism. It is part of wisdom to profit from

rational criticism, not so much because of what other people think of us as because of what they cause us to think of ourselves. . . .

Let us be in a position to defend ourselves . . . not by stentorian shouting of meaningless words but by logic that convinces. . . . If we put Rotary on the highest possible plane and keep it there, we shall experience no difficulty. . . . A grave responsibility lies on your shoulders and mine. . . . Rotary is a huge, powerful machine. Unguided, it could crash down the aisles of time a menace to all mankind. Well directed, it will become a humanizing instrumentality of which we need not be ashamed.

The words still reverberate with warning and with truth, and though the date beneath them is 1st January 1911, one feels they might well have been written — and certainly contemplated and slowly forged — over all the years since the original inspiration for the world's first Service Club had come to Harris during that lonely walk in Rogers Park in the first year of the century. He was writing more than a New Year's Day Message for Rotarians of then and now. He was writing on the first day of the modern era, with Armageddon growing impatient in the wings and Europe full of very real, brutal and three-dimensional "huge, powerful" machines about to thrash unguided "down the aisles of time", a menace and doom to all mankind and to the societies in which they were born. These blind machines were about to destroy their creators and drag a generation of innocent follies down to oblivion in their terrible wake.

It is easy now to forget that the First World War almost began in 1911 and not in 1914, in reaction to the Agadir Incident in Morocco between France and Germany. Indeed it was on 23rd August, the very day that the Second National Rotary Convention was in ferment on the waters of the Columbia over its aims and mottoes, that the Committee of Imperial Defence was also meeting in London and, among other matters of world crisis, was considering a memorandum by Winston Churchill which uncannily predicted, with astounding accuracy, the course of the first forty days of the war to come.

Harris had written in January: "The idea of having two or three hundred men in non-competitive lines looking out for your interests all of the time looks wildly seductive. If it worked out in practice as it does on the face of it in theory, we would soon corner all of the business there is in the world." His tone was ironic, of course, but it reflected precisely the situation which the Great Powers had once imagined they could create on the global stage — and of course failed to achieve with horrifying inevitability.

It is appropriate that the same first issue of *The National Rotarian* should carry a Californian advertisement, inserted by a member of the Los Angeles Rotary Club, for an "Ostrich Emporium". But if Harris were anxious for Rotary not to bury its head in the sand, his Rotary Manifesto — still more relevant than anything written about the Movement since, including much by himself in later years — loses none of its importance or significance from going unnoticed by the world at large at the time. After all, very few people in that year were in the slightest degree aware they had nearly been flung into the Great War three years too early. Churchill and Harris, in very different areas, showed awesome prescience of change and the future, buried under the public's natural preoccupation with other matters: the arrival of "ragtime" on dance-floors both sides of the Atlantic (helped by the composition of "Alexander's Ragtime Band"); King George V's Durbar in India, filmed for a three-hour cinema showing in "Kinemacolor" both in London and New York; the invention of animated cartoons; the launch of the *Titanic*; and, if we glance in the other direction, the revolution which threw out the Manchu dynasty and formed the first Republic of China. It was also the year of Chicago's greatest ever drive against vice and corruption, so an excellent time to avert Rotary eyes from their city of revelation.

In 1911, the long-simmering Vice Commission Report was published as *The Social Evil in Chicago* and, as proof of its thoroughness, it was revealed that the Commission members had convened no less than ninety-eight meetings to consider "special evidence". No wonder they were exhausted and quite indignant! They had even found things going on behind table-screens in ice-cream parlous, so not even teetotallers were safe from themselves, and concluded "The honor of Chicago, the fathers and mothers of her children, the physical and moral integrity of the future generation demand that she repress public prostitution".

In reprisal, an outraged Big Jim Colosimo had his enforcers make sure that his prostitutes — source of a staggering $5,400,000 turn-over per annum — went all round the city and suburbs in their tartiest clothes, ringing doorbells, renewing acquaintanceships and seeking rooms for the night. We can be sure that very few men were eager to answer the doorbell after that, and in fact the Chicago Protective League for Women sensibly condemned the whole thing a "monstrous mistake".

What Chicago Rotarians thought of this matter of high civic concern is not on record.

Rotary Number One kept a relatively low profile in 1911 and Paul Harris used the moment with advantage to turn Rotary eyes elsewhere in the country, and abroad. Certainly Portland, Oregon, was a nice long way distant from that very loud Report on Chicago wickedness. And the song that was often being conducted by Harry Ruggles in the Sherman House that year, "There are hands that will welcome me in / There are lips I am burning to kiss", while sounding suspiciously like an ill-timed local commercial, was in fact being chorused by all right-minded households across the land round parlour pianos. Redolent of homely, traditional and uxorious virtues, it was significantly titled "My Little Grey Home in the West". To Harris, with extension overseas in mind, it was also doubtless significant and encouraging that the song, like so much that was typically American, had come from England.

Ches Perry had his own methods and brought his extremely well-read mind into practical play. An item in that first number of *The National Rotarian* quoted the *Chicago Tribune* as claiming that reference to the Rotary Club could be found in the Bible, in the tenth chapter of the Book of Ezekiel. Those who looked, found references to cherubs holding wheels and that every wheel had "four faces; the first face was the face of a cherub, and the second face was the face of a man, and the third the face of a lion, and the fourth the face of an eagle". It is fanciful to imagine that the *Tribune* was referring to Rotary's four Founder Members, but more likely it was just poking fun.

Perry always viewed fun as something with a purpose, like everything else, and he exhorted his readers, "Does anyone know the reference?" He certainly did, and hoped that members would notice that the passage was describing the fall of the Temple and conquest by foreigners because Jerusalem was a city of blood and injustice. The Chicago Vice Commission Chairman might not be Nebuchadnezzar, but he would do. That Nebuchadnezzar would do for Paul's purposes was perhaps not so evident, but we may note that this was a kind of Babylon and that, in the lexicon of wickedness of W.T. Stead, scourge of Chicago, "Babylon" was always London. The coincidences of history kept a firm hand on the threads. This was the year London entered the Movement.

Perry had his own postscript to add to Paul's Manifesto, in which he gave an editorial reminder to readers of the four "Objects" which could now be accomplished as a result of having a National Association. These included "uniting all the Clubs at the proper time in some great civic or commercial movement which will make for something better throughout the Nation". In his very different way, he, like Paul, was raising the sights of Rotary. Unlike Paul, he wasn't frightened at what he saw.

Suddenly, the great milestone had been passed. Rotary was

never, could never, be the same again, though it was now to remain
the same for a very long time. It had ceased to be a Man; it was now
a Movement. Paul Harris had dreamed of a new transport for the
twentieth-century urban and business soul. His was a Herculean
labour, that of the creator. First he had had to imagine the vehicle,
then draw the blueprint and persuade others it would work, it
would move. Then he had to build the vehicle himself, painstakingly
and privately, in the secret ground behind the placid face, the
unblemished, unmarked, surface-wall of daily life. Few had shared
his secret; he did not fully acknowledge it himself till his subconscious showed it to him in all its awesome possibility. Yet he
had never wavered. Suddenly the Movement had started, and not
only started but was gathering momentum at incredible, terrifying
speed. All his inhibitions springing up and reasserting themselves,
Harris could feel the vehicle hurtling out of his control, the wheel,
that Golden Wheel, surge and pull and wrestle under his terrified
grip, as nervous reaction overpowered him. At that moment, his
hands were gently removed, prised free from a final last bid to grip
the rim, and another pair of hands, undeterred by the power and
the crushing speed, took the steering, settled to the controls. The
inventor leapt for safety and Chesley Perry, cool as ice, drove for
the horizon.

Paul was made President Emeritus. Thirty-two years later, when
Perry retired, he was offered the parallel title of "Secretary Emeritus"
and refused, with glacial amusement. Paul was of course the Founder
and Architect of the extraordinary prototype. Ches Perry was
Organisation Man supreme, before the species was recognised.
These were two of the most extraordinary men of the century and
their legacy is still to be assessed. The vehicle is now a juggernaut,
as Paul foresaw in that first editorial in 1911, though its image has
not changed in the public mind for decades. These men are the two
sides of the Golden Wheel. Thanks to Paul Harris, Rotary became
"Unknown, yet well known". Thanks to Ches Perry, it remains
even today, "Well known, yet unknown". We must even ascertain if
the transport had a soul on board, or whether it leapt with Paul.

That will become apparent, one hopes, as we explore the "unknown" in these pages. But now we are looking back at 1911. In
March of that year Arthur Sheldon was holding the Canadians in
Winnipeg's new Rotary Club in thrall. By July, he was over the
Atlantic and preaching the gospel in London; by the end of the
year, his voice boomed over Manchester. Before another twelve
months had passed — with Paul crowned, married and retired as
"President Emeritus" back home — Sheldon and his set of hand-
books on salesmanship were, in spite of the alien ground, sweeping

all before them in Mrs Jean Harris's home town of Edinburgh. And
Rotary was International.

CHAPTER SIX

Travels of a Medicine Man

In serving others I can profit most:
"I am a friend to man" — that is my boast.
  I do not crave a fickle nation's praise,
I do not rise to drink a selfish toast.

If men can say of me that I was true,
True to my better self as well as you;
  I ask no grander, nobler epitaph
When body-crushed I bid this world adieu.

The Rubaiyat of A-ro Tarian, 1913

The historical ways of Ireland, for good and ill, have always been a folklore unto themselves, and the coming of Rotary was no exception. In spite of his Bryan forbears — it might indeed be right to say in despite of them — "to win London" was ever the first objective across the Atlantic for Paul Harris and, according to official Rotary records, this is precisely what was achieved. The declaration which is carried on the cover of the Dublin Club's magazine to this day, that it is the journal of "No. 1 in Europe" is quite untrue, or at least as misleading as many of the Republic's road signs. Yet it will stay there for ever.

So which was first? Four Clubs were in fact founded in the United Kingdom (as still then constituted) in 1911: Dublin, Belfast, London and Manchester, in that order. The first two might as well have been formed by the "little people", however, for all that Harris and Ches Perry were aware of them. And in the following year, when the Third Rotary Convention was held at Duluth, Minnesota, it was London alone which came along from overseas to apply for affiliation — paying up the annual subscription of a guinea — and had its charter signed by Paul Harris, on what must surely have been one of the proudest days of the Founder's life, as World Club No 50. This charter was signed on 1st August 1912. Five days later the Duluth Convention opened and, on the strength of the affiliation of Winnipeg and London, the nearly 600 delegates changed the name of the organisation to the International Association of Rotary Clubs. Having signed London in, Harris was ready to retire, surrender to ill-health and strain, and accept the title of President Emeritus for life. He had seen the future, a future now guaranteed for him by the fact that London was the first Club overseas to form a Rotary Club. It was his dream of a lifetime come true, the summit of his ideal. By that time, of course, he certainly knew about Dublin — but Dublin knew little, and apparently cared less, about him.

Erin's islanders were accustomed to, and expected, Americans who treated them like charming, irresponsible gremlins, with lyre on lip and stout on heart; not as solid commercial folk dedicated to serving those less fortunate than themselves (could such exist?) — with regular "My Job" talks thrown in for good measure.

The same year Stuart Morrow arrived in Kingstown, Dublin's harbour, and knocked on Bill McConnell's door, Paul Harris was briefly back in Racine to bury the last of his Bryan uncles. It was his first visit there for forty years and would have brought again vividly to his mind the traumas, difficulties and miseries his maternal Irish forbears had inflicted on the family, and he would have been in no mood to wish Dublin rather than London to be Rotary's first Club overseas. The funeral would have also recalled to him the dreadful irony which still haunted him that Grandfather Harris, who had spent so much time and money bailing out Bryans had, after all, been a victim of the worst Irish joke possible: *he* had died on St Patrick's Day, which was thus one of Paul's saddest, most bitter anniversaries! Fortunately for Rotary, its gospel — or the Californian version of it — was brought to Dubliners by a seeming prodigal son. When they discovered he had returned to convert them on commission only, because he had failed abroad at everything else, they knew him without doubt as one of their own.

But the Founder could not have wished for a shrewder, more practical purveyor of his dream. As an authorised, self-appointed Medicine Man, Morrow instinctively knew from the moment of his arrival back in the Old World, how *much* of the new "elixir" would be palatable and in what dosage and strength. Paul had waited two years before introducing the Chicago Club to Rotary's service aspect. Stuart the Irishman from California didn't have the leisure for choosing his time of sobering revelation, but, as a fellow-Dubliner, he knew Europe's first Rotarians better than anyone else from the United States could have known them. Of the two sides to the coin, he kept the trading side uppermost for as long as he could, the boosting and business advantage. With today's almost instant communications, his task would have been immeasurably harder. Indeed, and this includes Rotary throughout the British Isles, Rotary might never have been launched there at all. Though good news still travels fast, faster than ever, it still barely keeps ahead of its creditors.

From today's viewpoint, it looks as if Rotary had chosen, for a Movement which aspired to hold itself apart from politics, the oddest time to appear in the romantic, rebellious and rackety backwater that was Dublin in 1911. Ireland was then (as it still remains) what it had been for hundreds of years, the "badlands" of the British Isles, where aspiring statesmen from London cut their teeth or broke their hearts, or both, the occasional one being murdered. All the big names had been associated with it, from Richard II to the Earl of Essex to Melbourne and both Churchills, Randoph and Winston, even though the latter typically was to come closest to grips with the Irish topsy-turvy reality, actively backing the North and signing a treaty which created the modern South.

But, though the world's headlines were soon to let Dublin on from her restless wait in the wings (after the First World War had made way for it), in 1911 the place was still historically "Hicksville". The Industrial Revolution had passed it by. Here was no centre of commerce, bursting with big money, ready to have business made respectable, even moral. True, the American cities which spawned Rotary One and Rotary Two had become very familiar with Dublin's most profitable export, Oscar Wilde, but to Chicago and San Francisco Oscar was a Londoner and his affectations typically English. In 1906, Bernard Shaw was merely voicing the romantic illusion of several generations when he observed that "Ireland is the only spot on earth which still produces the ideal Englishman" (overlooking the parallel romance which creates the exactly opposite illusion, if not so frequently). There were seven theatres, excellent hotels, beautiful parks and race-courses and Kingstown Harbour crammed with yachts, and all of these places were easily reached by the tramways or a brisk bicycle ride, a fairly new pastime in which young girls indulged as much as men. It was a charming town for the visitor and the rather staid well-to-do circles. But not so good for the "other half", many of whom lived ninety to a house with one tap for water and two lavatories in the back yard, also used by passers-by. Along with myths and bitterness,

Dublin's working-class tenements raged with tuberculosis. Yet in Phoenix Park, where the bird, being Irish, was destined to reduce itself to ashes time and again, the band played on. The whole of Ireland was then still part of the United Kingdom, of course — as it had been for over a century — but agitation for Home Rule was reaching its final peak and another of Stuart Morrow's Trinity College contemporaries, Sir Edward Carson (who still represented the College as a Member of Parliament at Westminster), was threatening to form a separate government in Ulster if the Liberals dared give Dublin independence.

In the year of Rotary's birth Edward VII had broken a chair in the theatre laughing at Shaw's *John Bull's Other Island*, but the old King had just died and no one was laughing now. Shaw himself was now more interested in the battleground of marriage as a subject for his pen (as a similar preoccupation was distracting Paul Harris).

But the Abbey Theatre, under Lady Gregory and Yeats, was overtly a theatre of revolution which had, incredible as it may seem today, rejected *John Bull's Other Island* in favour of works emphasising the cultural and historical separateness of Ireland from England. Possibly Harris was not unaware of this. But even if he did not know the fact that, in 1911, when Morrow was canvassing support for one sort of Movement in Dublin, the Abbey Theatre, travelling in the opposite direction, was canvassing support for a very different sort of Movement in America, he might well have been aware that in 1905, the year of the birth of Rotary, Sinn Fein came into being as the political wing of Irish rebellion. And he would have remembered those Fenian raids into Canada from Vermont when he was a boy. Both of which would have strengthened his resolve that London would be his goal, rather than such an obvious storm centre. For neither he nor Ches Perry chose Dublin, as we have seen.

The San Franciscan Rotarian whose own business had just failed in California and who, at fifty-six, was the oldest Rotary pioneer of all, was blazing an independent trail in the true spirit of the Wild West, and he was more than a trifle taken aback to find that the relatives and friends he had left behind twenty-six years before were less than ecstatic to see him. Dublin was seething, and packed enough already with more secret societies and sects than you could shake a shillelagh at, without another one trying to claim their attention. Rotary . . . what the devil was that?

And what indeed was Dublin? Even to a returning son, one long nurtured on the romantic American nostalgia for "Erin's Isle", the shock must have been considerable. For Dublin was not just the first town outside of the New World to have a Rotary Club, it was without doubt the most narrow and provincial, only just emerging from the state of a glorified village, half a colonial outpost still, half a frontier town. In mode of life, it was a city of diamonds and rags where snobbery was as rife as poverty and drunkenness. Thackeray's description of high society, made half a century before (he was shown around by Oscar's father, Dr Wilde), still held true: "Its magnates are tradesmen; brass plates are their titles of honour. O, that old humbug of a Castle! It is the greatest sham in Ireland." It had plenty of competition, both from people and the buildings they lived in.

The Castle itself, centre of constant and resplendent functions, was surrounded by slums through which the expensively dressed ladies and gentlemen — largely Protestant but strongly laced with Catholic professionals on the make — drove in their carriages. The few fine Georgian houses, and the many decrepit ones, housed the "better elements" (a favourite Harris phrase) at one end of a street and brothels at the other. When Morrow came home, the most notorious, Tyrone Street, had just changed its name to Railway Street, a sure passion-killer. Merrion Square, where Wilde been brought up (only fifteen minutes' walk from Shaw's family, but the two boys never met) was still grand, though Dr Wilde's hospital — before his great fame as an eye and ear surgeon — had been in a Dublin stable. Grand also was Fitzwilliam Square, but mere blocks away were shabby boarding-houses and tenements, soon inter-mingling with religious orders and thatched cottages, pubs, business houses, hotels, a few impressive public buildings, parks and then open countryside. Many Catholic charities were kept going by conscience-donations from the more refined brothels. Protestant charities were supported by gigantic bazaars, huge citified versions of village fetes, and one of the best supported was the Reformed Priests' Protection Society which existed "to extend a helping hand to a priest of good character who conscientiously abandons the Church of Rome for the pure faith of the Gospel".

All a sham, and though that part of sham which is allied to poetry, still a sham. The Abbey Theatre was not in an abandoned religious house, as the name might suggest, but was comprised of some buildings shoved together on Abbey Street, with their Irish vernacular renaissance paid for by a remarkable Englishwoman, Mrs A.E.F. Horniman, who had also sponsored Shaw's first full-scale London production, *Arms and the Man*. In 1911, Dublin had had its modern art gallery for only three years, on premises far more famous for having been the home of the creator of *Dracula*.

And all the rebels in rhetoric would soon be rushing to applaud the new King George V on his coronation visit to Kingstown Harbour. The river Liffey, about which Irishmen sighed abroad, took forty miles of twists and turns to cover ten, reflecting the pub conversations along its banks, and it was dark brown and smelly: hence indeed the name Dublin "Dubh Linn", meaning Black Pool.

Stuart Morrow would have found many grand new shops going up along Grafton and Wicklow Streets. On the other hand, a visitor of the time remarked on Dublin's delightful "frugality and lack of ostentation. . . . There is no money-standard in Dublin, for no one luckily appears to have any money". This is certainly endorsed indirectly by a theatre-mad young girl's comment: "Between Abbey Street and College Green, a five minutes' walk, one could meet every person of importance in the life of the city at a certain time in the afternoon." Whether of importance or self-importance matters less than the clear inference that an awful lot of people seemed to have no work to do. Some were, of course, too romantic to work. Most simply had no jobs and were destitute. Quite a few had no intention at all of working, jobs or no jobs, needing all their free time to train with the Irish Republican Brotherhood and plan the final break with England. The city was full of slums, slightly disguised by the rural nature of what was still basically a country town. A short morning's drive could bring one into the lush green countryside, where those who could afford to do so built their homes, away from the romantic phoniness, the naïve conspiracies, the social fantasy. Seeing these suburbs on his way into Dublin, an English official of the time wrote that they were "all neat, ugly, snug and middle-class". And it was in one of these suburbs that Bill McConnell, a successful young insurance executive, lived with his wife Ada. They had met in very correct circumstances at the Charleville Tennis Club, and she was Stuart Morrow's sister. Their cosy world was as much of a sham as any. Did they not know of the foreign scholars pouring into Dublin to write precious volumes about the Celtic Renaissance? Did they not know that the Irish Republicans were just starting an outspoken journal called *Irish Freedom*? Did they not know that their fellow-Dubliner Edward Carson was writing "I wish I could be in Ulster to know whether men are desperately in earnest and prepared to make great sacrifices"? Did they not know of those somewhat amateur, but ominous, plans for Dublin's disenchanted workers to form a Citizens' Army? Did they not know that John Redmond, leader of the Irish Party at Westminster had proclaimed "we shall have Home Rule before we know where we are", to which Carson had replied for Ulstermen, "they will not yield their birthright, not one inch, without a struggle"?

Of course we all live with sham assumptions. We know they are shams, and that without them life would become impossible. All the same, it is not surprising that Morrow aroused little attention from his brother-in-law's business friends and received, in the words of Bill McConnell, "cold water in liberal douches". Which was certainly the first and last time that water in any great quantity played a large part in the doings of Irish Rotary.

Of all unwelcome visitors on the doorstep, including debt-collectors and flag-sellers, near the top of the list must be the long-absent brother-in-law expecting house room and hospitality for an indefinite stay. Especially to a keen young business man like Bill McConnell, married only four years, to whom his wife's brother, a romantically moustachioed expatriate without a job, was a complete stranger. In deference to his wife and to her mother, who was doubtless pleased to see the return of a prodigal son, McConnell extended a reserved welcome. Irishmen who seek their fortune — and their Irishness — abroad, rarely return (unlike wandering Scots), being an entirely unsentimental race. John McCormack might sing gloriously about Mother Machree but he did so in America and Australia; in fact he was touring Down Under when Morrow made his reappearance in Dublin after a quarter of a century in California. He was not just broke, but bankrupt, and clearly expected his brother-in-law to use his influence among his insurance contacts to find him a job. But the political and economic climate must have quickly registered with him and this opening ploy was soon abandoned for his main ulterior motive, which was a personal Job Creation scheme, a scheme which was to launch upon the world a Movement the like of which had never been seen before — and by methods the rest of Rotary had never seen before.

McConnell himself must have suspected an ulterior motive from the start of his unpleasant New Year surprise, knowing that those wandering Irishmen who do return to their emerald green pastures usually have one. Indeed, viewing those wild moustachios, the police probably had an eye on Stuart Morrow, once they knew he had come back from the wilder reaches of the West. He had not, however, returned bearing either gifts or guns; he had brought a gimmick, and one that Bill McConnell was delighted to encourage, once he realised that it would get him off the hook finding work for Ada's brother.

Bill's business friends also became more amenable, once they appreciated that this brilliant lawyer of failed promise was not asking them to give him a job but inviting them to join an organisation which was already international (Morrow could be relied on to embroider upon Winnipeg) and which was intentionally geared to

1. (*above left*) The Founder, Paul Harris, at the turn of the century when he was a thrusting young lawyer.

2. (*above right*) Chesley Perry, the dynamo recruited in 1908.

3. Ches Perry in his prime.

4. The first four Rotarians: (*left to right*) Gus Loehr, Hiram Shorey, Silvester Schiele and Paul Harris.

5. The "little red school-room" in Wallingford, Vermont, where Paul Harris went to school, now commemorated as the Paul P. Harris Memorial Building.

6. Madame Galli's restaurant where Harris and Schiele decided to form Rotary.

7. Unity Building, Chicago: (*above left*) as it was when the Founder Members held their first meeting there in 1905, and (*above right*) today, viewed through Picasso's sculpture, *Woman of Steel*.

8. Sherman House, Chicago, in 1906 where the first Rotary Club lunches were held outside members' offices "in rotation". The meals cost 60 cents each!

9. The impressive entrance to the Chicago Club today. The Club still proudly proclaims itself, and rightly, as "Rotary One".

engendering more business amongst themselves. At this stage, of course, Paul Harris's Manifesto was unknown even to Stuart Morrow, who had left the United States before any of the 3,000 copies of *The National Rotarian* reached San Francisco.

The ease and speed with which Morrow adapted his technique from Job Hunting to Job Creation — the job in question being for himself and one for which there was no competition — suggest that Rotary "Extension" (the Morrow way) had been his purpose all along. At any rate, after only a few weeks, with Bill McConnell's help, he had convened a series of luncheon meetings with his brother-in-law's friends and contacts, and at a midday meal at Jury's Hotel on 22nd February 1911, almost six years to the day after Rotary was born, Morrow was confidently presiding over the first meeting of the Rotary Club of Dublin, his place in social history assured as the bankrupt lawyer who took Rotary to the world.

Things were cut and dried. After a few words, Morrow let William Lane (tailoring) and Thomas Ryan (jewellery) propose and second that "having listened to a statement of the history, aims and methods of the Rotary Clubs, now in operation in the principal cities of America, we approve of the attempt to establish a Rotary Club in Dublin". This was passed unanimously and it was then settled at once that the entrance fee would be 2 guineas, with the Organising Secretary taking half for himself in lieu of salary. There were nine Founding Members, including McConnell and Henry Jury, owner of the hotel, but Morrow was not not among them, since he was pocketing 9 guineas as Organising Secretary.

The whole proceedings would have given Paul Harris ten fits, though he would have approved of the moving spirit being another lawyer, especially when the Dubliners approved themselves a Rotary Constitution in March, six months before the Portland Convention described in the previous chapter had even met! As always, the Irish had their own way of doing things, however, and perhaps it is not surprising that such a convivial people took to a luncheon club as enthusiastically as they did to Guinness. Besides which, Ireland delights in producing the unexpected, and does so with monotonous regularity.

Since his personal knowledge of Rotarian ideals was confined to a relatively few months in the San Francisco Club, Stuart Morrow must have improvised brilliantly and persuasively, for the foundations he laid were sound. The Dublin Club still meets weekly in the same hotel and Bill McConnell was ten years later to become President of the British Association of Rotary Clubs. Dubliners were always, of course, cheerfully ready to overdo things, if allowed to, and one member that July tried to register himself twice under different Classifications. Presumably not enough of his colleagues were seeing double at the time, however, as he didn't succeed; but this was the day after Stuart Morrow decided to leave the Club to its own devices and move on, so maybe the member felt that all restraints were now lifted.

Morrow was in Belfast. One guesses that his recent experiences in California in straitened circumstances had taught him the invaluable instinct of when to shift to new territory and he was still without a job offer, from McConnell or anyone else. His personal Job Creation scheme clearly had to shift into a higher gear to enable him to decrease his cash-flow problem, and any bitterness he might have felt on learning that the Dubliners (with the approval of his brother-in-law) promptly appointed his successor at a salary increase of £25 per annum was mollified by his achievement in forming the Rotary Club of Belfast within a fortnight.

His motives were entirely personal and he was quite frank and open about them. Indeed, the interesting point to be made here is that he saw no reason to be otherwise. Rotary was a means, not an end, and the end was urgently selfish. Tendering his resignation to the Dubliners, Morrow wrote: "I find it necessary that I should take in more money to meet expenses." The only viable reason there is, of course — but the point is that these were his own expenses, not those of some charitable undertaking. Morrow was driven by an unstoppable combination of overdrive and overdraft, dedication and debt, allied to his enormous talent for persuasion. He was Rotary's Medicine Man, a figure familiar in early California, selling his amazing nostrum for the ills of the business life in one community after another, who, before he came, were probably unaware that they possessed any ailments at all.

Belfast was more responsive. Within two months, the Club had voted him an office and secretary of his own — an orphan girl, paid 5 shillings a week (the Chicago Club's secretary earned the weekly equivalent of $3, but then she wasn't an orphan). He also had a pay-phone. By January of 1912, membership had grown to 124, which is more than the Club has today.

The Constitution, which was accepted with surprising rapidity, was partly based on the Dublin precedent and partly on Stuart Morrow's developing inspiration. Business advantage predominated in the rules and procedures. Far from being coy about this, or feeling any need to be, Belfast members were required at each meeting to announce what business they had given, or received from, fellow-members — though, this being Ireland, the two categories seldom matched. It must be remembered that Stuart Morrow had never met Paul Harris and that his ideas of the practice of Rotary were derived exclusively from the customs of his San Francisco Club, where a paid assistant for "business getting" had been active for two years and where inter-member deals were not only reported but transacted during lunch and merchandise displayed in the dining-room not only on shelves but on the table, between the knives and forks. This was the apotheosis of "Boosting". The West Coast Rotarians had also sent a delegation to Washington to plead (successfully) for the next World's Fair to be held in San Francisco, celebrating their triumph with a champagne party of such exuberance that the doors had to be locked to prevent the public seeing them till they were in a more respectable state. To San Franciscans, this ranked as a civic service; a world away from the public conveniences of Chicago!

By January 1912, however, Morrow felt it was time to move on again, the Club becoming saturated with members, and his own commission for new recruits diminishing accordingly. Since Belfast business men showed no more inclination to offer him a job than had those in Dublin, the Medicine Man wrote his second resignation letter in twelve months and crossed to Glasgow in the spring. He must have left with some regret, since Belfast was a modern industrial city, thriving on one of the world's most important linen industries and giant shipyards, and he may well have felt more at home there than in the provincial Dublin of the day. Belfast was a big city, full of big business. Unfortunately, it was also a big bubbling volcano of big rebellion. As in Dublin, Rotary was just one more Club to join for a people that thrived on sworn oaths and conspiracy. The difference was that the Ulster societies were not furtive affairs and Morrow must have felt his efforts swamped beneath the Belfast Orange Lodges, the County Grand Lodges, the Unionist Clubs and the Women's Association, when the previous September these had marched 100,000 strong to assemble just two miles from the centre of Belfast and chorused enmity to Home Rule, pledging to take over the Government of Ulster, should it be passed. Safely in Glasgow, Morrow read of the 10,000-strong hostile mob, brandishing bolts and rivets from the shipyards and revolvers from the pawnshop, who poured on to the streets to howl protests against Winston Churchill when he came to speak in Belfast and decided he had timed his exit wisely.

Thus did Rotary come to Europe and thus indeed did it find its first footing outside the American continent. The first Club in the world had been formed by four lonely men; the first across the Atlantic by a man who was also lonely, and never more so than in the midst of the members he recruited and who failed in every case to recruit him in return.

He must have felt even lonelier when he learned that London and Manchester now both had Rotary Clubs, too. For, as we saw in the previous chapter, the Medicine Man had not been alone (as distinct from lonely) in precipitating Rotary's invasion of the British Isles. At the same time as he was selling Rotary — but not his personality — with increasing success to business men in the two main cities of Ireland, the Super-Salesman himself, Arthur Sheldon, was marketing Rotary and himself with sensational success in what was then still regarded by many as the civilised world's chief city, London. He and Morrow had reached these islands almost at the same time early the year before. Rotary in fact launched a two-pronged assault on the British Isles in 1911, though neither prong was aware of the other. But where Stuart Morrow was a returning prodigal in Dublin, dubious of his welcome, Sheldon was a familiar and much-welcomed figure on the London scene, where his representative, E. Sayer Smith, was busy setting up the Sheldon School of the British Empire, in Southampton Row, and Sheldon was publishing his series of little booklets on *The Science of Business* whose subtitle was *The Philosophy of Successful Human Activity Functioning in Business Building or Constructive Salesmanship*. We have only to reverse the order of words of that resounding line to "The Philosophy of Successful Business Building Functioning in Human Activity" to find ourselves sighting the heartbeat of Rotarian ideals.

Sheldon and Sayer Smith teamed up with a Boston Rotarian who was also a very familiar figure in London and already busy spreading the good word among business associates, Harvey C. Wheeler. Wheeler's firm, the Initial Towel Company, remains familiar to this day, of course, particularly within the confines of those establishments which, at that early period, appeared to be fast becoming Rotary's second home, the public lavatories. The Initial Towel Company's roller towels are still to be found at the Headquarters of Rotary in Great Britain and Ireland, while the officers of that body have often held Council meetings at the Russell Hotel, for many years the early home of the London Club — and also just a few yards up the road from Sheldon's branch office.

On 3rd August 1911, the Rotary Club of London held its inaugural meal at Simpson's in the Strand, a heavily sumptuous repast whose menu is still preserved with some awe in the Club archives. Six months before, Irish Rotary had come into being, though without Chicago's knowledge. Paul Harris, brimming with elation from his new twin-status as husband and Rotary President for the second time, knew only of London — until a member of the newly formed Club of Denver, Colorado, received a letter from a cousin in Dublin saying that *he* was a Rotarian, too. Snap! Denver sent word to Perry and Harris, who at first couldn't believe it. Soon letters from Chicago went in hot pursuit of the rogue Rotarian from San Francisco, who seemed to be conducting a one-man crusade on commission, at which Paul Harris's delight (how the rapscallion must have enjoyed the revelation!) matched Ches Perry's impotent fury, for by now Belfast was also under Morrow's wing.

The following month, at Sheldon's urging, E. Sayer Smith had established Rotary in Manchester. Indeed, by the start of the following year, Harris and Perry had heard that Sheldon had done even greater things, establishing Clubs in Paris and Vienna! No evidence exists for either fantasy, however, and one can conclude only that understandable euphoria and confusion had resulted from the sudden discovery by the Americans that two trail-blazers were at work in the same territory, selling the same product and with equally satisfactory sales.

From London, E. Sayer Smith was writing to Secretary Ches Perry: "Manchester is going good . . . its Membership has grown from eight to twenty-five in a month." The Bostonian Harvey Wheeler was writing: "I hope to be able to report Liverpool next, and then Birmingham . . . those of us who visit London will be made very welcome by English Rotarians." From north of the Tweed, Stuart Morrow (the only one of the three who actually would form Liverpool and Birmingham Clubs) was writing: "When I arrived in Glasgow a few months ago . . . I did not know a man, woman or child in the place. Today, however, the Glasgow Rotary Club . . . possesses a membership of 112 and a balance in the bank of about £200 (then worth $1,000)."

For all the organisation which, under Ches Perry, was rapidly being formed from the offices in the First National Bank, it was Paul Harris to whom the pioneers overseas reported. It was in his role as catalyst and connecting link between Morrow and Sheldon, between Ireland, Scotland, England and the United States, that the Founder performed his last great act of service before "retirement". His letter congratulating the Dubliners on forming their Club, written early in 1912, told them the address of the London Club. His correspondence with London told Sheldon and Sayer Smith about Dublin, Belfast and Glasgow. We may be sure that though the latter may have felt some chagrin, the former was inspired anew by that unexpected challenge, which he was to meet head-on by a sudden sweep down into England the following year. By September 1913 Morrow had formed the Liverpool Rotary Club (in less than a fortnight, the fastest formation in Rotary history) and one in Birmingham. He had formed the Edinburgh Club twelve months before, bringing its membership to 140 within three months. Two aspects of formation had not changed: as at Dublin, Belfast and Glasgow, Morrow had held an introductory meeting, had explained the Rotary Movement to his own, and his listeners' satisfaction, and had then been made Organising Secretary, taking for a salary half the members' entrance fee, which was still 2 guineas. Either he had given up the fast-fading hope that he would be given a job by Rotarians or he had resolved to make a full-time career out of forming Rotary Clubs.

Nor was this professional approach frowned on by either Harris or Perry. In the same issue of *The Rotarian* (as *The National Rotarian* had now become), which reported the Third Rotary Convention at Duluth, Minnesota, Stuart Morrow's photograph appeared, giving his address as 100 Bothwell Street, Glasgow, from which he offered "to undertake commissions or organise agencies in the British Isles for American businessmen . . . who would like to have such services from a reliable and competent man". While the Founder would have died rather than give his endorsement to such activity in relation to the formation of American Rotary Clubs, distance clearly lent enchantment to the view where "abroad" was concerned, and Ches Perry, functioning both as Editor and Business Manager of the publication, also had no qualms, once over his first shock, provided the practice remained a "foreign" one. *The Rotarian*, after all, was now "The Official Organ of the International Association of Rotary Clubs", the latest name for the Movement, which had been agreed at Duluth during the Convention of 6th-9th August 1912. This change of name had been proposed by a delegate from Winnipeg, and the official photograph of the delegates shows three defiant banners bearing the name of Winnipeg successfully shoving to one side the vainly flamboyant sashes labelled Chicago.

But the main sensation, as at Portland, Oregon, the previous year, was achieved by someone who wasn't there, this time the President of the Rotary Club of London, whose request for affiliation was granted, and his charter signed by Paul Harris, amidst acclamation. If the three delegates from Winnipeg felt slightly put out by this proceeding, their pride must have been salvaged when they learned that London's President was in fact a Canadian. There were at this time forty-nine Rotary Clubs chartered, forty-eight of which were in the United States and one in Canada, so that London was given the number "50". It also thus became recognised as the first official Rotary Club in Europe, a claim which Dublin still disputes (along with who won the Battle of the Boyne), on the basis of its having been formed by Stuart Morrow six months ahead of London, as indeed Belfast had been formed a few weeks before. Dubliners, however, paid no heed to the Shakespearian reminder that time has a wallet on his back, and by refusing, along with Belfast, Glasgow, Edinburgh and Manchester, to pay the required $1 per head affiliation fee to belong to the International Association, allowed London to step in front, where the records are concerned, and London remains there still. The fee of $1 equalled about 5 shillings in those far-off days, and it was not until Ches Perry later agreed that Clubs in the British Isles need pay only a shilling a head for affiliation that Stuart Morrow's progeny fell into line. From the viewpoint of Chicago, they put a black lining on the silver cloud, however, by agreeing at the same time to form the British Association of Rotary Clubs — a blow for Rotarian independence within the International Movement which, no matter how far and fast Rotary grew, was an innovation no other part of the world has ever dared to emulate.

Meanwhile, at Duluth, the Portland platform of the previous Convention was officially adopted for International Rotary and formed the basis for the first version of the Objects of Rotary, as well as confirming that membership of Clubs should consist "of one representative from each distinct line of business or profession". We have noted Ernst Skeel of the Seattle Club as the prime author of this platform, and he was also Chairman of a Committee which introduced and had adopted the first "Model" Constitution and By-Laws for all Rotary Clubs. This Committee, though not asked to do so, had also drawn up a first draft for a Code of Ethics. Though this Code was not pressed for the time being, the weary, prematurely middle-aged man from Racine doubtless welcomed it as giving him moral support for the address he was about to give to his fairly small audience. Small, that is, considering there were now just over 5,000 Rotarians to be called to Convention and that there was now a Club in Washington, the nation's capital. Echoing the over-optimistic hopes for the first Chicago gathering at the Congress Hotel, 3,000 had been confidently predicted. In the event, 500 came.

Quite a number came by boat, and Paul Harris came with them, on a voyage up the length of Lake Michigan, through the narrow channel that formed the border with Canada and down to the south-western corner of Lake Superior, where forty-nine miles of wharves fan out stupendously under the lee of 800-foot high cliffs atop which sit the boulevards of the city, where their Host Club then was barely a year old. Once again the Convention was being held at a great port and Paul Harris's friends noted that he had seldom been happier. It was a time of tremendous strain, but Jean was now there to sustain him, even though her home town, that other portside city far away on the Forth River, would soon be refusing to pay the fee to hear her husband.

It was the first of many journeys by water which Paul would make with Jean for World Rotary, but by far the most momentous. On the return trip, his hand would have been prised from the steering-wheel for ever, and prised by none other than the man he had put in charge of formulating the platform, drafting the new International Constitution and initiating progress towards a Code of Ethics, Ernest Skeel. We have noted that Skeel was to write within three years the main editorial content of the first issue of *The Rotary Wheel*, the British Rotary journal. He was to call his piece "Greater Rotary". For the moment, he was content with removing the Greatest Rotarian. Paul Harris was indeed elected the first International President. Nevertheless, just a few hours later he announced his "retirement" in favour of Glenn C. Mead, yet another lawyer, but this time, appropriately enough, from Philadelphia, home of Rotary's progenitor of two centuries before, Benjamin Franklin's Junto Club. And it was the hyperactive Skeel who proposed him.

Thus Skeel emerges as not just Rotary's first constitutional expert but the Movement's first king-maker and, more significantly, king-breaker. It might well have been expected that Rotary Number Two, San Francisco, would be in the lists. They did in fact have a candidate, but Skeel, from the rival West Coast Club, Seattle, put paid to that and also caused the rapid withdrawal of another rival candidature by the President of Duluth, the Host Club. As a result, no International President came from San Francisco till the Second World War. However, there has never been one from Seattle.

Accepting office before an audience of some 500, Mead declared: "The past of Rotary has been made secure by the sagacity, constructive genius and whole-souled devotion of the Founder, Paul Harris." Paul must have heard the tribute with mixed feelings, since the implication was strong that the future was none of his affair. Still, he was exhausted and glad to hand over, with the consolation of his new title, President Emeritus. He made one final address as President, hailing Rotary's spread to other nations and giving a fervent, fiery glimpse of the future (part of this address has already been quoted in Chapter One) but with emphasis on ideals of service, not business-getting. "The star of hope in the Rotarian ethical firmament must be high. It is hardly possible for it to be too high. . . . If we aim at the high mark, we may acquit ourselves creditably, even if we fall short of our full expectation." And with modesty that was transparently, almost heart-breakingly genuine, he proclaimed: "The grandeur of Rotarianism is in its future, not in its past. This is the matin, not the vespers, of Rotary. . . . Men will arise to the call, and the leaders in the days that are to come will be drawn from the ranks of those who are most deeply concerned in the ethics and the philosophy of Rotary."

When this address was duly printed in *The Rotarian* the following month, its final paragraphs were followed by Stuart Morrow's advertisements, inviting representative business men of Edinburgh to a meeting to consider forming a Rotary Club, for all the world as if he were unaware of the true reason for Glasgow Rotarians' not being at Duluth to hear Paul Harris. It was simply for the lack of "a guinea stamp", a sentiment soon to be shared by his tight-fisted Edinburgh recruits.

CHAPTER SEVEN

Wheels across the Sea

Here in the Zenith City
Of the great Unsalted Sea,
With zeal and zest
We greet each guest
Of the Club called "Rotary".
From England, Scotland, Ireland,
From Canada, too, they're bound,
From ev'ry state in our broad land,
They make the wheel go round.

Convention song, Duluth, 1912

Zenith City is an imperishable part of the folklore and fact of Rotary. Created by Sinclair Lewis as a typical Midwestern city, it is the fictional home of George Follansbee Babbitt, whom Lewis portrayed in his 1922 novel as the typical middle-class American business man of his era; and succeeded so devastatingly well, that Babbitt became the brand name for the butt of his satire. That satire extended through *Babbitt* to Rotary, of course, via the "Booster" Club to which his hero belonged. No reader could fail to identify Lewis's model. Not only, as noted, was it a name Harris and Shorey and their friends had almost selected anyway — and it is fascinating to speculate what would have then emerged as a symbol instead of a Golden Wheel — but "Boosting" was quickly established as a popular feature of Rotary's earliest Clubs, a custom whereby members continually praised their own and each other's products and services, openly touting for reciprocal business — and usually getting it.

The existence of this profitable ritual was advanced quite early on, in fact, as the real reason for the Movement's being called Rotary, and Harris knew it. When the Minneapolis Club was formed in 1910 (by Paul Harris himself, against strong opposition), the *Minneapolis Morning Tribune* observed:

> Everything is done in Rotation. Each meeting has a different chairman, each member of the club taking the place in rotation. If something especially good in the business world comes along, it is passed on to the next member if it can be of any service to him. Every endeavor on the part of the members is conducted in the same way, for the benefit of all.

It certainly gave a new meaning to "wheeling" and dealing, and though the reality of those early days has long passed into myth, such views are still pressed by opponents of Rotary, though with less and less conviction and sincerity. Paul Harris disliked the custom intensely but tolerated the practice, since it helped the Movement take hold in communities which otherwise might not have given his long-term ideals a second glance, which had to be cajoled from the accepted Victorian virtue of self-help to self-service before understanding fully what their Founder really meant by urging Sheldon's slogan of Service Above Self (no matter what Sheldon might have meant by it).

Yet Lewis did not pluck the name of his fictional Midwestern town (which he used in *Dodsworth* as well) from his imagination. Zenith was a popular name for Duluth, one of the three great cities of the author's home state of Minnesota. Duluth, at the head of the Great Lakes, is, next to New York, the second busiest port in the country. Lewis knew Duluth well and lived there for a time. So did lots of Rotarians in the summer of 1912, when that city played host to Rotary's Third Convention, and then was boosted into fame as the city where the Movement first proclaimed itself an international one. Lewis probably watched it happen. It was also where Paul Harris said goodbye to Rotary, the place where he confessed his exhaustion after the intense burst of creation that had realised his dream in so short a time. I have used the metaphoric description of seed-carrying for this extraordinary man — one cannot fail to do so — and we may note that Duluth, apart from its other distinctions, is famous for apparently having no pollen at all. It has thus earned its place in the Rotarian mythology. Duluth was where, on receiving word from London, Harris knew that the Movement was in essence the child he wanted. In the seventh year, he rested. Duluth was where he became President Emeritus. After Duluth, most of the world's Rotarians thought he was dead.

But how was it that Rotary caught on so swiftly and so powerfully in the British Isles, whether through official channels or through the persuasiveness of the roaming, and indigent, Medicine

Man? How was it that the delegates at Duluth could sing, with apparent utter faith and credulity:

> Your Union Jack's uniting
> With our Red, White and Blue.
> And as we sing
> God Save the King,
> You'll sing "America" too.

Part of the reason was, of course, that the two tunes were the same, and perhaps a few of the delegates were also aware that "Yankee Doodle" and the "Star-Spangled Banner" were also British melodies. But this made only the singing simple.

Previous chapters have given plenty of evidence that there was a fairly well-established cross-fertilisation over the Atlantic, by means of authors and lecturers, with a salting of rogues. This had gradually reached crescendo through the nineteenth century, from the lionising of Fenimore Cooper (who had begun by trying a poor imitation of Jane Austen called *Precaution*), through Edgar Allan Poe, whose mother was English and who was schooled in Great Britain, to Herman Melville, who was first published in London (by Byron's publisher, John Murray) and was for a time American consul in Liverpool, to Mark Twain, who received an honorary doctorate from Oxford at the same time as Rudyard Kipling. Kipling symbolises the passing of global power from the old to the new. He did so with eager American help, for his famous poem "Recessional" ("Lest We Forget") was retrieved from his waste-paper basket by the daughter of Charles Eliot Norton, the great Harvard scholar and friend of the literary mighty of both America and England, who had become a close friend of Kipling during the latter's stay at Brattleboro, Vermont, near Paul Harris's childhood home. We may note that the poet of empire, Kipling, was at this time gradually to give way his place in European admiration to the poet of democracy, Walt Whitman — and it was Whitman's great champion, G.K. Chesterton, who described the twentieth century as "This Rotarian Age".

But the worlds of entertainment dined voraciously from transatlantic tables also. That thriving child of entertainment, motion pictures, made silent films of *Vanity Fair, David Copperfield* and other classics; and they made *Raffles* the year Rotary was born! The stage world had long swapped stars also, from opera to vaudeville to honky-tonk variety. London paid Irving Berlin $1,000 a week to play and sing his own compositions and he wrote "The International Rag" in honour of his West End patrons. The Gaiety

Girls and Floradora Girls were as much household names in the United States as Gilbert and Sullivan had been, and if Harry Lauder went one way, Harry Houdini went the other. As always, popular art reflected the society it pleased. Before and since Jenny Jerome had married Lord Randolph Churchill, American beauty and wit had spliced with Ancient Britons. Bernard Shaw's heroines were far more recognisably American than English, and indeed his plays were more successful in the United States. In the year Paul Harris founded Rotary, *Man and Superman* took more money on Broadway than the Ziegfeld Follies.

Thus it is not surprising that investment by the British in the growth of their lost colony in Victorian times was now being reversed by way of importation of American business go-getting methods to the Old Country. The contrast between and compatibility of British and American social and business life were well illustrated during the first years of George V's reign by the works of P.G. Wodehouse, who produced in this period, just before the First World War, four plays, five novels, forty short stories and umpteen song lyrics, all of which met with equal success on both sides of the Atlantic. Indeed, in 1912, the year of Duluth, his book *The Prince and Betty* was published simultaneously in New York and London, though with different, if related, plots. Wodehouse's first collaboration with Jerome Kern (their most famous perhaps being "Bill" in *Showboat* much later) was, of all things, a show-stopper about Joseph Chamberlain and tariff reform — very much a business concern. To be a business man was rapidly becoming as respectable as being an aristocrat or politician, and this essentially Puritan ethic was most definitely imported from America. There was a major difference, however: whereas in the United States the notion of service and ethical practice had to be grafted on to successful business, in Great Britain those ideals already went hand in hand, at least in theory.

At Duluth Harris announced, "We are scientizing our methods of acquaintance-building to suit the rational requirements of men, and now we are going to scientize our service." The phrase was pure Arthur Sheldon who, coincidentally in London, was publishing his series of textbooks on *The Science of Business*, Lesson One of which pronounced, "It is high time that the searchlight of science be thrown upon the problem of successful human activity as functioning in constructive salesmanship", which Sheldon defined every few pages as "the art of securing progressively profitable patronage conditioned upon the principle of Service". In other words, He Profits Most Who Serves Best. Is it any wonder that the "hard-headed men" who were shortly to "do well out of the war" (in Baldwin's memorable phrase) threw open their arms to the new Movement? When Sheldon followed hard upon Morrow's departure from Edinburgh to hurl his tremendous oratory upon the shrewd Scots, many of them flocked to enrol in his course, receive his textbooks and, while noting, as one commented (with hindsight) "the most extraordinary mixture of wisdom and sheer balderdash", they rose to the persuasive fire of his words. After all, an Edinburgh lass had married the Founder, and she and Sheldon worshipped at the same shrine.

The mood was to be memorably enshrined in that runaway best-seller of the early post-war years, *The Man Nobody Knows*, written by an American advertising executive whose father was a clergyman. It enjoyed equal success in Britain, with its portrayal of Jesus Christ as "the founder of modern business" and the Gospels as carrying the essential lessons of good salesmanship, even interpreting "Let there be light" as a prophecy of neon signs which, though given notoriety by Broadway, were an invention of the British. This was not the Christ whom W.T. Stead had envisaged as coming to clean up Chicago, but then Stead was now at the bottom of the ocean with the *Titanic*. It was, however, closely related to a different Redeemer, the Christ of Science Himself, worshipped in the spread of Churches of Christ Scientist, that were to match the spread of Rotary Clubs around the globe, sponsored largely by business men, all based on Mary Baker Eddy's original First Church of Christ Scientist in Boston, Massachusetts. This was Science and Health as against Science and Business, but both drew on the Gospels for their respective sources of new truth and revealed laws of behaviour, being and action. From this movement had come one of the world's great newspapers, the *Christian Science Monitor*, in 1909. Its Editor naturally became a Rotarian the following year, when Boston formed Rotary Number Seven — 1909 saw Oakland, Seattle, Los Angeles and New York also in the fold! And in his first editorial — the newspaper's second, the inaugural editorial having been written by Mrs Eddy, then a mere eighty-seven years old — he announced:

> To count the various items of goodwill that went to build up the *Monitor* would be impossible . . . there was much more than buying and selling involved. There was the urgency of kindness in much of the work done. . . . There was honesty that rose above the claim of policy. Some might have seen confusion, but to the seeing eye, taking form among the clouds, was the vision of man serving man in a brotherhood of service.

This was only one year after Rotary reached its second Club, in San Francisco (Stuart Morrow's), so things were now moving fast.

Mrs Eddy's editor shared weekly fellowship with Rotarian Harvey Wheeler, frequently absent in London. Rotary officially became international through Boston, therefore, not San Francisco, despite that Morrow worked his wonders (as Harris said) ahead of anyone else in the British Isles. And the *Christian Science Monitor* followed suit; even today, London remains the only place outside the United States where the *Monitor* is published.

One aspect of early Rotary which did not survive long in the more formal procedures of the Old World was the Movement's Achilles' heel — "Boosting". Dublin, Belfast and Glasgow made heroic efforts to follow Morrow's guidance in this particular manifestation of "fellowship" — his old Club of San Francisco was very uninhibited in this regard, until it found itself boycotted by non-member firms for "over the top" excesses — but the practice faltered beneath the stern frowns at the Liberal Club on Princes Street, where the Committee of the Edinburgh Club met weekly. In spite of the fact that one of its sons had given the American business world its most indispensable adjunct, the telephone, Edinburgh was proud of the responsibility that one of its daughters had married the Founder of Rotary and named her marital home after an Edinburgh avenue, Comely Bank. Accordingly, its Rotarians quickly adopted and approved what they correctly perceived was the Paul Harris view of the proper business of a Rotary Club. After six months, they sent Stuart Morrow packing, to do his Boosting among the Sassenachs, though they strained themselves to give him a farewell present of 10 guineas for his trouble.

An indistinguishable mark of the sobriety with which Edinburgh welcomed Rotary is the fact that their list of Founder Members included only one man engaged in the trade of quenching thirst — and *his* Classification was "Mineral Water"! As time went by, this was to change. A far greater change in Rotary, however, was presaged by the vision of Edinburgh's first Club President and Secretary (after Morrow), R.W. Pentland and Dr Thomas Stephenson, respectively, who in May 1914 were to hold these same posts in the British Association of Rotary Clubs.

Why does everyone still hold it such a mystery, this unstinting welcome to Rotary in the Old World? Boosting may have been rejected, true, together with the mandatory use of first names, but this was surface matter. Below surface, business and social links were already cemented by the mason's grip. Farther up, the brash, exhilarating vulgarity of American politics was permeating our own. Lloyd George made small effort to hide his wheeling and dealing and could vary his accent with a facility any Tammany Hall ward boss might envy. It was significant that his private secretary for a time was a wealthy American, Waldorf Astor, whose Virginian wife, Nancy, became the first woman member of the House of Commons. The Northcliffe popular newspapers attempted to create sensational news as well as purvey it sensationally, just as the Hearst papers were doing in the States. Mammoth, screaming headlines told of the pursuit of Dr Crippen, a Midwesterner, of police gunfights with immigrants in Stepney — any American reader felt right at home in London. Winston Churchill's "siege of Sydney Street" (he had just become Home Secretary) took place within days of Paul Harris's Manifesto appearing in the *National Rotarian* in January 1911. So one could say, not too fancifully, that these two men, already bracketed in this book, took to the streets together.

Through Harris — this Don Quixote of the Western world and his proliferating Sancho Panzas — Rotary came to the towns and cities of Britain in the same milieux which were proving such fertile seed-beds in the towns and cities of America. Morals, social and political values, all were in question. Another American, Henry George, had already fuelled the brains of Socialists like Shaw, and union muscle flexed in parliamentary elections to tax away the landed gentry. Big business men were all in favour, it lifted the tax from them, and we find the fingers of the most famous politicians in the land almost caught in the tills of the Stock Exchange. The Marconi scandal involved greater names than Crippen, whom Marconi's invention had caught — two became Prime Minister, another Ambassador to Washington and Marconi himself became a Rotarian. Troops confronted strikers in London, Liverpool and Manchester. There were large-scale wildcat strikes, answered by lock-outs, in the year of the Portland Convention and the Portland platform half a world away. The charged atmosphere in Britain was very like that of Chicago in 1905. The world was shifting beneath the feet of business, so it was entirely natural, not mysterious, that Rotary had its first welcome from British business in precisely London, Liverpool and Manchester. As in Chicago, those six short years before, the slightly nervous men behind their office desks needed a new rationale and practical justification for the way they conducted their lives. Sheldon gave them the religion of Science; Harris gave them the religion of Faith. Morrow gave them a cocktail of both. All in the name of Profit; which always helps the medicine go down.

The historian must face facts on two levels at once. The level of what happened and the reasons why they happened are often sufficient, and sufficiently difficult, in themselves. History is a series of street accidents, and even eye-witnesses, depending on which pavement they were standing, or from which window they were watching, can give widely different accounts of each major collision. Unfortunately, the participants themselves are often the most reticent witnesses, their evidence the most unreliable. You do not ask the wounded to describe combat objectively; not till the scars are healed, anyway. By which time memory has faded and healed also. Romeo would have made a lousy historian if he had lived to retain his belief that whoever jests at scars never felt a wound. Any historian knows that the scars are far more important than the wounds, certainly far more informative. That they are sometimes funny also, is scarcely the historian's fault. The personal tragedies of Tweedledum and Tweedledee cannot stop us smiling.

So while the chapters following will recount the astounding growth of Rotary throughout the world properly through its milestones, turning-points, achievements, and the events which signalled them, time has been spent here examining some of the underlying reasons for the successful — and, more interesting still — *immediately* successful, transplanting of so essentially an American idea as Rotary. The concentration has been on the British Isles because it is there that Rotary first took root outside the New World. But a similar examination will not be needed for other nations it was to reach in the years after the First World War, because in their case most of the same reasons still apply. For Rotary transplated easily, not in spite of being essentially American but *because* it was essentially American — essentially *nineteenth-century* American, when the states were busy trying to unite and multiply and were doing so for the reason that it was a period when America was *Europe* transplanted. It began in the city through which many of the enormous tide of immigrants passed. And exactly the same phenomenon was true of San Francisco, where the tide from the Orient poured simultaneously in and the great torrent of European immigrants came to a halt at the Pacific, sharing with Keats's Damien "a wild surprise". As Paul Harris himself wrote, Chicago was "a social maelstrom where racial, political, and religious extremes met, clashing and ultimately merging into a semblance of homogeneity". Note the word "semblance". It is but another phase of European history set on another, cruder stage, the touring version of the original production, with subtitles. "In such atmosphere", said Harris, "The Star of Rotary had its rise." Indeed — and also its export success.

The names that appear amongst the first members of Chicago Number One tell the story: Schiele, Loehr, Ruggles, Chapin, Arntzen, Muñoz, Murphy — with English, Irish and Scots melding in the first surname of all, Harris. As Harris summed it up, perhaps rather too rosily: "The sparkling wit of the Irishman vied with the quaint humour of the Jews, to the delectation of the Members whose ancestry represented a galaxy of nations." No matter that, outside the Sherman Hotel, the sparkling tommy-guns of Irish gangsters were cross-firing with the quaint sawn-off shotguns of Jewish hoodlums.

Inside the Sherman Hotel boyish grins replaced gunfire, cigar-smoke floated overhead not gun-smoke. The Rotary Star was not a shooting star. It emerged in Chicago as the hope of a European community still not assimilated, with quite a long way to go. The term "melting-pot" was still being used to describe America three years later, after all, in the famous play of that name (by an Englishman). And we must remember, too, that Rotary reached out to a European world that itself was fluid as seldom before and never since. A.J.P. Taylor has noted that, even in 1914, Europe was still "a single civilized community, more so than even at the height of the Roman Empire. A man would travel across the length and breadth of the Continent without a passport until he reached the frontiers of Russia and the Ottoman Empire", while urban Europe shared a "common outlook in morality and philosophy". In the heyday of gang warfare, one had more difficulty travelling between north and south Chicago!

It was to this Europe that Paul Harris appealed through Rotary therefore, and not in vain. Of course, Paul aimed at London first; it was still the world's centre. And for all the precedents for Rotary mentioned in Chapter One, it was Joseph Addison in a *Spectator* essay in 1710 who had mentioned that "our modern celebrated clubs are founded upon eating and drinking, which are points wherein most men agree, and in which the learned and the illiterate, the dull and the airy, the philosopher and the buffoon, can all of them bear a part". Very much to the point, Addison continued: 'When men are thus knitted together by a love of society and not by a spirit of faction . . . to relax themselves from the business of the day by an innocent and cheerful conversation, there may be something very useful in these little institutions." He also cited the rules of one such club he visited: "None shall be admitted to the club that is of the same trade with any other member of it; none shall have his clothes or shoes mended, but by a brother member"; and a member's wife could speak to him only "without the Door". Though all Europe was a fertile ground for Rotary, the impending war would make it wait. But the most primed soil was British.

As a people — a "nation of shopkeepers", as Napoleon scathingly put it — who had won and lost more empires (today, we would call them take-over battles of commercial giants) than anyone else, the British felt they were uniquely placed to advise those who would do likewise. And advise they did, asked and unasked, for Rotary's next two crucial decades. Empires were their business, and vice versa. Since trade had, with demonstrable success, followed the flag, why shouldn't it follow the Wheel? Nor were these infuriating assumptions all that mistaken, in the eyes of the Movement's most sardonic observer. Only six years after Sinclair Lewis had mocked the "Booster Club" so effectively in *Babbitt* (he was awarded the Nobel Price in 1930), the author toured the British Isles and was able to take a first-hand look at how well the transplant had taken hold, flourished and evolved. "I have been accused of saying nasty things about the Rotarians," he admitted, during a 1928 interview, "but I assert that the growth of Rotary in Great Britain is more important for world tranquillity than all the campaigns of the reformers put together."

Meanwhile, to return to the last Convention before the First World War, perhaps Britain was rather *too* prime for the taste of Rotary One. Chicago was still fitfully smouldering over the fact that Clubs were multiplying all over the United States, and to have the formation, reluctantly acceded to, of a British Association of Rotary Clubs shoved in their face was really a bit much. Five British Rotarians had turned up at the Fourth Rotary Convention at Buffalo, another Great Lakes port, though at the opposite extreme to Duluth, and the London delegate told the gathering, "We came here as students. We go back full, live Missionaries." At the Fifth Convention in 1914 many Chicagoans saw with dismay how truly he had spoken.

For the record, this Fifth Convention, held in Texas at Houston (still at a port, if of a very special kind), gave the BARC "a hearty welcome", though the welcome was double-edged, since it added: ". . . the International Association of Rotary Clubs recommends to Mr. Morrow that any further work on his part . . . be done in co-operation with the British Association". Poor Morrow! But he was not the only Rotarian about to suffer the status of a non-person. Harris himself was no longer visible – his disappearance from the Rotary scene had been as complete as it was abrupt – but we can be sure the heartiness of the welcome was echoed from within the fastness of Comely Bank. Ches Perry made the motions, but his heart wasn't in it, as he candidly admitted in an article forty years later. The development, he wrote, "gave the North American Rotarians much concern" and he raised no objection "with the hope that the British and Irish Rotarians could be persuaded to give up their idea".

117

Not a chance, though it remains the only "territorial" association ever allowed. Two onrushing wars took care that its most particular distinction flourished behind the closed frontiers of battle. The Big One with Kaiser Bill was one, of course. As to the other, it would long be remembered that at Buffalo, the Dublin delegate, a gentleman with the evocative name of Sheridan, had asked his audience, "When are you coming over to see us?" and a voice from the hall had answered "1916"!

The playwright Sheridan, relation or not, would never have coined so sick a joke — even though his classic remark about a man having the right to sit by his own fireside, made while Drury Lane burned down, is very Irish — for even Rotary, already trying to ignore politics, would soon find it hard to cope with the thunderous tramping back and forth of 100,000 Volunteers in Dublin and Belfast respectively. How could you apply Classifications to a race where the Ulster Volunteers were commanded by a Dubliner, and the Irish National Volunteers by an Ulsterman? And in 1916, anyway, Dublin's only American visitor who mattered would be Eamon de Valera.

In later years Paul referred to Morrow as "the mysterious wonder-working Irishman", so he had known all along. It was a pity he didn't mention him at Duluth, but allowance must be made for his weariness, his readiness to hand over leadership and the priority his mind must have given to the following report received from the London Club, the triumph he so prized: "Though oceans may divide us, yet we are all united in the one great ideal of being happy ourselves and communicating happiness to those with whom we come into communion so closely as through the Rotarian cause." It was sweet music, balm to the heart-wounds of the Founder who was about to be removed, to let his hands be taken from the wheel.

Among the songs conducted by Harry Ruggles at the Duluth Convention — he was about to be elected to the first Board of Directors of International Rotary — was one containing the following lines addressed to the "Prince of boys" and "Father Paul" (he was called them both within four lines): "Take a little tip from Father / Take a little tip from me. . . ." This was presumably intended as a tribute and was perhaps accepted as such, since it was adapted from one of the hit tunes of the day — though no credit was given to the composer, a young Russian immigrant, still only twenty-four, but already world famous for "Alexander's Ragtime Band", perhaps a subliminal glance back at the Tsar, his court and Rasputin! Rotary has the Medicine Man to thank for providing the counterbalance to Sheldon's lack of tact and restraint. Even though Stuart Morrow had never met Harris, Perry or any of the other founding Rotarians, he had a greater practical sense of their aims and ideals than Sheldon and a greater success in conveying them. His farewell address to the Glaswegians was called "The Aims of Rotary other than Commercial" and, though he acknowledged primacy of the principles of Classification and sharing business interests, he added: ". . . it is distinctly within the province of a Rotary Club to take notice of dishonourable business methods, and non-ethical standards, with a view to their elimination".

This address, though no one in Chicago had yet met Morrow, and could learn much about him from the San Francisco Club, nevertheless reached Harris and Perry, who had it printed "without waiting to ask Mr. Morrow's consent" in *The Rotarian.* Harris and Perry knew, if no one else did (and even if one of them resented it) who had carried the brighter torch abroad and lit the farthest fuse. Morrow wasn't at Duluth, nor were any of the clubs he founded, but it was *his* work above all which had made it possible to call Rotary an International Movement.

As at Portland the year before, there was a boat trip, this time up the St Louis River, but it was mainly for Jean Harris and the other ladies — reports of the time refer quite brazenly to a Woman's Rotary Club of Duluth — and many delegates passed up the excursion to stay close to the action ashore those momentous days. For a true feeling of the occasion, we can combine this item with a contemporary description of the scene at the Commercial Club, that hot August of 1912 when Rotary became international, settled its Objects and Constitution and bestowed the title of President Emeritus upon the Founder, who himself had been a Rotarian for only seven years, and began as Conventions were always more or less to do, with the Mayor's welcome and the giving to Paul Harris not of the keys of the city but those "that would open every door of enjoyment" in Duluth, an ambiguous gift to a new husband. A delegate described "a large room, filled with tobacco smoke, banners on the wall, Paul P. Harris's stately dome looking up to the northwest through the shifting clouds, the ever alert Perry at his side. . . . One had to be there to catch the enthusiasms and to realize the sincerity of those dead-in-earnest men — pioneers blazing the way into a new era of commercial life". And up on the platform what was he thinking, that lean and tired, no longer so lonely man? He could bring himself to write of it only later and in the third person: "It was with a sense of relief, though, it must be admitted, with some sorrow, that Paul in Duluth yielded the creature of his imagination."

Paul Harris was fond of reading Wordsworth and perhaps the opening lines of "The Lost Leader" occurred to him as he left that platform in Duluth. But it wasn't quite for a "handful of silver" that he left, his "stately dome" disappearing from the thick haze of free cigars. Those cigars had been donated by the Duluth Rotarians to their guests; and their Club President, cheated of his aspirations to international high office, made a final and successful bid for dubious immortality in the Movement at the Convention Ball in the town's Coliseum, a most appropriate setting for despatching Rotary's first and finest gladiator. Stopping the band music and gathering the revellers in a circle on the dance-floor, the Duluth President spoke solemnly of "the great work accomplished by Mr. Harris" and then, on behalf of the entire Convention, presented the Founder of Rotary with a gold watch. As he contemplated this standard achievement gift for a minor clerk, we can well believe the official account in *The Rotarian* when it relates this "was a complete surprise to Mr. Harris, and he was so overcome he was unable to do anything but briefly and sincerely expressed his thanks". One hopes that, when Paul found himself in the privacy of his hotel room with Jean, a more fitting and trenchant response occurred to him. If so, we can be sure Mrs Harris was firm in her refusal to allow him to say it, though we can guess the "rapscallion" of the not so distant past would not have hesitated to say very definite things. The official account continues, with heavy-handed and distasteful jocularity: "It is now the proper procedure upon meeting Mr. Harris anywhere to inquire of him the time of day."

Let us hope he never gave it.

Duluth has two more distinctions, in Rotary terms. First, it announced agreement for a standard design of Monty Bear's Wheel which could be accepted by all Clubs. The second distinction lay some time ahead. Twenty-four years after it hosted the Third Convention at which the Movement became International by name, Rotarian William A. McConnell, OBE (holder of the Order of the British Empire), of Dublin, as the newly married insurance salesman "Bill" had now become — was invited to Duluth, or "Zenith City" as it still liked to call itself, to address a large Rotary gathering. Apart from declaring war "obsolete" and scorning Britain and America for "Re-arming" (this was three years before the Nazis marched into Poland and two months after they occupied the Rhineland), McConnell referred of course back to 1912, the year when "in this City of Duluth, Rotary...transformed the organisation into one of international scope".

He was mistaken, as we have seen. The Convention had indeed joyfully accepted and recognised the transformation, the Golden Wheel had rolled across the sea, but the man who had actually brought it about was Stuart Morrow, the Medicine Man. Yet not once, throughout a very long speech, did the speaker refer to his brother-in-law, that forgotten embarrassment who had turned up so unexpectedly on his doorstep at the start of 1911, looking for a job and bringing, as bait and collateral, a new Movement to the world.

Even at the Zenith, Nadir could be touched. Twice.

CHAPTER EIGHT

The Wheel at War — 1

Onward, Sons of Rotary,
　　Briskly march along,
Raise your joyful voices,
　　Lustily in song.
　　　　Sing Rotarian glories,
　　　　　Shout them near and far,
　　　　Till Rotary in all nations
　　　　　Becomes the guiding star.

Onward, Sons of Rotary,
　　March with steady swing,
Shoulder close to shoulder,
　　While you joyful sing.

Rotary Marching Song, 1915
(tune of "Onward Christian Soldiers")

The first time those words were sung was at the Sixth Rotary Convention, held at San Francisco in July 1915. It was the Convention of the first appearance of the Golden Wheel, the first Rotary Flag, the Code of Ethics — all of which we shall duly discover in this chapter — and the unveiling of the Movement's first Marching Song. America was not, of course, yet at war, but it was the first time Rotarians had met in Convention since the outbreak of the carnage overseas, and there was no doubt where their sympathies lay, notwithstanding Woodrow Wilson's counsel to the nation that it "must be neutral in fact as well as in name . . . impartial in thought as well as in action".

He did not know his fellow-Rotarians, however well he might feel he knew the Senate. He might be leading a country which believed it had forsworn foreign entanglements for ever, but he belonged, too, to a Movement which had already and irrevocably laid the corner-stone of an internationalism which would not be long denied. So did his then Secretary of State, Rotarian William Jennings Bryan (no relation of Paul Harris's grandfather), who was later to resign when Wilson decided to get tough with the Kaiser. Only two months before Convention, the *Lusitania* had been torpedoed with great loss of life; a British ship, true, but with many American passengers, on its way from New York to London and the first civilian passenger ship ever sunk without warning. Pro-Allied sympathies were strong and were not hidden, even at one of the largest banquets — for 1,900 — ever given in the United States, taking up an entire floor of the Palace Hotel. The Marching Song had come from Henry King of the Rotary Club of Boston which had stood as "Mother" to the London Club and had many British contacts. (Boston itself was closely connected with the tune's composer, of course, having seen the world première of *The Pirates of Penzance*.) No mention was made in the verses of Germany, but its import was plain.

Allen D. Albert, the new International President at San Francisco, was a journalist who had worked on several Washington newspapers and had served as a war correspondent during the Spanish-American War, so he well understood the world, and he reminded his audience of "the dust that is being blown over the scorched fields of to-morrow. About two million of boys and young men are said already to have died — enough to shadow the households of three Califor-nias. . . . What can we do as Rotarians? We can begin by understand-ing that peace is not to be had for the world cheaply. . . . With all our devotion to peace, we dare not forget that chains are worse than bayonets". This last was a quotation from Douglas Jerrold, the English journalist and playwright from whom Albert was fond of quoting. It is perhaps fortunate for Rotary (or perhaps not) that Jerrold died when Bernard Shaw was one year old, or perhaps he could have elaborated Shaw's wisecrack about Rotary's going "to lunch" by substituting the Movement for his native land in his remark, "If an earthquake were to engulf England tomorrow, the English would manage to meet and dine somewhere among the rubbish, just to celebrate the event", or characterised a Rotarian by his definition of a man so excessively benevolent "that he would have held an umbrella over a duck in a shower of rain".

So what would Rotary do when the shower became a rag-ing storm?

"Remember, remember always that all of us, and you and I especially, are descended from immigrants and revolutionists," Franklin Delano Roosevelt once advised that strange close-knit élite, the Daughters of the American Revolution. Those red-white-and-blue rinsed Madame Defarges, busy splicing their minks at the foot of a scaffold in readiness for their non-Anglo Saxon camp-followers, whom they regarded as liberty's queue-jumpers, badly needed the advice when the remorseless floodtide of the Second World War was only temporarily dammed by Munich. During the run-up to the First World War, however, Americans were still caught up daily in the last great waves of immigration, coming mainly now from Eastern Europe, the Austro-Hungarian Empire (still, incredibly, ruled by Franz Joseph), the Balkans, Syrians, Armenians, plus more Italians, Poles and Finns. This Euro-American society, primarily urban, was strongly reflected in the early Rotary Clubs and, as has been suggested, accounted for its export success, since what was then "typically American" was also typically European and was to remain so until Franz Josef's nephew was assassinated at Sarajevo and the throats of a thousand guns opened to four years of violent, deafening slaughter and 1914 brought the event from whose inevitability those immigrants had fled. Though the quota barriers were not law till ten years later, the self-destruct of the old European dynasties, prolonged and dreadful as it proved, marked the closing of that ever-open door on the Hudson. From the heart of the Austro-Hungarian Empire had come — along with much else destroyed — the death-knell of unfettered human traffic across the Atlantic. The death-knell also of American ideals of romantic love, via Sigmund Freud's anguished cry that America was a "gigantic mistake", and the fact that he had just sailed to New York on the *George Washington* and returned on the *Kaiser Wilhelm* was persuasively symbolic. The great man had also publicly lamented the lack of public conveniences in American cities, which made even more prescient in retrospect that first community service of Rotary One.

It is striking evidence of the more tolerant spirit of those pre-war years, incredible to us now — not simply that the American Rotarians fully recognised they were descended from "immigrants and revolutionists", and not very far descended either, but that the first great wave of Old World "immigrants" they welcomed to the Rotary fold were from the heart of that very Empire which every schoolchild in the United States was taught to scorn as a defeated tyrant — and the First Rotarians saw no inconsistency in this.

Nor did the tyrant.

Even as he was being hustled backstage, Paul Harris, with the ink still wet on his signed charter for the Rotary Club of London, knew therefore his vision was justified and only just in time. A few years later and this century's terrible tread of marching death would have obliterated his dream for ever. As it was, the almost obscene brutal selfishness that characterises modern society, both in national and individual form, was too late to abort the development of its most implacable foe.

While no British Rotarians were actually present at the 1912 Convention, the five who turned up next year at Buffalo were followed twelve months later by a figure whose presence aroused both anxiety and acclaim. This was Dr Thomas Stephenson of Edinburgh, a retail chemist who had taken over as his Club's Honorary Secretary after Stuart Morrow had left for England. At Houston in 1914 Stephenson came, however, with enlarged significance, as Secretary of the one-month-old British Association of Rotary Clubs, and carrying proxies for all eight! The fact that he also addressed that Texas audience on "Rotary in Great Britain and Ireland" shows that he also brought with him a thick Scottish hide.

Rotary actually had nine lives in Britain by this time, but the Rotary Club of Brighton was — carrying the tradition of Dublin and Belfast one step farther, rather like the whimsical, quirky Ealing films of later years — not only unknown to Chesley Perry and Paul Harris's successors as International President; it was even unknown to the BARC. When "discovered", it was even unknown how a Rotary Club could have been formed there, and its origins remain unknown today. Suggestions have been made that a genie escaped from the Royal Pavilion there and magicked the Club into existence. Another thought is that the ghost of the Prince Regent, frolicking about his bizarre oriental creation, took revenge for his father's loss of the Thirteen Colonies by begetting a maverick Club. Certain it is that the first, and not the least valuable, contribution of Britain to Rotary's evolving structure, was the emphasis it placed on a Club's "autonomy" within the Movement, by behaving at the start as if unaware that it was even part of a Movement.

Yet Boosting was there even in Brighton from the start, in a blatant form that had long been discredited in many American Clubs. Not only could its members be expelled for not putting business their fellows' way; one Founder Member resigned in a huff because his particular skills were ignored in favour of a rival's by another member's family — he was an undertaker. In another respect, it was very much part of the American template, however — its first Treasurer was a lawyer.

Dr Stephenson, whose own Edinburgh club had, a few years before, baulked at paying a guinea as an affiliation fee to the IARC, now did not hesitate to demand an affiliation fee of 40 guineas from Brighton to join the British Association! He didn't get it, negotiations dragged on throughout half the war years and Brighton did not agree to become a recognised Club until 1st January 1917 (it didn't accept the Standard Club Constitution until 1932). During these important and laboured negotiations, the flower of British youth perished in the Flanders mud, France and Germany fought each other to a standstill at Verdun, the murderous and futile slaughter of the Somme choked the trenches with blood and shattered bodies, the first tanks appeared, Jutland brought the great opposing fleets together and, just across the Channel from Brighton, 200 U-boats began slipping towards the Atlantic. They had been sent, following a gigantic miscalculation of the German High Command, to begin that orgy of destruction upon the high seas which was to force a declaration of war from a man very much like Paul Harris in his close, retiring nature and whom Ches Perry had suggested had the ideal Rotarian qualities, since he had said, "We are learning again that the service of humanity is the business of mankind . . . the men who serve will be the men who profit." This was Woodrow Wilson who had been invited to address the Houston Convention, where in the event delegates had to listen to Dr Stephenson's British declaration of independence instead.

The good doctor did not tell them that Stuart Morrow's original converts were voicing concern that the word "Ireland" did not appear in the BARC name. But then he and his fellow-Directors of the new Association were firmly of the opinion that Morrow and his activities were an unfortunate aberration anyway. Not only had he committed the incomprehensible gaffe of forming a Club in Dublin before Edinburgh, but, having remedied the error, the Californian dynamo had made clear that he fully endorsed Dr Johnson's view that the "noblest prospect" one ever saw in Scotland was the road leading to England. This "error" was carefully avoided by Rotary's World Leader in 1981, Dr Stan McCaffrey, another Californian, when he came to hold a goodwill meeting of the Irish Club Presidents from Ulster and Eire in Enniskillen — before even glancing at the Emerald Isle, he called at Edinburgh.

The British Association of Rotary Clubs was announced in 1914 to a Convention of 1,288 Rotarians, as against twenty-nine in Chicago four years before. They represented 110 Clubs, a total which had increased by another thirteen by the outbreak of war in Europe. For the next four years, even counting the eventual entry of the United States into the war, there was an inevitable divide between the Rotarian "immigrants and revolutionists" in the New World and the Rotary "colonials" in the Old. There was no civilian front line, as in the Second World War, of course, and large numbers of the United Kingdom populace not required for trench fodder lived lives whose essential structure and habits continued unaltered.

As for the Atlantic, at least until the middle of 1917 when Britain lost 600,000 tons of shipping in April alone and was spending £7 million a day during July to try to keep afloat, there was still a good deal of travel back and forth, for those who could afford it. But the great waves of immigrants had not struggled past the Statue of Liberty to turn right back for burial under a war memorial in a continent they had renounced, and American and British Rotarians might have inhabited two different planets.

Much as Chesley Perry deplored the formation of the BARC, therefore, without it Rotary would never have survived the cataclysm which now shook the globe, for administration of British Clubs from Chicago would have been impossible. That fuse of inspiration, lit by Harris, nurtured by Perry, fetched and carried by Sheldon and borne at hurtling speed through the British Isles by Morrow, would have sputtered to extinction for lack of tending. The dream of internationalism would not have survived. As it was, the Armistice found an exhausted world made, if not quite as "safe for democracy" as Woodrow Wilson pronounced, at least ripe for Rotary plucking — or "Extension". New World Rotary and Old World Rotary renewed acquaintance warily, found and reconciled differences and prepared for the tremendous launch through every civilised nation on earth. Whatever deviation from the American norm in organisation Perry found when the guns fell silent at last, he also found a Rotary which had survived siege and assault — and even, at one time, a national food supply guaranteed for six weeks only, an appalling thought which stunned the trenchermen of Chicago.

After another generation had matured enough to kill and be killed, Rotary's inbuilt and demonstrated survival kit — as much a mystery to its friends as its enemies — was to prove itself again, even more dramatically, in countries of every race and language, re-emerging even from under the crushing heel of a succession of savage totalitarian regimes. Yet it would never have reached those countries, all of them non-Anglo Saxon, had it not first found its proof under onslaught by U-boat and zeppelin in what *The Rotarian* always carefully referred to as long as possible as the "European" War. So completely absorbed in Rotary was Perry that, from some of his writings, it might be suspected he half-believed that European War to be a deliberate ambush of his Movement. Though he foresaw "the first war between nations as having large fleets of airships", he deemed it quite reasonable to expect that "by one concerted action the large nations of the world might agree that airships in war service should be permitted only for scouting, reconnoitering, carrying messages, etc., and should not be permitted to become men of war to sail over a defenseless city". Such naïvety is easy to mock today, but we must remember that in 1914 the combatants themselves expected the war to be over by Christmas. And we must allow for Perry's disappointment that the travellers' tales brought to Chicago of Clubs springing up in Paris and Vienna had proved all too soon to be as real as the Angel of Mons.

Almost at once, the outbreak of what used to be described as the Great War began to show how right Paul Harris's urge across the Atlantic had been. The British Association of Rotary Clubs was established and recognised by the International Association with barely weeks to spare before the Kaiser crossed into Belgium. Had this not been so, we may doubt whether the Movement would ever have become global as soon as it did. But that is only half of the debt owed by Rotary to BARC, for not only did the war's end find Rotary established *in depth* abroad — one or two Clubs could easily have shrivelled — but the dangerous times gave British Clubs a magnificent opportunity to show how Rotary Clubs could help their communities. The high words of Convention Resolutions and Committee sub-clauses were translated by pressure of events into concrete fact. Club members demonstrated by example the meaning of Rotary, translating the dream of Paul Harris by an instinct they understood imperfectly themselves. Because everyone else was helping too in the first civilian war, they understood only gradually what a splendid instrument Harris had placed in their hands.

Edinburgh Rotarians had supplied the impetus, inspiration, and the President and Secretary of BARC, and did not hesitate to set a lead when, in the words of Sir Edward Grey, the British Foreign Secretary, the lights went out all over Europe. In the first week after Great Britain had declared war against Germany, the Club Council had formed a War Committee and sent a donation to the Belgian Fund. By the end of 1914, the Edinburgh and Glasgow Clubs had begun recruiting a "Short Stature" battalion, and response was such that the two Clubs soon each recruited their own. Edinburgh's was called the Bantam Battalion and Alex Wilkie, a future BARC President, made uniforms for the entire 1,000-strong battalion in his own firm's workshops. They were called the 17th Royal Scots, and were soon in the trenches. The Club sent a New Year's gift to every single one throughout the war — those who survived. Rotarian Wilkie, whose "Wylkedin" line of weathercoats, suits and skirts for ladies, made up most appropriately in Harris tweed, were of high reputation and regularly advertised in *The Rotary Wheel*, again earned himself a place in Rotary annals three years later when he conceived the idea of offering a suit, free of charge, to the first fifty customers during Edinburgh's "Aeroplane

Week" who bought one or more £100 War Bonds at his store. In three days he took £5,000, enough to build two aeroplanes!

Those early leaders of BARC never lost the ability to startle their Movement with the unexpected. W.H. Alexander, the six-foot-four Ulsterman who became second President of the Association, in a letter to the Editor of *The Rotary Wheel*, playfully took Dr Stephenson to task for referring to British Rotary as "she": "British Rotary is, I think, neither feminine nor masculine. It is neuter." There was no reaction from Chicago to this deadpan assertion.

A morale-boosting speech to Edinburgh Rotarians in April 1917 by one of their members included the clarion call "Don't ask what can a Rotary Club do for me. Ask yourself what can I do for it". A generation later, President John Kennedy was to use the same formula in his inauguration speech, but it was then too late.

Nor were the families of serving men overlooked, as morale on the "home front" was soon seen as a top priority in modern war. Every Christmas, Edinburgh Rotarians took over several theatres to entertain the children of soldiers and sailors. Their ecstatic audiences totalled 6,000 in 1914; at the last treat in 1919, the total had reached an amazing 40,000.

At the other end of the besieged island, the "unknown" Brighton Club raised over £25,000 in War Weapons Week, but perhaps history will remember longest that, when America entered the war, the Club helped organise a mammoth sporting event which gave the south coast — and any U-boat captains with raised periscopes in the Solent — their first stunned look at baseball!

Half-way down the island, Birmingham (the sixth and last Club formed by Stuart Morrow) decided to set up a Trade Fair to rival that at Leipzig, and from this evolved the great British Industries Fair, from which in turn evolved the modern National Exhibition Centre, which plays host to 20,000 Rotarians from every country of the Free World in 1984 at the Seventy-Fifth International Convention.

The London, Manchester and Glasgow Clubs all formed groups of special constables and, among constant projects from all Clubs in the British Isles to entertain the troops, two were outstanding: the Eagle Hut in London's Strand for looking after troops in the capital (it contained 300 beds, a canteen, concert-hall, billiard-room, book-stall, bath and shower-rooms), and the Liverpool scheme for placing the homes of Rotarians at the disposal of American Rotarians with sons on active duty, so their families could get together during "furloughs" from the front.

In January 1915 BARC launched *The Rotary Wheel*, which is thus the second oldest national Rotary journal in the world —

today it continues under the name *Rotary* — and the indefatigable Dr Stephenson also undertook the editorship, on top of all his other duties. A glance through its pages for the four years of the war reveals the increasing involvement of Rotary in the life of the nation, for many of its articles were texts of Club reports or addresses given to Clubs by distinguished speakers — and, from politics, these included a multicoloured party spectrum, all the way from Neville Chamberlain (an early Birmingham Rotarian) to Horatio Bottomley, then the famous jingoist editor of *John Bull*, not yet known as one of Britain's most successful con-men. Topics were far-reaching and far-sighted and astonishingly free from taboos — profit-sharing with workers, decimalisation, the use of the new phenomenon of the motion picture industry, the sexual risks of women in offices, science and education, the mystery of sleep, the truth about venereal disease; nothing was barred. If by war's end Rotarians had enlarged their horizons by nothing else, these five sentences from *The Rotary Wheel*, selected at random, must have long stayed in the minds of its constant readers:

> Capital must be educated to understand that labour is something more than merely its paid tool.

> Where women do the work of men equally well, they should have equal pay.

> An Army Sock is the finest product that can be produced in the sock line. We are all glad that the Tommy gets in the matter of hose what he deserves — the best.

> The Jew is not a drunkard.

> The second way in which syphilis is transmitted is by kissing. In Russia, seventy-five to eighty per cent of cases occur by kissing.

The magazine also told of Manchester Rotary's Home for Belgian Refugees, of Belfast's Soldiers' and Sailors' Service Club, of Glasgow's Welcome Club, giving accommodation to 2,000 overseas soldiers every month, and of the apotheosis of Rotary achievement by the Bristol Club which, at the request of the Lord Mayor raised, in only ten days, £800,000 to pay for two battle-cruisers, one member actually showering the city with 50,000 leaflets from an aircraft of the Royal Flying Corps.

During a "Business Men's Week", many hundreds of thousands of pounds were raised by Rotarians all over the British Isles to buy ambulances and other needs of the front (London alone raised millions), while Dublin Rotarians, having bounced back from seeing their meeting-place destroyed in the Easter Rising, ran a gigantic sale to buy War Bonds, selling over 2 million items contributed by the city's stores.

The saga of Rotary in wartime Britain in 1914–18 included one personal heroic triumph and two personal tragedies.

Peter Thomason of Manchester was only thirty-three when he became the third President of BARC — in those days, the Rotary image was far from one of retired, elderly men — and in 1917 he was called up in the Royal Engineers, in which he served while still in office. To quote Roger Levy's *Rotary International in Great Britain and Ireland*, Thomason was "a man of great charm and dignity, and an exceptionally cultured and gifted speaker", and he enlivened many issues of *The Rotary Wheel* with reports he whimsically called "The Back of the Front". He was eventually wounded in action, but survived to serve his beloved Movement for fifty years.

As to the tragedies, one befell Harry Lauder, who was as famous and popular in the United States as in Great Britain. Lauder was a Glasgow Rotarian and not only entertained and addressed many Clubs but raised huge sums for War Bonds, touring the length and breadth of Britain, the United States and Canada. When his own only son, a major in the Argyll and Sutherland Highlanders, was killed in action, the famous entertainer buried his shock and grief in spurring his Rotarianism further. He visited the front himself, paid personally for a bagpipe band to tour in fund-raising concerts, launched single-handed a £1 million fund to help Scottish soldiers re-establish themselves in civilian life, and spoke to the Toronto Rotary Club in Canada pregnant words of warning which have never lost their relevance whenever the Movement has felt itself slacken:

> Men, until this war, we were asleep on the pillow of self-satisfaction. Ah, you know it, men, you know it! How we sat down at our well-filled tables and gorged ourselves till we could eat no more. Then, how we would walk to the mirror, pull down our waistcoat, look at ourselves in the glass and say, "Ah, I'm looking well!"
>
> But the scene is changed, men — the scene is changed!

The scene had also changed for another great Rotarian, though one no longer in any limelight. The BARC had met initially in Liverpool in 1913, soon after Stuart Morrow had formed its Club at breakneck speed, but when it moved to London the following year BARC found Morrow there, too. The "wonder-working Irishman" had, in fact, been invited by London Rotarians to instil new spirit into a Club that was flagging — an untoward development humiliating for the Movement's first Chartered Club in Europe.

And he succeeded. A year after Paul Harris had signed its charter, London had eighty-two members. By the third month of war it was down to fifty-two, at which point Morrow set up his "Rotary's London Bureau" in the Strand. In six months the Club had 125 members and was eagerly holding its Committee Meetings at his office. He was made a Board Member of BARC, and by October 1915 London Rotarians numbered 180. Morrow was now charging 2 guineas per member, and earning it, for he was saving London's face in the eyes of Chicago, and London Rotarians seemed quite happy with the arrangement, every member being well into making money out of fellow-members as well. In 1912 alone, £2,000 in deals had been made by "inter-trading"!

Then conscience descended upon London, perhaps the awareness of community service in the war effort for which it was soon to win a justified reputation. There were quarrels, and in 1916 Morrow made the perilous sea journey back to America. He left all his luggage behind and his good name with it. He went to Chicago and sought out Perry, from whom he received a cool interview. Paul Harris he did not meet; perhaps Morrow too had decided that Harris must be dead. He went back to California, and was soon immersed in war work the following year. The Medicine Man had no potion for himself.

As far as London and Rotary were concerned Morrow was as "dead" as Harris, though for precisely opposite reasons: one for being too idealistic, the other for being too unabashedly business-like. But both were to come again, to remind Rotarians on both sides of the Atlantic just how and what they were.

And the real luggage Morrow left behind was an offspring of Harris's brainchild, even while that child became a brainstorm in the Founder's mind. The genes were ineradicably the same, though the outward mannerisms and characteristics might be different. How the British Clubs developed was beyond the control of Perry, curtained and isolated by the lethal, U-boat-infested ocean and the thunder and smoke of war. But the Board of Directors of BARC operated loyally and conscientiously and reported regularly to Chicago Headquarters, and by the Armistice could report twenty-two Rotary Clubs in Great Britain and Ireland.

Had Ches Perry's intense earnestness been able to peer round their shoulders at every move, it might well have been more than British Rotary could take. As it was, the finally shared sacrifices and stress of war were to bring the New World and the Old much closer together in mutual admiration, which even the strains of peace could not undo, though the casualties of peace are never counted.

Leaving Europe to its murderous devices for the moment, let us watch how Rotary continued its spread through the United States and beyond, its almost irresistible energies, now halted by the Atlantic barrier, exploding backwards and sideways. Again, it was California which set the pace. Eager to prove that it could rise from the devastation of its earthquake just as magnificently as Chicago had flourished with new dynamism after its fire, San Francisco decided on the same method — the holding of a World's Fair in 1915, to be called the Panama-Pacific Exposition. At this Fair, however, San Francisco would go one better than its Midwest rival, for there would be a special Rotary building, on a site approved by Congress. And, at a suggestion from a Los Angeles Rotarian, the Golden Wheel was born. No metaphor here, for this was California: it *was* a wheel and it *was* of gold, solid gold (its inventor's name was even Golding). Bearing the message "California Invites the World", it set off on the 2nd May 1914 to roll round all the Clubs in the United States, Canada, England, Scotland and Ireland. Measuring fourteen inches across, the plan was that each Club as it received the Wheel, and "rolled" it onwards, would attach its own name by a smaller wheel to the outer golden rim. The intent was that, when the Wheel returned to California, it would bear 179 little wheels. When it came to rest at the World's Fair, it was fifty-four wheels short. Much of the world was otherwise engaged.

But there were worlds aplenty to conquer yet on Rotary's home ground, and 1915 saw the largest total of new Clubs yet affiliated in one year, fifty-eight, of which nine were in Canada and one was overseas in the opposite direction, out in the Pacific, in Honolulu, Hawaii, and by the time the 1916 Convention was held in Cincinnati, Ohio, the first "non-English speaking" recruit was announced. Rotary was now in Havana. It wasn't appreciated then, presumably, that Hawaiians had a language of their own also — that discovery was left to the popular songwriters, for Tin Pan Alley and Rotary arrived in Polynesia more or less in a dead heat, though the most famous Hawaiian song of all, "Aloha Oë", has been composed by the last Queen of the Islands, Liliuokalani, at the end of the previous century, before America had her deposed, annexed her realm, and made her exchange one type of royalty for another.

Havana was something very special. Ches Perry had seen four months of military service there and he hoped that Rotary Number One would be — seeing it must bite the bullet of internationalism — the instrument of success. Chicago's emissaries returned in failure, however — US troops were still going in and out of Havana like yo-yos at this time, while a relatively honest and efficient Cuban administration was being sought — but Florida Rotarians from

Tampa, choosing a moment of comparative stability, managed the coup in April 1916, bringing to birth the 226th Rotary Club in the world.

Perry wasted no time in attempting to capitalise on the event. He had already seen to it that an account in Spanish of the San Francisco Convention was distributed throughout Cuba and Central and South America. Translations now followed of "The Objects, Benefits and Obligations of a Rotary Club", "The Purpose and Scope of the Rotary Club" and the "Code of Ethics", but the Southern Hemisphere wasn't set on fire; not till 1918 did San Juan and Montevideo join, to be followed in 1919 by Buenos Aires.

While one can appreciate the International Secretary's very human wish to give free rein to his facility in Spanish, one can also doubt that it was strictly necessary. After all, the name of the Secretary of the new "Club Rotador de la Habana" was Albert L. Hoffman, not an ostentatiously Latin name, while the more satisfying sounding Señor Herbierto Coates, who set up Montevideo Rotary, was really an expatriate Englishman born just plain Herbert. But with his Headquarters staff in Chicago now increased to seventeen, occupying three rooms, Ches Perry had set up a special department of "Printing and Multigraphing" and was unleashing the torrent of Rotary literature upon members and non-members that has poured through the postal services of all continents ever since. Not only South America, but Africa, Australia and India were soon awash with pamphlets, leaflets and brochures from Perry's prized new multigraph printing-plates which, as he boasted, "we have preserved and which can be used again and again". And were, unmercifully. In beleaguered Britain, a contributor to *The Rotary Wheel* implied that British Rotarians cowered beneath the onslaught of paper even more than before the threat of torpedoes and bombs. "So voluminous and so frothy in its nature", he moaned,"that one is tempted to consign most of it unread to the waste-basket. But a sense of duty has led me to read some of it before doing so." Africa, India and Australia felt no such sense of duty (or perhaps sense of humour) and Rotary found no footholds there until more peaceful times had come and casualty lists had gone.

Winnipeg, Arthur Sheldon's first non-American capture, provided the International Association in 1917 with its first "foreign" President, Leslie Pidgeon, an ideal Rotary figurehead in that he combined the piety of being a Presbyterian minister – Jean Harris belonged to the same Church – with the reassuring, robust heartiness of an athletic six-footer, expert shot, hunter, golfer, swimmer and horseman. No one flinched when he spoke of serving the "International Christ", presumably as opposed to serving a Canadian

Christ — or even that famous Chicago version, invoked by Stead. As the United States made its decisive intervention into the European War, the Canadian declared, "America, Cuba, Britain and Canada — the countries of Rotary — are united as never before." He then told the Convention at Atlanta the sudden, sharp truth of the matter: "We believed we could go and attend to our own interests . . . and let the world beyond our shores look after itself. The present world catastrophe has awakened us from our dream."

But some, like Caliban, soon cried to dream again.

The BARC, through Dr Stephenson, sent a message of congratulations and welcome, as if to a graduating class, which in a way the Rotarians at Atlanta were, adding this lure: ". . . the War, far from proving a hindrance to the formation of Clubs, is to some extent a help". So it proved: attendance in 1918, at the second and final War Convention (where the US was concerned) was up by 52 per cent, and the number of Clubs registered a leap of equal percentage. In 1914, there had been 15,000 Rotarians and 123 Clubs. The Armistice was celebrated with 407 Clubs and nearly 40,000 members.

The Movement had indeed justified the somewhat patronising complacency with which it had viewed the war to end all wars, graphically symbolised by Perry's contribution to the Atlanta Convention. When President Pidgeon was uttering cries of noble exhortation as the first British Empire Rotarian to lead the Movement, Perry had coolly confined his Annual Report almost entirely to a discussion of *The Rotarian*'s circulation problems.

After graciously welcoming American Rotarians to the slaughterhouse of the Western world, Dr Stephenson confided to his British peers in his own magazine: "Our Rotary friends across the water will be none the worse for having, for a time at least, a real serious object to work for: it will show them, as nothing else can, of what their organisation is capable." This lofty note of condescension — probably a quite unconscious one and all the worse for that — was to cause plenty of trouble in the twenties and thirties. Meanwhile, as befits a true Scot, the good Doctor's main concern, it turned out, was fiscal. "Things are working towards a clear and definite arrangement as regards both affiliation fees and the standing of British Rotary Clubs," he reassured his readers, indicating the outstanding advantage of America's declaration of war. "All Rotarians should show their loyalty by coming into affiliation, leaving further adjustments to be made later. . . . Let it not be said of British Rotary that she failed in this most important action towards our latest ally."

But though some in Britain might deplore the lateness of

America's arrival at their side in line of battle – even Winston Churchill was to comment in *The World Crisis* about Woodrow Wilson, "All must respect the motives of a statesman who seeks to spare his country the waste and horrors of war. But nothing can reconcile what he said after March, 1917, with the guidance he had given before. What he did in April, 1917, could have been done in May, 1915. And if done then, what abridgement of the slaughter...!" – many sympathised, certainly in Rotary "over there", with America's dilemma.

John Galsworthy, later to write a brilliant introduction to a book called *The Meaning of Rotary*, sent a letter to a new Chicago literary magazine, *The Little Review*, saying with approval, "It seems you are setting out to watch the street of life from a high balcony where at all events the air should be fresh." He could have been describing America itself; he certainly could have been describing many Rotarians. Then, and now.

However, even in "Kaiser Bill" Thompson's citadel – and while Harry Ruggles conducted the Club choruses impartially, both saving the King and keeping watch on the Rhine – even on the streets outside, thousands of women, waving the Stars and Stripes, marched on Preparedness Day, their theme reflecting Chicago's long enthusiasm for the Scouting Movement, imported so successfully in the same year as the first Rotary Convention. Rotary and Scouting were soon to be closely intertwined by the reach of war across the Atlantic. Those marching women reflected the extent to which ordinary citizens were quite aware of what was coming and what should follow.

When it came and Wilson finally took the step, again in Churchill's words, "against his gravest doubts, against his deepest inclinations, in stultification of all he had said and done and left undone in thirty months of carnage", Leslie Pidgeon's immediate predecessor as International President, Allen Albert, was still in office, where his powerful, far-seeing guidance had already been given the previous year. Quoted from at the start of this chapter, that address contained other matter extending beyond the end of contemporary world crisis to the remainder of the looming, troubled century. In words of quite extraordinary power and vision, he placed Rotary in a global context it could not possibly attain by numerical influence for many years, yet with uncanny accuracy for today.

Clearly the close of the war now in progress must be made the occasion for drafting a new code of international law. Our responsibilities as Rotarians is to see that within the circle of our influence there is a sound and wholesome determination to sustain the new code. ... Wherever there are Rotary Clubs composed of men consecrated, as we are, to the gospel of peace, surely we will find there our opportunity to labour against the horrible and unendurable waste we have been witnessing. . . .

Thrilled with the spirit of Rotary, humble in the consciousness of God's boundless favor for America in a year when almost all the rest of the earth is stricken, it is my hope this day, and my prayer every day, that you and I may lift each other and Rotary into a larger Rotary that can make secure the blessings of peace for the poor of the world who have ever borne the burden of the wars of the world.

The Movement had come of age with a surge of energy and confidence while mankind seemed to teeter on madness and despair, an irresistible growth whose maturity had already outstripped the national will of the country of its birth.

CHAPTER NINE

The Wheel at War — 2

And soon we'll go across the seas and show the cruel Hun.
When Uncle Sammy starts to do, the job will well be done,
And Yankee boys will never stop till victory is won,
    As the world is marching on.

So, let us sing of Rotary from the ocean to the sea;
Let every jolly fellow join the golden Jubilee;
Democracy and Rotary are best for you and me;
    As the world is marching on.

Rotary Marching Song, 1918
(tune of "Battle Hymn of the Republic")

The words were by Rotarian Henry King of Boston again, who had made himself a sort of war laureate to the Movement. King had exchanged the music of Sir Arthur Sullivan for that of William Steffe, an obscure Southern composer of camp-meeting hymns. Rotarians were still marching "with a steady swing" but towards a tangible battle and a named foe, and the world was being made safe for Rotary as well as for democracy. For there was no doubt in many Rotarians' minds where the evil propensities of the Kaiser's Germany had sprung from: not just a lack of democracy, but a lack of Rotary. It was recalled in *The Rotarian* how even the rhetoric of Arthur Sheldon had fallen on stony ground there, and added: "Rotarians in Chicago, New York, Boston, Philadelphia and other cities went out of their way to show visiting German travellers those same Rotary Clubs which inspired Anglo-Saxons . . . business men in Germany did not seem able to comprehend nor be capable of appreciating the value to them and to their communities of Rotary ideals."

Nor was this fanciful. The same incompatibility between Rotary and dictatorial regimes of all kinds was to be tragically illustrated once again when Europe prepared for its second self-immolation in twenty years time. Rotary's absurdities and deficiencies have always been most graphically realised and pointed out by its own most devoted adherents, including its Founder, while its most powerful virtues have always been most clearly and promptly understood by opponents. One's enemies, as La Rochefoucauld long ago observed in one of his less pedantic sentences, always come nearer the truth in their opinion of us than we do ourselves; which is why, in behaviour and self-knowledge, we are usually our own worst enemies. It is both a weakness and a strength of Rotary that its members seldom have shown signs of appreciating this.

The International Board of Directors, meeting in Philadelphia following Wilson's declaration of war, announced rather pompously, at Perry's urging, that they would "place International Headquarters at the disposal of the Rotary Clubs in the United States in a special service to mankind in general and their own country in particular", and resolved to continue with their next Convention at Atlanta to help prove, as Perry had pronounced in an editorial, that Rotarians "can continue to be efficient business men and can at the same time be efficient patriots". Cynics might comment that this inferred a perversion of Sheldon's slogan in that now the business man would have the chance to make his biggest profits ever by serving his country best. War profiteers were indeed to abound, as they had already done in Britain, and some of them would be Rotarians, but a profounder truth was being hit upon: that America's most fearsome muscle-power lay in her industrial sinews. And, to be fair, American Rotary's will to serve the national community had been dramatically shown by the response of all Clubs to the 1913 tornado and floods which had devastated Nebraska, Ohio and Indiana. It was genuinely geared to plunge into the grim tornadoes whirling Europe to destruction. As always, in the future, it was geared to build and repair in the wake of international havoc.

So Atlanta became the "Great Patriotic Convention", as 1918 was to be in Kansas the "Win the War Convention", about which Woodrow Wilson sent Secretary Ches Perry a letter: "The service rendered by your organization in this time of national stress has been very great." Perry had also received from the Secretary for War the following endorsement about Rotary Clubs: "In the present emergency they have been especially effective, and their assistance and co-operation in supporting the many special activities made necessary by war are invaluable."

The year 1917 was a halcyon one for International Rotary: it brought the United States into the war and Brighton into Rotary. For the perspective of this book, both of course are of equal importance. In reality, the United States had been part of it, there was no doubt whose victory would benefit Americans most — and indeed a good many ships besides the *Lusitania* were sunk before the Germans offered Texas, New Mexico and Arizona to woo the Mexicans to fight their northern neighbours again, and then, with a staggering lack of restraint, torpedoed a US vessel called the *Aztec*. Equally, Brighton had really been part of Rotary, had been inspired and guided by it, shared its aspirations, while pretending it could lead a completely independent existence from BARC. Both the United States and Brighton had reality paraded several times before them, before either acknowledged its presence — though both then whole-heartedly embraced it.

In the same way, American Rotary's attitude to the war was mirrored by the Chicago establishment's view of British Rotarians. Even as Ches Perry was tut-tutting in *The Rotarian* that only one Club had been formed in Britain in 1914 (it was Newcastle upon Tyne), he put forward the preposterous suggestion, with utter seriousness, that Rotary should advise every nation in the world to rename its War Department a Peace Department: "If Uncle Sam will set the fashion it is most likely other nations will follow suit." Uncle Sam was basically in agreement, since the Rotarian in the White House was at that time still referring to the war "over there" as a drunken brawl. What we now call "even-handedness" was decreed the correct attitude, and Chicago Rotarians showed implacable neutrality by singing both "God Save the King" and "Die Wacht am Rhein" at every luncheon. They also showed home-town wisdom, since Big Bill Thompson, who had won the job on an anti-German vote (he was Irish), was in office so pro-German that he was nicknamed "Kaiser Bill".

That some American Rotarians treated the crisis with due solemnity was shown by a speaker who warned his fellow-members of the Birmingham Club — Birmingham, Alabama, that is — that "in order that we may appreciate to the fullest extent the importance of Peace as opposed to the European War, it is interesting to realise in how many ways, not before thought of, the conditions in Europe affect stationers in America". The speaker's business was, needless to say, in stationery. But so, after all, was the business of the diplomats, who often are themselves the last to realise that even bits of paper can have too high a price.

Hindsight makes sages of us all, yet it is important to recapture the general unreality of those times — on both sides of the Atlantic. As Bernard Shaw commented in his Preface to *Heartbreak House*, which, he admitted, represented "cultured, leisured Europe before the War", when he started the play, "not a shot had been fired; and only the professional diplomatists and the very few amateurs whose hobby is foreign policy even knew that the guns were loaded".

One who did was Winston Churchill. He recalled in *The World Crisis*:

> Men were everywhere unconscious of the rate at which the world was growing. . . . For a year after the war had begun hardly anyone understood how terrific, how almost inexhaustible were the resources in force, in substance, in virtue, behind every one of the combatants. The vials of wrath were full: but so were the reservoirs of power . . . the world on the verge of its catastrophe was very brilliant. Nations and empires crowned with princes and potentates rose majestically on every side, lapped in the accumulated treasures of the long peace. . . . The old world in its sunset was fair to see.

So it was perhaps some premonition which in 1914 led Rotarians for the first time to schedule their Convention earlier than August, that "awful month" (again in Churchill's words) when "more divisions fought on more days, and more men were killed and wounded than in any whole year of the struggle". Dr Thomas Stephenson, attending this Convention, as has been noted, to get his British Association recognised, commented on his return, with some awe, to his Edinburgh Club, "When an American begins to talk about his own business, nothing short of an earthquake will stop him."

Rotarians got their Convention in ahead of the earthquake that year; but even when it came, they still talked business, since it was somebody's else earthquake for three years yet. Only once during those three years of grace did they pause, at 11 o'clock on the momentous morning of 14th January 1915, on the roof of an hotel in Kansas City, Missouri, at which moment a group of senior Rotarians stood solemnly to watch a huge flag, specially made by the Kansas Club, rise proudly up the flagpole. The colours they saluted misty-eyed were not red, white and blue, however, but white, blue and gold. It was the first unfurling of the Official Flag of the Movement. The International President for that year, Frank L. Mulholland — yet another live-wire young lawyer, and only the fourth incumbent, but leader of a Movement already described by one journalist as "one of the greatest organisations in the world today" — did not manage to attend that initial ceremony, but at the San Francisco World's Fair later that year he saw that Official Flag flying high in the sky attached to a giant kite, with searchlight beams playing on it all through the hours of darkness.

The new flag was destined to fly in honour in most countries on earth in the next four decades, and at both Poles, too, and rush in regardless where often the Stars and Stripes would hesitate to tread. And the Europeans thought *they* were making history! All they were making was graves. And Woodrow Wilson was busy reassuring his foreign-born countrymen that same year that there was such a thing as being "too proud to fight".

Apart from food intake, however, and the fear, real or imagined, of future food shortage, the American Rotarians, once involved, threw themselves heartily into the Allied war effort, though the years while the conflict was still considered the European War saw two major developments in the Movement, now only irregularly in touch with the British Isles.

First, in 1915, the Committee Paul Harris had appointed way back in 1912 to consider a Code of Ethics — about which Seattle's Ernst Skeel had agonised some time (see Chapter Five) — finally came through with an acceptable draft at the San Francisco Convention, and from then on there was no looking back to a Rotary where business-getting was the prime concern. In Britain, Rotarians were seizing the opportunities of wartime to put Community Service into practice, while the International Association was putting it into memorable words. While today this Code is officially omitted from Rotary statutes and procedures, being considered too old-fashioned and out of touch in expression, it remained for long decades the corner-stone of Rotary principles and, though it goes on far too long and in too detailed a manner, getting more flatulent and laboured as it proceeds through eleven principles, its opening passage has a simplicity and grandeur that recall the preamble to the Declaration of Independence:

> My business standards shall have in them a note of sympathy for our common humanity. My business dealings, ambitions and relations shall always cause me to take into consideration my highest duties as a member of society. In every position in business life, in every responsibility that comes before me, my chief thought shall be to fill responsibility and discharge that duty so that when I have ended each of them, I shall have lifted the level of human ideals and achievements a little higher than I found them.

Its acceptance by the Convention was one of the Movement's finest moments, though it was done in a very offhand manner.

Similarly, the second major development was barely noticed, two years later, at the 1917 Convention, when in a few lines there appeared amongst many Amendments to the Constitution, the following Section 4 of Article XII: "This is a new section establishing an endowment fund, the principal of which is to be kept intact and the interest used to further the objects of this Association, with the Board of Directors as trustees of the fund." Commending it, the new President, the improbably named Arch C. Klumph, still enjoying the prestige of having personally been in the team that helped bring Cuba into the Movement, suggested: "It seems eminently proper that we should accept endowments for the purpose of doing good in the world." In fact, little use was made of this Amendment or its Endowment Fund for thirty years, when after the death of the Founder in 1947 it was to prove the ideal instrument for a lasting memorial to Paul Harris in the form of the Rotary Foundation (see Chapter Twenty-Three), whose world-wide and ever-growing network of scholarships is today Rotary's greatest and most imaginative claim to the advancement of true internationalism.

Yet it was natural the endowment clause should attract little note, for this Eighth International Convention quickly became "The Great Patriotic Convention", since Rotary's most eminent member, Woodrow Wilson, had just uprated the "drunken brawl" and declared war on what were called the Central Powers.

Rotary, being much larger in the United States than in Great Britain, and having been in existence that much longer, was at once recognised as a valued partner by the country's leaders, in contrast to Britain, where Lloyd George, Asquith, Churchill and Kitchener had certainly never heard of it. President Wilson sent a message, the Secretary for War sent a message, while American complacency took two swift blows to the chin, first from Major-General Leonard Wood, who bluntly told the Convention what war would mean in national service, fighting and lost lives: "You are going to send perhaps a couple of million men over the seas . . . this little call is only the beginnings." Nor did he shrink from reminding them that they stood at present protected "not by our own preparation or forethought, but by the struggling and bleeding lines of French and English". The general was unsparing: "It isn't flattering or pleasing, but we have allies strong enough to protect us while we do the plain, common sense thing."

What that common-sense thing was, he clearly spelled out, in words that were tragically forgotten when later crises shook the world and terrified Western civilisation, nearly death-wishing itself to extinction. "You can't prepare with words or with money or with men untrained and unorganized. . . . The sinews of war, the sinews that count, the big ones, are of a different type. They are the bodies and souls of men, trained and disciplined, and backed by a spirit of sacrifice, by a willingness to serve the right at any cost; and when a nation ceases to have that willingness it ceases to have a soul, and some other people will come and take its place."

143

If it had rendered no other war service, International Rotary, by giving such a prompt forum where those words could be spoken, had justified itself to its country of birth and to the lands where it had spread and, above all, to the shy, quiet figure who watched with Jean from the shade of Comely Bank and slowly regained his strength as the world drew near on fire, and his offspring grew to maturity to meet the challenge.

The fearsome facts of crisis were also brutally presented to the Convention at Atlanta – itself still bitter from being the only city laid waste in the Civil War on Sherman's march to the sea – by Pomeroy Burton, an American who was Managing Editor of the London *Daily Mail*, and who had returned to his homeland to find the majority of ordinary people "dangerously apathetic and oblivious to the acute peril which threatens them. It also finds this country astoundingly unprepared".

As in all moments of peril, Americans pledged themselves to their flag, recalling the recent words of their Rotarian in the White House on Memorial Day, a few weeks previously, the day when Americans remember those killed in battle: "The flag is the embodiment, not of sentiment, but of history. It represents the experiences made by men and women." In an excess of emotion, the Convention now heard the Stars and Stripes described as "that flag whose field, white like the snows of Valley Forge, is striped with regal red . . . the bending blue of its national sky all studded with stars whose blended beauty is radiant with the gathered glory of our past". Their other flag, that of International Rotary, had already been given similar treatment by Frank Mulholland (who was himself to go to France in February 1918) two years before: ". . . the main portion . . . is white, emblemising the banner of internationalism. . . . As the white stands for international amity and good will, so the blue stands for consistency of purpose, and the gold for the pure standard upon which rotates the wheel of eternal progress".

International amity would now have to be put into cold storage, though many there in Atlanta understood the probability that now even Rotary's "main portion" of white was, like the snows of Valley Forge, about to be striped with red.

Welcoming them to the dreadful arena, the BARC felt it constituted "recognition of the high humanitarian aims of the Allies . . . while deploring the inevitable sacrifice of valuable lives" in their "mutual service". And American Rotarians, the "frivolling and frolicking" behind them, bent to their task with a resounding energy, to Community Service that mirrored the example from Britain and even transcended it, by virtue of sheer size and numbers and the remaining ocean shield.

A War Service Committee was at once set up, to co-ordinate Club activities and to help and advise Rotarians how best they could help the war effort. The main effort, as asked for by the Secretary for War, was food conservation, and Clubs throughout the New World began to develop extensive fruit and vegetable garden allotments, with co-operation from local Scouts and other boys' groups. Philip R. Kellar, Managing Editor of *The Rotarian*, who was taking over more and more of the writing which Perry had once monopolised in early issues and who was a man of larger sympathies and understanding, wrote "Saving for Victory", urging a change in food consumption habits. Seattle banished all "meats and wheat" from their luncheons and even Havana announced breadless meals. War gardens became a tremendous activity. Perhaps it wasn't strange that Chicago, home of so much agricultural innovation and mechanisation, had within two months managed to get 200,000 vacant lots fertilised and planted, but Toronto — with, after all, a head-start — had a staggering 800,000! By the end of 1918, there were more than 10 million allotment gardens coast-to-coast, many of them under Rotary supervision. Rotarian Wilson even raised sheep on the White House lawn! Rotarians at Roanoke, Virginia, recorded a piquant aberration when one of them entertained the Club at his brand-new dairy farm. After an open-air symposium with "milkmaids and fairies", members "marched to their stalls" where there followed "the usual Rotary doings".

Turning from this Southern hospitality mixed, one hopes, with respectable horticulture, we note that Cleveland Rotarians harvested a superb potato crop of 1,500 bushels and distributed 1,000 signs reading WAR GARDEN — HELP GUARD IT. But nothing could top the project of Alburquerque, New Mexico, where Rotarians helped turn large areas of Rio Grande marshes into good agricultural land under the splendid slogan "United We Drain, Divided We Drown".

Clubs raised huge amounts to buy Liberty Bonds, and Paul Harris must have beamed to learn that his native Racine relied entirely on its Rotary Club to raise its quota of $4,000 — and not in vain, for the Club oversubscribed the amount in one day! Detroit Rotarians within ten days had raised over $1½ million, and were rightly held up as an example of Clubs everywhere. Clubs also subscribed enthusiastically to the "Smileage Books" Campaign. These had nothing to do with literature but were books of 100 coupons which gave admission to so-called Liberty Theatres in training camps, where top entertainers performed sketches and vaudeville acts. Indeed the nation's War Camp Community Fund was largely a Rotary achievement, and a great one, being the forerunner project of the later USO entertainments in the Second World War.

As often proved to be the case, what Chicago did today, the nation did tomorrow, and the most dramatic illustration of this came early on, when the city's Rotarians — their old neutrality thrown aside — developed the US Boys' Working Reserve, another attack on the threatened scarcity of food (by American standards). Rotarian Howard Gross, whose conception it was, maintained that "city boys are as anxious to whip the Kaiser as city men are. . . . Many are soft of muscle, but they could harden up by swinging a hoe, and our farmers are critically shorthanded". He persuaded first the Chicago Board of Education to release high-school lads for farmwork and then telegraphed his success to forty other cities. Within a month, it was in operation from Maine to Seattle, from Florida to San Francisco. Rotary One then persuaded Woodrow Wilson to let Rotarians form the nation-wide American Protective League, to combat spies and saboteurs, which enraged their Teuton-loving Mayor! The Clubs' total contributions to the three Liberty Bond drives totalled $7½ million, even though "Big Bill" maintained to the end that the world's largest German city had no business taking part in what the Mayor insisted on calling "the Federal Government's war".

Everywhere, Rotarians were actively building or sponsoring facilities for soldiers — work which was (to our ears) oddly termed "Concentration Camp" activities. Though not so oddly for Rotarians of Leavenworth, who raised $64,000 to erect a great community house as a permanent gathering-place for both soldiers and civilians, an interesting project for a location long infamous even then as the site of both the military prison and federal penitentiary. Denver members supplied an entire Soldiers' Club — canteen, rest-rooms, billiard-tables, the lot — and, anticipating the famous free concerts given in the Second World War at London's National Gallery, was mainly responsible for sponsoring the buildings of Denver's new concert organ, the largest in the country, giving free concerts throughout the year, at one of which its "virile and compelling tone" was produced by none other than Woodrow Wilson's daughter. In just one week, the San Antonio Club in Texas collected a library of 20,000 volumes for nearby Kelly Field.

Rotary ran many community War Chest collections, and at the Kansas City Convention of June 1918 endorsed the idea that all Rotarians would stop whatever they were doing for one minute at 11 a.m. each day to meditate and pray for the success of the Allied nations. This moment was called the "War Angelus" and delegates were instructed to draw everyone's attention to it daily by ringing bells and blowing whistles. They did so, at least for the duration of the Convention. For how long after, one can only guess, hysterically.

The Club in Chattanooga showed that there were similar industrial undercurrents to those which flowed in Britain through Rotary by giving a "Service Supper" in one of the city's main hotels, the guests being equally composed of trade unionists and employers. The Club in Champaign, Illinois, brought business men and farmers together to clear up "misapprehensions". While another striking example of post-war prescience was shown by a group of Clubs which adopted resolutions calling on the US Senate to expel Wisconsin Senator Robert M. La Follette for his anti-war pronouncements which "bring shame and disgrace upon the honor of our nation". La Follette was the man who single-handedly was to scupper Woodrow Wilson's plan for America to join the League of Nations and effectively cause Wilson's decline into disappointment and death.

Clubs comprising Rotary's District Eleven (as it was then called), which included Kansas, Missouri and Oklahoma, undertook to care for the welfare of soldiers training in all three states. Rotarians of Indianapolis took just a few weeks to find $15,000 with a maintenance fund of $1,500, to equip a lavish clubhouse at the huge army base nearby. When we read that the equipment included pool and billiard-tables, a popcorn machine, smoking stands, a piano, toilet supplies, plus a "Talking machine", a familiar chord is at once struck — of American Rotary's unparalleled generosity.

Members of the Club in Janesville, Wisconsin, birthplace of the composer and lyricist of "A Perfect Day", Carrie Jacobs Bond, daughter of the man who composed "Home on the Range", still a favourite in *Songs for the Rotary Club*, set up a uniformed committee of reserve militiamen from their membership to advise on soldiers' needs. Akron, Ohio, Rotarians went a stage farther, showing themselves also ahead of their time — by the distance of a world war — when they formed a "Home Guard". Senior Service Corps of men over forty-five were fast multiplying in many states, but Akron actually used that evocative name.

The generous impulse of Americans was not confined to their own shores. The Military Hospital Baseball League supplied two teams, one American and one Canadian, to play before more than 7,000 spectators for the benefit of the hospital in Dublin at the request of local Rotarians. And Rotary Number One, setting the pace as it continued so often to do, gave massive support to Chicago's "Rheims Restoration Fund", cocking another snook at Mayor "Kaiser Bill". Many other Clubs across the nation followed suit and "adopted" war-ravaged French and Belgian cities for post-war renovation. Most generously, *The Rotarian* permitted a full-page advertisement to Harry Lauder, in which he asked for money for his personal fund for Scottish soldiers. The International Board drew the line, however, at being asked to help supply "10,000,000 pairs of shoes for Suffering Russia".

Chicago was also way up front in what was perhaps the strangest manifestation of Rotary concern that occurred during the First World War, quite overshadowing all other projects, even that directed towards looking after the nation's boys (an enthusiasm much endorsed by Woodrow Wilson, and of course reflecting the eternal springs of the Movement, for Canada shared that concern equally). On 27th February 1918, it staged a spectacular parade, led by the splendid Chicago Band, whose conductor happily belonged to the Club. How Harry Ruggles must have envied Rotarian William Weil that day! The parade was to draw attention to support needed for soldiers' training camps, and it contained two contrasting floats: one showed a red-light emporium, the other "Uncle Sam's Recreation Club". One wholesomely pretty girl rode up front as "Miss Columbia", carrying a glass bowl for donations, guarded by a sturdy sailor-lad aglow with virgin strength.

It may have been this defiance of their Germanophile Mayor that so enraged "Big Bill" that he decided to found the Chicago Boosters' Club, a deliberate steal of one of Rotary's original possible names and formed with the aim of stealing the Movement's original impetus of "Boosting" – only this time the boost was for Chicago, to help Big Bill to recover some $4½ million he had somehow got rid of during the years of war, when citizens were looking elsewhere. "Throw away your hammer and get a horn," shouted the posters.

However that may be, the Chicago parade promoted Rotary's major theme throughout the time America entered the war – which was not the peril to the lives of their young men, but the peril to their morals (which makes another of the Mayor's posters "A booster is better than a knocker" have a piquant thrust in today's sex-jargon). When Churchill wrote of America's war declaration, he said, "No one stood against the torrent . . . pacifism, indifference, dissent, were swept from the path", but he could not have known that against the accompanying "roar of slowly gathered, pent-up wrath" International Rotary's sense of moral danger stood like a rock in those flaming waters. Chesley Perry reported to the Great Patriotic Convention that "More Allied soldiers in service on the Belgian-French line have been incapacitated through venereal disease than through gunshot wounds", and added news that was calculated to send a *frisson* through every mother's heart, that even

American soldiers in past wars "have been the means of staining millions of lives with horrible taints". He declared, with full backing from the Board of Directors: "We want to get the American people interested in protecting our boys from evil influences in home camps while they are training to protect us from foreign foes." To this end, it was proposed that an imperative duty lay on Rotarians to provide "wholesome amusements and recreations". Supporting Perry, the Immediate Past President of International Rotary, Allen D. Albert, now the Chicago Club's Chairman of its own War Services Committee and already known to favour "a new moral tone in the Army", said that older professional soldiers constituted "an unworthy leadership for the sons of the Rotarian of today" with "the filthy lewdness of their natures". Drink and venereal disease were the twin targets of the new moral tone and Perry promised that "grogshops and disreputable women will be driven away from the vicinity of the camps".

It was no idle threat. Rotary Headquarters in Chicago learned that a certain Army camp was to be moved by the War Department to a more salubrious locale because the nearest city was considered much too fast and loose and packed with vice. That city contained a Rotary Club (which was not surprising when one reflected where Headquarters itself was located) and, under Perry's goad, its members sprang into action, cleaned up the city's depraved areas, until it met "the requirements of the War Department for decency".

Perry's lead was welcomed by British Rotary, and the President of the Newcastle upon Tyne Club stated that "if America had done no other service than that of drawing attention to this International Evil, she would have deserved well of the Allies". In an address to his own Club's weekly luncheon (after the dishes were cleared away, one hopes), he explained to the amazed northerners: "Syphilis occurs in this way. An infected man or woman gives, during the most sacred of human functions, a vile disease to another human being . . . let me say quite definitely that sex intercourse is quite unnecessary before marriage." He then proceeded – he was also an Army doctor – to give members the benefit of a no-holds-barred clinical description of various venereal diseases, which quite took their minds off the horrors going on across the channel at Passchendaele, where 400,000 British troops were disappearing under a hideous avalanche of mud, rain and German cannonades to gain five miles of worthless ground. It was slaughter on a nightmare scale – a great morass of filth, agony and waste – but at least it was a slaughter of the innocents.

Down south, in the rogue Club which had only just applied for Rotary legitimacy, at four years of age, innocence was less abroad

— Rotarians in Brighton had several clinics under their eye, each of 200 beds, entirely devoted to victims of what the English called the French disease, and the French called the English disease.

The efficacy of the Club President's lecture was, however, rather cancelled out for those still able to get their copies of *The Rotarian* when they saw in the April 1917 issue an article by him in which he stated that women were divided in character between those who truly inspired their men and those who combined "opaqueness of mind with transparency of stocking". More shell-shock, perhaps!

As to the evils of drink, it was proposed at Atlanta that all membership Classifications dealing with aspects of the liquor trade be permanently closed though, to their credit, the Directors of BARC, when they learned of it, expressed their doubt that this could be applied to British Rotary. Indeed, the columnist in *The Rotary Wheel* tellingly observed: "Why should a man be banned from Rotary because he sells wines and spirits? . . . If the man who sells liquor is to be excluded from Rotary, then, *a fortiori*, the man who consumes it should also be rigidly kept out."

None the less, American sensibilities were respected, and when the "doughboys" were entertained in British Rotary homes, their considerate hosts agreed to remove strong drink from their presence — on such occasions, as Wilde's Gwendolen Fairfax almost observed in *The Importance of Being Earnest*, to do the right thing became more than a moral duty, it became a pleasure, a combination always attractive to the English.

In addition to the evil influences of flighty ladies and intoxicating liquors, the International Board of Directors passed resolutions inveighing against the ability of motion pictures to instil "thoughts of deceit, crime, disease, indecency or immorality" in the minds of the young. This may, or may not, have been connected with the fact that the Chicago film industry, for whom Charles Chaplin made his first two-reelers, had just collapsed before West Coast competition. Meanwhile, in London, young soldiers of all Allied nations flocked to Drury Lane to see that flagrant obstetrical masterpiece *Birth of a Nation*, apparently without any ill-effects.

And there was other reassuring news for anxious wives and mothers. When Frank Mulholland, now Past President, came over to visit the Western Front early in 1918, he reported that, though he had been with the soldiers in the trenches, in their billets and on leave, "I didn't see a single American soldier under the influence of intoxicating drink. . . . If anybody comes to you with any statement that our boys are going to the eternal bow-wows in France, you have my consent to look him in the eyes and tell him he's a liar."

The bow-wows of war, of course, were regrettably something Rotary could do nothing about.

But if some of the actions and statements of American Rotarians might seem to belong to an unreal world, the British were, as we observed in the previous chapter, ill-equipped to feel affronted, which explains to some extent the curious fact that they were not, it seems, so feeling. BARC's first President, R.W. Pentland, who, it will be recalled, had been once described by his fellow-Scots as "like the pianos he sells, Upright, Square and Grand", had sent this grotesque summary of war's drawbacks to Chicago Head-quarters: "The war has now lasted one hundred days, showing that the expenditure has been over seven hundred million pounds, or thirty-five hundred million dollars . . . and the sad thing is, that this money is more or less wasted, and *taken out of trade*" (my italics). Nor, after two years of carnage on a nightmare scale, were the reports getting any more basic through the Rotary filter. Only a few weeks after 60,000 British troops had been lost in one day on the Somme, the President of the London Club was telling Rotarians at the Cincinnati Convention, "We should think that life is a game . . . and the most glorious thing in the world is to win the game that you play fairly. No, there is something equally glorious, a gracious loser." In the course of this extraordinary speech, London's Presi-dent went staggering on with an orgy of alliteration − "Prosperity is produced by pluck, push, patience, perseverance, punctuality and peace" − then finished by telling his baffled audience, who had no more on their minds than that evening's Georgia Watermelon Party at the Zoo Gardens, that they were "human engines geared up to the highest pitch of efficiency, with intelligence as fuel, the steering wheel of right, the self-starter of reliability, cylinders of generosity radiating assistance, spark plugs of knowledge, water coolers of thought with grates of justice and chassis of intellect, the body of uplifting betterment, the axles of industry fitting into the cog of humanity, with sockets holding the spokes of business, held in place by the rim of business surmounted by a type of honesty". Since he neglected to add some such phrase as their being surrounded by the strait-jacket of self-preservation, we must assume he was also suffering from shell-shock and can only hope the subsequent water-melons bucked him up.

There is no reason to disbelieve the reported storms of applause which greeted these words. As Convention followed Convention, whether in war or peace, it soon became clear to a detached observer − or calculating participant − that the more baffled a Rotary audience was, the more likely it was to cheer, to be on the safe side. It was also better for the digestive juices. They were, after all,

151

getting well accustomed to the style now, from the prose that greeted them monthly on the editorial pages of *The Rotarian*, in which the ex-librarian and the ex-cement brick manufacturer, armed with the authority of his lieutenancy in the Army, greeted 1916, the year of the Somme, with the typical phrase, "the future is the rainbow of promise which holds the deeds that will be the heirs of our thoughts of today", a sentence that smacks more of cement than of the library. It is a pity that a man of such practical and piercing intelligence as Perry sought the mantle of the poet as well (such men often do, alas), since the unfortunate result had an effect upon all Rotary utterances which persists to this day, its being a Movement that attracts far more — and, indeed, is designed to — the practical man than the poet, though the confusion was natural, since both poets and Rotarians share the same thwarted sense of being unacknowledged legislators of the world.

And the privations of war did nothing to prevent the satisfaction offered Rotarians' digestive juices getting bigger and better. Even more so if you were too far away to read the menu, let alone savour it. British Rotarians saw copies of Perry's "Weekly Letter" now and then, and one of them mentioned that the Rotary Club of Greensboro', North Carolina, was offering a prize of "one bushel of genuine potatoes" for the best name suggested for the Club magazine. "That surely does not apply to Britain," wryly observed the anonymous "Searchlight" column in *The Rotary Wheel* (it was May 1917, when the Kaiser's submarines had brought Britain to the verge of starvation). "If it did, I would cable a dozen suitable names at once." Reports of International Convention menus seem to have caused surprisingly little envy amongst British Clubs, however. Georgia watermelons were nothing.

The San Francisco Convention report spoke warmly of the official reception in the St Francis Hotel (no echoes of Assisi here!) where delegates received their first taste of "the Californian brand of hospitality", described the morning after, with feeling, as "the brand that means abundance", and the whole Convention pro-gramme was described as "eminently practical, workable and full of meat". This was no metaphor, for the great Annual Banquet, held at the Palace Hotel, cost the San Francisco Club nearly $6,000 for the meal, which took two hours to serve and was labelled as so inspiring "that Frank Mulholland almost forgot his resolution not to make a speech". Digestive juices were revived after speeches by the appearance of "Miss Canada", who turned out to be a married lady from Vancouver draped in a Canadian flag. The flag was then presented to Rotary, but whether with or without Mrs Kelly inside it, we are not told. If not, she presumably either made a rapid, blushing exit, or Rotary Conventions were rather more exciting in those days than they later became.

With the United States at war, there was not a notable lack of food intake, and indeed a fiercer note had entered Rotary literature indicating an intention to preserve national standards: a Baltimore Rotarian included these lines in his exceedingly bloodthirsty poem, "America at War": "With cavemen fierceness battle we for home / We tear, we rend, to bring our loved ones food". But *The Rotarian* counselled more orthodox methods, urging Americans to study Mexican methods of growing corn and oriental methods of growing rice. The Rice Growers' Association entertained the Rotarians of Beaumont, Texas, with a meal consisting of cream of tomato soup with rice, red snapper steak with rice, rice jambalaya, tenderloin of beef with rice, and rice griddle cakes with syrup. British readers would doubtless have been content with the menu that was clearly available without the rice additives. And soon, in an effort to substitute national punch for paunch, the US Food Commissioner, Herbert Hoover, led American stomachs into a depression – as he was to lead the whole body politic into one thirteen years later – by issuing thousands of Food Pledge Cards which urged voluntary restraint. They urged Save the Wheat, Save the Meat, Save the Milk, Save the Fats, Save the Sugar and Save the Fuel. One pound of flour saved weekly per person meant 150 million more bushels for the Allies; one ounce of meat saved per person per day was the same as having 2,200,000 more cattle; an ounce of sugar saved daily meant 1,100,000 tons each year and so on. Eat more vegetables, urged Mr Hoover.

He could have Saved his Breath. Rotarians have never been great readers, in peace or war. But some small change was made. At the Kansas City Convention in 1918 the big meal was taken outdoors, in gigantic picnic style, and was literally a beanfeast, the beans arriving in a large auto-truck and baked to a guaranteed New England recipe, and 4,000 picnickers took home their bean-pots as souvenirs. Whatever else was eaten each evening at all the hotels is not detailed, but no less an authority than Chicago's own evangelist, Billy Sunday (now himself a Rotarian!), was quoted as recommending Kansas City to his fellow-members as a place "full of tabasco sauce and pepperino", and one feels sure delegates were not disappointed.

An article in *The Rotarian* which immediately followed the great beanfeast was startlingly entitled "The Hog's Part In The War", but guilty readers were relieved to see it was not a further diatribe from Herbert Hoover, but a piece about the vital part bacon plays in bolstering the spirit of fighting men, which also mentioned that

"In England, well-to-do people are standing in line for their food supplies and they, at least, are learning that the talk of famine is . . . a terrible possibility". On the opposite page was a poem reprinted from *Life* magazine:

> Little Herbie Hoover's come to our house to stay,
> To make us scrape the dishes clean, an' keep the crumbs away,
> An' learn us to make war bread, an' save up all the grease,
> For the less we eat of butter, the sooner we'll have peace. . . .

All of which must have seemed very bewildering to the rationed Rotarians who had already been fighting "over there" for three years. But all that emanated from the beleaguered islands was a slightly wry comment about a promotional leaflet "All Abroad For Larkland", issued by the Executive Committee for the Atlanta Convention, which described a Fancy Dress Carnival being prepared. 'It makes one's mouth water", was the comment, "to think that some 5,000 Rotarians and their friends will be frivolling and frolicking when we over here dare not even sit down to a modest dinner. But times have changed. Our American friends are our Allies, and it is now 'war-time' over there also. 'Larkland' may have to be modified after all."

It wasn't. Indeed, at the vast "Win the War" Convention the following year, Larkland was more in evidence that ever. At every possible moment (British Rotarians were astonished to learn) delegates and their wives broke into the new Rotary song hit, "I'm a Little Prairie Flower", whose lines went:

> I'm a little prairie flower,
> Growing wilder every hour.
> Nobody cares to cultivate me;
> I'm as wild as wild can be!
> I'm as wild as wild can be.

And at that repetition of the last line, the singer placed his or her index finger in the crown of the head and whirled rapidly round.

On the other hand, it may have been Rotary's war-dance.

Soon after, in Paris, a member of the Rotary Club of San Antonio, Texas, saluted the grave of Lafayette, intimate of Benjamin Franklin, who had led French troops alongside Washington's in the American War of Independence, and pronounced the electrifying news, "Lafayette, we are here!" The mouldering Marquis, who had risked imprisonment by his fellow-countrymen to join the Americans at the very start of their rebellion, was not able to reply, "And about time, too", but Rotarian Jack Pershing had certainly said the right and grand thing at the right time, even though America's military leader had arrived on this vast field of colossal battle fresh from the rather lesser assignment of chasing the bandit Pancho Villa — unsuccessfully — across the Mexican border.

Back in the United States another serviceman of much less exalted rank than the General was not so lucky in his timing and choice of words. In Philadelphia, home of Rotary's eighteenth-century precursor, Ben Franklin's Junto Club, Paul Harris was visiting his friend Glenn Mead, his successor in 1912 as International President, and joined him on an informal visit to the city's Rotary Army and Navy Club. This establishment was large and lavishly appointed and thoroughly in line with Rotary's pledge to protect the nation's youth in uniform. Philadelphia's Rotarians vetted all the ladies who partnered the pure lads at Saturday Night Dances from 8.30 p.m. till midnight (the girls were either their wives, daughters or mothers, or their employees), at which free ice-cream and cakes completed the romp. Turning from a conversation with Mead, a young sailor asked Mead's self-effacing companion one of the great histori-cal (and perhaps accusatory) questions of this century, "Are you a Rotarian?"

CHAPTER TEN

Paul Harris at War

And while I live,
        don't worry me at all,
Just keep off my toes, nor loudly call;
Have a thoughtful regard
        for my friends and me.
And don't take away our Rotary.

Burton Smith, Chicago Rotarian

Writing in early 1918, Rotarian Smith might have had his fellow-member — who also had happened to originate the Club, the name, and the Movement all those pre-war aeons ago — precisely in mind. Paul and Jean had met in Morgan Park, then a village outside the city limits, and it was there that Mrs Harris had gently but firmly led him back after his traumatic triumph and resignation at the 1912 Convention. When Paul had first come to Chicago the rising ground above the park itself, culminating in a ridge 100 feet above Lake Michigan, was starting to be developed as an exclusive residential neighbourhood. Its developers claimed "it counts among its residents some of the best business men of Chicago, and is blessed with having, generally, the right kind of citizens . . . saloons are *prohibited by law* . . . our children grow up surrounded only by good influences, while our families can go upon the street, or walk upon our beautiful greens without fear of insult or dread of meeting intoxicated persons". Mrs Harris deemed it the ideal spot to end her husband's rapscallion years of racketing round Chicago from one address to another in heaven knows what sort of neighbourhoods. The first fine houses were going up on the "Blue Plateau" overlooking the park in 1905, the same year Paul was founding Rotary, and he built his own home on one of the "best" roads there, Longwood Drive. If the Movement were to maintain its aim of attracting

the "better elements", its Founder should certainly go to ground in
an appropriate haven amongst them. Such people were also the only
proper and possible ambience for a pretty, and determined, young
wife of Jean's strict Presbyterian upbringing. After one of "Kaiser
Bill" Thompson's election triumphs, the comedian Will Rogers
sagely commented, "They was trying to beat Bill with the better
element vote. The trouble with Chicago is that there ain't much
better element." Alas, how regrettably true, but what there was
could be found around Morgan Park, on all sides of Comely Bank,
and the worst happening in 1914 was not the start of that far-away
European War but the annexation of this exclusive village "with all
the conveniences and advantages of the city, far from all its objectionable features" into Chicago's vulgar maw.

But the damage was more apparent than real and the Harrises
lived serenely insulated from the objectionable features of one of the
world's greatest and most exciting cities for thirty-five years. The
first half-dozen years were spent in a state of war — in succession,
Paul Harris's war with himself; then a war of Rotary concepts which
initially Paul could only watch as a demobbed casualty, living in a
state of siege others no doubt called connubial bliss; then under the
pall of world war, which Harris knew would be America's also one
day and was Rotary's from the opening thunder of boots and
wheels over Flanders, since the Movement in Britain, the crucial
beach-head to Rotary's internationalism, was in the front line from
the moment there began, in Wilfred Owen's lines, "the monstrous
anger of the guns" and "the stuttering rifles' rapid rattle"; then of
course the United States involvement, when in even the most withdrawn and remote of American homes one might catch echoes of
"The shrill, demented choirs of wailing shells" and see at "each
slow dusk a drawing-down of blinds". But Paul's chief war aim,
even before he had truly started to recover his own health, was that
Owen's "Anthem for Doomed Youth" should never be part of a
Requiem for Rotary. That was his war. He lacked equally the violent personal aggression of the pacifist, and the coward's dual need
to camouflage his conquest of himself and appease his fear of
victory. He was a worm who had learned turning at his grandmother's knee — it was a rotating movement, after all — and he
knew that wars were the delaying tactic of history, not its instrument. A man who had waited out his friends could easily wait out
his enemies, and he proceeded to do so.

Though already dead to many Rotarians — to some metaphorically, to large numbers literally — the exile of Comely Bank was
never entirely silent. Paul Percy Harris had, even as his mental and
bodily health teetered on the verge of exhaustion, summoned up

from some deep well of formidable conviction that would brook no stay the energy to stay on the bridge, though sharing the helm with other hands, and brook no opposition to the compass-setting he had determined for his brainchild from which he had never wavered. The Movement had spread well beyond Chicago, beyond his country's borders, beyond the seas. When he could do no more, he knew he had done enough. At only forty-four, he felt and looked twice that age. But he would not give lesser men, those who would never understand or would wilfully try to distort his vision of ludicrous size and wild ideals, the chance of seeing him die in harness, falter and fail and fall in the heat of the spotlight. If his colleagues thought they were dropping the pilot, and not before time, let them. Paul knew they would soon find he had set a course from which there was no deviation, try (and some would) as they might to wrest the wheel in other directions. He knew the channels and tidal forces, the rocks and rapids, Rotary must navigate better than they. He let go command, knowing better than they that, just in time, he had fashioned a craft that would survive — more important still, knowing better than they what it would have to survive; and yet even more important, *why* it would survive. It was his brainchild and he understood, better than anyone else, exactly what Rotary's true strengths were. He understood very well its weaknesses also, as he understood his own, but so fashioned its early growth that the former was sufficiently armoured against the latter.

He was a hero, a hero of service, there is no doubt about that. But he was not a fool. Rotary was his child, his only child. The birth of true brainchildren have more risk than most; the march of medical science has done nothing for them, except perhaps to pretend they don't exist. As with any other delivery, there had been exaltation, pre-natal tension, but then a long and deepening postnatal depression. Winding himself up to a tremendous last surge of effort, he had, against all personal inclination, let the spotlight pour full upon him, endured the mental agony of public parturition, like the royal births of old. After one great last effort the child was out of the brain's womb, the applause was like a sword, the peace was almost a death. Just in providential time, the stronge nurse was there to lead him out of the glare, and he and his "Bonnie Jean" built their lifelong home — with a rapscallion flicker, it was built on the only hill in Chicago. There on Longwood Drive near Morgan Park he had a view that in winter reminded him of his New England boyhood. And there, by staying in full view of everyone, he disappeared from sight.

He took a plate with him, an etched bronze plate with enamelled border, mounted on mahogany, a gift from the Rotary Club of Chicago, showing the text of resolutions adopted unanimously at the Club's Annual General Meeting. Presented under the guise of a testimonial, it read like a valediction, almost an epitaph, one step removed from an obituary. After several sentences beginning with "WHEREAS", it was "RESOLVED that the said Paul P. Harris be made and constituted, and he is hereby made and constituted, a life member of the Chicago Rotary Club, free from any requirement as to dues or attendance of meeting". After this patronising giving of life to Pygmalion by Galatea, the text stated that the plate was an expression of "appreciation and good will". A glance at the signatures is revealing. Of the missing Founder Members, Hiram Shorey was back in Maine and Gus Loehr dead; but Silvester Schiele's name is there, and so is that of Harry Ruggles, the song-leader, and Al White, the organ-maker, who had taken the seventh meeting to Rotary's first hotel lunch, and A.M. Ramsay, who had defeated Ches Perry to become sixth Club President. Altogether, fourteen old comrades signed. Ches Perry did not.

When he recovered from his breakdown Paul took slow steps back, taking guidance gratefully from Jean. He returned to his law work, nothing sensational, no crimes or divorce, but corporate, real-estate and probate law. He was persuaded to take an office in Ches Perry's growing Secretariat, but, doubtless to Perry's relief, attempted to play no part in administration. And almost no part in Rotary. Throughout the war years, and for long after, he appeared at no Convention. The "organisation men" of Rotary felt no need of him, though the percipient Secretary felt that one day a new need might arise (as it did). They dared not let him out of their sight. As he expressed the position laconically, and without ran-cour, to Jean, "We police one another without realising it." This well suited Perry, who strongly urged Rotarians to visit the con-valescent Founder and did all he could to build up the pedestal and do a Pygmalion in reverse to the figure on top.

One of the delights of visiting Chicago [Perry wrote to Clubs] is the oppor-tunity to drop in on Paul P. Harris, the Father of Rotary. . . . Paul is not these days in the most robust health, and he has not found it possible to travel much . . . he lives in a simple, domestic manner with his charming wife from Edinburgh, who is not one whit less pleased to welcome the visiting Rotarians than is her famous husband. . . .

There is something charming and delightful in this idea of Rotary having an ancestral home. . . . A long life to Paul Harris, and may his pursuit of the practice of law become more and more remunerative, so that he may have to do less and less law work, and have more and more time to entertain the visiting Rotarians — even until he shall do nothing else.

Seldom can the wish have been more candidly the father of the thought.

But if Paul Harris was the Father of Rotary, Ches Perry was certainly the Godfather. "His most characteristic point of superiority", Harris explained about Perry to a visitor, "is to be found in the fact that his wires are insulated. He is positively a non-conductor of calumny."

All wires from Comely Bank appeared insulated, too. All that Rotary heard from Paul Harris these days were annual messages read to Convention, over the preliminary chatter of the hall. They were curious, to say the least; in style and content, they bore no relation to the driving prose and sinewy thought which had produced the 1911 Manifesto in the first *National Rotarian*. They could not, even charitably, be compared to oracles from Delphi, because they were embarrassingly banal and besides, by definition, oracles are spoken. They were more like the work of a prose laureate of the Movement, who is expected to produce uninspired items on regular occasions which neither he nor anyone else expects to be read.

Nothing was reported in *The Rotarian* in 1913. In 1915, Harris told delegates twice in one message, "It's a real man's job to be a Rotarian", and added: "Men, your kind of men, big, hale, hearty, happy, manly men have found happiness in brotherly love, have stifled self in their confessed love to serve and have exalted truth." He then burst out, "I wish that it might be the privilege of all Rotarians to visit Secretary Perry's office and to see the wonders he has achieved there." But what was Rotary International supposed to grow and achieve, enchained in the First National Bank Building?

In 1916, the written message read out was, "It will be in keeping with the tendency of the times if Rotarians' activities narrow rather than broaden" and, staggeringly, "Faith, Hope, Charity and Clean Business, these four and the greatest of these is clean business. Charity sometimes destroys initiative and demoralises character, clean business never does." Was he mocking himself in the mirror?

The entry of America into the European War brought this message, in which recovery is signalled by the old strength of voice returning, a true, clear-sighted touch of the Harris of old:

Rotary's supreme purpose is to serve; never service more appropriate than on the present occasion. . . . Rotary, even in its most sanguine moments, has fallen short of realizing its own strength . . . we shall strike a mighty blow some day and we thenceforth shall know ourselves. . . . The Stars and Stripes and the Union Jack have at last been twined together. Though grown into National manhood and though bearing responsibilities of our own, this is a sort of home-coming celebration after all . . . Britain is being remade. The United States of America is to be remade.

Perhaps even Racine was being remade. Just over the border in Wisconsin, the birthplace of Rotary's Founder had formed a Rotary Club. He wasn't at Racine, either. But if Chesley Perry was at all disturbed by the old, vigorous, independent voice reasserting itself from Comely Bank, reassurance came from the Canadian Rotarians of Fort William and Port Arthur, who marked the advent of their new allies in war by presenting the General Secretary with an enormous bull moose's head for his office wall.

In 1918, as the war's end approached, Harris's message was carrying a salutary warning that Rotarians should not forget which nation had been their best ally in peace and war. The man to whom winning London to Rotary was "the grand objective" had not changed his loyalty. Urging his fellows to forget one-sided accounts of the War of Independence, he wrote: "Britain has demonstrated itself to be the fairest and, therefore, the wisest of all colonizers. . . . Such a navy as that of Great Britain in other hands might have seemed a menace to peace. . . . If it had not been for that same navy, this would have been a German world."

He also cautioned against thinking that the Armistice, when it came, would usher in a paradise of peace, safety and order: "The great march of human events is on and it will make no perceptible pause at the termination of the war. . . . Immediately following . . . will come the day of mental unrest, of clash of wills and ideals. No institution is so sacred as to be beyond danger. Even the home is being assailed. The happy-go-lucky age is past and we would not recall if it we could." There he spoke for himself, not for his fellows in the Movement, but his unsparing vision pressed on. For those to whom the Bolshevik Revolution was signalling Utopia, he gave blunt counsel: "Russia is an example of what a nation ought not to be, and of what may be expected of an unenlightened and oppressed people. They may have their Bolsheviki; we do not need them."

Finally, warning that the end of the war would only mean "we and the nations allied with us shall have embarked again on un-charted seas", he wrote this exhortation: "If there ever was a time for a greater Rotary, it is today. If there ever was a time when the will within struggled to burst its bonds, it does so now."

Yet his was to be a lone voice in a nation that began turning inward upon itself as soon as the guns fell silent in November. Or was he writing about his own stifled will? If he was, he would have been encouraged to pursue the renewed vein of resolution that seemed to be welling within him by a newspaper article which appeared in 1919, though unfortunately couched in terms again almost of an obituary, in the *Houston Chronicle*: "He organized a strange kind of club, from which men get nothing, but actually pay for the privilege of doing good." It was worth framing and putting beside that Chicago plate.

But, of course, no true victors were to emerge from that railway carriage in Compiègne Forest, only terribly tired men, some more defeated than others. On both sides, losses had been appalling and their manner nauseating; the stench hung over Flanders for years. Empires which had seemed a permanent fixture in global affairs were destroyed or emasculated; Holy Russia had gone and the Holy Roman Empire, and the red flag streamed like a screen of blood across the false dawn. Women and the working class now strode into the front ranks of affairs, the entire fabric of society in all countries assumed completely new patterns and shapes. Even those many institutions which appeared unchanged, were not. With one little noticed exception. The poor would always be with us, but far less poor. The rich also, but far less rich. The middle classes, however, who had neither commanded nor slaughtered each other, were on the rise (in the Soviet Union, of course, they ruled). And the field of opportunity lay wide before Rotary, spread-eagled for the taking. Middle-class morality was ripe for rape. At the moment of victory, at the Second Battle of the Marne before Paris, Marshal Foch had declared, "My centre is giving way, my right is pushed back, situation excellent, I am attacking." The exile of Comely Bank, had he been the force of ten years earlier, would have said much the same.

Yet 1918 brought not only the end of the Great War for Rotarians, as for everyone. It brought the end of Paul Harris's long night of eclipse, the rediscovery of some part of himself which had done that enormous deed so long ago. It brought the death of the past, but a past that had held much of mental torment and darkness, as well as echoes of triumph. He let it go, as he had let it go once before in 1912 at Duluth. When the storms had subsided, within and without, he looked about him and wondered how he had got so marooned high on that pedestal, how he had become one of those people invisible by their presence, a man it was impossible to ignore, unless he happened to be right there in the room with you.

News came that Gus Loehr had died, the volatile little "promoter" who had done so much to get that first meeting in the Unity

Building started. Much else was lost, too. Old standards, old moralities (in spite of all the Movement could do), good manners were
gone, perhaps good women were gone; certainly women as he knew
them, or thought he knew them. The old world was gone, on both
sides of the Atlantic. And many, many millions of young lives had
been lost, a whole generation and their seed with them.

But maybe one thing had found itself: Rotary. Behind all the
fustian declarations, the turgid rhetoric, the dreadfully sincere
incoherence of official oratory, basic simplicities and essentials
could be seen again as the red floods subsided and the terrible
thunder ebbed and ached out of the ears. Rotary, it was clear
now — whether Harris's Rotary or not — had come to stay, and
would survive. At the war's end the International Movement had
enlisted its 400th Club and, of these, twenty-one were overseas in
the British Isles and thus within the British Association of Rotary
Clubs. In the New World, Clubs were divided into twenty Districts,
each with a Governor; the BARC was divided into a further six
Districts.

The Kaiser had accomplished what Arthur Sheldon had signally
failed to do in his eager pre-war travels in Europe. A Club had been
formed on the mainland of Europe in Paris where all members,
whether from the United States, Canada, the British Isles or Cuba,
could meet while on war service. It was called the Allied Rotary
Club of France and it held regular Thursday luncheons in the
plush Hotel Continental, which set aside a "Rotary Room" for
the purpose.

A few more months of war might have brought forward even
more far-reaching developments, since not only had Rotary printed
and circulated a pamphlet, *Questions and Answers Concerning the
Present War*, to schools at 8 cents a copy in aid of the Red Cross,
but the question of forming a Junior Rotary had been seriously
considered, forty-three years and another world war away from the
first Rotaract Club.

When the last "War Angelus" sounded, the Rotary Club of
Chicago was meeting every day of the week, had introduced self-
service meals, and Ches Perry was writing to the British Clubs —
perhaps with just the tiniest malice aforethought — that he was in
correspondence also with men "who are interested in organizing
Rotary Clubs in China, Japan, India, France, Puerto Rico, and the
South American Republics, and also Sydney and Melbourne,
Australia". He added proudly: "We have learned that a Rotary
Club has been organized in Madrid." That knowledge was as much a
fantasy as had been the pre-war founding of Clubs in Paris and
Vienna. But Ches Perry was as determined in his own very different

way as Paul Harris had been, when Rotary's Founder was setting
about realising in hard terms his original Service Club "fantasy"
and, from the battlefront, Peter Thomason endorsed the dreams of
"that ideal letter-writer" in Chicago. He foresaw that when peace
came the British soldier would renew contact abroad made during
wartime – "so many of us will be bi-lingual, if not tri-lingual; and
we shall be having our travelling bags packed more often". He even
confidently forecast an IARC Convention being held in Britain
after the world had settled down again (and there he was right)
"and we should greet French, Belgian, and Colonial guests". No
doubt he had seen for himself also the impact made in Paris by the
Allied Rotary Club of France and, soon after the war, a French
Army lieutenant was telling Clubs he spoke to in Britain that
"Wherever a Rotary Club exists, it is like a little garden in a city,
where the flower of public spirit is cultivated". It was not till 1925
that Paris, Vienna and Madrid had their little gardens – in Madrid in
fact was founded continental Europe's first Club – but when they
were all in the fold, half the world was right in there with them.
Ches Perry's extraordinary powers of organisation, his insatiable
drive for "Extension", might betray him once too often into
premature claims, but those claims were held on to with mastiff
strength till he made them come true.

Paul Harris didn't interfere with the formulation of these plans.
He was invited down to New Orleans to speak to Rotarians in May
1917 when America's war was but a month old, and his words were
not the clotted clichés then stifling the air with patriotic fug. He
didn't say it was a man's job to be in the Army and fight the Hun,
and avoid wild women and drink. He said, "It's a man's job to be a
good Rotarian, and he who lives up to the precepts will be a good
neighbor, a kind friend, a loving husband, a companionable father,
and an asset to the community in which he lives." He knew men
had to be rapscallions first, especially when so many would die
before they could be anything else.

Of course, with a generation destroyed, the world looked to the
younger brothers and sisters of the fallen, of those who would never
be rapscallions. The dead of the United States alone numbered
116,000, for all the country's brief participation. The British, with
their Empire troops included, could count 947,000 crosses round
the swamplike abattoirs of the Western Front. On both sides the
losses were appalling. Again, in Churchill's matchless summing-up:
"In the sphere of force, human records contain no manifestation
like the eruption of the German volcano . . . nearly twenty million
men perished or shed their blood before the sword was wrested
from that terrible hand." And Rotary had earned its say in the

post-war world. Amongst all the Clubs in the United States, Great Britain and Ireland, Canada and Cuba, an average of at least 6 per cent were in full-time war service, thousands of others in war work on the home front, out of a 40,000 total.

The breach was there for Rotary to fill if it had the will. From the beginning, Paul Harris's concept of Rotary as a place where the "boy" in men could live again had never been changed. "The Members were boys again." How *could* it change? The concept was bound up in the unchanging past out of which Harris had brought forth his offspring; "to me, attendance at a Club meeting was very like being back home in my valley". Over in Europe, there was only the valley of death; in wartime America, the genius of Rotary was given an unparalleled opportunity to concentrate its ingenuity on nurture and welfare of the nation's boyhood. On this, Paul Harris and Ches Perry were in complete accord. "The life of every child", wrote Perry, soon after the American declaration of war and doubtless still obsessed with those perils of camp-life, "develops the same psychological problems as did the Garden of Eden. . . . Boys do wrong things because they do not think clearly. . . . If Rotary can find a way to make the boys develop into the men they should be, then Rotary will have given to the world another great age in the progress of the human race."

The recruitment of youth to the farms, eagerly led by the Chicago Rotarians, has been mentioned. The Boys' Club Federation had rallied under the cry "Feed or Fight"; then there was the slogan "Every Scout to Feed a Soldier", while the Woodcraft League proclaimed "The Hoe Behind the Flag". "Boy Power" — very different from our modern notion of the dread idea — sprang up like dragons' teeth, mobilised, under Woodrow Wilson's express order, into the US Boys' Working Reserve, with handsome bronze badges for the dutiful and good. "They can show themselves worthy of patriotic brothers who are fighting," said Rotarian Wilson, and only our disturbing hindsight notes the long foreshadow of the Hitler *Jugend*.

Rotary Clubs everywhere gave funds to form new Scout troops, for Baden-Powell's own brainchild, only two years younger than Rotary, had taken firm hold in the United States. Their proliferation in wartime was natural, after all, since "B.P." had come by his inspiration while observing and training the young Army scouts who did such valiant deeds for him at Mafeking in the Boer War. Many articles on Scouting appeared in *The Rotarian*. Rotary Number One had been one of the first "boosters" of American Scouting in 1912 and, when Chicago began the practice of choosing a "Boy Mayor" for a day in 1916, Rotarians were among the first to do him honour at a special luncheon. Rotary Number Two formed a Boys' Work Committee and two members of the San Francisco Club made up the original three-man Board of Trustees of the Area's Boy Scouts of America.

There were excesses, as was to be expected. "Rotary Loves Boys" was an unfortunate slogan that might have set training in the Concentration Camps back ten years, though it was not as bad as the poem "Dedicated to Rotary" with lines like

> The love of a woman is warm,
>   Her kisses as hot as the South,
> And glorious battle to storm,
>   The road to her amorous mouth.
> But what is the nectar you drink,
>   The fragile and beautiful span,
> By one indestructible link,
>   The love of a man for a man?. . .
> The highway to Heaven begins
>   With the love of a man for a man.

Perhaps Oscar Wilde had made more of a lasting impression than he (or Chicago) realised when he had paid his visit those long years before. Paul Harris would have found reassurance in reading the following verses (and Rotarians were prolific poets under the spur of war):

> My Rotary, you know I love you
>   And I long for you each day.
> My Rotary, I'm thinking of you
>   When I'm many miles away.
> I see the boys each week at luncheon —
>   My good old chums so true.
> My Rotary, I'm only waiting
>   Till I can get back to you.

Yet it was not all that strange. The armies of the First World War were the last innocents abroad, and war was still the only children's game one played with even more enthusiasm as adults than as boys, though rather less vindictively. The lines above were a despatch from the front. They could have been a despatch from Comely Bank.

No doubt the "war despatch" which subsequently gave Rotary's Founder the greatest satisfaction and pleasure was not from an American or, ironically, addressed to him, though *The Rotarian*

devoted a whole page to it. It was a letter written to Chesley Perry
by Rotarian Ernest Tickle of the Rotary Club of Liverpool (the
Club Morrow had formed at breakneck speed and where BARC had
been born). Tickle wrote that he had found Rotary inspiration and
idealism everywhere in the trenches — "over my Dixie can of army
stew, my gastronomic mind dwells on the Rotary luncheon" — and
the following passage is an astonishing tribute to Harris's ideal:

> Army life is hardly the environment for philosophic thought, yet the
> thought does come over one that in Rotary we have a force, still largely
> latent, which when our Movement *does* actually become truly and really
> *International* . . . then *nations* will learn, even as today's individuals and
> towns are realising, that each for itself is a basis for business, civil and
> national life which is fundamentally wrong and is rotten to the very core. . . .
>
> Let this be Rotary's grand aim through the coming years — then pos-
> terity will rise to praise and honour the names of Paul Harris and the faith-
> ful few who helped him raise the Movement his great heart planned.

Number 171193 Gunner E.W. Tickle of Number 88 Siege Battery
"somewhere in France" even recalled the fuss in his boyhood days
made about a book called *If Christ Came to Chicago*, and Harris
must have smiled his broadest wry and gentle smile, memories
pouring back in on him of those past days, when he read: "We may
humbly venture to assert Christ has come to Chicago . . . and
through Rotary is preaching a truly seven-day theology. God grant
the dream prove a real actuality." However Gunner Tickle rated his
own chances of survival, surrounded as he admitted he was by
events of "an absolute impossible atrocity with its unspeakable
horrors", we can fairly reckon that with this letter he ensured
Paul Harris's own. Even Rotary's, for it was living proof that the
Movement would come through its time of greatest trial. So would
Harris.

At the Armistice Paul Harris was a man of fifty; Rotary had just
turned thirteen. Thirteen often regards fifty as dead, and certainly
as not knowing what it is talking about. The following month,
the first of peace in the nation's capital, Washington, DC, *The
Rotarian* reported how Rotarians were guests of a Mr and Mrs
Hathaway "at their old colonial mansion", where they found "a
string band of fifteen negroes enlivening the occasion with old-time
melodies and buck-and-wing dancers added to the general merri-
ment. An oyster roast was on the programme", and afterwards
"the guests were met by Mrs. Hathaway who invited them to a
bounteous repast on the shady lawn".

Whether the city's best-known Rotarian, who had just finished making the world safe for democracy, attended, we do not know. What we do know is that neither November's nor December's issue of *The Rotarian* carried any message from Paul Harris.

It didn't matter. Though he sincerely believed the impulse of his Service Club had been divinely inspired, he did not hold any illusion — to adapt Captain Shotover's phrase from *Heartbreak House* — that the laws of God would ever be suspended in favour of Rotary because he had invented it, yet he had already had his victory in that letter from Gunner Tickle of Liverpool. Other words came back from it: "The war zone is hardly a place to expect a living revelation of the Rotary belief." But that's precisely where, against all expectations, it had been found, and he now knew that though the root might be trampled underfoot, scorned, pulled up, thrown aside and buried, it would never die.

CHAPTER ELEVEN

The First 21 — Edinburgh

Eyl! Eyl! Estan aqui,
Los Rotarianos,
Buenos compañeros.
Eyl! Eyl! Estan aqui,
Listos a probar el chow!

Uruguayan Rotary song

The tune had been written forty years before and there wasn't a Latin-American beat in any bar. It was, in fact, as genuinely Latin as the Founder of Rotary in Uruguay himself, "Herbierto" Coates. In other words, it was English. The song had first been sung in public in Boston in 1880 and was a Spanish version of "Hail! Hail! The Gang's All Here!", the collegiate — and later Democratic Party — anthem which was really the tune of the pirates' song in *The Pirates of Penzance*, composed by Sullivan.

Well, an historical case could possibly be made out of it, since Uruguayan independence from Spain had first been defended in 1806 by that British naval hero, Admiral Sir Home Popham, inventor of the flag-signalling system that had carried Nelson's famous message at Trafalgar, and both he and Arthur Sullivan's swashbuckling grandfather had later fought with Wellington in Spain. But it would be a pretty thin one. A much better case was the nearer truth, that the song came to represent perfectly both the spread of Rotary ideals around the world, a process which accelerated rapidly after the Armistice, and the British influence in much of that magnificent contagion, however well camouflaged. There was certainly a strong Yorkshire influence (what other Yorkshire kind is there?) in the articles written for *The Rotary Wheel* by William Moffatt, a Rotarian of Leeds who, throughout the inter-war years, exhorted the Movement to reach for ever more ambitious goals and also to be level-headed about its means and capacity to grasp them, rather in the manner of an insurance salesman urging larger but more realistic premiums. This was indeed Moffatt's profession, which brings him firmly into that group of lawyers and insurers who for so long formed the dynamic core of Rotary.

In August 1919 Moffatt wrote a piece on higher goals, which Paul Harris must have read in his Comely Bank retreat, sitting with Jean by the large picture-window overlooking his lovely autumn garden, with quiet pleasure. "Echoes of voices from beyond the sea come to us," wrote Moffatt. "They come from a new nation, and carry with them hints of abounding virility and high ideal-ism. . . . Rotary comes with a world idea. When our friends came from America they did not come to boast of America . . . they came as brothers from a far country, animated by ideals similar to our own. Race and history and nationality were forgotten, and we met simply as men. . . . Try to visualize what the International Rotary Convention at Edinburgh in 1921 will mean."

Try indeed. But who could? Even to propose it was an incredibly bold and imaginative stroke, the very first Rotary Convention held outside the borders of the United States! It had been murmured for several years, even the previous year, during the last August of the war when, at a splendid ceremony in the Waldorf-Astoria, New York, an American flag was presented to every one of the then twenty-two Clubs in the British Isles. It was the final gesture of the old thinking; Ches Perry stubborn, the Chicago spirit defiant. Today, they would be Rotary International flags, but then Rotary still meant the United States, or at least American Rotarians thought it did, so the spirit of Rotary gave British Clubs twenty-two Stars and Stripes. The proposal also arose to move International Head-quarters down to Washington, DC, so that Rotarian Wilson might have Secretary Perry's counsel at his elbow. Thankfully, for the future of Rotary, the proposal withered on the vine.

To others, Rotary's spokesmen gave an uncompromising back of the hand. In the first New Year of peace, The Rotarian pronounced a sort of anathema: "The people of Germany have within themselves the power to become like other human beings . . . the Germans may come to their senses more quickly than the Russians, and yet it is possible that they, too, will need a bath of blood to clear their blurred moral vision."

There were those who wondered if Rotarians had within them the power to become like other human beings and speculated if the dust which once had risen from beneath the rim of Monty Bear's first Wheel had done more than its share of vision-blurring, too. One

of them was Paul Harris and he lost no time in urging that the
Twelfth Convention should cross the seas to the city where his
wife "Bonnie Jean" was born. And it was he who insisted, albeit
behind the scenes, that Arthur Sheldon should give the main address
there. So it was that at midday on Wednesday, 1st June 1921, two
Cunarders, the *Cameronia* and *Caronia*, both packed from keel to
funnels with a total of over 1,000 Rotarians, plus their wives and
families, from Clubs all over the United States and Canada, set
sail for Great Britain and perhaps the most amazing — and certainly
the most significant — of all the Rotary Conventions ever held.

Thus began the first of the Movement's two great "21" events,
the Edinburgh Convention of that year. The second "21" occasion
was to follow five years later when the Movement celebrated its
"coming of age" in 1926. That year the Movement, we can say
looking back, received, as was proper, the key to the door of its
stupendous international future. In 1921, it was given the door
itself, the portal of the world. It is fair to say that both the world
and Rotary were overwhelmed.

Two Rotarians did not choose to join those shipmates of the
Golden Wheel, which was at last rolling over the Atlantic from which
the Kaiser's onslaught on Belgium had barred it seven years before.
Warren Harding, barely three months in office as twenty-ninth
President of the United States, was busy putting into effect America's
first quota restriction on immigrants, which confined those from
any one country to 3 per cent of the number of their fellow-
countrymen already resident (a quota the Mafia effortlessly ignored
in common with that earlier Volstead Act of Prohibition). He was
not aboard. Nor was Paul Harris. His time had not yet come again,
though he knew he would not have to wait long. And possibly he
was painfully aware of his own two Atlantic crossings in 1893,
during his years of "folly" when he had voyaged in squalor to
Liverpool as a seaman in a stinking cattle-boat. On the *Cameronia*
and *Caronia* the Cunard Line had even abolished second-class
travel: for this trip, there were no distinctions, and on both ships
every Rotarian travelled first class. And every Rotarian soon discovered, as they came up the gangplanks and on to the decks of the
higher reaches of the British Merchant Marine, that the definition of
an intoxicating beverage as one which contained more than half of
1 per cent of alcohol was one they could now legally put on ice
for the duration as they sang "Eyl! Eyl! Estan aqui!" in any language they wished, *buenos compañeros* to the last man. They were
led by the new International President, Estes "Pete" Snedecor, and,
since he was an old friend of his, Paul Harris felt the great occasion
was in safe hands. After all, had not Snedecor written two years

before, when considering the vistas now open to Rotary after the war: "What shall be the future organisation of International Rotary? . . . All Rotary Clubs will be affiliated directly with the International Association of Rotary Clubs, but will be divided into national or continental divisions, whenever there are a sufficient number of Clubs in a nation to justify a national or continental division." And in Edinburgh, a Committee was duly appointed to draw up a new Constitution for the Movement.

The pill — for those for whom it was a pill — was sweetened by Rotarian Sir Harry Lauder when he welcomed them to Scotland with these words: "Now we want to get very friendly with one another because we are all dependent the one upon the other . . . and we can do it by coming together in an atmosphere of kindliness with the glass of friendship always held up high . . . if we could drink it in wartime, surely it will taste all the sweeter in peacetime." Especially when, by a few days travel over the Atlantic, you could drink the real thing legally again.

Before we take a good look at the amazing goings-on at Edinburgh, let us look at the extraordinary world surround in which they happened and of which they were sometimes cause, sometimes effect, and the supreme symptom, before and after that June of 1921. For certainly Rotary was never the same again.

In the decade following the Armistice Rotary was to increase its membership by 300 per cent and put down roots in over forty more countries in every corner of the globe. By 1928, the Movement had proved that here was a plant which could flourish in both the stoniest and most luxuriant of soils. Like a mole carrying a magic nutrient which worked infallibly and yet which no one could understand, the Golden Wheel resumed an inexorable roll "underground" through a world riven by hunger, desolation, festering wounds and bewildered patriots, who had begun to sense that their victorious heels were firmly placed on the dying throat of their own dreams.

As noted, the original Golden Wheel, attempting to make a genuine journey through the world's Rotary Clubs, had been compelled to return to San Francisco with its transatlantic itinerary foiled by the "European War". The smoke of battle still hung in the air, and the appalling body-count had scarcely begun, when the Golden Wheel was on the move once more across the waters, much more powerfully as a moral, spiritual and ethical force than as a literal icon of service. But in 1919 the Atlantic was eschewed for other oceans; the flag of Rotary was raised over China, the Philippines, India,

Panama and Argentina. In the two instances where these new Clubs were not formed in a national capital, they were started in the chief port and commercial centre of the nation concerned, moreover one dominated by Anglo-Saxon business men. It was a Rotarian from the American West Coast port of Seattle — Rotary Number Four — who started Clubs in Manila and Shanghai, and it was two years before the latter elected its first "native", although it had at once the most exciting sounding of all Club magazines, *The Rotary Pagoda*. This first Chinese member of the Movement was one of his country's most famous and distinguished industrialists and politicians, Y.C. Tong, and it is regrettable to note that he was frequently referred to, rather insensitively, as the Movement's only "Celestial Rotarian", much being made of his apparent love of baseball! Still, soon he had enlisted the Chinese Ambassador to the Court of St James as a fellow-"native" member. Mr Tong is on record as saying, "I consider my membership in Rotary ... one of the greatest honours that I have ever received", and a great and exclusive honour it was to remain for some years, for even in 1924 Shanghai's 100 Rotarians included only ten Chinese — with ten British and eighty Americans as ballast. One of those eighty, however, was its first Secretary, George Treadwell, who was soon to return to the United States and was destined to become the first full-time paid Secretary of Rotary Number One. Nor was the value of his non-parochial background lost, for it was he who was to commission the University of Chicago's famous study of "the events and philosophy of Rotary" to which we shall refer in later chapters.

The Manila, Calcutta and Shanghai Clubs could be too easily dismissed as enclaves of "foreign devils". Almost invariably, the first Rotary Clubs in a country — Chicago, San Francisco, Portland, New York, Boston, Dublin, London, Havana, Montevideo, Lima, Manila, Shanghai, Panama, Melbourne, Calcutta, Buenos Aires — were based in ports. And the exception usually proved the rule; the lake port of Toronto, for example, was Canada's second Club, but its predecessor, as the then undisputed grain capital of the North American continent, was virtually the drydock of the plains.

Two factors were at once clear, therefore. The Movement appealed wherever there was a successful business ambience of variety and growth. Another vital factor was the presence of a strong multinational basis for recruitment, in which there was quite frequently a strong English-speaking element to take the lead. The latter qualification soon naturally lessened and disappeared, but at the beginning of Rotary's massive and rapid post-war expansion the most obvious place for a Rotary apostle to be found was a city where American, Canadian and British export and import merchants

173

gathered. For an increasing number of these men, home from home was not something you could accomplish by teaching the local barman to make a "highball" or his sons to play cricket, but by establishing a branch of the world's first Service Club — a concept which soon proved infinitely variable and miraculously adapted to assimilate local colour and conditions. Sometimes, it is true, local colour was not assimilated in any literal sense, which made the assimilation completely so in a metaphysical sense. Half the Rotary Club of Johannesburg, dedicated to "white" ideals, was American. The Rotary Club of Pretoria, announcing its success in breaking down race prejudice, produced as proof the fact that their Club, the second in South Africa, contained ten "Hollanders", eight Dutchmen, three Germans, two Jews, ten Colonials, four Scotsmen, one Irishman and about seven Englishmen. The Rotary Club of Calcutta was only a slight improvement on this state of affairs, its members including actually one Indian in addition to Europeans and twenty Americans, though it reported to *The Rotary Wheel* "in view of the great interest which Rotary in England has taken in Unemployment" that Calcutta Rotarians were represented on the Central Unemployment Bureau for Europeans and Anglo-Indians, and clearly regarded this as community service.

The pioneering Calcutta Rotarians did not know, of course, that a supreme practitioner of Service Above Self had preceded them to India four years previously, in the person of the little lawyer who had fought the Boers and Zulus for Great Britain and had then become dedicated to a life of poverty, celibacy and non-violent protest, and whose cause that same year of 1919 had directly brought about the death by British machine-gunners of 10,000 over-excited followers. His emblem was also a wheel, a spinning-wheel, and his name was Gandhi. "If I could popularise the use of soul force, *Satyagraha*," the Mahatma told Lord Chelmsford, the Viceroy, "I know that I could present you with an India that could defy the whole world." The Viceroy was Paul Harris's exact contemporary, and one can only conjecture that if the latter had been wearing those viceregal plumes, the two lawyers — though utterly different men — might well have found a workable understanding.

Small wonder that in the prevailing circumstances the self-styled "Founder of Rotary in the Tropics", an Englishman named Reginald Coombes, suffered a relapse in health before the Calcutta Club was one year old. He had written: "It was really in the darkness of a night in India that I first saw Rotary, exactly as men first see Christ." We have of course noted the parallel with religious revelation before in this history. It had been evident ever since the Movement evolved from Stead's sardonic vision of Christ coming to Chicago, but the

174

harsh stumble against the world and the flesh did not send even Paul Harris into the exile Rotarian Coombes judged necessary, when the Indian dark dissolved into revealing day, and he fled into charter membership of the second Club in Australia, forming then in Sydney. "Behold!" Coombes had written ecstatically as he surveyed Calcutta Rotarians. "There sits the stationer and the stockbroker, the barber and the barrister, the publican and the priest, communing together at one round table!" But what they were communing about was whether to share their new Club with native Indians. They decided not to and kept to their decision for two years, finally admitting an Indian only when they had found one with the status and respectability of one of the British knighthood (then being touted round the Empire, like Wimbledon tickets, by Lloyd George).

Clearly the spectacle had proved too much for Coombes. His fellows in Sydney included seven Managers and eight Directors. True there was a barrister, but he soon became Governor of New South Wales, vastly improving his Classification. There wasn't an "abbo" in sight. Everything was impeccably Anglo-Saxon in most cases; or imitative of Anglo-Saxon. Indeed, the first Clubs in Brazil, Argentina, Chile and Peru were all considered "a fine tribute to the American business spirit", though Latin-Americans not only found the practice of addressing each other by their first names more irksome than the British had, but the virtues of men of sixty "becoming boys" in spirit completely baffled those who had been brought up to regard formality and dignity as indispensable to the responsible conduct of social life.

In 1920, when the spread through Europe began in earnest, it certainly started with Spanish-speaking members, but the Old World lost no time in imprinting its own style on Rotarian practice and had no intention of becoming a transplant of an American image, while faithfully adhering to the Rotary service ideals. Meanwhile, elsewhere in the globe, far from the still ash-hot battlefields, the new non-European Rotarians in centres of world commerce were just as incomprehensible to the majority of British and American expatriates living there, as they were now the natives! And just as invisible.

Nevertheless, the Board of Directors of International Rotary ensured during the first post-war year that when Rotary did come to the European mainland it would arrive with a standardised emblem. Nearly sixty versions of it had already been discovered in use, and a special committee admitted with embarrassment that consecutive editions of the official magazine itself had carried on its covers Rotary Wheels with nineteen, twenty and twenty-seven teeth. A

Rotarian who had taught engineering at the University of Minnesota decided this was nonsense enough and took advantage of a stay in hospital following an appendectomy to redesign a Rotary Wheel from Monty Bear's original — which originally, it will be recalled, had aspired to no more than wagon-wheel status — in correspondence with sound mechanical principles. When the Golden Wheel arrived in Europe in 1920, it had twenty-four teeth, six arms and was technologically without flaw, and thus it has remained ever since.

For the one sabbatical year of 1919, however, the wheels of Europe remained solely political. Ches Perry permitted that first year of peace to be President Wilson's Year in Europe, deciding perhaps that one Rotarian was quite enough for the ravaged, punch-drunk Continent to absorb. The Chicago Secretariat waited in the wings while the stage was tidied up. The Movement would from 1920 onwards bring quite enough of codes, declarations of principle and noble resolutions in its own unique train. For the time being, Wilson's Fourteen Points were more than enough for weary, cynical Europeans, victors and defeated both, to cope with.

Cope with them they did, however, their intent being made clear by Clemenceau, the "Tiger", who sardonically remarked of the Fourteen Points that Christ himself had been content with only ten. Lloyd George, doubtless after a show of Welsh Chapel offence at such irreverence, contributed his own share of pragmatic sabotage, having followed up his victory over the Germans by an even more sweeping victory over the Liberals (his own party) in the "Khaki Election", leading a coalition party which was largely Conservative. We can find cynicism, if not derision, of the Fourteen Points even easier today when we read Number Six, which assured Bolshevik Russia "an unhampered and unembarrassed opportunity for the independent determination of her sincere welcome into the society of free nations". As it happened, Bolshevik agents had already walked in without knocking, and quite without embarrassment, and erstwhile friend and foe alike were concerned with stamping out mushrooming soviets in their own countries, so Number Six had little chance of getting anywhere, either as a proposal by the visitors or concession by the vanquished.

Indeed, the number of nations on the winning side of the conference table at Paris must have stunned the American leader, as he watched them all assemble to be photographed by his own official photographer, also his fellow-Washingtonian and Rotarian, George Harris (no relation of Paul's). Along with Britain, France, and Italy, there were Belgium, Romania, Greece, Poland, Czechoslovakia, Brazil, Canada, Australia, South Africa, India, the Hejaz, Portugal, Siam, New Zealand, Bolivia, Cuba, Ecuador, Uruguay, Japan and

Serbia. Serbia? Ah yes, it was a Serbian grammar-school boy who had started the whole thing, of course. Gavrilo Princip's bullets hadn't just killed an archduke and his duchess, they had destroyed a world.

History is a series of street accidents, as was observed in an earlier chapter. But this time, literally, young Princip had given up, was walking home. The Archduke Franz Ferdinand of Austria's car, taking a wrong turning, stopped to reverse out of a side road, bang in front of destiny's child. Bang indeed! American and British Rotary was right to focus on youth. Old continental Europe ignored it and an eighteen-year-old had sentenced his generation to death. Their elders now set about improving the road signs and ignoring the flow of traffic, a very easy thing to do in the splendid Hall of Mirrors at Versailles where the only view available was themselves in glory.

As to the democracy which had been saved by the slaughter, that would come into its own — such was the dream — in Wilson's League of Nations. Meanwhile, all those nations, each with victor's voting rights, might keep the Peace Conference dragging on for ever and there were a lot of jazz babies waiting to be born and have fun. Lloyd George, Wilson and Clemenceau settled terms with the Central Powers, the collapsed dynasties of Prussia, Austria and Turkey, and shunted all the other embarrassing and talkative Allies into committees, whose members enjoyed themselves thoroughly around Paris for several years and whose minutes were duly shredded by time. As the blind poet Milton wrote to his boss, the Lord General Cromwell, "peace hath her victories no less renowned than war". Those victories, as was to be the case twenty-five years later, were as always at the out-of-pocket expense of those who had stood triumphant on the battlefield. Congress, Commons and the Chamber of Deputies almost at once removed the Big Three from authority and ended their active careers on the world stage, more or less drastically. Germany paid over only a portion of the heavy reparations demanded and within ten years had not only borrowed back twice as much from the United States, but defaulted on the interest. The Kaiser enjoyed a Dutch Treat exile in Castle Doorn and died at eighty-two with his countrymen once more all round him, conquerors of Europe once again, blitzkrieging through the tulips.

Woodrow Wilson might well have recalled another Milton remark, made 125 years before Thomas Jefferson even started composing the Declaration of Independence, that "all men naturally were born free". It might have urged him to the reality that the aim of peace on earth was no new ideal and that there was nothing to which statesmen would not stoop to achieve it. By the end of 1921 the Big Three were all out of office, profoundly distrusted by the people they had led to what even their generalissimo Marshal Foch described thus: "Not Peace. It is an Armistice for twenty years." Wilson's League was duly formed, but America refused to join it and the world could hardly bring a paternity suit any more than blame Jefferson for Napoleon. Cause and effect has never been grounds for troubling a politician's conscience.

In May 1919, while the Peace Conference was in its final throes – at one point, Clemenceau even called Wilson "pro-German", and the affronted President replied, "Do you wish me to return home?", to which the Tiger answered "No", since he had decided to leave himself – British Rotary had a visit from its Past International leader, Arch. C. Klumph (see Chapter Nine), who said he was more convinced than ever "of the splendid part Rotary can play in bringing the two great English-speaking nations into a close and warm friendship which will link them together as a mighty team to preserve Peace, Justice and Honor among the nations of the world". He hadn't crossed the Channel, of course.

Estes "Pete" Snedecor – soon to bring the World Convention to Scotland – took a somewhat sterner view, however, during the same visit and deplored the fact that he found "a lack of conviction and, consequently, a lack of enthusiasm over the power and influence that Rotary might wield". But his opinion might have been soured by the discovery that he was mightily prone to seasickness, for by that time Rotary's two ambassadors had crossed a more crucial body of water than either the Atlantic or the Channel; they had gone over the Irish Sea. There they could observe the extraordinary circumstance that whereas, since 1911, the British Association of Rotary Clubs had increased to twenty-five, even with a world war on its doorstep, Ireland had still contributed no more than its two original Clubs set up by Stuart Morrow, those in Dublin and Belfast, though a number of attempts had been made to interest Cork. Ireland had other things on its mind. In charge of the whole Irish District (of two Clubs) Arch Klumph and Pete Snedecor found Bill McConnell, however, who, as Morrow's long-suffering brother-in-law, had been the Movement's first Rotarian outside of North America. They also found "the troubles"

For Dublin had other American visitors that summer, a three-man American Commission for Irish Freedom who had just paid an unrewarding visit to Woodrow Wilson in Paris; all he gave them was talk about "the great metaphysical tragedy of today". This trio caused quite a stir, making speeches from platforms draped with the republican tricolour and Stars and Stripes and even addressing the Dail Eireann, the Irish Government Assembly which met in Dublin's

Mansion House without any legal status whatever and with a President, the New York born Eamon de Valera, who had just escaped from Lincoln Prison.

Sinn Fein (which, it will be recalled, shared its birthday with Rotary), frustrated in its plans to be admitted to the Paris Peace Conference – where its leaders were reminded of their wartime claim that the Germans were "gallant allies in Europe" – were killing members of the Royal Irish Constabulary in the city streets and fomenting periodic strikes. Owing to one of these, the Rotary lunch for Arch and Pete could not be held in the usual hotel and took place in the basement of Woolworth's round a billiard-table. The visit was saved, however, by the guests' being entertained for dinner by Sir Harold Nutting, whose house, Arch reported, "is perhaps one of the finest, if not the finest, in all Ireland", and by their having lunch next day with the Lord Mayor of Belfast "at his beautiful country place". This hospitality helped the visitors forget the steel-helmeted soldiers on the Dublin streets and the tanks being unloaded on the Dublin quays. Alas, it helped others to recall with satisfaction the article which had appeared in wartime about Sinn Fein in *The Rotarian*, which was not disowned.

In Scotland and England a further round of gala visits awaited them, and Pete doubtless worried more about rough seas on the return voyage that year than about the fast-building tragedy of the Black and Tans on John Bull's Other Island, or than he pondered on the significance of the fact that the first Rotarian journalist in Europe, T.A. Grehan, worked for the *Irish Independent* and had written for his visitors' benefit: "Let it not be forgotten that the first Rotary effort outside of the continent of America was put forth in Ireland by an Irishman." Pointedly referring to the oblivion to which the establishment at Chicago had consigned Stuart Morrow, Grehan added: "I hope we Irish Rotarians will never forget the name or the man who bears it."

Anyone who read the newspapers of that time (or at any time this century for that matter) could scarcely doubt the state of health of any Irishman's memory. But in June 1919 Paul Harris himself expressed no public view about Morrow or the state of British Rotary. When the Versailles Treaty was signed the following month, the Founder of Rotary had a far more important and personal "Irish problem" to content with – the dying of his mother, the last of those feckless Bryans of Racine from whose voluble charm and extravagant penury his Vermont grandparents had "rescued" him and to whom he had been a stranger for forty-eight years. Cornelia Harris didn't even see him at the end, since she was now blind; but perhaps he saw her for the first time, a fellow-exile.

The rest of mankind, having shovelled the war-slaughtered millions out of sight, together with the nation where their war to end war had begun (Serbia disappeared into the new Kingdom of Yugoslavia), and rapidly ignoring the efforts of the peacemakers, began to emerge from the dark four years of self-immolation, glutted with blood, blinking at the gaudy, glittering twenties. For American Rotarians in general there was a far greater reaction to the signing of the 18th Amendment to the Unites States Constitution than any signing of papers at Versailles. In the words of a *Rotarian* editorial, "When John Barleycorn leaves the United States on July first, his departure will not create any stir in the American Rotary Clubs. The great majority of the Clubs have never known him." It was reported that 1 million gallons of hard liquor were stored away in Chicago on that day. The liquor didn't stay there for long. President Wilson had turned his attention from the wines of Versailles long enough to vote against Prohibition, but his fellow-legislators paid as little heed to his views on booze as they did to his views on Europe. It was in Chicago that his successor, Warren Harding, was nominated. And it was Chicago's Mayor, "Kaiser Bill" Thompson, who managed to get a law "banning" the speaking of English (as opposed to American) in the State of Illinois. Prohibition, not Rotary, was about to put the "Windy City" on the map of the world.

Early in the decade it was one of two cities that stood out in the chronicles of that time. Chicago established itself as the murder capital of North America, with prohibited armies of bootleggers killing each other and non-cooperative politicians, the gangsters gradually merging forces under an imported hoodlum from New York, Al Capone. With equal authority, Munich established itself as the murder capital of Europe, with prohibited German officers forming armies called "Free Corps", murdering republican politicians, and gradually merging forces under an imported hoodlum from Vienna, Adolf Hitler. Among the first terrorist victims was the man who had signed the Armistice terms for Germany and the Foreign Secretary who had agreed to carry them out. Munich did not have a Rotary Club, needless to say, till ostensibly calmer times, in 1928, when, like all other cities of the Western world, it was enjoying a tremendous boom in prosperity. Because business was good, times were good for Rotary though bad (at that moment, and briefly) for Hitler's political plans; but big business, wisely hedging bets, sponsored him as well as such institutions as Rotary. He was able to buy the celebrated villa which became Berchtesgaden and had time for the only love-affair of his life, with his niece, a blonde girl of twenty with (shades of Big Jim Colosimo and Sam Insull in

Chicago!) ambitions to be an opera star. There was room for only
one diva on Hitler's stage, however, and, baulked of a career, she
officially committed suicide.

As noted earlier, the first Club in continental Europe was formed
in a country not required at the peace negotiations, in neutral
Spain, at Madrid in 1920, not from any impulse from Chicago
Headquarters but as a second triumph for those same Rotarians of
Tampa, Florida, who had succeeded in establishing Rotary in
Havana during the war. Even as the first Club in the British Isles
had been founded in Dublin by a returned Irish expatriate from
California, so was the Madrid Club formed by a Spanish expatriate,
Don Angel Cuesta, who had returned from making his fortune in
California's East Coast rival state. It was hailed by sympathetic
Spaniards as heralding "a new social order". In Munich in 1920
those same words were being used by Hitler to proclaim the birth of
National Socialism along with the symbol, borrowed from his native
Austria, of the *Hakenkreuz*, the swastika. Thus the Wheel and the
Swastika arrived on the European scene cheek by jowl, determined
antagonists from the first, though this was not immediately apparent
among ordinary Europeans, who saw a number of superficial
similarities in their slogans and programmes. Indeed, did not this
Movement of Don Angel's hail from the sixth largest German city
in the world?

Post-war violence was not of course a European phenomenon
alone. Back in Houston, Texas, the home town of Colonel House,
Wilson's adviser, the President of the Rotary Club was murdered by
a Mexican terrorist who didn't realise that remembering the Alamo
was a strictly unilateral privilege. Nor did élitism in Rotary begin
with the infusion of some decadent European ingredient; it simply
reigned in Europe in its most frankly accepted form, and does so
still. Immediately after the Armistice, one of the most active
American Rotarians in Europe (apart from the US President), an
optician named Taylor from Mobile, Alabama, employed by the
Red Cross, expressed his belief that Europeans were not yet ready
to rise to Rotary ideals. "I do not believe that the time is ripe for
its introduction to any of the European countries except England,"
he wrote from his holiday suite in the Polish hunting-lodge of the
recently murdered Romanovs, amidst 800,000 acres of virgin
forest ("we are occupying the Czar's suite of rooms and have three
servants").

This was an élitist view. Europe was, on the contrary, more ripe
for ideals than for long years before the war. But they were no
longer prepared to accept them loftily handed down from a Messiah
who acted as if he had walked across the Atlantic. John Maynard

Keynes, the economist who would later become the most influential non-political figure in Western society until the men who made nuclear fission, looked at the Peace Conference and said, "Our power of feeling or caring beyond the immediate questions of our own material well-being is temporarily eclipsed. . . . Never in the lifetime of men now living has the universal element in the soul of man burnt so dimly."

As for the opportunity this presented to Rotary, the Founder sensed it correctly but for the wrong reasons. In his usual Message to the 1919 Convention, read as usual by Chesley Perry, he stated, with a sad regression from his recent brief emergence into the clear-sightedness of earlier years: "When the final reckoning shall have been made, it will be known that Victory, the prize invisible, was really won by the legions of unseen, unheard things. . . . Rotary is interested in the larger values, in the invisible. . . . Rotary, being invisible, spiritual, is intelligible to the higher order of things."

The higher order of things were in extremely short supply in post-war Europe, except for the lucky few who could put their feet up in an ex-Tsar's hunting-lodge. But when he wrote those words, Harris knew, as we have noted, that his mother was dying, the poor little rich girl who could never keep a dime, whose carelessness about higher things had thrust her son into an upbringing with grandparents whose Vermont rectitude was awesome — and it was the latter, not the former, who knew the value of material things. The old turbulent dilemmas had seized Paul's mind again, the dilemmas which he had created Rotary to resolve: the sustaining of practical ideals of service to others by means of whole-hearted acceptance of material success for oneself. The Editor of *The Rotarian*, whose emotions were not personally involved, proclaimed the new opportunity with candour when he said that the next Convention after victory should be devoted to "the greater task of making democracy safe for the world by fighting to save democracy from too sudden and violent social and industrial revolutions"!

There was no shortage of ideals nor of men to proclaim them. However, the survivors who ventured forth again upon the vast unmarked grave of Europe looked no longer to autocratic dynasties for their ideals but amongst themselves — not for princes of the blood, for the blood had proved to be everybody else's, but for men who knew what a pay-packet was, not knowing yet that it was still everybody else who would pay. And there they were, easily found, the rising middle classes with power in their pockets. So whether the new ideals were of Right or Left, it was more often than not the bourgeois which gave them birth. Elitism had not died, it had merely changed its uniform and its vocabulary and would flourish in the dachas of Moscow as in the villas of Antibes and the compounds of Cape Cod. The process had begun in Victorian times, but world catastrophe and the ruin of empires now left all doors open or swinging ajar on shattered or rotten hinges for the new princes of commerce. Demagogues battoned on them and the twisted gods that rose from those spouting ranks – knowing you cannot have soap-boxes without soap – drew fuel throughout the post-war decade from the bourgeois world of business.

The horror and holocausts which were to come from that bizarre collaboration were mercifully veiled in the early twenties, though Lenin, Mussolini and Hitler fully understood their needs and the need, above all, to wait. What concerns us in this history is that the opportunity offered by the newly courted and confident business man was fully understood also by the recluse in Comely Bank and by his apostles, and in their perception that there was no time to wait. Yet the language of the élite was still used, even by the man whose idea of a Service Club may yet be proved the last hope for mankind, and it is interesting that the term he chose came with uncanny instinct from the language of the nation where Rotary today grows faster than anywhere else on the globe. "What we need", wrote Harris in 1921, "is a race of Samurai".

John Pershing was, so to speak, Rotary's favourite Samurai at this time – and again the appellation is not inapt, for in 1905 when Harris and his three friends were forming Rotary Number One in Chicago, Pershing was seconded to the Japanese Army that was driving the Russians out of Manchuria. A grateful America invented a new super-rank for Pershing after the First World War, naming him "General of the Armies", and Rotary added its cheers by electing him an Honorary Member of its Clubs in Lincoln, Nebraska and San Antonio, Texas.

Rotary's home-grown élite regrettably quarrelled. The US President and his war-lord had a strong clash of views over the timing of the Armistice, the General feeling that he hadn't been allowed sufficient chance to win enough battles, but Wilson's successor, Warren Harding, who had accepted membership of the Rotary Club of Washington, DC, with flattering alacrity, made Pershing his Chief of Staff and then, while presiding over the reduction of the Navy, allowed Pershing to get on with organising the structure of the modern US Army which was to breed MacArthur, Marshall and Eisenhower.

So élitism, though it would not have been thought of in such terms, was not regarded as alien by the Chicago Secretariat. But noting that the Prince of Wales was an Honorary Member of the

Club in Windsor, Ontario (he was later Duke of another Windsor, of course), and that King Albert of the Belgians belonged incredibly to the San Francisco Club, *The Rotarian* crowed: "Thus Rotary has in its ranks the Chief Executive of the world's most powerful Republic, the heir apparent to the throne of the world's greatest Empire, and the King of the noblest little Kingdom in the world."

The triumvirate was brief, alas, for President Harding was not a Rotarian for long, but clearly he drew genuine inspiration from the Movement. Not a good speaker (he made hardly any election addresses in his campaign), he drew heavily for his speeches on Rotary's lexicon, particularly that part of it derived from Arthur Sheldon, telling the nation that service above self, allied to the idea that profiting most by serving the best was the only philosophy guaranteed to eliminate the twin curses of greed and graft.

It was an unhappy endorsement, for Harding's administration — though he was the last to know — remains a monument to graft and corruption, and when the Teapot Dome scandal broke (the notorious Dome being a naval oil reserve illegally sold into private hands), so did Warren Harding's naïve heart. In July 1923 he gave a further touching tribute to the Movement at its Fourteenth Convention in St Louis. Echoing that French lieutenant in England who had described Rotary's "flower of public spirit" (noted in the previous chapter), he said, "If I could plant a Rotary Club in every community throughout the world . . . I would guarantee the tranquillity and the forward march of the world." He added: "Then there will come out of the great despondency, and discouragement, and distress of the world, a new order."

A new order! It was a universal, atavistic dream — or nightmare, according to one's point of view — reaching down through the ages from Plato's *Republic* to Samuel Butler's *Erewhon*, even to the year of publication of the present book, which provides the title of the work whose writing killed George Orwell. Unfortunately for the twentieth century, while Harding was addressing words which, according to a contemporary journalist, resembled "nothing so much as a string of sponges" (Harding also has the dubious distinction of being the first statesman on earth to talk of something called "normalcy") to a Rotary audience of 6,000, an audience of 100,000 gathered at Nuremberg — yes, even then — to be spellbound by Hitler's exposition of a very different "new order". When a string of sponges is opposed to a train of delayed action mines, there's no contest. Harding, the applause of St Louis still ringing in his ears, was dead just over a month later.

Harding hadn't heard of Hitler. Nor had most Germans. But he had heard or was fast hearing, of his friend who was looting the

Veterans' Bureau, another who was stealing alien property, and his new deputy chief of the FBI who was not only a convicted murderer but a confessed German spy. Unkindest cut of all, he had heard of his fellow-Rotarian Edwin Denby of the Detroit Club, whom he had appointed Secretary of the Navy (a department in which Franklin D. Roosevelt had just served throughout the war under Wilson) and who was now implicated, also naïvely, in selling Teapot Dome. Not even Sheldon's scriptures could solace the small-town editor whose career had been financed and managed by the banker's widow he married and whose mistress was pregnant by him and about to write a best-seller about it. Surrounded by those who were profiting most where he had served his best, poor Harding "passed to higher service" (a phrase scarcely complimentary to the hereafter), as good Rotarians always do, leaving Teddy Roosevelt's daughter to pronounce (for her) the humane epitaph: "He was not a bad man, he was simply a slob."

After the insufferably self-righteous Woodrow Wilson, Harding, regarded as he may have been as a blinkered, good-natured slob, seemed almost lovable. He was succeeded by his extremely popular Vice-President, Calvin Coolidge, whose inimitable definition of the new order remains imperishably his classic slip of the tongue, that "posterity is just around the corner", his definition of the means to achieve posterity being "the business of America is business". By this he meant it was not the Government's business, which was to become as little involved as possible in either national or international affairs. From what he had seen of both as Vice-President, they seemed excellent things to stay out of. And keep quiet about, for, as Coolidge remarked when being harassed for press statements, "If you don't say anything, you won't be called on to repeat it", an inhibition which has never afflicted the leaders of International Rotary. Yet the prosperity of the United States, which had rapidly become the world's leading creditor nation — in other words, it was lending more cash to more people and nations than anyone else, heedless of the warning of Polonius to Hamlet that "loan oft loses both itself and friend" — became called Coolidge Prosperity, and Coolidge, who had taken the oath of office by kerosene lamp in a small town in Vermont, was hailed as the heroic symbol of wise and shrewd New England simplicities.

This no doubt helped the re-emergence and increasing confidence of Paul Harris, whose messages from Comely Bank to Conventions became longer, though he still stayed away in person. Suddenly, his style was in fashion again. Coolidge and he had been brought up in neighbouring towns and had attended the same local school, the only thing preventing their being schoolmates being Paul's unfortunate expulsion. That first name "Calvin" was splendidly apt for such a hero and Paul Harris, in his memoirs, was to praise Coolidge's "rugged honesty and his indifference to what folks thought of him as long as he could maintain his own self-respect". Clearly he saw an encouraging mirror-image here, and why not? Coolidge's own praise of Vermont, because of "her hills and valleys, her scenery and invigorating climate, but most of all because of her indomitable people", could have come from the Founder of Rotary's own pen.

Harris made a rare publicised appearance during 1922 in Washington, DC, when he laid a wreath at the Tomb of the Unknown Soldier, in whom again he may have found a mirror-image of his own self-made destiny. Yet two years later, when Racine Rotarians unveiled a bronze tablet in his honour in the city's park, he still could not bring himself to travel the sixty miles north of his home to attend the ceremony. The Message he sent implied that marking the place where he was born was far less important than to mark where Rotary was born. So at least he rationalised his reluctance in 1924 to return to the town where he had spent so few years with his parents before being despatched to Vermont. His Message to Racine — and for some men these messages still assumed the significance of communications from the spirit world — emphasised two themes which always preoccupied him: "Let us not fear the blazing of trails entirely new. I know of nothing in Rotary so sacred as to justify preservation at the cost of greater things." And he allowed himself a thinly veiled gibe at the rapidly accumulating administrative bureaucracy of the Movement at the expense of idealism. "There is a certain amount of spiritual energy which can be talked into men. Unfortunately, minor quantities only have, heretofore, been assimilated in forms preferred, and major portions vanished in thin air."

Certainly he himself often seemed to have done so. When it was announced that Calvin Coolidge had died, Dorothy Parker asked pertinently, "How do they know?" It could have been said of the Founder of Rotary had his strange life ended then also. But he outlived his fellow-Vermonter by nearly two decades and was no doubt delighted that his last great tour abroad in the 1930s should be made aboard the SS *Calvin Coolidge*. But this is to jump events, though even in 1924 the Movement was established in twenty-nine nations. Sometimes, it must be admitted, the word nation was extravagantly interpreted, since in that number was now included the twenty square miles of the British Crown Colony called Bermuda, where one of the early Rotarians was also busy founding the author of this book. Yet it was in Bermuda that the most significant event of the second "21" was to occur.

We shall come to that event in Chapter Thirteen. For the climax of this one — though we have been ranging our panoramic view on both sides of it — let us rejoin those Rotarians doing the "Pilgrim Fathers" odyssey in reverse as they disembarked from their Cunard liners at Glasgow and Liverpool respectively.

Paul Harris's trip to Liverpool, twenty-nine years before, had been such that, without it, he recalled, he "never could have believed that human beings could sink so low". But his battered old *Michigan* hulk was a far cry from the sleek *Caronia* with its whist drives, movies in the evening and grand costume ball. When Paul had arrived, he and his shipmates "were so exhausted that they could do nothing except sleep". Middle-aged Rotarians were made of sterner stuff, however, and were on the go from the moment the anchor-chain went rattling down into the Mersey at 7 a.m. The Lord Mayor — a Liverpool Rotarian — made a speech, Arch Klumph made a speech, patriotic songs were sung and three cheers were given for King George V and Warren Harding, bands played and the train for Edinburgh pulled out amidst wildly cheering crowds and a guard of honour of police constables and Boy Scouts.

Pete Snedecor led the *Cameronia* contingent ashore at Glasgow after a smooth trip enlivened by a Rotarian singing quartet who doubled in black faces every evening and trebled as the choir at Sunday service. "I Ain't Got Seasick Yet" was their most acclaimed number. Days were crowded with athletic events such as potato races, necktie races and "blind pig", the climax of the voyage being a colourful Mardi Gras Carnival. Appetites were good, as is testified by the fact that 20,000 linen napkins were disposed of, and there were only two complaints of ptomaine poisoning, though the final dockside breakfast was interrupted by an invasion of Highland pipers, a brass band, and 200 Glaswegian Rotarians serenading the mildly hung-over arrivals with "I'm a Little Prairie Flower" — the hit, it will be remembered, of Kansas City's "Win the War" Convention — which showed that even peace has its price. Again, Boy Scouts were on hand to carry luggage, and the visitors were bundled on to the Edinburgh train, each clutching a gift of heather and primroses, laced with bonbons, presented by bonny, blushing lassies. Over that week-end all the seafaring Rotarians were pouring into Princes Street, amidst more thundering bagpipes and roaring brass, while the amazed citizens "watched with the utmost curiosity", and after appropriate sightseeing, followed by special services in St Giles Cathedral, pretty girls in tartan accompanied the flags of Scotland, England, Wales, Ireland, the United States, Canada, India, Japan, Egypt, China, Sweden, Denmark, France, Spain, Mexico, Panama, the Philippines, Uruguay, Puerto Rico, Hawaii, Cuba,

Argentina, South Africa, Australia and New Zealand into the Usher Hall. This was Edinburgh's finest building, then only seven years old, having been finished just before the outbreak of war, and it provided this great international gathering with a magnificent setting worthy of the historic occasion which swiftly impressed itself on all. Here they registered, received souvenir programmes and badges of Scots plaid embossed with the Rotary emblem – genuine Golden Wheels blossomed on every lapel! All around them were banking facilities, postal facilities, information facilities, business-rooms and typing facilities, information facilities, plus, in case all got too much, first-aid facilities.

And refreshment facilities. Rotarian Warren Harding had sent a farewell message from the White House to the huge American delegation as it left New York, emphasising the "opportunity for very great service in the cause of good international relations in your visit to Europe. . . . I know the mission will do credit to our country and am sure it will make for that fuller understanding which all the world so greatly needs now". Such a sense of responsibility induces thirst, as Harding knew only too well – it was common knowledge that Prohibition stopped at the White House portico, emphasising the famed division between the legislative and executive branches in the US Constitution – and no doubt Rotarians found it encouraging that the Usher Hall had been built from funds bequeathed by a distiller.

CHAPTER TWELVE

Death of a Salesman

From the North, from the South,
　　from the East and West,
There spreads a mighty throng.
No creed, no code but to serve the best
　　Is the slogan that binds them strong.
Each for each other, and all for all,
　　Ready their task to see,
With hearty zest,
　　　　for any test
Whatever the task may be,
For he profits most who serves the best
　　Is the spirit of Rotary.

Songs for the Rotary Club

Well, it was a circus, no good pretending otherwise. And a very
enjoyable one. But a circus isn't all spectators. A circus demands a
sacrifice. That's what the bread is for, to encourage the sacrifice.
Whether the bread was occasionally dipped in the product of the
antecedents, colleagues and successors of Alexander Usher is
naturally not on record. What is on record — in a 600–page account
of the "Proceedings" (which is how happenings at Rotary events
are always termed) — is the bread, and there was plenty of it, lots
and lots of rhetorical bread, ranging from the sublime, through the
ideal and the pedestrian, to the ridiculous. It was when it reached
the ridiculous that the circus turned into a Calvary. Still a circus, of
course — indeed, its most extreme form — but the sort that nobody
watches. There are no spectators at Calvary on the day.

　　First to address the Convention, after preliminary welcomes by
local dignitaries, was the International President, in words which
showed great care and preparation. Pete Snedecor was acutely

189

conscious of the momentous character of their gathering and strove to make his listeners, undeniably in "holiday humour", equally so. "We are not here to be entertained," he told them sternly, "nor are we here to be momentarily thrilled by oratorical display." Arthur Sheldon, Super-Salesman of Rotary, sitting on a platform behind him, must have frowned at this, shuffling his own notes in preparation. As his listeners attempted to compose themselves into properly serious attitudes, Snedecor invited each one

> ... to take advantage of the exceptional opportunities here presented to broaden your vision, deepen your sympathies and enrich your lives with the lasting friendship of many interesting and cultured men and women. . . . We have espoused lofty ideals. We have committed ourselves to a rather ambitious code of ethics. We have entered the field of action and have taken our stand before the world with our standard of friendship and service floating high upon the winds of public opinion. The eyes of the world are upon us.

Certainly it seemed that Rotary had made a judgment of perfect timing in its first appearance on the international stage (it would not so expose itself for another six years) for the purpose of upholding the banner of bourgeois business virtues. A settled state of world affairs suddenly seemed more hopeful. The "non-violent" Gandhi had been elected leader of India's National Congress. Lloyd George, Churchill and Birkenhead had signed an Irish Treaty and Bill McConnell's Club was now in the Irish Free State. The most significant sign of all was that the most feared Dublin gunman of all, Michael Collins, had been offered, in place of a price on his head of £10,000, a contract for the same amount for his memoirs! Italy had held its first elections under universal suffrage that year and the Japanese royal family had actually sent Crown Prince Hirohito on a world tour. Lenin, Stalin and Trotsky had permitted capitalism to reappear in Russia (briefly), the United States had paid good money to Colombia for Panama and the Germans had finally agreed to pay even better money for causing the last war (also briefly). Snedecor was doubtless referring to the latter development when he said that "the nation which mistreats another must pay for it" but his general tone was conciliatory — even with the vigorous independence of British Rotary — when he declared, "Rotary conceives internationalism not as a group of families huddled into one room, but as a group of families living each in its own home in peace and in good cheer."

Snedecor's words were followed by Paul Harris's customary Message, still read faithfully by Ches Perry, though he can hardly have been happy with the trend of its sentiments, the emphasis of which is conveyed by this passage: "Much of the New World's material progress has been the result of the material help of the Old World. . . . We have accomplished much through the aid of British money but we have accomplished more, infinitely more, through the aid of British ideals." One of the latter, though Harris didn't repeat his oft-expressed thought here, was of course the ideal of Rotary itself. The Message ended: "This Convention will serve to cement in firmer and more friendly union the two great English-speaking nations, the first necessary step toward the attainment of the loftiest of all earthly aspirations, the brotherhood of man."

In spite of all the flags displayed in the Usher Hall, the only Rotarians actually present, besides those of North America and the British Isles, were five from Cuba and Paris and one from Calcutta. What these six thought of the Anglo-Saxon predominance one can only guess, but since their own Clubs, though ostensibly "Cuban" and "Indian", also reflected that predominance in their member-ships, they probably found nothing strange in it. In any event, the personal pronouncements of Snedecor and Harris paved the way towards the achievement of the main goal of the Convention, which was to start a thorough re-examination of how *World*, as opposed to *American* Rotary would be run. And foremost among the guiding principles agreed upon was the unequivocal phrase "that to the British Association of Rotary Clubs should be ceded the same powers as they now have under their present organisation so far as is compatible with the principles of the International Association". The original text had been somehow "lost" (by Perry perhaps, with unaccustomed inefficiency) but luckily not the gist of it, which was as just noted.

Messages arrived from other distinguished quarters to be read to the audience of nearly 2,500 in the Usher Hall. One of these was from the US Postmaster-General, Will Hays, soon to be despatched to Hollywood to improve the place after the Fatty Arbuckle scandal (where the corpulent comic was accused of causing a starlet to bleed to death after the violence of his love-making at one of the wilder parties), who was also a Rotarian. Hays urged the Convention to keep in mind that "there is ahead the greatest era of expansion and prosperity the world has ever seen. . . . There is a lot of business that is really sick, still staggering with the shell-shock of war and the debauch of extravagance, but . . . I cry continually for the common sense of courage and confidence, and I declare again, and shall continue to insist that we have less Thou Shalt Not". The glittering but sick world behind the silver screen, amok with its own debauch of extravagance, was soon to change that tune.

Baden-Powell, who had been invited to Edinburgh but was unable to attend in person, sent a message saying that "The Scouts' ideal of *Fellowship* and *Service* practically applies with equal force to that of the Rotarians". This was the perfect cue for a member of the Boys' Work Committee of Rotary International to rise to his feet. Had a cue been needed, that is. For his name was legion and there was a mighty buzz of anticipation round the hall as the massive dome of Arthur Frederick Sheldon, the Super-Salesman of Rotary, appeared. His selling slogan had passed into Rotary's lexicon, and Paul Harris was especially concerned that this should be the man to crown the great event with his legendary oratory, that which had sparked into life so many Clubs in America and Britain. It was ten years since he had last electrified a Convention — at Portland, Oregon (described in Chapter Five), when Ches Perry, even then the message reader, had relayed Sheldon's slogan in its creator's absence. This time the word was launched by a personal appearance. Alas.

Alas, the man who now rose behind the rostrum was a shambling caricature of the dynamic salesman who had stunned those first Edinburgh Rotarians in 1913. Of "the most extraordinary mixture of wisdom and sheer balderdash" noted then, the second quality had taken over and swamped the first. Rotarian W.B. Hislop, later to write a history of those pre-war Edinburgh days, recalled him as "an ugly, sloppy sort of man, on the lines of Dr. Johnson or G.K. Chesterton". The description is vivid; also, we might pause to note that where the first had been a famous clubman, the second, a decade later, would deliver a tremendous verbal assault on Rotary — but Sheldon was no Johnson and no Chesterton. It is interesting to discover what famous people he himself believed he resembled, and this we know from the *Character Reading* volume of his *Science of Business* courses, Lesson Nine, published in London the year before. In describing the three types of men, the "Mental", the "Vital", the "Motor", Sheldon let himself be classed as "Mental", along with Shakespeare, Michelangelo, Chopin, Froebel and Socrates. But with a warning, "the pitfalls of this type are nervousness and exhaustion, usually due to worry, overwork or mental strain". All those pitfalls were about to be brought into full public view of the Movement he had served so well.

What had happened? Simply another version of the modern tragedy — the salesman had been overwhelmed by the supreme error of his craft: he confused selling himself with selling the product, so that he came to regard the two as indivisible and of equal value. He believed that, as he had been the medium, so he had become the message; that by giving the Movement a slogan, he had given it a soul; that his words had granted Rotary its life instead of just its letter-head — though, to be fair to his influence and narrow genius, many Rotarians are still making the same mistake.

To Paul Harris, eager for news, it was later reported that his old friend spoke "as one inspired". Indeed, he nearly put the Convention to death, as the promised crown proved to be a thorny thicket of turgid emotionalism and half-baked theorising. As Roger Levy remarks drily in his fascinating *Rotary International in Great Britain and Ireland*: "The official record states that his speech lasted forty-five minutes, but if he did in fact deliver the text printed in the official report, it must have been more than an hour. It was received, apparently, with rapturous and prolonged applause. . . . " This, one imagines, was less for the speech than for the fact that it had ended.

For this was the moment when the Circus became Calvary. Nor was the thought a sacrilege. The analogy — more, the equation — had been precisely made by a Rotary clergyman in Canada two years before, celebrating the coming of the Armistice: "Never since the time when the Divine Rotarian went round the shores of Galilee . . . have men lived such days . . . for today we witness the triumph of those same ideals of righteousness for which Calvary's mighty sacrifice was made — those same ideals of brotherhood and service which are embodied in the meaning and purpose of Rotary."

The Movement, like its biblical precursor, required more than one Calvary. It was the logical and remorseless extension, after all, of the notion that the Founder of Christianity was the Founder of Modern Business Methods — the author of *The Man Nobody Knows* equated the words "Let there be light" with the fact that "the first and greatest electric sign was the evening stars" (he'd have been on firmer ground if he'd called them the first neon signs) — that the career of that Super-Salesman should come to a similar climax. For the major self-denial, which didn't seem to be noticed, of Bruce Barton's claim that "Jesus would be a national advertiser today . . . as he was the great advertiser of his own day" lay in the very title of his book. Sheldon didn't share rank in the pantheon with Paul Harris as a man nobody knew; at one stroke, he became the man nobody wanted to know.

Scriptural parallels abounded at the Convention, from the recommendation that boys could be inspired by a "Rotary" text that turned out to be indistinguishable from St Matthew, Chapter 11, verse 29 ("Take my yoke upon you"), to the Resolution unanimously adopted at Edinburgh for transmission to all mankind, which was identical with St Matthew, Chapter 7, verse 12

("Whatsoever ye would that men should do to you, do ye even so to them") — the latter professing a Golden Rule for the Golden Wheel while, doubtless out of deference to the non-denominational character of Rotary, omitting any reference to the author.

The Science of Business presaged what happened next to its author without any benefit of clergy, however. Following the dictum "He Profits Most Who Serves Best" came the corollary in Lesson Two: "The principle of Service is the sustaining power of the bedrock of satisfaction and the foundation of confidence." But — and the but was enormous and devastating —

> Just as one earthquake, if of sufficient magnitude, will destroy the bedrock and foundation underneath any given building, thus causing the super-structure of the building to crumble and disintegrate, so one error, if of sufficient magnitude, will shatter the feeling of satisfaction and the feeling of confidence . . . and destroy temporarily — and oftentimes permanently — the possibility of future business relationships.

He was a walking theatre for his selling methods, and always had been, and now he would give a dramatic illustration of how even their creator could fail catastrophically by ignoring his own rules. The crumbling and disintegration of the superstructure was almost at once paraded before the awed assembly. Calling his address "The Philosophy of Rotary", Sheldon confessed early on that one could simply say this was nothing more than the Philosophy of Service, but clearly the simple path was uncongenial, for he proceeded to plunge himself and his audience into a jungle of tangled prose and mangled metaphor. By way of allusions to a bewildering amalgam consisting of the Tertrum Organum, Aristotle, Sir William Hamilton, Einstein, the Self, the Individual, the Prince of Wales, Count Korzybski, the Omnipotent First Cause "and the noted Fichte", his talk reached an apogee with this extraordinary statement: "Human life, as a whole, may be symbolised by four equilateral triangles, the last three of which are of equal dimensions."

Before his audience could stagger up from this verbal haymaker, he floored them again with an appalling verse composition called "Niagara" — though it should have been "Nadir" — consisting (mainly, with prose deviations where rhymes had proved elusive) of couplets. A sample will suffice:

> Life is law, not luck, my brother,
>   and the laws are all God-made;
> right makes might, and wrong's undoing
>   is not very long delayed.

If your life is sadly troubled,
    seek the wrong you've done, my dear.
Never mind the other fellow,
    what he's done to you don't fear.
Be a man, be honest, loyal,
    ever faithful, ever true,
to whate'er the voice of conscience
    tells you clearly what to do.

One feels Harding in the White House was quite flummoxed by the news, / With his doxy in the basement and his desk awash with booze (the mode of composition is infectious).

It was the natural courtesy of the Scots — they had of course been exposed in the past to the long, vehement sermons of Calvinistic preachers who had cowed court and commoners alike — that doubtless helped hold ranks firm till Sheldon at last disappeared behind the rostrum. Then the Convention erupted into high jinks, and understandably so. Not only was the "Prairie Flower Song" bellowed with gusto — the spinning round in those kilts must have been a memorable sight "growing wilder every hour" — but "Old Macdonald Had a Farm" was given endless encores, the lyrics being largely devoted to imitations of ducks, chickens, cows and pigs.

On a more sublime level, right behind the Usher Hall, in the Royal Lyceum Theatre, Rotarian Sir Frank Benson (not Britain's greatest-ever actor but the only one to be knighted during an actual performance and with a "prop" sword) and his Company gave a performance of *Twelfth Night*, in which some might see a certain archetypal Rotarian who feels himself ever at the throne-room of destiny, "practising behaviour to his own shadow" and adjuring himself not to be afraid of greatness. Malvolio, letting himself be self-deceived to "let thy tongue tang arguments of state" and to "put thyself into the trick of singularity", might have been judged a cruel reflection of Sheldon's unfortunate speech, but at least it gave delegates a chance to relieve themselves with laughter at the image.

And there was even greater relief to follow. Possibly the most enduring achievement in Rotary terms of this pace-making Convention occurred during the second day, on a Monday afternoon, when Rotarian homes all over "Auld Reekie" opened their doors to entertain the visiting delegates and their families to tea. The principle of so-called "homestays" has become today such an integral part of International Convention that most Rotarians regard the custom as a typical American innovation to which the rest of the world has bowed sometimes reluctantly. Yet in fact this splendid

195

gesture of informal, warm hospitality took the Americans quite by surprise and was originated in the islands many visitors had been briefed to regard as "cold". Cold in climate perhaps, but far from cold in spirit, they discovered, and as they left this Athens of the North, many could exclaim, with Byron "Maid of Athens, ere we part,/Give, oh give me back my heart. . . ." Any shocks in the Usher Hall were quickly forgotten! As was their unfortunate perpetrator.

All ended with a great parade down Princes Street, whose floats included a stage-coach bearing a huge Rotary Wheel, a tableau of the Statue of Liberty and Britannia seated amidst her dominions, while the marchers included bands and delegations from every American state, every Canadian province, pipers and Yeoman Warders.

After the Convention Harry Lauder took some delegates off to sing them down the Clyde, while the remainder went to London to explain Rotary to their Majesties at a Royal Garden Party. King George V was heard to exclaim courteously, "I'd like to be a Rotarian!" but, on quickly being assured that his Classification was still open, he forbore to seize the opportunity. The Rotarians and their wives were then entertained at an enormous lunch by the London Club, saw the usual tourist sights and later spilled across the Channel to roam all over Europe, a lucky few meeting the harassed President of France.

Rotary celebrated the birth of the Irish Free State, immediately after the Convention, by electing as new President of British Rotary Bill McConnell, still famous as the very first Rotarian in the British Isles, who had still never yet been, by some Irish logic, even the President of his Club! Nevertheless, he had been Dublin's Secretary for eight years — almost since the departure of his brother-in-law for Belfast — and, together with his fellow-members, he had done much, so it was rumoured, by maintaining good relations with Belfast Rotarians, to bring about the Treaty which had, for a period at least, brought peace to his tortured country. If true, this indeed might have accounted for his ever-increasing absences from his native town in the year that followed!

Another after-effect of the 1921 Convention was that the Head-quarters of BARC was precipitately moved to London. A new Secretary was hired (see the next chapter) and implementation was at once put in hand of the twin objectives laid down and accepted at Edinburgh: the birth of a new Rotary Constitution which recog-nised that International Rotary was no longer, and never again could be, a series of branch outposts of the Chicago Club; and the determination to spread and entrench the Movement in Europe and beyond by way of Great Britain.

The British being what they are, a somewhat less than reverent view of these developments was taken by a regular contributor to *The Rotary Wheel* who took for the title of his column a quotation from Alexander Pope's "The Butterfly on the Wheel". A few months after the Convention the columnist wrote:

> The eagle eyes of Extension are turned (in proper devotional spirit) to the East. As the direction which the wise men come from, it is hoped that they will be made aware of the true inner significance of Rotary, and that we may soon welcome Norwich, Ipswich, Yarmouth, Lowestoft, Colchester, Bury St. Edmunds, King's Lynn, Peterborough, and Cambridge into the circle.

We can be sure Ches Perry was not amused. We can be sure Paul Harris was. And that both men had these same reactions at news of Rotary's "ghost", the original wonder-working Irishman whom Chicago officialdom had consigned to Californian oblivion five years before. Had they "faced West" that halcyon year of 1921, they would have seen him busy forming Clubs again. By concentrating on Edinburgh, they didn't at first notice how, with perfect timing, the snubbed Stuart Morrow had founded that year at Oakland, home of Rotary Three, the Soroptimist Movement — for women executives only, Rotary in drag. Yes, we can be sure Paul Harris laughed. Morrow's riposte would have greatly appealed to him. But at the same time he would have had a twinge of regret, for the ghost of Arthur Sheldon. The same age as Paul, who had recruited him at the same time as Perry, Sheldon, it had to be accepted, had receded abruptly into Rotary's risible past. Salesmen die many times before their death; super-salesmen taste of death but twice. Though a long-forgotten fourteen years were left him before fate, with exquisite unkindness, decreed that Rotary's Super-Salesman should die in a town called Mission.

CHAPTER THIRTEEN

The Second 21 — Denver

If you're anxious for to shine
            in the latest sort of line,
    As a true Ro-tar-i-an,
You must get up all the germs
            of the true Rotarian terms,
    And plant them where you can.
You must stand up at a table
    And discourse in accents able,
        Of the ethics of the business mind.
The meaning doesn't matter
            if it's only idle chatter
    Of the true Rotarian kind.

"Brighter Rotary" by R.F. Morse

The tune was still Sir Arthur Sullivan's, of course, from the comic
opera which succeeded *The Pirates of Penzance*, unknowingly
being parodied by the Uruguayan Rotarians as quoted at the start
of Chapter Eleven. Morse, a member of the Rotary Club of Black-
burn in Lancashire, England, published his parody of Bunthorne's
song from the first act of *Patience* in the October 1926 issue of
The Rotary Wheel. The original lyric had been a parody of Oscar
Wilde, far more subtle than the anti-Wilde doggerel written by a
Chicago journalist during the 1880s (recorded in Chapter One),
so this version, making fun of Chicago's most famous and durable
export, the Rotary Movement, was really loaded with a double
irony. It appeared in the same issue that recounted the RIBI Conference in Margate, which, while celebrating what I have called
"The Second '21'" (i.e. the twenty-first birthday of Rotary), had
had to be postponed from June to October because of the General

Strike. The more sober account of the Conference "Proceedings" declared optimistically that "We no more trouble about domestic worries like Constitutions and By-Laws — they are things of the past", but the more accurate state of affairs was mirrored, alas, in the Bunthorne parody.

Whether prompted by the parody or not, vengeance on behalf of Wilde was soon exacted by his fellow-Dubliner, and exact contemporary (as was Woodrow Wilson, who had died in 1924, thirteen days after Lenin and of very similar symptoms), Bernard Shaw, then seventy years young, who had something of his own to celebrate in 1926, the award of the Nobel Prize for Literature. In typical fashion, he announced that he assumed the prize was a "token of gratitude for a sense of world relief" that he had published nothing that year, but he soon proved that his output of talk was still non-stop, mischievous and devastating, and he decided to direct it at the twenty-one-year-old Movement. Four years would pass before he wrote his memorable postcard with the pithy comment that Rotary was going "to lunch", when asked about its future, but what he did say was quite enough to be going on with.

"Quite a large society has grown up in our midst of late years," he informed an audience in the Kingsway Hall, London, "a body called the Rotarians. Their object is to raise the employer, the business man, who is a mere vulgar tradesman . . . to professional rank, to make him an idealist, seeing that so much of the government of the world has passed into his hands, to try and make him worthy of his destiny. . . . I am afraid that the ideal with which the thing was formed never really has succeeded well in getting into the heads of the business men." And he professed that, as a result, he was "very sceptical about the salvation of the world coming from these gentlemen".

Probably to Shaw's surprise, *The Rotary Wheel* printed his attack, following it with a comment that the speech furnished only more proof that Rotary had reached a stage where the Aims and Objects programme was more necessary than ever. So perhaps here was yet another "wonder-working" Irishman. We shall soon see what the "Aims and Objects" were all about, but meantime let us pause here to note that the same issue of the magazine contained a percipient article asking whether Rotary was in truth "A Movement Without A Mystery"? Fortunately it wasn't, but the mystery was only just emerging from exile and hibernation at Comely Bank.

What met the Founder's eyes, blinking in the garish glare of the twenties?

President Wilson had brought his American dreams to Europe in the *George Washington* with the same devastating effect as Freud, in the same vessel, had taken his Vienna dreams to America before the war. Both sets of dreams encountered strong hostility in their initial impact; both inflicted long-term damage before time made their virtues more apparent. But, to the extent that Wilson thought of himself as a Rotarian in action, to him must be accorded the thankless role of John the Baptist – he didn't lose his head but his brain, which was perhaps worse – for he paved the way for the Angel from Tampa. Wilson was the unacceptable face of American idealism; from Madrid, the same news, the gospel of practical idealism, looked good.

Paris, perhaps a bit hampered by the presence in its midst of the Allied Rotary Club of France, soon founded an indigenous Club in the wake of Spain, when the soldiers started to go home. By 1925, Clubs had followed in Denmark, Norway, the Netherlands, Belgium, Italy, Switzerland, Austria, Czechoslovakia, Hungary and Portugal. And European Rotary had, in a few years, assumed such dynamic impetus that, to forestall any temptation to form a European equivalent of the British Association of Rotary Clubs (now grown to a "territory" of ninety-seven Clubs), Ches Perry ordered the setting up in 1925 of a branch of the Rotary International Secretariat in Zurich.

Perry came over in person to see this move accomplished to his satisfaction and Zurich's authority established. The man he put in charge, Fred Warren Teele, was one of a number of remarkable personalities who, having achieved great worldly success and prosperity, gladly put their gifts, at great cost to themselves and some discomfort, to the service of Rotary International, and the furtherance of a shy attorney's dream. Chesley Perry himself had been the first – a man of his enormous drive and persuasion could have won laurels in any field he chose. James Davidson, whose achievement for Rotary we shall soon discover, was another, and perhaps he was the most outstanding of them all. Fred Teele, who had been for some time a sort of roving Special Rotary Commissioner for Europe, was certainly of the breed, having resigned an $18,000 per year job with the Mexico Light and Power Company (and Presidency of the Rotary Club of Mexico) to run the new Zurich Office, for $5,000 per year. Its address has since changed, but that Headquarters for Europe has remained in Zurich ever since.

Though Perry wanted to give Europe a thorough once-over – and for Europe to be aware of it – he felt less than confident enough to leave a member of his Chicago staff behind to assist Teele, while he went on to declare formally Italy and France respectively a separate District of Rotary with its own Governor.

When he reached the true source of his disquiet, the British Isles, he was disarmed with a birthday cake (he visited London on the date of the founding of the Movement), an evening at the Savoy and a visit to the Apollo Theatre to see London's long-running, smash-hit Vivian Ellis revue, *By the Way* (later that year to repeat its triumph at the Gaiety in New York, as many British musicals still did regularly, a trend not resumed until recent times). But he still firmly declared (for all Europe to hear) the basic principles to which all nationalities of Clubs must adhere: "The unique basis of membership, the compulsory attendance rule, the intensive fellowship, the betterment of crafts, the aim for higher standards of business, and the high ideal of service to humanity."

Zurich, however, could but monitor events and regulate a form of organisational framework upon a process now well under way, a form of Rotary growth about which Perry could do very little. Moreover, his visits to Switzerland and London were rather over-shadowed that year by the Big Power agreements initialled at Locarno and signed in London, by which Germany was admitted to the League of Nations and agreed to maintain peace in Europe together with Belgium, France, Italy and Great Britain. Stanley Leverton, President of the London Club, promptly wrote to all Rotary Clubs throughout Europe proclaiming "the dawn of a universal peace", implying strongly that only Rotary could make the Locarno Pact work by "the advancement of understanding, goodwill and international peace through a world-fellowship of business and professional men united in the Rotary Ideal of Service" − which by now had become Rotary's Object Number Six (for the others, see Chapter Five).

Perry was upstaged, there is no doubt of it. He had had his cake and eaten it too, by taking back with him to 910 South Michigan Avenue and the seventy employees of his new Headquarters there the top tier of his London gift. Yet, had he known his literary history, he would hardly have been reassured by the fact that British Rotary's own Headquarters was now located in Norfolk Street, off the Strand in London, in the very same offices from which W.T. Stead had sallied forth some forty years before to plan Christ's possible "visit" to Chicago. Nor perhaps by the fact that London's enterprising new President, destined to make a global impact on the Movement, was an undertaker. That birthday cake was needed back home for solid nourishment. The pious Perry went back to find that the city where Rotary was born had had, in 1925, 16,000 more arrests for drunkenness than the whole of England and Wales.

Spain had been neutral throughout the war but had not escaped it unscathed. It had kept its troops from the trenches but was still profoundly affected by the conflict. King Alfonso's wife was English (the late Earl Mountbatten's aunt), but then so was the Kaiser's mother; liberal and radical elements hoped for allied victory, while Spanish generals hoped for Prussian triumph. Neutrality still meant a price to be paid by the war's end, U-boats had sunk sixty-five Spanish ships, and the revolutionary upheavals and murders which then convulsed the exhausted belligerents, convulsed Spain also. General Franco, the future "Caudillo", as Europe's first Golden Wheel went on display, was across the water in Morocco, forming the Spanish Foreign Legion. But Madrid had largely prospered from the war and Rotary, as elsewhere, offered the hope that commercial profit need not clash with social good.

As the Spanish journal *Nuevo Mundo* put it:

> It will be necessary for us to divest ourselves of the belief which every Spaniard holds, that in the struggle for existence each man lives unto himself alone. . . . As we were listening to Mr Cuesta, the thought came to us that we here in Spain are engaged in a merciless and cruel struggle, for this Code of Ethics . . . is above all a commercial code. . . . We believe that if it were possible to convert it into a law, more than one-half of the problems with which we are now contending and which make life so hard and bitter in Spain, would be solved.

A large claim? The first President of the Rotary Club of Paris expressed himself with typical Gallic fervour and florid eloquence: "The Rotary Club will flourish in France . . . when we can better make known its sphere and its aim and demonstrate its good work, inspired by the understanding that the peoples can gain by the creation of a society inspired by beauty and perfection." He inferred, of course, that this marvellous society would naturally be modelled on that prevailing in France, but it was intended, and accepted, as a compliment.

The Spanish and French attitudes polarised from the start the forms which the Movement would take in Europe, where Rotary has ever since been regarded as either a precious gem whose glitter and value could only be enhanced by its foreign setting or a gem which in itself could increase the value and transform that setting. Madrid believed that Rotary would immeasurably improve and humanise the commercial code, producing a diamond from the rough. Paris believed that it would add to this new business idealism an aesthetic quality which was the only facet it lacked; the diamond would now receive its polish. In the French manner. In both cases the perception was that of an élite.

This was also true in Italy, where the essence of the élitism stemmed from the fact that it was believed there to be of English origin and thus suitably exclusive, the wealthy business men of Milan conceiving Rotary as similar to White's, Boodle's or the Carlton. They would have been shocked to learn of its beginnings over spaghetti in an Italian restaurant. However, it arrived under the distinguished auspices of Sir James Henderson, who ran the Italian subsidiary of a Scottish firm in Milan. This native of Paisley moved to Italy in 1910 and died there in 1967, the English School in Milan being named after him to this day. No doubt the fact that he was a Scot made him especially suitable, because of the tremendous impact on Europe of the Edinburgh Convention.

The second Rotary Club formed in Italy was at Trieste. A few years before and it would have been the first Club in Austria, such were the shifting boundaries of the time. As for Austria's most active politician, he was busy in Munich, where his activities — partly journalistic, partly spying and agitation — were running parallel to those in Milan of a successful radical editor named Mussolini. Private armies battered and murdered socialists, or suspected socialists, all over northern Italy, but whereas Hitler's planned "march" on Berlin in the early twenties ended in ignominious defeat and prison (where he wrote *Mein Kampf* in great luxury), Mussolini marched from Milan to Rome in triumph — probably because he himself had the foresight to go by train.

Henderson wisely refrained from starting Rotary in Milan until "Il Duce" had gone south, but in fact the turbulent times continued to provide fertile ground for the Movement which profited, as we have noted, from the same preservative instincts which led European business men to support strong, centrally directed reactionary forces, whether normal or abnormal. In such times, who could tell the difference between them? "Rotary does good," said Mussolini, and the feeling was mutual. While Mussolini headed south, the new Milan Rotarians, their inaugural dinner accomplished, adjourned to La Scala to watch *Aida*!

Élitism was also much in evidence when Hungary formed its first Club, for not only were British Rotarians there in force, having just also launched Vienna, but Budapest's first Club President was a member of the Hungarian cabinet, Dr Theodore Koenig, Secretary of State for Finances. Vienna had no statesman as a Founder Member but it had one of international fame, the composer of *The Merry Widow*. Franz Lehár's hit-show of 1925 was *Paganini*, whose catchy tunes were doubtless hummed by Doncaster Rotarians, their Viennese midwifery over, all the way to Budapest and Prague and back to Yorkshire. Those Yorkshiremen had had quite a waltz!

It is worth our while to stop a moment here and go back over that last sentence. Up to 1921 the English county of Yorkshire had chiefly distinguished itself in Rotary by giving birth, at York, to the Movement's thousandth Club. Besides its pudding, the county's most famous product was, however, at Doncaster; a classic horse-race started by Colonel Barry St Leger in 1776 before he concerned himself with lesser matters such as leading his regiment against the American rebels. The dashing Colonel Barry was about to be supplanted, at least in Rotary annals, by the dash of the rather more prosaically named Frank Molloy (the Irish keep popping up in these pages), one of the first members of Doncaster's Club, formed only a few months after York. Molloy in fact deserves to rank with Stuart Morrow and Charles White (of whom more later) as one of the great Irish trinity responsible for making the Movement truly International. We already know what Morrow did, and shall shortly learn what White did. What Molloy did was to decide to go on holiday with some friends to Vienna, four years after joining Rotary, and such was his charm and persuasiveness that he had, in a very short time, formed the first Club on ex-enemy territory – and before he came back to Yorkshire, he had done the same in Budapest and Prague. Little wonder that he felt "ready for a holiday" when his vacation was over! Rotary had found another "wonder-working Irishman" – though not its last.

Perhaps this is an opportune moment for us to consider the form into which British Rotary had finally shaped itself and by which the BARC, launched in wartime Liverpool, had by the end of 1922 become RIBI (Rotary International in Great Britain and Ireland) with offices in London, a permanent Secretary, and an accepted permanent feature of the International Rotary landscape. It had also held two Conferences, the only gatherings of their kind in the Movement which were organised and controlled other than by the International Headquarters. These were in 1920 and in 1922, at Harrogate and Brighton respectively. Ches Perry kept an alarmed eye on the first, having to endure a very stormy sea-crossing to do so, but perhaps finding consolation on learning that Hugh Boyd, the Immediate Past President of the Belfast Club (who had played a major role in persuading other British Clubs to follow London's lead), had named his son "Chesley". Perry was also able to hear a forthright speech from the BARC President, Lloyd Barnes, an eloquent Liverpudlian (Liverpool again). Barnes affirmed the Rotary conviction that "there is, in the spirit of strife and the manifestations of industrial unrest now so general, clear evidence that civilisation the world over is failing in its ultimate aim – the moral welfare and happiness of mankind – because modern business and industrial methods . . . are permeated by selfishness and avarice", with the tactful addition that "in order that Rotary effort throughout the world may give expression to its highest ideals, international as well as national co-operation is necessary, and in this respect the International Association in Chicago has done a great work".

However, Perry was not present later that year at Leeds to hear words rather less congenial from the same person. This time Barnes pronounced his vigorous opposition to any attempt to dissolve the BARC (which Chicago was beginning to suggest), condemning it as "a policy contrary to Rotary ideals". The following year a London Headquarters was set up, complete with its first own professional paid Secretary, not a Rotarian, on a salary of £500 per annum. In due course, he was accorded membership of the London Club. Vivian Carter, a journalist who had been the pre-war editor of the famous illustrated weekly *The Bystander*, was well suited to the job, having been moved by the 1921 International Convention at Edinburgh to write articles for *The Times* in praise of Rotary which, he romantically hoped, would provide the uncaring, materialistic society he saw around him with an avenue back to higher things. With the zeal of a convert (and the spur of a natural vested interest in keeping his job) Carter attended the Los Angeles Convention in 1922, championing the BARC cause so effectively — no doubt encouraged by the talk he managed to have with Paul Harris as he passed through Chicago — that the emergent Constitution gave full acceptance to "territorial units" within the International Movement. "There was little or no apparent opposition, open or concealed," Carter reported, ignoring in his euphoria the fact that what was concealed would hardly be apparent.

It would be so later — no other "territorial unit" was ever to be granted status — but meanwhile BARC was to survive and flourish, though its name was soon changed to today's "Rotary International in Great Britain and Ireland". Nor did *The Rotary Wheel* hesitate to drive the lesson rather bluntly home to the Americans, publishing a fable in the style of Voltaire's *Candide*, in which the character of a "Wise Fool" declares:

> This Rotary was started in a far-off land by a few good men not many moons ago. In course of time, other good men, who dwelt in other cities in that far-off land, perceived that it was good, and started Clubs in their cities, and so the Movement grew. It is a good and wonderful Movement, with most marvellous possibilities, and every honor is due to those who nurtured it in its youth. It spread across the seas until it became so vast a thing that they who gave it birth . . . became amazed. "Unless we harness it," they said,

"this Rotary may take the bit between its teeth, so that we cannot hold it in control.". . . Their desire to keep the lusty youth tied to their apron strings is natural, but, unless Rotary is to be fettered, unless Rotary is to be endangered of its very life, these apron strings must go.

And Ches Perry took the hint, with reasonable grace, though, as we have noted in a previous chapter, with lasting regret.

And the international organisation itself accepted the suggestion of yet another "wonder-working Irishman", this time Charles White of the Belfast Club, and changed its name from the International Association of Rotary Clubs to simply "Rotary International", as it has been called ever since. "Thus", wrote White many years later, "the Chairman of a District in Ireland saved Rotary tens of thousands of words and hundreds of pages of print."

That he could not perform the same "wonder" for his own Association now reinitialled RIBI, to save everlasting repetition of its seven-word title, is just one more insoluble paradox of the Anglo-Irish conundrum. For at the same time as Los Angeles Rotarians were approving an instrument of reconciliation between Chicago and its sturdily independent "colony" across the Atlantic as the direct result of the work of a trio of Irishmen (White, plus Stuart Morrow's brother-in-law Bill McConnell, now President of the fast-disappearing BARC, plus the Irish-Canadian Rotary International President, Crawford McCullough), Ireland itself was saddled with five conflicting governments, one in the northern counties and four in the south, as a result of a number of treaties sworn to and instantly disowned.

But the conundrum at once demonstrated the extraordinary power and strength of Paul Harris's inspiration, for throughout the terrible civil war that engulfed southern Ireland and despite the tension with Ulster, Ireland's two Clubs, in the respective capital cities above and below the border, continued to work together in determined amity, a mighty example which has been followed to the present day by Clubs in every part of the Emerald Isle.

It is interesting to note that, even as the very first Rotary Convention in Chicago, back in 1910, had found its allure in competition with a production of *Salome* next door, so the immensely important Thirteenth Convention in Los Angeles in 1922 was held in the neighbourhood of a most exotic no-holds-barred production of the same work — based on original Aubrey Beardsley designs, too — being filmed in Hollywood. Being a silent film, as befitted unspeakable desires, it still starred the smouldering Russian actress refugee from Bolshevism, Nazimova, but apparently could not compete with the healthy charms of "Peggy O'Neil", the most popular song of many sung by obedient Rotarians in the Los Angeles Auditorium, though the lyrics were altered to praise "that Rotary Wheel" which "blends personalities, binds nationalities". As if in a last defiant trumpet-call, that year saw the composition of the song "Chicago", but that immortal tribute to the "toddlin' town" has, neither then nor since, found its way into a Rotary song-book.

There was a day's excursion to Hollywood by the nearly 60,000 present, and one suspects Vivian Carter was making an oblique reference to the dream-factory when he reported "we may know what are the heights of attainment above the valley of daily life . . . though we may not be able to make all the excursions into or towards the clouds that are prescribed by the guides". One eminent participant was the now ex-Postmaster General of Rotarian Harding's ill-fated government, Will Hays, the Rotarian from Indiana, whose message had exhorted the Edinburgh Convention and who had just come out West to take up an appointment as head of the Motion Pictures Producers and Distributors of America, intending to close down on ladies like Salome on celluloid with righteous wrath, a dedication perhaps not unconnected with the fact that he was in charge of a fund to raise millions of dollars for Presbyterian ministers.

This haunting of key Rotary Conventions by Salome is usefully allegorical in retrospect, for running ever beneath the smooth flow of fellowship, song and oratory, was the persistent counter-theme which seethed in Perry's brain: would the increasing number of non-American Rotarians one day insist that they would pay their tribute to the head of Rotary, its Founder Members and their ideals, only if that head were detached from the Chicago body? For the moment, all was well. The compromise worked, and indeed it was the British Isles' original Rotarian, Bill McConnell, now their President, who was asked to speak at Los Angeles for the non-American Clubs represented — those of Ireland, the United Kingdom, France, Canada, Cuba, Mexico, South America, Panama, Australia, Puerto Rico, the Philippines and China. In doing so, he pledged that his own Clubs would be "international first and British afterwards". While he spoke, his fellow-countrymen were holding their first election in the new Irish Free State on the basis of "Irish first and British never", while Rotarians in Belfast were in a city proclaiming "Irish never and British always". That election precipitated the Irish Civil War, while McConnell's Rotary pledge ended any threat of a division in Rotary, for it changed Rotary in the British Isles (now the United Kingdom and Irish Free State) into the form it would maintain, despite several subsequent rancorous disputes with Chicago, to the present day.

With a new Constitution securely established, and with the position of the British Clubs — for, in spite of blood and rhetoric, the Irish Free State was still in the Empire — firmly spelled out, Rotary sped confidently on to its twenty-first birthday. By 1925, the principles of ethical conduct in business, of internationalism (which Rotarians persisted in called "internationality", in the dreadful tradition of Warren Harding's coinage of "normalcy" for normality) and of community service were thoroughly established as integral parts of regular Club practice rather than a set of rules and ritual phrases. The last two had been dramatically given effect by the aid rushed to Japan from all corners of the Rotary world at the time of the great 1923 earthquake which devastated Tokyo and Yokohama and gave that amazing nation another chance to emulate Western, and particularly American, models by rapid reconstruction in the manner of Chicago and San Francisco after their disasters. Sixty-four per cent of the populace were left homeless and 200,000 perished. The subsequent rebuilding and expansion accelerated social change towards modern urban living, and the fact that much world assistance was seen being distributed by the Rotary Clubs of Tokyo and Osaka gave the Movement an immediate and lasting impact, which even survived the years of military dictatorship.

The most far-reaching change in Club organisation for practical Rotary service was developed rapidly in Great Britain in time for this coming-of-age anniversary under the direction of RIBI President Sydney Pascall, a sweet manufacturer who was later to become the first English leader of World Rotary and whose products were as well known all over that quarter of the world which was still coloured "Empire red" as Sir Thomas Lipton's tea. A devout church-goer and scrupulous business man (even as Rotarian Will Hays combined politics and the movies with religious devotion in southern California), he shared completely Arthur Sheldon's views on profits and service, and he set up an Aims and Objects Committee to study and recommend how the Rotary ideals could be regulated and administered on a clear and orderly basis. The report of his Committee was not only promptly accepted by the then sixteen "Districts" (as Rotary's administrative divisions had been called since 1912, when there were five in the United States, five in Canada and one in the British Isles) through the acceptance of the International Board of Directors in Chicago, but just as promptly by the other fifty-nine Districts which were now in thirty-five countries throughout Europe, Africa, South America, the Antipodes and the Far East, not to mention the United States and Canada. It is right to take note of the basic Aims and Objects outline, which was as follows:

An Aims and Objects Committee could not be fulfilling its full functions if it did not review . . . and deal with the principles underlying those Aims and Objects both subsequently and objectively.

This, therefore, led to the idea of a comprehensive Committee which should be responsible for the whole of the Aims and Objects and the propagation of their principles, with sub-committees to be responsible for the various main departments into which the Aims and Objects could be logically divided, for example Vocational Service (Business Methods), Club Service (Fellowship, Acquaintance, etc.), and Community Service, so that, under the main Aims and Objects Committee, both subjective and objective activities could be co-ordinated.

Rotary had indeed "come of age" for, with the addition of International Service, these Service Committees have been the operational framework upon which the deeds of Rotary have been devised and performed, in many languages, in all climates, on Club, National and International scale ever since. Thus, both the orthodox and unorthodox means by which Paul Harris's goal was reached overseas back in 1911 had been justified by the most "nuts and bolts" reckoning: Stuart Morrow's "unofficial" Club at Belfast had produced the man who gave Rotary International its name; and now the first overseas "official" Club of London, formed in Perry-approved style, had produced the man who gave Rotary its *modus operandi*, its work structure.

These two contributions to a World Movement which is still only beginning to realise the extent of its full potential may well be considered by social historians of the future to rank amongst the major gifts of Great Britain to twentieth-century civilisation. Fit to rank perhaps beside the other gift which came out of London that "coming-of-age" year, the gift first put on display at the Royal Institution: the world's first operational television set.

John Logie Baird was neither then, in 1926, nor later, a Rotarian, as was that other great innovator in communications, Marconi. The latter counts, in Rotary at least, as half a wonder-working Irishman, since his mother came from County Wexford, and he, together with Baird, bears the ultimate responsibility for the invasion of our homes by entertainment rather than old-fashioned domestic bliss. Thanks to his invention also, the Rotary Club of London, on the actual twenty-first birthday celebration of Paul Harris's meeting with Schiele, Loehr and Shorey, 23rd February, was able to broadcast a message to all the British Isles and Europe via the new British Broadcasting Corporation.

But London Rotary was not left out of television's early development, as it was a Club member who during 1926 first put Baird's invention on public display. Gordon Selfridge, who had brought another business ideal to London from Chicago, a version of Marshall Field's department store, had once complained to *The Rotarian* that his greatest struggle since moving to England was to "live down the popular disrespect of today for the shopkeeper". He further confessed that he hoped his epitaph would read: "He dignified and ennobled business." No doubt his joining London Rotary was a step in that direction, and his display of Baird's invention another. Whether his habit of opening up his Oxford Street store at midnight for the chorus-girls he fancied could also be judged another depended perhaps on which noblemen the girls eventually married.

Rotary International was still in a cocoon. The twenty-first birthday celebrations in Britain, though delayed, were as little affected by the General Strike, involving 2½ million trade unionists, as was Chicago by the birthday coinciding with the worst year of gang violence ever recorded anywhere, with seventy-six street killings and as many ghastly maimings, corpses at every corner, and with Al Capone complaining bitterly "I've been accused of every death except the casualty list of the World War" — a not inapt observation, since the gangster's favourite weapon, the Thompson submachine-gun, was named after, and manufactured by, one of Rotarian Pershing's wartime aides.

However, Rotary Number One, the original Club, did not entirely yield the limelight. One of its Vice-Presidents (nice title, too) was the original director of the Chicago Crime Commission, and it never forgot that the vocational service of another member, a prominent optician, had solved a spectacular crime through having made the last pair of glasses fourteen-year-old Bobbie Franks ever wore. Those glasses identified the victim after he was kidnapped and callously murdered by Leopold and Loeb, the wealthy young sadists who were saved from the gallows only by the magnificent oratory of Clarence Darrow in one of the most famous trials of the century.

Naturally, the men of those uppity Rotary Clubs over the West Coast ("Rotary expansion took on the proportions of a prairie fire, once Clubs 2, 3, 4 and 5 were organized" observes the historian of San Francisco Rotary, these Clubs being San Francisco, Oakland, Seattle and Los Angeles) had never shrunk from centre stage. And with more and more of America, indeed the world, turning its attention every day to the doings of Hollywood, Rotarian Will Hays, called variously "the czar of movie morals" and (by *Variety* magazine) "the biggest thing that has happened in the screen world since the closeup", devoted 1926 to making sure the film producers obeyed his ruling that they should not ridicule Prohibition. What better way to honour the Movement's "coming of age", after all? It was in the fine and worthy, not to say obsessive, tradition of protecting the morals of the young which Rotary had first made so manifest during the recent war. It also chimed in conveniently with the views of Al Capone; and it matched the mood of most of his fellow-countrymen for whom Prohibition had never been anything to laugh at. Indeed, it had long since driven most of them to drink — and in that one year 2,000 of them to death from poisoned booze.

Hays was not merely negative, however. That year he spent some time in making sure the world knew all about the twenty-three weddings of 1926 amongst the movie stars, and he looked away from their fourteen divorces and three separations. He also averted his eyes from the seventy-five "acting" schools of Hollywood which that year were taken to court by the District Attorney for teaching starlets an exclusively horizontal method. The year also introduced Hollywood's sizzling Clara Bow to the international silver screens as the "It" girl. That didn't bother Hays. Like Rotary's Aims and Objects, which overlay a seemingly intrinsically American product, that "It" tag — synonym for unmentionable sex — was a brilliant stroke of entirely English genius, and (as anyone who gave the matter a moment's thought would realise) a typical stroke at that.

If Rotarians seemed to be cultivating the art of looking away, they were doing nothing more than everyone else in that decade. While Rotary naturally thought of itself in particular as being that magic "21", the entire Western world was having a permanent slightly hysterical birthday party, and a sensational novel appeared in 1926 which gave its name to a generation, *Flaming Youth*. However, bright young things tend to hurt the eyes of their elders (who of course, as always, were holding the matches), and their elders (viewed as distinct from the age of the Movement) were busy birthday-partying in Denver. Where else, the cynic might note, should Rotary celebrate being twenty-one than in the city which minted 75 per cent of the coins used in America?

Looking away was a world epidemic, as pervasive as post-war flu. There was no published complaint or comment from Rotarians in Shanghai, when Chiang Kai-shek spent 1926 in crushing the city's Communist Party (the first in China), whose Founding Members included Mao Tse-tung. At the Denver birthday Convention, the representative from Tokyo's Rotary Club reminded delegates that his country sought "wisdom and intelligence from all nations", though he refrained from mentioning the pursuit of profits or that Japan was enjoying its first year of universal male suffrage. "You are going up the Rotary mountain from the west side, while we are going up the same mountain from the east side. I am sure we will meet at last." As indeed they did, fifteen years later.

As had been the case in Japan, the governments changed in Brazil, France, Germany and Austria which, like Britain, had a general strike as well. Spain and Brazil left Woodrow Wilson's League of Nations and Germany joined it; and while Mussolini suffered the indignity of three attempts on his life, Hitler found he couldn't meet his tax demands and asked for time to pay. One of those who would soon be helping Hitler meet those demands was Wilhelm Cuno, ex-Chancellor and head of the Hamburg-Amerika shipping line, who would also soon be helping form Hamburg's and Germany's first Rotary Club.

Upheaval and restlessness permeated every corner of the world between the end of the First World War and the onset of the Great Depression. Rotary came of age just in time to meet it, as it had reached overseas just in time before the First World War could prevent it. And the latest Message to be read out to Rotarians at their twenty-first birthday Convention from their Founder spoke the thought no one else dared utter: "Is Rotary coming or going?" wrote Paul Harris. "Is it morning or evening?"

One rather unexpected place the Movement had gone, the Convention learned, was to polar regions during the previous month, when a member of the Rotary Club of Winchester, Virginia, the appropriately named Lieutenant-Commander Richard Evelyn Bird, had made the world's first flight over the North Pole, taking a Rotary flag with him into instant international fame. At Denver, the magnificent feat made everyone ask each other "Who's this guy, Byrd?" Thanks to an avalanche of newspaper stories, everyone soon knew. But another question which plenty were also asking, and one less easily answered, for all the annual "messages", was: "Where is Paul Harris? Is he alive or dead?"

In answer, two special things happened for Rotary in 1926. Since Rotary had now attained its majority, perhaps Paul felt he could safely emerge from his exile in Comely Bank on to the stage again, even if in a small non-speaking part for the time being. Perhaps Jean felt he was ready and perhaps she herself wanted to play a part. Whatever the prime cause, emerge he did. Perhaps the organisation men realised they needed the magic of his presence, provided he wasn't given too many lines to say and played his allocated role. Chesley Perry certainly sounded defensive when he wrote in *The Rotarian* for June that year: "Rotary is not seeking to change human nature. Not at all. Rotary is merely trying to encourage humans to express their natural impulses." And, as an example, he fantasised: "People want to help me. I can prove it by letting the wind blow my hat off when I go out on the street. A half dozen men will chase it and retrieve it for me. The runaway hat takes them by surprise."

Did Perry sense Rotary's growth running away from him? Or the rising and dangerous gusts of world crisis? It was not six men who were wanted, but one. And in that same issue of *The Rotarian* the first instalment of an autobiography of Paul Harris appeared, though Perry, now Editor again, made sure that the Foreword stated "There is a vast difference between being the Founder of a Movement and being its Builder". The article was profusely illustrated, not only with photographs of Paul at various ages, but of his home at Wallingford, Vermont, and pictures of his Harris grandparents. Yet evidence was still required of Paul today, and that vitally necessary snapshot appeared with the final instalment in November. It showed Paul and Jean in Bermuda, on the first appearance of the Founder of Rotary International on foreign soil since Rotary's birth.

The exotic venue for Paul Harris's resurrection was shrewdly chosen. For, waiting his arrival in Bermuda, living in retirement, was none other than Dr Francis L. Patton, President of Princeton University during Paul's time there and immediate predecessor of Woodrow Wilson before the ivied halls lost the idealist of the League of Nations to the smoke-filled rooms of politics. Dr Patton was just the man, for all his eighty-four years, to renew his old pupil's self-confidence. Perhaps he reminded Paul of Emerson's words, "Every true man is a cause, a country and an age . . . posterity seems to follow his steps as a procession. . . . An institution is the lengthened shadow of one man", as if he would have needed reminding. What would have held him back was another passage from that same essay on *Self-Reliance*: "Expect me not to show cause why I seek or why I exclude company. . . . My life is not an apology, but a life. It is for itself, and not for a spectacle." What would have pushed him forward, none the less, was the passage that followed soon after: ". . . the great man is he who in the midst of the crowd keeps with perfect sweetness the independence of solitude". There was never any better description of Paul Harris and it pervades every subsequent description of him by Rotarians who were soon to meet him (and sometimes his handsome wife) all over the world.

Both Perry and Harris, after the success of that trial run in Bermuda, accepted that there was a Rotary job to be done and that only the Founder of Rotary could do it. The Movement, now numbering nearly 2,400 Clubs in thirty-five countries, needed to be shown who its Founder was — and was not — so that it could leave him behind. "Coming of age" is as much a crisis for movements as for men; in both instances, learning must come anew that maturity is the end of life, the beginning of living; it is realising that you can never depend on others for your birth. And Rotary, expanded as it was, was bursting to be born.

There was something else, just as important. It was time for Rotary International to take leave of the parochial hot-house of its Secretariat in the heart of Chicago, where the Movement was as much in peril of being isolated from itself as Paul Harris had been in its affluent suburbs. That same year, Ireland's great poet-playwright of "the troubles" had likewise decided to leave the source of his inspiration, Rotary's first-born in Europe, for much the same reason. In his later autobiography Sean O'Casey recalled how in that summer of 1926 he "felt that if I stayed in Dublin, life would become embarrassing to meet. . . . All its streets led into one square where everyone met, where hands were shaken, shoulders clapped and drinks taken to everyone's health". Chesley Perry never demonstrated the great awareness of his administrative genius more dramatically than now when, against his own cold instincts, yet knowing what was generous and right for the Movement to which he was more obsessively than ever dedicated, he persuaded Harris to come forth. For both men, it was a sacrifice.

John J. Arnold was the first President of the Rotary Club of Hamilton, the capital of Bermuda, and it was his historic honour to be the first non-American Rotary Club President to welcome Paul Harris, now aged fifty-eight. Jack Arnold, as he was known, was not island-born. He was a Canadian and became the first non-Bermudian to sit in the island Parliament (the author's father was the second, and was also to become Hamilton's Club President). As he grasped Harris's hand in March 1926, Arnold was touching the greatest moment of his life, had he but known it. For he that was lost, was found. Paul Harris had chased after Ches Perry's hat for him, blown off from a head grown several sizes too large for him. He would catch it and restore it, without rancour, for he had appeared on the island of Shakespeare's *Tempest*, like Prospero exiled by one who had

> . . . new created
> The creatures that were mine, I say, or changed 'em,
> Or else new form'd 'em; having both the key
> Of officer and office, set all hearts i' the state
> To what tune pleased his ear; that now he was
> The ivy which had hid my princely trunk,
> And suck'd my verdue out on't . . .
>   . . . like one

Who having, unto truth, by telling of it,
Made such a sinner of his memory,
To credit his own lie, he did believe
He was indeed the duke. . . .

though Perry was not the Duke, never had been, never would be, and knew it probably better than Harris himself.

On Rotary's twenty-first birthday, then, this was the best gift of all, wrapped up in the bright colours of a semitropical paradise. Paul Percy Harris was alive and well on one of the last British colonies — a drop in the ocean, that navigators' corner, that galleons' grave, round which the Spanish Plate fleet had turned right for home. That's what mattered for Rotarians. No matter that what mattered most for their "Rotary-Anns" was not resurrection, but a brazen, glamorous, incredible death 800 miles north-west, where New York wives queued eleven blocks to weep over the lying-in-state of their favourite dishwasher, Rodolpho Alfonso Raffaelo Pierre Filibert Guglielmi di Valentina d'Antonguolla, and millions more all over the world threw their dreams in despairing throes on the catafalque of that handsome son of a sheikh. Who lived if Valentino died, his impotence covered in cloth of gold?

Well, Paul Percy Harris, for one, who called up a quotation from Goldsmith to characterise his travels as "a man who leaves home to mend himself and others". And the tango went on regardless, with the newly born compensation of the Black Bottom. For the year had followed the twenty-first tradition and had brought Rotary and Rotarians the key of the door, with an ever-increasing awareness on the part of friend and foe alike that only Paul Percy Harris could turn it.

CHAPTER FOURTEEN

Travels of a Boy Wonder

O lad of mine,
O lad of mine,
   We'll stand as one
In rain or shine,
Each night and day
I'll always say,
   "You're the best boy in the world"
O lad of mine.

Songs for the Rotary Club
(tune of "Sweet Adeline")

Though the first invitation for Paul Harris to start his travels for Rotary filtered through in 1926, there was not an immediate follow-up to the Bermuda visit. It was not until 1928 that Paul and Jean allowed themselves to be urged upon their odyssey to visit the wide-scattering cousins of Paul's brainchild, a pilgrimage which would occupy them, with brief respites, for the next eight years.

By the time they started, not only Germany was firmly in, but Java and a clutch of Latin-American nations, Costa Rica, El Salvador, Ecuador and Bolivia, shortly followed in Europe by Greece and in the East by the Federated Malay States, among many others, right to Hong Kong. The previous year the world had shrunk by means of physical communication in two more stages: the first telephone service across the Atlantic had been opened, and the first solo flight over that same ocean had been made by Rotarian Charles A. Lindbergh. In a few years, shrinkage would proceed at an almost alarming rate. Rotarian Bernt Calchen would pilot the plane which took Lincoln Ellsworth over the Antarctic, Byrd and Piccard took the Rotary flag over both Poles and into the stratosphere, and the daughter of

Rotarian John Johnson of the Rotary Club of Hull, England, became the first woman to fly solo from England to Australia, which she did in twenty days (part of it while the RIBI Conference for 1930 was taking place in Edinburgh). Amy Johnson later paid tribute to the Rotary Clubs which had received her along that route across the Orient, most of which were founded by the subject of this chapter, a Boy Wonder sixty-six years old.

Shrinkage had also occurred over the Southern Hemisphere, in rather bizarre fashion, since a flying route was pioneered from the United States to Argentina by two young American aviators, who had just completed the flight when they were killed in an air collision. In commenting on their funeral, the President of the Buenos Aires Rotary Club reported that "we, as Rotarians, while deeply regretting the sad occasion, are glad to recognise that it developed feelings in fullest accord with the Sixth Object of Rotary" — that is, international service.

Feeling perhaps that the Sixth Object was getting a bit dangerous, Fred Teele resigned from the Zurich office in 1928 to return to business (Perry's "mole" followed suit, returning to Headquarters), and a Dane, T.C. Thomson, took over as Special Commissioner in Europe, asserting that "the Sixth Object is a special European object, for in Europe . . . mutual understanding and friendship is [sic] today not very prevalent" and calling for "a powerful chain of Rotary initiative from country to country the world over".

His call was certainly answered in spectacular fashion, though not only in Europe — indeed, not mainly in Europe. Both Greece and the Malay States were brought into the Movement by one extraordinary man, Big Jim Davidson, and it is highly arguable that no other man could have done it, or certainly done it over such a short space of time and at such an early stage of both Rotary and the twentieth century, before the "post-war world" after the Second World War, the headlong growth of communications and, above all, the sweep of multinational corporations across the globe had cast the commercial veneer of nations much in one mould, making all races and creeds superficially much more fertile for Rotary Clubs than fifty years ago. It was thanks to Big Jim alone that Amy Johnson found all those Rotarians waiting along her route through the East to Australia.

For Paul's travels were one of two which began in 1928, within months of each other. Since one took in the West and the other the East, one representing consolidation and identification and the other pioneering, we shall consider them in successive chapters, this one and the next, taking Jim Davidson's first, because — in spite of

Paul's serious coronary the following year (which, typically, did not deter him) — it was the massive and assertive Davidson, not the frail-looking, retiring Harris, who would die first; by fourteen years, in fact, and die moreover as a direct result of his journeys for Rotary.

Half-way through his own eight years' odyssey Paul Harris discovered that on the other side of the door he was busy opening was a world twice as large as he, or anyone else in Chicago, had imagined. Without Jim Davidson, that revelation would not have come about. A Rotarian six years older than Paul, Big Jim took ship just three months after the Harrises, to begin three years' constant travelling. Describing Jim Davidson as "the Marco Polo of Rotary", *The Rotarian*, in a commemorative article appearing in October 1979, said: " . . . the Davidsons were off on an adventure whose importance they could never have guessed . . . taking in tens of thousands of kilometres and completely redrawing the world map of Rotary". Redrawing it, one might say, in an exercise-book, for this was at heart a *Boy's Own* adventure, to use the name of one of the most popular boys' magazines at the turn of the century. And the journey was the culmination of, and set an immortal seal upon, a decade of Rotary absorption with the whole concept of boyhood through the twenties. Before, therefore, we can fully appreciate and understand Jim Davidson's success, we must assimilate two factors, philosophical and practical: the reason he went and why he succeeded.

James W. Davidson, one of the biggest dealers in farming real estate in the Canadian West, an author, travel writer, foreign correspondent, Far East expert, also a one-time roving diplomatic trouble-shooter in the early years of the century, adored the romance of travel and adventure, and it began with his love of the circus. From his youngest days Davidson wanted to belong to one, and a lifelong friend recalled Big Jim driving to watch his first circus in a horse-drawn farm-wagon. To the end of his life, photographs show him at his happiest playing an old cornet in any circus parade within reach, and in any country. He climbed 7,000 feet to reach a mountain circus in West Bengal; he tried to ship home a sacred white elephant from Bangkok to a friend's circus in Canada. A Boy Wonder, indeed!

Lillian Davidson, his wife, who wrote a book about their three-year journey, understood her husband well. "Often", she wrote, introducing her narrative, "I have felt a pang of regret at inducing him to give up the foreign service and the life he loved so well and enter into a humdrum business existence. So, now I am happy to see him back in a work . . . to which he is so well-adapted and finds so congenial. . . . Like Huck Finn, Jim regards it as 'tough but interesting'."

Sixty-six might not seem to many the ideal age for anyone to start behaving like Huckleberry Finn, America's ideal boy, but the chance was seized on by Big Jim, for he belonged to a band of men who believed no age was ever too late for the purpose, either to start or continue — he was a Rotarian, belonging to a Club which preserved the boy in men, and like all right-thinking wanderers, Mark Twain's great creation seemed to him the patron saint of rapscallions. Paul Harris, in *My Road to Rotary*, recalled that "the grand splurge of the year, more dazzling even than the County Fair . . . was circus day". He, with Jim Davidson, remained a boy in love with a circus all his life — but he sublimated an urge he felt unseemly into another urbanised circular emblem. And for that Golden Wheel, Jim Davidson became the star performer.

"We swung to the east . . . Our glorious expedition was on its way; great explorers were we; our fame would spread far and our names be long remembered. . . . How could there be adventure in tracing a known course?" The words are not Jim Davidson's, they are Paul's, recalling those rapscallion adventures in Vermont, many passages of which could have been lifted complete out of *Huckleberry Finn* — published, incidentally, the year the eighteen-year-old Paul was expelled from the Black River Academy (recorded in Chapter Two). Paul's actual journey then was only in the hills around Wallingford and he got lost: in truth, he was Tom Sawyer to Davidson's Huck Finn. Mrs Davidson was right and no doubt remembered well that "tough but interesting" was how Huck had described *Pilgrim's Progress*.

Before chronicling Davidson's progress, which we can regard as the apotheosis of the boy factor in Rotary, it will help to examine how that factor had come to assume, and maintain triumphantly, its predominant hold on the minds of a fast-growing group of sober-suited bourgeois business men in the second decade of this century. Where lay the well-springs of Rotary's absorption with boys which Paul Harris — like Perry, childless — was to tap so powerfully and enduringly? This is not the same thing as our modern concern with "youth" which infers — sometimes, but seldom, correctly — that the puerile objects of our communal attention have genuine adult awareness and basic, if somewhat hidden, responsible aims. Edwardians were engrossed with the subject and state of boyhood, as an intrinsically distinct condition, to a degree of intensity which seems extraordinary to us today and, far from being regarded as a preliminary to adulthood, "boyhood" was regarded as self-sufficient and desirable in itself. Mark Twain's master creation,

Huckleberry Finn, was an early harbinger of this change. No doubt the intensity was the more strong because of its complete turnabout from the Victorian attitude towards all stages of growing up, which was simply to ignore them. Children were dressed and treated as stunted adults, in every sense, and only impinged on one's attention from advantages of size, convenient for going down mines or up chimneys, or into pockets and second-storey windows — and in this latter role, the juvenile thieves were not even called boys but "snakesmen". Dickens's Artful Dodger was a premature adult rather than an immature one, and Oliver Twist's black topper, frock-coat and cravat as a professional mourner were in fact quite normal everyday wear for children. They were regarded, at best, whether in Fagin's grip or Dr Arnold's, as apprentice men, and small mercy was shown to those who faltered in the apprenticeship. The cry then was "Boy for sale!"

Charles Dickens created many memorable child characters, but our interest and sympathy with them, as clearly were his, are not inspired by their virtues as admirable children but their stoicism as heroic small adults. None of them remain children still defiant at the story's end, in contrast to Mark Twain's Huck Finn, the first boy to assert that growing up was a defeat not a victory, adulthood a craven surrender to expediency. When Aunt Sally offers to adopt and "sivilise" him, Huck vows to "light out for the Territory ahead of the rest", because where civilisation is concerned "I can't stand it. I been there before". No Dickens narrative ends thus, but he was very much of his time and had been dead fourteen years when *Huckleberry Finn* appeared. He had portrayed triumph over boyhood; Twain portrayed, for the first time, boyhood triumphant.

No wonder that the most virulent critic of Twain's book when it first appeared was Louisa May Alcott, who had her own safe idea of what "little men" should be. When women go around saying that men never truly cease to be boys, they are whistling in the wind for a rude noise that never comes; most of them would run a mile from a real boy, and those who do meet one seldom marry his ageing counterpart. "Mother's boy" is a contradiction in terms; so are women in Rotary.

When Bruce Barton in *The Man Nobody Knows* claimed Jesus for the world of commerce as the first modern salesman, "the great advertiser", he drew on Jesus' famous statement that his chief priority must always be "my Father's business". What mystified Joseph and Mary (Jesus being twelve years old at the time) did not in the least puzzle Barton, to whom business was business as boys will be boys. Many American business men have never lost that belief, nor have most other successful men, and it was a belief in which Paul Harris never faltered and on which Rotary thrived. Thrived perhaps as a last hope, for a real playground is a far rougher place than a firing-range: One makes boys, the other only men, and after two world wars and countless small ones, known and unknown, which have collectively killed even more people than their betters, perhaps we can all more readily say we cannot stand civilisation either, having "been there" just once too often.

Meanwhile, till that belief prospered and extended, as far as the business and professional classes were concerned — and they were the ones who dominated the Victorian world, of course, and indeed both created that world and were created by it — boyhood (girls didn't count, anyway) was just the unmentioned and unmentionable necessity of existence, like the rituals of sex . . . adults, regrettably, could come from no other source. They shared the view of Ambrose Bierce, the sardonic American author and journalist (who, like Twain, had begun his journalistic career in San Francisco) that "the fact that boys are allowed to exist at all is evidence of a remarkable Christian forbearance among men".

We are discussing here a change in Anglo-Saxon attitudes, needless to say, since it was in the Anglo-Saxon matrix that Rotary was begotten. And the abrupt, rapid and sensational change in the status of boys came about with a sudden rush of typically Anglo-Saxon double-think and prurient hypocrisy, culminating in the show-piece of the Oscar Wilde scandal. The result was that "the love that dare not speak its name" was able to be shouted from the housetops, or at least from the newstands. Paradoxically, boys moved into respectable consideration through some of them becoming the openly avowed sex-objects of respectable men. Via the lurid spotlight of Wilde's three trials, and others like them which are not now so well, or so often, remembered, attention was focused on boys as a separate species, sufficient unto themselves. The comic side of what he was doing for the boy species, at terrible cost to himself, did not escape Wilde. When an actor friend of his showed great embarrassment at alluding to the impending court proceedings, Wilde quickly put him at ease. "Don't distress yourself," he said. "All is well. The working classes are with me . . . to a boy."

The man who got to the heart of the matter was our old acquaintance, W.T. Stead, long returned from excoriating Chicago and threatening its citizens with a disapproving Redeemer, but still crusading, and now editing *The Review of Reviews* from the rooms overlooking the Thames that would one day house the Headquarters of Rotary in Great Britain and Ireland. It was there that he wrote on Wilde's conviction:

It is impossible to deny that the trial and the sentence bring into very clear relief the ridiculous disparity there is between the punishment meted out to those who corrupt girls and those who corrupt boys. If Oscar Wilde . . . had ruined the lives of half a dozen innocent simpletons of girls, or had broken up the home of his friend by corrupting his friend's wife, no one could have laid a finger upon him. The male is sacrosanct; the female is fair game.

And there we have it. The male was sacrosanct. The sacred basis of Victorian society, male dominance, reacted against a mortal threat, but it was reacting too late. The Victorian world was apparently still secure behind all its dust-heavy codes of behaviour, its narrow, complacent assumptions. But only apparently, and we can return appropriately to Mark Twain for his remark about a well-known inn: "It used to be a good hotel, but that proves nothing — I used to be a good boy." It was Huck Finn speaking.

Having failed to smother the emergent species with scandal, the Anglo-Saxon world did a complete turnabout as the old century tipped over into the new. Only ten years from the trial of Oscar Wilde, a Club "like an oasis in a desert" was formed in Chicago, the town which had scorned Wilde as typical of "clowns with pansies", a Club which had "meetings very different from the meetings of other clubs . . . far more intimate . . . the members were boys again", a Club called Rotary. These words of Paul Harris take a powerful edge when we find him being apostrophised in a poem as a "Prince of Boys", published in the same issue of *The National Rotarian* which shows us Chesley Perry still respectfully making his Annual Report personally to Paul, beginning "Dear Sir".

In between, what had happened? Well, the male was still sacrosanct, but it had become the male as Boy. No mention was made that Rotary's "Prince of Boys" had been married to a Princess for two years. But then no one realised — or perhaps Rotarians were only just beginning to — that the Princess was about to whisk the Prince of Boys up on to her white horse and ride off with him to their safe castle in the suburbs. Peter Pan's Wendy, in fact. Americans were to succumb to James Barrie's "lost boys" in Never-Never Land, who couldn't and wouldn't grow up, as completely as the British, in some ways more so. And 1905 saw both Rotary appearing in Chicago and Peter Pan on Broadway. Mark Twain wrote to its leading actress: "It is my belief that *Peter Pan* is a great and refining and uplifting benefaction to this sordid and money-mad age." One has but to substitute Rotary for Peter Pan (or Huck Finn) and there we have Paul Harris's identical dream.

Bernard Shaw ridiculed Barrie's invention as much as he was to ridicule Paul Harris's later on, and for the same reason: he held that both encouraged their partisans to hold as attainable quite impossible goals. But Shaw, as he often was when at his most perceptive and entertaining, was outvoted by common humanity in both cases. Peter Pan exported with immediate and huge success to the United States and spread there from city to city like wildfire (it opened in San Francisco only ten days after the earthquake). After all, there were redskins in it and its original title had been "The Great White Father", the Indians' name for the United States President. Similarly, as we have seen, Rotary had huge and immediate success, spreading across America, and exported to Britain with equal ease and triumph.

The Anglo-American triumph of boyhood in the Edwardian era was sealed by the formation of the Boy Scouts, which Baden-Powell founded in 1908 and which made an enormous and durable impact across the Atlantic from 1910 onwards. It was no surprise that the Movement which had been formed to preserve the boy in men was at once drawn to the Scouts. In Chicago, many Rotarians became involved in Scout organisation, and San Francisco followed suit. With the example of Rotary One and Two, the pattern spread all over the United States. It was this Scouting influence, allied to pressures of the day, that moved the 1917 "Win the War" Convention in Atlanta to establish a Committee on Boys' Work for the purpose of guiding and co-ordinating Club efforts in this field. By 1919, that Committee was reporting great progress and the man in charge at Headquarters laid down objectives with a very modern ring. Those objectives were divided into Redemptive Work and Creative Work. Redemptive Work included plans to help "boys who have gotten into bad habits and under bad influence . . . boys in reform institutions; boys in unwholesome surroundings . . . boys who are growing up physically defective in ways which may be combated successfully if promptly attended to". Creative Work included "the giving of sex-hygiene instruction . . . physical development and practical education, including vocational training and guidance". The Rotary Club of Blackwell, Oklahoma, was praised for ensuring that boys who wanted to leave school for work in their mid-teens would instead stay on and finish their education.

The April 1919 issue of *The Rotarian* carried an article by a Boy Scout executive in Indiana, Rotarian George Wyckoff, which spelled out the new partnership unequivocally. After referring to the war service of Boy Scouts in America — listing war gardens, the sale of one in twenty-one of all Liberty Bonds, aid to the Red Cross, and collecting nearly 21 million feet of black walnut for gunstocks and aircraft propellers — he stated: "Truly the Boy Scout is a Rotarian, as the Rotarian is a real Scout. It's your game, Fellow Rotarians. Come on in!"

And in they came. A poem in the same issue rhapsodised

O, but I like you,
You sun-tanned boys,
You brown-clad boys of mine.

while Wyckoff himself found a quotation to drive his theme home: "When God made the first man, he made the world significant, but when he made the first boy, he made it interesting." It was on the evidence of very similar remarks that Wilde had spent two years in gaol, two years that killed him, but time had passed and war, the great equaliser, had just killed his eldest son.

Ches Perry no doubt drew lessons from the rapid adoption of Scouting round the world, which quickly outdistanced Rotary in this respect. In spite of the number of flags at the Edinburgh Convention of 1921, representatives of only six countries were actually present, the overwhelming majority of whom were from the United States. We have already noted that Baden-Powell could not attend. The reason for his absence was that he had held already his own enormous gathering the year before in London. This was the first great international Scouting Jamboree, at which the Duke of York — the future King George VI — was present, and no less than twenty-seven nations attended that! It was a further sign to Perry that Paul Harris, with a matchless instinct, had struck precisely the right chord of response from the very beginning.

Rotary and the Boy were an equation seldom in doubt from then on. In October 1917 *The Rotarian* had declared, with no trace of self-consciousness or embarrassment: "The boy holds an important position in the world. . . . Rotarians, enlisted under the banner of the highest ideals of service to the world, should be interested in boys; most of them are." And casting fears of Freudian slurs to the wind, in January 1921 it published an article which roundly asserted: "Ever since the time when Adam and Eve went forth from the Garden of Eden to people the Earth, the problems of boy life have been with us." Presumably one could be raising either Cain or Abel and not know till too late, or more likely, realise one was raising both at once, but the statement is not for scriptural or psychological analysis. Instead, it would have been best to adapt Mark Twain's warning notice prefacing *Huckleberry Finn*: persons looking for a motive would be prosecuted, those looking for a moral would be banished, and those looking for a plot would be shot.

Twain, to whom incidentally Bermuda became just as important as it was later to become to Paul Harris, had died just a few months before Rotary's first Convention in 1910, but his classic novel about boyhood triumphant was a milestone in the change of attitude in society towards boys and made that change both manly and respectable. He also, by his humorous approach, leavened and refreshed it with a dash of typical impiety, writing in the copy that he autographed for young Winston Churchill on 21st January 1901, "To be good is noble; to teach others how to be good is nobler, and no trouble". With such sentiments around, no wonder Queen Victoria died the day after, to be succeeded by a splendid fifty-nine-year-old boy.

From complete disregard, boys had leapt to high visibility via such *fin de siècle* scandals as Wilde's. After a brief garish prominence as a focus of nightmare vice, this aspect went underground again, but never more were boys consigned to an Anglo-Saxon limbo, fit preoccupation only for poets, pederasts and over-anxious pedagogues. Men were often nicknamed "Boy" for entirely virile reasons, and when the First World War turned the Lost Boys into the Lost Generation, followed by a decade when young women did their fashionable best to look like boys, Rotary's absorption with them as a species to be nurtured, protected and advanced in their own and others' esteem, became inevitable.

Altogether, 1921 proved a halcyon year for affirmation of Boys and Rotary as a team. The lead editorial in the January issue of *The Rotarian* was entitled "About Boys". In its March issue Paul Harris himself recounted how he had endeavoured to rescue "an embryonic negro burglar" of fifteen at the urging of the Boys' Work Committee. As a counter to this, the Rotary Club of Selma, Alabama, entertained 120 farm-boys at their weekly luncheon, "all white boys in the county" being eligible. Meanwhile in Canada, Rotarians of Toronto, Ontario, raised $8,000 in eight minutes for two Boys' Clubs, while in Saskatoon, Saskatchewan, "the most complete survey of boy life" was made. In July *The Rotarian* was advocating censoring the more steamy motion pictures for boys in an article by the catastrophically named Orrin G. Cocks. From Montevideo "Herbierto" Coates reported that thirty newsboys had been taken for a picnic (being English, Herbierto made sure the programme included "sports, drills, bathing and grub"). Shanghai raised a Boy Scout bugle band and supplied tents and uniforms. Mexico City Rotarians donated, equipped and endowed a recreation area for deprived youngsters, and Puerto Rican members organised health and educational facilities for the young. In Cienfuegos, Cuba, a troop of over 300 Boy Scouts was formed. Belfast raised £4,500 for the Scouts. Aberdeen adopted fatherless boys, sons of war dead.

Brighton set up a Benevolent Fund for educating poor students through an allocation of 10 per cent of Club subscriptions. Auckland, New Zealand, sponsored a boy's band to give monthly concerts at the local prison, while Australia's Sydney Club had as its first President Sir Henry Braddon, who directed his major efforts towards helping boys, and whose much-quoted saying on the subject soon became Rotary lore: "One way in which Rotary develops the individual is in preserving the boy in him. Deep down in the heart of every good fellow there is a boy." In his posthumous memoirs, Paul Harris was still quoting Sir Henry approvingly.

But Rotary One lived up to its reputation for boosting the biggest, brassiest and best by staging a mammoth parade of 50,000 boys down Michigan Avenue (though New York had anticipated them the year before) to inaugurate Boys' Week, an annual celebration that was to continue for over forty years. They even had a message from President Harding, who informed them that "the boys of today will be the men of tomorrow", though of course that promise was contingent upon their staying out of the crossfire of the bootleg gangs of Capone and Bugs Moran.

The Movement's key message of the year when Rotary introduced itself to the world at Edinburgh, however, was perhaps that received from the author and editor (of Edgar Allan Poe) Roscoe Gilmore Stott, of the Franklin Club in Indiana. "I know nothing on earth that equals the potential worth of a dirty-faced, freckled nosed, uncombed, sparkling-eyed lad," he wrote in the July *Rotarian*. Complacent, patronising and corny as it was, Huck Finn was ever more recognisable, and the sentiment sufficed to inspire a dedication to Boys' Work renewed at Edinburgh and followed by Clubs all over the world to this day. In this, as befitted a famous Army Scout, Baden-Powell blazed a trail which Rotary and Rotarians have never failed to acknowledge.

There were voices of dissent, notably from the very articulate English Rotarian, William Moffat, whose name has already appeared in this narrative. During his year as Chairman of the Yorkshire Clubs in 1923 he had boldly declared in an article, first appearing in Britain, then reprinted in America:

The main plank in the present Rotary programme seems to be Boys' Work. I deny that Rotary is fitted to do Boys' Work in any new, unique or even large way. . . . I do not deny that Rotary can do good service among boys. I do not wish to discourage one single Rotarian from putting his heart and soul into Boys' Work. . . . *But I most emphatically deny that this is Rotary's chief job.* Boys' Work is a Rotary incidental, not a premier function.

10. (*above left*) The amazing Stuart Morrow, Paul's "wonder-working Irishman", who took Rotary beyond the New World.

11. (*above right*) Harry Ruggles, the initiator of Rotary songs, who is also credited with popularising community singing in the United States.

12. Rotary International President, Estes Snedecor (*right*), is greeted by Rotarian William Logie as he arrives to attend the Edinburgh Convention in 1921, the first ever Rotary Convention to be held outside the United States.

13. (*above left*) Arthur Sheldon, Rotary salesman supreme and inventor of the motto "He Profits Most Who Serves Best", before his debacle at the Edinburgh Convention.

14. (*above right*) Jim Davidson, the "Marco Polo" of Rotary who travelled throughout the Middle and Far East on his Club-forming mission.

15. King Albert I of the Belgians opens the first Rotary International Convention on the Continent of Europe, held in Ostend in 1927.

16. Paul Harris being hosted in South Africa by Generals Smuts and Hertzog.

17. One of the first television broadcasts: Paul Harris (*second from left*) and Chesley Perry (*second from right*) share more history-making in 1940.

18. Paul and Jean Harris in 1941, the year of the Chicago Club's great Business Exhibition.

19. Paul and Ches, the men who made Rotary, chatting together at Comely Bank in 1942, the year of Ches Perry's retirement.

Paul Harris would never have agreed with him, yet Moffat represented that robust, steady streak in Rotary which has always made it shrink from going "over the top". His voice was heard just in time, for at the St Louis Convention, held later that year, a motion to make Rotary responsible for all children's work in the United States was defeated, to be replaced by Resolution 34, a milestone resolution which firmly directed each Club towards Community Service, "based upon a real community need" and requiring "the collective co-operation of all its members". This latter clause at last spelled out the real purpose of having in membership a complete cross-section of business and professional men — the "Classification" system — and set the Movement firmly on its future path. It certainly reflected Moffat's call for Rotary as "representative men to reshape the modern world on straighter, sweeter, more merciful, and more humanistic lines". Yet, for all that, the longest Resolution still concerned Rotary's policy and planning for Boys' Work and urged "the Clubs in their respective communities to awaken the public to the challenge of the boy".

Boys' Work became the predominant Rotary activity during the twenties, as far as community service went, followed closely, especially in the United States, by help for crippled children, an offshoot of the major project, since concern for avoiding psychologically crippled lives formed a major motivation, the scars of distorted wartime values being succeeded by the wicked lures of prohibition temptations, being followed in turn by the damage of the Depression years, "Boys' Work has gripped the heart of Rotary," proclaimed *The Rotarian*, and that grip held. Indeed, amongst rank-and-file Rotarians it quite eclipsed the Sixth Object of Internationalism for the time being.

George Olinger of Denver, Colorado (where the "Coming of Age" Convention had been held), was twice Chairman of the Boys' Work Committee of Rotary International during these years and a Rotarian representative on the International Boys' Work Council as well as the organiser of his own Boys' Work Foundation throughout the Rocky Mountain Region, and of the Highlander Boys of Denver, numbering 10,000 youngsters at one time. As the twenties went on, Olinger was aware of a waning enthusiasm in this field among some Clubs and, in the January 1928 issue of *The Rotarian*, he announced his undiminished faith that "today boys are no longer personal property but individuals, individuals with sacred personalities to be guided skilfully into the achievement of the unguessed buried potentiality" — an unfortunate choice of adjective perhaps for a man whose Classification was undertaker.

Yet his enthusiasm was not misplaced and had much relevance

to the success certainly of one of the two Rotary voyages commencing that year, ten years after the Armistice. It is significant
that Jim Davidson, in his first letter back to Perry from Istanbul
rhapsodised, "This place is everything that you can imagine the
Orient of your boyhood's dreams to have been", which gives us
an excellent reason to consider his journey before that of Paul
Harris. Another reason is that the latter's was not fatal to the
traveller.

So not one, but two, momentous journeys for Rotary com-
menced in 1928. Paul and Jean travelled westward over the Atlantic,
sailing from Montreal in the *Laurentic* in May; and three months
later James W. Davidson, six years older than Paul, sailed with his
wife and daughter from that same port on the *Duchess of Atholl*,
only heading in the opposite direction. The Boy Wonder was
on his way.

Inspired after his first meeting with Paul Harris in 1921, Rotary's
"Marco Polo" had gone to Australia and New Zealand, in partner-
ship with a fellow-Canadian colonial, J. Layton Ralston, to inaugurate the Movement in the Antipodes. By 1928, however, Ralston
was well launched on the political career which was to make him
successively Canada's Minister of National Defence, Minister of
Finance and then his country's Defence Minister again during the
Second World War, so Davidson made his greatest voyages for the
Movement on his own, along with his wife Lillian, and daughter
Marjorie, for company. In contrast to Ralston, Davidson had
already had a number of outstanding careers by 1928, enough for
several lifetimes of most men. After he had pursued circuses in his
boyhood, his travelling propensities came to the fore again when,
as a theatrical manager, he arranged speaking tours for the greatest
explorer-adventurer of all time, H. M. Stanley, the celebrated "dis-
coverer" of Livingstone and the Congo. While Paul Harris was
boldly investigating the remoter byways of Chicago during the 1893
World's Fair (along with W. T. Stead and "Christ"), Jim Davidson
was away on the top of the world, sledging in the frozen wastes of
north-east Greenland with Commander Robert Peary's expedition,
looking for the North Pole. He then became a war correspondent
for the *New York Herald*, as Stanley had been before him, and
covered both sides of the Sino-Japanese War of 1894–5, becoming
fluent in Japanese and writing a classic book on Formosa, which
had just become part of Japan (as it remained until 1945). He
lived in Formosa for nine years, but could not still his wandering
feet for long. Having been decorated by the Emperor of Japan, he
was commissioned by the Tsar of Russia to write a book on
Manchuria. He had not quite finished it when the Russo-Japanese

War of 1904—5 broke out, but he had plenty still to do as Inspector-General of US Consulates all the way from Port Said in Egypt to Tokyo, the very same route he would later traverse on his great Club-forming mission.

A roving investigator for US presidents long before doing the same job for Rotary, Davidson probed Manchuria and the Trans-Siberian Railway crises between Russia and Japan for Presidents McKinley and Teddy Roosevelt, managing at the same time to court his future bride, the daughter of a San Franciscan business man, in Shanghai and Kobe, the great port which then comprised Japan's only real international community. It was not till after marriage "settled" him in Calgary that he joined that town's Rotary Club in 1914. The settling did not last long.

After being called one of Rotary's Special Commissioners for his pioneering work with Ralston in the cities of Melbourne, Sydney (see Chapter Eleven), Wellington and Auckland, Davidson, who had vowed to convert Australians to Rotary "dead or alive", returned to say "we doubt if Rotary was ever subjected to a greater test" though he held to his view, shared strongly by his friend and admirer "that prince of real fellows, Paul Harris", that the Movement's chief global virtue was its strengthening of the ties between the English-speaking nations and that there was "no service that we can render of greater benefit to humanity in general than to promote harmony and good fellowship among all Anglo-Saxon groups".

This narrow view rapidly broadened, along with the Movement, as the twenties saw Rotary take root throughout Europe and South America, and — now grandly titled Honorary General Commissioner for Rotary International — Davidson carried out, from 1928 to 1931, the greatest mission of his career. He set off for the East again (via the Orient Express) at the age of sixty-six — with a grant of $8,000 from the Board of RI — to lay the groundwork for, and, where possible, establish Clubs in Athens, Istanbul, Cairo, Jerusalem, Baghdad, Damascus, Bombay, Teheran, Delhi, Madras, Ceylon, Burma, the Malay States, Singapore, Java, Bali, Sumatra, Siam, Indo-China, Formosa and Hong Kong. It was a huge undertaking for one man, almost too stupendous for the restricted concepts of the boardroom in Chicago, whose contribution of $8,000 came to look more and more of a pittance. But there was no complaint from Big Jim, who journeyed more like Rotary's Pro-Consul than its Marco Polo, taking with him testimonials to Rotary from the just-elected leaders of the United States and Great Britain, Herbert Hoover and Ramsay MacDonald, from the Foreign Secretary and Nobel Peace Prize-winner Austen Chamberlain, plus two kings and many public figures. Nor from Lillian, for love of whom he had given up his life of roving political adventure in his country's foreign service. She was glad to see him in his element again, though it was to cost him a personal outlay of a quarter of a million dollars and, in the end, through exhaustion, his life itself, though he gave both willingly.

No other man could have done the job, and once again Paul Harris and Rotary were in debt to a man who gave of himself entirely to the cause of World Extension. By and large, to those vast areas of the globe, in the process of emerging from Western dominance and the long thrall of European imperialism, Jim Davidson was the ideal embodiment of this new Movement. He was a figure recognisable, acceptable, respected and understood by the new professional and business élite coming to the forefront of affairs in the non-white nations. Big Jim spoke to them in a Rotary vocabulary neither Perry nor Harris would have known how to use and probably would have deplored — and they responded. He sold them the acceptable face of commercial imperialism: just as it had done elsewhere in the world where the pioneers had gone, the Club came first matched to its new context. The Gold of the Wheel was welcomed; the service could follow later.

Stamford Raffles, a descendant of the eminent naturalist and founder of Singapore, was a member in Kuala Lumpur. The Delhi Club's first President was the manager of Burmah Shell Oil and, before a few weeks had passed, all but five of the first twenty-eight members were off to Simla to join the viceregal court through the hot weather. In Rangoon, Davidson wryly recounted, he tried to explain Rotary's ideals to a group of prominent Chinese and Burmese merchants: "I was asked to explain in what way Rotary would help business. I replied quite definitely that it would not add to their business returns in any way. [They] arose as one man and departed, wondering doubtless just why they had ever been called together."

Big Jim took such disappointments in his massive stride, waiting through temperatures usually in excess of 100° F while the process of oriental decision-making dragged on at a slow tempo until it either ended negatively, or the conclusions were subsequently forgotten or denied. The Rangoon Club he finally formed consisted, he confessed, of "business men, officials, educators, professional men, engineers, scientists, etc., a true cross-section of the community", then the telling phrase, "together with a few representative Burmans". It was the old story of Calcutta and Shanghai; for all his efforts, the founding Rotarians were more often than not mainly British or American. He consoled himself with the reflection that one day Rotary might be made available "to a larger number in these countries . . . allowing perhaps representation in each vocation from each different race". In Malaya, indeed, there was proof this could work: though racially Clubs were fully integrated, with Malays, Chinese, Indians, British and Ceylonese working freely together, barristers, for example, were elected, one each, from the Chinese, Indian and European communities.

In Indonesia he found the Dutch became willing Rotarians, provided class distinctions were observed. The Batavia Club had fifty-nine Dutchmen, eight Javanese and three Chinese, the Dutch being all top government officials, bankers, shipping executives and brokers. The Djakarta Club included both the Dutch Governor and the local Javanese Prince whose court customs much resembled those made familiar to us in *The King and I* musical. In the actual land of that musical, Siam, Big Jim incorporated six princes into a Bangkok Rotary Club, including the Minister of Communications, the Minister of Foreign Affairs and the Ministers of Education and Health, but his top business recruits of thirteen nationalities were all non-native, since the Siamese, he learned, were "real aristocrats and prefer that others shall do their hard work for them". Not a Rotarian ethic in sight, therefore, but he found that the Chief Minister promptly discarded all his glittering medals and decorations for a single Rotary button — neither Big Jim nor Rotary ever received a greater tribute.

Hong Kong presented him with little problem, for its commercial community was completely interracial. Having begun with an ideal to promote harmony amongst scattered Anglo-Saxon groups, Jim Davidson then ended his three-year mission by proclaiming Rotary's main object as "a better understanding and friendship among different nationalities". He also claimed, with justification, that, as a result of his efforts, "Rotary was now a worldwide organisation, for now practically every city of importance from the Mediterranean to the China Sea and the Pacific had its Rotary Club".

As his journey progressed, Davidson had learned that Rotary had to adapt and compromise in order to achieve acceptance. His task was far more formidable than that which had faced Morrow, Sheldon, Teele and, latterly, even Perry in Europe, for in the countries from which the United States had drawn its populations and heritage many common assumptions awaited the arrival of the Service Club Movement (see Chapter Seven), since Chicago Number One sprang from a racial mix that was Europe transplanted; in many ways, Rotary was already a European idea, with European precedents. The oriental mind — as also those of Middle Eastern and African cultures — was, on the contrary, alien ground.

Frighteningly so, in retrospect, for almost anyone other than Davidson. He had to battle with autocracy old, courteous and maddeningly friendly (Siam); new, courteous and maddeningly unhelpful (Turkey); discourteous and unhelpful (Indo-China); with communities where no work, business or otherwise, was done by men at all; where often business centres were linked only by the most luxurious trains in the world routed across barren, impoverished landscapes teeming with ignorance and disease; communities where far too many nationalities were in business (except the native, who didn't care) or far too few (also excepting the native, who still wasn't interested); and everywhere with endless flights of stairs to officials, insufferable heat, and the excruciatingly slow pace of life, thought and action about which Lillian approvingly quoted Kipling:

> Now it is not good for the Christian's health
>   to justle the Ayran brown,
> For the Christian riles, and the Aryan smiles,
>   and he weareth the Christian down;
> And the end of the fight is a tombstone white
>   with the name of the late deceased,
> And the epitaph drear: "A fool lies here
>   who tried to hustle the East".

Jim learned, or tried his best to learn, not to hustle the East, but his tombstone was only briefly postponed for all that.

Before plunging under the baleful skies and screaming, fetid inertia of Asia, Jim had earned his full measure of Rotary immortality by founding Clubs both in Cairo, which had almost more business interests and nationalities than could be crammed into Rotary Classifications, and Jerusalem, where the only two firms were Shell Oil and Thomas Cook, and where the Jews, the only native business men, were emigrating in greater numbers than those coming in. And before returning to Canada, Davidson revisited his old Far East haunts, starting with Formosa, where he had come as foreign correspondent in the 1880s (and now was able to set up the island's first Rotary Club), then Tokyo, China, the Philippines and Korea, where the Rotary Club of Seoul had been founded by the Japanese Governor-General, Saito, shortly to become Japan's first military Premier, abolishing his country's last party government on the slide to the Second World War. Most astonishing to our modern eyes is to read of his most cherished of all visits to old haunts, that to Manchuria. Here he casually refers to visiting no less than three already established Rotary Clubs, in

Dairen, Mukden and Harbin, watching baseball games and seeing young girls in Western short skirts and silk stockings. An observation on their Russian neighbours gives a depressingly familiar insight into the unchanging paraniac mentality of Communist rulers: "It was interesting to note that the Soviet government maintains a guard on the boundary, not to keep people from entering Russian territory but to keep those within from escaping."

Big Jim had only two real failures, in Turkey and in Indo-China. Both were, for different reasons, unexpected. Mustafa Kemal, the great, ruthless Ataturk, had just disestablished Islam as the state religion, abolishing polygamy, the fez, the Arabic alphabet itself — not to mention Islam's prohibition of liquor (he was not teetotal) — and the thorough Westernisation of the nation should have made this most bourgeois of Western ideas more acceptable than anywhere else in the Middle and Far East. But along with an eager grasp of Western customs went a paradoxical suspicion of Western motives. The Prefect of Police approved (or said so), the Minister of the Interior approved (or said so), but no signed permission for Rotary Clubs materialised. Presumably Mustafa Kemal, whom the Davidsons admiringly compared to Mussolini and Teddy Roosevelt, did not approve. In contrast, a few weeks later, Greece's durable strong man, Venizelos, personally received Davidson, gave approval, and the Athens Club was formed, including both allies and enemies of Venizelos, a striking witness to the non-political characteristic Rotary was determined to assert for itself.

Davidson's second great failure, Indo-China (this included the territories known today as Cambodia, Laos and Vietnam), was unexpected because it was a French possession. Not only were there long and sentimental ties between the United States and France, but the first Rotary Club in Europe, whilst unofficial, had as we know been the Allied Club in Paris during the 1914—18 war. Davidson had conferred with Rotarians in Paris and had letters from the Minister for the Colonies to the Governors at both Hanoi and Saigon. Yet not the slightest interest was forthcoming. Indeed, Rotary's Sixth Object, its internationalism, which was what Davidson's trip was all about, firmly labelled his mission impossible from the start. Davidson was no sentimentalist and spelled the facts out clearly: "The French colonist believes that his people are those who have made great sacrifices in developing these Asiatic colonial possessions and therefore any special benefit . . . should come to the Frenchman rather than to men of other nationalities. . . . This policy has kept Saigon and the other cities very exclusive, and trade and the professions are restricted to the French. . . . Consequently, there is little in the spirit of Rotary to appeal."

This experience was in painful contrast to Big Jim's shining example in promoting the Sixth Object in Asia. This was Singapore, where the Club he had formed needed only a year to accumulate more nationalities than any other Rotary Club in the world — no less than eighteen, including, in alphabetical order, American, Arabian, Armenian, Chinese, Dutch, English, French, German, Indian, Irish, Italian, Japanese, Malayan, Persian, Romanian, Russian, Scottish and Swiss. Lillian summed up the great achievement in *The Rotarian* for January 1933: "Today one may take any of the great steamers which carry passengers between Great Britain and Japan and . . . find a Rotary Club at every stop; in fact, excluding Istanbul and Saigon, there is a Club in every city in Asia to which Western men commonly travel. . . . It is my husband's belief", she concluded her account, "that nowhere in the world can Rotary render a greater service than in Asia."

Was he right? Has time proved the Boy Wonder right? Why should it do so, and how did it do so? I think, viewing his transformation of the world map of Rotary, and the aftermath, we can venture conclusions ourselves.

The reasons so far suggested for the rapid spread of the Rotary Movement in lands beyond its birth are relevant only for roughly half the world. The essentially European traditions from which it sprang, albeit transplanted to the New World melting-pot — applied as dressing and spice to an Anglo-Saxon ethic — suffice for its superficially astounding ready acceptance among the white races of the Western nations, including Latin-America, of course, where the cultural compost merely differed in being mulched in from Southern European Catholic hotbeds rather than Northern Europe's Protestant forcing-house. These reasons will not be sufficient for the Middle East, and even less so for the Far East. As indicated in earlier chapters, the examples of Calcutta and Shanghai immediately after the First World War showed that the Rotary idea could take firm root in the top dressing of European business and professional classes which prevailed in the great commercial centres of the Orient at that time. But for such roots to take hold below topsoil, there needed to be an appeal to the Eastern mind at depth. That mind, however, as we have learned, sometimes to our chagrin, as this century blusters, battles and blunders on, remains beneath the veneer of polite custom and trading practice utterly different from those of America and Europe, as different as when they were encountered by the original Marco Polo, for that matter, even though we tend to forget the oriental origins of today's Western obsessions, not with meditation and the martial arts, but gas and coal, paper money and bombs. The more we go East, the farther West we go.

234

In the present writer's view, it was Rotary's solid foundation on promotion, recognition and encouragement of the Boy in Man that was the talisman to which the East responded as much as the West. This was, and remains, the universal lodestone of Rotary's appeal, legitimising for grown men the renewal of the "gang". George Olinger listed in 1929 the virtues of what a gang provides for a boy:

1. "Pals" of his own age and kind.
2. An enlarged, shared circle of interests.
3. Unselfishness and good citizenship.
4. Loyalty to a "gang's" standard and ideals.

These things were essential elements supplied by membership in Rotary, and combined in Olinger's statement that "Well-directed and properly motivated gang life is an essential part of every boy's larger education". They were the essence of the instant world-wide success of Baden-Powell's Scout Movement. And, more than Codes of Business Practice, more than the Golden Rule (though this was itself Confucian), more than international understanding or community endeavour, they were, and always have been, an essential part of man's urge to join Rotary. It was as true of the world of Aladdin as it was of Peter Pan, and it is an instinct all too easily perverted to causes of conquest and tyranny, as Nazi Germany was all too soon to show. Rotary gave the instinct an acceptable, respectable, even prestigious, outlet, and this is what brought the response of the Orient to the Boy Davidson's adventure — and that response could be given so readily only to a man such as Davidson. A Pro-Consul reliving his young past, in love equally with the East and with Rotary, for the equal appeal each made to the boy in him, Davidson understood it was that very appeal of the boy which alone could lure the East into Rotary — as Kipling's *Kim*, through whose boy's eyes has come, say Indians themselves, the best portrayal of India ever given by a Western author, helped rescue the lama from their shared enemies, causing that mystic to say: "Just is the Wheel! Certain is our deliverance!"

Just was the Wheel, certainly. Because right on target; for Eastern promise is the promise of our youth, where its magic lies, where the day begins. Nostalgia for the Boy in Man is no lament for lost innocence. We are never less innocent than when we are young; boyhood is the time of extreme realism, when even our fantasies are closest to the knuckle. It is only as we grow older that we erect a wall of innocence — of not-seeing — around our lives to sustain us against cruelty, disappointment and decision. We do not mourn childhood for lost happiness, but for long miseries, sharp pains, joys, discovered guilt and strength to bear them all. It is only in age we cry we do not know; in boyhood, we know it all.

In "shades of the prison house" Wordsworth strikes the precise analogy. Our prisons are packed with wards of innocence, a terrible and ruthless innocence to which the law has condemned them for life, though wilful naïvety put them there in the first place, the naïvety of consequences. Boys accept consequences along with truth. Girls do so also, of course, but the years give them no refuge. Women are far less innocent than men; life gives them far more of the consequences.

To recapture the careless bravery of boyhood is thus a universal longing to which men of success of every race and creed and political belief are happy to admit, and grateful are many to a Rotary formula and concept that provide for its aspiration. In terms of world humanity, the slaughter of the innocents is always self-slaughter. Those who renounce innocence can survive only as fools or madmen or great generals and statesmen who wield the innocence of others' dreams. It is only innocence which cannot see crime in the garden, deceit at the door, the corruption and nakedness of emperors. Boys have the stuffing knocked out of them because their elders feel they may otherwise never outgrow reality. Paul Harris gave middle-aged men of success a chance to put the stuffing back in. Not too much at first, that would be unbearable; but a chance to put aside the hermitage of innocent respectability that locks us alone; to serve the victims of jungle life, not excluding themselves; and to encourage those who spurn the false god of innocence, like Mowgli and Huck Finn. We are all bravest when young.

Just was the Golden Wheel, then, and it was seen to be so. And Davidson rolled on across Asia for three exhausting years. Eight months after Lillian's final account had been published in *The Rotarian* the editorial page was announcing his death, and declaring, "No words here can possibly appraise such a man, nor his service to Rotary." Fortunately, our words now *can*, however, for Asian Clubs are increasing at such incredible speed that by the end of the century — the present International Secretary, Herbert A. Pigman, confidently predicts — membership in Clubs of the Far East will exceed 600,000, making the preponderance of Rotary decidedly oriental. Back in 1930 it was Singapore, not Saigon, that was showing the way and knew the future, both for Rotary and the East. And Jim Davidson who knew how the world would wag. There is still no Club in Saigon today; there are ten in Istanbul.

At the International Convention of 1934, held in Detroit, all the excitements, singing, robust heartiness and ringing declarations and rhetoric were suspended briefly while a gigantic portrait of Jim Davidson was spotlit behind the platform and Allen Albert stepped forward to pay a tribute to the great servant of Rotary who had suddenly died the previous July. Albert had been International President in 1915, had like Davidson been a journalist and war correspondent, and had long held a sombre, realistic and far-sighted view of the world (see Chapter Eight). His phrase all those years ago, when Kaiser William trampled over Europe, about "the dust that is being blown over the scorched fields of tomorrow", perhaps echoed in his mind now as, coincident with the Convention that late June, there was news, for those who cared to read it, that Hitler was supervising the treacherous slaughter of Ernst Roehm and all his old Brownshirt thugs and storm-troopers in the so-called "Night of the Long Knives".

Ten days later the Nazi's own newspaper, the *Völkischer Beobachter*, took time off from official excuses for the massacre of over a thousand "traitors" to assure loyal Nazis they could still remain members of Rotary without fear of taint. Indeed, to the contrary, said Goebbels's mouthpiece: "The Rotary Club . . . is no secret organisation with special rules. According to its aims and objects and past practice, there is no reason whatever to distrust it . . . opportunity is offered for past members upon request to par-ticipate in its activities and thus spread enlightenment as to the character and aims of our movement."

Against this monstrous corruption of the uses of Rotary Extension in the Germany of the 1930s Allen Albert could speak with un-feigned admiration of Davidson's monumental accomplishment on the other side of the world:

> Adventure is to the adventurous. The Davidsons underwent hardships that might well have daunted even a Peary. . . . Davidson had several fevers. . . . His daughter was dangerously poisoned by insect bite. Every traveller knows how the next land beckons, and since the next land meant Rotary to the Davidsons, their stay in the East lengthened on and on, despite the mishaps, the perils. . . . Everything about him was big — body, head, brain, voice, laugh, straight look of the eyes, heart, purpose, ideal, love of Rotary. . . . His faith was vast . . . by steamers on ocean and river, by rail, automobile and aeroplane, by pushcart, camel and elephant . . . to more than two thousand other men in their offices and counting rooms . . . he was a torch-bearer. . . .

In that month, other torch-bearers were burning books in Berlin, lighting the way to the next roaring rally for *Lebensraum*. But now the world had a choice, though it didn't know it. And from Athens to Hong Kong Big Jim Davidson had made that alternative possible.

CHAPTER FIFTEEN

Travels of a Boy King — 1

Hurrah! It's Rotary today!
Old pals, new friends will meet;
We'll sing a song of cheer, then pause
For prayer before we eat.

Forget your cares, Rotarians!
Take time to count your joys;
Let bankers, merchants, doctors, all
Once more be happy boys.

Songs for the Rotary Club

Years afterwards, upon hearing the news of Paul Harris's death, Vivian Carter, who had been Editor both of *The Rotary Wheel* and *The Rotarian*, recalled: "I never met a celebrity less conscious of being one, or less concerned to live up to the tradition woven around him. ... A fancy of his was to sit in a dark corner and listen, and talk — when drawn out — slowly, deliberately and reservedly on almost any topic raised. His philosophy — strange as it may seem to those who associate Rotary with flamboyance and exuberant optimism — was that of a sceptic."

A decade after his death, a Past President of the Aberdeen Rotary Club in Scotland remembered: "I asked the great man if I might take his photograph. He readily assented, but pointed out that as the light was rather bad, it might not come out; and he produced from his pocket a photograph of himself and told me to tell my friend that this was the one I took. Paul Harris visited Aberdeen three years later — again without notice. When I shook hands with him, he gave me a sharp look and then said, quite casually, 'Hello there! How did that snapshot turn out?' "

From these two reminiscences we can gauge not only much

239

about Paul Harris's character, but the surprise and delight which accompanied the impact about to be made by that character on the fast-expanding Rotary world from 1928 to 1936, during which time, and taking two serious heart attacks in his stride, the Founder of Rotary undertook to give back to the Movement, which Ches Perry had now nursed into being on all the continents and over all the seas of the world, its original birthright and basic, simple dynamic, and he did it by being nothing more — and nothing less — than his straightforward, essential self. By the time his travels were over, Rotary was unified more securely than would ever have been possible otherwise. It had been born once for a close and tight-knit group in one place at one time; it had to be born again for hundreds of varied groups, speaking dozens of languages, allied to many loyalties and varying cultures, across the sprawling, brawling twentieth century. On the doorstep of mankind, as it drew in its breath to shout weakly at catastrophe, the First Rotarian politely presented himself. And did not spare the self he presented.

Nor did he cosset himself with any false dignities. After his dress-rehearsal appearance on the world scene at Bermuda in 1926 (described in Chapter Thirteen), the intervening twelve months were a time of preparation. He started appearing, often with "Bonnie Jean", at Rotary gatherings. He even crossed his personal Rubicon by making a major speech at a District Conference in Racine! The effort is not to be underestimated. Paul Harris had come to terms with his past, his *own* terms, to the inestimable benefit of thousands of others in many lands. He had turned what for many of his fellow-countrymen would have been a lifelong psychological liability into an asset for the world, what might have been a personal crutch into a global escutcheon. Americans often regard their past with an extraordinary love-hate bordering on mania; no other people search for their roots with more diligence, none travel farther to escape from them. Many cultivate their origins as devotedly as they tend their cannabis plants. The American author Thomas Wolfe was at this time in the process of writing — in Europe — the first draft of his famous novel *Look Homeward, Angel* (a quote from Milton, which continues "and melt with ruth"), which bore the suggestive subtitle *A Story of the Buried Life*. For Harris, half the "buried life" was at Racine; the half he preferred not to dwell upon. Yet he had no time for ruth — that is, self-pity. One feels he had wisely decided that searching for one's roots is an overrated, when not positively indecent, pastime: those which lie nearest the surface prevent all mature growth; those lying deepest are discovered, sooner or later, in other people's drains. And Paul Harris was going for growth.

He also now literally assumed the new starring role Ches Perry had planned for him, by appearing in the first Rotary film ever made, *A Visit to the Home of Paul P. Harris*. This showed him at Comely Bank about his daily routine, and acted as a trailer for his looming world travels. Perhaps also it was made to convince Rotarians abroad that they would shortly be seeing the real thing and not an impersonator of a long-dead legend. The million Rotarians round the globe today regularly receive films and "slide-sets" from Headquarters but it is safe to say none will ever be as historic as this silent movie "short". Its director was a real original, too: Rotarian Charles "Chic" Sale of the Scarsdale Club in New York. Chic Sale was, like Harry Lauder, an extremely successful vaudeville star and one of the first headliners in Hollywood's comic "talkie" films, but he was destined to achieve lasting international fame when he published his little masterpiece *The Specialist*, all about "the champion privy builder of Sangamon County" which the *Times Literary Supplement* hailed as "shrewd and amusing . . . too genial to be offensive". We can be sure Paul vastly enjoyed his company but doubt if his pious consort ever permitted the book into the Comely Bank library. It is still in print today, in its umpteenth edition. To Jean Harris's relief, the film did not indicate whether or not the residence of Rotary's Founder possessed "the average family three-holer". The *TLS* book reviewer's term "innocently Rabelaisian" fitted Chic Sale and Paul Harris, though not the rapscallion's wife.

When Big Jim Davidson and Paul Harris began their travels in the same summer of 1928, they were both well aware that they had quite different roles to perform. Big Jim's giant performance was on a scale — especially considering his health and age — that is still difficult to grasp today. He was, in the modern vernacular, doing his own thing. Mark Twain had written, in the thin disguise of Huck Finn, that he had had quite enough of "civilisation", and so it was with Jim Davidson. Admirers of Twain's greatest novel will always remember its classic closing words: ". . . Aunt Sally she's going to adopt me and sivilise [*sic*] me, and I can't stand it. I been there before". Big Jim's beloved Lillian, for whom he had given up all his former roving life, knew better than Aunt Sally, of course, and Rotary owes her also a considerable debt. We must not forget, however, that when, early in *Huckleberry Finn*, the boys form a gang, it was Tom Sawyer, and not Huck Finn, who was elected "first captain".

So now we can consider the "first captain's" travels, those of the President Emeritus, who had stayed in the shadows for so many years. When Davidson, before commencing any of his journeys for

Rotary, had been taken by Ches Perry to meet Paul Harris, the introduction for the admiring Big Jim had been to "the Founder of Rotary". And when Harris modestly demurred from that description, Perry persisted and went even further, in a burst of uncharacteristic but utterly sincere, fervour. "Rotarians come to see you, Paul," he firmly declared, "in about the same spirit they go to visit the source of a great river." The tribute was as spontaneous as it was generous – and indeed, undeniably true. Harris never forgot that moment, treasuring it above all their divergencies in approach, in the past and future, to the cause they shared. That river, thanks to Jim Davidson, was about to be extended by many thousands of miles and, however strong the tribute, would lead to many tributaries. Far too many, in Perry's view. Psychologically, philosophically as well as geographically and historically, mankind was developing the concept of Rotary in an exhilarating number of different ways. Some tributary streams were more shallow than Chicago's, some were deeper, some plunged carelessly towards rapids heedless of Perry's warning cries, others moved far too sluggishly, some seemed to rise and fall with political tides, others disappeared for long periods underground before reappearing with a jaunty gush in unexpected places. It was time they should all be reminded of their single living source, in Perry's view.

It was not Paul Harris's, but he appreciated the sincerity of Perry's anxieties and, willing as he was to play the part his old friend was thrusting upon him, he kept his personal motivations to himself – for the present, anyway. Yet one motivation would become transparent. His delight in accumulating evidence that, like him, Rotarians all over the world were boys at heart, and accepted him as their Boy King. Indeed, for part of his Pacific travels, he would be accompanied by George Olinger, champion of the Boys' Work Committee who had recently proclaimed: "Don't wait until you're a man to be great: Be a Great Boy!" In his understanding of boyhood, Harris could also understand Perry's concern about the way some of the younger Clubs might behave, with not quite enough parental respect for Chicago. As the writer who was arguably America's best-known Rotarian of those days, William Allen White, Editor of the renowned *Emporia Gazette*, in Kansas, had memorably expressed it: "Every generation has been frightened by what it begot. . . . This ancient terror of offspring, this fear of wise childhood, comes because we cannot mirror ourselves accurately." As much as he could, Harris was determined to still Perry's alarm, or at least prove it exaggerated.

Even at this distance, we can sympathise with Ches Perry's quandary, and the ambivalence he must have felt in releasing the man he revered, but whose competence he distrusted, loose into the Rotary world. For those who have to live with it, there is only one thing more uncomfortable than an idea whose time has come, and that is the continued and embarrassing presence of the man whose idea it happens to be. Perry's position was akin to that of a taken-for-granted guardian of a girl whose looks are suddenly and sensationally in fashion — and at the top of the fashion at that — but whose progress and irresistible rise as the belle at every ball is rather marred for her suitors and escorts by the fact that "her mother comes, too". Or in this case, of course, father. For there is one thing that proud fathers cannot tolerate, and that is anyone who tampers with their handiwork, even though in their deepest hearts they appreciate, better than anyone, that such tampering is the ultimate, indeed the essential, tribute that a suitor can pay. This situation faced Chesley Perry with a dilemma that, to be fair, was not entirely of his own making, though none the less welcome for that; it was the dilemma's resolution which was so tiresome. An essential part of Harris's parental genius was his tolerance. He could watch his beloved brainchild grow with the proper awe of every father; where he differed from most was in the lack of any jealousy of his daughter's suitors. His was no heavy parental hand. Far from owning a fierce possessiveness, he gave his daughter wings and encouraged her to fly in the infinite air. Perry's was the heavy hand of the cloister, which Harris had ensured would come too late. Perry's recognition of this — and it was his particular genius to acknowledge that recognition — also almost came too late. As the equally proud, but far more possessive, stepfather of Rotary, he had every reason to hope and believe that when Harris, drained to a nervous exhaustion, had stepped away from the spotlight into the soothing, cool retreat offered by Jean and Comely Bank, the Rotary "household", of which he, Perry, would then take full command, would look to no other head. He settled to a twenty-four-hour-day absorption in ordering its affairs, paying its regular bills, hiring and firing household staff, moving house when required, watching over childhood traumas, growing pains, friends, education, first jobs and careers. Yet, to weld this metaphor to our previous one, the house Perry had charge of was a house on wheels. Golden Wheels. It was a homely vehicle turning into a streamlined juggernaut, and though Perry had the nerve and cool to control it, he was becoming increasingly aware that he had lost the steering he had once seized from Harris.

Paul Harris had not an ounce of envy or malice in him, yet he must surely have allowed himself an inward smile of satisfaction at what Headquarters in Chicago saw with alarm was a zestful child growing rapidly out of her clothes with a speed none had anticipated. What *he* saw was the maturing adult growing suddenly *into* hers. Ches Perry could cope, and cope magnificently, with a household even of such phenomenal growth as was now clearly on his hands; what he had not bargained on was a house which had suddenly become many mansions. But this was exactly what Paul had foreseen, of course. Rotary, his Rotary, was not lost at all; it was found. When he had let his hands be prised from the steering-column all those pre-war years ago, he had already locked it into the future.

The truth was, no one could replace the Founder. Usually, revolutionary movements — and it cannot be stressed too often that the Service Club Movement, so complacently accepted today, was always (as its emblem had indicated from the start, whatever Monty Bear thought) revolutionary — if they fail to devour their young, at least play down the role of their Founder until he is no longer around in person to discompose them. Perry had journeyed powerfully, and with an immense and deserved authority, to Europe and Great Britain. And still, members, new and old, asked him where was Paul Harris, who was Paul Harris, was he ill, was he dying, was he dead? It was unnerving.

Perry and the Rotary International Board of Directors bowed to the inevitable. No one could reassure like the Father, no touch could unite like that of the Founder. No presence could re-establish and locate the foundations of the building, suddenly housing so many mansions, like the architect. Perry, the great builder, had nonthe less built to another's plans. Architect and builder were the names Harris had tagged on to himself and Perry. He never changed his view. Perry, for his part, never sought to challenge it; if the thought ever crossed his mind that Harris, travelling round the world, might undermine his authority, it did not stay long. These two extraordinary men, though their characters denied intimacy with each other, thoroughly understood each other's roles and destiny. Both had no other aim in life but to serve their Movement.

Paul's new role was now upon him, as he began, from 1928 to 1936, his second period of service to Rotary. As before, it was carried out mainly alone, for now it was the turn of Jean Harris to have a nervous breakdown. The character of this strange, beautiful and forceful woman, her influence on her husband and on Rotary, and her conduct after his death, will be examined in a later chapter. For the present, we may note that the motto on her grave in Edinburgh — shared not with her husband, of course, but her brother — reads: SHE HATH DONE WHAT SHE COULD. This quotation is not given attribution on the headstone, but it is in fact from St Mark, Chapter 14, verse 8, and refers to the woman

who came to Jesus in the leper's house and poured expensive
ointment over His head, arousing much indignation amongst those
present at what they regarded as a waste of money which could
have been spent on the poor. To which Our Lord made his famous
response about the poor being always with us, adding, "She hath
done what she could: she is come aforehand to anoint my body to
the burying." The inscription is almost top-heavy with implications,
but we shall examine these later. Meanwhile, leper or not, anointed
or not, Paul Harris was still to be a long time burying. "Bonnie
Jean" had quite a wait; and had he known that she would then
decide to dig him up again, "doing what she could" with a vengeance,
he would surely have thought it hilarious. For time was to demonstrate that as he falteringly survived at home, protected by her
warm and steadfast strength, he waxed robust as he travelled and
Jean sickened. Back home, he would be stricken again and she
would bloom. The pattern never changed.

Paul and Jean set sail from Montreal in May 1928 on the SS *Laurentic*, and they were given a rousing send-off by local Rotarians, who
in August were to perform the same office for the Davidson family
when they too embarked down the St Lawrence River, aboard the
Duchess of Atholl. This first stage of Paul's travels, however, was
to be completed even before Big Jim sailed, yet he was still in strange
territory on his return to Chicago in July, and he found International
Headquarters — with a room set aside for his personal use — moved
to 211 West Wacker Drive, taking up two floors of the new nineteen-
storey *Chicago Evening Post* building, part of a vast new development along the Chicago River, facing on the opposite bank the
rising Merchandise Mart, the largest business building in the world.
It was a long way, in just eighteen years, from one room in the First
National Bank on La Salle Street, next door to the Chicago Club's
office, and was eloquent of a phenomenal growth which had barely
begun. What the Founder thought of the transformation scene, we
do not know. Perhaps Ches Perry felt that a home-coming to such
palatial surroundings, following a triumphant tour of Europe,
would impress upon Paul Harris the need for him to step forward
once more into the limelight. If so, it proved to be a case of too
much too soon, since the following year Paul was felled by a massive coronary.

For the time being, however, it was glory all the way during the
first stage of his travels, his two-month tour to Europe; and it was
"Bonnie Jean" who was felled. A "nervous disorder" can be many
things, especially when a woman is forty-seven; medically it may

not be very important, strategically it can be vital. Certainly Jean Harris must have had many reservations about Paul's re-emergence from their settled and cosy hermitage at Comely Bank. In the event, she played no part in his grand tour, staying with her numerous relatives in Scotland in the bosom of the Kirk. Her brother, the Reverend John Youngson Thomson, was the Minister at Greenock, twenty-one miles down the Clyde from Glasgow, where their liner had docked, and Jean did not stir from there while her frail-looking husband revealed his living self to the Rotarians of the Old World and spoke at more than fifty Clubs in the United Kingdom and Europe in ten weeks. Perhaps Jean drew Paul's attention to the fact that buried at Greenock was "Highland Mary", the mistress who briefly succeeded the original Bonnie Jean in Robert Burns's affections, leaving Jean with the poet's twin bastards. At all events, Paul hastened off on his own to visit Ayrshire and the Burns country, no doubt quoting to her some favourite lines,

> There's not a bonnie flower that springs
> By fountain, shaw or green;
> There's not a bonnie bird that sings
> But minds me o' my Jean.

though both knew that the original Bonnie Jean disapproved of rapscallions quite as much as her modern version and married the bard at length to domesticate and finally bury him. Did either reflect that Mrs Burns's maiden name had been Jean Armour, of the same family whose later generations were to put Chicago on the map with the largest meat-packing company in the world? More immediately, did either reflect that what was happening was that Paul, on his own for the first time in eighteen years, was off on his second "folly"?

There is every sign that Paul enjoyed himself hugely, not to say blasphemously, worshipping "at the shrine of an immortal" amidst the very scenes of *Tam o'Shanter*, that rollicking, spooky tale of a drunkard who watched witches and warlocks dancing in the Kirk and took a fancy to one of the dancers, a girl with a "Cutty Sark", which did not mean she was carrying a model sailing-boat but that she was wearing only a short chemise. In the Kirk, indeed! And — even worse! — Paul wrote gleefully of how, as he "sat at the table where Bobby [Burns], Johnnie, Tam, and their companions were wont to sit, the thought came to me, 'What a wonderful nucleus for a Rotary Club' ". This was blasphemy compounded! Paul continued: "What a Rotarian he would have made, this man who so loved the companionship of his fellow-men that he combed the countryside for yokels with whom to commune." Scarcely the model for a Rotary Extension office, in Ches Perry's eyes (was that cold, commanding figure also reckoned a yokel?), or in the eyes of any of the makers of Rotary Rules and Constitutions which laid down guide-lines for desirable recruits. Nor can one envisage Paul Harris combing the countryside for yokels to chat with – in 1928, that is.

The man of advanced middle age who gambolled – there is no better word – about Ayrshire in 1928 was in spirit and fact the young lawyer who had delved eagerly into every aspect of Bohemian life in Chicago during the Gay Nineties, the college graduate who had lived from hand to mouth all over the United States and in Britain and Europe for five gloriously impulsive years, the boy who had been expelled from the Black River Academy. Grandmother Harris would have been most distressed; Grandfather Henry Bryan would have roared with laughter, especially since Ayrshire's greatest son, and the man who would make the most lasting impact upon the twentieth century, was to turn out to be not Robbie Burns at all. That man was a forty-seven-year-old professor of bacteriology who, even as Paul Harris gambolled, was in London observing a bacteria culture on his laboratory window-sill being killed by a green mould. But while Fleming was making a name for penicillin, Harris was near making a name for himself on a coach-tour of the Lake District, chatting up three pretty girls, one of whom gave him a lozenge for a coughing fit, after which "we became a happy party forthwith".

It was a perfectly respectable name, of course, that he was earning for himself. This was no figure of pathetic or tragic ridicule playing out a sexual farce, no elderly man of distinction besotted with young beauty – nothing like Aschenbach in *Death in Venice*, that sad pre-war creation of Thomas Mann, Founder Member of the Munich Club, who would shortly become the first Rotarian to win the Nobel Prize for Literature. This was a man rediscovering the springs of his own unquenchable youth and eager to share that discovery with everyone and anyone. The girls he met in the coach had no doubt been properly counselled on the matter of not accepting sweets from strangers, but nothing would have been said to them about not offering their own.

So for two months, off on a lone "folly" for the second and last time in his life, Paul had his marvellous, and marvellously happy, innocent party. A studio portrait done of him at the time by a London photographer, Reginald Baines, tells its own story. Instead of gaunt, tired features, seemingly raised with exhausting effort above a thick overcoat whose weight appears too great a burden for those coat-hanger shoulders, we are confronted with a sharp, vibrant face, alert with warmth and a knowing humour, eyes keen with an ironic but quite unmalicious enjoyment of himself and everything they see. One even doubts that he is wearing a Rotary badge. If he is, it is hidden beneath the perky orchid blossoming not only through his buttonhole but, one feels, throughout his whole being. He is a boy again.

The extraordinary truth is, that although this tour had been planned for two years, hardly any Rotarians in Great Britain, Ireland or on the Continent had been told Paul Harris was coming. There are several possible explanations for this. Perry and the Board of Directors may have been especially concerned about Jean's health. It was accepted that Paul's own health and well-being depended a great deal upon Jean, and they might have thought that they were putting enough of a strain upon his slow but steady climb back to equilibrium as it was. They also knew how he felt about a personal spotlight and were anxious that the desired effect upon Rotary's first Clubs abroad of the Founder's appearance in their midst should not be placed in jeopardy by his sudden panic or a repetition of his 1912 collapse, this time in full view of the world. On the other hand, too many flourishes on the heraldic trumpets — "making ready the way", using the sort of scriptural parallels which so easily sprang to mind in relation to Rotary and its Founder — might set him on too high a pedestal, either for Perry's comfort or his own, thus throwing years of careful structuring of organisational discipline into unseemly disorder. In other words, the manifestation of the fact of him, carefully controlled and underplayed from Chicago Headquarters, could serve to unite the fast-multiplying Clubs (there were nearly 3,000 of them, reaching now into Yugoslavia and Romania, not including those Big Jim Davidson had in the making), but, out of such control, it could result in an upsurge of evangelistic fervour far too destabilising for the Movement's current stage of development. In 1928 few could be aware, in Churchill's recollection of the time (he was then Chancellor of the Exchequer under Rudyard Kipling's cousin, Stanley Baldwin), that "the high-water mark of Europe's restoration" after the Locarno Pact was coming to an end, since "old antagonisms were but sleeping, and the drumbeat of new levies was already heard" and that "Europe was tranquil, as it had not been for twenty years, and was not to be for at least another twenty". But men of perception, very like Perry, applying himself to Rotary administration each and every day and often into the long hours of the night, could sense the fast-approaching chasms about to open under the stock-markets' frenzied, hysterical whirl spun to a nightmare pitch, dancing to death. Members of Rotary Clubs would be amongst those business men most affected by the financial earthquake; the Movement needed an urgent renewal and strengthening of its foundation.

To that extent, therefore, sending Paul was a gamble. And when Jean opted out as soon as the *Laurentic* berthed across the Atlantic, Perry must have been assailed by grave misgivings. He need not have been. Paul failed neither Ches Perry nor Rotary, because he did not fail himself. Because once again he was allowed to *be* himself. No advance notice delighted him; he detested fanfares. On the other hand, he also knew perfectly well that no one really enjoys the prospect of entertaining an angel unawares; it is a host's perpetual nightmare. Far better to dine with the devil you know than the angel you don't, and Paul's welcome round the world was in direct proportion to people's surprised and joyous recognition that he was indeed the devil they knew, being one of themselves. And his clear goodness helped them understand why they had become Rotarians, that theirs was a bearable secret after all. They hadn't realised there was a void until he filled it; they hadn't appreciated that the legend in his own lifetime was in fact themselves.

Even so, lack of warning of his coming could have meant a Second Coming, had he any ambitions to be a cult figure. As it was, his effect, again in New Testament terms, was more a resurrection and reinforcement of failing or neglectful and careless hearts. Suddenly he was a presence among the Rotary Clubs of Europe, galvanising *their* will to be themselves. And they knew him for their leader, for he had forsaken all to follow *them.* Unaffectedly modest, direct and simple in speech, his impact was unsensational to a startling degree. He purveyed the *idea* of Rotary simply by being there, he embodied its *ideals* in his manner quite as much as by his matter, but what he spoke of when called upon were the uncomplicated aims from which he had never wavered and which he had never intended to complicate: to reach for the essential friendliness of men and the unforced exercise of their essential goodness in concert.

He had no desire to make history. That indulgence was being very capably handled that year by Rotarian Senator Arthur Capper, of the Topeka Club in Kansas, who had introduced a Joint Resolution into Congress the previous month, urging his country to accept the invitation of France's Minister of Foreign Affairs, Aristide Briand, that their two nations agree to the "renunciation of war as an instrument of national policy", a resolution later that summer to become the Kellogg-Briand Pact, a pledge outlawing war eventually, which was signed by sixty-three nations. The US Secretary of State, Frank Kellogg, himself referred to it as an "international kiss" and time was soon to prove it a kiss in the dark, but in 1928 there was sufficient euphoria in Europe, in the light of American world peace initiatives and incredibly generous loans, not to say glamorous gangsters, to create an ideally receptive ambience for Rotary's American Founder. The King of the Belgians and the King of Italy were already Rotarians; so was a much more genuine autocrat, that pioneer of broadcasting John Reith of the BBC who allowed no one near a microphone who was not in full evening dress. That was history enough.

Vivian Carter, quoted on Harris at the beginning of this chapter, had by now built such a reputation as Editor of *The Rotary Wheel* that he had just been invited to Chicago to assume direction of *The Rotarian*, but he stayed on a few extra weeks in London to welcome Harris, of whom he also wrote: "If Chicago still deserves its reputation for hustle, none of its citizens lived up to it less . . . [his] movements, like his speech, were slow, quiet and unobtrusive . . . one could place him more easily in an old-world English village."

The rapscallion had had quite enough of the reclusive life for the moment, however, and he took to the great cities with unabashed glee. His "maiden speech" in Europe was to the Rotary Club of Birmingham on 4th June, an occasion which he was alone in regarding as a failure (no doubt exaggerating the standard of Club guest speakers) but where he enunciated the greatest Rotary ambition of all, one that only now, nearly sixty years later, is being seriously attempted: "I am not going to attempt to affect religious or national feeling, but I feel there ought to be some place where men can meet on an honest plane, without respect to those other considerations, and I want my Rotary to be that sanctuary."

From there, he was off to Belfast and then Dublin, where his favourite "wonder-working Irishman" had started Rotary overseas seventeen years before. Luckily, Ireland had at last entered a phase of relative calm, owing to the absence through murder and executions, mainly by fellow-countrymen, of its great names in the bloody struggle for independence from Britain. But Harris was introduced to one survivor, the Irish President, William Cosgrave, one of the rebels in the wartime Easter Rising which had demolished the Headquarters of the Dublin Rotary Club in 1916, and learned that the Rotarian making the introduction had once hunted Cosgrave as an officer in the British Army! Harris left convinced that all Irishmen were "wonder-working" but would not have been pleased to learn that his fellow-Rotarians among them thought of him "more as an apparition than the living founder", possibly because so few of their own new nation's founders were still alive. Perhaps it was to fortify the "apparition" that he was given two shillelaghs, one by the Dublin Club, one by the journalist who covered his visit. "It is easy to imagine", said the Dublin Club's report, "the heart-breaking disillusion which would have burst over us if a trace of the charlatan or the egoist or the spellbinder had been discovered" — in other words, if Paul Harris had combined into a stereotype of an Irishman. Fortunately, although Rotary was "too big now to suffer permanent damage even from its Founder", Paul was judged on balance "a man worthy of the cause".

Then it was back over the Irish Sea to the port where his love affair with all things British had begun midway through the "folly" period, thirty-five years before. Unaware perhaps that Liverpool was to a large degree an extension of Ireland, Paul was briefly disconcerted — having received many written pleas to pay the Club a visit — to find that he had been double-booked with another speaker on the great day, but quickly recovered (perhaps it was a spur) to deliver what he, and many others, regarded as one of his finest speeches on "Rotary and Its Critics". His listeners remarked on his "enthusiasm, his humour, his oratory . . . full of fire, softened with pathos and eminently practical . . . he seemed to radiate power with his every gesture . . . it was this suggestion of unbounded energy that impressed us most". Was this the recluse who had so long been self-exiled in his Comely Bank retreat outside Chicago? The appalled hermit who had shrunk from appearing at large meetings? Now, with every day, more years fell from him. With the poise, came again the air of relaxed authority that took himself and his Movement less earnestly than anybody else. "There are two kinds of criticism," he said. "There is the constructive critic and the destructive critic. The constructive critic is the Rotarian critic of other people and the destructive critic is the critic of Rotary." The tight, challenging smile swept over his audience and, after a hover of caution, the waves of laughter rose. His sense of fun was infectious; to many, and for the first time, came the realisation that the essential principle of belonging to a Rotary Club was nothing less than enjoyment.

Paul's energy redoubled. He seemed tireless, addressing meetings, large and small, from London to Leeds, Nottingham to Plymouth, from Bristol to Cardiff, often several in one day. Many Clubs were still surprised when he appeared; many more were surprised by his physical appearance. At 8.15 on the morning he reached Wales he had breakfast at Cardiff, then raced through London and spoke at a Canterbury lunch with words of a "breezy and at times highly humorous nature", and in the evening dined in Paris, gaily unmind-ful of pouring rain and the lack of a visa — deprived of "Bonnie Jean's" gentle reminders, he had forgotten to obtain one. Nothing daunted, he addressed the Rotary Club of Paris the following day, where he remarked the presence of "fifteen or twenty foreigners, most of whom were Americans".

By this stage of his European travels, of course, word had been sent that he was coming and Rotarians had flocked to the capital from all over France to hear him. There were twenty-one French Clubs at this time, ranging from Lyons to Marseilles, from Le Havre to Perpignan, from Bordeaux to Antibes. He was greeted with typical Gallic charm and fervour and cheerfully accepted the request to shorten his speech "because of the necessity of its being translated" whether for the benefit of the French or the Americans, is not clear. The Club President, who had conducted the luncheon with appropriate gusto, paid his distinguished guest the ultimate compliment by informing him that he had compelled him to leave the hospital bedside of his son, who had just suffered a skull fracture, to lead the hospitality, and the two parted in floods of tears, "as mists dispel the sun", Paul commented. After an obligatory visit to Versailles and the American war cemetery, Paul was thankfully on the train to Zurich. That summer Paris was so crowded with politicians talking about how to word the Kellogg Pact, and American expatriates trying to find which police cell Scott Fitzgerald was in or where he was drinking each day or fighting with his wife or Ernest Hemingway, that there wasn't a room to be had.

Since he had made a point of seeing the British contingent off while he was in London, the Founder of Rotary was of course perfectly well aware that the Nineteenth Convention of Rotary International was even then taking place 4,000 miles away, in Minneapolis, Minnesota, without him. The Board of Directors were taking no chances of his first reappearance stealing their own thunder in the second largest auditorium in the United States, but it did not trouble him. The Convention-goers would hear a Paul Harris Message as usual, prepared by Paul before he left, read by Ches Perry, and this time it contained these words:

> When civilization was young, men were content to eat and drink and live and die in the monotonous levels of life until there was born one whose eyes were frequently fixed on the distant hills. He was discontented with the dead levels of life, and often absented himself from his fellowmen. In course of time, it was learned that it had become his custom to climb the distant hills. . . . Though dead level men continued to proclaim reformers impractical dreamers, yet, somehow, the spirit of the hilltop began to get its grip on men whose abodes were on the dead levels.

It is difficult to believe that those 9,448 Rotarians and wives present, representing forty-four countries, paid a great deal of attention to these words. The reading of the Founder's Message had become an obligatory ritual – to adapt Voltaire, if the Movement hadn't had a Founder, it would have been necessary to invent one, which was largely what had happened – but those who listened could hardly have been in any doubt as to who had lifted his eyes and who were the "dead level men". There was, after all, only one hill in sight of Chicago and Comely Bank sat on top of it.

Still, most of the audience had never been to Chicago and the play that was to bring Chicago to the stages of the world, *The Front Page*, was still in rehearsal for later that summer. Far more familiar to the delegates than Paul Harris were the names of Chicago Rotarians Sheldon Clark and George Lytton, who the previous year had been official judges at the notorious second "long count" heavyweight championship bout between Jack Dempsey and Gene Tunney. At Minneapolis, Chicago itself figured in talk as the city where the Republicans were busy nominating Herbert Hoover for a presidency which would lead America into the Depression and Al Capone into gaol. Depression of the economy and suppression of gangsterism were not what delegates would have gathered, however, from the Message theme "Whither Are We Going and Why?" Nor were they what Paul meant. He knew exactly where he was going and why. He was seeing at first hand the flowering of his Rotary dream in Europe, and the only "why" he needed was his intention to enjoy himself in the process. What if most of those in Minneapolis would still not be sure whether Paul Harris was alive or dead, in hospital or worse? In the excitement of welcoming the first German delegation to a Convention, they were probably not too bothered. Nor was Paul, who was newly out of his Comely Bank gaol and alive as he hadn't been for years.

A tremendous reception awaited him at Zurich, where Rotary was already in the headlines, thanks to local Rotarian Walter Mittel-hozer, chief pilot and President of the Adastra Aviation Company, having just published an account of his pioneering flight, with three companions, on a hydroplane from Zurich right down across the African continent to Cape Horn. But Paul Harris's welcome owed nothing to Fred Teele's successor at the Zurich office, T.C. Thomsen, seemingly one of the few who still didn't know the Founder was coming – perhaps a Chicago-inspired ignorance, since he was to appear only fleetingly at Basle the next day to make sure Harris caught the train to Strasbourg. He wasn't missed, since a fellow-Rotarian from Chicago appeared and escorted Paul on a tour of "indescribably beautiful mountains and along gem-like lakes", keeping a welcoming party at Berne waiting two hours for the ravished rapscallion, who was not unduly contrite and enormously grateful to his guide, only recently sent over by Perry to give Thomsen some backbone at No 2 Pelikanstrasse. Swiss hospitality was lavish in the country's capital, though the Rotarians made sure Paul left for Basle in time to catch the train.

From Strasbourg, where he found a Club just getting organised, it was not long before Paul was sailing down the Rhine to Cologne, by which time he felt well into the heart of Europe, and knew it for a very different Europe from the confident continent of kings and emperors he had last visited over thirty years before. While the Paris he had recently left had been also playing host to the nego-tiators of the Pact of Paris outlawing war, the recent elections in Berlin had just welcomed its first Nazis into the Reichstag – only twelve among 491, it is true, but they included both Goebbels and Goering. They did not yet include Hitler, who not only had no visa (like Paul) but no passport either, having renounced his Austrian citizenship and been refused German naturalisation, a stateless condition he was to sustain unperturbed for another four years. Chamberlain at Munich and "peace in our time" was ten years away.

Harris travelled round a Europe where the swastika was as yet no bigger than a Brownshirt's fist, and seemingly abustle with rising prosperity like his own country. Soviet Russia, now Stalin had got rid of Trotsky, seemed to have put aside fomenting unrest abroad to concentrate on expanding its industry and murdering its farmers. Mussolini announced the destruction of the Mafia and death duties, a twin achievement which seemed to many Italians well worth the parallel destruction of universal franchise and free trade unions. Just a year before, San Francisco's Honorary Rotarian, King Albert of the Belgians, had welcomed Rotary's Eighteenth International Convention to Ostend, telling his huge audience of over 6,000 how "the great Rotarian ideal" would enhance international relation-ships, and this first European Convention of Rotary had finally accepted Britain's Aims and Objects plan into the whole world-wide scheme of the Movement.

It seems remarkable that neither then nor later during his official trips to Europe did Paul Harris visit Italy, though he spoke fondly throughout his life of his trips there to buy marble during his first "folly" years. By now, Italy had twenty-two Clubs and was already publishing two Rotary journals, one of which, *Realtà*, was printing the best speeches given to Clubs and had become a much-quoted "highbrow" review; so one would have expected him to be much attracted to the country which had given his brainchild such a warm welcome. Perhaps the organisers of Paul's itinerary felt that his informal, self-effacing manner might seem a let-down to the florid, colourful mode of Italian Rotary, whose style and élitism were unsurpassable. The Movement had become positively cluttered with royal highnesses, including the Duke of Aosta, the Duke of the Abruzzi, the Prince of Piedmont, the Count of Turin and the Prince of Udine, before King Victor Emmanuel III (one year younger than Harris) had himself joined, together with Crown Prince Umberto, destined to be Italy's last monarch.

Nor was the flavour entirely aristocratic in terms of senior members of the royal family. A non-Rotarian guest that summer at the Rotary Club of Venice observed with awe that he was surrounded by "thirty men who represented the acme of Italian culture.... There was the head of the greatest flour-manufacturing plant in Italy. There was the leading banker of the country. This man was famous in yachting circles. That man was a merchant prince of great wealth . . . only one of them was just a plain citizen of Venice" and, had the visitor known Venetians better, that plain citizen probably reckoned himself superior to the rest, even including the Club President, who happened to be Mussolini's Minister of Finance.

Moreover, Italy was a preserve which Ches Perry appeared to have allotted to himself. He was a frequent visitor and may have decided on Paul's not coming there after a visit the previous autumn when Perry had been granted an interview with Mussolini in Rome, after which Il Duce had expressed "his cordial satisfaction" to the press and Perry had expressed nothing. Or possibly Perry had been deterred by the news of the discovery by Austrian Customs officials, a few months before, of five freight cars loaded with machine-gun parts on their way from Italy to Hungary, an abortive smuggling effort which had shocked the League of Nations and scandalised Europe. Club activities in Italy often reflected the social status and cultural interests of members in their concern for community welfare, so that, though magnificent gifts to hospitals were not uncommon — Genoa, Leghorn and Milan were outstandingly generous in this respect — far more frequent were projects connected with furthering art exhibitions, music recitals, preservation of great sculptures and paintings, and so forth, an emphasis natural in the home of the Renaissance and only proving, after all, that Rotary service was infinitely adaptable. Of greater significance perhaps, in the light of Perry's session with Mussolini, was the successful Italian Rotary effort to have the next International Convention at Dallas agree to their Resolution that "Rotary affirms the duty of every citizen to address his activity towards the general interest, and first of all towards the progress and prosperity of his country". Doubtless the patriotic emphasis of such a Resolution kept Il Duce happy with Rotary for the time being. As would the official account of the growth of Rotary in the peninsula, in which Italian Rotarians announced that "Fascism is no longer a party, but the nation itself", and the participation by Clubs both in Mussolini's campaign to make farmers grow more wheat and drain the swamplands and to improve the national road network over which the automobile tyres of the Pirelli brothers — both members of Milan Rotary — purred increasingly.

With such diplomatic ballast, Rotary in Italy could get on with its idealistic and artistic contributions to the community (its position was soon to seem unassailable when the son of Count Ciano, Minister of Communications, and Member of the Rotary Club of Leghorn, married Mussolini's daughter and became Il Duce's Foreign Minister). Moreover, the new political alliance with Hungary — notwithstanding that arms-smuggling attempt — no doubt had the knock-on effect of encouraging Hungarian Rotary also. Though in founding the Budapest Club Doncaster had appropriately, and with typical blunt honesty, given that first Balkan Club two Rotary wheels of brass (Yorkshire vulgarism for money), the Movement had spread there not through commercial channels but entirely academic ones, in the university cities of Debrecen, Pécs and Szeged. As ever, Paul's wide-flung seeds were finding the appropriate nourishing beds in which to burgeon, however they might vary from the Chicago conception.

At all events, the Movement was now well entrenched in Italy and Hungary. In Germany, there might still be time for his personal appearance to influence the manner of growth. So Paul Harris turned north. The Rotary Club of Cologne had, like that of Strasbourg, been in existence for only a few weeks, but the calibre and financial status of its membership soon made him acutely aware, if he hadn't been before, of the higher social status and income level of most Rotarians in Europe compared with those of North America and the British Isles. For example, Cologne's Rotarian élite included the President and a professor of the 600-year-old University (abolished by the French under Napoleon but refounded after the First World War) and some of the most prominent business tycoons in the country. Whether concerned over the élite aspect or not, however, he may have reflected how strange it was that Cologne was the third and not the first German Rotary Club, since it boasted a traditional bulwark of the Movement, the oldest Chamber of Commerce in Western Europe. The city also contained industrial giants like Otto Wolf and great bankers like Schroder, who were cultivating friendships with the city's Nazi Gauleiter, Dr Robert Ley, a chemist who was rather too fond of drink and destined to be the future administrator of "Strength through Joy".

But after a happy three-day visit to Dutch Rotary Clubs, in company with Anton Berkade, the paternalistic biscuit manufacturer who had introduced the Movement to Holland nine years before, after a visit to America, Paul was back as the guest of Rotary's most important acquisition since the Armistice – the first Club in Germany, at Hamburg. For this visit, Special Commissioner Thomsen had at last appeared on the scene to brief the Founder, and we can be sure his advice was similar to views he had expressed in *The Rotary Wheel* earlier that year – for example:

> The last and most important development of Rotary is the opening up of Clubs in Germany . . . and let us hope that Europe is approaching the dawn of a new era . . . the time has come for realising to the full some of our mistakes, and for making up our minds not to repeat them . . . now that we have raised trade and other barriers between many countries and practically are living – or rather starving – in water-tight compartments. . . .

One cannot but feel that the Dane sensed strongly the black undercurrents already flowing beneath the superficial surface of calm which now overlay the immediate post-war turbulence of Europe. The President of the Hamburg Club, Wilhelm Cuno, was not there to welcome Paul. Cuno, General Manager of the thriving Hamburg-Amerika Line, was, as we have noted in a previous chapter, one of those being courted by Nazi treasurers, like his peers in Cologne, but he was hedging his bets in masterly fashion, naming his new ship the *New York* and even now was still absent in Minneapolis, telling the Convention there, "in spite of our keeping away from political and religious questions, our living of Rotary ideals means to sacrifice ourselves, not only in our daily life, but also in our duties as obedient citizens, as devoted men of our nation. . . . "

Paul soon noticed a striking similarity in the behaviour of "the highest ranks of cultural and business life in Germany", in Hamburg as in Cologne. Neither group had the slightest intention of asking him to speak. Since he could scarcely rise without invitation, he had resigned himself to this strange Teutonic gag, but Thomsen was enraged. No Club President being there, the Dane reached across the table and seized the gavel, hammered for silence and introduced Harris himself to the astonished members. Equally astonished, Harris was slow to rise in the silence, said very little when he did and hastily resumed his seat. Of this disturbing episode in his triumphal tour, he wrote soon after: "Was it that the German Rotarians were averse to hearing speeches? I am satisfied it was not." His astonishment had not blunted his irony, which might have had an even sharper edge to it had he been aware that the widow of a Hamburg industrialist had just rented her holiday villa at Berchtesgaden for the equivalent of $25 a month to a stateless radical, an ex-corporal of a Bavarian regiment, who wanted somewhere quiet to dictate a book to Rudolf Hess, all about his struggles, admiration of the British Empire and hatred of Jews.

The day following his visit to Hamburg Paul Harris was back in England, and the embarrassments there and at Cologne were forgotten in the excitements of the most stirring day of Paul's solo travels. Landing at Grimsby in Lincolnshire, the great fishing port which had once been the chief landing-place for Thomsen's Viking ancestors, Paul proceeded to make two great speeches on 5th July — he had spent America's Independence Day on the North Sea. One was to 2,000 Rotarians in Clumber Park, seat of the Duke of Newcastle, and the other at eleven that night to a second huge gathering at Doncaster.

He was a man come into his own. Peter Thomason, wartime President of the then British Association of Rotary Clubs, who had interrupted his period in office to serve in the trenches (see Chapter Eight), called the occasion "a day of ecstasy". Paul had walked across the Park through a lane of cheering crowds and spoken from a platform in their midst, a riveting, magnetic figure in the slightly old-fashioned cutaway coat that suited his lean figure, turning this way and that so that all could see and hear him. Typically, "he hardly mentioned Rotary", said a reporter. He didn't need to; after all, he *was* Rotary. His words were "drily humorous, whimsical, splashed with witticisms, abounding in jokes . . . yet through them all shone the spirit and the personality of the man himself".

Back in Scotland where he was reunited with his "Bonnie Jean" who had been spending her time attending religious conferences with her brother and brother-in-law, he found himself slightly upstaged by the beautifully timed entrance of canny Harry Lauder into the Glasgow Club just as Paul was well launched into his address. Quite correctly, Paul referred to this slyly as "an intrusion" by the little music-hall knight, but he didn't let it put him off his stride. At Edinburgh, Paul sat for a portrait bust and then set sail for home from Greenock.

He was still briefly his own man, for Jean stayed behind, and Paul wrote in his report, as he crossed the Atlantic: "while I had been on the herein described Rotarian debauch, she had been on a mild-mannered Presbyterian orgy. . . . I had hoped that she would remain in Scotland for two or three months longer".

Some hope! Jean Harris had doubtless taken full note of the change his travels had effected in her husband and took ship after the rapscallion only a fortnight later. He had, after all, just come back from Germany, and perhaps the terrible news had reached her from Berlin, not of Goering and Goebbels, but of her fellow-Scot, Ramsay MacDonald, the Labour leader, a great supporter of Rotary and the common man, who had sent a message himself to Minneapolis: "Today we are striving as we have never striven hitherto to find the way to peace." What MacDonald was striving for in Berlin that summer, however, was not so much the peace of nations as peace of mind, by getting back some pornographic letters he had written to a former girl-friend. He apparently succeeded, thanks to his companion; and since that companion was Oswald Mosley, about to launch Fascism in Britain, it is perhaps scarcely surprising. But it enabled MacDonald to undertake a second term as Prime Minister the following year with a clear conscience, if that is not a contradiction in terms.

By 1932 Paul Harris was again in Europe and again on his own. But before that he had recovered astonishingly quickly from the heart attack of 1929 (suffered about the same time as seven more famous heart attacks in the St Valentine's Day Massacre which made Capone King of Chicago), though it could have served as excuse enough — his own or that of others — to explain his continued non-appearance at great Rotary International gatherings, including even the 1930 Convention in Chicago, held but a few miles from his front door, which celebrated his brainchild's Silver Jubilee. The managers of Headquarters indeed planned that it should. But once brought back from exile, once subjected to the invigorating experience of that first stage of his travels in Europe, he was not so easily shunted aside again. Perhaps Ches Perry realised this when he passed over the duty of reading Paul's Annual Message to the Jubilee Convention Chairman, this explanation having been given: "Paul has felt that he would be able to deliver his message in person. To our most sincere regret, however, the condition of his health again makes that impossible."

Or maybe Chesley Perry had seen the Message beforehand, for the words rang with a renewed and uncompromising vitality of vision. They told his audience bluntly that Rotary was in danger of seizing up with too many rules, of not being ready to change as it grew. A favourite ideal was "Can more than one Rotary Club be successfully maintained in a city?" The answer had traditionally always been "No", but "The Rotarians of the City of London . . . scrapped a useless precedent that stood in the way of their natural and proper growth, thereby putting themselves in numerical ascendancy of the entire Rotary world." The Message added: "Rotary is a social movement and as such is in danger of the blighting efforts of precedent. It has already suffered from the plague."

Worse was to follow. It was suddenly discovered that Mr and Mrs Harris were in the hall and the whole audience cheered and stood as they were escorted to the platform. The International President for that year, Gene Newson, hastily stepped forward to the microphone to say "Gentlemen, it is regretted greatly that Paul can't speak to you this morning" — but he was too late, and the voice of Paul Harris rang out to a Convention for the first time in eighteen years. The face was thin and pale, but the words, slowly and deliberately chosen, were those of an unrepentant rapscallion still: "I have tried to think what is there that I can say to you in a sentence or so that will be of more interest to you than any other thing that I might possibly say." He soon thought of it. Behind him and around him the organisation men held their breath, and one likes to think that Perry smiled a quiet smile. Suddenly, Paul challenged them: "Well, how do you like it now?" He belonged far more with the men on the floor than with those on the platform and they knew it. A storm of applause greeted his mischievous query, and he barely got another sentence out as concern for his health became overpowering and he was hauled out of sight.

Seventeen of the original Rotarians of 1905 were still around and most of them posed for a group photograph. It unfortunately included neither Paul Harris nor Silvester Schiele, who had shared that memorable spaghetti dinner at Madame Galli's. But still, it did include Harry Ruggles, the "song" man, and Al White, the man who had taken "Rotary One" out of rotating offices and into the Sherman Hotel.

All of which suggests that Paul attended the remainder of the sessions only sparingly, for health reasons certainly, but also perhaps because he was more conscious than most that Rotary was rejoicing in a mirage. True, hats were off to mourn the "passing" of eighteen Clubs because of the Depression, but no reference was made to the nation-wide stock-market loss, now rapidly mounting to $50 billion, nor to the rising tide of unemployment in the United States, then passing 10 million and still going up, nor to the fact that Chicago itself was bankrupt, nor to the national concern over catastrophically rising crime-rates, epitomised by Capone's daily drive through cheering Chicago crowds in his new armoured car. Rotary's home town was $300,000 in the red, and a lot of that red was on the sidewalks — or on garage floors over which Capone's business competitors were hung from meat-hooks and "persuaded" with cattle-prods.

Of course, Chicago Rotarians themselves were not deluded, even while attempting, in the cause of soothing anxieties, to delude others. As taxpayers, they knew that Capone's various rackets were costing them $136 million a year, or $45 for every man, woman and child in the "Windy City". As a concerned electorate, the members of Rotary Number One couldn't help knowing that the recent primary elections (first stage in the American system for choosing party teams to fight for the White House) had become known by everyone as the "Pineapple Primary" because a lethal blizzard of hand-grenades, or "pineapples", had been lobbed into homes and offices to convince wavering supporters and beach the floating vote. Voices were even raised in the US Senate that American troops, who were stationed at that time in Nicaragua to prevent civil war, would be better employed in Chicago. And though Chicago Club President Floyd L. Bateman was busy assuring the Rotary world that visitors would find the city "safe and healthfully stimulating", his fellow-Club member Frank J. Loesch, heading the city's Crime Commission, was coining the celebrated label "Public Enemy" (a tag which the strutting, vicious, puffed-up millionaire hoodlums hated) as part of his lifelong crusade against the glamorisation of crime, political corruption, wholesale intimidation and brutal destruction, for which he later received the Chicago Rotary Merit Award. As Special Assistant Attorney-General, Loesch had once told the Club, "the alliance between crime and politics is shown by the fact out of 149 gang murders . . . there has not been a single conviction". But his name was not among the Convention speakers.

One name that was there in 1930 served to remind Jubilee celebrants of the heroic work Jim Davidson was doing in the Orient. This was Rotarian Prince Iyesato Tokugawa, head of the family which as Shoguns had once ruled Japan for two centuries, and Paul Harris agreed to have his picture taken with this head of the Japanese House of Peers. As for Harris himself, he knew for sure that the success of his 1928 trip abroad had made a lasting impact on the Movement back in its country of origin, and that his compatriot fellow-Rotarians were proud of him, when the entire Silver Jubilee Convention rose to its feet and remained standing till their Founder – himself "found" once more – had left the hall. The lesson was not lost on him, or on Ches Perry, or on Jean.

CHAPTER SIXTEEN

Travels of a Boy King — 2

Rotary Bruder, auf zur Arbeit!
Rotary Bruder, auf zur Tat!
Wo helfen du kannst, greif zu!
Erst kommt der Dienst dann Du!
Rotary Bruder, auf zur Arbeit!

Rotary Hymn by Dr Fritz
Lohner-Heda/Franz Lehár

Before Paul's first post-war trip to Europe concern had been growing, and it had found strong vocal expression in the islands of
Rotary's original foreign foothold, that some way had been lost.
Two English Rotarian clergymen expressed the view in candid
terms. In Halifax, Yorkshire, the Reverend L.J. Hines had said,
"Very soon Rotary will have to prove to the world whether it
means anything, not as a stunt, but as a going concern. One of the
greatest challenges to Rotary is to prove that the future of the
world can be entrusted to middle age." Barely had Ches Perry
harboured happy visions of ancient times when such heresies might
be burned out at the stake, when the Reverend T.W. Riddle of
Plymouth, Devon, pronounced, "The Rotary Movement on the
whole . . . is a little elderly, somewhat self-righteous, very diffuse,
alarmingly incoherent, by no means certain as to its goals, and
distressingly dubious as to its route." Now, however, in the wake
of Paul's European visit and as the Depression loomed large, the
Rotary faith took new heart. The President of the Dublin Rotary
Club was saying, "there is a change of feeling in Ireland, and the
barriers which have hitherto separated those of differing classes and
creeds are being broken down . . . the fact that in Rotary men
differing in religion and in politics can meet week after week on a

common footing of friendship, and can work together without friction, is one of the most hopeful signs of the times".

From Vienna, Elsa Carlyle Smythe, an Australian working for a campaign to celebrate "Good Will Day" amidst old enemies, wrote: "I can assert, and with profound conviction, that if ever the country dance of hate ceases in Europe, one of the strongest factors in stopping the music will be the quiet, steady influence of the Rotary Club." If this were indeed likely to be the case, it was undeniably providential that the next Rotary International Convention was held at Vienna, source of this rather overripe tribute. But Paul Harris was not there. It was as well perhaps that he stayed at home in 1931, for had he travelled in the British Isles first, as he always did, he would have found that his Movement's most prominent political enthusiast, Ramsay MacDonald, the British Prime Minister, was busy yet again severing connections with an old love. This time it was not just a Berlin flapper, but the entire Labour Party, which proceeded to expel him when he ventured to form a National Coalition Government (consisting chiefly of the Tory class enemy) and then to cut the dole money for more than 2 million unemployed, provoking riots in London, Liverpool and Glasgow and a naval mutiny at Invergordon! Many recalled Disraeli's famous saying that England did not love coalitions — which is presumably why that great leader became a Christian — but " Dizzy" had overlooked the coalition of misery, at which the English excel. As for Herr Hitler, he was forgetting that (with good historical reason) foreigners hated British coalitions even more than the British did, since British strength in war is forged from them, had always been, and soon would be again.

However, excitement and upheavals were not lacking outside the huge picture-window at Comely Bank either, where Paul and Jean sat, one each side, for part of every day. Not only was the drama of Al Capone's conviction and final removal from the Chicago scene being enacted (Capone claimed indignantly that because of the distasteful publicity, he'd received a letter from a suburban housewife in England offering him £100, plus expenses, to come over and bump off her neighbour!), but a less vicious, though far greater, crook, the London-born Sam Insull (see Chapter One) was seeing the Depression bringing dramatic collapse to his financial empire. Even so, at a public hearing, the banks admitted that Insull's credit was still better than the "Windy City's". Because people needed cheering up, this year also saw the apotheosis of jazz which New Orleans in the twenties had sold up the river to Chicago. Louis "Satchmo" Armstrong had already made some of his finest recordings with several versions of his group, the "Hot Five", and was about to embark on tours to Europe, while Chicago-born Benny Goodman's star was rapidly rising through various orchestras, raising him to the throne of King of Swing. A public opinion poll of 1932 showed that the average citizen of Chicago was mostly aware of names in the following fields: (1) film actors, (2) gangsters, (3) athletes, (4) politicians, (5) musicians, (6) big-business executives, (7) stage actors, (8) radio actors, (9) journalists, and (10) film directors. Plenty of headline drama there, without looking to Europe.

Still, we may doubt that these were Paul Harris's priorities, for just around the corner from Rotary Headquarters on Wacker Drive the *Chicago Times* described a constant derelict population of 1,500 haunted, jobless men, waiting for food, all of whom "carried huge rolls of old newspapers or lay covered by the sprawling black and white sheets". And an English visitor to New York, G.K. Chesterton, brought him even more perturbation with a terrible blast at Rotary:

> It is a form of comradeship that is gross, common, vainglorious, blatant, sentimental and, in a word, caddish. . . . There is something vulgar about such companionship. It lacks spiritual dignity. . . . Why is there this debasement of human friendship?. . . Two Rotarians complimenting each other are like two savages rubbing noses. . . . Without the admiration of something better than ourselves or each other, we become a mutual admiration society and a very paltry collection of snobs.

The vehemence of this diatribe can be only partially ascribed to the barbarous habit of breakfast meetings (Chesterton had a nice appreciation of the time and place for dining), to which even then Americans were addicted, for it was at one such function that Chesterton had made his speech. And only partially to the contrast which Chesterton sensed between complacent Rotary affluence and the surrounding gloom of business failure and social despair. For, running throughout his address, was the theme of hostile Catholicism: "The Catholic Church exists, among other things, to maintain the concept of human dignity in what may be called 'This Rotarian Age'."

Such sectarian vehemence can be attributed to the fact that, for part of his visit, Chesterton was undertaking a lectureship at Notre Dame University, famous Catholic establishment of advanced education and very superior football teams. But the impact of shock was as calculated and effective as those delivered by Oscar Wilde in the 1880s. Like Wilde a big man (of six feet two inches), Chesterton much enjoyed deliberately tempting, and then not living up to, the fond hopes of his detractors. Wilde in San Francisco drank everyone else under the table. On a similar speech-making visit, so did Chesterton. And when the latter returned from the West Coast, he quite demolished Clarence Darrow in debate, leaving the great trial lawyer (Paul Harris's erstwhile office neighbour and recent convert to Rotarianism) floundering. And however virulent – if somewhat theatrical – he was in voicing his opposition to Rotary, he more than compensated for it in another speech he made during the same visit in 1931. In this he uncannily predicted that the next world war would happen "when Germany tries to monkey about with the frontiers of Poland". Yet his more profound prophecy was his gibe about Rotary, since the twentieth century has seen it translated into an accolade more accurate than Chesterton dreamed of.

This brilliant star convert to Rome was an ideal choice for delivery of such an anti-Rotary broadside in the land from which the Vatican derived most of its revenue and where its most well-known adherents were the Irish and Sicilian mobsters – who were also unfortunately based in Chicago. Rome's antagonism was based in part on the widespread confusion that existed in Europe between Rotary and Freemasonry (and indeed many European Rotarians belonged to both), as a result of which priests, by a directive of the Sacred Consistorial Congregation, were now forbidden to join Rotary Clubs. The hostility was to come to a head twenty years later, before being laid to rest, but meanwhile this speech would have caused much distress to Paul Harris's "Bonnie Presbyterian". Chesterton went on to compare Rotarians unfavourably with "the great saints and heroes of the Franciscan order". But even St Francis (whose name, after all, was given to Rotary Number Two) would have been hard put to it to greet the broadside with the mild smiling tolerance of Paul Harris, who agreed there was much to criticise, took the label as a compliment and deftly turned the tables on G.K.C. by naming his next book *This Rotarian Age.* And today, a Jesuit priest has held office as a District Governor in Italian Rotary.

In March, the extraordinary man who had truly and single-handedly justified the validity of that label "Rotarian Age" in the Middle and Far East, at last came home to his adopted country, Canada. Big Jim Davidson, accompanied by his wife and daughter, was given a tremendous welcome by Rotarians in Vancouver, at a gathering of over 600, conscious of their historic place in cheering the safe return of the "Marco Polo of Rotary". Even the cool, calm breast of Ches Perry was stirred and he hastened northward across the continent to be present. Davidson was persuaded to return to

Chicago with the General Secretary, to give a report on his journey in person to the Board of Directors and to meet once again his revered "source of the great river". But the plan for him to go on from there with Perry to make a triumphant appearance in Vienna (a plan which had no doubt contributed to Harris's decision not to attend, and thus allow Davidson his proper limelight) proved not possible of fulfilment. Big Jim's task was done; his life nearly so.

Life was nearly over that year also for another English visitor to New York, also on a lecture tour, on whom the city had an even more drastic effect. There the fifty-seven-year-old Winston Churchill (like Chesterton, only six years younger than Paul Harris) was run down by a taxi, whose hapless driver – Churchill, as usual, was crossing against the light – came within a very black ace of handing the Western world to Hitler on a plate.

Perry therefore went on to Austria without the distraction of either Big Jim or Paul (making another unscheduled appearance on the platform) to throw awry the controlled running order of events – as Paul's unexpected, though brief, speech at Chicago had done the year before. The "builder" was back in his role of reading the Founder's Message, which included this passage: ". . . the world is not so much in need of great production as it is in need of a right-about-face in its view of life. The glorification of the material has been tried and found wanting". Ches was probably relieved Paul was not present to make any mischievous elaboration on the theme. In the event, the glamour of Vienna, host to the 1931 Convention, quite overwhelmed the personalities present and the Austrian Government issued the first stamps ever minted in honour of Rotary. An aura of sweetness quite literally held the stage as the fifty-seven nations represented (another eleven had sent no delegates) unanimously elected its first European International President, Sydney Pascall of the London Club, who was also at that time the most famous sweet manufacturer in the British Empire. The Convention highlight was a gala performance of *The Merry Widow*, which had happily burst upon the world in the same year as Rotary, conducted by the composer himself, Rotarian Franz Lehár of the Vienna Club, at the Theater an de Wien, the same theatre where the famous melodies were first heard in 1905. Lehár himself was not of course Austrian at all but Hungarian and, not to be outdone, the Rotary Club of New York enrolled that year another Hungarian-born genius of operetta, Sigmund Romberg (composer of *The Desert Song, The Student Prince*, etc.).

A message from Ramsay MacDonald followed right after Paul's, never mind that in the eyes of his fellow-politicians he was no longer the powerful and influential statesman Rotary took him to be: "... the fact that Rotary's aim is to promote mutual understanding encourages me to hope that the work of the Convention in the economic sphere will have important results, for I am convinced that it is only by accepting the principle of give-and-take that we will succeed". MacDonald's notion of give and take was soon apparent: it was to give the British no chance whatever to increase their relatively small stockpile of armaments, to inhibit French rearmament, and to take away all constraints upon the Germans, who were to be allowed to increase armaments without limit – including matching the British submarine fleet up to 100 per cent – which was almost a prescription for suicide.

Though this was Rotary International's twenty-second Convention, it was the first truly to merit the name, and those who attended it were throughout made deliberately conscious of their growing internationalism. The venue was a city redolent of the history of many nations and past empires – the organisers called it, in fact, Rotary's own Congress of Vienna, though the tyrant-shadow lurking offstage was a good deal nearer this time than Elba – and though English was the official language, most of the speakers were European and many tongues were spoken. Sydney Pascall accepted his presidency in three, while T.C. Thomsen – now an Honorary General Commissioner for Rotary – reappeared from Copenhagen to speak in no less than ten! A special presentation was put on to demonstrate the usages of Esperanto at the instigation of Sir Charles Mander, a Past President of RIBI, but, though this universal language has always possessed a strong and persistent lobby in Rotary, it has never won official approval for use in the Movement. This is certainly not because the first book explaining Esperanto was written in Russian (the language of its inventor), or because its publication coincided with the start of Lenin's university career, both in law, in student agitation and immediate expulsion – though any of these reasons might have sufficed had Rotarians been aware of them. Since Western nations have long understood from St Paul that speaking with the tongues of men and angels avails them nothing without charity, it has naturally occurred to many Rotarians from time to time that the pentecostal gift cannot but advance the cause of those with impeccable charities already in mind. But others have never forgotten that some of the world's longest and greatest hatreds have been sustained between men who understand one another, and that some of the cruellest wars in history have been fought between armies with nothing in common but the same language. And so Rotary Conventions, like so many others, have continued to enjoy the benefits of simultaneous translation facilities, those with ears to hear accepting headphones,

willing victims to the all-conquering alienation thrust upon us by
the communications industry. In Vienna, of course, everyone spoke
Lehár. Unfortunately, Hitler spoke Wagner.

In spite of a fervent address on disarmament by the distinguished
British statesman, Viscount Cecil of Chelwood, a principal founder
of the League of Nations and future Nobel Peace Prize-winner,
hindsight shows us that the most prescient words uttered at the
Convention were from a Viennese Rotarian, Count Coudenhove-
Kalergi, founder of the less ambitious but no less unsuccessful Pan
Europa Movement, who declared, "The union of Europe has
become essential, for only by this means can Europe combat the
three dangers which threaten her existence: a new war, general
misery and Bolshevism. The three are intimately related."

Among other speeches we may note with interest that of a
Rotary International Director, Howard Selby of Florida, in which
he described a visit he had made to the Havana Club in Cuba:
" . . . the social aspects of the visit were most delightful but the
ignorance of some of us at least toward Cuban history was appalling.
Since that visit we have learned . . . to better appreciate the idealism
which permeates the life of our Cuban friends". This bonus of
Rotary fellowship did not, alas, mean that the speaker understood
better the services of Secretary Perry there during the Spanish-
American War — if Ches were blushing, he blushed in vain — but
neither did it mean that Selby was aware of the ruthless dictatorship which then terrorised the island under Machado (whose brother
was at the Convention as both a Havana Rotarian and International
Director of the Movement), even though Florida was as full of
Cuban refugees from the tortures, repression and executions as they
are today, two dictators on.

We may also note the speech given by Rotarian Shinjiro Matsuyama, a member, oddly enough, of the London Club, since he was a
Councillor at the Japanese Embassy there. He was remarkably
frank, for those who had ears to hear (as indeed was the author of
Mein Kampf, for those who had eyes to read), by stressing that, if
the League of Nations was to do any good, it would not do so by
emphasising disarmament but by underlining economic problems.
"Peace cannot be assured simply by Disarmament," he said. "Economic conditions are the root of the trouble. . . . The record of
the history of the world shows that most countries in earlier times
took advantage of their arms not merely for defensive purposes,
but very often as a means to advance their economic prosperity
and expansion." He was drawing a blueprint. Three months later,
the Japanese Army invaded Manchuria in response to a Chinese
economic boycott, driving through Mukden where Jim Davidson

had been hosted by the Rotary Club earlier that year and, in effect, beginning the chain-reaction of the Second World War.

But Congress, just like that previous historic Vienna Congress in 1915, danced! And why not? Lehár's latest operetta, which was also performed for the Convention, was *Land of Smiles*. And with sessions in the great Concert House, a reception and dance at the former Imperial Palace, the Hofburg, performances by the State Opera and Vienna Symphony Orchestra in the park, all-night roistering in starlit wine-gardens till dawn, topped by a "coffee-party" in the grounds of the Summer Palace of Schönbrunn, Rotary was at last made to feel thoroughly at home in Europe. Fortunately, the ravished 4,000 at the Convention were mostly unaware that the generous *Gemütlichkeit* was being indirectly sponsored by the Bank of England which had just a week before loaned 150 million schillings to the Austrian National Bank, thus staving off the country's imminent economic collapse, though not the Government's. Indeed, Chancellor Dr Karl Buresch, who personally welcomed the Rotarians, had been in office for only twenty-four hours when he did so, a sign of the importance Vienna attached to the coming of this immense world gathering.

"Viennese hospitality – who has not heard of it?" exclaimed Sydney Pascall, when at least the waltzing had to stop. All fifty-seven nations represented there had heard of it soon enough when the Rotarians returned home, but most did not hear the rumblings of financial disaster that would soon spread from Austria right through Europe, bringing political disaster in its wake. Next time the International Convention was to come to Europe, only six years later, Rotary was dying fast under the Nazi boot – along with much else. Three-quarter time beat in ghastly, but unperturbed, counterpoint, with no-quarter time.

It was not, however, in its lack of foresight regarding totalitarianism that Rotary suddenly found itself vulnerable. It had, after all, come into the arena of international understanding as a secondary – if, in the long run, far more important – "avenue of service". Its primary goal had always been the bringing of ethical business practices into the trading and commercial worlds of capitalism, and this was where its claims seemed all at once absurd. No sooner was it claiming some advances for its much-discussed Code of Ethics than its leading figures found themselves as much surprised by the collapse of the world's stock-markets as any lesser breed "without the law", as Kipling had expressed it of old-fashioned empires.

As the Movement had multiplied its colonies of compassions, recruits in the world's great cities and centres of commerce had always been culled from the top echelons of business. Yet just before Rotarian Herbert Hoover announced "the final triumph over poverty" and then forgot to duck, as the whole boiling mess of the Great Crash poured in a torrent of disintegrating fortunes through the windows of the Oval Room and flooded the White House, Rotarian Alberto Pirelli, the newly elected President of the International Chamber of Commerce, declared: " . . . the scientific study of production and marketing, the forecasting of the movements and supply of raw materials is undoubtedly flattening out the curve of the so-called business cycles . . . we are every day getting farther and farther away from periodically recurring extremes of panic and prosperity". Alas, the only sure flattening out was soon being done at his Milan factory, while the seemingly unstoppable spin of the Golden Wheel was everywhere being battered by bursts of exploding punctures and flying rubber.

It was true that, just as the primary impetus for the Aims and Objects of Rotary International had come from England, so did the essential aims and objects of Roosevelt, about to take the Depression by the scruff of the neck, derive from the English economist, John Maynard Keynes. But Keynes was no Rotarian, and most Rotary business men were as self-deceived as were most non-Rotarians about the financial and political future. Indeed, they had only the dubious and depressing enlightenment of Sir Oswald Mosley, whose Blackshirt Fascist thugs were smashing through the East End at this time. He told them in the pages of British Rotary's new literary journal *Service in Life and Work* that the United States had now substituted for Lincoln's government of the people, by the people and for the people, the New Deal's "government of the people by the bankers for the Jews", while in Britain liberty meant only "the futile self-advertisement of parliamentary debate, while industry declines and unemployment rises . . . the liberty of the great press lords to stuff the people's minds with lies, in order to destroy dynamic movements [he referred, of course, to Fascism not Rotary] and to keep things as they are in the interests of a comfortable few who batten and grow fat on the decadence of a nation".

The words are sadly familiar today, only they are heard more often through more media. Our financial soothsayers, all too available now, are no different from the augurs then and indeed in ancient times — and they still prophesy according to the way the wind blows, with neighbouring oracles, just as the Greeks and Romans did of old, having precisely opposing rules even for that! If one gazes into the crystal balls of a stockbroker's eyes long enough, whoever he is, one tends only to see red.

In the year 1932 alone, when Paul and Jean Harris resumed their travels for Rotary, twenty-seven Clubs and 2,000 members vanished from the international roster under the economic blizzard, and only five years remained before the first totalitarian fist smashed down. Yet in between came a golden pause of progress for the Movement, a brief era of seeming tranquillity in the West which was heralded by a Club being formed in Latvia ten years after that country gained its independence from Lenin's Russia and just ten years before Stalin's Russia swallowed it back. And within that pause, while Latvia blossomed in the eye of the storm, the Founder of Rotary, between the ages of sixty-four and sixty-eight, did some "wonder-working" of his own.

Coming back to Europe in 1932 Paul was aware that his job this time was the business of re-establishing the Movement, and not just himself as four years previously. Not just the credibility of the Movement, either, but that of Chicago, for Hollywood was now at its zenith and the world saw the United States through the eyes of the "picture palace", which probably had more truth in them at this time than at any other. The previous year, Al Capone, trapped at last on income-tax evasion, had finally been sent to prison for ten years, but the first, perhaps the best, film about his rise and fall, the great movie classic *Scarface* — a nickname no one had ever dared use in Capone's hearing — was making the reputation of Paul Muni (Austrian-born, Chicago-educated) and *Public Enemy* was doing the same for James Cagney. "Service Above Self" and "He Profits Most Who Serves Best" were in danger of being eclipsed by two other phrases, also both born in Chicago, "Never Give a Sucker an Even Break" and "Taken for a Ride", but the Rotary slogans unfortunately never made the movies!

In the first issue that year of *Service in Life and Work* these lines appeared:

> They are starving, they are freezing in Chicago,
>   There is too much oil in Oklahoma;
> In Nebraska, broke and beat,
> They are burning "surplus wheat"
>   And the wind wafts Chicago the aroma.

But another aroma had at last vanished. With Capone gone, "Kaiser Bill" Thompson's reign as Mayor of Chicago was over, too, and the *Chicago Tribune* gave him a candid farewell: "For Chicago, Thompson has meant filth, corruption, obscenity, idiocy and bankruptcy. He has given the city an international reputation for moronic buffoonery, barbaric crime, triumphant hoodlumism, unchecked graft and dejected citizenship." Just before the start of Prohibition, he had also been Honorary Chairman of the Rotary Club's first Boys' Week Committee, but his subsequent career had rather over-balanced the scales in his disfavour. Meanwhile, Ches Perry's Head-quarters on Wacker Drive was part of a city development that had built over and obliterated large parts of the city which had provided the seedy background of some of the worst incidents of the gangster-ridden years, so there was new hope.

Chicago now also redeemed itself in another spectacular way, for as Paul Harris started on his travels again, Franklin Delano Roose-velt was nominated as Presidental Candidate in a great Democratic Convention there (where his cousin, Teddy, had also been nomi-nated, as had Abraham Lincoln). So, from the city which had profited most from the evils of Prohibition and then been bank-rupted by the Depression, came the first signs that the bad years were over, though, during the subsequent campaign, Chicago's new "clean-up" Mayor, Anton Cermak, was gunned down in public during a political rally by a maniac trying to assassinate Roosevelt. Or was he? Granted the scene of the killing was not Chicago, but Miami; yet not far away was Capone's sumptuous island mansion, where he had "retired" just before arrest and where he was to spend the last years of his life. And in December of that year Cermak's personal bodyguard shot Capone's closest aid in revenge.

Meanwhile, in Europe's twilight, Paul used a visit to the Hague, where he was a delegate to an International Congress on Compara-tive Law (having left "Bonnie Jean" in Scotland once more – a Law Congress scarcely smacked of "folly"), as a springboard for a series of appearances in Northern European Clubs. Though the world-wide Depression had now cost Rotary International the demise of twenty-seven Clubs, Extension was more than compensating, and Paul went forth as President Emeritus of a Movement that now reached into Latvia, Estonia, Poland – and the then free port of Danzig – as well as Romania and Yugoslavia. With the new Clubs Jim Davidson had brought into being, the third decade of the century found itself looking with many a wild, and often inaccurate, surmise, at over 3,500 Rotary Clubs across the globe. In turn, Paul visited Hanover, Berlin, Riga, Tallin (Estonia), Helsinki, Stockholm, Göteborg, Copenhagen, Oslo and Bergen, full of the renewed energy he had displayed on his last European tour and even more of the mischief. Danish Rotarians had had the privilege of witnessing the first appearance of Harris the actor since his "folly" days at the People's Theater in Denver, when they persuaded him to play a beguiling blonde maiden in a local sketch. This was long before Copenhagen won its reputation for more dubious transvestite casting. But his most important act on this stage of his world travels for Rotary was to initiate the planting of Trees of Friendship, a happy notion he continued to the end of his life in every country and clime, and which he persuaded Sydney Pascall to emulate when the Englishman started off on his own presidential travels that year. Ironically, the first Friendship Tree he planted was at the great Tempelhof aerodrome in Berlin, a city already under unofficial siege by 400,000 storm-troopers trying to intimidate the eighty-five-year-old Hindenburg to yield government to the impatient Nazis and where the Reichstag's control had come briefly under Goering, who promptly dissolved it. Even as Harris was planting his tree, Hitler was about to bury the Weimar Republic. Today, the apotheosis of Harris's gentle custom lies in the forests of Rotary Friendship Trees planted by the race Hitler was already planning to bury in their millions, the State of Israel.

Yet Paul missed nothing that others did not miss (or pretend to miss). In England that autumn, speaking to the Rotary Club of Burnley, Hannen Swaffer, one of the twentieth century's most cynical, and influential journalists (notorious for his remark "Freedom of the Press in Britain means freedom to print such of the proprietor's prejudices as the advertisers don't object to") proclaimed, "the principles of the Rotary Club are the principles upon which the modern world is being rebuilt", a statement he must have known to be utter rubbish. What *was* being built to shape the modern world, as everyone involved in foreign affairs knew perfectly well, were Hitler's future U-boats which, though banned by the Treaty of Versailles, were surfacing in "secret" shipyards of Finland, Holland and Spain.

The following year marked another break in his Rotary travels, but Paul intervened notably all the same on the international scene by strongly advocating and seeing launched a Spanish edition of *The Rotarian* for Latin-American members. Then, early in 1934, the day before the twenty-ninth anniversary of the day he founded his Movement, Paul took Jean with him on another tour of England, Wales and Scotland, though as before Jean took time off to stay with her numerous relatives near Glasgow. But this time she wasn't alone in keeping an eye on the resurgent rapscallion. Also stringing along were Ches Perry (who spent the Atlantic crossing playing table tennis with Jean) and that year's International President, the Canadian John Nelson, together with other high-ranking Rotarians. This was because of alarm again on both sides of the water that, according to one point of view, RIBI as the sole territorial unit in the Rotary world was becoming a constant factor of disunity and discontent in Rotary Clubs of other nations. It was a case, on the one hand, of the irritation of Ches Perry and the International Board of Directors that their word alone did not automatically become the Rotary Law in Great Britain and Ireland; and on the other, of the World Movement's being now too big (though only one-eighth of the size it is today) for control to be arrogated to one Headquarters in the Midwest of the United States. It was, in fact, the old argument about the special position of the British Isles — crucial to the issue of devolution versus centralisation — which had been aired at the Edinburgh Convention in 1922, and supposedly settled the following year (see Chapter Eleven). But this time there was no melodic or comic intervention by the revered Sir Harry Lauder to smooth over dissension and pique, and Perry and others rightly considered Paul Harris's own position on the matter suspect. After several days of luxurious debate at the Mayfair Hotel in London Paul felt that "suspicions had been dispelled, the atmosphere had been cleared", but he was wrong, deceived by his own simple, generous-minded idea of Rotary. Teeth went on grinding in Perry's Chicago office over British "obduracy", and their echo grinds there still. An International Committee was in due course set up, but the *status quo* still existed before such concerns were obliterated by the Second World War. Only to return later, when the world had once more been made safe for committees.

Leaving Perry and the others to brood over the possible future of an entire "territory" of rapscallions, Paul escaped with relief to take Jean to see the original Wallingford, the town which had given its name to the Vermont village where he grew up, and which proved to be a charming little place by the Thames in the lovely Cotswolds, dating from pre-Roman times and subsequently defended by Alfred the Great and knocked about more than somewhat by Cromwell. After which he embarked on a tour of Rotary Clubs all over the British Isles, omitting only Ireland, where the great survivor De Valera was now President and the IRA were naturally in arms again to oppose their old leader, who had therefore formed a new force called the Blueshirts, to distinguish them from all those Brown- and Blackshirts running amok on the Continent.

Paul and Jean received a rapturous reception in Edinburgh, to which Jean had often told her husband she would willingly crawl "on her hands and knees". Here she was born, here brought up on Comely Bank Avenue, and here she would die. Meanwhile, the Lord Provost gave the couple a grand banquet and the Rotary Club gave them lunch, at which Jean received an inscribed silver salver and Paul delivered an eloquent oration in praise of his wife that brought a standing ovation thundering through the dining-room of the North British Station Hotel.

Free of their Chicago chaperones, Paul and Jean now sailed to South Africa, where in seven days they covered 3,000 miles visiting Cape Town, Johannesburg, Pretoria, Durban, Pietermaritzburg, East London and Port Elizabeth, planting Trees of Friendship as they passed. A great Rotary Conference was held at Cape Town, addressed by the Governor-General, the Earl of Clarendon, and General Jan Smuts, the famous soldier-statesman who still had much history to make. Unfortunately, the General used the occasion to make some rude remarks about the United States in general and Chicago in particular, to which Paul replied with mild but impressive force.

From South Africa Rotary's First Couple returned to Britain for more Club visits, chiefly in Scotland again, though at smaller and more remote Clubs, and Paul discovered that while they had been south of the equator, far more pointed and personal remarks had been made about Chicago, directed without equivocation at the Rotary Headquarters there. RIBI President John Crabtree, who had been called by the Editor of *The Rotary Wheel* "the finest brain in Rotary", had said in the course of a speech to the RIBI Conference that while he accepted there must be a strong central authority for Rotary International to preserve its fundamentals, Chicago Headquarters

... has never thought out what are the Rotary fundamentals ... and thus we see that an inordinate emphasis is laid upon legal details of administration, to criticise which has come to be regarded in some quarters as tantamount to heresy ... the Board of Directors of Rotary International, handicapped by languages as it is, and changing almost completely year by year, has very little power to initiate policy, often repudiating the policies of its predecessors; and thus the real governing power is assumed by a few men of character.

Paul fully understood that for "a few men" one read Chesley Perry, and he knew that Crabtree was right. But he kept his own counsel. And he used the opportunity offered by the influential contacts of the London Club to acquaint himself with the realities of the situation in Europe. One of the most distinguished commentators on the international scene was the journalist and noted broadcaster Henry Wickham Steed, lecturer on Central European History at King's College, London, former Editor of *The Times* and a most successful innovator in the field of propaganda during the First World War (the Germans had declared Wickham Steed's "new weapon" as effective as poison gas), and Paul had a most interesting dinner with him. As a result, we can be sure that Rotary's Founder would have returned to America with a very clear idea of what was really happening, and about to happen, in Europe, for Wickham Steed had already addressed Rotarians in the RIBI quarterly journal *Service in Life and Work* with these extraordinarily prescient lines:

> The world is very small; it is shrinking rapidly, and no nation can any longer be a law unto itself. We have to stand or fall together. We are, for instance, confronted as a world with an extraordinary change which has grown up in Russia. I warn you that unless we can create a civilisation juster, better, and giving fuller opportunities to individuals to exercise freedom, our old Western civilisation will probably be doomed and will deserve to be doomed. If we, after the lesson of the Great War, cannot stand together with other nations and take the risk of pulling our weight and using our restraining power so that no nation shall make war, then we shall deserve all we get. . . .

And they were lines with just as much urgent applicability after the Second World War — indeed, at this very day — as after the First.

Paul would have observed also that British Rotarians had another, far more sinister, phenomenon to disturb them during that summer than suspicions of Ches Perry's motives in Rotary administration, for the German Embassy in London was busy sending out speakers to Clubs all over the islands to expound the virtues of the new Nazi rulers of the Third Reich and to "explain" their blatant and vicious persecution of the Jews. Many British Rotarians were vigorously protesting, and their anger centred upon a particularly obnoxious racialist speech made by the German Attaché to the Birmingham Club. The Birmingham Club President did not help matters by explaining, "I do not suppose that a large proportion of the audience agreed with Dr. Randolph, but all of us were delighted to hear him."

As delighted no doubt as the International President of Rotary, John Nelson, was for the privilege of a pleasant, civilised chat with Mussolini in May and with the Austrian Chancellor, Dollfuss, after the harrowing RI-RIBI row in England. Shortly afterwards Mussolini had the first of his many chats with another special visitor, the German Chancellor, Adolf Hitler ("I don't much like the look of him," murmured the portly Duce), and Dollfuss was dead from a Nazi bullet in the throat.

The Detroit Convention of Rotary in 1934 was notable for one other event besides the tribute to Big Jim Davidson described in Chapter Fourteen. Paul Harris was awarded the Silver Buffalo Citation by the President of the Boy Scouts of America, who said of him: "No man has accomplished more distinguished service to boyhood." The Founder of Rotary promptly had a second heart attack, though this was probably less for the unexpected honour than because of the immensely strenuous tours he had taken during the previous six months. Yet, on a cold morning in the following January, he and Jean were put on a train for the Far East by Ches Perry, who appeared on the station platform, to Paul's expressed surprise, "beaming almost to the point of being radiant with jollity and good cheer".

The train gone, Perry went, as usual, back to his desk to work far into the night, while Paul and Jean sped towards the Rockies and the West Coast, where they took the SS *President Coolidge* to Hawaii. Without the distractions of playing table tennis with Ches Perry, Jean was violently seasick and Paul found himself alone at meals with one other survivor, a Japanese Director of Rotary — and time has proved this fact a harbinger of Rotary's future. He also found himself enraptured — shades of the girls he had met in the Lake District in 1928 — by a girl at an adjoining table and the "sweet ripple of her laughter", but was disconcerted when his Japanese friend informed the girl's mother of his delight.

At his Honolulu welcome, Paul found himself draped with a very special garland of flowers called the "Ilima" wreath, a measure of the great esteem with which he was to be greeted throughout his Eastern journey, for the last person to be so honoured had been the US President, Franklin D. Roosevelt, the year before. Japan came next, where he dined in Tokyo with Rotarian Admiral Viscount Saito, now Finance Minister, whom we met in the last chapter and who was shortly to be assassinated. Visits to Rotary Clubs in Shanghai, Hong Kong and Manila followed, and then the Harrises sailed for the Antipodes, where Jim Davidson had begun his stupendous pioneering voyages for Rotary fourteen years before.

In the vast reaches of Australia, the fourteenth nation to join Rotary, and to a lesser extent in New Zealand, Harris now encountered Rotary organised on a scale resembling that of South Africa (and, of course, India, though Paul never visited it). In 1935, Australia had been divided into two Rotary "Districts", one of which included the states of Victoria, Tasmania, South Australia, Western Australia and part of New South Wales, and the other the larger part of New South Wales plus Queensland. A glance at the map may make this division seem disproportionate, but one should appreciate that in 1935 the largest state, Western Australia, covering an area of 2 million square miles, was represented by only two Clubs! Even ten years later, when the continent was divided into four enormous Districts, a Governor had to be prepared to travel at least 40,000 miles to visit all his Clubs.

After Jim Davidson's visit with Colonel Ralston in 1921 (noted in Chapter Fourteen) it had taken six years to accumulate seventeen Clubs and form Australia's first District (that is, covering the whole continent), and ten years after Big Jim brought Rotary to the South Pacific, Australia still had only thirty Clubs. Subsequent to this, the world Depression had closed down many, but by the time the Harrises arrived there were about sixty Clubs. No doubt Paul was amused to contrast this circumstance with the situation in London, which had made the extraordinary progression from being Rotary's smallest District (with one Club) to being the smallest District with more Clubs than any other in the world, as it remains to this day.

Paul's visit had the effect Ches Perry intended — an effect far more needed round the Pacific than across the Atlantic — and the sight of Rotary's Founder, a legend alive, produced a great surge in membership. Clubs no longer felt they were outposts of the Movement nor uncertain of their relevance to the great ideas and developments being generated in Chicago and London. Indeed, the Rotary Clubs of Perth and Sydney, at opposite ends of the southern coastline, sometimes now had far less sense of their relevance to each other. Even Clubs which were relative "neighbours" felt this, as Australia's official Rotary history makes clear: Adelaide members "knew very little about Rotary and there was no one to advise them, because the sponsor Club, Melbourne, was 500 miles away and they didn't know much about Rotary either".

There was no parallel of course with the sister dominion, Canada. Distances in Canada were as vast, but at almost every point an American Club was not too far away. When Paul arrived "down under", Canada had already supplied three International Presidents to the Movement, while Australians had to wait till after the Second World War to provide their first. This was to be Angus (later Sir Angus) Mitchell, and, as Governor of one of the two Districts that year, he was one of Paul's principal hosts.

Paul's strong sense of irony was given much to feed on from the moment he disembarked at Brisbane, where he was met by a delegation which decided he looked tired and decreed that a drive out in the country would do wonders for him. Arriving on a hilltop, they proceeded to give him a conducted tour of their new crematorium, an inspiration Paul wryly dubbed as "absolute genius"! Having been shown the ovens and other delights of "the culinary department", Paul was taken back down the hill to begin a non-stop round of speeches, interviews and receptions with an unending procession of high dignitaries in luxurious settings which tended to belie the Australian reputation for disdain of such formalities.

What Paul brought to Australia was his unselfconscious notion of what Rotary was for — fun and friendship. Contrary to popular conception, the starch was all on the Australian side, until he managed to disassociate the awe and mythology about himself from their minds, after which they learned fast. He had only to pooh-pooh the notion that Chicago was dominated by gangsters ("I haven't been shot or shot at, or even held up, in forty years") for Australian Rotarians to stage a mock hold-up of his party, complete with pistols and sawn-off shot-guns, not once but twice. Even the occasion when the ceiling of an hotel in New South Wales fell in on Jean while she was dressing for yet another grand occasion became an oft-repeated comic anecdote.

A tour of three weeks over the North and South Islands of New Zealand completed the Pacific stage of Paul's global travels for Rotary, and on his way back he made sure the route included Vancouver in Canada where he could report in person to Jim Davidson's widow on the arduous but inspiring journey of nearly four months — planting his Trees of Friendship from Tokyo to Tasmania — he had made along part of the trail of her husband's great mission. More travel was in store for Paul. Though he was sixty-seven years old and had suffered two heart attacks, there was still one more continent that Ches Perry wanted him to visit. He did not hesitate. In January 1936 Paul and Jean left for three months in South America.

As a warm-up for the Latin arena, Paul had sandwiched in a visit to Mexico the previous year, where tiredness from his Pacific journey no doubt accounted for a somewhat lack-lustre and platitudinous address, a throwback to the style of his earlier days of eclipse, but he did have the pleasure of hearing the six "Objects" of Rotary rendered down into Four Objects, partly, it was stated, in the cause of "a simpler and more logical fashion, which appeals to the European mentality":

1. The development of acquaintance as an opportunity for service.
2. High ethical standards in business and professions; the recognition of the worthiness of all useful occupations; and the dignifying by each Rotarian of his occupation as an opportunity to serve society.
3. The application of the ideal of service by every Rotarian to his personal, business and community life.
4. The advancement of international understanding, goodwill and peace through a world fellowship of business and professional men united in the ideal of service.

The wording has not been altered to this day. Paul must also have been relieved that it was not only the European mentality which approved, for Luis Machado from Havana rose to move the adoption of the new phraseology on the grounds that "it would simplify the understanding of the aims and objects plan, particularly in the Latin American countries". Perhaps it was also in the cause of Latin-American understanding – where great leaders were expected to show themselves in some style, after all – that Paul, during his brief rest after Mexico, allowed himself the uncharacteristic pomp and circumstance of journeying by private railway carriage to Cleveland, Ohio, to celebrate the silver anniversary of a Club he and Ches Perry had set up together back in 1910. Ches rode with him.

The countries of South America now had 193 Clubs and nearly 5,500 Rotarians ready to receive the Founder. However, two which had joined the Movement together in 1927 had to be bypassed in the cause of discretion over valour, since they were still technically at war (most fighting had stopped the year before but a peace agreement was not to be signed until 1938). These were Bolivia – which at La Paz had the highest Club in the world – and Paraguay, though the Rotarians in La Paz and in Asunción, Paraguay, were living up to the highest principles of Rotary in action by looking after each other's prisoners of war. All the same, whether it was because so many Wild West outlaws had sought refuge in South America, such as Butch Cassidy and the Sundance Kid, or simply because of the world-wide reputation of the city of Rotary's birth, both Paul and Jean were obliged to obtain no less than twenty-five authenticated certificates, formally stating that neither of them had ever been under arrest, before they could head south. This, in spite of the fact that Al Capone, now safely tucked away in Alcatraz, had recently revealed himself as a patriotic statesman, issuing a warning from "the rock" that Bolshevism was "knocking at our gates. We can't afford to let it in. . . . We must keep America whole and safe and unspoiled". Clearly, keeping South America that way required that strict vetting procedures be applied to everyone, even to the Founder of Rotary, who came out of Chicago. The same regrettably did not seem to apply to those who came out of Berlin, he was to find.

As if this weren't enough indignity for a daughter of the Kirk, the waters of the South Atlantic proved no more hospitable than those of the South Pacific twelve months earlier, and a severe storm left Paul pacing the deck by himself again. By some administrative slip-up which no Rotarian of any official standing at all would tolerate today, the spacious cabin promised had turned out to be a cubby-hole jammed in the bow of the ship, and Jean suffered terribly from seasickness. Paul for once lost his usual equanimity and said a few intolerant things into the gale.

One wonders if it had occurred to Paul, as it certainly occurs to anyone viewing these travels today, that it was rather strange that the super-efficient Ches Perry should always pack him and Jean off on their longest travels during the worst months of the year for ocean weather. It was certainly no comfort whatever to the implacably level-headed Jean to know that Lord Nelson had also suffered from seasickness, the usual maddening comfort offered, much less that she and the Admiral were both clergymen's children.

In Panama, Paul started right away planting a Tree of Friendship; which was just as well, since the Panamanians were busy trying to prise loose some of their obligations to the United States under their Canal Treaty. The President of Panama and his entire cabinet assembled to meet the Founder of Rotary, after which a special private train was available to waft them over some of the most spectacular mountain scenery on earth to Bogota, capital of Colombia, where a request from the President and Foreign Minister to welcome Paul personally did not prevent a harrowing cross-examination by the authorities about their right to be there at all. To this day, Colombia is the only nation in the world to have Paul Percy Harris's fingerprints in its criminal records.

Paul and Jean were delighted to find themselves guests of the American Minister, William Dawson, who himself was a bit of living history, as he had been the first Rotary Club President in South America, courtesy of Herbierto Coates, all those long years ago in Montevideo. Then it was back over the Andes and down the coast to Ecuador where, at Guayaquil, Paul was accorded a great reception and received the Order of the Sun, one of the country's highest awards. Unknown to themselves, the Harrises were doing a service to the United States as well as to Rotary, for Ecuador was infested by Nazi agents at the time, stirring up anti-American feeling with considerable success. But their minds were more on the past than present. They were reminded forcefully that they were now in the land of the Incas when they went on to Peru, where yet another Order of the Sun awaited them, as well as visits to the tomb of Pizarro, founder of Lima and destroyer of Inca civilisation, and to the University of San Marco, the oldest university in the Western Hemisphere, founded two years before Philip II of Spain married Bloody Mary of England and seven years before Elizabeth I succeeded her wretched stepsister.

In Lima Paul and Jean were feted by Rotarians, one a recent Ambassador to Washington, Federico Puzet, and there Paul planted his Tree of Friendship at the entrance of a Rotary-sponsored public playground, which he officially opened. They stayed with President Benavides — by the standard of the time, a reasonably benevolent dictator — at his seaside home before sailing on down the coast to Valparaiso, Chile, making a triumphal progress en route in their ship the *Santa Inez*, for, at every port of call, Rotarians swarmed aboard to take the couple sightseeing and to Club luncheons. Of these stops, the most significant for Paul was at Arica, which the League of Nations had awarded to Chile in 1929 while decreeing it a free port for Peru. The two nations had been in dispute over the port ever since they had fought the War of the Pacific during 1878-83 over the sodium nitrate deposits from which Alfred Nobel manufactured his nitro-glycerine, and even the League did not mend matters. But, as Paul was delighted to discover, "it occurred to the Rotarians of Chile to send Christmas greetings to those of Peru, and Peruvian Rotarians sent New Year's greetings in reply and through this simple wedge was opened a channel through which cordial relations have been resumed". This was presumably the first time that the custom of exchanging Christmas cards between acquaintances who are not on speaking terms with one another was introduced to South America, though it had been long established in Anglo-Saxon cultures.

Rotary Clubs had started in Chile the same year they were introduced in Italy; and Paul found the then nation's leader, President Allesandro, to be not only of Italian descent but a fervent admirer of Mussolini, whose autographed photo graced the presidential office. He also found him disconcertingly not "at home" when he called, but was later granted an audience at which Allesandro agreeably professed equal admiration for Franklin D. Roosevelt and Il Duce. Indeed, like F.D.R., he had succeeded in taking his country out of the Depression, a circumstance mirrored by the fact that Chile had by now roughly one-third of all the Rotarians in South America, 1,500 in fifty-three Clubs, and was about to play host to Rotary's first South American Regional Conference, with delegates pouring in from all over the continent, to attend receptions, balls, dinners and luncheons galore both at Valparaiso and the luxury beach resort of Vina del Mar, where the Harrises stayed.

There had been a time, and not all that long ago, when many South Americans had harboured dark suspicions, in the wake of colonial memories, that Rotary was just another exceptionally ingenious device aimed at furthering the selfish business interests of Yankee entrepreneurs, but their experience of the Founder and his wife was, in Paul's own words, "helping them become convinced otherwise", and he could testify "how wonderful was the joy with which they embraced it". And embraced the reticent couple literally and often no doubt. For Paul was now in territory made familiar to him in France and Germany (and he would have found the same in Italy, had he gone there) of a Rotary made up from the community's élite. Not only had he and Jean at last been given the ship accommodation they expected, but luxury hotel suites awaited them ashore. He unfeignedly relished it all. "I say without reservation", he later declared, "I consider South American cities to be among the most beautiful in the world", and further elaborated, "I must admit with equal frankness, even at the risk of appearing disloyal to my own countrymen, that the upper strata of South Americans are ahead of us in many respects." The upper strata stood and cheered him, the Minister of Foreign Affairs gave him the Order of Merit, and the local shellfish laid him low for two days, with doctors advising him to cancel the rest of his tour. He ignored the advice and was soon planting a very special Tree of Friendship, to which ceremony all nine South American nations with Rotary Clubs had sent sacks of native earth to empty round the roots. It was moving, it was tremendous, it was an overwhelming vindication of his dream. As horticulture, it was questionable.

After the excitements of Valparaiso they had five days to relax on the transcontinental train journey (private carriage – he had not rehearsed in vain) to Buenos Aires, where their first dinner engagement was at the famed Jockey Club and a grand reception was given in Paul's honour by the United States Ambassador. Here they also visited perhaps Rotary's most remarkable project south of the equator: the Instituto Cultural Argentino Norteamericano, established by the Buenos Aires Rotarians, where 3,000 students learned English and discussed cultural differences and similarities between North and South America. During their stay in Argentina's beautiful capital Paul and Jean took a brief journey across the Rio Plata (the river Plate, where the drama of the Graf Spee, Nazi Germany's pocket battleship, was to be played out in three years' time) to visit Rotary's first Club on the continent, that of Montevideo in neighbouring Uruguay, where the English-born "Don Herbierto" Coates had established the Movement in 1918 and where he was still active and eagerly waiting to greet his idol. Coates introduced Paul to President Gabriel Terra of Uruguay. But perhaps the most significant moment again was the planting of a rather special Tree of Friendship, this time in the grounds of Crandon School, founded by an old friend of the Harrises, Mrs Frank Crandon, of Evanston, Illinois, a suburb of Chicago that today derives its chief fame from being the modern Headquarters of Rotary International.

Then it was on to Brazil, where the now familiar lavish entertainments and banquets awaited them, followed by planting of Trees of

Friendship in Santos, São Paulo and Rio de Janeiro, and still more luxurious hotel suites, which were beginning to pall on Paul and Jean, though they were now resigned to accepting the élite treatment. A meeting with President Vargas, who had just introduced martial law after an abortive Communist uprising, followed, before the couple sailed northward for home.

Paul Harris now had one more decoration, Brazil's Order of the Southern Cross, to add to his already overburdened chest. But he must have glimpsed signs in Brazil of another sort of cross, the hooked swastika, which was beginning to make its unabashed appearance among the large numbers of Germans in the southern provinces of Brazil, along with ever-increasing numbers of young Fascists, who — with black, brown and blue already spoken for — were marching about as the Greenshirts. However, wrote Paul, in elegiac vein, Jean and he "felt that the gods had been kind in granting us a great adventure; that our lives had been immeasurably enriched by contacts with our fellow creatures living below the equator". In other words, ten trees for four medals seemed a fair exchange.

They soon discovered that their fellow-creatures carrying on with their lives above the equator had not been idle in their absence. Germany had reoccupied the Rhineland, at once showing as cruelly foolish and false all that "dawn of a universal peace" which Stanley Leverton of the London Club had written about so confidently ten years before, telling fellow-Rotarians throughout Europe (see Chapter Thirteen) that only Rotary by advancing "goodwill and international peace through world-fellowship" could make the Locarno Pact work. Locarno had been strewn to the winds and, unknown to the general public, the world's first radar stations were going up along Britain's south coast, while its citizens mourned the death of King George V and the renouncing of the throne by Edward VIII who could not rule, he said, without "the help and support of the woman I love". And British Rotarians, led by the sweet magnate and Past International President Sydney Pascall, with the assistance of Rotarians from the United States, Canada and South Africa, had formed a seagoing "Club" on the maiden voyage of the *Queen Mary*.

Meanwhile Stalin was busy exterminating what was left of all his original revolutionary fellow-leaders after amazing purge trials where they had "confessed" complete betrayals of communism. For his part, Mussolini had sworn allegiance to Hitler, as had Japan, and then ordered the invasion of Abyssinia, his pilots spraying poison gas, destroying towns *con brio* and enthusiastically hurling black chieftains out of high-flying aircraft. In Tokyo,

Paul's recent dinner companion, Rotary Viscount Saito, had been butchered during a February snowstorm when 1,500 Army mutineers, whose troops had reached the Great Wall of China, massacred most of Japan's leading statesmen. In Palestine, Arabs had called a general strike against increasing Jewish immigation. In the Pacific, Australia, New Zealand and the United States faced with alarm the fact that all naval treaties had suddenly become void. Finally, in Paul's homeland, a German-born carpenter, Bruno Hauptmann, had just been sent to the electric chair for the kidnap-murder of Rotarian Colonel Lindbergh's baby, and Franklin Roosevelt, about to become President again by the greatest margin in history (losing only Maine and Vermont), was preparing to follow Paul's example and make headlines by appearing in Buenos Aires.

And Rotary in Europe that summer of 1936? As Alessandro Ubertone, Italian Rotary's present Editor has recently written: "Although Rotarians were persons occupying responsible positions in Italian society, they were not of the same mould as the early Christians and no doubt they felt that it would not be very comfortable to hold Rotary meetings in catacombs." An indefatigable Germanophile, Rotarian Ernest Atkins from the English Club of Wandsworth, reported himself "nearly blinded by the blaze of decorations" at a Rotary Conference at Salzburg and announced himself convinced that the German-Austrian District "is leading European Rotary at the present time", especially since Franz von Papen, the Nazi Minister to Austria and future inhabitant of the dock at Nuremberg, "in most interesting conversation, gave me assurance of Hitler's desire for peace, and especially for friendship with France", which he had proved by "allowing" 300 Rotarians and their ladies to cross the border for the occasion. Atkins could not have known that the egregious Count (who survived even Nuremberg) was busy giving the Austrian Nazi Party 200,000 marks a month at this time, and had conducted an even more interesting conversation with the United States Minister in Vienna, confiding to him that Hitler was determined to grab south-eastern Europe. The once-proud Rotary Clubs of Spain, the first to form on the European mainland, had abruptly been stunned into silence by the shattering opening salvoes of the Civil War, in which a dress rehearsal for the Second World War was being enacted – a silence which was to last forty-four years. At a European Advisory Meeting in Zurich of Rotarians from most European nations, Chairman Kurt Belfrage of the Stockholm Club announced, "Rotary has no political problems whatever . . . our Members must never forget that they as Rotarians have not to spread national hatred, but international understanding and friendship", and the Swede concluded with a statement of devastating complacency: "When the individual Rotarian pronounces his opinion, may he therefore do it with the modesty, the tolerance, and the broad mind which belong to all sincere neutrality and which are the signs of nobility of all good civilisation." Dr Goebbels might have chosen a different adjective to precede the word "civilisation": "doomed".

Paul and Jean had been struck by other deplorable matters since their return to America, and they sent urgent word to the Twenty-Seventh Convention of Rotary International, meeting at Atlantic City, that they were "almost shocked at the drabness of our cities". Over a period of eight years they had visited the British Isles, Europe, South Africa, Hawaii, Japan, China, the Philippines, Australia, New Zealand, and Central and South America, and their minds were naturally filled with the colourful and exotic sights and sounds of a world filling up with Golden Wheels. They were bound to have been dazzled, bound to feel dull for a while when it was all over. But they knew that they had threaded a great bond of affection for Rotary's Founder, which would hold the Movement together, however precariously, during the three violent nightmare years of terrifyingly swift descent to Armageddon.

Yet could the Rotarians of Europe be considered less clear-headed and more cowardly, more morally blind, than other Europeans? Or indeed than other peace-loving citizens anywhere in the world, where none other than Lloyd George, the mighty leader of Great Britain against the Kaiser, had just paid a visit to the new *Reichsführer* and come away enchanted, the wizard bewitched, announcing to a world pathetically anxious to be reassured that Hitler was "a great man"? When Ramsay MacDonald's successor (Stanley Baldwin again) had deliberately sent to the Mediterranean a British fleet with not enough ammunition to stop Italian troop-ships bound for Mussolini's new African empire? When France agreed, and signed a pact with Berlin, not to disturb Il Duce? When Baldwin's cousin, Rudyard Kipling, on his seventieth birthday, wrote to Paul Harris's friend Wickham Steed, to say that he thought the world insane? When more nations than ever before, far more athletes than ever before, and many more thousands of spectators than ever before, were pouring from all over the world into Berlin for the 1936 Olympic Games, deeming them correctly the most spectacular sports event ever held? Franz Lehár's "Rotary Hymn" (in its official English translation)

> Fellow Rotarians, you are wanted!
> Fellow Rotarians, up, to work!
> Whoever can help, grip fast,

Service comes first, Self last –
Fellow Rotarians, you are wanted!

was being drowned out, in Vienna as elsewhere, by the rather different hymn composed by a Protestant minister's Nazi son, Horst
Wessel, murdered in a street brawl with Communist gangs in Berlin,
which was being sung everywhere in growing volume:

Raise high the flags!
Stand rank on rank together,
Storm-troopers march with steady, quiet tread!

For this had been the period which was soon to be preserved in
literary aspic for all time by the title of Robert Graves's book about
the between-war years, *The Long Week-End.* And in those terms,
the world was now at Sunday morning, half-dreading the possible portent of the bells, half-asleep still, half at hymn and half
hung-over.

CHAPTER SEVENTEEN

Death of the Boy

We're full of vivacity, fire and pep,
But we'll join the procession
and fall into step.
The boys of our town are waiting today,
Waiting for men to show them the way.

"The Boy Speaks" by John E. Wilson,
The Rotarian, 1934

Boy into Youth into Man. In the thirties all civilisations were
macho civilisations; indeed, most still are. Their heyday in Europe
and the Anglo-Saxon world had been the Victorian era, when young
men had gone forth to win empires from savages by means of beads,
Bible and bullet, whether it was the public schoolboy striding the
veldt or through the Afghan pass, or the American Wild West full of
adventurers called "Kid" this or "Kid" that, or named after places
and towns, like the Cisco Kid or the Sundance Kid — the most
notorious of them being, of course, Billy the Kid. Not many lived
much beyond boyhood, yet all of them attained immortality. Many
of the Wild West gunmen were not raised on the plains or anywhere
near them — the Sundance Kid came from Plainfield, New Jersey,
Billy the Kid from New York's East Side — but were lonely men of
the big city transplanted to the companionable loneliness of the
desert, to which they soon added the companionship of the "Wanted"
posters. Such as it was, it was all they knew, and most died early,
lonely deaths. It was only then, as dead "kids" — indeed, the first
"dead-end" kids — that they made friends with the world. As we
have noted before (in Chapter Fourteen), this was the spring of
Rotary which Paul Harris carefully tapped, taking the consequent
tide at full flood and diverting it craftily, gently, into his particular
quiet pool of fellowship. Pistol-packing Peter Pans were much more
acceptable to wives when thy confined their activities to having

"lunch out" with the boys rather than nights out with them. Yet that boyhood could not survive the decade of world Depression that ended in a thunder of burst balloons. It was the last party, and there were those who saw the end of the party sooner than others. And few there were, even amongst them, ready to give a "growing-up" talk to the boys entering puberty while there was still time. There were even fewer to be found in the Rotary Movement. Another movement had them in plenty, however, drawing inspiration from the dark places of savage heritage common to all races.

In his classic *The Golden Bough*, Sir James Frazer describes the initiation rites into manhood to which a number of primitive tribes subjected their young boys. It was a ritual of death and resurrection, "the ceremony of killing a lad at puberty and bringing him to life again. The lad dies as a man and comes to life again as an animal". The world was about to see a great deal of that going on, as the 1930s died in a fusillade of pain, fright and frightfulness. Of one tribe in New South Wales, Australia, Sir James writes: "The youths on approaching manhood are initiated at a secret ceremony, which none but initiated men may witness. Part of the proceedings consists in knocking out a tooth and giving a new name to the novice, indicative of the change from youth to manhood." Basically, not such a different procedure was being followed from 1932 by those tribes forming themselves into the New Order that would "last for a thousand years", and whose most promising recruits were those who joined the *Jungvolk* at ten, taking an oath in the presence of a "blood banner", and proceeding via the Adolf Hitler Schools and the National Political Institutes of Education into a six-year disappearance within the walls of four *Ordensburgen*, the Order Castles of the ancient Teutonic Knights. Inside those romantic, fearsome walls they underwent rigorous physical training and Nazi instruction. The castle from which they graduated, and finally emerged reborn as men, was located at Marienburg, right next to the Polish border. They would therefore be the first in, so to speak, and the last out, for troops of Hitler Youth fought in the rubble of Berlin when the Russians were only a street away from the Fuehrer's bunker. And Youth wore a death's head on its cap: the animal that came to life in the 1930s was a killer.

But while all this could have spelled the end of Rotary, it didn't. A superb instinct for survival, an instinct which fuels the shifts, adaptations and accommodations of all great Movements, ensured that Rotary had, with perfect timing, arranged that it was well prepared with guide-lines to see it through this traumatic period from a source whose lack of bias was beyond question and whose intellectual and professional qualifications were beyond dispute.

The University of Chicago had been founded — ten years after Oscar Wilde had made the city self-conscious about culture — by the ruthless genius who had made citizens like Paul Harris self-conscious about business ethics, John D. Rockefeller. It was indeed the beneficiary of the oil emperor's first conscience-salving operation, to the tune of $35 million. And in 1934 the University undertook a study of the organisation which had been specifically dedicated by Paul Harris to laundering such ruthless, unprincipled methods as those by which Rockefeller had built the Standard Oil colossus. The irony must have given immense pleasure to Paul, who served on the Committee of the Rotary Club of Chicago which recommended that this study be made. In a sense, the study could have been called Rockefeller's Revenge — the first and greatest of the Victorian "robber barons", now aged ninety-five, was thriving in the Florida sun when the Report on Rotary was published in 1934 — although the University Study Team soon discovered, "it was evident . . . that Chicago Rotary should be studied in relation to the international setting and in front of its international background if it was to be understood". This comment, made in the foreword to the Report, gave early warning to Chicago readers how completely the parochial, inward-looking members of Rotary Number One had been outwitted and outmanoeuvred by their quiet but determined Founder.

The published Report, entitled simply *Rotary?* (query included), resulted from the initiative of that same George Treadwell who in 1919 had been one of the first Rotarians in the Shanghai Club (see Chapter Eleven) and its first Secretary. The following year, business taking him back to America, he had become the first paid Secretary of the Chicago Club, a position from which he did not retire until 1947, the year of Paul Harris's death — and about half-way through his term of office he suggested the investigation by the University of Chicago. The resultant Committee, which — this being Rotary — spawned another Committee, which spawned another Committee which did the work, was primarily outlining a survey of Rotary's past, of how it had become what it was. It was therefore called the Forward-Looking Committee. "The service ideal, psychologically considered, is a reflection of the reaction of conscience against the unadulterated pursuit of profit," said the Report, biting enthusiastically the hand that had nourished into existence the University which employed its authors and researchers. The Report's findings were in the highest traditions of objective academic study and were received by thoughtful Rotarians, for many of whom John D. Rockefeller was as mighty a legend as Al Capone, who lived, after all, just the other side of the almighty dollar, with delighted shock.

Partly, this was the very human pleasure taken by citizens of impeccable conduct and upright, even staid, personal lives, who are told that they are really rather wicked old devils at heart. Mainly, it was almost relief at confirmation of what many had suspected for some time: that Rotary was rather like an old-fashioned, over-upholstered automobile, badly needing a service but in which no garage was interested and which was about to find itself caught mid-track in the middle of a murderous and noisy Grand Prix race called the Mid-Twentieth-Century Homicidal Holocaust.

The original battle against the "unadulterated pursuit" of profit was now won, the Report implied, and it was time to make sure that the baby did not go down the plughole with the bathwater. "The inhibitions of Rotarians about profits reflect no credit on Rotary. If the search for profit is 'selfish' and unworthy, then all of American civilisation and the entire social and economic order of the western world are selfish and unworthy, for they have been created by business profits, developed by profits, and preserved by profits." With this declaration, bold and unequivocal, the University raised a standard for the Movement it would have hesitated to raise for itself, for Rotary was now placed in a similar political context in the land of its origin as it had always at once been placed in Europe, Africa, the Middle and Far East and in Latin America.

Since Rotarians were business men, they were in the main Republicans (which meant in the United States precisely the opposite to its meaning elsewhere), and in the White House the voters had now installed the wealthy "class traitor" Roosevelt, who had the year before recognised Stalin's government and whose Democratic Administration was pulling the United States out of the Depression by means of a programme of blatant National Socialism (which also meant precisely the opposite to its meaning elsewhere). North America now seemed to have taken to its heart Rotary's view of profits as a dirty word just as Rotarians were re-discovering their virtue as a prerequisite to service. However, one outstanding exception to the generalisation that Rotarians were Republicans was of course Rotarian Roosevelt himself, who saw the Movement (he had joined the Albany Club while Governor of New York State) standing for "inherent honesty, fair dealing, orderly justice, the rights and worth of the individual to society and of society to the individual". In other words, what his enemies called the "creeping socialism" of his famous New Deal was a mani-festation through politics — and what was, for a time, a benevolent dictatorship — of what had once been the basic impulse of Paul Harris's Movement. This was "Vocational Service", a term in regard to which Rotary, on the other hand, said the University Report disconcertingly "had no clear meaning and has not acquired any". Rough talk, but rougher was to come when it stated, "ethics, like charity, begins at home, and if Rotarians are unwilling to discuss setting their own houses in order, they cannot hope to set other people's in order", and it claimed that Chicago Rotarians certainly were guilty of this reluctance.

This is not a hindsight view. The authors of the University of Chicago Report were, after all, living in the midst of the Roosevelt upheaval — the very Auditorium where Mary Garden had performed her operatic Dance of the Seven Veils next door to Rotary's first-ever Convention (see Chapter Five) was to house in time the Roosevelt University; and all round the "Windy City" the gales of farming reform were sweeping across the great agricultural heartland of America — and they could, and did, provide a running commentary of comparison.

> The point which the Committee has been striving to make as to the importance of Vocational Service . . . has received striking confirmation in the march of events in these few past brief months since this study was initiated. . . . Suddenly, we find the United States Government using its strongest methods to do just that to which the Rotary Business Methods Committee met such resistance: to bring all the members of the same vocation into cooperative action . . . the New Deal presents the greatest challenge and opportunity that Rotary has ever had.

Not all Rotarians welcomed the revelation. For a bourgeois committee's terms of reference to be hijacked by the State was, many felt, a form of piracy if not tyranny. To replace infinite discussion and debate by brutal decision was to remove the life-support machine of the democratic process, the aqualung of bores. But religions, even secular ones, need not die simply because they are proved true, as Wilde maintained. He did not, as Shaw did, understand the value of committees, which, like all other primitive forms of life, can reshape and reform themselves infinitely. Which is what Rotary was being urged to do by the Chicago investigators. And that is what the Movement promptly did, and has done ever since, growing ever in strength. Yet it helped Rotary know its worth: the compliment of the New Deal may have been a back-handed one, but it was an enormous compliment just the same.

Even Paul Harris was a bit taken aback by the bluntness of the Report, though he had been foremost among those urging for one in the first place, insisting that the University was given a completely free hand to research where it liked, question whom it liked and state its conclusions as fully as it liked and in whatever manner it liked. And of course the great University (it was just seven years later that it took over production of the *Encyclopaedia Britannica*) would not have undertaken the study otherwise. None the less, Paul counselled that "Rotarians should be especially heedful" of its "deliberate, thoughtful criticisms" and expressed the hope that the Report would "serve to shake complacent clubs out of their complacency, indifferent clubs out of their indifference, and to arouse all clubs to a higher sense of responsibility".

In an official review of the published Report, Past President of Rotary International, Allen Albert, who even before the First World War (which people were beginning to doubt really *had* been *the* Great War it was still commonly called) was turning Rotarians' eyes to reality by telling them that "peace is not to be had for the world cheaply" (see Chapter Eight), was still present to fulfil his recurring and priceless role. He had no reservations about the Report and urged that it be read throughout the Movement and its lessons learned. He even urged that "our brothers in the British Isles [should] procure a corresponding study on the part of great political scientists in King's College, Cambridge or Oxford . . . that we who are responsible for the leadership of Rotary in this day might have counsel of the seers of our day". Neither of the English universities obliged, which was probably just as well, since the counsel of the "seers of our day", at Cambridge anyway, were at this time preeminent only in incubating some of the greatest betrayers of Western civilisation this century was to know, or find out about, students like Philby, Burgess, Maclean and Blunt, to mention the known few at the uncovered tip of the garbage heap. But Allen Albert — Rotary International President in 1915, and with thirty years of service to his beloved Movement still before him in 1934 — enthusiastically announced the value of the "vivisection" of Rotary which had taken place "as impartially and coolly as though it were on the operating table" all the same. More, Albert not only commended the Report's findings, he even ventured so far as actually to urge Rotarians to open the Report and *read* it! He well knew how much of the imputation of philistinism levelled at his fellow-members had fed fiction from fact, and he added firmly: "If we are the back-slapping, bread-throwing, crude company we have been pictured here and there, such a statement as this will hardly penetrate into the thickness above our ears. If we are anything better, especially if we are earnest men who seek to serve our fellows, we shall have here something of a range-finder for the Rotary of tomorrow." A range-finder, he implied, for something better than hurling bread-rolls, by which Rotary could not live alone.

The University of Chicago research team lofted a mirror. Gazing into it, a Rotarian could see a close reflection that was as reasonably satisfactory as any middle-aged business man had a right to expect. The interest and excitement was into the two alternating backgrounds the mirror showed behind his barbered image. One showed a domestic landscape glowing and vigorous under the benevolent thrust of New Deal reform. Here was a portrait of national acceptance of Rotary's "vocational" principles — responsibility towards those less fortunate than oneself in the national community, responsibility towards employees, customers, business competitors, youth and the old. Though the term was not then in use, the world's first announced "caring society" was showing lustful life. The other background, swirling in and away on the mirrored horizon, now darkening the first, now being withdrawn like a tantalising silken net played out by fate — mischievous angler as ever — showed a glowering scene abroad in which the Rotarian saw no clear way at all but incomprehension, which he nurtured complacently. *Rotary?* pointed out that, while both perspectives were central to the Movement's outlook, it was also getting out of touch with both. Even as, for Rotarians who had coined the modern sense of the phrase, "Vocational Service had no clear meaning and has not acquired any", so International Service (the famous Sixth and now the Fourth Object), while "the most recent and talked about of major Rotary activities . . . has scarcely been carried into effect at all".

Small wonder then, like the great frightened majority of the Western world, that so many of the men who would be boys again, even if only once a week, were tempted to grasp their dreams and ideals in both hands at the mirror-face and step boldly into looking-glass land, long before they reached the key paragraph near the end of the University of Chicago Report which stated: "The problems of Rotary are in a peculiar sense the problems of modern industrial civilisation. The future of that civilisation depends upon the capacity of business leaders to deal intelligently, generously, and broad-mindedly with the economic and political aspects of the world crisis which is threatening it with dissolution." After all, Rotarians round the world — in 1934, numbering 150,000 in seventy-seven countries and geographical regions — could look upon it as a Report strictly applicable only to the Chicago Club, Rotary Number One, which had boldly commissioned it.

Allen Albert knew better and said so; the Report itself said as much. Indeed, the very commissioning of the Report acknowledged the fact, if only by the obstinate persistence of the belief of many older members that Chicago still had the soul of Rotary under lock and key — metaphorically at the Sherman House (where the Club still met), at 35 East Wacker Drive, and more literally, at Comely Bank — and that the western shores of Lake Michigan held the Rome, Mecca, Canterbury, not to mention Buddha Gaya (containing the modern version of the Bodhi tree in Paul Harris's own garden) of the enlightened bourgeois world. Yet when we read the proceedings of the Twenty-Fifth Annual Convention of the Movement in Detroit that year of publication, only eleven lines in over 600 pages refer to the Report, speaking of it as "an interesting contribution to the Movement as a whole" although "not in any sense official". John Nelson, the Canadian who was that year's International President, did certainly "commend it to the consideration of our members everywhere", but by adding at once his observation that "it is regarded as of such news value by many leading newspapers that it is commanding considerable attention in their reviews of interesting books", he ensured that few of the nearly 3,000 in his audience bothered to open it.

Nor is this to imply rebuke. Most Rotarians tended, then as now, to approach books about themselves with all the enthusiasm and respect they would pay to a parcel bomb. That such a book should first be rendered harmless by the expert attention of newspaper reviews made it twice damned in Rotary eyes, since an editor could commit only one offence greater than not writing about their Movement, and that was writing about it. On the other hand, as all the best, and most well-bred book reviewers can effectively dissect the qualities of a book without actually reading it, they leave no obligation on the busy public in their turn to do more than simply be aware that the book has been reviewed. The public need not read the review any more than the reviewer has read the book, and so, by the end of the process, everyone need know as little about the huge mystery as maybe the author does himself, and the word is rendered safe — and often successful.

Allen Albert was on the programme, but only to deliver his splendid tribute to Big Jim Davidson (noted in Chapter Fourteen). The following year, Albert was appointed Chairman of a new Commission on Rotary International Administration, a direct result of the University of Chicago Report, but this only highlighted the inward-looking "isolationist" reaction of most Rotarians — the Commission's job was derived from just three pages of the Report, those dealing with election of Club officers. This was broadened to include the investigation of current electioneering practices among candidates for the International Presidency each year. The gesture to international implications was thus made; in practice, all those implications were ignored.

Rotary wore the aspect of the time, of course. Its ignoring of international storm-clouds, indeed the threat to its own existence, by extracting from *Rotary?* only an impetus to decide the best way of choosing an international leader, was no more an about-face from reality abroad than was the United Kingdom's drawn-out hassle in high places about which king — more vital even, which queen — should follow the passing of King George V, a controversy taking place at about the same period. And Allen's Commission was needed. The uninhibited, brash, rough-and-tumble showbiz wheeling-and-dealing of American national politics had had its apotheosis in Chicago for many years, so it could scarcely be expected that the style would not rub off on the administration of that city's most famous export. Candidates for the International Presidency had openly avowed their rival claims for many years, with supporters "lobbying" enthusiastically at Conventions — and if Rotarian Franklin D. Roosevelt had himself ruthlessly and rumbustiously made his way to the White House so recently, why should Rotarian aspirants to glory shirk the same style?

The answer was obvious in the aims and ideals of the Movement, of course, but the practice continued for many years, though it was admitted by few, until the Commission's recommendation was accepted that "the office should seek the man, not the man the office". The method was then adopted, and it is one that has continued to this day, of appointing a Nominating Committee of distinguished Rotarians from many nations to recommend a presidential candidate each year, from names submitted by Clubs all over the world. The method did not eradicate unseemly practices or guarantee perfect results. On the contrary, the post-war years have found on the Rotary hustings some impenitent lobbyists, and the Nominating Committee has even, in all innocence and stunned surprise, found itself recommending a former officer of Hitler's dreaded *Schutzstaffel*, the SS! But on the whole it has proved to be a sane, civilised and workable practice, and in fact it has no more than adjusted to international needs a method already in use by Rotary Number One itself, including the proviso that even the fortunate President Elect of the Nominating Committee could be challenged "from the floor" by other candidates before election was confirmed.

So *Rotary?* was helping Rotary put its house in order before the coming mortal storm, and this was important, indeed crucial, for its survival. But essentially it was American housekeeping. The University of Chicago was pinpointing a vital weakness when it zeroed in on Rotary's internationalism — whose essential lack of real depth was typified by its translation into "internationality" — as another example of aims being honoured more in speech than

by their observance. Here the Movement failed to follow the
example set by Rotarian Roosevelt who, when asked why he still
consorted with undesirable "city" political machines (especially
that of Chicago), replied, "they may be sons of bitches but they
are *our* sons of bitches". One feels certain that had Paul Harris
been given to such language, he would have used it to urge Rotary
to watch more what was happening to their fellows in Clubs abroad.
Rotary? as best it could, did this for him.

Yet its conclusions were realistic and pessimistic. The book
reported that to the question circulated among Chicago Rotarians,
"In what specific ways could the Club render more effective International Service?", the numbers of those who replied, "All of us
will soon be forced to take an active part in world affairs", were
fully equalled, if not exceeded, by those who replied along the
lines of "Generally speaking, none. I would avoid trends towards
socialism and internationalism", or of "Not mixing gratuitously in
the problems of other countries and people". Fascism and Nazism
were not mentioned by Chicago. But then neither were they mentioned by a party of thirty British Rotarians, led by the Torquay
Club, who toured Germany that same summer and wrote of visiting
a Munich which "still quivered with the convulsion that had shaken
it a few days before", though they "were struck by the evident
desire of all with whom we came in contact to be understood by us.
Their attitude, despite an obvious reticence, was an appeal to us
to suspend judgement". Judgment had certainly been suspended
by everyone (and remained so until the findings of the courts of
Nuremberg over twenty years later), and by Hitler most of all, for
it was a mixture of cool calculation and vengeance that brought
about the wholesale murder of all his old "storm-trooper" friends
of the SA, *Sturm Abteilung*, many of them homosexual thugs,
including its leader Ernst Roehm, his principal aid in launching the
Third Reich. During that week-end of slaughter, 30th June-1st July,
centred upon Munich, over 1,000 died, just before the British
Rotary group arrived, including the priest who had helped him
write *Mein Kampf*, an event which the British Rotarians quaintly
described in *The Rotary Wheel* as using shocking methods "so alien
to our own conceptions of ordered government. But", went on the
account, "we perceived in the welter in which they are involved the
strivings of a great and richly-endowed people to find a form of
government suited to the genius of their race".

History records, alas, that they found it — for a certain dark side
of that genius, anyway. Rotarian P. H. W. Almy had the wit to quote
Shelley's lines "Wild Bacchanals of truth's mysterious wine,/King-
deluded Germany", and to refer to a revival of the "spirit of

Arminius" (a tribal leader in Germany who inflicted a defeat on
the legions of Caesar Augustus in AD 9), but then buries his perceptions in Rotary platitudes, concluding: . . . "their domestic politics
do not concern us. As Rotarians we know neither race nor politics
nor creed. We embrace all these; we try to see the worthiness of all;
and we seek for all a common denominator in Fellowship and
Service". Alas, "Pa" Almy, a kindly Torquay solicitor, was destined
to face disillusionment head-on when he later served as RIBI President in the last year of "peace", that of Chamberlain at Munich.
Another group of British Rotarians, arriving a few days later,
while admitting to "not understanding the drastic action that was
taken on 30th June", felt that "the country is without question
endeavouring to build up the physique of the youth". Boy Scout
morality was still in ascendancy over its motto.

Still, it was a point of view, though not perhaps one shared by
the young man whom Hitler, on that 30th June 1934, had found
in bed with Roehm's second in command, Edmund Heines, later
described by William L. Shirer in *The Third Reich* as having "a girl-
ish face on the brawny body of a piano mover", and who was at
once taken out and shot in the drive of the Hanslbauer Hotel, just
outside Munich, where the perfect physique of large numbers of
youth had been discovered in room service to most of the Fuehrer's
old, and doomed, friends, and had promptly shared their fate.

But since most of Germany was befuddled by what was going
on, not excluding most of the murdered victims on that "Night of
the Long Knives", the visiting Rotarians from Britain could scarcely
be faulted for sharing their apprehensive confusion, especially since
a German delegate to Rotary's International Convention in Detroit,
which had ended only the day before, had announced: "The Rotary
work for youth in Germany is to be treated somewhat differently
from most other countries . . . the National Socialist Movement
requires the supervision of the entire education of the coming
generation . . . that work is by no means a particular Rotary work."

Prominent amongst Rotarians who thought differently was a
recent Past President of Rotary in Great Britain and Ireland, Herbert
Schofield, a man of large personality, build and intellect, an
educational pioneer who was world famous for his work at the
Loughborough College of Technology. Chairing a discussion on
Youth Service at Detroit, he tried to urge delegates away from their
fixation with "Boys' Work Committees" towards considering those
young people of seventeen and eighteen now out of school but
without jobs. He had heard the German sentiments echoed by a
Chinese Rotarian from Shanghai who, after describing a previous
anarchic student period (dictating who ran the colleges, the dismissal

of teachers, putting professors on trial and smashing up their offices, which seems a remarkable prefiguration of the more recent Cultural Revolution), stated that "China at present is ruled by the Kuomintang. . . . Any movement that is not in accord with Kuomintang principles is not allowed to function. This is why . . . the students are under better control."

Neither the "solution" of Hitler nor that of Chiang Kai-shek appealed to Schofield, but he had an uphill fight to persuade the largely American Convention that there was any problem at all. Boys' Work and Boys' Clubs were what delegates wanted to talk about; "youth" to them represented an unruly older group whose reactions were unfathomable and whose unwillingness to work was a root cause of the Depression. Boys, on the other hand, would be boys — and, later, if they behaved themselves, maybe Rotarians — and in the protective guidance of that innocent maelstrom of pre-pubescent energy lay one of the prime duties of the world's first Service Clubs. As for those few years later, when rapscallions turned into ruffians, and, even more alarming, young adults, that was a matter for politics, religion and, if all else failed, the police — certainly not for Rotary discussion. Schofield fought to turn their eyes outward, to broaden the area of legitimate Rotary concern. The economy, the politics, of the world must provide hope of one kind or another for its youth, he realised; they must be groomed to be the national strength not its weakness. The totalitarian regimes were realising this: "Czechoslovakia used to have an outlet for young fellows to go to Russia and Poland. . . . Those outlets are definitely closed by political barriers." He came nearer home: "You have sent a large number, and we have sent a smaller number, to Russia, to help with the industrial reorganization in that country. I know something about Soviet Russia. It is not going to be very many years before no more of your and our executives are going there. They are getting ready to organize within their own vast borders. That outlet will be closed. These national barriers are closing round."

It was no use. The New World was closing down its own national barriers in isolation after all. The Convention reverted enthusiastically to considering Boys' Work, Boys' Clubs, Boy Scouts, Boys' Weeks, and, with surprising vehemence, how to keep girls out of it, all these things, just as their mothers were being kept out of Rotary Clubs. It was all very reminiscent of First World War days, when Conventions were far more concerned about protecting their soldiers from bad women than from bad generals. Yet perhaps the most surprising suggestion from "the floor" was to promote the sanitising effect of music: "Of the thousands of criminals, racketeers, gangsters and hoodlums arrested in the United States," declared Henry Cox, a college instructor from Omaha, Nebraska, "no one single man has yet been found who has had four years of membership in an adolescent band or orchestra." Here clearly was a believer (with Congreve, not Shakespeare, as is often supposed) that music had charms to soothe the savage breast, a belief that should have taken some hard knocks a month later when Hitler's enjoyment of a performance of Wagner's *Das Rheingold* at the annual Bayreuth Festival was vastly improved by his receiving a running commentary, between the acts, of the murder of the Austrian Chancellor Dollfuss by Viennese Nazis. Naturally Rotarian Cox had never heard of these goings-on, but any historian — or connoisseur of opera and the movies of Cecil B. De Mille — could have told him that where music and breasts are concerned, ever since the first tom-tom sounded, the result has been conflagration and intended to be so.

Two strong notes of warning were sounded. Schofield awakened a positive and sympathetic response in Robert Mohler of Kansas, who roundly declared: "Unless we find a better social and economic order for these hundreds of thousands of young men, I fear that Rotary will not have served in this day and age as it should have served." Schofield's own most forceful words were: " . . . if the capitalistic system is not going to deal with this question, the next generation is going to deal with the capitalistic system".

But the theme of boyhood had a card waiting up its sleeve, at sight of which even Herbert Schofield had to throw in his hand. The Boy Scouts of America had sent their President, a Rotarian, to Detroit, to honour Paul Harris with the Award of the Silver Buffalo, for "no man has accomplished a more distinguished service to boyhood".

Even so, it was already too late. Boyhood would be a long time adying in the Movement, but the first knell had sounded, and gradually the conception of "Youth Service" would take its place. The University of Chicago Report had already urged Rotary's need for "more of the ruthless characteristic of youth".

It was the same need already identified by the New Chancellor of Germany who, not for the first time, was cleverly tapping the same sources of strength as Paul Harris. And he had but to build on an already firm foundation, since, long before Hitler had been democratically voted into the same office that Rotarian Cuno had held a decade earlier, the Weimar Republic had boasted the largest national youth organisation in the world, 10 million boys of various groups who belonged to the Reich Committee of German Youth Associations. And their new leader under Hitler was Baldur von Schirach, a young man who looked like an American college boy and who, despite his name, was in fact more American than German, numbering among his forbears two signatories of the Declaration of Independence.

And with the death of the Boy, innocence was in its long last throes during these last few years before the Second World War. The occupation of the Rhineland in 1936 was followed by the invasion of Austria in 1938, after which came Czechoslovakia, then Poland, then civilisation itself was struggling for survival. In Churchill's words, though, the inevitable step had come that terrible 30th June in 1934, when it was clear "that conditions in Germany bore no resemblance to those of a civilised state. A dictatorship based upon terror and reeking with blood had confronted the world". Two weeks after the massacres of that Saturday afternoon in Munich and Berlin, the Fuehrer explained why he had acted thus: "I did not wish to deliver up the Young Reich to the fate of the Old Reich — I gave the order to shoot." So it was Bang, You're Dead, and nobody argued. And as Hitler's Youth flourished, Paul Harris's Boy withered. Not all at once, of course.

None the less, the Nazi Movement had succeeded in transforming Germany's Youth into men, their boys into Youth. Visitors to Berlin in the thirties frequently saw in its wooded outskirts groups of Hitler Youth scrambling through the trees, climbing obstacles and racing over the fields, carrying heavy army packs and rifles too. They were strong young men, ruddy and handsome, confident and happy. They had been happy boys and were now happy young lads, being transformed into happy, confident men.

How did youth fare through the 1930s with Rotary, whose special dedication to them has been constantly noted, as a Movement brought into being by one man's boyhood? In Germany, youth had been commandeered. How did Rotary cope elsewhere? In 1933, the Rotarians of Göteborg in Sweden gave a series of lectures to the young unemployed, and Spanish Clubs co-operated in a scheme to suppress the supply of pornographic books and photographs reaching boys and girls. The Shanghai Club sent a large donation to help poor Russian children in Manchuria; the Ipoh Club in Malaya formed the first library the town had ever known, for use by youngsters only; Madras Rotarians funded scholarships impartially for groups of Hindu, Muhammadan and Christian children. In Avignon, France, the Club formed a special holiday camp for sons of European Rotarians; Prague Rotary undertook to look after groups of English boys studying at the world-famous Czechoslovak Bata Shoe Factory; in Italy, Verona, Turin and other Clubs embarked on a programme of sponsoring young students at famous universities. The Club at Azul, Argentina,

donated a library of 3,000 volumes to educate juvenile delinquents
— in the city gaol; in Juxtepec, Mexico, Rotarians paid for dental
care of all local schoolchildren; at Sonsonate, El Salvador, Rotarians
continued their annual tradition of providing 400 new suits for the
poorer boys and young men of the town. Many Clubs in Brazil
concentrated on the care of crippled children, following a long
tradition established by Chicago's No One Club. And Hungary in
August played host to hundreds of boys sent by Rotary Clubs all
over the world to the International Boy Scout Jamboree, held near
Budapest, presenting every single one with a 400-page volume of
photographs illustrating Hungarian life, omitting presumably the
activities of the country's leader, the rabidly anti-Jewish "General"
Gombos (while Minister of Defence, he had promoted himself from
Captain), who was very busy setting Hungary on the path to dictator-
ship which would begin with Gombos's transportation of arms from
Italy and end with Eichmann's transportation of Jews to Auschwitz.

Let us skip three years to see what was happening when European shadows first started gathering for Rotary with the outbreak
of the Spanish Civil War. The future of Spanish Youth was now, of
course, spoken for, from 1936 till 1939. Over in Italy, Clubs were
still concentrating on education where young people were concerned, Vicenza sending a student to Belgium. In Yugoslavia, the
Pancevo Club had the interesting idea of introducing an essay
contest for schoolchildren, the topics being "King Alexander and
World Peace", "Characteristics of the League of Nations" and
"War as a Last Resort". Romanian Rotary Clubs undertook to look
after the children of poor families in their respective towns for
eighteen months, and the Austrian Club of Graz provided books,
clothes, shoes, meals and holiday gifts for a local school (more of
Graz later). In France, as Civil War was suddenly detonated to the
south of the Pyrenees, Clubs everywhere rushed to adopt the
children of Spanish Rotarians, now abruptly turned into refugees,
orphans or both.

But away from the cauldron of the punch-drunk old warrior
continent, what of those lands where that great Boy Wonder, Big
Jim Davidson, had rolled the Golden Wheel? With a sense of horrified approval, remembering the city's unsavoury reputation in those
times, we discover that the Rotarians of Port Said, Egypt, were
finding "suitable shelter" for the numerous boys and girls wandering
homeless in those garish streets and dank, dark alleys. In Jerusalem,
Rotary started a battle against seemingly impossible odds by
campaigning against lethargic local authorities to stop young people
drifting into the popular career of professional beggary, a future of
peculiarly Middle Eastern promise; while at the other end of North

Africa, the Rotary Club of Casablanca took a number of orphanages under its wing and bought blankets and beds for them, staging a special showing of the film success *The Story of Louis Pasteur* to impress hygiene upon schoolchildren.

Farther along the Davidson trail, the beggar-child problem — then as still today — was also exercising the consciences of Calcutta Rotarians in concert with the Bengal Government; the Rotary Club of Malacca gave young people in their city a large playground and sponsored holidays; Penang Club members in Malaya promoted sports for the young. In Manila, capital of the Philippines, Rotarians struck deeper into the youth "problem" by publishing a series of careers guidance booklets that became required reading throughout the island (they had been read to Paul and Jean Harris at banquets the year before). Chinese Rotarians took the view that, where youth was concerned, safety lay in numbers — the Hangchow Club presented a silver spoon to each new child born to one of its members, while the Tientsin Club placed a flag by the lunch-plate of each proud father and demanded a donation to Club funds for every pound the baby gained in weight, a custom explained to a surprised group of boys and girls visiting Paul Harris that year in Chicago by a Tientsin member who happened to be in the vicinity. In Shanghai, Rotarians judged that many of their youth problems resulted from overcrowding and promoted new homes with more light and air, a solution soon tested the following year when Japanese planes mercilessly battered the city to ruins. In the meantime, the proud parents of many of those bomber pilots, in Tokyo and other cities, were preparing summer camps for the athletic sons of Rotarians.

As might be expected perhaps, those Clubs which Jim Davidson, with Ralston's help, had first founded in the Pacific, were foremost in placing their accent on youth. Naturally, much effort in Australia and New Zealand was directed towards outdoor recreations, but Newcastle, New South Wales, members provided them especially for young deaf-mutes. The Sydney Club developed a succession of gymnasiums converted from, of all things, "unused" police stations, thus making certain that they stayed unused. The Goulburn and Wollongong Clubs, one inland and one on the coast, gave annual seaside holidays to about seventy underprivileged children to build up malnourished physiques. For their part, Brisbane Rotarians also gave underprivileged children Christmas holidays at the seaside (during Australia's high summer, of course). In New Zealand, the "neighbour" a thousand miles away across the Tasman Sea, all Clubs combined to support a Rotary Health Camp for sick and crippled children on a beautiful island site, and the Auckland Club organised a job service for the handicapped. The Christchurch Rotarians formed a group of twenty-four Maori children into a superb choir which toured the country giving concerts for a fund for crippled children. Indeed, it seemed that Clubs in the Antipodes, because of the natural chances their magnificent climate and scenery gave to youthful recreation, were more acutely aware than Rotarians elsewhere of those youngsters to whom normal exercise was denied through physical handicap.

Rotary had started in South Africa at the same time as it had in Australia and New Zealand. But in 1936, fifteen years of the Movement had resulted in only eleven Clubs there, as against twice as many in New Zealand and forty-nine Clubs in Australia. Yet, in spite of the fact that this was the year in which true apartheid measures made their first ostentatious appearance with the setting up of a separate electoral roll for black people in Cape Province (though they could vote only for whites), Rotarians made this year one of shining achievement, especially in the field of youth. The Johannesburg Club set up a youth hostel for the whole of the East Rand, a part of the world where Rotary's wheel really *was* made of gold. The Pretoria Club spent the equivalent of thousands of dollars to set up and staff a dental clinic solely for the use of poor children who could not afford to pay for care; and in the Transvaal Rotarians organised a series of careers talks in schools. It may have helped that, in the early part of the year, Paul Harris's old friend George Olinger, an inveterate traveller and campaigner for Boys' Work (see Chapter Fourteen) and now retired from his inevitably thriving business as a mortician, had travelled around in South Africa with his wife at his own expense, speaking the Rotary Boys' gospel at every single Club.

It was, of course, the year Paul and Jean Harris made their triumphant tour of South America, as described in the previous chapter, so if we continue along the path of the sun in another ocean hop, west over the Atlantic, we shall not be surprised to find Rotary activities at full pace on that continent during these twelve months.

In 1933, Ches Perry had already deemed their Clubs so important that a special Spanish edition of *The Rotarian*, called *Revista Rotaria*, had begun monthly publication. Now in 1936, counting the nations and islands of Central America and the Caribbean, there were 282 Clubs in the old empires of Spain and Portugal. Compared with the number of Clubs in the United States at this time, 2,557, this seems a modest amount (it was just over half the number of those in Great Britain and Ireland), but when we consider that Chile, with fifty-six Clubs, was only eight Clubs behind France, which had more

Rotarians than any other nation on the mainland of Europe, a different perspective of importance emerges. Indeed the election of a South American as World President of Rotary was only four years away.

Recognising the priority of love and care lavished on the young in all Latin countries, it is no surprise to find Central and South America alive with projects directed towards youth. Mention of a few must suffice. Both Santiago (Chile) and Lima (Peru) found Rotarians forming a "Protective league" for the sponsorship and support of poor students. In João Pessõa (Brazil), a Rotarian donated sufficient funds to endow and maintain a school for the poor, which he named the Paul Harris School. In Argentina, the Rotary Club of Santiago del Estero established a society called "Friends of Education" which enjoyed wide influence. In Mexico City, a doctor in the Club devoted every Saturday to the care of the young; and in Cuba, the Rotarians of Antilla set up a research unit to discover the cause of an epidemic of stomach disorders amongst the children in rural regions of the country. And it was in March of 1936 that the Rotarians attending their first Ibero-American Conference in Valparaiso, with Paul Harris as guest of honour, placed a plaque of commemoration upon the great "Christ of the Andes" statue (which itself had been cast from melted-down cannons) that signalled peace on the border of Chile and Argentina. Paul was to make reference to this occasion at the Nice Convention of Rotary in the following year (see the next chapter).

It was Paul's tour of South America, in fact, which was to prove the most decisive for the Rotary Movement of all his journeys round the globe. The Founder of Rotary, as we have seen many times, was the epitome of traditional Anglo-Saxon reserve (many regarded him as "typically" English, even the English); no personality could have been in greater contrast to the flamboyant, demonstrative characters who peopled the Rotary stage south of the equator in the New World. Yet his impact upon those cultures so vastly different from the Vermont Valley back in the Green Mountains near Elfin Lake which fashioned the boyhood ideal that in turn fashioned Rotary, was dramatically proved not by the activities directed towards youth just described, but by a far more extraordinary phenomenon. During 1936, from the old Spanish Main all the way to Cape Horn, generals erupted into power, dissolved democractic institutions with varying degrees of severity, turning the entire continent into a nest of totalitarian regimes. Yet, in contrast to the Old World, not one of those regimes attempted to regulate or dissolve the new Rotary Clubs sprouting everywhere. Nor have they since.

In North America and Great Britain and Ireland, the prime emphasis on boyhood was being slowly but remorselessly smothered by the twin oppression of the thirties: unemployment and the ever more certain approach of another world war. The lost generation had given birth to the dole generation. In Europe, there were over 30 million unemployed, in the United States 10 million were without jobs, and of this horrendous combined total more than 13 million were young people, a generation of youth trained by trade, craft, natural skills and education for careers at all levels, but who had never drawn wages or salaries in their lives. Between them, Europe and the United States had as many idle and vagrant as India, where Gandhi was attempting to alleviate the situation in 5,000 remote villages by his celebrated campaign with the spinning-wheel which, however uneconomic in producing cloth, at least gave an occupation to many with nothing to do. Germany, Austria, Bulgaria and other European countries found a solution not in spinning-wheels but in pickaxes, carried on the shoulder like rifles. Labour Camps for Youth were formed increasingly, some voluntary, some compulsory, and their ultimate aim was becoming ever more obvious to travellers with clear minds. But it was not the way of the United States and Great Britain, which had begun counter-action against the unhealthy nationalistic nature of the Labour Camps by starting exchange visits of sons of Rotarians between their two countries, the very first on record being the visit of four boys from the state of Georgia to England, reciprocated in 1935 by four English boys visiting Georgia. By 1936, "youth exchange" was in full flood across the oceans of the world, with young American and Australian men and women visiting China and Japan, Danes going to South Africa, and every country in Europe criss-crossing in youth exchange visits. England, thanks to the spur of Ernest Atkins of the Wandsworth Club (see the next chapter), favoured exchange with Germany.

The hope all this engendered had, alas, come too late to save this generation of the dole from the ordeal of their fathers. After the return of five young Czechoslovaks from the Rotary Club of Portsmouth that summer of 1936, one of their fathers wrote: "We are very much obliged to the Portsmouth Rotarians for their kindness, which I am sure will leave the most beautiful memories in the young souls of our boys for the length of their lives." Neville Chamberlain and Munich were soon to change that view, and shorten both memories and lives.

In the 4,000 communities in seventy nations all over the world where Rotary Clubs had been formed by now — 1936 saw the addition of Fiji and Sarawak — community help of every kind was being given by members, according to local needs, though some parts of the world gave social occasions rather more priority than others. Because of their temperaments and natural gregariousness, it is not surprising for instance that the French and Italians put "fellowship" high on their schedules. But 1936, with the start of the Civil War in Spain, cast an inexorable shadow over the Movement in which men were boys again the better to understand the problems of youth.

At the Atlantic City Convention Paul Harris spoke clearly of what he saw ahead: "There is an immense amount of conceit in the world; and bombastic speeches of supposedly patriotic order deceive the youth of all countries into the belief that the intentions of their countries alone are honorable, and that in war, their countries alone are invincible. Such misleading propaganda does not make for security, it makes for trouble." Paul may have been thinking back to that supreme moment for him, two years ago at the Detroit Convention when, just back from his trip to South Africa, he had been awarded the Silver Buffalo for "distinguished service to boyhood". The citation added significantly, "In this case, international in character". Present in that 1934 Convention audience had been a Past President of the Rotary Club of Belgrade, Milan Stojadinović, who was also a member of the European Advisory Committee of Rotary International. He was later to tell the Convention, in pledging his support of the Fourth Object of Rotary: "The Rotary Clubs in Yugoslavia try to advance international understanding, goodwill and peace. . . . This task often places the Rotarians of Yugoslavia in a difficult position, namely, they are trying to be internationalists when all around us we find extreme nationalism."

At that Convention of 1934 Rotarians had learned of the first "Institute of International Understanding" held by the Club of Nashville, Tennessee (today, rather more famous as the centre of a truer internationalism, for good or ill: that of the pop-music world). Now, at the 1936 Convention, that initiative was adopted for Rotarians of all countries. But again too late, for Rotarian Stojadinović who, from his remarks quoted above, might have been presumed to be in the forefront of such an initiative, was no longer a delegate. He had become in the intervening two years Prime Minister of Yugoslavia and, a sycophant of Mussolini and Hitler, conceived of himself as the Fuehrer of his country and was soon to welcome and support the invasion of Austria and destruction of Czechoslovakia.

But the gulf between ideals and reality never surprised the Founder of Rotary, a fact which made him different from almost all others in the Movement he had conceived, for he remembered the Chicago in which he had conceived it, with enormous determination but utterly without illusion. The fact that Rotary's setting was expanded from the anarchic "Windy City" of 1905 to a world about to be wracked by tormenting hurricanes of misery and disaster and of colossal ferocity did not alter the intent of his straightforward, simple faith one iota. Like Churchill, he could but wait and warn and cling to waning hope that the lemmings could be turned back from the sea even yet.

Momentarily sighting a false dawn at the 1937 Convention at Nice (see the next chapter), Paul was in good company, for that year Churchill was to find himself the companion of that same Rotarian Stojadinović at a dinner in London in honour of the Yugoslav Premier, during which festive meal Lord Halifax announced his acceptance of an invitation to go hunting in Germany with Goering at his great estate at Karinhall (soon to be filled with the looted art masterpieces of Europe), an invitation the lordly Master of Foxhounds accepted with joyful alacrity; sport, if not love, could find a way perhaps! As Rotarians knew only too well, the ceremonies of eating had their sacrilegious, as well as sublime, motivations. In 1938, however, with Clubs being established in both China and Japan, countries now at each other's throats, with new Clubs in Cyprus and the Anglo-Egyptian Sudan, while at the same time they were being closed down in Austria, Italy and Germany, Paul chose a cautious line at the Convention, veering between giving a warning and making an effort not to antagonise the isolationist line he saw appearing amongst the Movement's "organisation men", Ches Perry in particular. He had also listened to these words of the Movement's first French President:

> It is natural to expect Japanese Rotarians will be carrying on as loyal Japanese, and Chinese Rotarians as loyal Chinese, just as you and I are each loyal citizens of our own countries. But what of co-operation towards international understanding? . . . When bitter fighting is in progess, naturally passions are inflamed on both sides, and thus for the moment it unfortunately does not seem there is much that Rotary can do. We are continuing to maintain our contacts and to explore every possibility. . . .
>
> The first duty of every Rotarian is to be a loyal citizen of his own country, and this is possible, even though one is devoted to the cause of international understanding. We sincerely regret that the Rotarians of Germany and Austria, in the face of circumstances, felt that the only decision they could take was to disband their Rotary Clubs. . . . But even though the former members of Rotary Clubs in Germany are no longer Rotarians, they are still our friends.

And Paul knew how many questions this left begging. In the audience were nine delegates from China and six from Japan, and one could hardly expect many possibilities being explored besides mutual mayhem when Chinese Rotarians were dispersing and fleeing before the Japanese invaders in all the principal mainland cities. Those Tientsin Rotary fathers of the year before, flags, families and all, had scattered into the hills in mortal terror. The Rotarians of Shanghai alone were trying to disperse funds from Clubs round the world to over 1 million refugees and the Peking Club was already witnessing the setting up of a puppet Chinese government under Japanese bayonets.

Herbert Taylor's Four-Way Test (see the next chapter) did not equip Rotarians for such circumstances. Rotary International President Duperrey had already that year witnessed personally "the union of Austria with other Germanic lands in the German Reich", but he made no report to the Convention on the reactions of the Rotarians of Linz (formed in 1927, the year *Mein Kampf* was completed) when the Fuehrer revisited his home town (it also had the distinction of being Eichmann's) on his triumphant progress to Vienna. It was in Linz, however, that Hitler signed the document proclaiming Austria as a province of the Reich.

> One not infrequently hears some Rotarian inveigh against Rotary for its so-called lackadaisical policy in international affairs . . . he declares that it is high time that Rotary abandon its Pollyanna politics and take position in international affairs worthy of full-grown men. He demands that the forces of Rotary International be mobilized and its influence brought to bear to the end that international marauders be brought to justice in order that democracy may survive. . . .
>
> We cannot break faith with our Rotarian friends, wheresoever they may live, whatsoever countries they may owe allegiance to. We simply can't do these things in Rotary; there are enough things to be done that are entirely constructive. To succor the distressed, the innocent victims of war, pestilence and famine is constructive; that is quite within our line. Rotary should be outstanding above all others in the sorely needed thing — international good manners.

It was a brilliant performance. Without wishing to panic delegates (members from China and Japan still sat in the audience, which this year numbered nearly 10,500) he succeeded in telling them the world was changing. Without any indication that he shared them, he listed devastatingly the causes of concern for world events which Perry would have preferred to ignore. In one classic sentence which perhaps summed up his most lasting and profound feeling about

Rotary, he drew delegates' attention to the fact that world affairs were no longer in the hands of men with even a pretence of protocol, that the world was teetering on barbarism, though even he could not have forecast the cynical disregard of international pledges about to cascade its filth upon mankind, or the end of honour among thieves, or the deliberate elevation of homicidal killers to power, or the extermination — far from battle — of so many millions.

By the outbreak of war in Europe Rotary International, in spite of closures by the Axis powers, had grown to encompass over 200,000 members in eighty-eight countries, and indeed the 5,000th Club was chartered in Rockmart, Georgia, USA. Among these there were two new countries: French West Africa, now Senegal, and the island of Guam in the Pacific, a dependency of the United States. Guam was destined to be the first island occupied by the Japanese after Pearl Harbor in December 1941 — only five days afterwards, in fact — and its liberation by US forces in 1944 saw some of the Pacific's bloodiest fighting. It was from Guam that the US Air Force launched some of its most devastating attacks against Japan in the closing months of the war, before the atomic age began and abruptly brought surrender. The island has an even more lasting claim to fame. It was here that the last Rotary Club was formed before the Second World War began, and this Club was the first to be re-formed after occupation by the enemy when peace returned.

What Paul Harris told the Rotarians at the 1939 Convention is quoted in the chapter that follows. His most significant utterance to be noted here lay in the key phrase he had just used at the San Francisco Convention in 1938 (which had first played host to the Convention in 1915, when the First World War had already begun) half-way through his speech. He had called Rotarians "full-grown men".

CHAPTER EIGHTEEN

Birth of the Man

If all the Boys of the World
  Agreed to be Sailors free,
  What a fine bridge their boats could be!

So, what a fine circle
  Round the World it would be
  If all Mankind to join hands would agree!

*Lines by the French poet Paul Fort
quoted by RI President Elect Maurice
Duperrey at the Rotary Convention, Nice*

There was another guide to the world's Rotarians during the 1930s, written three years before the University of Chicago Report but which has long survived it in the minds of most Club members. It was *Rotary*, without a question mark, written by a Rotarian of the Chicago Club, Herbert J. Taylor, for his own use when he sought guidance in prayer after leaving his Classification of "Packaged Groceries; House-to-House Sales" to take over a bankrupt firm called Club Aluminum. "One morning", Taylor recounted (often), "I leaned over my desk, rested my head in my hands. In a few moments, I reached for a white paper card and wrote down that which had come to me — in twenty-four words." Those words were a formulation he called the Four-Way Test, and they went thus (with capitals):

1. Is it the TRUTH?
2. Is it FAIR to all concerned?
3. Will it build GOODWILL and BETTER FRIENDSHIPS?
4. Will it be BENEFICIAL to all concerned?

Taylor made all his employees memorise this "code" and claimed that it enabled him to pull the Aluminum Company out of the red. Since he began by ceasing to make exaggerated claims for his product in his advertising, the objective observer would say he was simply following sound business practice, but, to Rotarian Taylor, he had managed — through a flash of inspiration from Above (he was deeply religious) — to encapsulate the Rotary Code of Ethics in an easily remembered formula.

In so doing, he violated one of the first principles Paul Harris had ever felt about his Movement and maintained throughout his long life, that Rotary was neither a religion nor a substitute for religion. To many Americans, however, business is often either one or the other, if not both, and, since most Rotarians are business men, the confusion is understandable — in the United States anyway. Abroad, it was not necessarily so. As Roger Levy states in his history, *Rotary International in Great Britain and Ireland*, "This was a piece of home-spun morality with which R.I.B.I. Rotarians were never unanimously comfortable", though it has duly appeared since all over the world on desk-sets, wall-plaques, illuminated scrolls and ashtrays, and in all Rotary literature, translated into every major language on earth. As for being a neat summation of Rotary's Code of Ethics, it was of course nothing of the sort. It was a needle's eye through which successful men could enter the kingdom of heaven, of which Rotary was a possible ante-room. It was a *Boy's Own* version of morality and we can be grateful that it wasn't brought to the world's attention until 1939 when Herbert Taylor became President of the Chicago Club; thus no harm was done until it was too late for the harm to be serious.

Taylor's life coincided well with Rotary: he was born in 1893, the year Paul Harris had taken his first look at Chicago, and he became World President during the Movement's Golden Jubilee, during which he seized the opportunity to distribute 400,000 copies of his Test. He was reputed to recite from memory twenty-one chapters of the Bible each day, in the light of which one cannot but feel that he would have done Rotarians a better service by urging them to read the Ten Commandments. Certainly if everyone followed the Four-Way Test human communication would become utterly impossible. As might be expected, its author was devoted to his self-proclaimed "hobby" of Boys' Work, personally sponsored one of the largest camps for boys in the United States and pioneered dozens of what were called "Interdenominational Christian Youth Projects", which, to anyone else, would appear a contradiction in terms, like his Test. Paul Harris came to regard him, at least for publication, as "a great man and a great Rotarian", but the Movement was spared delay in maturing from boyhood during the decade of the Depression and rise of dictatorship by his not coming to prominence until 1939, when Rotary's greatest crisis of survival was full upon it.

In the present chapter we can follow the progress of that maturation, reluctant as it sometimes was, by studying Rotary in a part of the world which was near enough to the totalitarian menace to feel its dire threat and yet was sufficiently distanced from Europe to share the natural hesitations of the whole International Movement — namely, the British Isles. In so doing, we shall chart the amazing and horrifying rise to power — through consent of the terrified — of the monster who came so close to destroying Western (and Eastern) civilisation. It will not be done through recapitulating the whole familiar story — even though that cannot be told too often — but from the standpoint of its reflection in Rotary affairs, especially those of RIBI. That "territorial unit" of Great Britain and Ireland, about which such controversy had arisen in the rest of the Rotary world, was the first Rotary seed-bed to have flourished outside North America and it was continuing to do so, despite the Nazis, when the rest of Europe, Rotary and all, had gone under.

Fittingly, it all began on the Ides of March. It was then, on 15th March 1933, that Hitler's democratically elected (a point often forgotten) first cabinet devised the plan by which the Reichstag (Germany's parliament) would vote Hitler unlimited power for the next four years. Next morning, conscription was introduced. Seven days later, total power was his, achieved by the simple expedient of his ordering his intimidating thugs to surround the Reichstag deputies, arrest all the Communist members and detain the more troublesome Social Democrats. To chants from the stormtroopers, threatening "Fire and murder!" (which came, anyway), the deputies voted 441 for Hitler, ninety-four against. The Fuehrer had said shortly before, "We have no scruples, no bourgeois hesitations. . . . [My enemies] regard me as an uneducated barbarian. Yes, we are barbarians. We want to be barbarians. It is an honourable title." Professor Alan Bullock, the chronicler of Nazi tyranny, has summed it up thus: "The street gangs had seized control of the resources of a great modern State, the gutter had come to power." At the time, the British Ambassador, Sir Horace Rumbold, minced no words in his report to London: "Prominent socialists and communists have been surprised at night and murdered in their beds, or shot down at the doors of their homes . . . the windows of shops owned by Jews were smashed and their contents looted. . . . One of the most inhuman features of the present campaign is the incarceration without trial of thousands of individuals whose political antecedents have rendered them obnoxious in the eyes of the new regime." Sir Horace — whom Anthony Eden was later justly to call "one of the best Ambassadors this country has ever had" — rightly regarded these concentration camps (of which there were already at least fifty even in 1933) as "a new departure in civilised countries". He added, "the speeches of Nazi leaders would be regarded in most civilised countries as deliberate incitements to violence", which they were, of course; and concluded, "I have the impression that the persons directing the policy of the Hitler Government are not normal. Many of us have the feeling that we are living in a country where fantastic hooligans have got the upper hand."

Yet, largely, the rest of the world ignored the warnings, partly because the First World War and its terrible losses still loomed large in their minds and also because they could not credit that such bestial horrors could occur in the twentieth century. Although (on the very morning after the Nazis had encouraged workers to participate in great May Day celebrations in Berlin) all trade unions had been abolished, the Labour Movement's *Daily Herald* in Britain still kept making as many excuses for the Nazis as *The Times* — which was even removing from its columns any passage possibly "offensive" to Hitler. Everyone hoped that the reports from Germany were exaggerated, that power would have charms to soothe the savage breast, and even the *Jewish Chronicle* hoped "the Nazi chiefs may acquire in office that sense of responsibility which they could not feel when wooing the passions of the rabble". Why listen to warmongers like Winston Churchill? The Nazis were clever enough to allow people to travel freely in and out of Germany. Unemployment was rapidly vanishing there, ordinary citizens felt an understandable new national pride, most of them being unaware of what was going on but at the same time being conscious that other nations were once more treating Germany with respect and some awe. In August 1933, 90 per cent of them — over 38 million — voted in a free plebiscite to let Hitler have complete dictatorial power. Even as these lines are being written, British media are marking — as is happening in other parts of Europe, including Germany — the fiftieth anniversary of Hitler's coming to power, which underlines the macabre fascination that the Nazi regime still exerts on the public.

Why should Rotarians in Great Britain and Ireland have reacted any differently from the vast majority of their compatriots? Why should Rotarians anywhere? The town of Rotary's birthplace, after all, had witnessed the same phenomenon, on a concentrated scale, much earlier; and, no less than their fellow-citizens, the Chicago Rotarians regarded Capone and his gangsters with the same mixture of incredulity, terror and resigned tolerance as the world now treated Hitler and his. Tolerance of Capone and his predecessors by Chicagoans was the result of its being sometimes hard to discern any basic differences between ruthless big business and ruthless big crime. In Capone's words: "The very guys that make my trade good are the ones that yell the loudest about me. They talk about me not being on the legitimate. Nobody's on the legit."

He was right. It was precisely because almost nobody was "on the legit" that Paul Harris had started his Movement. And gangsterism stayed Rotary's near-neighbour for many years. The son of Vivian Carter, now a retired Wing Commander in the RAF, clearly recalled for the present writer the death of Tony Lombardo, Capone's "prime minister" at the head of the Unione Siciliana and ruler of some 15,000 Sicilians in Chicago alone. Lombardo and the then British Editor of *The Rotarian* shared a liking for the same restaurant, just a block or so away from Rotary Headquarters at East Wacker Drive, and it was near there, while on his way to lunch, that Lombardo was filled with dumdum bullets one midday rush-hour, while hundreds gaped and "saw nothing". Vivian himself had luckily lunched elsewhere that day but he had quickly learned to accept, like other Chicagoans, native or adopted, the facts of life in that turbulent city.

Kenneth Allsop, in his definitive book *The Bootleggers*, states the unavoidable parallel:

> Capone had been one of the most powerful men in the world. In 1931, Mussolini had been dictator of Italy for nine years . . . it was only months before Hitler became Chancellor and constituted the Third Reich; Stalin had been supreme head of the Soviet Union for seven years . . . all of them were part of the same pattern of that darkening time, an age when enforcement of policy by gun, cruelty and oppression, in contempt of the theoretical canons of law, became naked and ubiquitous.

The evidence that James Doherty, a crime reporter on the *Chicago Tribune* during Capone's heyday, gave to Kenneth Allsop, has a startling ring: "I can't believe he was all-evil, like he's been painted. . . . Sure he was a cold-blooded killer, but he had his good side. I see him as a victim of his time and circumstances. Capone was tolerated by the public because — let's face it — he was giving them a service they wanted."

Much the same was being said now on Hitler's behalf. It was the reason why, at the beginning, many German business men could, without rupturing their consciences, support both National Socialism and their Rotary Club. And outside Germany as well. It may crystallise an uneasy facing of past realities to recall that in the mid-thirties the most popular Nazi slogan familiar to the public was *Gemeinnutz von Eigennutz!*, which translates into another alarmingly familiar slogan, "The Common Interest before Self", almost Rotary's war-cry since 1910. Everyone forgot, if they even then knew, how Hitler had bragged of his lack of scruples and bourgeois hesitations. Scruples and bourgeois hesitations were what Rotary Ethics were truly all about. Hitler was well aware of this and knew where his enemies lay. But he waited five years before striking at the Golden Wheel.

Meanwhile, across the Channel, at the Fourteenth Annual RIBI Conference in 1933 at Scarborough, Yorkshire, Dr Leslie Burgin, MP, an Honorary Member of the Luton Club and a practised survivor in politics, being a Liberal who managed also to be Parliamentary Secretary to the Board of Trade in Ramsay MacDonald's National Government, stated that the new leaders of Germany were no more alarming than examples of what he perceived as "a pulse running through the whole universe which may be symbolised as the desire to begin afresh. . . . Some of the movements towards dictatorship in former Spain, present Italy, and modern Germany, to say nothing of the United States of America, are instances of the recognition of the necessity under certain conditions of a combination of plan and drive".

The equation of Hitler's methods with those of Roosevelt was a frequently recurring simile at that time, and by no means confined to commentators outside of the United States, many of whom indeed do not hesitate to use it today. Many found the catchphrases New Deal and New Order interchangeable. Dr Burgin spoke of a new world, however, which Rotary could help build, where "suspicion dies, hate has no place, revenge and resentment perish, and comradeship takes pride of place". This was not quite the New Order Hitler had in mind. His ideas of plan and drive had been witnessed at first hand a few days before by a group of Norwich Rotarians who had had a number of members in Germany for the workers' May Day celebrations (unaware that on 2nd May Hitler had arrested and efficiently murdered most of the top Labour leaders". They reported back that the new Nazi Chancellor "had given the nation hope", while their Club President doubted "whether there was any other way in which a nation could be pulled together than by preaching intense nationalism and pride of race". Norwich Rotarians were told that "while no doubt injustices had been done to the Jews", reports reaching England were much exaggerated, although "some who were working against Germany and were not desirable would be driven out". That these happened to include the likes of Rotarian Thomas Mann (a non-Jew) was not, it seems, noticed.

A few months later, Rotary International President John Nelson got a warm welcome from the Rotary Club of Berlin when he announced that "the helpful offices of Rotarians are available to assist the national spirit to its best form of expression". The Nazis beamed their official blessing on the Movement on hearing such reassurance, but many Jewish Rotarians thought it wiser to resign all the same, less for their own sake than that of Rotary. And the puzzlement of British Rotarians continued when they read the comments of a member of the Frankfurt Club, the London Editor of *Die Frankfurter Zeitung*. This individual admitted that "very deplorable things have happened in my country", but added that "the constructive part has begun. . . . Hitler has already proved . . . that he is a statesman".

Rotarian Ernest Atkins, who was to be so reassured by the wily Von Papen three years later in Salzburg (see the previous chapter), was even then gushing in *The Rotary Wheel* about a group of eighteen German and Austrian Club members visiting London who, he claimed, were "always charming and courteous in every circumstance, and even when most bitterly attacked, they yet defended their country with dignity and firmness, patiently explaining the difficulties and the terrible position that had caused so much controversy. It was impossible to hear them, to see them . . . without being absolutely convinced of their integrity". The German visitors were later entertained by the Manchester Club, which played "Deutschland uber Alles" for them before luncheon, so they must have felt they had plenty going for them, as this tune was not, to the certain knowledge of those present, yet in the Rotary song-book.

Yet the actions and attitudes of these British Rotarians were not in the least out of tune with majority opinion at that time. In October of that year, when Hitler was completing his first twelve months as Chancellor and busy preparing for a November election which would convert the Reichstag into nothing more than a collection of Nazi cheer-leaders (and by a massive 92 per cent of the popular vote), there was a by-election in Fulham, lying just across the Thames from Ernest Atkins's Wandsworth. Eleven days before, Germany had contemptuously withdrawn from the Disarmament Conference as well as the League of Nations, both unmistakable signposts of Hitler's intentions (which he bothered less and less to conceal). These sinister facts were ignored by the electorate, who overturned a safe Tory seat and brought in the Labour candidate with a 5,000 majority and a 26.5 per cent swing, largely the result of a promise made by the then Labour leader, George Lansbury (grandfather of today's international star of theatre and films, Angela Lansbury), who declared, "I would close every recruiting station, disband the Army and disarm the Air Force. I would abolish the whole dreadful equipment of war and say to the world 'Do your worst'."

The Nazi gangsters, now firmly consolidated in dictatorial power, needed no second invitation, and Britain's National Government of the time — to Churchill's great disgust — bowed to the obvious nation-wide pacifism, fearful for their parliamentary seats. Besides, no word of alarm was heard from the Rotarians of the free port of Danzig, just two years old, where the Nazis had also taken over the government in June, although exchange visits were made with the Club there. A certain troubled note was sounded by Bristol at the news that Munich Rotarians had expelled the Nobel Prize-winner Thomas Mann because he was a Jew (he was not, in fact, but it made a useful excuse), but, by and large, the tight little island maintained a tight little Rotary. Scots District Chairman Patrick Smith called the Rotarian Prime Minister, Ramsay MacDonald (of the Hampstead, London, Club), "the great architect of peace in our time", while inordinate pride was taken in the fact that HRH Prince George, later Duke of Kent and royal patron of RIBI, had made use of the Rotary rest-room at the British Industries Fair.

The next lodestar of enlightenment for British Rotarians came at their 1934 Conference from the eminent journalist and broadcaster on international affairs, Vernon Bartlett, who, after all, had been lucky enough to have had a personal interview with the Fuehrer the year before, after which he reported that Hitler had promised that all the concentration camps were about to be demolished. "Until Movements like yours", Bartlett scolded the Conference, "have taught individuals to understand that these foreigners are normally decent individuals like ourselves . . . we shall not begin really to get the governments to act in the interests of world peace." Some Rotarians felt suitably cowed, others less so when they recalled the speaker's description of Hitler's "large, brown eyes — so large and so brown, one might grow lyrical about them if one were a woman". Or colour-blind; since Hitler's eyes, doubtless hypnotic, were in fact blue.

In 1935, the indefatigable Germanophile, Ernest Atkins, reported on a great meeting at Wiesbaden of Rotary International District 73, at that time consisting of all the German and Austrian Clubs. These had mainly discussed how to improve international relations, since, even Atkins quaintly admitted, there was a "limitation of opportunities for Community Service in Germany". Probably the most significant feature of his printed report, however, was a photograph he took of this "harmonious" International Conference at work: dominating the proceedings and the entire hall was an enormous swastika draped at the end of it. Atkins, typically, saw nothing incongruous in this.

A much grander Rotary European gathering took place that year in Venice, in the great Palace of the Doges, where Rotarians from twenty-two countries marched up the Stairway of the Giants, past the colossal statues of Neptune and Mars, for their meeting in the Chief Council Chamber, possibly the most splendid room in Europe. Here 1,500 delegates sat before Tintoretto's 800 portraits crowding his huge canvas of Paradise and listened to the Duke of Genoa — a Rotarian like all the Italian royal males — welcome them on behalf of the King, followed by a representative of Il Duce. The blaze of medals, flags and priceless masterpieces stunned those present into a proper sense of "the dignity and influence to which Rotary has attained", in the words of a British delegate. The reporter went on, with unconscious irony: "Those who doubted the wisdom of holding the Conference in Italy, under existing conditions, reckoned, literally, without their host. Not a dissonant murmur was heard; the spectre of politics was banished from our midst; the touch of Rotary had made the whole world kin."

Unfortunately, there were no Rotarians in Abyssinia, which was possibly why Mussolini himself was not present, being too busy preparing the invasion of that country which took place within three weeks. The dictatorial personal touch had already made itself felt, however, for that excellent and social sailor, Commodore Kruse, of the liner *New York* (built, it will be remembered, by the Rotarian and former German Chancellor Wilhelm Cuno [see Chapter Fifteen], one of Hitler's old creditors in the past), has taken part in a mid-Atlantic rescue, and when Rotarian Kruse of the Hamburg Club returned to his home port, Hitler came on board to greet him personally.

That crucial band of water called the Channel, was, however, while protecting the British from too uncomfortably close an acquaintance with the dictators' progress, also keeping them immune from some of the grander delusions of those who lived too close to the surface parade. At the Margate Conference of Rotarians in Great Britain and Ireland in 1935, delegates were lectured on "The Rotarian's International Obligation" by Sir Norman Angell, the distinguished economist and campaigner for peace, on whom fate had already paid two most unkind tricks. He had invented "The Money Game", a card game devised to teach the public the elements of economics, in 1928, just when genuine players all over the world were about to be dealt the worst losing hand in stock-exchange records, and had then received the Nobel Peace Prize in 1933, the year Hitler became Chancellor of Germany. Now, as co-President of the Worldwide Movement against War and Fascism, he enjoyed enormous prestige. His honesty about the futility of war and the possibility of maintaining any sort of practical "parity" of weapons as an insurance for peace certainly took him many steps above the impractical, often politically motivated, unilateral disarmers of today. In 1933, his famous 1908 classic about the stupid myths of war, *The Great Illusion*, had been revised and published again (five years later, Erich von Stroheim was to pinch this title for his classic anti-war film), and now he chose the Rotary platform to suggest a remarkable anticipation of Nato:

> In International affairs, we make force an instrument of the litigants; whereas force, in civilisation, must be the instrument of the law. . . . The problem which faces civilisation — work in which you as a Rotarian must assist — is to transfer power from the hands of the litigants to the law, the law that there shall be no more war. In so far as our armies and navies shall exist at all, they shall be combined and pooled to resist the war-makers, so that there shall be always such preponderance of power against the maker of war that war will not in fact be made.

And he roused his audience with a burst of heavy biblical idiom: "Have faith and act upon the faith, and ye shall be served; doubt and act upon that doubt by doing nothing and assuredly ye and your generation and nation shall perish utterly." He also used a catch-phrase that was taken up by the press everywhere, "Faith, Hope and Parity", a reference to "parity" in naval strength between Britain and Germany which Hitler was cleverly manipulating at the time as an excuse to build pocket battleships like the *Graf Spee*, launched earlier that year.

The speech made a tremendous impression, combined with that of the following speaker, the Reverend A.J. Costain of the Colwyn Bay Club. Costain, who, after disarming his audience with a witty dissection of a typical Rotary Club ("a man can succeed in life by qualities that are not truly social . . . not that we despise success, because we have all succeeded in some small measure — we may not have reached astral splendour, but we may have come to aspidistral comfort"), suddenly struck fire:

> We are in the Rotary game, and we want to play it, but I want to say something more . . . I think we ought to make the Rotary game a little more worth playing. . . . We have too high a regard for the rules of the

game. I want to suggest that it is possible to be too much concerned for
Rotary and too little concerned for the things for which Rotary stands. . . .
    I am quite ready to admit that Rotary cannot commit itself to every-
thing, but I ask, Is there nothing to which Rotary can commit itself? . . .
We have been talking of Youths' and Boys' Clubs from this Rotary platform, and making in England a brave new world, and all the time, if you
listen over your shoulder, there comes the mocking laughter of the War
God. . . . I hope Rotary is going to take its life in its hands and say . . .
that peace can only come by the rule of law and justice and by the nations
banding themselves against any nation that dares to break the peace.

The lack of resolution of the British Government, extremely
busy "doing nothing", including the despatch of a fleet without
adequate ammunition to the Mediterranean, to move sanctions
against Mussolini's appallingly brutal invasion of Abyssinia, showed
that Margate heard the heart of Europe rather clearer, alas, than
Westminster. We may also note that a Special Search List of about
2,300 names drawn up by Himmler (headed by Winston Churchill's,
of course) of prominent persons the Gestapo were to round up
immediately Britain surrendered, included Sir Norman Angell's.
Which showed that someone in Berlin was listening to the heart of
Margate very closely indeed, and was aware of the Rotary Conference Resolution which resulted directly from Sir Norman's speech
that "the time urgently calls for action declaring to the world that
Rotary stands for international collective security and peace".
    Good resolutions, as Wilde observed, are cheques that men draw
on a bank where they have no account, but at least the record
stands. And it was symptomatic of a change slowly spreading
through the nation; for George Lansbury, whose potent message of
pacificism had proved so effective two years before, now resigned as
Labour Party leader before the scorn of the far from pacific trade
unionist Ernest Bevin (later, as Minister of Labour and National
Service in Churchill's wartime Government, to give the world its
first glimpse of the post-war Welfare State at a speech to London
Rotarians), who told Lansbury he was tired of having Lansbury's
conscience "carted about from conference to conference". Attlee,
a major in the First World War, took Lansbury's place.
    In 1936, many German and Austrian Rotary Clubs sent messages
of condolence on the death of King George V, and the Governor of
the Austro-German District 73 shook hands with a Falmouth
Rotarian during a War Memorial service, though the Englishman,
who had lost two brothers in the First World War, had taken an
oath never to touch a German's hand again. This tale Governor Otto
Kroeger took all over Germany on his return, for it illustrated so

well "Rotary's all-uniting and atoning spirit". There was an escalation that year of "international youth exchange" trips between parties of British and German students, culminating in a plan to celebrate Coronation Year by building an International House of Youth in London which would match similar buildings noted all over the Third Reich, for "in Germany, Youth has been given a definite place in the State". The plan came to nothing, though Berlin Rotarians eagerly responded to invitations for their young people to visit London (they returned by air later).

This was the year in which many Rotarians' plans came to nothing, or were changed, the biggest change occurring when the said need for a coronation in twelve months' time made it necessary to switch the venue of the next International Convention from London to Nice (postponing the first Convention held in England for a further fifty-seven years, till Birmingham won the honour in 1984). It also changed many plans for travelling to Spain, where Civil War broke out in July, at once isolating 745 Rotarians from the rest of the world, sixteen years after Spain had been the first nation to establish Rotary in Europe. Professor J.H. Nicholson of Armstrong College, Newcastle upon Tyne, told a Rotary Rally, "In the solution of world problems of today, Rotary is . . . one of the few bridges between democratic England, Fascist Italy and Nazi Germany." A further view was offered by a Past Governor of Rotary District 73 (Austria and Germany), Robert Burgers, an executive of the German Bank and Discount Corporation, who, perhaps unconsciously echoing the Fuehrer, spoke of "The new order of life" which was approaching — here came an ominous military metaphor — "on many fronts" but which, he warned, would not consist "merely of a fresh collection of recipes and rules of procedure . . . we have lost faith in forms, as such". No one could say the moving finger wasn't writing clearly enough, it was just that so few in 1936 were reading exactly what it wrote.

Some did, appreciating their former word-blindness. The Torquay solicitor, "Pa" Almy, whom we have already noted earlier in this chapter as leading the British Rotarians into Munich practically on the heels of the "Night of the Long Knives" two years before, now a sadder and wiser man, wrote in *The Rotary Wheel*: "The Armageddon of the Apocalypse was foreshadowed not as a conflict between rival dynasties but between rival beliefs, and the struggle now being waged in Spain might well be the prelude to this Armageddon."

As we can better appreciate now, the Spanish tragedy was the bloody first act, not the prelude. This had already happened in March, when the German Foreign Minister had summoned the

Ambassadors of Britain, France, Belgium and Italy to his office to propose a twenty-five-year pact of non-aggression, starting with a demilitarisation of both banks of the Rhine. Even as this discussion kept some of Europe's top diplomats busy in the Wilhelmstrasse on the morning of 7th March, Hitler, overriding the doubts of his generals, was sending 35,000 troops to reoccupy the Rhineland and build a wall of fortifications. The French could easily have thrown them out, but hesitated and looked to Britain, who looked away. Lloyd George, the man who had humbled the Kaiser, only counselled, "I hope we keep our heads." Lord Lothian, who as Lloyd George's one-time Secretary had helped draft the Treaty of Versailles, now being so flagrantly violated, only commented, "After all, they are only going into their own back-garden." Which was to be expected since his lordship was the first to make respectable the term "appeasement" in a letter to *The Times*.

Churchill warned the House of Commons: "It will be a barrier across Germany's front door which will leave her free to sally out eastwards and southwards by the other doors . . . and will enable the main forces to swing round through Belgium and Holland." He bombarded the Government with warnings, which were ignored. In fact, the only advice he gave in 1936 which *was* followed was in a memo to Sir Thomas Inskip, the Minister for Co-ordination of Defence (a job Churchill wanted for himself but was refused), in which he advocated the appointment of a Ministry of Supply to plan national civil and munitions production, and even this suggestion wasn't followed for three years, the first Minister of Supply being none other than Rotarian Dr Leslie Burgin, the same whom we have already met at Rotary's Annual Conference in 1933 explaining that all Germany wanted was freedom to "plan and drive". When Churchill took over the running of the war, he soon replaced Dr Burgin with the dynamic Lord Beaverbrook, who knew all about plan and drive.

As a matter of fact, British Rotary did make a lasting impact on the world in 1936, with a Club project, little noticed then, but which has since benefited millions in every country — alas, many of them victims of the coming war. A Past President of the Rotary Club of West Ham, London, E.A. Johnson, OBE, suggested to his Club the idea of providing white sticks for blind pedestrians, and the notion — an obvious and simple enough idea, yet it always needs a genius to think of such things — was now spreading fast, though West Ham had begun distributing the sticks several years before. It was a great Rotary achievement and a project the Movement was admirably fitted to carry out, and swiftly.

The pity was that there were no such aids available for the blind politicians nor for the blind populations they were leading. Nevertheless, the Rotary Clubs of Europe were holding successful meetings everywhere and in inter-country social activities were setting a model for the rest of the Rotary world. After one such meeting between Clubs fron Austria, Hungary and Czechoslovakia, the Secretary of the Rotary Club of Baden-bei-Wien, noted enthusiastically: "The sincere wish was expressed for a closer co-operation of the three countries on the vast field of International Service. The Baden-bei-Wien Club was thanked for its increasing endeavour to surmount national borders by spreading mutual understanding and goodwill." And during the singsong — legacy of Harry Ruggles — during visits of German Clubs to Britain and vice versa, it was found that the song most popular with, and equally well known to, both sides was "Tipperary". This preference might perhaps have puzzled that Scottish nobleman who immortalised the view that writing a nation's songs was more important than its laws.

This was the moment when A.A. Milne chose to make the first of three appearances in the pages of *Service in Life and Work*, the quarterly journal published by British Rotary. A journalist and playwright whose works had appeared in *Punch* (where Christopher Robin had made his first appearance) since 1906, the year after Rotary was founded, his career had reached its apogee with *The House at Pooh Corner* in 1928, though he was still active and successful. He had tried ever since to "live down" his four children's books (his autobiography devotes only eight pages to them) and he resented identification only as the creator of a toy animal who announced, "I am a Bear of Very Little Brain, and long words Bother me" (much as Conan Doyle loathed Sherlock Holmes and Lewis Carroll had vainly tried to escape from Alice). Thus he welcomed the opportunity to advance his pacifist views about the Nazi threat, which certainly reflected those of much of the social and political establishment:

It is difficult in these days, when, as it seems, each morning brings us in view of a new crisis, for the average man to keep a clear head. . . . It is perfectly true that a compromise or surrender in face of an armed threat is not a pleasant thing to stomach; but if the alternative is (as it certainly will prove to be) the torturing and dismembering of men, women and children whose only wish is to live their lives peacefully and happily, then it must be remembered that the alternative also is not a pleasant thing to swallow. . . . The remedy of war is almost always worse than the disease. . . . It follows that in almost any crisis which arises I am opposed to a policy which carries with it a threat of war.

So were lots of his readers, probably most of them. And the unpleasantness of the Rhineland reoccupation and the outbreak of Civil War in Spain was partially offset for those many lucky Rotarians who received an invitation from Otto Kroeger, still brim-full with the discovery that he had been able to shake a Falmouth Englishman's hand again, to attend the Eleventh Olympic Games in Berlin that August. These were the most spectacular Games yet staged and they were staged by masters, who took down all the anti-Jewish slogans for the duration and gave thousands of visitors to their capital an impression of blinding dazzlement of the Third Reich. A Rotarian of the Deptford Club was moved to voice this comment in the columns of *The Rotary Wheel*: "What *organised* attempt is being made by British Rotarians . . . to understand the condition of German Rotarians today? It cannot be denied that a proper attempt at understanding of other countries' problems constitutes the unavoidable obligation of every real Rotarian."

Quite a number of English visitors to the Olympiad doubtless followed this obligation by attending the "Italian Night" dinner which Goebbels gave for 1,000 guests near the Berlin suburb of Wannsee, not far from the home of a young officer, Count von Stauffenberg, destined eight years later to place a bomb next to Hitler that failed to kill the monster in the famous 1944 plot of the generals. Meanwhile, in a laudable effort to understand the British, which many Americans found more difficult than understanding Germans, the Rotarians of Portsmouth, Virginia, sent to the "original" Portsmouth and Southsea Club a lavishly engraved parchment which expressed their deepest sympathy on his father's death to "King Edward VIII, who holds a warm spot in the heart of every true American" and for whom they prayed "that he may have a long and successful reign".

The reign lasted 325 days, and the coronation that took place in 1937, following the abdication crisis, was that of King George VI and Queen Elizabeth. And it soon became apparent that the valiant efforts of British Rotary to come to terms with the Third Reich were also to have a brief reign. That coronation summer, a German guest speaker reassured the Burton-on-Trent Rotarians in Staffordshire that "National Socialism is not an export article", a declaration doubtless heard with relief, since at its following luncheon meeting the Club heard an eminent rabbi describe the oppression of the Jews in Germany as combining all the refinements of cruelty that other oppressors had been able to think of, to make the position of German Jews utterly hopeless. After his speech, it was reported, "the two points of view were keenly discussed".

At Dorchester, six former prisoners of war who had fought for the Kaiser and had been interned locally, returned to give that city's Rotarians a devastating insight into the "new" German mind. "The climate has a great influence on the thinking mind of man," declared these philosophers, "and that is one of the reasons that English people cannot think like the German people." This statement was followed by an intriguing display when all six Germans jumped to their feet, on sharp command, to give the Rotarians a Teutonic version of "three cheers", flinging their arms stiffly forward in the Nazi salute and shouting "Heil! Heil! Heil!"

At the end of the year, the forty-two Clubs in Germany were disbanded, the resignations led by the Governor, Kroeger, the same who saw now that he had learned too late how to shake the hand of an Englishman again. Clearly the weather had taken a long turn for the worse. The Golden Wheel was about to take its spokes underground, or have them broken.

At this crucial juncture Rotarians were fortified by the second appearance of A.A. Milne in their journal, his article being entitled ominously "Realism in High Politics". Like many of his compatriots, the man in flight from Winnie the Pooh was beginning to be less certain about the possibility of easy options in this new world of the dictators; like boys all over, he was wondering why the "grownup" statesmen were not getting things straight. "To every amateur student of High Politics", wrote Milne ironically, "moments come when he puts down his newspaper with the feeling that he has been attending an early experiment in Television, at which the voices of the speakers have filtered to him through acres and acres of cottonwool. . . . This, he says to himself despairingly, cannot be real life. . . . If a real Eden were talking to a real Ribbentrop, a real Chamberlain writing to a real Mussolini, surely they would give some greater impression of reality than this." Like Pooh, he was beginning to ask for a little butter on his bread, especially if that bread were clearly going to be the bread of affliction. And he justly complained:

> We amateurs of peace are told to take a realistic view. But would real people in real life spend hours discussing agreements and contracts and leases unenforceable by law with men upon whose word they could not rely? Obviously not. Yet at this moment those three "realistic" nations, Germany, Italy, Japan, are signing a Pact. . . . With pomp and ceremony and a hullabaloo in their national papers, Mussolini and the German Ambassador will fix their seals and sign their names to some document, and to some high promise pledge their words of honour.
>
> Germany! Italy! Japan! The three nations which have openly and deliberately and shamelessly violated, in the great cause of realism, every treaty which they have signed!

To many readers, the narrative at this point will have a bitterly familiar ring. But we have never moved forward as much as we care to think; and we may remind ourselves here that Milne was now writing to Rotarians when the BBC had already been running the world's first regular television service for a year, and that it was twelve months also since Britain had welcomed the arrival from the United States of that indispensable aid to modern independent thought, the gallup poll — a more subtle form of tyranny, which was prepared to bide its time.

As noted, 1937 being Coronation Year meant that Rotary's International Convention, originally planned for London, came to Nice, thus pushing the world size of the Movement right under Hitler's nose, which might well have impelled the easily irritated Fuehrer to close down the German Clubs six months later. Certainly the French gave the Convention, which brought over 6,000 Rotarians to the Riviera from more than sixty-five nations, a resounding, demonstrative welcome, those of the host country being especially pleased that a Frenchman, Maurice Duperrey, of the Paris Club, was for the first time to take office as the Movement's World President, and perhaps grasping at the rather fragile straw that it was a German Rotarian, from Stuttgart, who had selected the Frenchman's name for nomination (both blissfully unaware that inside three years German jackboots would be tramping down the Champs-Élysées). The President of France himself, Albert Lebrun, opened the Convention in the Municipal Casino at Nice, accompanied by a number of members of his cabinet, including the Foreign Minister. The Premier, Léon Blum, head of France's first Popular Front Government of Socialists and Radical Socialists, was not present, but he had already made his contribution by suspending a series of sweeping left-wing reforms, not of course because of the Rotary visitation (though it helped) but because capital was leaving the country at an alarming rate and he had had to devalue the franc.

The Nice Convention had the exalted title "An Adventure in International Understanding and Good Will". It was a brave gesture, since the nationalities present were already squaring up to each other, often bloodily, beyond the shelters of the Casino walls. The French Premier had pledged the workers of France "to resist Hitlerite aggression"; France and Britain were already facing Germany and Italy on the opposite side in the Spanish Civil War; and, capping all, Japan was bombing China (and nearly killing the British Ambassador in the process). Nevertheless, there was a formal Franco-German luncheon, Franco-Italian dinner and Latin-American dinner, the Americans and British taking pot-luck elsewhere, it appears. Not that in France they would have had far to look!

Indeed, during this very summer Churchill took Anthony Eden and Lloyd George to lunch at a favourite restaurant of his just outside Nice to discuss informally the dangerous world situation, and Eden and Churchill met frequently there. No doubt Ribbentrop got to hear of it, for he asked Churchill to drop in for a chat at the German Embassy in London, where he said Hitler wished above all to be friends with Britain, provided Britain let him do what he liked in Europe: "The Fuehrer is resolved. Nothing will stop him." To which Churchill replied, "Do not underrate England. She is very clever. If you plunge us all into another Great War, she will bring the whole world against you like last time."

Ribbentrop scoffed, but down at Nice there was no such scoffing as that, for it was agreed to have a campaign of fund-raising from 1st January 1938 to 1st July 1939, with the aim of collecting $2 million for the Rotary Foundation, an endowment (see Chapter Nine) fairly moribund since its inception in 1917 by Arch Klumph, "for the purpose of developing international understanding". The French President told the Convention: "You belong to the most diversified ranks of industry, commerce, agriculture and the liberal professions. In each of them you endeavour to be an élite. . . . Thus you constitute, in the heart of your respective countries, centres of influence, of mutual understanding, on which governments may count in their work of international drawing close together." The Foreign Minister, Yvon Delbos, told them: "Setting aside all that can divide in order to seek for what can bind together, you have banished from your programme questions of religion, controversies which are strictly political, and doctrinal debates. You are in this animated by the same spirit as the French Government." Affecting not to notice raised eyebrows, he continued: "Your task is more difficult in Europe . . . where the harmony of international life remains subject to severe trials."

Rotarian Otto Fisher tried to explain tactfully why Club recruitment was slower in Austria and Germany (forty-four delegates) than elsewhere: "Soon after the organisation of the first Clubs, we had in Germany the interior political movement in 1933 which, of course, took possession of all the strength of our men." Rotarian Guido Carlo Visconti de Medrone contented himself with asserting proudly that "some very distinguished personalities in our country" had joined Italian Rotary (twenty-three delegates), but hastily switched to describing a visit to China and Japan, adding "as you sow, so shall you reap" rather obliquely. In any event, it was the Far East that was reaping, though not in the manner he implied. But actual events were not mentioned by either the Chinese (fourteen delegates) or Japanese (thirty delegates) representatives. Fong

Foo Sec instead brought Nice Rotarians up to date on the latest achievements of Chiang Kai-shek's dictatorship, which, instead of a New Order, a New World or a New Deal, was producing a "New Life" in which "Rotary sweetens our lives". Kokichi Uyeda announced that Rotary well accorded with his country's ideal of "benevolence and self-sacrifice", but, he disarmingly confessed, "in the matter of international understanding and friendship, Japan has much to learn from Europe and America". It learned fast.

Rotarian Armando de Arruda Pereira closed the international round table part of the Convention, which had become a series of personal testimonials, in the manner of a staid evangelistic gathering, with some ornate Latin flourishes: "Rotary in Brazil has done wonderful good . . . to brothers in that huge area." Then he thrilled his hearers by widening his focus:

> Notwithstanding the fact that we Rotarians speak different languages, we all understand each other even if it is only by mimic or a sweet smile, because we all understand one language — that which is spoken by our hearts. . . . The world is undergoing weary days. Every now and then the dark cloud of unhappiness and sorrow floats at a distance in the midst of clouds of smoke and dust. Rotarians, Rotariennes! It is up to us to pull down and brush away all of this from the international scenery. With the sunshine of our friendship, we must unfold and spread a permanent rainbow of brotherly feeling, of gay spirit and happiness.

He made no references to the "New" element introduced in Brazil (nineteen delegates) by Paul Harris's recent host, President Vargas, who had just proclaimed a "New State" with all the totalitarian trappings of his Nazi friends (see Chapter Sixteen), but in his reference to "international scenery" as if it were all part of a flimsy stage décor, he touched closer to the truth outside the Municipal Casino than anyone.

Including Paul himself, still so bedazzled by his South American travels that the Founder's own major address centred upon an emotional dithyramb to the enormous statue "Christ of the Andes" towering over a pass in the Andes Mountains near Mendoza on the border between Chile and Argentina. "May such monuments be erected on border lines between countries throughout the world," he suggested, and quoted the words written on a plaque affixed to the twenty-six-foot-high figure: "Sooner shall these mountains crumble to dust than Argentines and Chileans break the peace sworn to at the feet of Christ the Redeemer." This statue had been put up after the settling of a border dispute back in 1902 between

Chile and Argentina by the timely intervention of Edward VII of England. But Harris made no mention of this reality nor of the fact that it was himself and other Rotarians, attending a Rotary Regional Conference in Valparaiso, who had put up the plaque just the year before, thirty-four years after the event. The monuments of modern Europe were the Maginot and Siegfried Lines and Rotary had no plaque to place on these. "It is a time for a renaissance in our thinking on international affairs," Paul concluded. "Rotary is blazing a trail over which many of the present generations and generations yet to come will follow. . . . Now that art, music, literature, science and industry each has had its renaissance, it is time that human relationships . . . have their renaissance and Rotary is leading the way to that happy event."

With that speech at Nice, in the presence of the last President of France before De Gaulle and of Rotarian Charles Jourdan-Gassin, Chairman of the Organising Committee of the Nice Club and the man who was to do most to keep Rotary alive during the German Occupation, Rotary's Founder made clear that his original dream had lost none of its vigour. He did, however, allow himself to be persuaded, after the Convention, that it was not really wise of him to attempt to visit Clubs in Italy, Yugoslavia, Bulgaria, Romania, Czechoslovakia, Austria and Hungary, as he had optimistically planned. He paid a final visit instead to Clubs in the British Isles, and in July left Britain and Europe behind for ever, a wiser man.

Rotary in Great Britain and Ireland, which had sent nearly 400 delegates, plus their wives and families, to Nice, had their own witness in their RIBI President, Verrall Reed, whose talk, entitled "Mind Your Own Business", was an all too accurate reflection of the attitude of mind the Axis powers were quite properly counting on, and at the end of the following year, Sydney Pascall, the sweet manufacturer who had presided over Rotary's great Vienna Convention in 1931 (see Chapter Sixteen), was still permitting his memories of the waltzes of Franz Lehár to obliterate the stamping choruses of the Horst Wessel song in 1938, for — after twelve months during which Hitler had annexed 10,000 square miles of Czechoslovakia, invaded and taken over Austria itself, and led Chamberlain by the nose to the shame of Munich — he could still write in *The Rotary Wheel*:

If we would judge fairly, there is much to admire in the policy of Hitler. He has largely achieved the unity of the German race, has given his people a new hope in life, order in place of indiscipline, security instead of fear and uncertainty. . . . It would be foolish to belittle the benefits and only defeat our desire for understanding and co-operation with the German people.

His view was no doubt welcomed by one Franz Schneiderhann, an obliging Austrian who was a past member of both the Vienna and Salzburg Clubs and long-time director of the Vienna Opera, and whose elevation to the Board of Rotary International at Nice — his supreme moment in the Movement — had been abruptly truncated by the suppression of Rotary in the Third Reich. This versatile musician, adept at any tune, it seems, was now able to defend his country's subjection by claiming in an address to Rotarians at Wolverhampton: "If the German Government had not fulfilled the wish of the men who had called them in, there would have been within a week a bloody revolution and a bloody civil war in Austria."

As if these sentiments were bloody likely, the British called on their last resource, football, and sent an amateur football team, inspired and sponsored by the Rotary Club of Islington, on an eight-month world tour. There was no attempt to arrange fixtures with Berlin or Moscow, however — Hitler had wrung the ultimate tribute from sport with the 1936 Olympics — but the team began in Holland, went on to Switzerland, then on through Egypt and India to Burma, Malaya and Singapore. The soccer stars of the Golden Wheel then achieved the amazing double of a goodwill visit to Canton while the Japanese bombed it, followed immediately by a sporting visit to Tokyo to play the Japanese national team! Politics could, it seems, play no part in even a Rotary football eleven. A brief visit to play Hollywood stars in California was followed by a triumphant tour of Canada before the team returned to Islington, to find that during their absence trenches had started being dug all over Hyde Park. Yet, reported their Rotarian manager, "not one incident marred our perfect goodwill trip".

The notion that sport was closely related to politics and war was not new, but the notion that it could take the place of either *was*, and didn't last long, though it is now very much in vogue again. Summing up what their football team had accomplished at this perilous moment of world history, the Islington Club reported that the players had, amongst other achievements, "Made friends of all nationalities on and off the field of play; shown the traditional grit and courage; demonstrated English sportsmanship, leaving an opinion of English youth as every patriotic Britisher would wish it; and left on the native mind [native!] the impression that English youth values the friendship of any fellow player on the field". Had it been a professional squad, schooled in accordance with modern team and spectator standards, we should probably have had the Second World War a year sooner. As it was, the team's trophies were shown on television, to the glory of Rotary and of Great Britain. By way of an unhappy postscript, Islington itself was devastated by the very first bombs to fall on London on the first night of the Blitz.

The century, alas, was a long way away from that Christmas of 1914 when British and German troops had played soccer between the trenches; for that matter, it was a long way away from it even then. It was perhaps also more immediately regrettable that the soccer players had not included Prague on their schedule, for an embarrassing scene might have been spared Chamberlain and Lord Halifax at 10 Downing Street in September when, after news of the Munich meeting, Rotarian Jan Masaryk confronted the Prime Minister and his Foreign Secretary in their cabinet room, and told them in shaking tones, "If you have sacrificed my nation to preserve the peace of the world, I will be the first to applaud you. But if not, gentlemen, God help your souls!"

This display of unfortunate Middle European emotionalism would have been much deprecated (had he known of it) by the Chelmsford Rotarian who wrote to the *The Rotary Wheel* in November about "the friendly feeling created at Munich" and counselled that "mainly a Rotarian in his private and business life should spread abroad the fact that peaceful solutions are possible in this world. By thus becoming a centre of sanity and stability, he can counteract the panic growth of the idea that war is inevitable".

Munich could now also give the Rotarian time to address himself and his Club to more serious, less melodramatic matters. The Kingston upon Thames Rotarians, for example, had in hand a very serious debate on the motion that "in this country today there is widespread mis-use of leisure which is deplorable". It was not quite in the same league as the notorious 1933 Oxford debate at which undergraduates had voted never again to fight for King and Country, but it was equally irrelevant, though rather more intriguing. Just what deplorable activities Britons were getting up to in their leisure hours, such as going to Noël Coward plays and joining the dole-queue, was not specified, but Hitler in fact had long ago had the same conviction about the German people and had since 1933 been rapidly prepared to direct his countrymen's undoubted energies in more positive directions. This of course commended him to many Britons, who honestly could not see what all the alarms and excursions were about in some excitable quarters. Such as Czechoslovakia.

But a change in the mood of British Rotary was becoming evident, all the same. At the 1938 RIBI Conference, President Tom Warren, one of the most impressive of British Rotarians ever to take office, then Director of Education for Wolverhampton, and later to be the first President of World Rotary after the war, spoke sadly and generously: "I say *Auf Wiedersehen* with affection and regret to the German and Austrian friends I have lost — as Rotarians, that is.

I hope with all my heart we shall one day have them back again."
Soon after, when the Clubs in Italy and Czechoslovakia were also
crushed, the National Council of Italian Rotary adopted the following Resolution, which was read out to all of Italy's thirty-four
Clubs: " . . . that the Objects of the Association in Italy find their
best expression and most efficient realisation in the programme and
policy of the regime and in the tenacious and farseeing work of
Il Duce".

In Graz, second city of Austria, the Rotary Club had lasted just
ten years before a wild, shouting mob of 10,000 Nazi thugs ran
horrifyingly berserk in the town square, tearing down the Austrian
flag and raising the swastika banners which were to terrorise Europe
for the next seven years — years that would seem almost as long as
the "thousand" which Hitler had promised these brutal and exultant young men of the Third Reich.

Meanwhile, with so many Clubs lost in and devoured by the
whirlwind, Ches Perry was asking Clubs all over the still free world
to send aid to the Rotarian refugees pouring into France from the
twenty-nine shattered Rotary Clubs of Spain, the cream of that
country's professional and business men. In April the following
year Tom Warren's luckless successor, President Almy, wrote to
every Club in Great Britain and Ireland asking them to give assistance to their local National Service Committee, so that Rotary
should "pull its weight". As in 1938 one ex-Foreign Secretary, Sir
Samuel Hoare, had addressed the Conference, so now did another in
May 1939, of rather different calibre, namely Anthony Eden, who
was soon to take office again under Winston Churchill and indeed
one day to be Prime Minister himself. At the Conference, as "Pa"
Almy's guest, Eden spoke with the moral authority of one who had
resigned from Chamberlain's government, chiefly in protest against
its acquiescent policy towards Fascist Italy, when he said:

We have had more than enough of gangster tactics. If we oppose methods of
snatch and grab, it is because this practice among nations puts a stop to
progress in every sphere. Under our eyes the world now remilitarises itself
physically, mentally and materially. We all put on uniform again. This
must seem to many of us a melancholy prospect . . . not because the British
people are decadent or soft, but because they know that war, when it is not
unbelievably degrading, is unspeakably stupid.

It was a bracing dose of realism which the nation needed and no
organisation was better suited than Rotary to disseminate. "We all
put on uniform again" was a graceful tribute to President Almy's
support of National Service. But Eden understood and applauded

the real strength and real business of Rotary, as he proved by his concluding sentence: "Do not be afraid of your idealism," he told his audience of over 3,000, who were gathered for this last pre-war Conference under the great onion dome of the Royal Pavilion at Brighton, once a paradise for escapism. "It should be some comfort for you to know that we realise that such a Movement as yours has the true expression of the inward mind of the free peoples of the world."

History was to show that it remained a true expression of many peoples who were not free also, but it was not until after the war that news emerged of many Clubs which had continued meeting clandestinely in both Germany and Japan throughout the years of global conflict and at great personal danger. Meanwhile, in the technicolour grandeur of the Prince Regent's magnificent "folly", all was politics in the "phoney peace", or at least advice from politicians, and no one dared to say that Rotarians did not discuss such things, when day by day the foundations of lives still holding desperately on to normal routine vibrated uncontrollably to the heavier and heavier tramp of jackboots across the old battered borders and thresholds of ancient races and peoples.

After Anthony Eden, who called out from the platform as he left, "We may meet again on some other occasion later on. Meanwhile, may I wish in all sincerity godspeed to you and to your Movement", Leslie Burgin was back once more. No longer the "Doctor" but the "Right Honourable", being now Minister of Supply, the Luton Rotarian was also no longer the complacent Conference speaker of 1933 who had assured delegates that the "pulse running through the whole universe" was no more than Hitler's natural desire to "begin afresh". Instead he made a rousing declaration that "in this great period of trial" all Rotarians must ask themselves "whether their conception of service was being translated into the maximum output of prayer, thought and action that it was possible to ask from the Rotary Movement as a whole". As key business men, they could "exert great influence". He begged them as Rotarians "not only to be aware of that influence but to use it".

The most startling transformation paraded for the delegates, however, was the U-turn offered by Lady Astor, the "Virginia creeper" to all totalitarians who wished her adopted country ill. It was an astonishing recantation, in effect. Only the year before, her country house, breeding ground of the "Cliveden set", had been establishing its reputation as a top people's watering-hole for appeasers of Hitler. Ribbentrop had been a guest there, and it was at one of her house parties that Chamberlain was persuaded into incautiously admitting that neither Britain nor France, nor probably Russia, would intervene if the Nazis attacked the Czechs. Now, she described dictatorship as "a ghastly thing" and roundly declared to the Rotarians, "unless the democratic free States are prepared to make sacrifices as much as the totalitarian countries . . . we may lose all that our forefathers lived and fought for, and we may go back into the dark ages". She may well have been made aware that Jan Masaryk, the Czechoslovak Minister in London, whose father had been the founder and first President of Czechoslovakia, and who had resigned his post in disgust at Chamberlain's betrayal, was a member in exile of the Rotary Club of Prague and was almost certainly in the audience! And her researches may have also reminded her that Thomas Masaryk, a philosopher as well as statesman, had first become famous in 1881 as the author of *Suicide as a Mass Phenomenon of Modern Civilisation*, forty-seven years before the West's betrayal of the nation he created had proved this possibility the most sad and prescient title ever penned. Nor did its prescience end with his nation's vain sacrifice (by its friends) before the gods of war who were now — according to custom — busily making mad those they intended to destroy. The little nation Thomas Masaryk had single-handedly forged into life only twenty-one years before Rotary met beneath the Prince Regent's onion dome would have but a brief rebirth before its second sacrifice under Soviet tanks in 1948, when Rotarian Jan, as Foreign Secretary, would be found dead in the courtyard beneath his office window as another "suicide", witness to his father's terrible foresight.

A few months after that 1939 Conference in the Brighton Pavilion Jan Masaryk wrote in *Service in Life and Work*, "the democracies need a new coat of paint. They must be made more alert . . . [but] the preservation of democratic institutions is infinitely worth while. Intellectual freedom is the most important. . . . Rotary Clubs, for instance, have been stopped in totalitarian countries", and this he instanced as a definite condemnation of totalitarian philosophy. This was a tribute Paul Harris must have received with proud, if sorrowful, gratitude. Though now a Foreign Minister in exile, Jan Masaryk, as with many other European Rotarians (see Chapter Twenty), still had a "home" within the great International Movement; as indeed so did his Prime Minister and lifelong friend, Eduard Beneš, who became a member of the Putney Rotary Club for the duration.

In the next issue of *Service in Life and Work*, A.A. Milne made his last bow for Rotary with his finest contribution. Gone was the pacifist at all costs who had claimed in the same journal three years before that "Heil Hitler!" was only an irrelevant, mindless remark

that a German made even when just buying liver sausage and that
war was no remedy for anything. He expressed contempt for the
pacifism of Munich: "It is time that we cleared our minds of a
good deal of cant about autocracies. We plead in their excuse 'the
right of countries to choose their own form of government'. No
country ever 'chose' autocracy. Russia didn't; Italy didn't; Germany
didn't; Spain didn't." And, as for its being "bad form" for an
Englishman to comment on them (a national virus from which we
are not free even in the 1980s), Milne wrote scornfully: "This is
nonsense. We can comment on cannibalism, we can comment on
slavery, we can comment on tyranny. And when one particular
form of slavery, such as flourishes in a totalitarian state, is not only
an indecency in itself, but a menace to the rest of the world, then
it is our duty to comment." And he tellingly made the parallel
noted before between the likes of A. Capone and A. Hitler: "If
we say, and say rightly, that we are now more humane, more alive
to and shocked by the evils of the Rule of Force, we are leaving out
of our reckoning the individual gangster . . . in a totalitarian state,
the gangster may easily be the autocrat." And democracy at last
was taking steps accordingly, for Hitlerism, Mussolinism, Stalinism,
whether regarded as a genuine political doctrine "or merely as an
excuse for autocracy, they are, they must be, a danger to the peace
of the world".

Milne called his essay "What Are We Fighting For?", but he
might well have used the title of his own autobiography, also
published in 1939, *It's Too Late Now*. For the twentieth century
was coming to a rapid and cataclysmic maturity, faster and faster.
Not only had the Boy died, he was become a Man. At this time
Christopher (Robin) Milne was eighteen and about to spend six
years on active service with the Royal Engineers in the Middle East
and Italian campaigns; and, as if in retaliation for having left behind
for ever the "bear with little brain", he was eventually hospitalised
at Bari with a head-wound. It was the Man who came back. The
ex-soldier who had once owned Winnie the Pooh later said that his
father's subtitle for *It's Too Late Now* was *The Autobiography of
a Writer*, "but it isn't really that at all. It is the story of a boy".
Just like Paul Harris's *My Road to Rotary* was to be, in fact, the
story of a boy.

We must end this chapter before it began, to show that the insights
and perceptions of reality reached with such slow and painful
puzzled anguish over six years by British Rotarians could have been
attained long before. Many of them had travelled the Continent

frequently during this time on their business affairs, but none foresaw that evening of 31st August 1939 when a group of SS men, outfitted in Polish uniforms, staged the "raid" on a German radio station which gave Hitler the excuse he required to claim he had started the Second World War in self-defence. During 1932 — when the Nazis were still in a minority in the Reichstag (Hitler, be it remembered, was never himself elected to that parliament but ran for Chancellor from the start) — one of those business men struck up a friendship with a young German who eagerly avowed himself "a Hitlerite", and that young man's correspondence appeared in the pages of an early issue of *Service in Life and Work*. Below are some extracts:

> We are all very pleased by this gentleman-like attitude which you have shown to your former enemies. I got the impression that you do not like war because war is wrong and nonsense. . . . Very many people in England think of the Hitler-movement as a typical "warlike" German movement. What a bad knowledge of German sentimentality, German misery, distress and poverty they must have! . . .
>
> The Germans do not like war, even if they march in very great numbers in the streets and deliver speeches which do not seem to be peace-like. I told you already that I too am a pacifist. . . . It is impossible for a youth to have the same view of life as a well-meaning and well-disposed elder man. . . . Youth in Germany thinks the fight for the absolute independence of their home country their duty. Home country expects everybody to do his duty. I thank you especially for your words for me and my comrades. You said it yourself, a very difficult but a very great task is waiting for us.

But the young might impose on "well-disposed elder" men in a way they could not do on their peers elsewhere. The answer to the Hitlerite soon came from a young Englishman, Lyall Wilkes, in a subsequent issue of the same Rotary journal:

> Having fought to make the world safe for democracy, the world turns round and decides that democracy is not safe for the world. . . . Lately I have heard many people talk of the noble ideals and aspirations of youth. I believe more sheer nonsense has been written about this subject than anything else. For we find today that youth the world over is outplaying the older generation in every form of persecution, tyranny, and injustice. In what youth today are we to believe, what youth are we to admire? The young people in Germany who demand the expulsion of liberal-minded or pacifist professors from the University lecture-rooms? The young Hitlerite who does not hesitate to beat defenceless Jews and Socialists? Whenever Mussolini is particularly belligerent or bellicose he is so because he knows

that the youth of the nation will enthusiastically support him. And the young people of Spain and Russia lend their aid readily to any form of religious or racial persecution.

And this indeed was what the young Hitlerite had meant by the ominous words "a very great task is waiting for us".

What that "very great task" was we know now to our horror and the youth of today to its incredulity, even though the nightmare is over and has been documented down to its grisliest detail. It was time to grow out of the idealisation of boyhood, the worship of youth (which youth itself had not sought); to realise that the bringing out of the boy in man was not necessarily to bring out the best in him. It was rather the beast in him that lingered nearest the nursery. Hitler did not deify youth, he degraded it. In Nazi Germany there was no nonsense of allowing Wordsworth's "shades of the prison house" to close in on the growing boy, but to throw those gaol doors aside and set the beast free.

Nor did Paul Harris deify youth. He was well aware that the "rapscallion" had a dark as well as adventurously unbiddable side, and he urged Rotarians to the discovery of the boy in themselves so that they should know themselves better and thus be better prepared to help the succeeding generation. The between-wars world, in which flaming youth seemed to come into its own everywhere for the first time, pretended to set youth on a pedestal; in reality, it was set on a pyre. The inheritance the young came into was dubious; for many it was a holocaust. It was not their world at all, it was their fathers' world, and when they came to man's estate they found that estate mortgaged to the hilt. A bloody hilt. But many Rotarians made the same mistake then that they make now. Youth are not the leaders of the future, they are its fodder, the vanguard of the past; and it was part of Rotary's duty to see that the overdue payments they inherited did not accumulate into a Wagnerian immolation.

Past President Tom Warren of RIBI took a realistic outlook with him when he went off to the Rotary International Convention in Cleveland, Ohio, in June 1939. He told delegates how, even the previous September during a visit to his married son's house, after listening on the radio to the rantings of European statesmen, he had said, "I am sorry, son, but we have got to go home, and I think possibly the next time we see you, you will be in uniform." But Tom concluded with a fierce hope: "Rotary helps me to join other men in steadily revolting against that damnable, unclean beast that we call war."

The eighty-four British Rotarians who had come to Cleveland

heard a Message from President Emeritus Paul Harris which displayed the old clarity of vision that cut through cant with ruthless unsentimentality and was employed just as skilfully as any preface by Rotary's old antagonist Bernard Shaw (this was probably why Paul never took umbrage at Shaw's comments). He admitted wars were wicked and shameful, but first called on delegates to remember "that what we call civilisation has made its greatest advances at the point of a sword". That was history and had to be accepted, and no nation carried an unstained scabbard in that regard. But it followed that to protect that civilisation required the sword also, and we could not shrink from it, although "we cannot end war by means of war". Already, Paul looked beyond the terrible conflict: "I am convinced that what Rotary has done in a small way, nations can do in a large way. To me our Fourth Object is the way out. Now is not the time for its abandonment nor its suspension; now is the time when it is most needed. It will carry further than the guns of the most formidable battleship." Rotary's Fourth Object was, of course, its stress on promoting international understanding, and it was doubtless the clarity of this vow and intent which kept the embers of Rotary glowing clandestinely in most of the main belligerent nations (on both sides) throughout the six dark years to come.

Yet some bewilderment almost at once set in when Ches Perry rose to make the Report of the General Secretary. At Nice, it will be recalled, a campaign of fund-raising under the auspices of the Rotary Foundation had been agreed, with the aim of collecting $2 million "for the purpose of developing international understanding". Now, Ches Perry stated, "No appropriation" had been made during 1938–9 for carrying on the promotional work of the Rotary Foundation. And further bewilderment must have been felt by the British delegates when they heard the following:

> It is generally understood that there is a struggle going on in the world. . . . Rotary should be energetic and fearless in stating and restating its Objects. . . . Rotary should do this openly and without hesitation, but, at the same time, without permitting any Rotary Club or any group of Rotary Clubs or Rotary International as a whole to become involved in any political situation, in any conflict between governments or within countries.

Among those listening at Cleveland were delegates from Polish Clubs. There were ten Clubs formed by then in that unhappy nation, and the last words history records of the Rotarian presence there appeared in the bulletin of the Lodz Club, which had been formed in the year Hitler came to power. As if in malevolent revenge, the bulletin was issued on 27th August, reminding its members that their Rotary District Governor would be visiting them the next day. Whether or not he arrived we shall never know, for only three days later nearly 2 million Germans had come thundering over the border from East Prussia, and within a fortnight it was the German Army Group South whose Blitzkrieg of Panzers were Governors in Lodz, which at one stroke, in one day, lost not only its Rotary Club but — for the long and awful duration — even its name.

British bewilderment and, for a time, growing anger with the ambivalent approach to the second world crisis, as exemplified by Perry's seemingly clinical comments, were soon to provoke severe strains between Rotary International and RIBI, resolving itself into a straightforward Anglo-American confrontation and hinging largely on whether anyone has the right to turn someone else's other cheek. Meanwhile, if not in Cleveland, the "unclean beast" was loosed, and the President of British Rotary at the outbreak of war called for all Clubs in Great Britain and Northern Ireland (those Rotarians south of the border were very sensitive about this point, being non-belligerents) to carry on as before, though practical steps to aid the war effort had already been taken (see Chapter Twenty).

President Almy had also sent a Resolution to the Rotary International Convention at Cleveland, Ohio, which was presented to it by Tom Warren. It was from the Rotary Club of Hull, and it read as follows:

1. We desire to place on record our continued adherence to the collective principle as the only enduring basis of world peace.
2. We urge that steps be taken by the nations of the world to call a World Conference for the purpose of constituting a Society of Nations which could be all-inclusive in membership.

The Convention voted it to be withdrawn by an overwhelming majority, but not before Rotarian Carl Miller of Iowa Falls, Iowa, speaking on behalf of an "international assembly" group, had made a disturbing comment on the motives of those who had urged its withdrawal: "The fundamental issue is whether or not Rotary International shall lift its voice corporately on behalf of the fourth point in its program . . . for the great issue of international peace." He went on:

The issue today is not merely the Hull Resolution, but whether, when the opportunity presents for Rotary to raise its voice, will Rotary raise its voice or will this policy hinder the raising of that voice. We know there is a danger implied in a raising of the voice of Rotary International. There is danger in living. We know that there is danger that some might be hurt. But we feel that it is better to speak, when we are so impelled, than to worry about treading on certain people's toes.

There is a juncture in the existence of an individual, in the existence of an institution, of an organization, when the individual or the institution must decide whether to live or whether merely to exist, whether it is better to preserve the body and let the spirit die, or whether it is better to make that spirit live, even though the body or a part of the body dies.

The Rotary voices of Hull and of Iowa Falls were heard more clearly later, six years later in fact, when another sort of Conference — undreamt of then — also met in San Francisco, this time to formulate and sign the Charter of the United Nations, a Conference in which forty-nine Rotarians were invited to participate. But by then it was a different world — what was left of it — and a different Rotary world, and Ches Perry had retired. For now, he made sure the voice of dissent from the floor with the "established" view was overwhelmed, and the distant call from Hull ignored. But it was not a lone voice. Carl Miller's words deserve to be inscribed in stone and neither his name nor his warning should ever be forgotten. He was not entirely alone, even so, and an echoing cry gave an answer back over the Atlantic.

The Editor of *The Rotary Wheel*, W.W. Blair-Fish, the man who had succeeded Vivian Carter when that remarkable man had gone off to Chicago to edit *The Rotarian*, only to tangle once too many times with Ches Perry and suffer a nervous breakdown (not the first, as our early chapters have shown, to have been so affected by Rotary's "builder"), wrote an editorial which spoke for all of Rotary International, in a manner Paul Harris could not but approve and Perry not thank him for.

If any Rotarian should be thinking sadly at this moment . . . that all the peacetime organisation and effort of Rotary was like a pretty toy — a spare-time hobby of grown-up men, which war has made to look ridiculous — let him think again. . . . Let us resolve consciously to serve in this war as much for the sake of all that we know to be decent in Germany as in ourselves. Let us still maintain and spread through war our Rotary principle of world fellowship and world law as the only means to peace. Let us stand for a peace of unrevengeful justice and of fellowship re-established.

This was not a philosophy for boys, not even for men who were boys only once a week.

Another voice had been added to that of Paul Harris and Carl

Miller at Cleveland, that of Miss Violet Ilma, organiser of the American Youth Congress and editor-publisher of *Modern Youth*, who represented the authentic voice of young people, called to a Rotary World Convention for the first time. Paul Harris must have sat forward in his chair, eyes glistening in appreciation, as the young lady quoted, to him and over 9,000 others present (including, still, Chinese and Japanese, since, in spite of China's blasted cities and destroyed armies, war had not been declared yet by either side) from Ralph Waldo Emerson: "To keep the young soul, add energy, inspire hope, and blow the coals to useful flames; to redeem defeat by new thought, by firm action — that is not easy, that is the work of divine men."

It was not only the work of men, it was what the war ahead was to be all about. And at their first Club luncheon in September, after Britain's ultimatum over Poland had expired, the Rotarians of Watford — already the site, unbeknown to most of them, of one of the key underground tracking stations with which the Royal Air Force would baffle the Luftwaffe and win the Battle of Britain — all stood with raised glasses for a solemn declaration, and drank a toast to the future of German Rotary.

No one applied the Four-Way Test to Armageddon.

CHAPTER NINETEEN

The Wheel at War — 3

These things which Rotary believes
    And men and nations strive to teach
Are not those goals which skill achieves
    But such as lie in easier reach.
The world will change its worse for good
With universal brotherhood.

So mind not what the cynics cry.
    Pay little heed to wisdom proud.
Still hold the Rotary banner high
    And serve the truth and not the crowd.
Still keep for all mankind to see
The spirit that is Rotary.

"Greeting to Rotary" by Edgar A. Guest, 1940

Edgar Albert Guest was Middle America. He was middlebrow
Middle America, and when he wrote the verses quoted above he
had been a member of the Rotary Club of Detroit (the fifteenth
Club to be formed) for twenty-five years. He had worked on the
Detroit Free Press for twenty years longer than that. Today, he is
largely unknown outside the United States but his city isn't, and
the reason can easily be ascertained from the fact that it was
founded by a Frenchman named Cadillac. Detroit remains the
"automobile capital of the world" that it became largely through
the single-minded efforts of a close friend of Eddie Guests' with
whom he shared lunch-counter meals in his younger days: Henry
Ford. Ford was the hero of Eddie Guest's poem which runs:

Somebody said that it couldn't be done,
    But he with a chuckle replied

That maybe it couldn't, but he would be one,
Who wouldn't say so till he'd tried.

And the site of Ford's first world-famous assembly plant is at
Dearborn, a town named after the same major-general who also
gave his name to the forest on the other side of the Michigan peninsula, which grew into Chicago.

The Chicago-Detroit axis was thus the backbone of Middle
America, and Henry Ford and Paul Harris take their place in history
as the two poles of that axis, pioneers in their own country who,
by representing and exporting Middle America — the one in thought,
the other in action — all over the world, together brought the
United States to the forefront in the space of two generations. In
1911, Ford established in Britain his first overseas branch, as did
Paul Harris. In 1915, when the Rotary Movement delivered itself
of its Code of Ethics (see Chapter Nine), Ford chartered a "Peace
Ship" to take himself and like-minded evangelists across to tour
Europe's belligerent capitals, determined "to bring the boys home
by Christmas"; though this extraordinary venture did not stop him
from embarking on war production, his methods being as vital to
the success of the First World War as to the Second.

Henry Ford's relationship, directly and indirectly, with Nazi
Germany were as ambivalent and uncertain as Rotary's — and,
indeed, as all other onlookers of the free world. The Youth Leader
of the Third Reich, for example, claimed that he had been converted
to anti-Semitism through reading Ford's book *Eternal Jew*, but the
Kaiser's oldest surviving grandson, Louis-Ferdinand, who was foremost in the abortive plot to kill Hitler in 1941, was spurred to a
large extent by democratic values he had learned while working
five years on Ford's assembly line at Dearborn (he was also a guest
of Roosevelt at the White House during his honeymoon).

The link between Henry Ford and Paul Harris was this poet of
Middle America, Rotarian Edgar A. Guest, and at the time he wrote
the lines quoted in 1940, Eddie's old friend was already building
the two square miles of floor space called Willow Run, the "longest
room on earth", to make Liberator bombers. Guest's homespun
moral philosophy was that of most American Rotarians, but he
wrote with the assembly-line methods of Ford. It was not by chance
that in the same year in which the International Convention at San
Francisco produced the Code of Ethics, Eddie Guest really came
into his stride, and he was to maintain it for the rest of his life (he
died in 1959, at the age of seventy-eight). Writing at least one poem
a day for 365 days a year, he commanded a devoted audience of
6 million readers, and collections of his verse broke sales records

for books of poetry. The citizens of Middle America (no matter where they actually lived) referred to his text over cornflakes as fervently as Gladstone had consulted the Old Testament Prophets. Nor did he write just for their comfort, as his poem "A Little Brass Tag", a brutal account of the return of a soldier's body to his family, shows clearly. He thrived on the fact that Americans have never accepted the fallacy that great poets run deep, nor that brooks must all babble. They do not believe that to be understood is to have failed (unless, of course, they are in politics); to put one's own banality to the test and say what millions think takes courage and a certain technique. Rotarian Eddie reaped his rewards. Byron awoke one morning and found himself famous; Eddie Guest got up each day and found himself read. He had joined a nation of heroes which takes the truth at breakfast. In Europe, truth is ever a late riser; in the United States it shines with the dawn's early light. In the phrase which Rotarians have co-opted for themselves, Americans are a busy people; if you don't make them think with their cornflakes, you've lost your chance.

When Paul Harris, during his last year, was putting the final touches to *My Road to Rotary*, he appended a prayer which lay closest to his heart at the end of the final paragraph: "God grant that my vision of the faults of men and of nations be dimmed and my vision of their virtues be brightened." This closely echoed a verse Eddie Guest had written years before:

> Let me be a little kinder,
> Let me be a little blinder
> To the faults of those around me,
> Let me praise a little more.

And certainly the practice of true Rotary ideals, as opposed to their increasingly convoluted statements in turgid constitutional documents, had been well summed up in a poem by Guest called "Sermons We See", in which we might be listening to Paul himself:

> I'd rather see a sermon than hear one any day;
> I'd rather one should walk with me than merely
> tell the way.

It presents no difficulty for the more sophisticated Europeans and Latin Americans, the business men and politicians of the Levant and Asia, to find such homely sentiments an easy target for mockery. But while most "great" poets lived private lives very different from the magnificent uplifting fire of their immortal stanzas, Rotarian Eddie Guest was throughout his life the same man who had munched sandwiches on a counter-stall in 1895 with the night engineer at the Edison Company plant, spending his days visiting hospitals, homes for the aged, orphan asylums, chatting to lonely or troubled families in their homes, giving informal talks to schoolchildren. And though that one-time night engineer was likewise mocked when he hired (out of his own pocket) that "Peace Ship" to Europe, having just blithely driven his millionth car off his revolutionary assembly line, it was the same man who was to lead the way in turning Detroit into the "arsenal of democracy" during the Second World War, while remaining a man of simple and unpretentious tastes who still liked nothing better than to don overalls, get covered in grease and solve a problem on the machine-floor beside his assembly-line workers, for while no one else may still have been able to build a car with his own hands, Henry Ford could.

As "celebrities", these men were ciphers, and they wished to remain so. All were of the temperament that prefers to be "lost in a crowd". Ches Perry had a magnetic presence and dominated every Rotary Convention. Paul Harris seemed to come on and off the scene almost apologetically. Yet even as Henry Ford had "put America on wheels", so Paul Harris's own Golden Wheel now carried forward the service conscience of America and the world. These two men, Henry Ford and Paul Harris, were the muscle and morality of the Middle America that was about to contribute so incalculably to sustaining the world's epic struggle against Hitler, following Britain's epic fight and triumphant defence under Churchill, thus setting an example to the world of unselfish service in the cause of rebuilding man's faith in man.

Rotary has never claimed as much for itself. It is part of its strength, as well as of its weakness, that it has not done so. Yet through its greatest trial it emerged stronger and larger than ever, even in the midst of fire and holocaust and the aftermath of hate and ruin. The source of that strength can still be found in the verses of Edgar Albert Guest, even though the banality of their truth may make them unpalatable to those who hold out for too fastidious a demarcation line between art and life. Eddie Guest's middle name gives a little-known secret away. The poet laureate of Middle America and of Rotary was in fact born in Birmingham, England. Whether literary scholars like it or not, therefore, this unpretentious chronicler of Middle America values, of essential Rotary values, filtered by Rotary International through most of the nations on earth, became in effect the last, least-known internationally, but probably most influential of English Lake Poets − though his lakes were St Clair, Erie and Michigan rather than Borrowdale, Coniston Water and Windermere.

It didn't matter that Henry Ford had remarked, following the ignominious failure of his "Peace Ship" journey, that "History is more or less bunk". Assuming that he was not referring to his ship's accommodation, he could afford to say so, as a man who was, more than most, to change history overnight himself. Several times. So was the Movement that Paul Harris had founded thirty-five years before. Which is why Edgar Albert Guest was quoted at the start of this chapter. The present chapter and the next three will portray the truth of his lines, minding not "what the cynics cry", and demonstrate the incredible survival of the Movement through the Second World War, not only in the countries of the victors but in those of the vanquished, when Clubs (which began the war in 1939 with 4,967 and ended it in mid-1945 with 5,385, an increase of 418) were able to show not just their admirable fitness for community service, even when the stakes were life and death, but clear evidence of their destiny as vehicles of post-war internationalism.

The Second World War has been too well documented and re-hashed in books, films and television, and of course on far too large a scale, for the present writer to try to describe, in the same sort of detail, Rotary's actions and reactions during it as was given for the period of the First World War (discussed in Chapters Eight and Nine). But this chapter will consider the opening scenes of the drama carefully, while the following three will provide more of a montage for the Rotary years from Pearl Harbor to Nagasaki. Beyond the guns, Rotary International at first seemed to regard the war as an aberration. But only seemed. One can easily feel superior about this, and it is salutary to recall that when Eddie Guest's pal arrived back home with his "Peace Ship" in the First World War, one passenger − having enjoyed the round trip − pompously announced to the press that he was resigning because so many passengers were cranks and fools. Ford, on being baited by the newspapers for comment, said drily, "The situation seems to be improved by resignations."

Rotary International soon understood that it was fighting for its life, long before most of its member nations understood the stakes. There was no "phoney war" probationary period before annihilation such as the wavering governments of Western Europe were allowed until the summer of 1940, as Stalin − whose forces had swept in at Poland's back door while Polish lancers galloped to challenge the Panzer tanks pouring in a flood of steel through the front, across the so-called "corridor" — divided the spoils of conquest with Hitler, much to the latter's surprise. Already 116 Clubs had been buried in Germany, Austria, Italy and Spain, soon followed by Czechoslovakia's thirty-nine, and now Poland's ten, while barely a gasp of breath remained for the six Rotary Clubs of Lithuania, Latvia and Estonia as Russia surged to the Baltic. The eight Clubs of Finland survived for a time, since, to the world's astonishment, and certainly Stalin's bafflement, the Soviet hordes were held at bay in the wild lakes and forests of the Mannerheim Line until March the following year.

In Spain, no single decree abolished Rotary as such, as had happened deliberately with the warring Axis powers. Franco determined to maintain neutrality and rebuild his shattered country after the Civil War in which 1 million Spaniards had slaughtered each other, but he forbade societies with "international connections" and he also forbade meetings of more than a dozen people at a time. Between such pincers, the Movement, whose Fourth Object was looming more and more important, could not hope to survive. Yet neither did it die. Rotary went into hibernation wherever totalitarianism swamped the earth. In the following six years nearly 500 Clubs were buried beneath the global landslide of death, destruction and terror. But apart from where the Russian Bear planted its smothering paws after the final atom-shrouded silence, Rotary re-emerged.

From the International President of Rotary, the headmaster of a private school in New Jersey, Walter Head, came a message for the stunned nations of Europe: "Rotarians everywhere are shocked and saddened by the outbreak of war. . . . Our memories of the conflict of 1914-18 are still poignant; also we remember the high resolves which followed that tragic period . . . the unbelievable has happened. . . . Rotary seeks to spread understanding and goodwill throughout the world. When this has been completely accomplished, war will cease." It is an aim Rotary still pursues. To a reporter who came to interview him at his Montclair Academy for boys, President Head confided what he regarded as the curse of the world: lack of communications between ordinary peoples. "In world trade," he pointed out, "adaptation and change are always at work to develop methods of saving time in transportation and communication. On the other hand, the importation and exportation of ideas from one country to another — the outstanding hope of saving civilisation — still goes on in the same way as it did in the ancient world . . . Babel's curse is still upon us." Not upon himself — he spoke French, German and Spanish fluently. But he omitted to reflect upon his forbears. His home town of Revere, Massachusetts, was named after the man who had brought to American rebels warning that "The British are coming!" and he was directly descended from John Hancock, who had signed the Declaration of Independence (side by side, as we have noted, with the ancestors of Hitler's Youth Leader). The global conflict that these two incidents heralded, which had changed the course of history more than any other, had regrettably been between peoples who both spoke English.

Yet when the International President met his Board of Directors there was already one empty chair, that of Jerzy Loth, Rotarian of Warsaw, last seen amidst the ruins of the city by a "March of Time" photographer who had been approached by Loth as he filmed the waves of Stuka dive-bombers, disintegrating buildings and streets filled with fires, rubble and corpses. Rotary International Director Loth had been concerned only to send his greetings via the photographer to Walter Head and Ches Perry. Then he walked away through the choking dust. He would not see Chicago again. Only ten Rotarians escaped, twelve were executed, the fate of most of the remainder not being known for certain, though some news emerged (see Chapter Twenty-One). A number of them, however, were called upon by the civic authorities to serve on specialist committees when an effort was made to restore some semblance of normal life under the Nazi Occupation, at least for the next three years.

From Paul Harris came not a word in public. Chesley Perry was heard from but certainly not in a way that Europe, and especially Great Britain, expected.

Of course the "establishment", the "organisation men" of Rotary, had every excuse for not appreciating the mortal peril in which the Movement stood. Bernard Shaw, while not retracting one syllable of his notorious statement that Rotary was going nowhere but to lunch, had deigned to grant an interview to *The Rotarian* the previous February, in which he reassured members that they were not, on the other hand, going to find the bread of affliction on their menu. "There is not the least chance of a war happening in the near future," he confidently declared, giving as his reason that "the airplanes of A, B, C and D would bomb the cities of E, F, G and H so effectively that the white flag would be hoisted at approximately the same time in the several capitals." Showing that even the sage of Ayot St Lawrence was as subject to widely held delusions as lesser beings, he told Rotarians that if war had been going to happen "it would have happened during that fortnight last September" (i.e. at the time of the Munich "peace in our time" crisis). Certainly Shaw was deadly accurate when he said, "Formerly it was possible for one side to think —

for a year or two — that it had won. The single redeeming feature of
the next world war, when it happens, is that this will not be possible. In reflecting upon that, perhaps you may find some particle
of hope."

Perhaps readers of *The Rotarian* felt that particle of hope enlarged
and that Winston Churchill echoed Shaw's opinion when the
impending saviour of the Western world sent an article stating that:
"Now is the time to make it plain to all men, and to all nations,
that the systematic and deliberate butchery of noncombatants by
air bombing will bring reprisals and the retribution of overwhelming
force." But while Churchill, who had just delivered the manuscript
of *A History of the English Speaking Peoples* to his publishers
(though he was unable to spare time for proof-reading for another
seventeen years), might have felt the need to give comfort to the
New World which in a short time he would call "to the rescue and
the liberation of the Old", he had held high office during the First
World War and knew that no war-lord really believes retribution
possible, certainly not a German one. Of the Kaiser's War he had
written (as was partly quoted in Chapter Ten), "In the sphere of
force, human records contain no manifestation like the eruption of
the German volcano. . . . To break their strength and science and
curb their fury, it was necessary to bring all the greatest nations of
mankind into the field against them", and he was well aware it
would soon be necessary again.

As for Shaw, theatregoers in the United States and Canada during
1939-40 had plenty of opportunities to see his play *Geneva* (starring Barry Jones, who ironically was to play a conscience-stricken
professor threatening London with an atomic bomb in the post-war
film success *Seven Days to Noon*), in which he has England's
Foreign Secretary tell "Battler" and "Bombardone":

> When you ask me what will happen if British interests are seriously menaced,
> you ask me to ford the stream before we come to it. We never do that in
> England. But when we come to the stream, we ford it or bridge it or dry it
> up. . . . We have no speculative plans. . . . I warn you — I beg you — do not
> frighten us. We are a simple well-meaning folk, easily frightened. And when
> we are frightened, we are capable of anything, even of things we hardly care
> to remember afterwards.

Geneva's tour of North America ended with a run at the Henry
Miller Theater in New York during January 1940, but we may
doubt Ches Perry ever saw it, or had read any of Churchill's (or
Shaw's) writings apart from those contributed to *The Rotarian*. Perhaps he could not have been expected to anticipate the devastation

from the air of Rotterdam and Coventry, or the retaliation on
Hamburg, Cologne and Dresden; but he might have recalled the
burning of Washington by the redcoats in 1812. Perhaps he recalled
the latter too well and the recent disputes over Rotary in Great
Britain and Ireland. At all events, in October, with the war one
month old, and a Polish government in exile already announced in
Paris, an American merchant ship *City of Flint* was reported captured by the pocket battleship *Deutschland*, and Churchill's famous
radio broadcast was made describing Russia as "a riddle wrapped in
a mystery inside an enigma". Even so, the only European news
Perry found to issue to Rotarians everywhere was that the (then)
seventeen Rotary Districts of Great Britain and Ireland would now
be considered directly responsible to his Headquarters and that
their leaders would now be called "Rotary International Representatives" rather than "Governors" as elsewhere. In fact, RIBI called
them "District Chairmen" – and it still so regards them.

Much worse was Perry's releasing of an "official" RI statement
to the effect that the war was definitely *not* to be regarded as "a
Rotary war" and that "Rotary Clubs must keep out of it". It continued: "We feel that Rotary Clubs should not become involved
in national and international politics, should not become propa-
gandists for or against any cause of national or international concern."
Erupting in fury, the Editor of *The Rotary Wheel* in Britain replied
in print:

> What the autocratic promulgators of that statement entirely fail to realise
> is that they are not thereby keeping Rotary *out* of politics but are on the
> contrary plunging Rotary dead into them . . . this bland declaration is
> nothing more nor less than a declaration of American national policy; and
> it is (as it has always been) especially noteworthy that American policy . . .
> is the one national brand which, under the title of international, Rotary
> not only can adopt but is expected to adopt.

The peculiar stress and danger of the time had spurred his cry, but
it echoed a chord of division and ambivalence within the World
Movement which had been present many years; indeed, is not done
yet.

Rather than react so provokingly against what was undoubtedly
a reflection of the Neutrality Act of the United States, which had
been operative for two years and was now reinforced by a General
Declaration of Neutrality signed by all the American Republics at
Panama on 2nd October, the wise and moderating influence of
Tom Warren was brought to bear. He had made a speech of poignant "farewell" to German Rotarians (noted in the previous chapter)

and was now wielding greater influence as a Vice-President of the International Board. His Club at Wolverhampton sent President Walter Head word that "the spirit and service of Rotary will during the stress of war conditions be more necessary than ever before . . . the Club expresses the hope that all Clubs throughout RIBI will similarly continue to give our country the benefits of Rotary throughout the war period". One result of his message was that the Rotarians of Augusta, Georgia, sent Tom Warren a token sum of $100 for the Red Cross.

There was no need for any ambivalence outside of communications to Chicago Headquarters. The General Council of Great Britain and Ireland sent the text of a Resolution to all Rotary Districts in France and the British Empire. This recorded the Council's view that "it is now clear beyond doubt that Great Britain and France are fighting in this war for the preservation of precisely those principles to which Rotary is dedicated. It is our belief, moreover, that the present emergency calls upon Rotary more urgently than ever before to justify its idealism".

From France and the Empire response was largely enthusiastic in support. We can be sure also that, when he heard of it, the World President of Rotary did not dissent. Between himself and Ches Perry and many American Rotarians the same split of opinion existed as obtained between President Roosevelt — who fully understood the menace of Hitler — and much of Congress and the American people, who liked to quote Thomas Jefferson's warnings against "entangling alliances" and urged isolation within a "Fortress America". Straddling both areas of dissent was so well known a Rotarian as Charles Lindbergh, who announced that "the security of our country lies in the strength and character of our people, and not in fighting foreign wars".

Perry might grow coldly furious during the midnight hours, in his office on 35 Wacker Drive, at the thought of the generosity of Augusta Rotary to the British Red Cross, but his International Board was not an American Board and amongst those who could not attend its next meetings were: Tom Warren in England; Emile Deckers of Antwerp, Belgium; Richard Currie of Johannesburg, South Africa (whose government under General Smuts had voted to fight with the Boer's old enemy and one-time prisoner, Winston Churchill); and Jerzy Loth, who had disappeared in the flames of Warsaw. And whatever Perry's thoughts on the war, how could Rotary "keep out of it"? In January a new statement was issued, which Perry had no choice but to accept:

In these catastrophic times, the Board feels that it should re-emphasize to

Rotarians throughout the world that Rotary is based on the ideal of service,
and where freedom, justice, truth, sanctity of the pledged word, and respect
for human rights do not exist, Rotary cannot live nor its ideal prevail. . . .
The Board, therefore, condemns all attacks upon these principles and calls
upon each Rotarian to exert his influence and exercise his strength to protect them. . . .

One who was already doing so was Herbert Schofield, the English
Rotarian educationalist who had vainly tried to warn the 1934
Detroit Convention of the Nazi menace to youth (see Chapter
Seventeen). His Loughborough College was already running National
Emergency Courses, including one for those young men "desirous
of securing the requisite qualifications for consideration as pro-
spective Commissioned Officers". Another so doing was Field-
Marshal Baron Carl von Mannerheim of Finland, member of the
Rotary Club of Helsinki-Helsingfors, rather more strenuously
holding at bay the might of the entire Russian Army. While a
Lausanne Rotarian (and Lieutenant-Colonel), Marcel Pilet-Golaz,
had become President of Switzerland, entrusted to preserve that
remarkable nation's neutrality from the bloodthirsty threats of
dictators to the north and south. Rotary's first martyr to freedom
was undoubtedly Thomas Mann, expelled from Munich. Second was
the unfortunate and intensely loyal Jerzy Loth. For a time it
seemed that the third would be none other than another member of
the Helsinki-Helsingfors Club, the great composer Jan Sibelius,
listed missing after a Soviet air raid, but he was subsequently reported unharmed.

However much Perry wished otherwise, the inevitable could not
be staved off, as he had managed twenty-five years ago (see Chapter
Nine), when Rotarians could be persuaded to think of the conflict as
the "European War". He could even try suggesting that all nations
suddenly call their War Department the Peace Department (an
uncanny anticipation of Orwell's *1984* notion). But it was not 1914
again, and the Rotarian who was this time in the White House knew
very well that "over there" was no drunken brawl amongst worn-
out decadent empires and that, metaphorically speaking, the vicious
fights were not taking place in another town, another place, but
that blood was running down the street just a block away. So did
the other New World governments which, at the Pan-American
Conference at Panama, had decreed, with absurd confidence, that
the ships of belligerents could not come any closer than 300 miles
from their coasts. They were two months too late, since Hitler had
ordered twenty-one U-boats to sea in August and despatched the
Deutschland to prowl the North Atlantic while the *Graf Spee*

headed for South America. In 1914, Perry had to be concerned only with what was happening to Rotarians in the one country outside North America which had formed Clubs, and an Anglo-Saxon one at that. Now, the despatches came from all over the world.

With a Rotarian as President of the country, Swiss Rotary Clubs were determined to keep faith both with patriotism and their Rotary commitment, and the Zurich European Office of RI promptly started losing its staff to military service; all Clubs lost members to the general mobilisation but kept regular meetings going for those who could attend. Two Rotary District Governors were called up for war work in France, while Maurice Duperrey, who had welcomed the Convention to Nice as World President in 1937, had three sons-in-law and three nephews at the front line on the Saar, which everyone was expecting to explode any minute on to Hitler's thinly held borders while his main forces crushed Poland, leaving twenty-three divisions to be easily overwhelmed by 106 French divisions and four British. If they had attacked. Nothing happened, in fact, and tourist boats continued to ply the Rhine between twin phalanxes of soldiers building equally useless steel and concrete bunkers in full sight of one another. The Rotary Club of Strasbourg was the first to cease continuing its luncheons, feeling a bit too close to the frontier and the dreaded grey uniforms.

The Scandinavians seemed to find stimulus from the neighbouring slaughter in Poland, the Swedes reporting new recruitment to Clubs, while the Danes, unaware they were next on the Fuehrer's shopping-list, actually formed three new Clubs. The first Rotary war victim in Belgium was a member of the Antwerp Club who was returning from a visit to New York Rotarians when his ship struck a mine and sank. He survived but lost all his personal belongings. It was, alas, a British mine. This did not stir up anti-British feelings amongst the Belgians, however; a Bruges Rotarian put his hotel near the coast at the disposal of any other Rotarians in the country who, noting ominous signs, felt they would be safer nearer the Channel.

Across the Channel, after the hair-raising moment when an air-raid siren went off just fifteen minutes after Chamberlain's declaration of war, nothing much changed during the "phoney war" period except that the luncheon helpings got progressively more skimpy, though the ubiquitous Spam had yet to make its appearance. The Newcastle upon Tyne Club, formed during the early months of the First World War, was pleased to find itself providing RIBI's leader, President Tom Young, for the first three years of the Second World War, since the British held no more Rotary elections until 1942 (to celebrate perhaps the retirement from office of its arch-foe, Ches Perry, in that year), and their leader sent a message to

20. Four world-famous Rotarians: (*left to right and top to bottom*) Guglielmo Marconi, Franz Lehar, Albert Schweitzer, Carlos Romulo.

21. Pope John Paul II accepts the Paul Harris Award in 1981 from the then RI President, Rolf J. Klarich, of the Rotary Club of Helsinki-Helsingfors, Finland.

22. (*above left*) Rotary road sign in Chile, South America.

23. (*above right*) The famous "Christ of the Andes" monument on the border of Argentina and Chile, erected by the Rotary Clubs of Chile in 1936.

24. Rotary marker, a Paul Harris monument in Portugal, located on the western-most point of Europe.

25. Interactor (a member of one of many Clubs for those aged between fourteen and eighteen sponsored by Rotary) in Paysandu, Uruguay, eagerly carries flags of all nations to a Rotary International rally.

26. The modern Headquarters of Rotary International in Evanston, Illinois, a suburb of Chicago.

27. The Paul P. Harris Room preserved at RI Headquarters, where the Founder of the world's first Service Club Movement worked almost till the end of his life.

28. Comely Bank, the home of Paul and Jean Harris, where hospitality was extended to Rotarians from all over the world.

all Clubs to "carry on". This they did, discovering at once two areas in which to employ Rotary "clout" in every community: counteraction against the panic and large-scale dismissals of employees by firms large and small; and action against an outbreak of scandalous profiteering, particularly amongst the suppliers of black-out curtains.

Rotary's other great opportunity in the British Isles resulted from the flood of refugees, about 60,000, from Germany, Austria and Czechoslovakia who had arrived in England. Following the example of Manchester Rotarians, many Clubs set up hostels and employment centres to take care of them, and their numbers were soon to be drastically increased. As for the only bit of "combat" actually going on, more than half of Britain's Clubs became linked with the minesweepers patrolling the North Sea, making themselves responsible for maintaining contact with the lonely crews when they came ashore.

One report might well have reconciled Ches Perry to the effrontery of Stuart Morrow in forming the first Rotary Club outside North America all those long years ago when the General Secretary had been only one year in the driver's seat. Like all their countrymen in the twenty-six counties of Eire, the now independent Republic of Ireland, Dublin Rotarians (though then still a part of the British Commonwealth) decided that not only wasn't it a Rotary War, but it wasn't an Irish War either – and so the self-styled (erroneously) "No. 1 in Europe" joined Cork in becoming the only two Clubs across the Atlantic (excluding, of course, the Axis countries themselves) to opt out of Europe's greatest period of trial.

With a commendable display of disinterested (if ingenuous) fellowship, the Rotary Club of Bangor in Northern Ireland still urged that the 16th Rotary District (combining both parts of Ireland, as it still does, though now called District 116) should operate as though nothing had changed. As if in reward for such disinterest, one of its members, Frederick Price, was elected Chairman of the District until 1942; and as if in reward for the ingenuousness, his home was the first building to be destroyed in Northern Ireland by enemy bombing.

Rotary was at war outside of Europe even in 1939, and reports came in from two sources: countries of the British Commonwealth; and the Far East, where the seemingly never-ending ruthless struggle between Japan and China continued.

Australia and New Zealand (now with eighty-four and twenty-five

Rotary Clubs respectively) declared war on Germany a few hours after Great Britain. "When the United Kingdom is at war, Australia is at war," declared the Australian Prime Minister, Robert Menzies, without a moment's hesitation, and by the end of 1939 the Australian Imperial Force was on its way to the Middle East, while training of air crews for the coming great air battles over Britain and Europe was well in hand. Rotary Clubs set up recreational facilities for army camps and the Adelaide Club was foremost in setting up a Fighting Forces Comfort Fund and a Business Advisory Committee to advise the dependants of fathers fighting overseas.

New Zealand soon backed up Australia's three divisions with another, the forces combining once more, as in 1914-18, into the famous Anzac Corps, which was to play such a critical part in the campaigns in Crete, Greece and the Western Desert. Back home, New Zealand Rotarians played a major share in establishing the Federal Union Movement which, in its advocacy of collective security and a diminution of national sovereignty in the cause of internationalism, was a clear harbinger and pace-setter for the United Nations, in the birth of which Rotary was to play such a significant part.

South Africa now had thirteen Rotary Clubs, and all supported the declaration of war against Nazi Germany which followed two days after Chamberlain's on 3rd September. There was much sympathy for Nazi principles amongst South African politicians, or at least a feeling that Nazi aggression was none of South Africa's concern, but Jan Christian Smuts (who incredibly had once been State Attorney to Paul Krüger, leader of the Boers against the British in 1899, and was now to become one of Churchill's great intimates) carried the nation with him into supporting the one-time mortal enemy, Britain. Consequently 325,000 volunteers joined the Commonwealth forces in Abyssinia and the Middle East, nearly half of them non-whites.

The incoming Governor of Rotary District 55 (including South Africa), a Founder Member of the Cape Town Club, was also Colonel of the Duke of Edinburgh's Own Rifles, and he found himself caught travelling in the United States when the regiment was mobilised. This Rotarian, called Cecil James Sibbett, did not hesitate, at once buying a passage on a cargo boat from New Orleans to Cape Town, a month-long voyage, and sailing to take command of his regiment, a patriot unquestioning. It befitted a man who had in his youth been Assistant Political Secretary to the legendary Cecil Rhodes, founder of Rhodesia, of the Rhodes Scholarships and a towering figure in the history of southern Africa — indeed,

Rhodes was the man who invented the phrase "painting the map red" to describe the spread of British imperialism from Cairo to the Cape.

In 1939, down in the Cape of Good Hope, however, Rotary was unaware of the proximity of danger, of how close nearby at one moment the *Graf Spee* was lurking, and felt far enough removed from the possibility of enemy contact to continue basic support for the community, now in fact more essential than ever. A crèche for coloured children was provided at Stellenbosch, and the Rotary Club of Springs provided a swimming-pool for the Far East Rand Hospital at one-quarter normal cost. Rotary, in fact, was everywhere providing an enormous stabilising influence.

In Canada, where Rotary had placed its first step outside of the United States, the response was never in doubt; only the width of a lake away, Ches Perry watched resignedly and kept tight-lipped vigil. All the same, there was a delay in the move to arms. Determined to assert an independent line in world affairs, Canada had refused to join sanctions against Japan when it had attacked China in 1931, or against Italy when that nation had invaded the hapless Abyssinians in 1935, so it waited until four days after South Africa had done so before lining up with Britain and declaring war. An anguished cry reached Perry from Rotary District Governor Gerry Moes of Hamilton, Ontario: "When war actually began, I had the horrible sensation that the bottom had dropped out of Rotary. Its most cherished Object, that of international goodwill through understanding, appeared a completely futile effort." After he had realised that it was only civilisation the bottom was dropping out of, the Governor took heart, possibly recalling also that he lived in the centre of his country's steel industry and Hamilton's warlike past, for this was where 700 British troops had routed 2,000 Americans (capturing both their generals) in the War of 1812.

Despite that Canada had been the last of the great Commonwealth nations to declare war, Canadian soldiers were the first to reach the "home" country and were well involved in the battle for France the following year. Canada was also, like the other dominions, training many thousands of air crews. Rotary tightened ties already strong. The Minister of National Defense was the Rotarian from Halifax, Nova Scotia, Colonel Jim Ralston, who, together with Big Jim Davidson, had founded the Movement in Australia and New Zealand soon after the First World War (see Chapter Eleven). And when in 1940 the two giant North American neighbours formed the Permanent Canadian-United States Joint Defense Board, it was another Rotarian from the Regina Club in Saskatoon, Dr H. L. Keenleyside, who was made its Secretary.

Nor did Canada throw its doors open only for air crew trainees. In Britain, at the start of hostilities, the term "evacuees" applied solely to schoolchildren who were taken out of London, an obvious prime target for the Luftwaffe; soon it had a wider application, as Hitler's hordes engulfed the Continent. Thousands of families sent their children to Canada, and the present writer, attending Bishops College School in Lennoxville, Quebec, at the time, found, to his rather casual amazement, that in his last term he was a prefect with authority over new boys with resounding names like Rothschild and Eden (the Foreign Secretary's nephew). (In recent years, other "new boys" of my last school year have reappeared on the cultural and political horizons of Great Britain, such as the prominent Labour MP Greville Janner and the orchestral conductor George Hurst. At this period, my elder brother, Teddy, was becoming a Flight Lieutenant at Moosejaw, Saskatchewan — one of only two in his class of fifty to survive the coming battles of Africa and Europe — so we were beneficiaries of both halves of that huge country's hospitality.)

Rotary's ever-strengthening international links once more showed their quiet power when Canada's then total of 160 Clubs issued a blanket invitation to all Rotarians in Great Britain and Ireland, and later France, suggesting that they send their threatened children over the Atlantic to the care of Canadian Rotary families for the duration, a spontaneous and generous offer accepted on a wide scale, though for some, thanks to the ever-growing number of the wolf-pack U-boats, the journey to safe harbour was not completed.

Under the British flag, the Second World War therefore immediately affected Rotary right across the globe. And Rotary Clubs were very glad to be so affected, the amazing durable Commonwealth link gaining immense reinforcement from the Movement in whose Extension and growth through many nations Britain had played such a part. Indeed, since the world atlas then showed that Empire "Rhodes" red over one-quarter of the world's surface, the partnership, however unacknowledged, was inescapable. Paul Harris relished the fact; Ches Perry bore up under its burden grimly, perhaps with a nightmare vision of the centre of Rotary International slipping from East Wacker Drive to Tavistock Square. In any event, it was as a citizen of the Empire and Commonwealth that Big Jim Davidson — by then a naturalised Canadian — had made his amazing journey across the Middle and Far East (recounted in Chapter Fourteen), forming Rotary Clubs among peoples of many languages, colours and religions, through the glorious and convenient circumstance that the vast majority of them still dwelt under the unifying umbrella of the Union Jack.

The regrettable appeasement symbolism of that umbrella at Munich was transitory, since Churchill was soon to snap its folds shut, revealing the snarling bulldog beneath. For that matter, Churchill himself had never been taken in by the umbrella's apparent meekness, though no doubt acquiescing in its right to inherit the earth, for as First Lord of the Admiralty – which he became, at Chamberlain's invitation, at 6 p.m. on the day war was declared – he entertained the Prime Minister and his wife to dinner, and after talking with him on unusually social and intimate terms, recorded, "What a pity Hitler did not know when he met this sober English politician with his umbrella at Berchtesgaden, Godesberg and Munich, that he was actually talking to a hard-bitten pioneer from the outer marches of the British Empire!" Actually, whatever Hitler thought of Chamberlain (and he referred to the British and French leaders after Munich as "little worms"), he had a healthy and realistic regard for Britain, together with its dominions and colonies, and told his astonished generals of his genuine admiration "of the British Empire, of the necessity for its existence, and of the civilisation that Britain had brought into the world" and his belief that he could "make peace with Britain on a basis that she would regard as compatible with her honour to accept". He most sincerely hoped that he would not have to fight the British.

It was perhaps not all that strange. For Hitler could not possibly forget that it was another Englishman named Chamberlain at the turn of the century whose philosophic and historical writings had first proclaimed the Germans as a Master Race, inciting them to their dreams of world conquest and virulent hatred of the Jews, through several generations. Born in 1855, and thus only one year senior to Bernard Shaw, another worshipper of dictators (with whom Shaw shared an abhorrence of Rotary, of course), Houston Stewart Chamberlain – whose uncle, a field-marshal, was also named Neville! – became a demon inspiration, first to Kaiser William, who declared him sent by God, and then to the Nazis, whose party he joined in 1923 in its very early rough-house days and whose leader he in turn proclaimed had been sent by God to lead the German people to their great destiny (even though Hitler was in gaol at the time). Though a naturalised German since 1916, a son-in-law of Wagner, and holder of the Iron Cross – the Kaiser's personal gift – this warped, neurotic genius from Portsmouth was, at the outbreak of war, still being hailed in Berlin as "the spiritual founder" of National Socialist Germany, which indeed was the case – after all, he had even obligingly "proved" that Jesus could not possibly have been Jewish! Small wonder that Hitler found himself, at the crunch, reluctant to wage war with England, especially an England led, of all things, by a Chamberlain!

And Hitler was right in his appreciation of the latent strength of the Empire and Commonwealth, which showed their force in Rotary not only in the great dominions but in the colonies, large and small. In Ceylon the war effort was early off the mark, the island having an eye on Japan. But Europe's crisis engaged it too, and the Rotary Club of Colombo, when the war was still but a few months old, had already formed a Jewish Refugee Relief Committee, and one of its members, Abraham Gardiner, told the Thirty-First Convention of Rotary International, meeting in Havana, "England's cause is right", a view he assured delegates was also held by none other than Gandhi, whom he knew well.

Sir Stanley Spurling, Founder Member of the Rotary Club on the island of Bermuda — where Paul Harris had begun his tentative re-emergence into public Rotary life in 1926 (described in Chapter Thirteen) — and incoming Governor of Rotary District 174, which included the entire State of New York (appropriately, the "Empire" State), told Convention "everything we hold precious is at stake" and revealed that the island had full voluntary mobilisation of its young men.

The only part of the British-controlled world which was unaffected by any direct menace during the war was Palestine, held by the British under mandate from the League of Nations since 1922. Paradoxically, the titanic onslaughts all around it, unleashed first by Italy and then Germany, gave Palestine six years of peace after a decade of increasingly bloody strife between Arab and Jew, a decade which had shown the influence and innate stature of Rotary at its best, for all factions kept their membership. Both sides held their fire against each other now, though the Zionist organisations announced full support for Britain against the nation that was trying to exterminate their race, and both Jews and Arabs volunteered to serve in British army units. It was in this service that Moshe Dayan lost his eye and gained that famous eye-patch. The war years, however, brought Palestine not only peace but tremendous prosperity, as its industries negotiated fat contracts to supply Montgomery's famous Eighth Army, and the Rotary Club of Jerusalem — like those of Cairo and Colombo, a Jim Davidson "baby", of course — exemplified the spirit of Rotary internationalism as no other Club could. There, Arabs, Jews and British members continued to meet, as they had met each week in fellowship all through the bitter years of civil violence, and for that matter still do.

The fellowship in the Club of Haifa was perhaps more fraught.

It had been formed three years after the Jerusalem Rotary Club, in 1932, when restrictions on Jewish immigration into Palestine had been eased (the High Commissioner that year even became a member himself of the Jerusalem Club), and by 1940 Haifa had forty-eight members including, as well as Jews, Arabs and the British, Frenchmen, Italians, Germans, Egyptians, Russians, Bulgarians and Romanians. There was a third Club there which balanced on an even more precarious tightrope, namely the Tel Aviv-Jaffa Club, which alternated its meetings between Jaffa, an Arab town, and Tel Aviv, a predominantly Jewish one. If the Jewish members thought oppression of Rotary had been left behind in Europe, they were soon disillusioned when Arab Rotarians were threatened with death if they kept lunching with Jews. But the Arabs still came, and no Rotary Club ever closed in Palestine, or in Israel, as it later became. An American war correspondent, visiting the Jerusalem Club, reported in amazement:

> I had heard about Rotary in Jerusalem, but it was a minor, albeit pleasant, shock to find it here. Jerusalem, even for a newspaper correspondent, is a very foreign place. . . . Here is an American heading an oil company, an Arab architect with an international reputation, a Jew merchant whose family has been active in Palestine for 400 years . . . the Membership Committee was headed by a Jew, with two Arabs and one Britisher . . . the Committee which invited speakers had an Englishman for Chairman and two Arabs, one Pole, one Jew, three British as Members. On the Community Service Committee were an Arab as Chairman, and four Jews, two British, one Swede and one American.

The Jerusalem Rotary Club must also have on record the most unique Committee minute of any Club in the Movement anywhere. It was recorded during 1940, and stated that "Rotarian Wadsworth agreed to arrange for a buffet luncheon to be served on the Dead Sea. He also extended an invitation from the Sodom and Gomorrah Golfing Society to use their links without fee". One feels that the hand which wrote it was laconic and British.

Had Erwin Rommel and his Afrika Corps reached their goals and not been thrown back at El Alamein, perhaps such minutes would have been less cool, less "laid-back", as we say today, but probably we should never have known anyway. As the guns besieging Tobruk rumbled for the second time along the North African coast, and their many uniformed members vanished from lunch on urgent business, and Monty stuck Rommel's picture up in his caravan, the Rotarians of Jerusalem — mindful of the fate of their fellow-Clubs in occupied Europe — prudently destroyed most of the Club's documents.

We consider the battles raging between China and Japan last of all because, as yet, neither of those countries had even declared war on each other! Since the start of what was still referred to as the "China incident" in 1937, Japan had destroyed the Chinese Air Force, completely driven Chinese armies out of much of eastern China with enormous losses, stunned world opinion by her brutal bombing of civilians at Canton and horrifying mass atrocities on the fall of Nanking, and occupied all the principal Chinese cities, including the capital. Chiang Kai-shek, withdrawing into the vast eastern regions of China (allied temporarily with his future Nemesis, Mao Tse-tung), still controlled the rural areas from which guerrillas mauled the arrogant and pitiless invaders, who could still afford to withdraw two divisions to train in jungle warfare on Formosa for the coming attack through Malaya to Singapore and, at the same time, fight the Russians to a standstill in yet another undeclared war on the Mongolian border. Small wonder that the United States judged it wise to move the Pacific fleet from San Diego, California, to Pearl Harbor, Hawaii, in April 1940.

The true wonder came two months later, when the World Rotary Convention met in Havana, Cuba, in an extraordinary demonstration of both its strength and weakness (from the same evidence, according to one's standpoint). Ches Perry had judged this a good time to resign and, in a proposed "final" speech, to an audience which included delegates from both China and Japan, he declared with a straight face that at least half of China's twenty-five Clubs were functioning "in more or less a normal way", while those Chinese Rotarians who – for reasons he left unspecified – had had to leave their home cities had formed such "informal" Clubs as the Outport Rotarians' Tiffin Club in Shanghai, and the Vagabond Rotarians' Tiffin Club in Hong Kong. In Japan, on the other hand, that country's forty-three Clubs were "carrying on actively".

Rotarian Komatsu of the Tokyo Club came to the platform to confirm this fact, explaining to delegates how all the money sent from Clubs around the world at the time of the Japanese earthquake of 1923 had been used to build an orphanage where young women were given courses in domestic sciences and "in cultural training such as flower arrangement, tea ceremony, music, painting and so forth". Above all, however, his Club had "naturally been interested in all endeavours to promote international fellowship and understanding". Komatsu concluded: "Let us be zealous and earnest in our efforts to safeguard Rotary, so that each step taken in this critical hour may redound to the enhancement of its influence and usefulness. . . . Let us avoid any action which might be interpreted as casting stones of blame. Let us not lose sight of the fact that the peoples of the world do not possess the same psychological approach to the problems of life." Or, he might have more pertinently added, to the problems of death, for he was Managing Director of the Asano Shipbuilding Company, a firm named after a famous eighteenth-century samurai who had killed himself after being insulted and whose forty-seven retainers had avenged the insult and then also killed themselves, according to the warrior code of Bushido. Their graves are venerated to this day in a temple in Tokyo, and the story of Asano had much to do with the type of fanatic soldier who was about to maraud across the Pacific.

It is interesting to note that the Japanese view of the psychology of nations expressed to that Havana Convention in 1940 is entirely different from that expressed by the eminent Japanese psychiatrist who, as these lines are being written, is World President of Rotary for 1982-3. Dr Hiroji Mukasa, on the contrary, holds that the psychological problems of people in any nation are fundamentally the same, and he takes this message to bolster Rotary's Fourth Object of international unity wherever he travels. Whether historical retreats or psychological advances account most for this change of emphasis, it remains an intriguing and encouraging turnabout.

The Rotarians in Havana knew nothing of Asano, however. And for once even the great veteran Allen Albert's vision of reality was blurred when he introduced the speaker with the words "Of all the men I know, Takashi Komatsu's smile is supreme". Though indeed, at that moment, it was!

It was from Paul Harris, now seventy-two, that the cold douche came:

> If we would be realistic, we may well keep in mind the fact that the developments in Europe are not new and unprecedented, nor is the shock on the nerves of the American people without precedent . . . we must view present-day developments, not as isolated matters, but rather as a chapter only in the long history of world affairs . . . we must remember that we are living in a predatory world, that our own beloved countries have been no exceptions . . . the neutral countries of the New World, who have profited so much from their own lawlessness.

Harris had the same panoramic view of history as Churchill. But it was not what the Rotarians had come to hear, and their gift of a large box of Havana cigars went not to him but to Chesley Perry as a farewell gift.

Perhaps the most symptomatic feature of the Havana Convention lay in its reflection of the internal evolution of the Movement, not in its reaction to world events while the war was still "phoney".

Thirty-five years before, Rotary had been founded, not by the frail old man of seventy-two up there on the platform lecturing them, but by the brisk thirty-seven-year-old lawyer on the make, which he had then been. Until the First World War, most of his co-pioneers, in both North America and Great Britain, had been drawn from that same age group. Their chief non-Rotarian guest speaker at that Convention was Walter B. Pitkin. His is not a name to conjure with now, yet he was the author of a book whose title retains its enduring and potent magic of conjuring unreality as much today, when it has passed into the language, as when it first appeared on the dust-jacket of his work, namely *Life Begins at Forty.*

The triumph in Havana was Perry's, not Paul Harris's. The sixty-eight-year-old General Secretary, his bearing as upright, immaculate, military and intimidating as ever, was relishing that triumph on the scene of his brief military career as a lieutenant in the Spanish-American War of 1898, that three-month phenomenon which bore as much relation to the events in Europe and China as did Teddy Roosevelt's Rough Riders to Guderian's Panzer juggernauts. It seemed a fitting moment to close his career at full circle. But there was little thought or apparent appreciation on his part that life, and a way of life, was in fact now ending for thousands half that magic age of Pitkin's.

CHAPTER TWENTY

The Wheel at War — 4

We are a little tired
Of being admired.
The sincerest form of flattery of our nation
Would be imitation. . . .

The epic message much sustains
Our courage — but, when war is made,
Kind hearts are less than aeroplanes
And simple faith than foreign aid.

W.W. Blair-Fish, Rotary Service, 1940

When Poland had reeled back before the stunned world's first unbelieving glimpse of the terrifying Blitzkrieg in action (a concept, incidentally, invented in Britain by Captain [later Sir Basil] Liddell Hart, General J.E.C. Fuller and others, but taken up and put into practical and profitable production by others to our disadvantage, following the customary fate of British innovations), Rotary International President Walter Head had prudently decided against a planned presidential tour of Europe. Most observers expected, and the German High Command most certainly feared, that France, with its overwhelming strength in men and arms, would smash through Germany's sparsely defended western flank. Indeed, we now know that the much-vaunted Siegfried Line was nothing more than a "construction site", in the estimation of Hitler's own generals. But the French Government, advised by the timid General Gamelin, and encouraged by British appeasers still active at Westminster, froze into inaction. Churchill fumed and Colonel Charles de Gaulle commented acidly, "Peering between the battlements of our fortifications, we shall watch the enslavement of Europe."

"Please convey to Clubs my deepest sympathy and best wishes," cabled President Head. "Have most sympathetic appreciation of difficult situation for Clubs and Rotarians in France." The Paris Club replied: "French Clubs thank you for expression of sympathy. Filled with confidence, they will bear the ordeal, preserving attachment to Rotary principles." While the Club at Le Havre, busy looking after all British officers and men passing through the town as well as welcoming "all members who may find themselves at any time in the neighbourhood" (there would soon be all too many), replied: "We wish, with all our hearts, that this visit may be merely postponed and that it may take place soon." Another cable received with appreciation at Rotary Headquarters in Chicago, read: "Rotary Council for Denmark, Iceland, Finland, Norway, Sweden, declares its utmost desire to carry on in order to help humanity."

On 9th April 1940, two months before the Havana Convention but only four days after Neville Chamberlain had gloated at a Conservative Party rally that Hitler had "missed the bus", the Wehrmacht, heady from its Polish conquest, sprang north upon Scandinavia. It was almost over in twenty-four hours; and another sixty-two Rotary Clubs had disappeared. Denmark, through sleight-of-hand brilliance, was lost to the Nazis by the time its amiable citizens were finishing breakfast, as were all the main ports and cities of Norway before darkness fell. In spite of a mauling by the British fleet and momentary reverses at the hands of an Allied force of Norwegian, British, French and, yes, Polish troops, Major Vidkun Quisling, whose name was rapidly to become a synonym for traitor, was able to declare himself Prime Minister of occupied Norway on 15th May, and Sweden accepted terms for neutrality. One month after the attack on Norway, and exactly one month before the Rotarians began arriving in holiday mood in Havana, Guderian's armoured columns tore into the vitals of Luxembourg, the Netherlands and Belgium, and raged towards France. Another fifty-three Rotary Clubs were engulfed.

It was Chamberlain, not Hitler, who found the bus leaving without him and was left walking home through London's black-out, after a howling, derisive House of Commons had dismissed him. He had called for sacrifice, and Lloyd George, Europe's saviour in the First World War, suggested that Chamberlain should sacrifice himself for a start. "In the name of God, go!" shouted Leopold Amery, an old colleague of his (echoing Cromwell, three centuries before), whose own son was to be hanged as a traitor shortly after the war. Chamberlain went and Churchill, only two years younger than Ches Perry, began his historic leadership of the free world. In five days, the Dutch had surrendered and on the same day that

Quisling in Oslo became "Prime Minister", the French Premier Daladier telephoned Churchill to tell him "We are beaten!"

German tanks, dive-bombers, daring parachutists and airborne troops completed the conquest of Europe in six weeks. By 5th June Belgium was engulfed and Britain had accomplished the miracle of rescuing one-third of a million soldiers from the beaches of Dunkirk right under the noses of the baffled Blitzkrieg generals, and to the far from speechless rage of the Fuehrer. Four days later, the Rotary Convention opened to the news that German Panzers were on the banks of the Seine.

On Monday, the following morning, as Mussolini — earning himself Churchill's epithet, "the jackal" — decided it was safe enough to join in by declaring war on France and Britain, President Walter Head told the perspiring, sun-tanned delegates, "To those of you who are wondering about the fate of Rotary in such countries as Holland, Belgium, Denmark and Norway, I can only say that we know nothing specific at the moment", though he could have hazarded a reasonable guess.

On Wednesday, Ches Perry was delivering his General Secretary's Report, in which he acknowledged the newspaper headlines about Europe in only the most cursory manner, though he did say that "with regard to the Rotary Observance Week, special pamphlets adapting the general plans for the week to conditions in the CENAEM (Continental Europe, North Africa and Eastern Mediterranean) region were prepared in English, French and German. . . . It will be understood that many of the Rotary Clubs in CENAEM region have had to adapt their activities". He also ventured to observe "a considerable decrease in the amount of correspondence received from the Clubs in the region", but reference to the great sums sent by Clubs in Great Britain and Europe for Polish and Finnish relief was the nearest he came to current affairs. Europe's howls of torment fell on deaf General Secretarial ears.

This attitude could have come as no surprise to Tom Warren, who had made the perilous journey to the Convention with Reginald Coombe, President of the London Club. Together with a delegate from Hungary, they were the only three Rotarians from Europe present! Warren had addressed the Convention the day before, sketching in lightly a picture of wartime conditions in beleaguered Britain. He had ended his address by saying that RIBI, like the psalmist, was lifting its eyes to the hills and that "prominent among the peaks in the hills is the peak of our grand old Rotary". He refrained from any reference to the fact that the peak was, for the moment, surrounded by clouds, but the temptation must have been strong, because he had just heard the RIBI Message to Convention read out, along with messages of "fraternal greetings" from all over the world, and he knew it had been grossly censored. After the wishes for a successful Convention, the actual Message from RIBI had made reference to "British Clubs, alas, otherwise engaged in International Service". Perry did not judge these sentiments fit for the ears of delegates, and removed them.

That rather typically British "throw-away" line had clearly irritated Perry and so he had had it deleted from the record, either spoken or written, an extraordinary piece of vindictive vandalism. His great farewell moment was not to be spoiled. As Roger Levy comments in his history of RIBI: "The British might believe that their cause was International Service, but they must not be credited with having said so." Tom Warren made no direct reference to this, but permitted himself a little gentle irony in his speech to the delegates sitting before him in the opulent, exotic Grand Salon of the Centro Asturiano, one of the largest Clubs in Havana, on whose ornate facade blazed the name of Rotary in blinding rainbow neon. "It is almost sacrilegious of me to see the lights of Havana, because we have now developed cat's eyes, and I will have to get my eyes attuned to the blackout when I go home again." To the "home fires burning" he would have been able to add in a few months time. But with admirable restraint, he made no attempt to make or imply any melodramatic reproach, in private or public.

The roots of the Grand Alliance to come were burgeoning in the slowly awakening soil of at least part of America, and one of its main nutrients was the Rotary Movement which, for ten crucial years, had been an entirely Anglo-Saxon phenomenon, and to whose development key figures in British Rotary, as these pages have shown, had made such far-reaching contributions during the 1920s. Even Churchill, whose personal rapport with the wheelchair-bound Roosevelt was soon to become so vital to the prosecution of global war against the Axis powers, summed up this period in *The Gathering Storm* in these words: "So far no ally had espoused our cause. The United States was cooler than in any other period. I persevered in my correspondence with the President, but with little response." The trouble of course was that the Americans, from Roosevelt downward, were proud that Winston Churchill, through his mother, was half-American; unfortunately, this was the half they distrusted. In the same way, it had been the very English-ness of the Thirteen Colonies that had so irritated George III; and Tom Warren had a great sense of history and a good sense of Americans. Wilde had said that Britain and America were separated by a common tongue; in fact, they were soon to be separated far more drastically by a special relationship.

Meanwhile, as distinct from the official "platform" stance, the two Englishmen were besieged with sympathisers, and London President Coombe reported:

> I suppose Tom Warren and I were being asked every minute of this Convention what the Governors could go back and tell their individual Clubs, as they distinctly came forward with the idea of doing everything possible to help us. . . . I was deeply moved by the sympathetic desire of the American women to mother our children, and I shall never forget the longing of these Governors and friends to get us into the United States and safe from harm.

The two Englishmen even went through the absurd prescribed ritual of electing an RIBI member to the International Board of Directors. Tom Warren took the chair at a "fully" attended meeting of British delegates, with Reg Coombe as Secretary. Warren then called for nominations, whereupon Coombe nominated Warren and then took over as Chairman while Warren seconded the motion, after which Warren resumed the Chair and declared himself elected "unanimously". Goering in the Reichstag couldn't have done it better.

All resonance of Europe's anguish could not be stifled, of course, despite the obstructive Perry. The Governor of Rotary in Finland was there, since he was in the United States to organise Finnish relief with the former US President Herbert Hoover (Rotarian of the Pine Bluffs Club, Arkansas), and Finland still had seven of her eight Clubs left, the exception being in Viborg, formed in 1931 and now ceded to Russia. The Rotarians of Assen in the Netherlands, having compiled a list of families willing to take soldiers into their homes to "read, write, and enjoy a cup of tea", suddenly found they had soldiers in plenty amongst them for the next five years, though tea was not high on their list of demands. The Rotarians of Ghent were preoccupied with restoring their thirteenth-century Church of St Nicholas when this community project became overwhelmed by the grey hordes pouring through the town towards the British trapped at Dunkirk. The Paris Club proudly contributed Rotarian Raoul Dautry to the doomed French Government as a hapless Minister of (largely non-existent) Armament, while twenty-nine other members of the Club were called to action, many never to return (see the next chapter). But soon all would be inaction and Rotary on the Continent of Europe would go silent.

Meanwhile, the scenes in Havana's huge and palatial social Clubs were reminiscent of the "sound of revelry by night" Byron had described in his poem *Childe Harold*, in relation to the Duchess of Richmond's Ball before Waterloo, when

> . . . bright
> The lamps shone o'er fair women and brave men;
> A thousand hearts beat happily; and when
> Music arose with its voluptuous swell,
> Soft eyes look'd love to eyes which spake again,
> And all went merry as a marriage bell;
> But hush! hark! a deep sound strikes like a rising knell!

Such it was in the Centro Asturiano, where hundreds of couples danced on the marble floor of the huge main ballroom beneath a soaring azure dome or did the rumba at the vast Casino Deportivo by the moonlit shore to fourteen orchestras. The most talked-about headline of the Convention did not tell of the surrender of King Leopold of the Belgians or of the dramatic entrance of Rommel's 7th Panzer Division leading the fearsome columns of steel and thunder and fire from Belgium into France. It read "PERRY STEALS SHOW IN LUNCH WITH ROTARIANS", and carried an account of Ches Perry's speaking in fluent Spanish about his fight for "Cuba Libre" back in 1898, his speech "interrupted repeatedly by thunderous applause by admiring Cuban Rotarians".

Away from the massive ballrooms of the magnificent Clubs, many delegates spent their evenings sampling the colourful noisy gaiety of Havana night-life, in an exotic ambience described officially as "the spell wielded by the tropic nights, a magic of deep ebon-black skies and bright stars, gently waving palms, and a soft, caressing breeze bespeaking mystery and romance", which was liberally available in the many glamorous Havana night-spots run by the nation-wide Crime Syndicate in America whose headquarters was the comfortable cell at Dannemora maximum security prison in New York State, where "Lucky" Luciano, challenger and then inheritor of the mantle of Capone, ran his vice empire undisturbed by incarceration (he was released two years later for a special reason, of which more later). On Thursday and Friday, delegates reluctantly dispersed — out of 3,719 nearly 3,000 were returning to the United States and Canada — and on the day the Rotarians left Havana, 14th June, the Champs-Élysées shook to the tramp of German boots, while across in Poland, near Cracow, a camp for political prisoners was formally declared open. Paris fell and Auschwitz rose and Rotary went home; the world had had a very busy week.

Meanwhile, the first known Rotary fatality of war outside of Europe and China turned out to be a member of the Club in High Wycombe, a pleasant but unremarkable town in the Wye Valley of the beautiful Chiltern Hills north-west of London, which had thus far featured in history only as an entry in the Domesday Book and as the location of an inn, the Red Lion, in front of which Disraeli, the great Victorian Prime Minister of Empire, had made many impassioned speeches on two of his four unsuccessful attempts to get into Parliament. And the first continent outside of Europe and China to be touched by the opening salvoes of Armageddon proved to be the least likely one, South America. The link between the two was the advent upon the high seas of the German pocket battleships.

Two of these warships, the *Deutschland* and the *Graf Spee*, had been sent to sea even before Hitler's attack on Poland, to play havoc with British shipping in the North and South Atlantic respectively. On 23rd November, the armed merchant cruiser *Rawalpindi* was reported sunk by the *Deutschland*, between Iceland and the Faroes. Her gallant commander was Captain E.C. Kennedy, a Rotarian of High Wycombe, retired some years from the Royal Navy, who had answered the call for volunteers at once, writing to the Club Secretary just before sailing, "I send the Club my very best wishes, and look forward to the day when we shall have seen this show through, and we will all meet again." His loss was, of course, the first of many to the World Movement, but the news would have struck hard at Paul Harris (Churchill described Kennedy's action as an "heroic fight"), since the High Wycombe Club had given Paul such a wonderful reception on his last visit to Britain four years before. Indeed, the Reverend Wilfred Float, who conducted Captain Kennedy's memorial service, had played host to Paul at that time and was a long-standing friend. Thus, the news which shocked Britain into sending most of her Atlantic fleet out for revenge, brought home to the frail old man at Comely Bank at an early stage the heart-breaking reality of another world war and another crisis for his beloved Golden Wheel.

Four days after Captain Kennedy's memorial service, the *Graf Spee*, having sunk nine cargo vessels over a wide area below the equator, including the Indian Ocean, appeared off the coast of Brazil and was at once sought out by three less well-armed but daring British warships, based in the Falkland Islands. Nor was this the first time those now headline-making islands had been the focus of world attention: the German admiral, whose name the *Graf Spee* bore, had died near there when four out of five of his cruisers were sunk in a running battle with a British squadron in the First World War. News of the *Graf Spee* was extremely depressing for the Rotary International Secretariat, for the next Convention was still at that time due to be held in Rio de Janeiro, a plan already put in jeopardy by a decree enacted by the Brazilian Government restricting all organisations whose headquarters were located in another country, and President Vargas was treading an ever more cautious path as regards the war, with a large German population and the ever-growing Nazi Greenshirts marching about his cities. Vargas had sent one son to be educated in the United States, another in Germany and Italy, hedging his bets.

The fate of the Convention was probably decided by the sea battle which followed on 12th-17th December 1939, when the *Graf Spee*, planning to intercept any British merchant ships emerging from the river Plate into the Atlantic, was herself intercepted by a heavy cruiser, *Exeter*, and two light cruisers, *Ajax* and *Achilles*, and by midnight of that Wednesday was badly damaged, putting into the sanctuary of Montevideo harbour for repairs. On the following Sunday, watched by thousands — who had come across the river from Argentina, over the border from Brazil, and had even flown down from the United States — the *Graf Spee* sailed a few miles down river, where she was scuttled by her captain, after which he went ashore in Buenos Aires on the other side of the great river, took an hotel room and shot himself.

Thus Uruguay, with a pro-British people but a German-trained Army, in whose capital "Herbierto" Coates had first established Rotary in South America at the end of the First World War, again proved crucial in the development of Rotary in South America. The extraordinary events on the river Plate captured the world's headlines (even, grudgingly, those in Soviet Russia), kept Churchill jubilant in the Admiralty War Room for an entire day, earned Grand Admiral Erich Raeder, Commander-in-Chief of the German fleet, an outraged telling-off from Hitler, and of course gave Montevideo Rotarians a grandstand view of history. The sinking of the *Graf Spee* also, whatever their leaders might say, brought the people of South America off the fence. As Churchill wrote to Roosevelt, without the British warships, "South American Republics would soon have many worse worries than the sound of one day's distant seaward cannonade". It may be that those republics remembered that it was the deliberate shield of British sea power 100 years before which had enabled them to break free from Europe and achieve independence, and that in effect the same service had been performed again.

Thus it was that the 1940 Rotary Convention was now moved from Rio north to Havana, to be on the safe side. Ches Perry could also now deploy his Spanish to good effect, and not have his "final" appearance on the platform spoiled. It was Tom Warren, however, chairing the Nominating Committee for the next President, who made certain that the choice fell on a Brazilian, Armando de Arrudo Pereira, of the Rotary Club of São Paulo, thus ensuring that the seventy Clubs of Brazil remained in the fold. Today, São Paulo alone has nearly half that number of Clubs and has itself played host to the International Convention (1981), while Rio had its moment of Convention glory offered again, and confirmed this time, in 1948.

Pereira was an inspired choice. An engineer and historian and a true cosmopolitan, he had divided his education between his home city, and Genoa, Italy; Farnham and Birmingham, England; and New York, USA. Well acquainted with Paul Harris since the early 1930s, he had translated Paul's *This Rotarian Age* into Portuguese and had been the Founder's principal host during the Harrises' tour of Brazil. During his one-year term as Brazil's Rotary Governor (known in Rotary then as District 72) he had increased membership in his country by fifteen Clubs. As a result of his international upbringing, he was fluent in five languages, speaking French, Spanish, Italian and English in addition to Portuguese. His election enlarged the global perceptions of all Rotarians, reminding them that he was a prominent citizen of a nation which covered half a continent and was roughly the same size as the United States. In 1942, as we shall see, his country showed a rash but encouraging faith in Allied arms.

The inspiration which Tom Warren guided as Chairman of the Nominating Committee – and it was the first time that the World President had been chosen in this fashion – was twofold: Pereira was not only a Brazilian, he was the first South American to achieve Rotary's international leadership. Cuba at once awarded him its highest honour, the Carlos Manuel Cespedes Cross. In Brazil, all talk of restraints upon the activities of Rotary ceased, and, soon after, Vargas appointed a Rotarian of the Rio de Janeiro Club to the Supreme Court. So it was that Pereira's appointment resulted in yet another, and timely, dramatic illustration of the respect that now came almost automatically Rotary's way from world leaders. Where the dictators of Europe were concerned, this respect had worked to Rotary's detriment and destruction. In South America, it had the opposite effect and ensured Rotary's survival and accelerated its growth.

Having a leading citizen of São Paulo as Rotary International's President did much to bring the most powerful of Latin-American dictators off his fence. The German language could be heard all over São Paulo, and indeed all over the southern part of Brazil. At one time, moreover, there had been more Italians in São Paulo than Brazilians; 200,000 Japanese had settled nearby; the first, and strongest, revolt – with nearly 50,000 rebel soldiers mobilised – against Vargas's role in the 1930s, had come from *Paulistas*. That

combination could have been decisive when Vargas was faced with a
Paulista President of Rotary. Yet Vargas had played host to Paul
Harris and been impressed; he was not insensitive to the happy
coincidence of the Founder's first name being the same as that of
Brazil's largest city, or to the fact that that city was often compared
to another, where large populations of Germans and Italians also
lived, and was popularly known as "the Chicago of South America".
It was enough on the scale. In two years' time Brazil would have
25,000 troops fighting the Germans in Italy, their bravery bringing
lasting honour to their country. When he addressed his acceptance
speech to the delegates in Havana, Pereira said, with Latin emotion
and passion, "In the Americas we have fought for our rights and
liberty", knowing that in his native land there was no parliament,
nor were there elections or a free press. Yet he knew also that
Vargas was rapidly developing the industry and mineral resources of
Brazil, and that, in the words of Hubert Herring's definitive history
of Latin-America: "Vargas had appointed himself father of his
people, a role in which he delighted, and on the whole the people
enjoyed it."

Possibly this appealed to someone else at Havana as he listened to
Pereira's speech, someone else who had delighted for so long in a
similar role. At all events, Ches Perry shortly afterwards announced
that he was withdrawing his resignation as General Secretary and
would soldier on.

Perry's decision was greeted with mixed feelings in many quarters,
not without cause, and the extent of his influence in persuading the
International Board of Directors — which that year consisted of five
Americans, three South Americans (including the President), and
one Rotarian each from England, Canada, Switzerland, China and
the Lebanon — to maintain an official distance between themselves
and the war was proved by another censorship of a message from
Great Britain, this time his refusal to publish a cabled appeal from
the Rotary Club of Preston, Lancashire, in *The Rotarian*. The
appeal, looking for a more concrete response than expressions of
"sympathy", read: "We Rotarians in Great Britain tender our
sincere thanks to all American Rotarians for their sympathy in the
fight for the rule of law as against force, and sincerely hope for a
continuance and intensification of their moral and material support
to Great Britain and her Allies in their days of trial." Perry replied
that the Executive Committee of the RI Board had bluntly refused
the request, with his clear approval. Should it be published, said
Perry, with his customary air of patronising condescension, "it
would at once be definitely taken as being an official expression of
Rotary International. . . . Unless we are ready to now abandon the

international ideal of Rotary, which has been maintained for over a quarter of a century, we must act discreetly and logically". But the Preston Rotarians were not looking to Rotary International Headquarters for discretion, they were looking for valour. One Preston Rotarian announced with bitter disappointment that the war had weighed RI in the balance and found it wanting in true, vigorous leadership, refusing to fight for what it professed. It deserved to be submerged, if it remained content to sit with arms folded while "the lamps of Rotary were going out one by one".

Perry had not repeated the mistake of announcing to the world that this was not a "Rotary War", but he had done the next worse thing. Fortunately for Anglo-American cohesion in the Movement, response from individual Rotarians and Rotary Clubs right across the United States made it clear that while Perry may have spoken for the Rotary "establishment", he had not done so for its members. Most importantly, he didn't even speak for his own Club of Chicago, since its great Secretary, George Treadwell (whom readers will recall as first Secretary of the Shanghai Club before he returned to Chicago in 1920, and later as the man who inspired the investigation of the University of Chicago called *Rotary?*, described in Chapter Seventeen), pulled no punches in an article for his Club journal *Gyrator*, in lising a Rotarian's duties in the world crisis:

> As a leader and executive dedicated to the principles on which human liberty is founded . . . he must checkmate those who play the game of force and barbarism, consciously or unconsciously, with their class, religious, or racial hatreds of Jews, hatreds of capitalists or of Britain or France, or hatreds of any nations that stand for genuine self-determination of peoples, for individual and collective human liberties.
>
> Reduced to its stark essentials, this is a world battle between Golden Rule civilisation and barbarism. It must be a battle without compromise against Germany, Italy, Russia and Japan. . . .
>
> The time has come when Rotary leadership must rise to meet the world challenge to its tenets. . . . If we cherish the German, Italian, or Danish Rotarians who believed in Rotary ideals, our best way of restoring them to our fellowship is to fight the ideologies that have engulfed them and thus free them to return to the service of Rotary's Objects. . . . Rotary asks Members to subscribe to its ideals and must offer to those who oppose them a chance to withdraw from the organization by issuing a clear and definitive statement of its stand, and ask for Rotary Clubs' commitments to it. It is time for all men to stand up and be counted in our Rotary world.

This was a splendid challenge, from a voice not heard from Rotary before and not heard since for some time in the post-war world, much to the distress of many Rotarians. Its courageous exhortation did much to save Anglo-American Rotary from fragmentation, and could easily have been interpreted as a direct challenge to the General Secretary.

Perry did not choose so to regard it. But the man who has once "resigned" a post, no matter for how long or with what distinction he has held it, and then reconsiders his decisions and tries to resume, never again is accorded the respect he owned before. Though Ches Perry was to hang on for another year, his day was done. Once a man has been called indispensable, the worms start licking their lips. Paul Harris had long ago welcomed new generations of architects to add wings to his original structure; his "builder" had tired of building, but would not only let no one else share new blueprints, he refused to look at them.

The final defeat of official indifference to specific cries for help, of unresponse to the agony abroad, came in June 1941, when the temper of the Thirty-Second Convention of Rotary International in Denver, Colorado, was very different from that in Havana. And for this the major credit must go to the presidency of Armando de Arrudo Pereira. As a South American public figure of universal esteem throughout the continent, but with lifelong sympathies with Europe, he united the will of Rotary and disarmed those suspicious of its being dominated by an Anglo-American conspiracy. The Brazilian President Vargas had given permission for American bases in Brazil, and airstrips were being laid out from Amapá in the north, just over the border from French Guiana, down to Caravelas, for flights to Africa, though the United States was of course not yet in the war. These bases continued the line of those made available to Roosevelt by Winston Churchill in September 1940, in exchange for fifty old-age destroyers, which extended from Newfoundland through Bermuda and Trinidad down to British Guiana. Vargas wrote to Pereira, in words of support but canny ambiguity: "Your meritorious efforts towards world fellowship, to benefit all men of goodwill, are not only inspired by idealistic aims, but are based on reality. These Rotarians, who are scattered so generously on all continents, do not lose sight of the interests of their respective nations. . . . Love for country is a dogma of respect which is necessary to the true appreciation of the highest human aims." Ambiguous or not, the good, clever and pragmatic Doctor benignly watched the formation of fourteen more Rotary Clubs in Brazil that year; one of them at Santa Cruz, one of the new American bases.

And the farce of having a Japanese delegate no longer prevailed. In fact, George Treadwell had referred to Japan as an enemy, though he had written twelve months before Pearl Harbor. At last, it had been recognised that Japan was an enemy to Rotary, in its brutal assault upon China, and the charade had been dropped that the Movement played no part in the Far East conflagration. Japan itself had abandoned the pretence, following its new partners in a tripartite pact, Italy and Germany, in suppressing all its forty-four Rotary Clubs. Indo-China had been occupied and General Hideki Tojo had taken over as Premier, a post in which he was to lead Japan into the world war, thence to defeat and his own end on the gallows. One Japanese Club, in Uwajima, must hold the record for the briefest existence on record, as it was barely formed before being disbanded. (It was re-formed in 1965.) The list of newly formed Clubs also included Formosa, but in this instance the name referred to a town in Argentina.

China, on the other hand, managed to have three delegates at Denver, which was two more than they had at Havana, and one of them was elected to the Board of Directors. The interesting thing about that Rotarian, Yen Te-ching, moreover, was that he belonged to the Club in Nanking, a city which was at the time serving the Japanese invaders as a puppet capital, much in the manner of Vichy in France serving Hitler. Meanwhile, the Rotary Club of Chungking, Chiang Kai-shek's capital, still carried on amidst the air raids, moving their meeting-place on top of an air-raid shelter. Altogether, China still had twenty-five Clubs, amidst all the terror, destruction and death, though only twelve of these held meetings in their original towns, the others meeting as refugees in the Outport Rotarians' Tiffin Club of Shanghai previously mentioned. Throughout the war, in fact, Rotary in China never closed down. That happened only when peace came and brought bloody civil war. Today there are no Rotary Clubs at all on the Chinese mainland, and the present rulers will not allow their reintroduction, whereas in Japan the Movement thrives mightily. On Taiwan (Formosa), however, there are nearly 100 Clubs, keeping Rotary in China alive.

Ches Perry still dug his heels in. President Pereira called his own main speech "The Rotarian Amid World Conflict", yet before the Convention was over, he was pressured into intervening in the proceedings to state that "the speeches you have heard during this week express the individual thought of each program speaker and not the official opinion of the organization".

But not even Rotary's honoured "builder" could play Canute any longer in June 1941, and his hastily flung-up dam crumbled before the weight of inexorable events. Eddie Guest's fellow-native of Birmingham (and the same Birmingham, for only twelve years separated the two men), poor bewildered Neville Chamberlain, had died the previous November, just six months after giving way to Churchill as Premier, and one month after the Battle of Britain had driven off Goering's Luftwaffe and given Hitler his first setback. In the RAF squadrons to whom, in Churchill's deathless phrase, "Never in the field of human conflict was so much owed by so many to so few", there were, besides British and Commonwealth pilots, 200 Polish and Czech flyers, thirty-nine from Belgium and twelve just escaped from France. Helping to thwart "Operation Sea Lion" was also a significant nucleus of United States airmen, who formed the Eagle Squadron against the strenuous opposition of their Ambassador, Joseph P. Kennedy. Kennedy was convinced Britain was about to lose the war and his son, the future US President, John F. Kennedy, had just published an account of British diplomatic blunders entitled *Why England Slept*. It was, however, the American public which was sleeping, for *The Rotarian* proudly announced in October that one-third of the new Japanese cabinet were Rotarians.

Not all the combined lullabies of those who thought like Joseph Kennedy and Chesley Perry could make the sleep last much longer, however. Roosevelt obtained from Congress vast sums to build up the US Army and Navy, to sell munitions to any republic in the Western Hemisphere, and then to finance the great Lend-Lease aid programme to the benefit of Great Britain and Soviet Russia. With France in his pocket, Hitler looked south-east and in turn swallowed Romania, Hungary and Bulgaria, all of which joined the Berlin-Rome-Tokyo Pact, and then from these new borders sent his hordes pouring down into Yugoslavia and Greece, arriving in Athens on 27th April.

Hitler had rescued Mussolini's forces in Greece. He was too late to do so in Africa, where British troops captured Italian soldiers in tens of thousands in Eritrea, Abyssinia and Libya. But the British were then forced into another Dunkirk-style evacuation from Greece and its islands and duelled with the Afrika Corps back and forth across the Libyan Desert. Roosevelt appointed Rotarian Frank Knox of the Chicago Club as Secretary of the Navy (one development even Perry could not ignore). Rotarian Cordell Hull of the Carthage Club in Tennessee as Secretary of State, and Rotarian Henry Stimson of the Huntington, New York, Club as Secretary for War, completed a very committed trio. Roosevelt then thought it was time to deal with another Rotarian, though one of a rather different commitment. On April 23rd, as the Nazi divisions tramped down the borders of south-east Europe and roared along the Mediterranean coast, Colonel Charles A. Lindbergh turned publicly and damagingly against the country which had sheltered him and his family after the kidnapping of his baby son in 1932. At the first

mass meeting of the America First Committee, a cheering crowd of
30,000 in New York heard him denounce the British Government
for having "one desperate plan. . . . To persuade us to send another
American Expeditionary Force to Europe and to share with England
militarily, as well as financially, the fiasco of this war", and for
encouraging "the smaller nations of Europe to fight against hopeless
odds". Two days later, President Roosevelt, also in public, denounced
Lindbergh as a defeatist and an appeaser. Three days after that,
Lindbergh resigned his commission, a resignation promptly accepted
by Rotarian Stimson.

The Royal Navy had by now destroyed or demobilised half the
Italian fleet; but when the Thirty-Second International Rotary
Convention met at Denver in 1941, Rommel was at El Alamein,
poised to strike at the Suez Canal, many British cities were blackened
and shattered, over 14,000 civilians had been killed in London
alone, and in May even the House of Commons Chamber had been
destroyed, fortunately when not in session. Germany's most powerful warship, the *Bismarck*, had been sunk in May also, but in
revenge for the five-minute sinking of Britain's fastest and largest
battleship, HMS *Hood*. With huge losses to submarines in the Atlantic (the author vividly remembers watching convoys assemble off
Bermuda, strung across the horizon as far as the eye could see), it
was fast becoming a poisoned lake. In the three months to May
U-boats alone had sunk 142 ships, while Germany's battle-cruisers
had destroyed or captured thirty-nine ships. The chance was very
real that the British Isles would starve to death. That possibility
indeed loomed very close and real also for Bermuda itself, assemblage point for the convoys, after the merchant ship named after
Eddie Guest's birthplace, the *City of Birmingham*, was torpedoed
and sent to the bottom on her way from New York to the island,
laden with desperately needed food.

Rotary had brought its Convention to Denver before, of course,
to celebrate its twenty-first birthday in 1926 (noted in Chapter
Thirteen), trying at the same time to ignore the rude things Bernard
Shaw (like Henry Ford, an ex-employee of the Edison Company)
was beginning to say about it. What would Shaw have said in June
1941 had he known that the opening symphony concert, broadcast
over the radio from one coast to the other, consisted mainly of the
works of Hitler's favourite composer, or that the top officials of the
Movement had been accommodated by Ches Perry in an hotel called
Broadmoor, also the name of Britain's famous mental asylum? A
certain amount of unreality was unavoidable, with the awesome
presence of Pike's Peak nearby recalling the days of the city's
founding during the "Pike's Peak or bust" gold-rush of 1859 (a

Rotarian article about the occasion was even called "Along the Convention Trail"); with delegates in a euphoric daze following the tremendous impact of Wagner's *Lohengrin* and *Tannhäuser*, played for an audience of 10,000 in the great open amphitheatre under the stars in the foothills of the Rocky Mountains; above all, with Rotarian banker Julius Tausz going round telling everyone that Rotary Clubs were hale and hearty in Hungary, even though he himself had wisely not gone back to Pécs since leaving home for the Havana Convention, and must have known that German troops had been moving freely about his country since the previous September, and had indeed invaded Greece from there. The sad truth, of course, as most delegates knew in their heart of hearts, was that the fifteen Rotary Clubs of Hungary, the seven Clubs of Romania, the thirty-four Clubs of Yugoslavia, the eight Clubs of Bulgaria, and the four in Greece, had all functioned until the last possible moment. Indeed, the last independent Bulgarian government (though strongly pro-German) had included four members of the Rotary Club of Sofia, holding the portfolios of Foreign Affairs, Finance, Commerce and the Interior and Public Health. But the totalitarian avalanche buried them all, as Hitler extended his sovereign power through all their countries to encircle the final victim (now that Britain had eluded him) and gave the plan of attack the code-name first of "Otto" and then "Barbarossa". The assault on Soviet Russia, the Fuehrer told his generals, would make the world "hold its breath and make no comment". His plan was to defeat, destroy and systematically, efficiently, to murder a nation.

What the delegates at Denver could not possibly suspect — any more than most other people, including the German public — was that the day before the Rotary Convention opened, on 14th June 1941, Hitler had conferred with the commanders-in-chief of his Army, Navy and Air Force, together with his top field generals, all of whom had been called to Berlin from their jumping-off posts on the eastern borders of Finland, Poland, Slovakia, Hungary and Romania, for a final briefing and pep talk from their exultant Fuehrer. During a break for lunch in the huge Reich Chancellery, Hitler had explained that his guests were to forget any nonsense about rules of war and the Geneva Convention where Russia was concerned; their job was to lay down a gory-red carpet not just of victory but of terror and annihilation by force and famine. As the truth dawned as to what he meant, some generals were appalled, but none dissented. They may indeed have been the first to "hold their breath", but, when they let it out, they made no protest.

The first Rotarian to learn of "Barbarossa" — though it was now as an ex-Rotarian, since the Italian Clubs had dissolved — did so the following morning while his ex-fellows were registering at their Denver hotels. Count Ciano, Mussolini's Foreign Minister and son-in-law, was told by Ribbentrop as the two Secretaries of State were idling in a Venetian gondola on the way to lunch. Though loftily explaining that "every decision is locked in the impenetrable bosom of the Fuehrer", Ribbentrop nevertheless assured the Count that "the Russia of Stalin will be erased from the map within eight weeks", a prediction that history was to treat with the same distinction as that of the panicking French generals who warned their folding government that Britain was about to have her neck "wrung like a chicken". The impending victim this time, not waiting to hold its breath, was doing – as it had always done – plenty of its own burying, and the Rotary Clubs of Latvia, Lithuania and Estonia disappeared without trace as Russia moved to the Baltic. Sweden, carefully grading its neutrality, had refused passage across its land to the British; now they let the Germans through, to march into poor Finland and line up on its border with Russia. Almost two years before, when German and Russian armies had divided prostrate and bleeding Poland between them, the predators had dined together at Brest Litovsk, where Stalin suggested strongly that Hitler's advance should stop. It did, for the present. And at the celebration banquet, the Russian commander toasted General Guderian with the immortal phrase, "To the eternal enmity of our two countries". The Russian's inadequate grasp of the appropriate German word *Freundschaft* (friendship) had emerged as *Feindschaft* (enmity), but neither side thought it worthwhile correcting the truth.

From darkened Whitehall, the man whose state of mind had recently been described by Hitler to a Reichstag braying in Teutonic ecstasy as one which could "only be explained as symptomatic either of a paralytic disease or of a drunkard's ravings" cabled gloomily to Roosevelt: "In this war every post is a winning post – and how many more are we going to lose?" Fortunately, neither the US President nor the American public shared Hitler's opinion of Churchill and a new biography of the British Prime Minister became an instant best-seller. The Navy Secretary, Frank Knox, of the Chicago Club, told the *Chicago Daily News* that the book about Churchill "becomes almost necessary reading for anyone who wants to keep himself or herself intelligently informed on world affairs".

When Paul Harris stepped to the microphone at Denver, he was aware that about a dozen men of those listening to him had risked their lives by sea journeys to attend the Convention, coming from Australia, New Zealand, China and South Africa. He was also aware that when the last President of Rotary International not chosen by a Nominating Committee, his fellow-Club member in Chicago, George Hager, had toured European Clubs in 1938, the itinerary had included Sweden, Finland, Estonia, France, Belgium and England. Of those fourteen nations, Rotary now survived recognisably in only six: Finland (partially), Denmark (cautiously), Sweden, Switzerland, Vichy France (unoccupied French territory) and England. In a year, two of those would have gone from the list, as German rule tightened in all France and Denmark. The delegates, on their side, were certainly conscious that most of them were seeing a legend in the flesh for the last time. In trouble with his health again, Paul Harris was an old seventy-three. From his painfully thin frame, his gaunt features, pared to the skull with that huge, unmistakable dome, cheek-bones sharp against the tight-drawn skin, thrust forward from rounded shoulders like an emaciated eagle. "Watchman, what of the night?" he cried out to the startled delegates, answering himself, "The morning cometh".

The religious connotations, never very far from Rotarian prose and practice, he exploited shamelessly. Following his quotation from Isaiah, he went on: "God grant that the morning come soon to our dear friends in Great Britain and on the Continent and in China who are bearing the heaviest load of sorrow. In the darkness of this hour, may we remember that morning is bound to come." Less realistic than Churchill who, even when the tide of war began to turn, told his countrymen that they were not faced with the beginning of the end but the end of the beginning, Paul did not give the watchman's full reply, which was "The morning cometh, but also the night". When a saint cites scripture for his purpose, he does so more selectively than the devil, who presumably is less well acquainted with the text.

When Paul Harris struck his prophetic vein, he was unerring and uncannily so. "It is not the part of wisdom to cause our neighbours to fear us. It is the last thing in the world to hope for," he said, at once, unconsciously pinpointing the weakness of Hitler's view of his giant eastern neighbour, a lack of wisdom which in a few days was to lead directly to the appalling decision which would seal the Third Reich's doom. But when he added, about the Rotarian countries of the New World, that "these countries, having no purpose to serve other than the preservation of peace throughout the world, are in an especially good position to wield an important influence in peace conferences", with a voice which could insist "that a new order in international affairs be set up, and that friend and foe have equal voice in the councils. . . . " Paul predicted precisely the important role Rotary would play in the setting up of the United Nations Organisation.

The Denver Convention delegates found themselves faced with an array of speakers of outstanding quality, with eloquent, impressive and memorable things to say to them, things that are equally eloquent, impressive and memorable today, and indicative of the tremendous turnabout of Rotary world awareness that had taken place since Havana in 1940. The loss of so many Clubs to totalitarian regimes brought American Rotarians into stark confrontation with both the powerful internationalism of their Movement and the dire danger it was in. The threat to freedom and civilisation was made brutally clear to Americans in Rotary six months before it took Pearl Harbor to do the same for the rest of their compatriots. And with their peril, Rotarians began to glimpse their power.

Barclay Acheson, a Canadian who knew the world well, having done relief work in Russia after the First World War (his committee had then included the wives of both Lenin and Trotsky), as well as in the Middle East and China, stood in the great open Red Rocks amphitheatre when the strains of Wagner had died off under the stars, and said: "I have watched propaganda at work. I am probably more aware of it than you are . . . [and] often thought of Milton's old concept of armies of evil and good struggling unseen in the air about us. There is no question in my mind but that an unseen battle of ideas is going on for possession of the earth."

This was one of the first public statements on the true agony of modern times, still often denied or ignored today; but still needed, as were his ringing, scornful denunciations of those who thought real progress came only from totalitarian societies. "My contention is that the failures of free people are not failures at all. Ours are the problems of success; ours are the problems of the most accelerated pace of human advance the world has ever seen." Above all, Acheson, as a non-Rotarian, was able to make dramatically clear to Rotary where its destiny lay, in terms which, in contrast to the more platitudinous Constitutional declarations, had a direct impact:

> Each socially-conscious Rotary Club is like a growing cell in the body politic; if those growing cells fail, the social order withers and dies, but if they put forth creative efforts in solving social problems, we advance. . . .
>
> The harmony of the world should be like the harmony of an orchestra, each playing his own instrument and his own score, but all brought together by the great ideals of Rotary, free men united in service and good fellowship.

Another speaker, who spelled out Rotary's duty with more precision, and with all the authority of an ex-International President, was a dynamic lawyer from Nashville, Tennessee. He and fellow-Club members had held the first "International Institute" ever in the Movement back in 1934. Will R. Manier Jr was a man impatient of empty phrases and fond of testing those of others to gauge their emptiness or otherwise ("I have seldom had an original idea, but out of many years of Rotary experience, I have had the opportunity to test many ideas that have been suggested by others"), and when he took office had promised significantly, "I shall not undertake to take myself seriously, but I shall undertake to be your task-master, too, and I hope we may put Rotary in high gear." That he was accepted by Rotarians, even before his election, as being of world status, is evidenced by the fact that his nomination had been proposed by an Englishman and seconded by a Frenchman, and that a motion to make the vote unanimous had been proposed by a Spaniard and seconded by a Tokyo Rotarian. It was Manier who had taken Rotary's last Convention on to European soil, presiding at Nice in 1937, and now at Denver he minced no words, paying scant heed to the Rotarian tradition of non-involvement in political affairs and national disputes. He had won the Distinguished Service Order in the First World War and had read *Mein Kampf*, and he proceeded to detail to the Convention exactly what Hitler had planned and carried out, and vigorously shattered once and for all the Movement's cherished idealism of Youth by pointing out one similar pattern in all the totalitarian states, whatever their ideology: "In every one of the dictatorial countries, the dictator and the government have sponsored a youth movement; and the dictatorial regimes rest on the youth of the country, whether it be in Communist Russia, Nazi Germany, or Fascist Italy." Sparing his audience nothing in puncturing the "isolationist" dream, he told them, "Neither oceans nor forts nor tanks nor planes are a complete defense against the penetration of ideas; and the totalitarian idea is threatening us even in this hemisphere . . . inevitably, no matter how little we will like it, we are going to find ourselves actual combatants in this war." Though, in his view, he added with great percipience, Americans, little though they might realise it, had been in effect already engaged in the war for several months. He then made a courageous statement which, from anyone else, might have brought cries of resentment. We can be sure it brought glowering looks from Perry, behind him on the platform:

> While I have always said that it was no concern of Rotary what form of government existed in any country, I have seen the Rotary Clubs destroyed or disbanded in Germany, in Austria, in Italy, in the countries absorbed by Germany and Italy, and finally in Japan. . . . Rotary, as well as Rotary

International as an organization, has a stake and a very real stake in the victory of the democracies of the world war which is now in progress. I therefore feel that every Rotarian and every Rotary Club may properly do everything they can to ensure that victory, not only for the sake of the Clubs and the Rotarians of their own country, but for the sake of Rotary International itself.

It was a brave commitment and its record gives Rotary an honoured place amongst those who saw the way ahead and the clear path of duty for free societies against the threat from across both oceans, accepting the cautious lead of Roosevelt, already "that man in the White House", whom Manier confessed he personally disliked.

The speech must have thrilled Paul Harris; but the moment that electrified the Convention and was never forgotten by those who were present, came when Second Vice-President Tom Warren, who had come at great risk to the Havana Convention a year before, spoke to the delegates in a crystal-clear broadcast live from an underground BBC studio "somewhere in London", which was picked up on short wave at Long Island and relayed to Denver by the Mutual Broadcasting System. Tom Warren had heard Will Manier's talk and urged the Convention to "look upon his bold and rugged contours and you will see why Gibraltar still stands". In the words of the official account, "tremors coursed up and down more than one spine" as Warren's voice came to them across more than 4,000 miles. Thousands across America also heard this outstanding British Rotarian, himself destined to be World President in the year of that victory which now seemed so distant, as his message rekindled faith in his beleaguered island and new confidence in the strength of his beloved Rotary:

Though we live on a fighting front, perhaps because of it, Rotary was never stronger, never more virile than now, when the spirit of service has become an amazing reality. . . . The Rotary side of the epic story will be worth the telling when the proper time arrives. . . .

To you Rotarians of the Commonwealth, I offer the salutations that pass between brothers in arms. . . . We have sworn to hold fast, whatever the cost. One has to live here to realise that cost. But the alternative can never even be contemplated. . . . The Czechs, Yugoslavs, Poles, and other friends of yours and mine illustrate by their crucifixion the hell's brew to be quaffed by decent peoples, if we fail . . . Churchill proclaims we shall fight, if necessary, to the end, on this our own, precious island. We know it. . . .

We are now learning in extremity that, unless Movements like Rotary can spread and unless leaders and followers are sincere unto sacrifice, there is little hope of saving the world's sons and daughters from the hell that has been ours these many years. Tyrants thrive on the complacency of decent folk. Rotary must no longer be complacent. We can be an ever-growing power in the world. Our principles are right. By following them, regardless of cost, we shall endure. Without this, we shall fade. . . .

I suggest to the Convention that it takes its future boldly in its hands.

Under the presidential guidance of Armando de Arruda Pereira, citizen of a nation which had once briefly threatened the very existence of Rotary within its borders, the Movement had come a long way round, had grown and matured enormously during the twelve months since Havana. When the broadcast ended, Pereira, tears unashamedly streaming down his cheeks, rose and urged the audience, many of whom were as emotionally moved as he, to tell Tom Warren, "the message that we all have in our hearts" and say "We are with you, Tom". The only British Rotarian there was Past Club President Ted Spicer of the London Club, who reported, "You may imagine that to me it was most impressive and rather made a lump in one's throat, when the whole immense audience rose and said those words."

Pereira's own volatile President in Brazil had made the prophecy not long before, which now began to come true. "Patriotism in Rotarians", wrote Dr Getulio Vargas, "grows stronger through their contact with men of all countries of the world. For this same reason, the fecund activities which they have performed for the sake of universal unity and concord have produced the best results and slowly but surely, with the reaping of new and brilliant harvests, the prestige of the institution will increase."

And so it proved. And its modern influence right round the world can possibly be dated from the extraordinary moment in the Municipal Auditorium of Denver when, having heard the voice from embattled London clearer than any other from the platform (the public address system, as usual, was not functioning properly), nearly 9,000 throats cried out their full-hearted response: "We are with you, Tom!"

The year before, as Rotarians began leaving Havana, German soldiers were marching through Paris. This time, as Rotarians began to pack up in Denver and queue for trains and planes for home, Hitler sent 150 divisions storming into the Soviet Union, supported by a screaming onslaught of 3,000 fighters and bombers from the skies, across a 2,000-mile front extending from the Arctic Ocean to the Black Sea. It was the most enormous military operation in history and it caught the Russians completely by surprise (though Churchill had been able, from espionage reports, to send the coldly dismissive Stalin clear warnings of what was about to happen, including the exact date). Within a month, the German Panzers — once more, as in the Low Countries and France, with Guderian in the lead heading for Moscow — were 300 miles into Soviet territory, killing and capturing thousands, and destroying masses of planes on the ground. It was Blitzkrieg on a gigantic scale, and the world, as Hitler had foretold, did indeed hold its breath. But comment was plentiful. General Franz Halder, Chief of the German General Staff, noted in his diary that Hitler would be master of Russia in a few weeks. In Washington, the American General Staff told correspondents exactly the same thing.

In Denver, far above the great Red Rocks amphitheatre, the final spectacular moment of the Convention had been the sudden illumination of a huge red star against the mountain. The instinct of Rotary seemed as sure as ever. Except in one respect; but then this failure of perception was shared by almost everyone else. Like a malevolent conjurer, the God of Battles was misdirecting the audience's attention away from his next trick, the biggest surprise of all, the Magnificent Appearing Act. In July, the Commander-in-Chief of the Japanese fleet, Admiral Isoroku Yamamoto, had sold a certain idea to his country's war council and a special training programme was begun, causing the withdrawal of Japan's most modern aircraft-carriers out of the Pacific into home ports, and causing much puzzlement in Manila and Hawaii amongst radio-operators who could no longer intercept their signals. Japan's envoys were talking peace and sending missions to Washington for the purpose. Was Midway threatened? Wake Island? (As the name of the first implies, these islands lay about half-way between Hawaii and the Philippines and were used as staging-posts for the long Pacific flights of the US Navy.) No, it was decided, more likely Russia. Tojo would emulate Mussolini and put the boot in from behind after Germany had slammed the Soviet forces stumbling into shock defeat. No one thought for a moment of Honolulu, with its romantically named harbour. After all, it was nearly 3,500 miles from Japan. Five months later, on November 10th 1941, Vice-Admiral Chuichi Nagumo, commanding the Fast Carrier Strike Force, slipped out to sea and disappeared to the north, his fleet including six carriers with the most advanced naval aircraft in the world.

The Rotary Club of Honolulu showed that someone was thinking of the US fleet which crammed its harbour, however, by presenting the sailors with a brand-new water-fountain to amuse them on shore leave.

CHAPTER TWENTY-ONE

The Wheel at War — 5

It's a long way to Reconstruction,
It's a long way to go;
It's a long way to Reconstruction,
But the only way I know.
Goodbye, Selfish Interests,
Goodbye, *laissez-faire*,
It's long, long way to Reconstruction,
But our only hope lies there.

F.L. Billingham-Grieg — Editor,
London Rotarian

With such new versions of well-known "community song" numbers did the Rotary Club of London enliven its spirit and bolster its morale, as the war-clouds piled higher and heavier, the bombs rained down and rumours flew about of piles of German bodies being washed up on East Anglian beaches, the result of abortive invasion attempts. It testified to two important aspects of the Movement during the war — at least, in all those nations threatened by the world conflagration: a spirit of militancy and a superb determination to consider the post-war problems of the world, even when it seemed almost ludicrous to others to think Rotarians would play any part in it, or even that the British nation would continue to exist at all in recognisable form.

But far from proving irrelevant, the Rotary Movement was proving an oasis of calm fellowship in the storm of destruction pouring down upon the cities of the United Kingdom. It reminded members of peacetime values to which they had dedicated their lives, and it also served to give others a sudden, heightened appreciation of those Rotary values. Almost every member of Churchill's

Coalition Government came to address the London Club and one cabinet minister in particular made a speech of global importance about the post-war world, which we shall consider in the next chapter. A streak of what the British call "sheer bloody-mindedness" actually resulted in larger Club attendances at the height of bombing raids than in peacetime. The Rotary Club of West Norwood eventually held the record of being bombed out of its meeting-place more than any other Club — which was eight times! The Hull Rotarians had five changes of venue, four of which were destroyed in two successive nights of intensive raids; while the Plymouth Club resignedly witnessed one dining-place after another being annihilated until, gazing round the rubble of one of Britain's most devastated cities, members realised no such places were left!

Bernard Shaw, whose scribbled postcard had made him the eternal gadfly of the Movement, once observed of the British that they thought they were being moral when they were only being uncomfortable. But the experience of British Rotary in the Second World War took his point rather nearer the truth of this mysterious nation — which, together with the concept of fair play, has given the "professional foul" to the world — by showing how often the British seem to be uncomfortable when in fact they are being heroic. Hitler had an intuitive glimpse of this danger and showed it in his hesitations at Dunkirk, but his nature was too unstable to grasp the gleam. The British had spent so many generations looking foolish on foreign beaches that they could play the part to perfection when it mattered. The strength of their Empire was never that it was admirable, but that it was completely absurd.

If Hitler was confused by the British, it is not surprising that plenty of Americans shared his uncertainty, though with their familiarity with Noël Coward's brilliant satirical song about "Mad Dogs and Englishmen" going out in the midday sun, it is strange they never contemplated what other traits the two might have in common when cornered. As far as Rotary was concerned, up until the end of 1941, American Clubs had divergent views about the courage and stamina of British Clubs, reflecting roughly the opposite ideas of Paul Harris and Chesley Perry, and indeed — as Britain was to learn later when Roosevelt and Churchill differed over post-war aims — the diversion of prejudice existing in the US President's own mind when he was engaged, though in fast failing health, at the Yalta summit and seemed to distrust his great friend, the "Former Naval Person", more than he did Stalin. From the Rotary Club of Dallas came a letter which said: "The desperate fight England is making for the sacred liberties of mankind has the earnest sympathy of every sound-thinking American." And from the Saranac, New York, Club came this rousing reassurance: "America is back of Old Britain with every gun, every dollar, and, I believe I can safely say, every man, for we know and realise that your fight is our fight." On the other hand, from Sand Springs, Oklahoma, came the following:

> We hear that civil liberty in England is about abolished, and that the nobility still dress for dinner, and we just can't understand this nobility stuff. . . . I saw the King on his visit here and he looked like a very ordinary individual to me . . . [the English] have lost every battle, have seen thirteen nations overcome, so can it be wondered at that it is frequently said here that the British simply won't fight . . . 75 per cent of our people oppose sending American boys out of the Western Hemisphere to die in the battles of Europe.

As it was only about 150 years or so since Europeans had sent their boys regularly into the Western Hemisphere to die in the battles of America, this seems a bit ungracious, as does the reference to the King looking like an ordinary individual when such a state of affairs was supposed to be the essence of New World democracy. It was perhaps fortunate that the writer was unaware that the figure of Britannia was modelled on one of Charles II's fancy women, who is pictured showing her well-turned ankle to prove it, Lady Frances Stuart's legs being as famous in her day as Betty Grable's were about to become to US servicemen everywhere.

However, within a month of that last letter being written, the writer was to be confronted with the fact of global war, which is that if you won't go out of your hemisphere to meet the enemy, he will quite happily come to you. Blair-Fish, the outspoken Editor of the British *Rotary Service* magazine, unwisely rammed the obvious point home with a long editorial entitled "Now Is the Lesson Learnt?", in which he added insult to injury by commenting, "Neutrality is treason to civilisation." It was his last editorial for Rotary, since, in disgraceful and complete contradiction of all the Western world was supposed to be fighting for, the RIBI General Council dismissed him. For the next five years the magazine was apparently produced by a being from another world, since no editor's name appeared in its pages, and British Rotary's hierarchy had, partly at least, proved Sand Springs, Oklahoma, absolutely right.

One Rotarian was not in the least surprised when the news of "Barbarossa" had broken across the world. Field-Marshal Mannerheim was helping to make that news, as he had made headlines since November 1939. Indeed, his Club of Helsinki-Helsingfors which, against all difficulties, had managed that year to hold a District Conference and to auction sixty pounds of coffee — now very scarce in Finland, and sent there by the Rotary Club of Plymouth, Michigan — to help fund a new children's hospital, had two birthdays to celebrate that December amongst its members. One, the composer, Jan Sibelius, was two years older than Paul Harris; the other, Field-Marshal Mannerheim, was amazingly one year older than the ailing, ageing Paul, when he led a Finnish Army out through the forests to retake the Karelian isthmus which the Finns had been forced to cede to the Russians in 1940, eagerly seizing the opportunities offered by "Barbarossa". When they had triumphantly recovered their lost territory, Mannerheim called a halt and refused the help with which the Germans could certainly have captured Leningrad. But that was in the north amidst the wastes of a freezing December, just after Mannerheim's troops, operating in 30 degrees of frost, in conditions so cold that tank turrets became solid and immovable, had surrounded and destroyed two entire Russian divisions.

Five days before, from the other side of the world, news had undoubtedly reached Mannerheim of that other tremendous engagement fought in the brilliant sunshine of the South Pacific, where Japan's Fast Carrier Striking Force under Nugamo, after a deliberately confusing voyage, had halted 500 miles north of Hawaii in order to launch its great surprise attack on Pearl Harbor, slumbering on a sunny Sunday morning. The crews of the great warships moored two-by-two in "Battleship Row" were preparing their 8 a.m. ceremony of hoisting the colours as the dive-bombers and the torpedo-launchers appeared before their unbelieving eyes. Then the high-level bombers struck, and for the loss of nine fighter planes, fifteen dive-bombers and five torpedo-bombers, the Japanese carriers had put the entire battleship force of the US Pacific fleet out of action.

About ten miles from Pearl Harbor the Rotary Club of Wahiawa-Waialua decided to forgo its regular meeting on the following Thursday; indeed, it did not meet again until a month later, on 8th January. When the first bombs fell, the Club Secretary had to restrain his children from running into the streets to watch the show, for the enemy aircraft were flying along their bombing-run directly over his house. But he and every member of the Club had their defence jobs to do and posts to man. "Funny", he reported later, "we did not seek shelters. We had work to do and it was done. Every Member of our Club did his share." This was true of all the six Clubs then formed in the islands, and counters the received wisdom that the Americans were completely unprepared for the notorious raid. Rotary certainly wasn't — the Editor of the Wahiawa-Waialua Club Bulletin, Harry Shaw, was soon in uniform as an army captain and in charge of all censorship for the islands.

The Japanese had also struck at the Philippines, Hong Kong and Malaya, and were bombing Singapore. Churchill, who just two days before had with reluctance declared war upon his old friend Mannerheim and Finland, after an exchange of friendly letters, now wrote to the Japanese Ambassador stating that he had the honour to be "with high consideration", his obedient servant, to let him know that Britain and Japan were also at war. Britain in fact declared war upon Japan before Roosevelt did — Japan, of course, had not declared war at all. By the end of the year, Hong Kong and Manila had fallen, as had the Dutch East Indies and many Pacific islands. Britain's two great battleships, *Prince of Wales* and *Repulse*, which six months before had hounded the *Bismarck* to blazing destruction, were now themselves sunk by Japanese planes.

The famous Outport Rotarians' Tiffin Club in Shanghai and its equivalent Vagabond Rotarians' Tiffin Club in Hong Kong were submerged by the conquerors. So were the eight Clubs of the Philippines, though the Manila Club managed two meetings before going under, one on the Thursday after Pearl Harbor (which the Hawaiian Clubs passed up) and an historic one on 30th January 1942, when a "rump" meeting of members was held in the cramped, stinking tunnels on the island of Corregidor, a fortress built in Manila Bay during the Spanish-American War, where, amidst the sounds of battle overhead and the cries of the wounded in the dank darkness all around, a revolver-butt served as a Rotary "bell" to bring the meeting to order and elect General Douglas MacArthur as Honorary Member. The extraordinary scene was witnessed by Carlos P. Romulo, a Past President of the Manila Club and Past Vice-President of Rotary International, who had also just seen his own extensive newspaper buildings blown sky-high in the "open city" which soon became the world's second most devastated capital of the Second World War. Rotarian Romulo, who was to win the Pulitzer Prize for his Far East despatches and become one of MacArthur's aides, had already made a name for himself by warning Rotarians in Bangkok, Thailand, back in September, that their government would shortly surrender to the Japanese within five hours of an ultimatum, a prediction proved correct to the minute! A few months after the Corregidor Club meeting, a naval lieutenant of the Rotary Club of New Jersey was in command of the torpedo-boat flotilla which sank two Japanese cruisers while rescuing MacArthur from the Philippines on the orders of Roosevelt — taking Rotary's most famous new recruit to Australia and supreme command.

Romulo had also caused an unwelcome sensation amongst the Rotarians of Singapore by prophesying exactly the fate which had now engulfed them, as the Japanese astounded the British by bicycling through the "impassable" forests of Malaya and, with much inferior numbers, capturing Stamford Raffles's great city from the undefended north, taking 60,000 prisoners in the process. The five Clubs in Ceylon survived, however, as that island (now Sri Lanka) escaped invasion. Meanwhile, inspired by the example of Chungking, Rotarians in India held a successful District Conference in Calcutta while Japanese bombers attacked in waves.

An enormous segment of the legacy of Jim Davidson now seemed lost for ever, but the seeds he had planted were soon to show how durable they were amidst despair, desolation and brutal occupation. Soon a report was smuggled through from Foochow, China, that not only was the Rotary Club there still managing to function under the noses of the occupation force but had recruited eight new members! In Japan, out of forty-four Rotary Clubs in existence in 1940, as many as twenty-six continued to meet throughout the war, known to each other simply as Day-of-the-Week Clubs. By meeting on their usual day but calling themselves by that day's name, they contrived to avoid the displeasure of their military rulers. The most famous of them all, the original Club in Tokyo, was addressed by their ageing Founder, a banker called Umekichi Yoneyama, who had brought the idea to Tokyo in 1920 from Dallas, Texas. He sadly told the Tokyo Club, "I only find my heart full of deep emotion. When I think of Rotary's contributions to the nation all these years, the Club's history may be said to be coming to an end in glory. . . . The Wednesday Club to be formed is intended to continue without interruption the fellowship we have developed and cherished in Rotary. It will be your organisation just as the Rotary Club has been. I hope you will endeavour to make the best of it." The Club members had a lot to make the best of on 18th April 1942, five months after Pearl Harbor, when Japanese forces stood triumphant all over southern Asia, threatening India itself and causing the Australians to consider evacuation of their entire northern coast, for on that day their fellow-Rotarian of St Louis, Missouri, Colonel James Doolittle, led sixteen carrier-based planes on Tokyo's first bombing raid. Tokyo was not to be bombed again until 1944, but this morale-booster for the Allies was badly needed. With under 200,000 soldiers — less than one-fifth of the number it was using against the Chinese — Japan had overrun the Philippines, Hong Kong, Malaya, Singapore, Thailand, Burma and the Dutch East Indies, not to mention almost every island across the vast South Pacific.

An editorial in the January 1942 issue of *The Rotarian* stated clearly: "Rotarians face the challenge of events resolutely. As have their fellows in other lands, Americans will rise to their responsibilities as loyal citizens and give freely of themselves and their substance, though the cost be blood, sweat and tears. . . . We dare not let our idealism die. . . . There can be no looking back. The furrow will be long — and it must be straight." Yet the same magazine had to report, possibly as a reflection of the Republican Party's conviction that Roosevelt had deliberately "provoked" the Japanese attack, that the Board of Directors of Rotary International had turned down a proposal to form an Emergency Advisory Committee to guide US Rotarians on national-service activities, and when International President Tom Davis invited all Clubs in the United States to submit their views on the idea to him, less than 3 per cent bothered to reply. The RI Board nevertheless had to accept the fact of war and stated, in a guide for action issued to all Clubs, that "every Rotarian will be a loyal and serving citizen of his own country, and that as such he will do everything within his power to bring this war to a speedy end".

No such cautious exhortation to rally round the flag was needed by Chicago's alternative face, that of Al Capone, who though he no longer attended his own board meetings in Chicago, was still very much in the news. He had been released from prison in 1939 and was attempting a dignified retirement on his Miami estate, where he granted occasional interviews, one of which was to a famous British journalist of the day, Trevor Wignall (who had written a biography of the present writer's grandfather and had excellent credentials), to whom he opined he would never return to Chicago. "I'm finished with that burg," he said. He was in no way feeling rejected by his country, however, and set Rotarians an example after Pearl Harbor by at once offering his services to the War Department "in any capacity to aid the national defense effort". Though he might well have contributed valuable advice on how to deal with the global gangsters terrorizing mankind, his offer was ignored. It may possibly, by the publicity it attracted, have acted as a spur for the RI Board declaration, however, overriding Ches Perry's reluctance, for Capone was still a potent Chicago hero.

Nor was Capone's offer unrealistic. In eighteen months' time, his old rival, the New York crime tsar "Lucky" Luciano (as we shall see in the next chapter) was to have his own similar offer enthusiastically accepted by the Allies invading Sicily, eager to use his contacts with the island's Mafia chiefs, an arrangement which proved outstandingly successful in speeding conquest and lessening British and American casualties – while increasing crime and ensuring the success of the post-war boom in drug smuggling.

That Board Meeting was Ches Perry's last. Finally, Perry had to accept that he had been overtaken by events, and no doubt wished that he had carried through his plan to leave Rotary's world stage at the Havana Convention in 1940 when the going was good and he had his big box of cigars. Pearl Harbor told him he had left it too late. With uncharacteristic indecision, he began to dither from January on, giving notice that he would take a leave of absence before retirement after the RI Board Meeting in January; but still he stayed. Then he announced that his leave would start on 1st March; he still stayed. On 1st May, after writing his final Report to the Board, which he customarily delivered in person at the Convention, but now left behind to be printed with other reports in a handbook, Chesley Perry really did empty his desk at 35 East Wacker Drive. His ostensible reason for doing so was that he had no wish to cramp the style of the man who would at long last become only the second General Secretary that Rotary International had ever had. But, though his Report was this time only in a printed handbook with others, his farewell letter was read aloud from the platform in the Maple Leaf Gardens of Toronto by International President Tom Davis: "From afar, I salute you and say take over and carry on." He could not keep out of his last words, try possibly as he might, a note of that lofty patronage he had held like a sword all his life between himself and his colleagues.

It would have been too much, Perry knew, to maintain that patronage of his at the Thirty-Third Convention of Rotary International. For it was held in the fiercely loyal British Commonwealth city of Toronto – whose Huron Indian name aptly means "place of meeting" – and in June 1942 Canada's second city still had a population almost entirely British in origin, with vivid memories of its parliament being burned down in the War of 1812 by the Americans (when the British took a torch to the White House in reply). Indeed, its mace, then stolen, had been returned by Roosevelt only eight years before! Toronto was also in the home province of Crawford McCullough, Rotary International's President in 1921, whose soldier son had recently been killed on active service. Ches Perry could no longer disregard the fact that greater international events were, even if only for the time being, superseding the Rotary Movement and his own controlling hand on the Golden Wheel. Toronto also would have flaunted before him two galling reminders of the days when Rotary first had become truly international through the link of the British connection and control had begun to slip from solely American hands. First, Perry arrived to find that the huge National Exhibition Grounds, designated as a recreation and hospitality area for more than 6,500 families, had been requisitioned by the Canadian Army. Secondly, the entertainment in the Maple Leaf Gardens was headed by "the sweetheart of millions the world over". It was not Mary Pickford of Hollywood this time (though "America's Sweetheart" was in fact a local girl, Toronto-born Gladys Mary Smith) but Gracie Fields of Rochdale, Lancashire, famous comedy singing-star of the music-hall, variety stage, radio and films, whose hit "I'm the Girl That Makes the Thinga-m'bob That's Going to Win the War" celebrated the women who were performing prodigies of effort in producing war materials in Britain's factories. Ironically, she was at this time fast slipping from favour in her native land because of her conspicuous and continuing absence abroad, but to Rotarians in Toronto she was the "one and only, incomparable star", singing "inspiring and soul-fitting music".

In the field of inspiring and filling souls, "Our Gracie" had a strong rival in Jean Harris, who was ushered to the microphone to urge the Convention to "acknowledge the Eternal Power", and to ask God to give them "wisdom, judgement, discernment, love for all". It may have been in reaction to this Presbyterian resurgence that Paul Harris's speech tended to the frivolous when he said that the world must stop finding things to fight about, admitting "my fealty most naturally adheres to the bald-heads. Long may they live and become the dominant race. Their judgement is generally mature and kindly and one seldom sees a baldheaded man in an insane asylum".

Perry, whose hair was receding but whose head was not of Harris's eggshell dome proportions, had had enough. During this, his third and, so to speak, final "positively last appearance" — even if only in printed form — he metaphorically bowed to the inevitable (although no one in this life ever really saw that extraordinary man bow) and, in his own firmly restrained but effective way, rose to the occasion (though he made no reference to his successor, Philip C. Lovejoy — whose name, right out of Restoration comedy, might well have been his sole Rotary recommendation, had he not been also Perry's assistant since 1930). "Despite the losses which the organization has sustained," Perry reported to delegates, "Rotary International today has more than 5,000 Clubs with a Membership of more than 200,000 Rotarians, who are meeting the challenges of the day by intensifying the normal program of Rotary." Yet the tale he had to tell, though unemotional and unembroidered, was far from "normal", and referred to the six Rotary Districts in Asia from whom "no recent word has been received", to the Clubs in the United States, Canada, Australia, New Zealand and South Africa who were sending funds, canteen equipment, food and clothing to the bombed cities of Britain, to the manner in which all the community services of Rotary all over the world were being adapted to meet national emergency wartime needs — without the attendant moralising which had sometimes accompanied such activities in the First World War (described in Chapters Eight and Nine) — and to the Relief Rund for Rotarians which was helping Rotarians of all nationalities in the most unlikely places, including "Lithuanian Rotarians who are now in Siberia".

Though two-thirds of those at Toronto who were reading or hearing about their seemingly indestructible General Secretary's Report for the last time were from the United States, his audience still included Rotarians from enemy-occupied countries who had somehow made the hazardous journey through U-boat infested seas to Canada. And Tom Warren, whose broadcast from London had so electrified the Denver Convention the year before, was there in person, with four colleagues, who had made the hazardous voyage (it had taken six weeks) via Lisbon, to tell shocked delegates that one in every five homes in Britain was now damaged or destroyed. One of his companions, the President of RIBI, then uplifted their hearts and faith by telling of the great role Rotary had played in wartime Britain. He was well qualified to do so, since he, Tom Young, had held office for three years (RIBI had had no time to spare for elections since 1939) and could give such first-hand experiences as a recent fire-watching stint during a bombing raid in Newcastle upon Tyne when he saw twenty-seven homes vanish to rubble in a few minutes. In sum, his heartening message was "the genius of Rotary in Britain was in educating the individual in the ideal of service and directing him to channels through which he could express it in personal effort".

Union Jacks had draped the stage, and the whole audience had risen at Gracie Field's bidding to sing "Land of Hope and Glory". But perhaps the most emotive and influential moment of the 1942 Convention — as at Denver — was a broadcast, not this time from Britain but from "somewere in Australia". It was Carlos Romulo once more, relaying the good wishes of Rotarian Douglas MacArthur to the Convention, and spelling out uncompromisingly to those who had once been told it was not a "Rotary War" what Rotary stood for: "Rotary is an idea and a dream — the idea of peace and the dream of its realisation, a lasting peace predicted on freedom which recognises the dignity of the human soul . . . wherever that freedom which dignifies the human soul is threatened, there Rotarians are in peril, and where freedom perishes, there a part of Rotary lies dead."

Such categorical declarations of Rotary faith would not have been to the taste of the retiring General Secretary; he had striven against their expression in both world wars. His was not, however, a denial of world reality, nothing so simple; everything he had thought and done throughout his thirty-two years of devoted service at the dynamic organisational heart of Rotary International had been from his fierce loyalty to the purity, as he saw it, of the Movement's origins. And he remained a giant of a man, however coldly authoritative his nature, however much the polar opposite of Paul Harris, however unyielding and dogmatic he had been, and still remained, to such apostasies (in his mind) as Rotary International in Great Britain and Ireland. Though it found very different expression, his life-commitment — as it had been since the age of thirty-eight — to Rotary had been uncompromising, he had been indeed a celibate Savonarola who had devoted every waking hour (of which he had had more than most) to Rotary, and he let the passion of that blazing motivation show tantalisingly through in the text of his final Report as General Secretary, in a way Paul Harris himself had not done for years, in the process; he showed exactly why Harris had selected him for Rotary in 1908, knowing Perry's destiny better than he knew it himself. And in almost the last words addressed to a Rotary Convention as General Secretary, Chesley Perry wrote:

> In the days when the world was at peace, Rotarians were convinced that the Rotary ideals and the Rotary program of service were greatly needed. Now, in a world darkened by hatred, death and destruction, how much more needed are the things for which Rotary stands! A crucial year — perhaps the most difficult that has ever confronted the organization is ahead. The efforts of the R.I. Board alone cannot bring Rotary International satisfactorily through that year; the District Governors, no matter how earnest, cannot of themselves do so. It is for every Rotarian to demonstrate the value of Rotary, the virility of Rotary, the vision of Rotary.

It was an impressive credo for the Movement and one which proved, as he let the reticent guard slip for the first time in over thirty years, that he understood exactly, even if he had sometimes hidden the fact from himself as well as others, what Paul Harris's ideal had been, and remained, its simplicity and strength.

Chesley Perry had not changed his essential views one iota since assuming his post full-time in 1910. At seventy, he was still the same man who had then said, "Rotarians must develop their full potential not in collective action but in persistent, persuasive action as individuals", and "The best way to reform the world is to reform oneself". But one thing Chesley Perry could not reform was his style as General Secretary, though it seemed increasingly irrelevant as the war news poured in. During the four days of the Toronto Convention, the German armies captured Tobruk and roared towards Egypt, while the Panzers encircled and battered down Sebastopol and headed for the oil fields of the Caucasus, and the Japanese established airbases on the Aleutian Islands to strike at Alaska. Perry was confirmed in his belief that it was past time for him to go. With a Rotarian now Supreme Commander in the Southwest Pacific, another, Admiral Ernest King, of the Lorain, Ohio, Club, as Chief of Naval Operations and Commander-in-Chief of the US fleet, and a third, Major-General Lewis B. Hershey, of the Angola, Indiana, Club, running US Selective Service, there were priorities of command transcending those from the eighth and ninth floors of 35 East Wacker Drive.

Out before the platform party (for the first time in thirty-two years without Perry's presence), out in the vastness of the Maple Leaf Gardens, by means of escape or exile, had somehow come a few Rotarians from China, France, Hungary and even one from Czechoslovakia. This latter nation, the catalyst and victim of appeasement, had been the chief vain sacrifice of Chamberlain and Daladier in their efforts to placate the ravenous Nazi appetite before the beast which had entered the soul of Germany turned its infected jaws snarling on the whole world. Now the lone Czech Rotarian represented the nation which had provided the world's conscience with yet another dreadful sacrifice just eleven days before the Convention, when in revenge for the assassination of "Hangman" Heydrich, Hitler's golden boy, the little village of Lidice was razed to the ground and all its male inhabitants executed.

Asked to pay a tribute to Perry in a later issue of *The Rotarian* that year, the rapscallion from Racine surfaced mischievously: "What will Rotary do without Ches and what will Ches do without Rotary?" asked Paul Harris rhetorically, betting on Ches to find his way through. "Verily, I believe that Ches will gallantly survive the crisis."

He did, of course. He proved his character by surviving his indispensability, that smiling herald of oblivion. Survived also "a fitting memento and a suitable decorative scroll" which a Convention Resolution granted him; also the suggestion that he might care to be called General Secretary Emeritus, an offer he firmly refused. His retirement became official on 30th June 1942, but by that time his compatriot Rotarians were more concerned with the fact that eight German agents had managed two days before to land on Long Island from a U-boat. Also that Hitler had made Erwin Rommel, the so-called Desert Fox, a Field-Marshal and called

him home to give him his baton for driving the British back again
into Egypt where, on the day of Perry's departure, the Afrika
Corps paused at El Alamein, almost in sight of the Pyramids and
only sixty miles from the Nile. Here it was joined by a jubilant
Mussolini, prepared to take the salute at a march past of Axis
troops in Cairo in fifteen days.

The course of events of the Second World War, even though nearly
forty years have passed since its tremendous conclusion, and
smaller wars have filled us with horror in the intervening period, are
familiar enough to even the youngest generation of readers through
books, films and television, for any detailed recapitulation to be
required here. From the autumn of 1942 on, the worst crisis was
past, the tide turned against the Axis powers, and though some of
the most barbaric cruelties remained to be perpetrated by the
licensed malevolence extended by both German and Japanese
rulers (the Italians were soon to realise the ghastly company they
were keeping and to be subjugated in turn by their erstwhile allies),
from this time forward their best and most experienced commanders fully understood that neither Nazi gangsterism nor the Japanese
military clique could do any better than hope for the most favour-
able terms possible for peace. Confronted with terms of unconditional surrender, the Nazi conquerors of the Long Western Siesta
of the democracies and Soviet Russia's complacent unpreparedness
fought every inch of their retreat, often murdering local populations
as they did so. But the merciless venom shown in horrible atrocities
committed by the Japanese troops had their counterpart in the
incredible bravery shown by their soldiers in battle, and both had
their source in the more poisonous aspects of their racial, religious
and warrior-caste teachings. The Nazi perversion of slavery, medical
"experimentation" and mass genocide that methodically extermi-
nated millions, on the other hand, manifested a horrible sickness
of the Western soul which even today we hardly dare face. Over
12 million, half of them Jews, were systematically starved, tortured
and killed, not in battle but in cold blood, as part of deliberate
Nazi policy, coolly documented and pleasurably described.
   No one who dies, especially if he dies in pain and terror, dies
any less for being part of a small or giant statistic. But those who
remain count the cost and wonder if it is fully paid yet. As each
year passes, we see ever more clearly that while the First World
War might reasonably be considered as a conflict to do with "making
the world safe for democracy" (with all its faults, inadequacies and
injustices admitted), the Second World War was fought for nothing

less than the soul of man, whatever else we thought at the time. Boundaries and territories were the stakes, as always through the ages, but never before had damnation hung so palpably over the smoking earth. Faith brought us through, faith in God and man; and for tens of thousands, and many thousands more inspired and helped by them, a large part of that faith lay in Rotary.

We have already noted the extraordinary survival of Rotary Clubs in the heart of Japan, even in the midst of war, when most of their compatriots were swayed by the insidious sickness of deceptively easy conquests, though for non-Japanese members of their Clubs, things had been uncomfortable even a year before Pearl Harbor. James Young, a foreign correspondent who had lived in Japan for thirteen years (indeed, had met his American wife there, at a Rotary function), was a member of the Tokyo Club, but this had not prevented his arrest without trial in 1940 because Japan's generals disapproved of his despatches to the prestigious and influential International News Service, and his imprisonment for sixty-one days until he was deported — fortunately before Britain declared war on Japan.

The Rotary spirit remained alive even in occupied Manila, which became the most battered capital city in the world next to Warsaw. After swearing in General MacArthur as a member, the Club President had made his way back to the city from Corregidor and the Bataan Peninsula, and he and his fellows kept a Rotary Club alive all through the years of Japanese internment — even advertising in the Santo Tomas Internment Camp Bulletin for new members!

But whether or not Clubs survived in clandestine form, individual Rotarians held as civilian internees or as prisoners of war continued throughout the years of conflict to keep in touch with Clubs which were still free. A world-wide Relief Fund for Rotarians was organised and administered by Phil Lovejoy, Ches Perry's successor at 35 East Wacker Drive, and the 200,000 or so Clubs still beyond the clawing reach of tyranny held symbolically "sparse" lunches, sending the money thus "saved" to the Relief Fund. This Fund in turn sent parcels to captured Rotarians in camps within enemy territory everywhere, sometimes "adopting" special camps. Even in 1942, Rotarian soldiers held prisoner were receiving parcels of tinned meat, fish, dried fruit, chocolate and cheese, and they had belonged to Clubs in Burma, Poland, France, Belgium, Britain, Australia and New Zealand. Incredible as it may seem, before the terrible days of the "Final Solution" set in, even the members and families of German Jewish Rotarians received these parcels, and many were saved from death by starvation by this help before the holocaust.

The nineteen Clubs of Norway had been extinguished almost

completely. Crown Prince Olav, who had escaped from his country with other members of the Norwegian royal family, told Rotarians at a meeting in New York, "I know that their beneficent influence has been so great, that the Rotary Clubs were the first Clubs that were dissolved after the invasion." The Oslo Rotarians transformed themselves into a ski club, a ruse which worked for a couple of years until their ski cabin was confiscated and they transformed themselves once again into a group of small "bridge clubs". Most Clubs had similar huts in the mountains which could become the headquarters of "sporting" organisations. Other Clubs were not so fortunate, especially in Stavanger, where the District Governor found Gestapo headquarters set up directly opposite his home.

Many of those who heard the Crown Prince speak were members of the New York Overseas Rotary Fellowship, consisting roughly of seventy refugee Rotarians from Belgium, Poland, Czechoslovakia, France, Austria, Yugoslavia, the Netherlands, Finland, Denmark, Latvia and Spain. Indeed it was a Spanish Rotarian, Mariano Font, who had organised this association of Rotarian exiles, modelled on a similar association formed in London (of which, more later). Font also built on his experience of running a regular luncheon Club of Spanish exiles in Paris, after the start of the Spanish Civil War, before the surge of Nazism had brought him across the Atlantic. One of his present members was a recent Past President of the Paris Club. Others were a machine-tool maker from Belgium, an opera star, a stockbroker from Milan and a famous French film-maker. The professions and businesses represented included medicine, textiles, leather, music, timber, cosmetics and publishing. Few intended to become American citizens: all were bound by the comforting oasis of Rotary fellowship and by the determination to see that their international friendship would one day help rebuild the shattered civilisation of a European continent which had learned a tragic, costly lesson. Theirs was the spirit which would spread International Rotary across the world at a stupendous rate and on an awesome scale.

In the Netherlands, which endured one of the most oppressive Nazi occupations under the repellent Austrian "quisling", the young Viennese lawyer, Dr Arthur Seyss-Inquart — who first betrayed his homeland to the Germans, then stamped an Austrian SS heel upon Holland with terrible butcheries and mass deportations and finally ended up as the last "Foreign Minister" of the collapsing Third Reich before being hanged at Nuremberg — Rotary survived throughout the Occupation, under the guise of drinking clubs and similar social gatherings. An outstanding example was at Nijmegen, situated at the northernmost point of the Siegfried Line, at one of the Rhine crossings Montgomery tried to grab during the great parachute drop at Arnhem, where in fact a great future Secretary of Rotary in Great Britain and Ireland, Major Victor Dover, MC, was to be captured. In this vital strategic town Rotarians met regularly throughout the Occupation, at an hotel largely taken over for the housing of German officers.

The Gestapo first sent watchers to monitor meetings – the pattern was always the same – and then confiscated money, membership lists and assets of all Dutch Rotary Clubs, though in many cases these were hurriedly hidden. Out of approximately 1,100 Dutch Rotarians ninety died at German hands before the five-year nightmare was over, ten in concentration camps. All Clubs received official notice of "confiscation of assets" and received ominous warnings similar to that given the Rotary Club of Amsterdam by the city's SS Group Leader – "Should it be found that any assets have been left undisclosed or not been fully disclosed, measures on the part of the Security Police must be anticipated". Anticipations were not difficult; and the fact that, in spite of them, Rotarians still continued to meet clandestinely all over occupied Europe was an extraordinary testimony to the strength of the Movement's basic ideals.

Rotary had given early warning of its incredible hardihood by forming new Clubs even under the first shadows of German conquest. Over one month after the Netherlands had capitulated and Queen Wilhelmina had escaped to London with her government, a new Rotary Club had been chartered at Bussum, thirteen miles from Amsterdam, and survived for three months before all Dutch Rotary Clubs were shut down. The French had formed the Menton Rotary Club exactly one month before war was declared and this was permitted to operate for some time, since it was located in the unoccupied zone under Vichy. The same applied to the Club of Les Martigues et Etang de Berre, which was not formed until 1940!

One French Rotary Club formed in 1939 which managed to stay in being throughout the war, although finding itself at times very much in the midst of hostilities, was Dakar, in what was then French West Africa (it is now the capital of Senegal). Until November 1942, when the British and American forces under Eisenhower invaded Morocco and Algeria (eventually, together with Montgomery's Eighth Army, to take more Axis prisoners than were captured by the Russians at Stalingrad), all the French possessions in Africa were considered part of Vichy France, and General de Gaulle's Free French forces, backed by the Royal Navy, bombarded and landed troops there but were driven off by Vichy defenders. The local Rotarians, however, were never forced to suspend their meetings, even when, two months later, the farce of Vichy was ended and the Germans overran the entire French mainland, driving all Rotarians there into either a sporadic, furtive existence or outright oblivion.

When complete night descended, it was the blackest night, and those communities which before victory found themselves directly in the path of battle were often so disorientated that it took up to five or six years for them to re-form when peace returned. This harsh state of affairs shattered the Clubs of Caen and Moulin, for example, for years. As for members, they suffered, endured, perished or disappeared, as did individuals everywhere as the Nazi oppression increased with the notorious *Nacht und Nebel* (Night and Fog) order, which legitimatised random murder and "disappearances" to torture and death in Germany to keep down resistance. Rotarians were amongst the first Frenchmen to form or gallantly support the "Combat" underground group, and were often caught, tortured and executed accordingly. A member of the Paris Club became publisher of the *Editions de Minuit* (Midnight Books) whose contents the Gestapo considered subversive — rightly — but the books continued right through the war, different bits of each volume being printed all over Paris in spite of random raids and arrests.

Another Rotarian ventured into print with more tragic results. Past Governor Louis Renard, of the Poitiers Club, ran for two years an underground typewritten newspaper, but was finally traced and arrested, deported to Germany and, sixteen months later, beheaded. After the war, French Rotarians published a memorial booklet in his honour. Another District Governor, who fought with the Maquis, was on the run for two years, the Gestapo ever snapping at his heels while he hid in the homes of friends or in farm buildings. He was never betrayed. Above all, Rotary itself was never betrayed, at whatever risk. Clubs with Jewish members made arrangements rapidly to transfer their property to non-Jewish members for the duration. Even if the member was taken and did not return from the holocaust, at least this preserved his home, land and business from confiscation, for his family.

Rotarians in Germany itself quite naturally kept an extremely low profile, though holding themselves in readiness to emerge once more when the nightmare had passed. Indeed, one of them was to emerge quite spectacularly upon the world scene when war ended, as we shall see. In Austria, Rotarians, like all citizens, were under much closer surveillance than in Germany, in spite of the vaunted "unity" of the two nations under the Austrian-born Fuehrer. Even so, some of the Vienna Club managed to meet twice a month in each other's homes throughout most of the war, in spite of the terrible risks. They desperately wanted to maintain the fellowship, though there was nothing they could actually do.

Even in Poland, Rotary survived in spirit, though many members were imprisoned, murdered or both, sometimes killed at work, sometimes in their homes. The man who had sent out the last news of Rotary from Warsaw before the city was engulfed in blood and terror, was also the first to send word out after peace was declared. Jerzy Loth (see Chapter Nineteen) wrote that "although Rotary was persecuted, we kept together faithfully, maintained friendly relations and helped those who were in need. I can only tell you that we went through hell". He had lost a daughter and brother and six other relations, and the Germans had robbed him of all his possessions, destroying his home and business. Warsaw's Past President had been murdered, so had their District Governor.

In Czechoslovakia, 15 per cent of all Rotarians were executed or died in prison or from the effects of brutal treatment. Six members of the Prague Club alone — their most famous member was of course in London — were executed after vile torments, two of them perishing in gas chambers with their entire families. Hope survived of the inextinguishable ideals of Rotary, none the less: the exiled President Beneš had been made an Honorary District Governor before he fled. A Prague Rotarian deemed it of such fundamental importance that Eduard Beneš should one day wear his emblem of the Golden Wheel that he hid it from the Gestapo, concealing it indeed on his person through several terrifying Gestapo "sessions". And after the war Beneš did in fact receive it.

Miraculously, Rotary survived throughout the war in Denmark, even after the Germans dropped the mask of friendly partnership in 1942 and took over the state fairly blatantly. However, in the late summer and autumn of 1944, when Himmler's Gestapo dungeons were full of Hitler's senior officers and generals, men who had led the German armies to extraordinary achievements being tortured and strangled with piano wire from meat-hooks in revenge for the failed attempt on Hitler's life in July, discretion prevailed. News also came that Eisenhower's armies were on the Rhine, that Montgomery might well be about to drive across the Ruhr industrial complex straight to Berlin, that the Russians were at the gates of Warsaw, Romania and Bulgaria were out of the war, and that the long-patient Finns were turning on their German occupiers. Kaj Munk, the playwright-priest whose outspoken sermons had long angered the Nazis, had been found dead by the roadside and most of Denmark's police force were now being deported to Germany. Peter Heering, Secretary of the Copenhagen Club (and head of the famous cherry brandy firm) decided that Rotary lunches should simply be discontinued for the time being; as in Norway, many Clubs became "bridge clubs".

The miracle of Rotary's survival was just as great in Finland, of course, so long "on the side of" Germany from lack of choice. But though the Danish and Finnish Rotarians still kept meeting, there was little as Rotarians they could actually do, and the Swedes soon came to consider themselves as guardians of the Golden Wheel through the nightmare years on the Continent of Europe. "If we Rotarians have any duty in the world today," wrote Governor Akmgren in *Rotary Norden*, "it is not to let ourselves be overcome by the confusion and darkness which prevail. . . . Rotary ideals are the drops which can and will wear down the stone walls which now separate peoples." And his fellow-Rotarian Harald Trolle spoke in similar terms of long-term commitment: "I believe, in spite of everything, that even if Rotary's voice has now been officially silenced in many places and is only weakly heard in other places, its way of thinking can be the seed from which crops of mutual understanding can eventually grow." Meanwhile, Norwegian Rotarians queued to escape over the border, and Swedish Rotarians' hands were everywhere to help them do so.

As the deepest hours of despair seemed to drown all hope, it was estimated at 35 East Wacker Drive that 10,000 Rotarians lay in thrall under the New Order of Europe. They were not to know that, as Winston Churchill had said of the British nation when it seemed about to crumble before the insane war-lord at whose word even the ruthless Prussian commanders trembled, Rotary was being proved in its finest hour.

This finest hour was most vividly illustrated by its most tragic moment, which occurred in the hell of the Theresienstadt Concentration Camp in Czechoslovakia. There had come a Jewish Rotarian and his wife. The man had been forced to leave his beloved Club in Bavaria, then the couple were forced to leave Germany itself for Holland, where one of Seyss-Inquart's cattle-trucks had gathered them up in his terrible purge of Jews (which included, of course, the famous Anne Frank family) and deported them. In the camp hospital, the man's wife watched her husband slowly die of maltreatment and starvation, and survived to write the following:

> There he lay with many fellow sufferers, hungry, pestered by vermin, tormented with pain, a broken man.
>
> Then one day a new patient arrived, just as wretched, and was put in a nearby bed. After the two men had talked together several times, it developed that the new arrival had been President of a Czech Rotary Club. An inner light illuminated the faces of the two men. They grasped each other's hand

and, in whispers, began to exchange memories of their years in Rotary. They joy increased when a third companion, who had overheard part of their conversation, was recognised as a Rotarian from Vienna.

Now a better time began for these men, doomed to die. They knew that before long they would perish from hunger. Each day their limbs grew more and more swollen. No wonder, with the tiny portions of pitiful food given them! Nevertheless, they felt their troubles less as they talked of the days in their beloved Rotary Clubs. Naturally they had to employ the greatest caution, for had the Nazi commander . . . suspected three former Rotarians were together, the hardest punishment would have followed.

The appearance of the three emaciated men was pitiable as death approached. My husband was the first to be released from his torment. Before he became unconscious, he clasped again the hands of the two strangers. The Czech followed in a week, the Austrian after ten days.

Thus the tie of friendship which surrounds all Rotarians improved the last days of these three victims of Hitler's barbarism and, amid misery, grief and privation, led them in spirit back to better and happier days.

Rotary's greatest trial was Rotary's greatest triumph, and Madame Else Dormitzer's sad recollection became the eloquent vindication of all Paul Harris had planned and dreamed and known all along, never wavering in his faith. Thanks to his inspiration so long ago in such a very different time and place, a German, a Czech and an Austrian, in the deepest extremity of filth, disease and terror which Nazi sadism and insane hate could devise, had drawn the poison that ran molten through the veins of the Third Reich, had lifted the Golden Wheel above the swastika, had deprived Hitler of the European soul.

CHAPTER TWENTY-TWO

The Wheel at War — 6

He that stepped forward to follow the flag . . .
You'll find now, with thousands, shipped home
in a bag,
Just a little brass tag.

"A Little Brass Tag" by Edgar A. Guest

The call comes clear to Rotary;
A call to take the lead;
To weld the nations with good will
By word and thought and deed.
Oh, Rotary, in brotherhood,
Thy purpose is fulfilled;
God make thee strong till in our world
Thy spirit is instilled.

Rabbi Raphael H. Lavine,
Songs for the Rotary Club

In the midst of horror and brutal annihilation there were three magnificent gleams, pointing to the survival and triumph to come of Rotary's internationalism. In 1943, Sweden — which then had forty-one Clubs — organised its Rotarians to play the major role in taking care of 32,000 homeless, orphaned and undernourished children from Finland, which was the nation worst afflicted by war shortages of all those not actually under Nazi rule. A survey which appeared in *The Rotarian* commented: "Sugar, spices, coffee, tea, wheat flour, and conserves are mere memories in Finland . . . as for fruit, children under 10 years wouldn't even recognize a banana in a picture." While as for bread, "the starving Finns are thankful to have a mixture that is about 60 per cent potato flour, 25 per cent cellulose (sawdust), and 15 per cent mixed grains. . . . Finnish children last year picked 10 million quarts of berries in the forests during the summer months . . . canned without benefit of sugar, however, they made an unpalatable dessert. . . . As for eggs, while the English ration permits about one egg (with shell) per month, in Finland the hens don't lay anymore because there are no hens". Until the end of the war, Swedish Rotarians brought these children back to health and gave them homes.

Another shining light came from Switzerland, the valiant little nation which had already been insolently "incorporated" into the Third Reich on the maps of the Wehrmacht (and was uncomfortably aware of the fact) but which preserved its independence and neutrality intact by announcing complete mobilisation from August 1939, and plans to demolish all their factories, public utilities and mountain tunnels if invaded. The Swiss also ostentatiously announced the preparation of a mountain redoubt for prolonged resistance if the Germans tried to come. They didn't come; at least, the Wehrmacht didn't. The most powerful Germans who came in the end were conspirators planning to kill Hitler, meeting (they hoped, vainly) in secret at Berne and Zurich. The twenty-five Swiss Clubs took in children on holiday from both occupied and unoccupied France and from Belgium and the Netherlands in the darkest days of the war, giving them clothes, food and outdoor exercise, and a precious glimpse of what life in a sane, peaceful world could be.

The third beacon shone from the five Clubs in neutral Portugal, where the Movement had arrived in 1925, five years after Spain. Though their country was infested with Nazi spies, Portuguese Rotarians managed to keep fellow-members in France and Belgium supplied with parcels of food and coffee throughout the long years of war, often in conditions, in the later years, that made the difference between life and death to the recipients, between irrational hope and suicidal despair.

No such gleams, alas, could irradiate the souls under Japanese occupation as their troops swarmed over the countries of Middle Asia. Malaya, Thailand, French Indo-China and the Dutch East Indies did not provide the feast for the wolves that the European continent provided, but 35 East Wacker Drive estimated that nearly 1,400 Rotarians lay in thrall under the Greater East Asia Co-Prosperity Sphere, Japan's equivalent of Hitler's New Order. Rotary — and many Rotarians — were obliterated, but some Clubs managed to meet in secret throughout most of the war, as did the Manila Club, already noted. Not in the East Indies, however, where Rotarian

Club Presidents and District Governors were horribly tortured and callously starved in concentration camps. The widow of a Past President of the Batavia Club wrote: "My husband died after three years of internment, hunger and dysentery. I never saw him again after 11th May, 1942; he lay sick in this town for many months and I did not know; even if I had known, I would not have been allowed to see him." Her tragedy was commonplace in a world gone seemingly mad; though this first impression, to those who endured the un-endurable, gave way to acceptance that sanity was not the preserve of the victim. There is no lack of evidence from previous eras of man's inhumanity to man; it is defined by history. The shock of this century has been to discover there is nothing inhuman about it.

Rotarians in Burma had met furtively in small groups, but surveillance by terror squads − the Japanese equivalent of the Gestapo were the Kempeitai − was too constant and close for any regular meetings, even camouflaged, to be attempted. Rotary's greatest survival story was enacted, of all places, inside the dreaded Changi gaol in Singapore where, with a courage and determination their military commanders had not shown, the city's Rotarians did the memory of Big Jim Davidson great credit in not only hold-ing regular meetings themselves but in organising the "rump" of the Rotary Clubs of Malacca, Seremban, Kuala Lumpur, Ipoh and Penang into "host Clubs" for a month each in turn, somehow even managing to keep minutes of their proceedings.

After October 1943 the Kempeitai (who had been amusing themselves by executing batches of Chinese citizens of Singapore on the island beaches at dusk) had time to take a more active interest in Changi, and no more meetings were possible. Rotary consultations continued, however, during the confusion of camp mealtimes, in languages which Rotarians knew their captors would not understand. In 1945, the Clubs in Changi started meeting once more and were challenged no longer − the practice was an act of outstanding bravery and psychological perception, for hideous reprisals could have resulted from an enemy nearing defeat.

The gleams of hope in Asia came in those areas where Japanese armies did not gain a foothold. Even under the threat of invasion by land and sea, the worth of maintaining the Rotary ideal never faltered and in proportion, as Clubs in the occupied lands of Middle Asia were submerged in silent agony, the number of Rotarians in India and Ceylon doubled, as did their Clubs and, when famine struck India, alleviation on a grand scale was organised by Rotarians who proceeded to "adopt" particularly hard-hit villages. The Poona Club − whose name had come to symbolise a caricature image of the British Raj (erroneously, since people who might know that

Churchill had once ridden polo ponies purchased from the Poona Light Horse would probably be unaware that this haughty-sounding outfit was composed mostly of Indians) — adopted a village with sensational results, for none other than Mahatma Gandhi arrived to bless the project! Indeed, Gandhi at this time seemed to be presenting himself to the world as something of a Rotarian *manqué*. Indian colleagues relayed his pronouncements to Conventions; he became a frequent contributor to *The Rotarian*. His statement, "To my mind, as soon as a man looks upon himself as a servant of society and earns and spends for its sake, his earnings are good and business ventures constructive", might have derived from Arthur Sheldon's Sales Course. Poona was also one of the places where Gandhi was held in detention during this time, not everyone having forgotten his advice to Britain to surrender after Dunkirk, since "Hitler is not a bad man". But there were many British Rotarians who had once held a similar view of the Fuehrer, after all, and not everyone had forgotten that either.

While many Rotarians in Europe struggled to keep their idealism, both collectively and in terrible loneliness, even when it seemed both pointless and hopeless, those three gleams from Switzerland, Sweden and Portugal meanwhile kept morale alive in the lands where the Germans and the hated Gestapo seemed permanently entrenched. The greatest Rotary beacon sweeping back and forth across the enslaved continent, however, was fuelled by the Clubs in Great Britain and Ireland, which included both European and British members, where no German soldier was ever to set foot except as a prisoner of some British commando raid across the Channel and no Nazi parachutist landed, apart from Luftwaffe pilots who had had to bail out and Hitler's deputy Rudolf Hess, who in May 1941 made his bizarre flight to Scotland in order to explain to the King, via the Duke of Hamilton, that he was "on a mission of humanity and that the Fuehrer did not want to defeat England and wished to stop the fighting". Churchill learned of this weird visitation while watching a Marx Brothers film — he might have been less surprised if Groucho had sloped in with a message from Roosevelt — and had Hess put in the Tower. The Fuehrer was reportedly speechless with rage; the next night, Churchill's beloved House of Commons was destroyed.

The degree to which Hess misunderstood his unwilling hosts is no better illustrated than by the fact that, as early as the previous November, when air battles over Britain were tailing off, the Rotary Club of London had been selected by Churchill's cabinet as the forum where the first announcement (by Ernest Bevin, Minister of Labour and National Service and future Foreign Secretary under the immediate post-war Labour Government) was to be made of post-war plans for the Welfare State, the continuation of what had been started indeed by Churchill himself (of utterly opposite party political beliefs to Bevin) together with Lloyd George before the First World War. Bevin, founder and General Secretary of the largest trade union in the world, the Transport and General Workers, had failed in two attempts to enter Parliament, but when Churchill became Prime Minister he wanted Bevin in his War Cabinet and found him a safe seat. Though two years were to elapse before the famous Beveridge Report was published (its proper title was *Social Insurance and Allied Services*), many of its ideas for the post-war world were already being worked on, and Bevin clearly appreciated that the Rotary Movement, as the world's first Service Club, had been filling gaps at the local community level, as regards the handi-capped, those in want, employment conditions and youth care, with which the State should concern itself much more. In his famous speech to the London Rotarians (including many from Europe who had fled from the swastika tide now lapping at the Channel), Bevin spoke in the Connaught Rooms, ironically just round the corner from the Kingsway Hall where Shaw's first "going to lunch" barb had been delivered thirteen years before. The fact that a fellow-Socialist was now delivering such a water-shed address to the London Club was a complete rebuttal, at last, of the Shavian gibe. Outlining the causes of war, the Minister said that probably the biggest contributing factor "was the failure to provide an economic basis for the development of resources with a view to securing for humanity a new start" and went on:

> Unemployment has been the devil that has driven the masses in large areas of the world to turn to dictators ... the common people do not become "rights" and "lefts" and "middles" out of sheer wickedness. As the masses marched the streets of Europe, and indeed of this country and America, under their different banners, they were but demonstrating the outward and visible symptoms of economic disorder which led to their arguing the different theses of their different political outlook, and what indeed were they striving for but to find in the world, somehow, social security?

And then to those crowding the tables, men whose Movement still based its motive power on Sheldon's durable sales slogan "He Profits Most Who Serves Best", the great trade unionist declared:

> If profit can be the only motive, the natural corollary is economic disorder, and economic disorder will bring you back to the same position you are in

now, ever recurring, and future generations will again pay, in the same form or another, the bitter price we are paying now. . . .

I want to give you a new motive for industry, for life. . . . I suggest we accept social security as the main motive of all our national life. Begin there. . . . In Rotary, you accept service as the mainspring of your whole organisation and being; and does not service give the greatest satisfaction in life? . . .

I feel it in my bones that things can never be as they were. The old age has passed; the new age has to be built, and what greater tribute can we pay to those who are suffering at the moment than to be able to say to them, "This time it is really not in vain".

At that historic moment, Ernest Bevin was giving the counter-point to the magnificent speeches of Churchill which were rousing the spirits of his own countrymen, as well of those in Europe and the free world. Churchill was persuading mankind that the war could be won; Bevin was persuading them how the peace could be won. The London Clubs, as we shall see, responded with unexpected enthusiasm to both clarion calls, determined both to win and to survive.

It was no accident that the War Cabinet had chosen the Rotary Club of London as the forum for Bevin's speech. It was the finest witness possible to Rotary's genuine internationality and to the spirit which was even then keeping Rotary alive under the crushing weight of Axis oppression and seeming invincibility both in the West and East. It was a turning-point not only in Rotary's perception of itself, but in the world's perception of Rotary, a change marked even more dramatically two years later. Meanwhile, writing about the speech in the Labour Party's newspaper the *Daily Herald*, even such a left-wing journalist as Hannen Swaffer declared, with some awe: "The significance of [Bevin's] utterance lay in the warmth of its reception. . . . Looking around at the great gathering and its receptiveness yesterday, it was forced on me how millions [*sic*] of people, formerly comfortable and well-fed, are now blundering towards a new conception of life and its meaning. . . . The fact that such a gathering could applaud such a speech, was in itself a comment on the changes now going on in men's minds."

It was even more a comment on Swaffer's distorted view of the Movement; though to be fair, the then celebrated and influential columnist — invariably well fed himself, and frequently well watered — shared the view of most of the public. In calling his column "Rotary Applauds a New World", he recorded a changed perception which from now would grow and grow. For Bevin's speech, and his deliberate choice of venue to deliver it, was neither the first nor last witness to Rotary International's new status in the eyes of world governments. London at that time was packed with Europe's governments-in-exile and exiled royalty, which alone made of the Rotary Club there a miniature United Nations. But soon, the Past President of the Rotary Club of Katowice, Poland, Casimir Zienkiewicz, formed the Inter-Allied Outpost of Rotary Clubs of Europe, to which refugee Rotarians from not only Poland but Czechoslovakia, Denmark, Norway, the Netherlands, Belgium and France belonged. Eduard Beneš, exiled President of Czechoslovakia, belonged to it, but he also belonged throughout the war to the Rotary Club of Putney (the owner of the celebrated Bata Shoe factory had by then travelled somewhat farther, exchanging membership of the Zlin Club in Czechoslovakia for that of Trenton, Ontario). Here, Rotary International was throughout the war directly in the front line in the most literal sense, where, as nations fought to preserve the freedom of the West and gathered forces to return and reclaim their lands and peoples, Rotary – in the many diverse realisations it had taken in those nations – gathered strength to return with them to retake the high ground of men's minds. The front line continued after the Normandy invasions with the advent of the V1 and V2 bombs, and Rotary in Britain paid a sum in lives no less than did Rotarians living under the Occupation. Air raids, after all, killed 60,000 civilians altogether during the war, two-thirds of them in London. The Rotary Club of Chelsea lost President, Vice-President and Secretary during one night of bombing. During the same night, the Vice-President and Secretary of the Czech leader's adopted Club at Putney were also both killed. It was a casualty list repeated many times all over the United Kingdom, and in August 1942, the Duke of Kent, RIBI's first and only royal patron, was killed in an air crash when serving with the RAF. He had been an enthusiastic patron of the Movement in Great Britain and Ireland for eleven years.

Each Rotary International President, as the war years went by, both before and after Pearl Harbor, made a point of touring the besieged British Isles and did much for Rotary's reputation, both within and without the Movement, each time they did so. To extend the Swaffer tribute, Rotary was not only applauding a new world but acclaiming the guts of the old. In 1944, the new RI General Secretary, Philip Lovejoy, accompanied the President of that year, Richard H. Wells, a prominent business man of Pocatello, Idaho (immortalised as the town where July Garland used to sing heart-rendingly that she was "born in a trunk"), and discovered the enormous courage of the Rotarians who were not content simply to "carry on" but to expand their numbers, having added twenty-seven Clubs since the war began. Lovejoy wrote graphically of his visit: "Every Rotarian, every person in Britain, lives and works under tension . . . overworked, blitzed, rationed, how does the British Rotarian let down? Quite right. He goes to Rotary. . . . He finds refreshment in the good fellowship, the conversation, the discussion of Rotary's enduring and universal principles, the talks by beekeepers, ornithologists, statesmen and world travellers. Never has he appreciated Rotary more." And the community work went on as well, the hostels for servicemen, canteens, care of homeless families, orphaned children. He described for the other "231,000 Rotarians of the world" the food shortages, clothing coupons, the five-inch limit of water in each bath, the limited supply of almost everything except Brussels sprouts, the extraordinary amount of work every man did apart from his job. He cited, in particular, Percy Reay of the Manchester Club (one of RIBI's outstanding Rotarians, later described by Roger Levy in his history as "a quiet Scot whose statesmanship had been of inestimable value to the Movement", who was destined to become RIBI President in 1948; indeed, he remains active still), who, in addition to his clothing business, ran eighteen Red Cross hospitals. He learned of what he termed the universal "heroic silence" kept about homes destroyed, whole families of Rotarians being killed overnight.

No doubt Lovejoy was told also of the British anti-aircraft gunner, in one of the merchant ships plying the U-boat infested Atlantic, who was given two cases of grapefruit by a Rotarian in the Canadian port of Halifax, which he had then auctioned in England for the Red Cross for £727! Though Sigmund Freud and his large family had been British residents since 1938, when they fled the *Anschluss*, Freud himself had survived only twenty days of wartime Britain, otherwise we might have been offered some fascinating insights on this amazingly lucrative auction, which seemed to prove that the British at least are tempted not so much by forbidden fruits as unobtainable ones. The General Secretary said nothing about nylons, though he bore the perfect brand name for them.

What Philip Lovejoy did *not* include in his account was news of a *Report on Postwar Reconstruction* just then published on behalf of all the Rotary Clubs throughout the London area, whose individual Reconstruction Committees had been set the task of submitting their respective studies and conclusions.

Though three years had passed since their collective thinking on this subject began, spurred by the watershed speech made to the original London Club by Ernest Bevin in 1940, that powerful character's impact was still clearly discernible, since the startling recommendations included:

industry controlled "for the purpose of limiting profits and speculation" and organised "to afford an adequate standard of life for all employed in it";

nationalisation of all banks and public utilities, including transport;

social security for all and the world freed "from the control of currency by financiers and vested interests" by bringing "the distribution of credit and regulation of currency under national and international control";

all land dealings under government control and the production of goods planned to give employment to everyone;

a State medical service; and

the immediate introduction of a ten-year plan "to merge all existing educational establishments into a single State system . . . private enterprise in the provision of educational facilities to be made illegal".

These were scarcely reflections of the common public image of Rotary then or now, but were strong indications of an increasing involvement of the Movement − in Britain anyway − in public affairs, an influence soon to make itself evident in the international councils of world leaders as the United Nations began to take shape.

It was as well that Lovejoy's predecessor was not making that tour, as Ches Perry would simply have seen confirmed all his worst fears about the wisdom of permitting the "territorial unit" of Great Britain and Ireland to maintain its independent administration. Even that unflappable demeanour might have been shaken by such evidence of the English-influenced New Deal philosophy of Roosevelt coming home to roost with a reinterpretation of Vocational Service in Rotary from the Conscience of Business to the Conscience of the State. Fortunately, Perry was preoccupied in fashioning a new life and new career in the Movement for himself. At the age of seventy-two he was now married to his former long-time secretary, Peggy Schafer, and was about to become President of the Rotary Club of Chicago. So perhaps Lovejoy kept this startling Report from him for a time; as also the news that Al Capone's personal armoured car, from the days when "Big Al" ruled Chicago, was somehow being exhibited at British fairgrounds all over the country, until it was withdrawn from view when American servicemen protested that it gave a false impression of Chicago and of their homeland which "no longer had gangsters". In any event, whether or not Chesley Perry would have pretended to believe that America no longer had gangsters, any British Rotarian post-war reconstruction report inspired by Ernest Bevin would have placed itself automatically beyond the pale of consideration, had Perry become aware of two things the blunt Mr Bevin himself claimed the United States *did* have: "Your newspapers are too big and your lavatory paper too small."

In June 1942, the same month as the old era of Rotary was ending in Rotary with Ches Perry's exit at the Toronto Convention, which·Rotarian Bata attended (having set up his new shoe factory in Ontario), its new era was begun in London with a great gathering of all nations, sponsored by British Rotary and under the chairmanship of Sydney Pascall, elected, of course, at the glamorous and glittering Vienna Convention as President of Rotary International in 1931. The topic was post-war youth – assuming there would be any – and the countries represented were Australia, Belgium, Canada, China, Cuba, Czechoslovakia, Denmark, the Dominican Republic, France, Greece, Guatemala, India, Panama, Poland, South Africa, the United Kingdom, the United States and Yugoslavia – plus the Soviet Union! Its Report went to the Education Ministries of the United Nations governments (Churchill sent Harold Macmillan, future Prime Minister, as his official observer) to form, as Roger Levy asserts, "the kernel of the body that came to be known as UNESCO", the first most publicised arm of the United Nations Educational, Social and Cultural Organisation. (The present writer was honoured to write and compère the first broadcasts to Europe about UNESCO after the war over the Voice of America, while at Harvard University.) Post-war reconstruction was a primary concern (unexpectedly radical) among British Rotary Clubs throughout the years of conflict, for their faith never wavered in victory, and this was at RIBI District and Club level. The concern was also true of the United States and Canada, and it was also constantly discussed by members of the Inter-Allied Outpost of Rotary Clubs of Europe. The result was that when the San Francisco Conference was called in 1945 to draft the Charter of the United Nations, Rotarians were included in thirty-six of the fifty national delegations and, by special invitation, Rotary International sent a special delegation to act as consultants.

Perhaps, however, the apogee of world recognition of the great latent power of the Golden Wheel came the following year, when the first meeting of the UN General Assembly was held in London. Tom Warren, who had now become the second Englishman to be elected World President of the Movement, at once stated that this milestone in the history of mankind should be the "touchstone for a gesture of international goodwill unique in the history of Rotary". Whereupon, on 16th January 1946, RIBI on behalf of International Rotary was host at London's Caxton Hall to all the UN delegates. The diversity of representation was even greater than when Rotary had been midwife to the birth of UNESCO, the nations there being (again alphabetically) Argentina, Australia, Belgium, Bolivia, Brazil, Canada, China, Colombia, Cuba, Czechoslovakia, Denmark,

Dominica, Ecuador, Guatemala, Haiti, Honduras, Iraq, Lebanon, Luxembourg, the Netherlands, the Philippines, Saudi Arabia, Syria, the United Kingdom and Yugoslavia. Many of the delegates were Rotarians anyway, giving the event a double prestige.

The factor which in the event marred this great moment for the Movement was the absence of delegates from either the United States or the Soviet Union. This calamity – for it was nothing less in the long-term view – had been prefigured the previous June, at the Thirty-Sixth Convention of Rotary International, held one month after VE day had been announced by Truman and Churchill (just to be different, Stalin waited another twenty-four hours before making his own announcement to the Russian people, no doubt so that he could claim that Soviet forces fought the Germans longer than the Anglo-Saxons). The Convention was held in Chicago, birthplace of Rotary and of the diehards of Rotary – and was marked by the second lowest registration recorded since the Second Convention was held in Portland, Oregon (described in Chapter Five). Indeed, there were eight *less* in attendance than at Portland, and rather more were attending the weekly meetings of the Chicago Club where Ches Perry was now President! It was not perhaps coincidence that the Movement's foremost "internationalist", Tom Warren, had therefore the smallest Convention audience of his career to listen to his acceptance speech as incoming President. Philip Lovejoy justified the poor attendance by quoting a directive from the US Government, issued in January, which stated that there should be "no meeting of more than 50 persons from outside the trade area of the community in which the meeting is held" unless the War Committee of Conventions gave permission. As Lovejoy piously observed, Rotary International was "always desirous of conforming to the spirit of a regulation". And he proceeded to break down even the 141 delegates accordingly into four sessions, so that Tom Warren found himself, at the greatest moment of his life, addressing only fifty Rotarians. Nevertheless, Warren told them, unconsciously echoing Hannen Swaffer: "We are going into a difficult year. We seek nothing less than a new world. . . . Rotary was an infant in 1918. Rotary couldn't have much effect at that time. In 1945, Rotary is a grown power, aged forty years. And this powerful auxiliary, if used aright, can seek the truth this time, and make that truth known."

But world recognition in 1946 of Rotary's achieved internationalism was ruthlessly lacking at this supreme moment in the very country which had given it birth forty-one years before. Thus, with only a year to live, Paul Harris was denied realisation of the summit of his dream (for the first time, he sent no Message to the

Convention), and it must have saddened him greatly. The spirit of Ches Perry was proved far from gone at East Wacker Drive (as was the spirit of Rotarian Woodrow Wilson): the Immediate Past President of Chicago's Rotary Number One had stooped to conquer. Rotary International was never again to approach that universal recognition and understanding which it had seemed poised to achieve.

Returning to May 1943, the time of the Thirty-Fourth Convention of Rotary International, we find that delegates were subjected to an uncompromisingly realistic speech by Carlos Romulo again, by now a colonel on General MacArthur's staff. "Do you realise", he told the nearly 4,000 delegates at St Louis, Missouri, amongst whom now sat that far from ordinary Rotarian from the Chicago Club, Ches Perry, "that so far in the Pacific, America is a defeated nation, crawling in the dust of defeat, with Japan as the victor, the lord, the conqueror? . . . From the tip of Burma to the tip of Java, Japan is still our master."

Fortunately for the tone of the Convention, which was hoping to put aside such negative worries under their slogan "Rotary Serving — In War — In Peace", there was plenty of upbeat exhortation also from the platform, especially from "Bonnie Jean" Harris, whose evangelistic fervour positively bloomed in these crisis years. She did not suggest this time, as at Toronto, that delegates should acknowledge "The Eternal Power", and instead of asking for God to give Rotarians wisdom, judgment, etc., she told the 4,000 earnest and enthusiastic listeners in the Municipal Auditorium that she hoped God would treat them with mercy. With those words of comfort, she yielded way for her husband to come carefully forward to grasp the lectern.

The 1943 Convention was a truncated one, only three days long, and relatively austere, in comparison with the huge patriotic pageant of Toronto. The US Office of Defense Transportation had asked the Rotarians to avoid week-end travel, emphasising that 2 million soldiers a month were now being moved about the country, while their wives were requested to restrict their shopping to between the hours of 10 a.m. and 2 p.m. so as not to swamp public transport. However, since General George C. Marshall, Chief of Staff of the War Department, praised by Churchill as "a rugged soldier and a magnificent organiser and builder of armies", had recently accepted membership of the Rotary Club of Uniontown, Pennsylvania (it was the fourth Rotary Club he had joined during his Army career), the Convention found the slogan engraved in stone outside the Auditorium, "Where the torch of democracy may be rekindled", a happy augury.

Others found it saddeningly ironic, since only shortly before the Convention, the Movement had chartered its first Club in the Dominican Republic, the Rotary Club of Ciudad Trujillo, the capital city once called Santo Domingo by the brother of Christopher Columbus (it is the oldest European city in the Western Hemisphere), now renamed by General Rafael Trujillo, who had established the most brutal dictatorship in the New World and the longest-running in modern times, lasting eventually from 1930 to 1961. Trujillo himself had also become the latest Honorary Rotarian and, making the chief speech at the Club's inauguration, he pronounced: "I consider that the international function of Rotary is to collaborate in the crystallisation of one of the most urgent needs of America: spiritual and material unity of the entire continent for the purpose of protection, progress and peace within an absolute equality of deed and right. . . . I extend my cordial greetings to all the Rotarians of the world." He also extended the gift of a gavel to the Convention and this was enthusiastically pounded at St Louis, as enthusiastically as his secret police were constantly pounding political opponents in torture dens all over the Republic, and even abroad when they fled, while Rotarian Trujillo amassed a personal fortune of $800 million.

The Rotarians of Havana sponsored the new Club, but in later years Cuba was to prove one of those most determined to topple Rotary's only member with a dictator Classification. In 1961, Rotarian Trujillo was to be machine-gunned in his car in typical gangland style at the age of sixty-nine on his way to meet one of his mistresses. No Rotary "two black balls" ended his association with the Movement but twenty-seven bullets, and Ciudad Trujillo became Santo Domingo again, with the Club renamed accordingly. But Rotary International had to endure its most embarrassing Rotarian for twenty-eight years.

Carlos Romulo's rather alarming pronouncements seemed combined with "Bonnie Jean's" view of a salutary apocalypse in Paul Harris's first words, the Founder assuring his audience that "the question as to whether or not there is such a place as hell is no longer a matter of speculation. There is a hell and it's in the here and now". He was not referring to St Louis, however, but to the admired fighting spirit of Rotarians in Great Britain. "It is not remarkable", he conceded, "that under such circumstances, some of our overseas friends wondered whether Rotary was worth salvaging. All wonder is now passed; Rotary in Britain is stronger, more human and kindlier than ever before. . . . Rotary has stood the test of fire and blood and manifestly is destined to endure."

All quite true. But seen from a nearer, more practical viewpoint, it would have been more accurate for Paul Harris to say that Rotarians in Britain had learned the lesson shared by all their compatriots and the refugees in their midst from all over Europe: that those who turn the other cheek to a tyrant will find his biggest kick already aimed there; while those who turn their blind eye to history have already forgotten who gouged it out in the first place. European Rotarians in exile soon found they had exchanged the bread of affliction for Brussels sprouts, but being Rotarians, they put service above self and bore it stoically. Others, outside the Movement, like General de Gaulle, were not so forgiving, then or later.

The 1943 Convention soon had the words of Paul Harris confirmed when delegates heard over the radio at noon that day Winston Churchill speaking to the United States Congress, the second time the British Prime Minister had been invited to address the American legislators but the first since America had entered the war. Churchill's words were a counter to Romulo's: "The African excursions of the two Dictators have cost their countries in killed and captured 950,000 soldiers. In addition, nearly 2,400,000 gross tons of shipping have been sunk and nearly 8,000 aircraft destroyed. . . . There have also been lost to the enemy 6,200 guns, 2,550 tanks and 70,000 trucks. . . . Arrived at this milestone in the war, we can say, 'One continent redeemed. . . . ' " His vision was more far-seeing than Romulo's, probably because he knew more of the facts of the situation. The Japanese had now suffered more serious reversals and greater losses than the general public knew about. Their élite carrier force under Admiral Nugamo, which had devastated Pearl Harbor, had tried the same tactic on the British bases in Ceylon and failed, receiving such damage that it never regained its potency and its Admiral went home. The US Navy inflicted, in its turn, enormous losses on the enemy in the great battles of Midway and the Coral Sea, not only preventing an invasion of Australia but sinking half of Japan's aircraft-carriers. Indeed, one month before Romulo spoke, Yamamoto, the Japanese naval commander-in-chief, had been shot down over the sea. In terrible fighting, all the far-flung islands of the new Japanese empire were being regained, and the names of Admirals Nimitz and Halsey were being added to the American pantheon.

In the province of Kiangsi the Chinese had also inflicted tremendous casualties on the Japanese Army, while in India, though driven from Burma and racked by malaria (which at one time was putting no less than 12,000 men on the sick-list each day), the Fourteenth British Imperial Army under General Slim was slowly being forged from British, Indian, Australian and New Zealand troops (under the overall strategic direction of Admiral Lord Louis Mountbatten), a force which in fifteen months would drive the enemy from Burma and defeat them in the greatest single land battle of the war against the Japanese Army, inflicting nearly 350,000 casualties.

Of the European side of the global war, the day after the Americans ambushed Yamamoto, the SS in Warsaw decided to get rid of the 60,000 Jews still left in the walled-in ghetto where they had been driven after the Polish invasion. Accordingly, SS Brigade-führer Juergen Stroop attacked them with tanks, flame-throwers, artillery and dynamite squads, but the Jews fought back from vaults, cellars and sewers with smuggled arms and the planned three-day action took four weeks. It was not till 18th May – on the very day that Carlos Romulo was delivering his warning to Convention – that Stroop was able to make his own final report: "Today, one hundred and eighty Jews, bandits and subhumans were destroyed. The former Jewish quarter of Warsaw is no longer in existence."

This curtain-raiser to the "Final Solution" was mercifully not known to the Convention, but one of the reasons for it – that the German Army needed the extermination camp trains to transport their troops away from new Russian offensives – was becoming known. Not only had the Wehrmacht surrendered at Stalingrad, but Leningrad had been relieved and the Germans with their Italian and Balkan allies had lost some 500,000 men. Hitler was shortly to lose another 500,000 men in the greatest tank battle in history – indeed, the greatest battle of the war – at Kursk, where seven of his prized Panzer divisions were totally destroyed.

The Allies, having crossed from North Africa to capture Sicily (with a little help from an unexpected ally, "Lucky" Luciano, Capone's old gangster enemy, who mustered Mafia aid on the island), now battled up the Italian peninsula, and Italy surrendered, the King abruptly dismissing Mussolini from power. Twelve months later, the Anglo-American forces entered Rome, while over 3 million of their brothers-in-arms began the Normandy invasion, and the Russians recaptured the Crimea and Ukraine, stormed into the Balkans and across the Polish frontiers. In the north, that most cunning of all warriors, Rotarian Mannerheim, made terms with Russia and took Finland out of the war.

At the Thirty-Fifth Convention, brought back to Chicago for the third time after fourteen years, Paul Harris stepped forward to speak and found himself being decorated with the Heraldic Order of Cristobal Colon (Christopher Columbus) by the President of the Rotary Club of Ciudad Trujillo of the Dominican Republic! It was the special gift of the appalling Trujillo, "a ruler who lives and practices the Rotary ideal", he was informed, and the photograph which we have of the occasion shows the Founder of Rotary looking suitably bewildered and discomfited, knowing, as everyone present did, that the Dominican President had disposed of all his rivals quite as permanently as did Hitler and Stalin of theirs, had put up 1,870 monuments to himself in his capital city, and had made his two sons respectively Chief of Staff of the Armed Forces and Vice-President. Paul, now a fragile seventy-six (he had had another operation in 1942), reading his prepared text, found that he was telling delegates that "there are no great fundamental differences between men and between nations. None are entirely good, none entirely bad. The great mischief-maker is misunderstanding. . . . As soon as is consistent with safety, the conquered nations must be restored to productivity in science, music, art and literature". The sentiments were basic to his conception of Rotary, but the utterance was unfortunate with that tyrant's bauble round his throat. His mind, as he knew, was on the past as much as the future, for his official thirty-ninth birthday greeting that year to his Movement, which *The Rotarian* published next to a facsimile reproduction of his handwritten note, quoted once again Robert Burns's statement that all men would brothers be, for A'that. At least it pleased Jean Harris, who, as Paul grew weaker, was now saying her own piece more confidently at each year's Convention.

Another year and victory came at last, with Hitler dead in his bunker and Russian armour crunching over the ruins of the Reichstag. In the Pacific, MacArthur took back the Philippines; and the Allies brought the Germans to total defeat in the West, the RAF having flattened Dresden and Hamburg, which suffered even more devastatingly than had London, Bristol and Coventry during the Battle of Britain.

In the midst of the Allies' military triumphs the Movement suffered a sad blow when the Rotary Club of Albany, New York, lost its most famous member, President Roosevelt, in April 1945. To the end, he had conducted his country's war and territorial manoeuvrings with allies, and present and future enemies, with the aid of a massive globe in the Oval Room at the White House, weighing 800 pounds and reaching fifty inches in diameter, made for him specially by a firm run by Rotarian Earle Opie of the Chicago Club.

That same month brought death also to Mussolini as well as Hitler; the former being shot by Italian partisans with his mistress and hung upside-down with her in Azzano. His son-in-law, the sardonic and opportunist Count Ciano, who had helped engineer Mussolini's dismissal by Rotarian Victor Emmanuel in July 1943, had already been shot dead sixteen months before by Fascist partisans. Thus, when peace came, the Rotary Club of Leghorn found itself deprived of one of its most socially prominent and embarrassing members, for which they were profoundly grateful.

As the evil empire of the Third Reich was collapsing, mercifully well short of its intended thousand-year lifespan, German Rotary's most distinguished refugee, Thomas Mann (thrown out of the Munich Club, of which he was a Founder Member, it will be remembered), broadcast a message to the ordinary non-Nazi citizens of the country he had fled eleven years before. While still in Munich, he had given a memorable description of the Movement:

> In the Rotary Club, men of all tongues and of all climes have united, men who know well the eternal values in the sphere of the individual, in the sphere of art and culture, men who are determined to defend it against the accusation of materialism; men, however, who are equally determined that they will permit no false romanticism to interfere with their will to serve and to work for a better human organisation.

And now, from his new homeland (he had just become an American citizen) he spoke these words to the ruined nation of his birth, to the shattered heart of the Nazi world, which Munich had been:

> The war aim of the Allies is a secure peace; the setting up of a worldwide system of collective security, within the framework of which a free and democratic Europe is comprised: and inside of this Europe, a free and democratic Germany must some day resume its reponsible and respected place.
>
> I say "some day"; it is clear to me, as it must be to you, that this day cannot be tomorrow nor the day after tomorrow. . . .
>
> The Nazis have talked to you a lot about Europe. Even today they assert that they are defending Europe's culture as well as her soil — they, the hangers and flayers of Europe's peoples! . . .
>
> The German is no devil, as many assert. Likewise he is no archangel, fair-handed, in shining Aryan armour, but a man, like everybody else; and he must learn to live again as man and brother among his kind.

The great writer's broadcast reached the ears and inspired the faith in a future of reconciliation of many Rotarians in Germany, who indeed began to form "ex-Rotarian" Clubs wherever they could as soon as the dust had settled over their streets, littered with masonry and unburied bodies, in the wake of the final surrender of Admiral Doenitz, the U-boat commander whom Hitler had named as his successor but who had inherited only a waste-land of lost, shifting masses, bewildered mothers and children, vacant-eyed old people, uncertain, unarmed soldiery, ill-equipped, many of them barely in their teens, wandering vaguely along the road, climbing their way through ruins, picking a path through the skeletal remnants and mountainous rubble of the Third Reich. From this dull, hopeless chaos of the once-arrogant who had inherited the earth in their mouth and nostrils and eyes, Rotary still sprang. In Stuttgart, Hanover and Hamburg, the Golden Wheel appeared again in threadbare lapels — unofficial, of course, but insistent, with a strength that was still peculiarly German.

Ernest Atkins, the Wandsworth Rotarian, ever the unreconstructed Germanophile who had let himself be dazzled by the wily fox Count von Papen at the Austrian Youth camp before the war and been misled by his enthusiasm for exchanges of British and German Youth (see Chapters Seventeen and Eighteen), no longer had Von Papen to deal with. That shallow but durable schemer, described by the French Ambassador in pre-war Berlin as "superficial, blundering, untrue, ambitious, vain, crafty and an intriguer", was busy defending himself at the Nuremberg trials — surviving these too, even though his inept intrigues had done more than anyone else to let Hitler come to power. Hence Atkins, still in thrall of his beloved Germany, and now a member of the London Club, pleaded in *Rotary Service*:

It is now that Rotary can take a tremendous part in the international super-creation of states; perhaps a greater one than can any other non-political organisation. . . .

We must recreate German Rotary without further delay, and so place little cells of democracy in every town of Western Germany. . . .

We want these men. We want them in Rotary, but far more, we want them in the ranks of democracy, fighting to retain a free Europe. . . .

Freemasonry has been re-established in Germany. English and American officers visit German Masonic Lodges. Is Freemasonry greater than Rotary in breadth of mind and vision? . . .

This is Rotary's great chance. Dare we lose it? It is not only the rebirth of German Rotary which is at issue, it is the peace and security of Europe, of England, our own land. . . .

If Rotary is afraid to tackle this job, then its Members are unworthy of their professed ideas and we are luncheon Clubs and luncheon Clubs only. God grant for the peace of mankind that we prove we are more than this and prove it *now*.

Rotarian Atkins was not as blinkered as perhaps he had been before. His faith in Germany was genuine enough but he also appreciated the threat of Russian talons wishing to claw beyond their area of occupation. While many Americans also understood this — Churchill having by this time made his "iron curtain" speech at Fulton, Missouri, in which he had also said, "the safety of the world requires a new unity in Europe, from which no nation should be permanently outcast" — the Board of RI in Chicago was doubtless put off by Atkins's candid references to Freemasonry and to "our own land" (it was a permanent bugbear of Rotary International that the public often believed it synonymous with the Masons) and it declared nothing could be done while there was still military government in Germany and Austria. Which was rubbish, of course, since it was to present no obstacle in Japan, as we shall shortly see.

But Atkins need not have worried. Thomas Mann's broadcast, we may be sure, also reached the ears of another Rotarian in Germany, but one who had chosen to remain there, though twice arrested by the Nazis. It was this man who in himself — though he was far from young, being indeed only eight years the junior of Paul Harris — was to form the image of the "new" German in the minds of the victors. A Founder Member of the Rotary Club of Cologne, formed in 1928, the same year as that in Munich, he had helped entertain Paul Harris on his visit that year (see Chapter Fifteen) and was one of those who took the Founder of Rotary to the top of an observation tower to view the breath-taking panorama of the city, all illuminated for an important exhibition, whose central feature was the famous Gothic cathedral. Of all that Paul Harris then saw, only the cathedral miraculously remained amidst 600 acres of waste-land after the 1,000-bomber raids had left the building, like St Paul's, surrounded by waste and rubble. Nicknamed *Der Alte* (the Old One), that Rotarian led his country back into the family of nations. The rubble of Cologne was grassed and planted over into mounds of cultivation, which can be seen today. They are called the Adenauer Hills.

In Japan, as we have seen, the Rotary Clubs had not been dispersed; they had merely suffered a sea-change into Day–of–the–Week Clubs, the Japanese being far more tolerant towards their own Rotarians than they were of those in the lands they occupied. After the dropping of the atomic bombs on Hiroshima and Nagasaki, both of which had Rotary Clubs, it remained only for the Movement to seek permission to be re-established, for which the word of Rotarian (and post-war dictator of Japan) General MacArthur would be required. This was obtained by the remarkable third

General Secretary of Rotary International, George Means (though he was still Assistant to Phil Lovejoy when he achieved this feat), who had been grandly informed by MacArthur that authorisation by Washington would be needed. "The word 'authorization' bothers me, General," said Means. "Rotary cannot operate if it must be subject to the authority of governments." The modern Shogun contemplated this blow, and eventually recovered to say: "If I didn't think Rotary was the noble institution that it is, and as it is internationally known to be, and if it would not be of great benefit to the Japanese people, I would not want to see it here. The whole thing is up to Rotary."

And up to a very special type of Rotarian, the sort perhaps that Japan alone could produce. Takashi Komatsu was the speaker who had made an extraordinary address at the 1940 Havana Convention (see Chapter Nineteen) about the need for Rotary to avoid any action which "might be interpreted as casting stones of blame". None other than Allen Albert had then said "Takashi Komatsu's smile is serene". It was about to become more serene than ever as its owner now resurfaced in Tokyo, alive and well, to travel round as George Means's interpreter with the task of looking over the Day-of-the Week Clubs and confirming their enthusiasm to welcome Rotary back. It is not surprising that the Occupation authorities, however, not only had Komatsu still under suspicion at this time but under surveillance, and they kept a careful watch on the trail along which he led the resolute Means towards his end. It was perhaps significant that when the revived Tokyo Club drew up its first list of recommended members, that list – though it included 75 per cent of the Day-of-the-Week Clubs – did not include Takashi Komatsu. The serene smile was soon back in favour, none the less, and indeed soon back in the international hierarchy of the Movement.

Evidence of George Means's remarkable success was given the present author at the RIBI Conference in 1983 when the International President of Rotary was guest at the Annual Conference at Blackpool of RIBI and there presented a Special Presidential Citation (though he could have made several, it was the only one Dr Hiroji Mukasa, an eminent psychiatrist, chose to make) to Group Captain Leonard Cheshire, VC. The award was, of course, a tribute from the Movement to the work of the Cheshire Homes, residences where care is given to the incurably disabled. It was at the same time a magnificent gesture for a Japanese Rotarian to make to a man who had flown as an observer when Nagasaki took the second, and far more powerful, atom bomb.

MacArthur accepted Honorary Membership of the revived Tokyo Club, announcing that the organisation was "sorely needed in this time of so much world unrest". Thus Rotary became the first non-religious international organisation readmitted to Japan after the war and Japan has now become the fastest growing region in the Rotary world. Hiroshima and Nagasaki today have six Clubs each.

Rotary's revival in Italy began with a very different type of US commander, General George Patton, who wore two pearl-handled revolvers and thus felt the need for fewer words. As early as 1943, when he and Montgomery had retaken Sicily between them, Patton had been approached by Rotarians in Palermo and asked if Rotary Clubs could please now start again. In contrast to MacArthur's windy rhetoric, Patton had simply replied, "Go ahead". Since he had used the same approach with the gangster Luciano, who had as noted come in the train of the US Army to re-establish Mafia control over Sicily, he doubtless felt a counter-influence highly desirable.

But Rotary in the Italian peninsula had to wait till 1947, and meanwhile, Rotarian Guido Carlo Visconti, a member of the same famous aristocratic line which had produced Dukes of Milan and one of the great film directors of our time, gathered enough signatures from Italian senators to persuade the King to dismiss Mussolini. When the Rotary Club of Rome was given back its charter, the chief guest was Premier Alcide de Gasperi, his Foreign Minister Count Sforza and half of his Ministry. Beside him sat Italy's new District Governor for Rotary, who ran the gallup poll.

The *annus mirabilis* for the Golden Wheel came in 1949. In that year Japan's Prime Minister, Shigeru Yoshida, was guest speaker at the first post-war meeting of the Rotary Club of Tokyo, when it formally received its charter bringing Japan back into the Movement. The same year saw Rotary started in Germany again, with the chartering of the Rotary Club of Frankfurt. The same year also saw Rotarian Konrad Adenauer become the first Chancellor of the German Federal Republic, and that irrepressible Rotarian, Carlos Romulo, become President of the United Nations General Assembly.

The following spring, the Rotary Clubs of Japan held a Conference in Kyoto, which proclaimed this Resolution: "In the true spirit of Rotary ideals and of the new Japanese Constitution, which resolves not to resort to arms, we call upon our fellow Rotarians around the world to join hands in the determination to discover ways of peace and understanding." And the same spring, on the other side of the globe, the Rotary Clubs of Germany, meeting at Baden-Baden, proclaimed this Resolution: "We regret every attack which in disregard of human rights was directed towards a neighbouring nation. Now a new start can be made. Rotary International, in true Rotary spirit, has stepped out ahead of politics in that it permitted the establishment of Rotary Clubs in Japan and Germany before the statesmen could unite on treaties of peace."

It was not a case, as the British journalist had called it, of Rotary's applauding a new world. A new world was applauding Rotary. Forty-five years old. A late developer perhaps. But a survivor. And now, matured, full-grown, how it bestrode the world!

CHAPTER TWENTY-THREE

Once Every Fourteen Hours

Great Movements find the man,
The man the hour . . .
The emblemed Wheel became a passport far
                                    and wide,
Symbol of action,
Mark of accomplishment . . .
Progress unparalleled is seen
In Rotary's lengthening years;
Its growth phenomenal,
Its program rich and timed to current needs:
An annual harvest of good works and leadership,
Thousands of times repeated . . .
These forces of fraternity
Have breached estranging walls of custom, time
                                    and distance,
In Friendship's name . . .
As Paul would have it be.

"Paul Harris, Founder of Rotary" by Rotarian
Vernon Boyce Hampton

The poem above, introducing this chapter, was published in 1968 to
commemorate the hundredth anniversary of the birth of Paul
Harris. The aspiring poet (who paid for the printing), a Past Governor
of Rotary District 723, was a schoolteacher who fondly believed
his poem would "become part of Rotary's living literature, historical,
contemporary, challenging and inspirational". It hasn't. But its
subject transcended the sincerity of his votary, and the above
selection of observations from the poem are true and summarise
well the achievements of the Golden Wheel, forty years on. And

this chapter will deal with those forty years, even though the last one ended when Rotary had but reached half its present age, and though in that second half the Movement since 1945 has multiplied itself four times. When VJ day was declared, there were 5,441 Clubs around the world and the international membership numbered 247,212. Thus, during six years of the most terrible war ever known, Rotary had managed to introduce approximately 1,000 new Clubs and 40,000 members. Today, the 20,000th Club is a landmark left behind and the total world membership rapidly nears 1 million.

Yet, as H.G. Wells wrote, "History is, and must always be, no more than an account of beginnings." It is also true that the most interesting parts of any biography are those concerning the growth to manhood, the discovery of "vocation". Since "Vocational Service" has been the major ingredient of Rotary, just as Paul Harris intended it to be from the start in 1905, any attempt to encapsulate all its triumphs, its value as counsellor and comfort to statesmen, its potency as viable for such men as they tread their paths of glory as for the rest of us, would soon become not a chronicle but a catalogue. A catalogue, moreover, no longer listing only feelings

> Of unremembered pleasure: such, feelings too perhaps,
> As have no slight or trivial influence
> On that best portion of a good man's life,
> His little, nameless, unremembered, acts
> Of kindness and of love.

in serene Wordsworthian anonymity, though many Rotarians still believe this is the correct and modest destiny for their Movement. The catalogue from now on would be of larger deeds on an ever larger scale. Thus far the catalogue has been extremely impressive, but the chronicle is over — the casting, the first sketch played in front of friends, the move from amateur to professional, the development from miracle plays to the Theatre of the Absurd (i.e. history). And now, Paul Harris's favourite philosopher (who also progressed from the hermit hut to the stage), Ralph Waldo Emerson, is completely vindicated, for no institution was ever the lengthened shadow of one man more than Rotary International; Rotary's history and Paul's biography (history and biography are one and the same, held the Sage of Concord) walked hand in hand. Eighteen months after the end of the Second World War, Paul Harris was dead.

But he had taken his great Movement to maturity. In the years since mankind stepped back from self-immolation Rotary has not so much matured as expanded mightily. First came the survivors, trooping with undiminished spirit out of the long shadows of the Occupation. In the first twelve months of peace Clubs were re-admitted officially from Belgium, Burma, Czechoslovakia, France, Greece, Luxembourg, the Netherlands, Norway, the Philippines and Singapore. By the end of 1949, Austria, Germany, Italy, Japan and Korea were back in the fold. It was rather akin to the observation made by Sir Winston Churchill's distant cousin, the adventuresome and very brave journalist Anita Leslie, who recalled in her memoirs, *A Story Half Told*, published in 1983, that the swallows which made their regular Maytime journey back to Germany from Africa in 1945 flew in and out and around all the bombed buildings searching for places to nest, puzzled that almost all their familiar haunts had disappeared in the desert of rubble. But find new homes they did. And so did Europe's Rotarians, such that by 1953, when the dynamic George Means — outfacer of MacArthur in restoring Rotary to Japan — succeeded Philip Lovejoy as General Secretary of Rotary International, world membership was fast approaching 400,000 and there were nearly 8,000 Clubs.

Such a huge organisation could be run no longer from two floors at 35 East Wacker Drive, regarded as the fountain-head of the Movement for twenty-five years. Indeed, the move to East Wacker Drive from South Michigan Avenue (see Chapters Thirteen and Fifteen) had in itself been seen by some as signs of elephantiasis in the Movement, though it was then half the size it was to become by the end of the war. In 1927, when Stanley Leverton, of the Rotary Club of London, was at Headquarters as a member of the International "Extension" Committee (whose function was to foster new Clubs around the world), the visit rather overwhelmed him, leading him to comment to his colleagues, "As a nation, of course, America thinks big and acts big. I am wondering if you sometimes act too big. The impression I have formed in Chicago leads me to wonder how long this organising on such an enormous scale will continue. Is there not a danger that you will over-organise and over-develop?"

His doubts were soon assuaged into such a conversion that it was his brainchild — the so-called "Leverton Plan" — which permitted the greatest outburst of growth of all, when he conceived the idea that one Club, especially a large Club formed to serve a great city, could share recruiting rights within its limits with new Clubs formed with smaller geographical areas inside those limits. Leverton's immediate concern, first put forward in 1933, was obviously with London, but its applications were clear in other vast — as we call them now, in characteristically ugly parlance — conurbations, like New York, like, even, the holy of holies, Chicago! Ideas do not spread like wildfire in Rotary (there are too many wind-breaks formed against them), so it was not until the St Louis Convention of 1943, ten years later, that the Leverton Plan became part of the Rotary Constitution; yet in time for the post-war explosion, all the same.

But there were Clubs which did not re-emerge and have never re-emerged, those which have fallen beneath the crushing weight of the Iron and Bamboo Curtains, though those in Czechoslovakia came back briefly to life after a false dawn of liberation until the Communist *coup d'état* in 1948 and the murder of Rotarian Jan Masaryk, hurled from his office window into the courtyard of his foreign ministry on 10th March. Lost were the thirty-nine Clubs of Czechoslovakia then, together with the ten Clubs of Poland, Latvia's two, Lithuania's two, Estonia's three. Then there were Bulgaria's eight, Romania's nine, Hungary's fourteen — all were lost. The twenty-five Clubs of mainland China soon vanished into oblivion too, along with the four of Manchuria. And though Yugoslavia heroically shook free of the Russian manacles and regained its destiny, its once thriving thirty-four Rotary Clubs have never returned.

Yet the Rotary bell, placed by the Club President wherever Rotarians meet for their weekly meal, seemed to sound a tocsin of survival round the globe. Two miraculous survivals can be recorded from the many, these two occurring on opposite sides of the earth, from the Eastern War and the Western War. The bell of the Cebu Club, from the island of Cebu in the Philippines (founded in 1932), turned up shiny and undamaged in the crowded Manila internment camp, sitting in full view in the camp's broadcasting studio, with the Japanese completely unaware of what it really was. The bell of the Rotary Club of Kristiansand (founded in 1924), on the southern tip of Norway, was also discovered intact in the cupboard of the Gestapo headquarters in Stavanger, where it had remained, apparently also unrecognised, for five years. Throughout the horrors of the totalitarian Occupation, both in lands of piling heat and heaping snow, possession of these bells would have meant arrest, if not instant torture and death. The mysteries of their survival are perhaps very human ones, but they are no less miraculous for that.

When the Second World War ended, the world's first Service Club Movement was forty years old, but the doubts and hesitations which are traditionally supposed to accompany that milestone of existence were blanketed out by the relief and celebrations of victory. The psychologist author of *Life Begins at Forty*, who had addressed the Havana Convention in 1940 (see Chapter Nineteen), might conceivably have had plenty to say directly to its members on this significant birthday also, but chose not to. Instead, Professor Walter B. Pitkin, of Columbia University, contributed an illuminating article to *The Rotarian* on the brilliant successes being achieved in rehabilitating war-handicapped soldiers, proceeding from there to praise the realistic, non-self-pitying approach which accelerated the adjustment of so many of the brave young men. His subject-matter was still essentially the same, of course. Most people — at least, in the Anglo-Saxon sphere — regard their fortieth birthday as the worst of all handicaps (though whether in spite of, or because of, Pitkin's famous book title, is arguable), far worse than losing a limb from a bullet or bayonet or hearing from a bomb-burst. Worse because though artificial aids can restore mobility and sound, none can restore youth. And indeed Professor Pitkin used his article to make a profound comment which the Movement would have done well to ponder closely, had it been in a mood for self-examination, and this was rather too much to ask in the climate of global excitement which closed a shell of camouflage over his words. We shall remove their camouflage presently in the next chapter, which is the last of this history, but for the time being leave the words to watch their time.

For Paul Harris himself, the relief and celebrations were drowned in his own grief at losing his closest friend a few months later, the coal-merchant Silvester Schiele, his neighbour for so many long years, on 17th December 1945. No one knew Paul better, or Rotary better; no one saw more clearly how the Movement would develop when the terrible war was at last over. "Rotary is bigger," Schiele acknowledged, "but Rotary is not yet better than the man in whose brain it was born."

But did even Schiele guess there would be nearly 1 million Rotarians forty years on? Or where they would be? For administrative purposes and organisational convenience, the Movement is now divided into six regions. By the end of 1982, those regions, in round numbers, had enlarged to the following totals: the United States, Canada, Puerto Rico and Bermuda had 379,000 Rotarians; Latin-America and the West Indies had 86,000; Europe, North Africa and the Near East had 163,000; the Middle East, Asia and the Far East had 163,500; Central and Southern Africa, Australia, New Zealand and the Pacific Islands had 62,000; and Great Britain and Northern Ireland, together with the Republic of Ireland, had 60,500. The ten nations with the largest number of Rotary Clubs (again in round numbers) were: the United States with 6,100 Clubs; Japan with 1,500; Brazil with 1,200; England with 1,100; India with 1,000; Australia with 950; France with 680; Argentina with 600; Canada with 500; and the Federal Republic of Germany with 475 Clubs. The rate of "Extension" has multiplied five times since the end of the war, increasing by about 500 Clubs annually. Indeed, it is now an astonishing fact that once every fourteen hours a new Rotary Club is formed somewhere in the world, and an even more astonishing fact that 70 per cent of Rotary International now exists *outside* the United States!

But the biggest triumph still belongs to Big Jim Davidson, and Paul Harris always knew this would be so. Most Rotarians had long forgotten their own "Marco Polo" who had taken the Movement to Asia and the Far East on his own broad back, but Harris made special reference to him in that last Message he wrote for *The Rotarian.* "When Jim's health and strength were failing", wrote Paul, as his own failed rapidly, "he spent three years in completing the span of the world. . . . After reporting to Rotary International's Board in Chicago, Jim returned to Canada and died." In 1982, when the figures above were compiled, the heritage of Davidson's great sacrifice in Asia had reached 163,500 Clubs. It has been projected that within fifty to seventy years that number will have risen to include 600,000 members, and Asia will be by far the largest segment of the Rotary world.

Which seems to prove that, after all, it was by the surest instinct that the tree Harris planted in Chicago had reached out its tendrils first in 1908 to the shores of the Pacific. Most of his fellow-members, as we saw, were dedicated to keeping the Golden Wheel in the New World. Paul in his deepest heart yearned for it to return to the Old World. Having conquered both of those worlds, the Wheel now rolls at an ever-accelerating pace towards an even older world. Midway between them all, of course, lies that oldest world of all, where the Wheel and the Garden of Eden were one. But Paul Harris himself was never complacent, and though his Message to Rotarians was entitled (presumably by the Editor of *The Rotarian*) "The Best Is Yet to Be", his warning in 1945 was abrasive and challenging:

> Is everything all right in Rotary? If so, God pity us. We are coming to the end of our day. . . .
>
> No, thank God, everything is all wrong. There probably is no part or parcel of Rotary which cannot stand improvement. . . .
>
> I like to think that the pioneering days of Rotary have just begun. What's 40 years in the life of a great Movement? There are just as many new things to be done as ever there were. Kaleidoscopic changes are taking place, many of them without our will. Even to hang to the fringe of this

fast-changing world is about all most of us can do. Rotary simply must continue to pioneer or be left in the rear of progress.

Few listened, for the huge explosion in Clubs and membership was about to take place. The old man was deemed a maundering Job.

Yet he was right. The world forgot its guilt much faster after the Second World War than after the First. The crime being so huge, it could not do otherwise. I remember my brother Teddy telling me how all RAF officers like himself, resting from long months of battle, had "tours of duty" which involved taking turns to bring back the bodies of dead pilots to their bravely grieving families. Since the bodies themselves had almost always been destroyed in a plane crash, inextricably mashed into the wreckage, the coffins my brother reverently escorted and saluted were usually filled with stones. This became a parable of the post-war world wherever the totalitarian holocaust had passed. No one knew where the bodies were buried, only the coffins. All the lost and bereaved could say, with a new terrible meaning to Yeats's line, was, "Tread softly because you tread on my dreams." But, alas, that's what dreams are for.

Thus man manoeuvres his past to manure his future. The late beloved in their final wooden conformity were consigned to mass graves as surely as those rags and bones which were soon bulldozed into yesterday when the fighting stopped. The memory was too terrible to forget, but its burden soon exceeded the baggage allowance for sane travel; just retribution would have gelded the world. The victory parades soon over, following each other like lemmings we marched breathless behind the drums of the defeated into the pace-maker years, where everyone found a heart who could afford it. You either kept up or were swept up. Rotary followed Paul's advice and strode forward with the rest in the building boom that rose over the killing-ground. Science may indeed be the record of dead religions, but if religions prove to be true they deserve no better and technology, in the event, gave rich compost to more faiths than ever before. And in the rising clamour of new liturgies, more and more men, repelled by so many muddied altars, lured to the Golden Calf, turned to the Golden Wheel instead.

So it was that under George Means the Rotary International Secretariat, Headquarters of the World Movement, was moved out of central Chicago at long last into a custom-made building erected on an undeveloped site in the northern suburb of Evanston. Here, the symbolic first spadeful of turf was turned, an event sandwiched neatly for the historian between the death of Stalin and the coronation of Queen Elizabeth II, and by August 1954 "1600 Ridge Avenue" was open for business. It is there to this day and nearly 1 million men in 158 nations know the address as well as they know their own, for it is every Rotarian's second home. It is set on an attractively landscaped corner of a very busy intersection, for Evanston has been a city in its own right since 1892 and the home of one of the great American universities, Northwestern. Rotary Headquarters is also right in the heart of Cook County, the last bastion of the old-style Irish-American politicos whose votes took John F. Kennedy into the presidency by a knife-edged margin. Within this imposing porticoed three-storey limestone building works a staff of more than 300 men and women from over thirty countries, administering the enormous commonwealth of practical compassion and multinational community service which is what those million individual members in their 20,000 Clubs have now become.

If, in moving away from East Wacker Drive, the Movement thought it was at last exorcising the associative spirit of Capone, gangsterism and political and business corruption which Rotary had done so much to combat, however, it was mistaken. No Tony Lombardo has been gunned down in the midday streets just a block or so from its new Headquarters, true enough. But it was there in a suburban Evanston that in 1930 the Business Men's and Women's Pistol Club had been formed by the Mayor and the Chief of Police (themselves later proved associates of a North Side Crime Syndicate running illicit liquor, gambling, prostitution and "protection") to fight back against the criminals with naked fire-power from under respectable armpits which till then had harboured nothing more lethal than deodorants. These good citizens were only putting into practice the flip-side, so to speak, of the Golden Rule which both Harris and Perry held to be the heart of Rotary motivation, that is to say when doing unto others as they might do unto you, be sure to do it to them first. Said Police Chief Freeman, "We are equipping merchants and professional men and women for war against crime. . . . We are arming the members with .38 calibre police automatics, and they will also be instructed how to disarm gangsters." One hopes that at meetings of the Evanston Rotary Club of that time which had then been in existence for ten years, "artillery" was checked at the door, but the episode illustrates clearly yet again that the origins of the Movement, both in central and outer Chicago, drew up plans that were battle-plans in a war that was physical as much as philosophical, and front line in both aspects.

As for Evanston in more peaceful days, though walking alone after dark is still not encouraged, the new Headquarters remains in the mainstream of the good fight. The present General Secretary, Herbert A. Pigman, only the fifth incumbent, successor to Harry Stewart, who in turn had succeeded George Means, sees no essential difference in the function of the Secretariat at Headquarters from what it has always been. "The original purpose remains", he says, "communications and administration, even though the Secretariat has expanded from a roll-top desk in Ches Perry's office on South Michigan to eight thousand square-metres here at Evanston."

And he is of course right. In spite of the post-war outburst, Rotary has expanded, not grown. And the fact that Rotary International remains centred at Chicago (never mind the change of venue, to every Rotarian Headquarters is "Chicago") means that, no matter how many languages can be heard chattering away on Ridge Avenue, most of the key executive positions remain filled by Americans. And though membership dues are paid in all the world's currencies, they are realised in the universal currency, the almighty dollar. A huge amount now of almighty dollars. In 1982, Herb Pigman was administering an annual budget of over $15 million.

An even greater sum was being disbursed from Evanston in furtherance of an idea Arch Klumph had put forward in 1917 (see Chapter Nine) when, presiding as the sixth President of Rotary International at the Atlanta, Georgia, Convention, he had success-fully recommended the setting up of an Endowment Fund "for the purpose of doing good in the world" two months after the United States had entered the First World War. The Rotarians of Kansas City, Missouri, started contributions with a gift of $26.50 and other Clubs followed, but the notion was rather swallowed up in the immediate national and international crisis and remained a half-forgotten Amendment to Article XII of the Constitution until eleven years later. In 1928, the persistence of Arch Klumph achieved the actual establishment of the Fund "to be administered through the Rotary Foundation". This was the year, it will be remembered, that both Paul Harris and Jim Davidson set out on their travels round the world, one to reinforce the message of Rotary, the other to implant it, and this time the Fund had the more concrete goal of furthering the Sixth Object of Rotary — now the Fourth — that is, advancing the cause of international understanding, which Klumph then saw as being best achieved by the spreading to all nations of the enlightenment of Rotary's Code of Ethics. "When the Rotary campaign for ethical business conduct spreads through-out the world and is accepted," he wrote, "one of the greatest and most serious hidden underlying causes of jealousy and war will have been removed." Klumph, averting his eyes from the deposit of $26.50 from the Kansas Club, though by then it had no doubt accrued substantial interest, called for an ever-increasing avalanche of gifts and bequests from both Rotarians and non-Rotarians that would one day reach (he boldly forecast) the staggering total of $10 million. Unfortunately, his optimistic call had barely gone out when stock-markets crashed all over the globe and the more assertive governments took their cue instead from the ethics of Chicago's *alter ego*, the thriving enterprises of Al Capone.

In 1937, the Foundation tried again, setting a more ardent goal of $2 million and reverting to the tactic of twenty years before when it was vague in purpose, an editorial in *The Rotarian* stating only that the Foundation was "so set up that its strength can be used with effectiveness at points where the fabric of our society may be weakening". Response was still far from promising and, when Paul Harris reached his biblical span the following year, the "Paul Harris Seventieth Birthday Remembrance Fund" was established and it was announced that Clubs in the United States, Canada, Newfoundland and Bermuda had sent contributions amounting to $100 for every year of the Founder's life. Which sounded better than $7,000.

In 1947, assets of $500,000 were announced by Arch Klumph, who said that $100,000 would go to aid war-affected Rotarians. He then once more announced that the Foundation was setting a target of $2 million, but he was addressing an audience largely indifferent to his scheme, fine and fantastic as it was, and mostly unaware either of who he was or indeed who Paul Harris was. It was not the Founder's life but his death that would release the dam.

Harris died in January 1947, and it soon became known that he had requested no flowers and, moreover, had made it clear he wanted no statue or other memorial in granite or bronze. Should anyone desire to honour his memory, their money would be much better spent towards the goal of better understanding between nations. The Rotary International Board of Directors had approved the Foundation's new $2 million plan only the week before, and now, as contributions began to flow in spontaneously from all over the country, requesting that the gifts be designated in memory of the late Founder, Klumph wasted no time in renaming his life-long project, so long still-born or frustrated after brief growth, the Paul Harris Memorial of the Rotary Foundation, with the precise object stated of enabling graduate students to pursue their education for one year in a nation other than their own.

Within twelve months, ten students — called at first "Paul Harris Fellows" — were enjoying the benefits of the Foundation, and the fund had swelled to over $600,000. Suddenly, there was no stopping it: the extraordinary man who single-handedly had wrought the shape of Rotary and its essential aims and philosophy by making it the sublimation of his life, brought about the Movement's greatest achievement by the sublimation of his death. By 1982, more than $120 million had been contributed by Rotarians all over the world to provide one year's advanced study to over 12,600 young men and women, each one chosen by a Rotary Club to send abroad, each one taken care of and befriended by a Rotary Club in the "foreign" country in which he or she had chosen to study. Thirty years after the notion of a Foundation Endowment Fund had come into existence, it took identity and motive as a memorial to one of this century's most remarkable men.

Each of Rotary's Districts selects candidates from names submitted by Clubs and are allowed to apply for one or more scholarships according to the amount that District has contributed during the previous year to the Foundation. Since 1965, the Foundation has also funded Group Exchange Teams, made up of cross-sections of business and professional men from one District who spend six or eight weeks exploring the life of men in similar occupations in a District of another nation. The following year, the second District sends a group of similar professional and business men on a return visit to the first District. As of 1983, at the time of writing, women have been included in these exchanges. The graduate students and the groups being exchanged share one common denominator: none nominated to benefit from the Foundation Awards can be either a Rotarian or related to a Rotarian.

One thing has changed, however. The students are no longer called Paul Harris Fellows. That name was soon given to individuals honoured by being presented with a Paul Harris Fellowship Award, a means of raising funds for the Rotary Foundation which has proved enormously successful. Any Rotary Club which gives $1,000 (or its equivalent in any national currency) to the Foundation has the right to present a Paul Harris Fellowship Award to anyone of its choice, man or woman, Rotarian or non-Rotarian, and the success of this scheme, with the educational opportunities it has brought to nearly 13,000 graduates and nearly 8,000 Group Exchange Teams, has more than compensated its beneficiaries for the loss of their old title. Sometimes called "Awardees" or "recipients", their most widely accepted compromise name has simply been Paul Harris Scholars, categories of which have today broadened to include Undergraduates as well as Graduate, Vocational Students (where experience is more important than academic achievements), Teachers of the Handicapped, and Journalists.

Though the Paul Harris Fellowship Awards provide approximately 75 per cent of all contributions to this most successful and widely known of all Rotary activities, they have also provided ammunition for acute dissension within the Movement, sporadic but none the less significant. Rotarians in Great Britain and Ireland and, to a large extent, on the Continent of Europe, tend to place the major emphasis of the Award on the honour it bestows on those who receive it. It is conceived as a merit award, to be given as a mark of high esteem and accepted as such. Rotarians elsewhere, treating it principally as a money-raising gimmick, cheerfully buy it for themselves, often their wives, not seldom their entire families. The extreme manifestation of this tendency undoubtedly occurs in the Far East, and in Hong Kong and Japan there are entire Clubs whose every member sports a Paul Harris Fellowship button in his lapel. Some Clubs even make it a condition of entry that new members contribute the $1,000 which will permit them to wear this treasured button! Needless to say, this latter practice has no official sanction from Rotary International Headquarters, which nevertheless welcomes the flood of money which is rapidly making the Far East Clubs a major source of Foundation Funds, as indeed these are becoming the prime growth area of Rotary itself.

The principal concern of Chicago (or "Evanston", as today the Movement's Headquarters is more frequently referred to) is to have the largest increase of funds possible for Foundation purposes. The principal dismay at such an attitude is undoubtedly registered by British Rotarians, who maintain that this crude "buying" of honours is a deplorable practice and detrimental to the public image of Rotary, a complaint which perhaps comes oddly from a nation which barely blinked an eyelash when the so-called "Lloyd George Fund" came into blatant operation in 1918, a year after Arch Klumph's first inspiration, with the aim of selling knighthoods, baronetcies and peerages to wealthy war profiteers so as to raise £4 million as quickly as possible for the Welsh Wizard's future election expenses, an enterprise which resulted, incidentally, in such an appallingly corrupt Honours List in January 1919 that it was deliberately camouflaged by tacking on a knighthood for the most famous Rotarian of the day, Harry Lauder (not that Sir Harry knew, of course). Nevertheless, Rotarians in Great Britain and Ireland are extremely sensitive on the issue, and, by an ironic twist of fate, their feelings were clearly mirrored by Sir Harry's greatest avowed disciple, the American entertainer Danny Kaye, whose solemn pleasure at being presented with a Paul Harris Award at the San Francisco Convention in 1977 swiftly turned to astonishment when he saw the same Award promptly being given to more than twenty other individuals by an International President blithely unaware of the impression he was creating — until Mr Kaye stormed out of the Convention Hall and refused to perform further for the puzzled audience.

Today, it is finally being accepted that a new Award, for merit only, must be created by Rotary for those they wish to honour other than by banking their gifts, and this new Award may indeed have come into existence by the time the present book appears.

Foundation scholars are selected not only for their obvious worthiness in their field, but for their judged capacity to be good "ambassadors" for their homeland in the foreign country where they will study and travel, and this fostering of international understanding amongst the youth of the post-war generations has won for the Movement, with those of all nations who understand the Foundation or are even aware of it, universal praise and deep respect. Many of the first Foundation Scholars have since become men and women of influence and high position in industry, the professions and politics, and their year as a Foundation Scholar, they admit, has had a profoundly formative effect on their view of the interdependent world we all inhabit today.

Whereas the very highest disbursement for a scholarship in the year when the Foundation took life from the Founder's death, 1947, was just under $3,000, the average Award (at time of writing) requires to be at least $13,500 per scholarship, and thus it is not surprising that roughly 90 per cent of funds received has to be spent on deepening and broadening the international experience of the young — a clearly much-needed counterpoise to modern youth's amazingly nomadic habit, in their knapsack hordes, of bravely but anarchically trying to engulf the world. Yet the three aims of the Foundation — the wording, but not the sense, has since been pared and refined — were declared as:

1. the promotion of Rotary Foundation Scholarships (sic) for advanced study;
2. the fostering of any tangible and effective projects which have as their purpose the furthering of better understanding and friendly relations between the peoples of different nations; and
3. the providing of emergency relief for Rotarians and their families wherever war or other disaster has brought general destruction and suffering.

And evolving under the third aim there has now developed, adjusting to the contemporary social climate, a concentration on the needs of the Third World, and this emphasis is utilising the other 10 per cent.

The Foundation scheme under which this is accomplished, is called (and was so named by Clem Renouf, a small-town lawyer of Queensland, Australia, who launched it during his presidency of Rotary International in 1978-9) the Health, Hunger and Humanity Programme, mercifully abbreviated to 3-H. This scheme, in one tremendous imaginative lap, extended the local community service projects of Rotary Clubs to encompass whole nations and geo-graphical regions of the world, so that the essential Rotary ideals remain unaffected: the giving of individual personal service, aug-mented, when needed, by a financial back-up, which again comes from voluntary contributions from Rotarians. It should be remem-bered, when one contemplates the vast sums involved and the scale and scope of the Foundation established in memory of Paul Harris, whether for education, professional training, group exchanges or 3-H projects, that almost every single penny is found, and found on a voluntary basis, from within the Rotary Movement. Several great pharmaceutical firms, commencing with one in Canada, have donated vaccines for measles, diphtheria, polio, tetanus and other diseases, and volunteer medical teams, formed by Rotarians, have taken these to the Philippines, into the countries of Central America − often under conditions of extreme personal peril − and into Africa. In Malawi, polio is not only fought but its effects are miti-gated by a two-year programme of corrective surgery on its victims and by teaching the people how to continue this work and to design and manufacture simple braces and crutches from local materials. To the teeming miserable refugee camps of Hong Kong and Thai-land have gone Rotary doctors and dentists from the developed world in year-round relays, taking unpaid time-off from their busy practices and regardless of discomfort, the risk of contracting disease themselves and dangers from political upheavals. Many of those who have gone, and taken their wives with them to help the world's afflicted in some regions where even sanity and sanitation take a low priority as against sheer survival, have been volunteers of advanced years, eagerly emerging from the secure comforts of retirement to offer their skills in the cause of tending the great wounds still festering in the hot continents. The leprosy clinic of Lambaréné, run by that controversial and saintly genius, the late Dr Albert Schweitzer (philosopher, theologian, musician, mission doctor, Nobel Prize-winner and, symbolic of reconciliation, Honorary Member of two Rotary Clubs, Colmar in France and Passau in Germany), has been rescued, restored, rebuilt and restaffed by the concerted effort of Rotarians all over Europe, with German Rotar-ians playing a leading role. This was the true signalling by Europe of the end of nightmare, a magnificent witness by European Rotary that the nation of Bach, whose true genius Schweitzer had restored to mankind, had risen whole from the banal and tawdry Götterdämmerung by which Hitler, the worshipper at a warped and morally diseased Bayreuth, had nearly torn Wagner's genius, and his country's, from the world.

The final stage to date of the developing Paul Harris Memorial Fund has been the setting up of the Rotary Foundation Endowment for World Understanding and Peace, which will project and protect the ideals of Paul Harris perhaps even beyond his own most daring imaginings and hopes, ensuring secure financial support in perpetuity for ever more ambitious, ever more imaginative endeavours of Rotary service from all nations to all nations, so ranking it among the world's largest foundations. An ocean of compassion, and the honour of the first drop of $26.50 will remain for all time with Kansas City, as will also the honour (see Chapter Nine) of first flying the Official Flag of Rotary.

Paul's horizons were always boundless, but so was his transparent humility. In his first published writing for Rotary in 1911, he had declared, when there were still, to his knowledge, less than thirty Clubs in the world: "Rotary is a huge powerful machine. Unguided, it could thrash down the aisles of time, a menace to all mankind. Well directed, it will become the humanising instrumentality of which we need not be ashamed." And in the last interview he gave before his death, he told the interviewer who had asked him the question he had heard a thousand times, not counting the times he had asked it of himself, about whether he had foreseen the growth of his Movement, "When a man plants an unpromising sapling in the early springtime, can he be sure that someday here will grow a mighty tree? Does he not have to reckon on rain and sun and the Smile of Providence?"

And Rotary Clubs are still places where "men can be boys again?" Yes, but to a wide variation of degrees, depending on which part of the world Rotary is formed. After a hideous war when many thousands paid for their membership with disgrace, flight, imprisonment, torture and death, Rotary could never be the same again in such externals. Where frivolities come naturally to the place and occasion, no one revels so late in life in such childish nonsense as a Rotarian. As the older generations in the Clubs pass, however, and their concerns grow more serious in a serious post-war world where "peace" has still managed to bring death to 10 million people, even without benefit of nuclear fission, the virtues of youth regained have been increasingly experienced at one or two removes. This preoccupation with youth was inevitable, given the culture from which Rotary grew. After his visit to Chicago and points West,

Oscar Wilde had written: "The youth of America is their oldest tradition . . . to hear them talk, one would imagine they were in their first childhood." That remark appears in *A Woman of No Importance*, which Chicago was very anxious to stage, though in vain. It was in a later essay that Wilde continued his theme, stating that American young people "spare no pains at all to bring up their parents properly and to give them a suitable, if somewhat late, education. . . . In America, the young are always ready to give to those who are older than themselves the full benefits of their inexperience". Such as in Vietnam. In the Rotary Movement, where old dogs are for ever under the delusion that they can teach young ones new tricks, this was an American obsession that proved too readily exportable, since no one likes to grow old, except at the expense of the young; hence history.

The long involvement, sometimes obsession, with Boys' Clubs and Boys' Committees has now been replaced, and improved upon, by the forming of Clubs called Interact and Rotaract, both sponsored by Rotary Clubs and, to a greater or lesser extent, supervised by them. Interact Clubs are for boys and girls in the "intermediate years" (hence Inter + Act as the name) immediately prior to university. In different parts of the world, this means different specifications in terms of schooling, but the average age span of members is fourteen to eighteen. Rotaract (telescoped from Rotary-in-Action) is for the age group eighteen to twenty-eight and — after some hesitation — was also constituted for both sexes, the strange Rotary logic being that the older male and female animals get, the less they can be trusted with each other. Rotary is still for men only. Both these organisations were formed in the sixties, that decade when youth seemed set to take over the world on every continent. It was less flaming youth than youth with a torch in its hand, both figuratively and literally. In Paris, they fought society from piled barricades; in Washington, they paraded with their guitars in the cause of Civil Rights; in Tokyo, students threatened the lives of visiting statesmen of the West; in Peking, they drove professors from universities into the paddy-fields; in London, rather than thumb their noses, they put pins through them and were mainly content to make the country "swing"; in Guatemala City, they laid siege to the private homes of government ministers. The principal difference between this manifestation of outrageous youth and that which had brightened the twenties was that in the case of the latter rebels, they had aped, as best they could, the depravity of their betters; rebels in the sixties, on the other hand, aspired to the mindless anarchy of hooliganism in dress, manners and personal appearance. The so-called "upward mobility" in an increasingly classless society which the Western world's hyperactive reformers loudly trumpeted, became in reality a downward swagger which depended for its impact upon there being a class structure to horrify (and to slip back into when pubescent drives became as boring to their possessors as to their onlookers). Those young men and women who did not slip back into the shock-proof bourgeois world, instead slipped farther into another characteristic they shared with their unconscious models of the 1920s — promiscuity and drugs. The miracles of modern science and the developing skills of the Do-It-Yourself craze brought these to a poisoned peak of availability; the "kicks from cocaine" of forty years back were swamped by a saturation of young bodies with cannabis, heroin, barbiturates, amphetamines, mescalin, "uppers" and "downers" of all kinds, while different varieties of the contraceptive pill replaced the Lost Generation of the twenties with the Lust Generation of the sixties, from which the Welfare State had removed even irresponsibility. Easy virtue and illegitimacy became meaningless terms with the advent of the one-parent family, a literal concept of supreme idiocy which was morally, economically, socially and — above all, because as we talk we live — grammatically, a contradiction in terms.

Exactly as the Rotary Movement had developed a response to the casual amorality of the business world in the early years of the century, so it formed Rotaract and Interact Clubs as a practical response to the amorality of youth as the century nudged into its third quarter. And young people everywhere, conscious as anyone that their "swinging" was beginning to take place at the end of an infinite length of rope which the guilt of their elders was giving them, have responded with enthusiasm. Adopting goals identical with those of Rotary, Rotaractors have displayed community service drives fully equal to those of their sponsoring Clubs, often surpassing them in variety and originality while usually enjoying themselves far more, being less inhibited by tradition and far more aware of the principle which directed and inspired the thinking of Paul Harris more than any other, the only principle in fact that he, unlike Ches Perry and most of his fellow-Rotarians of the Chicago "establishment", was perhaps prepared to evolve into dogma: that doing good for one's fellow-man can be enormous fun, a principle shared by most religious communities, and certainly by Christian ones until the Puritans got their stifling hands on it.

Today, again rounding up numbers, there are 4,000 Rotaract Clubs with 80,000 members in eighty-nine countries, and over 4,000 Interact Clubs with 91,500 members in seventy-eight countries. Interact is strongest (at the time of writing) in the United

States, where it is closely interwoven into the school system; whereas the fastest growth area of Rotaract today is in Great Britain and Ireland. But they are both rooting well all over the world and, while maintaining a fairly close benevolent eye on Interact Clubs, most Rotarians are wise enough to intrude as little as possible into the affairs of their Rotaract offspring, disconcerted as they are liable to be by the insights occasionally offered by young people into Rotary effectiveness — and often, horror of horrors, by women Rotaractors — and disinclined as they are to court rebuff by having their advice rejected or even their own deficiencies in understanding of Rotary revealed. In effect, with the rapid growth of Rotaract, we have come full circle to the spirit of 1905; the spirit of the New England rapscallion has found joyful, untrammelled rebirth.

The years since the Second World War in Rotary have also been highlighted by two great reconciliations, one within the Movement and one without. We have seen during this history how the relationship between Rotary International, as administered from Chicago by Chesley Perry, and the Rotary Club of Great Britain and Ireland, as founded by the free-wheeling enterprise of Paul Harris's "wonder-working Irishman", Stuart Morrow, as well as through the more orthodox channels on guidance from Headquarters, had undergone periodic strain, culminating in the first great climax of polarisation of attitude between Perry and Harris in 1912. It was then that Paul signed the charter for the formation of the London Club, after which, worn out to the point of exhaustion, he retired to Comely Bank, leaving the field clear for Perry. The subsequent war in Europe came too quickly for that brilliant supremo to do anything but watch from the sidelines as the Clubs in the British Isles formed their own Association.

After the great Edinburgh Convention of 1921 (outlined in Chapter Twelve), a generous attempt had been made to regularise the situation by delegates whose ears still rang with the bagpiped hospitality and cheer of the newly knighted Sir Harry Lauder, who then combined his role as one of America's favourite entertainers with that of being its favourite Rotarian as well. During the war he had been the only non-American member of George M. Cohan's "Over There League" (progenitor of the Second World War's USO entertainers for United States forces) and had celebrated the war's end by being the only non-opera and non-ballet star to perform at the Manhattan Opera House. The success and euphoria of Edinburgh had not a little to do with the decision taken at the Los Angeles Convention in 1922, whereby permission was given not only to British Clubs to continue as a self-governing "territorial unit" (a unit described in 1914 as "a valuable ally to the International

Association . . . to the end that by strong and active co-operation the cause of Rotary would be furthered in Europe"), but extended to include the assemblage of similar units elsewhere in the form of a "national or territorial administration", fullest control being granted to such units "over all matters which are exceptionally national in their scope".

The 1927 Convention at Ostend — the first on the Continent, addressed by King Albert, himself a Rotarian ("I think I am alone in the classification to which I belong") — applauded the royal acclaim for "groups of individuals, working close together like you do for a common purpose" and decided that some Rotarians, not more than a Channel away, were not working closely enough, and, in the gleeful report of Chesley Perry, "action was taken to eliminate national units from the administrative scheme of Rotary International". However, even Perry accepted that "legislation established one exception" in a passage in which one can clearly detect the grinding of General Secretarial teeth. Thus RIBI remained.

In 1934, Chesley came with Paul and Jean Harris to London to debate the matter again (see Chapter Sixteen), but had to return frustrated without the prize. The last great effort from Chicago to get rid of what Headquarters saw as the anomaly of RIBI — there were many in RIBI, on the contrary, and not only there, who saw the international control of Chicago as an anomaly — was begun in 1960, just after Ches Perry had died and perhaps therefore as an unconscious tribute to his memory. If so meant, it did not succeed. Though mounted on the argument of membership "per capita" dues — since RIBI, governing itself, paid far less in annual dues to International Headquarters than did Clubs in the rest of the Rotary world — the quarrel, as Roger Levy's perceptive and indispensable history of RIBI points out, was "at first sight about money. But in fact it was about power".

Through eight years the last great upsurge in argument rose, punctuated increasingly by accusations, from one side or another, of legislative chicanery, accusations of bad faith, threats of abolition and threats of secession, more or less plainly stated. In 1964, the International Board met outside of the United States of America for the first time ever, but the meeting in London — whether intended to be reassuring or intimidating — ended in a spurious glow of mutual admiration and euphoric confusion at the Savoy Hotel on America's Thanksgiving Day at which the World President Charles W. Pettengill spoke of "the gratitude of the Pilgrim Fathers for the first harvest in a new land. Rotary has had its harvest too: we are grateful for that, and the part which your Clubs have played in bringing it about", which left everyone scratching his head.

The following year, confusion was cleared when Headquarters cast off all restraint and ambiguity, threw aside soft words and flourished the big stick, publishing a report entitled *The Territorial Unit Form of Administration* which amounted to a demand that RIBI be abolished. It was the situation of Lord North and the Thirteen Colonies in reverse and produced a like reaction, led ironically by an Irishman, John Little of the Belfast Club, the first Irishman to be President of RIBI for forty years, his predecessor Charles White (also of Belfast) having provided the Movement with its title of Rotary International, as we have seen in earlier pages. John Little wrote unequivocally in the Rotary journal: "It aims at the destruction of R.I.B.I. for the sake of domination"; and later that year, Austrian Past Rotary Governor Wolfgang Wick, one of the world's most eloquent and influential Rotarians, asked at a great European Conference in Amsterdam, "Where would Europe be without Britain, where would R.I. be without R.I.B.I.?"

By 1968, sanity had prevailed. The presidency of Rotary International was in the very capable and compassionate hands of Richard L. Evans (and Wolfgang Wick was one of his Directors). Evans was now faced with a typically forthright broadside from that old editorial firebrand W.W. Blair-Fish, whom we saw summarily gagged and fired by RIBI in 1941 for his unambiguous views on what he regarded as Chicago's hypocritical stance on the war. This splendidly polemic writer now came out of the wings to centre stage with a searing article, "Centralised Control: R.I.'s Inveterate Vendetta", and he crystallised sentiments widely shared in the British Isles. Evans was the man for the dangerous hour, hailing as he did from Salt Lake City and high as he stood in the counsels of the Mormon Church, whose founder, Joseph Smith, like the Founder of Rotary, progressed from Vermont to Illinois, and whose central principle was "Teach them correct principles, and let them govern themselves". Evans ordered that two nominees from RI and two from RIBI should sit down together and thrash out the dispute. Which they did in three days, in Roger Levy's words, "in an unprecedented atmosphere of fellowship and determination". RIBI's territorial unit was now written into the International Constitution itself for the first time, and its right to govern its own affairs *where they appertained only to British and Irish Clubs* was accepted, while the authority of Rotary International was accepted as overriding where matters of World Rotary were concerned.

Nearly twenty years later, with the balance of Rotary shifting inexorably out of America, and in particular towards the East, regional administrative offices have been set up not only in Zurich, but in Stockholm, Sydney, Tokyo and São Paulo. Many Rotarians believe that the Golden Wheel will soon make a complete turn back to 1922 and that the impracticality of administering 1 million men in 158 countries from a green corner of a northern Chicago suburb will be fully appreciated and that RIBI, having regressed from being model to near-pariah, in the minds of the more diehard Rotarians, will become a model again.

The great reconciliation without the Movement has come between Rotary and the Church of Rome. The first evidence of this came in 1929, and arose, paradoxically enough, in Spain, where Rotary had founded its first European Clubs eight years before. For reasons now largely unknown, but certainly due in part to careless statements by some European Rotarians which were widely misinterpreted, the Spanish clergy became strongly opposed to the Clubs there, and their sentiments spread rapidly through the Catholic hierarchy, culminating in a decree from the Holy See that it was "not expedient" for Catholic priests to join Rotary Clubs or to be present at their meetings. This decree was serious news in many parts of Europe (the ex-German Chancellor, Wilhelm Cuno, the Hamburg shipowner who had supplied funds in early days to Hitler and was a prominent lay Catholic, was much disturbed) and it rang alarm bells, of course, for the predominantly Roman Catholic members in Latin-America. Part of the problem lay in interpreting the term "Service", as in Rotary Service, as indicating a quasi-religious organisation, and in a quite erroneous identification of the Rotary Movement as part of World Freemasony, a centuries-old antagonist of the Vatican. The International President of Rotary that year, Tom Sutton, was fortunately himself a Roman Catholic, and he went as soon as possible to Rome in an attempt to clear up misconceptions there. He saw Cardinal Gaspari, Secretary of State for the Vatican, and believed he had convinced Father Rosa, Editor of *Civiltà Cattolico*, to cease that paper's virulent attacks on Italian Rotarians and the Movement itself. Sutton came away convinced that his mission was accomplished and so informed the first journalists who interviewed him on his return. But he was mistaken and the "promised" article in *Civiltà Cattolico* praising Rotary never appeared.

A few years later, shivers went right through European Rotary after an article appeared in Paris in *La France Catholique*, in which it was stated that there was secret collusion between Freemasonry and Rotary and that Paul Harris had formed Rotary from the inspiration of his membership of a Masonic Lodge. None of this was true but the effect ricocheted as far as Lithuania, where the attack was reprinted in *Rytas*, the official organ of the Lithuanian Christian

Democrat Party. Fortunately, the attack was disproved to such effect that the Editor of *Rytas*, leader of the Catholic Party and a former prime minister, promptly agreed to join the Rotary Club in Kaunas, that country's second city.

Happier auguries appeared when in 1933 the Rotary Club of Paris gave an official reception to Monsignor Baudrillart, Rector of the Catholic University of Paris and President of the Catholic Institute (also a future cardinal); and when Count Franco Ratti, a member of the Rotary Club of Milan, was revealed not only as Minister of Public Works for the Vatican but a nephew of His Holiness Pius XI. Better still, the Pope himself soon after performed the marriage sacrament which united the Count with the daughter of Senator Crespi, a fellow-member of the Milan Club.

But the situation remained bewildering to and traumatic for many Roman Catholic Rotarians and would-be Rotarians and it began to resolve itself on pragmatic lines, with local priests being given discretion by the Vatican on whether or not to discourage Rotarian membership to their laity, depending on local conditions. This was the principal reason why, though the first Rotary Club outside of North America had been formed in Dublin, it was several decades before Ireland could produce more than the three Clubs of Dublin, Belfast and Cork. And it was not until 1975 that the Dublin Rotarians could accomplish the daring move of inviting the Deputy Grand Master of the Masonic Order in Ireland to explain Masonry to its members, thus killing two long-standing bugbears at once.

In January 1951 all seemed to go into reverse for a time, when the Holy Office of the Roman Catholic Church once again decreed that no priests could join Rotary and that "the faithful should be aware of secret, seditious and suspected organisations". But, in contrast to 1929, there was an immediate counter-surge of protest from both Catholics and non-Catholics, in the press and in public utterances, so far in twenty-two years had the worth and prestige of the Movement spread across the globe, proved in peace and war. Once again, by chance, the International President of Rotary, Arthur Laqueux of Quebec, was a Catholic, and the French Canadian deplored the decree in no uncertain terms. He was joined by Monsignor John E. Noll, Roman Catholic Bishop of Fort Wayne, Indiana, also a Rotarian, and Australian Catholics declared the decree "quite incomprehensible".

A supposed association with Freemasonry — condemned since 1730 by six papal bulls — was widely blamed, the suspicions emanating largely from the conduct of some South American Clubs, which it was rumoured had adopted an anti-religious stance;

specifically, Rotary was considered to be linked with the then current persecution of the Church in Mexico. By a supreme irony, the decree which had struck the Rotary world like a bombshell was published just a week after the Movement's repentant scourge, Sinclair Lewis, had died in Rome, and some recalled that their other terrible opponent, G.K. Chesterton, had, after all, died a Catholic convert.

Faced with the surprise and indignation of many Rotarian Catholics, in particular the 3,500 in the Clubs of Italy itself, and also an increasing swell of observations abroad linking the Vatican "persecution" of the Movement with that of Nazi Germany and Soviet Russia, coupled with remarks on the wartime ambivalence of the Vatican towards the Fascist dictatorships and the Jewish holocaust, steps backward began. Bishops were instructed to make local investigations by *Osservatore Romano*, the Vatican newspaper, which professed itself authorised to state the following: "In some nations, because of a prevalent Masonic influx, the action of Rotary Clubs has conflicted with the activity and the ends of the Church. It must be said, however, that such has not been the case in other nations where . . . the attitude of Rotary has shown itself in practice tolerant and benevolent towards religious interests." The Vatican was clearly embarrassed by the violence of world reaction and hastily proceeded to indicate that its strictures applied only to Spain, the Netherlands and "some" South American countries. The fuss soon died away but in 1959 the Catholic Truth Society still felt able to include Rotary in a pamphlet entitled *Forbidden & Suspect Societies*, on this evidence:

> Since Rotary is neither secret, nor seditious, and has never yet been formally condemned by the Church, the implication is clearly that it is in some way suspect and deserving of caution. And we can easily guess the reason for the Church's suspicion. By presenting itself as a guide to good living, in complete independence of any denominational creed or moral authority, Rotary encourages the all too common view that man is his own sufficient guide in interpreting the moral law, that any creed will do, and that no particular religion is obligatory.

Rotary was not, all the same, now bracketed with Masonry as a Society Banned Under Pain of Sin and Excommunication, but with the YMCA, as a Society Banned Under Pain of Sin Only.

But this was the final effort. In November 1970 Pope Paul VI agreed to address gatherings of European Rotarians in Milan and Rome, and in March 1979 Pope John Paul II spoke to 5,000 Rotarians attending the Seventieth Rotary International Convention, asking them "to convey to all your colleagues throughout the world the expression of my esteem for the efforts you are making on behalf of humanity". His Holiness paid special tribute to the Health, Hunger and Humanity Programme during a special Vatican audience, and made this remarkable tribute: "In your efforts and endeavours for the good of man, you can be assured of the understanding and esteem of the Catholic Church."

Misunderstanding was over, and in 1981 this remarkable Pontiff accepted the Award of a Paul Harris Fellowship, shortly after the attempt on his life. Moreover, in 1982, he accepted Rotary International's World Understanding and Peace Award. The mutual tributes had been paid, reciprocal honours given, and the rift healed, sixty-three years on. Since then, an Italian Roman Catholic priest has accepted without hesitation the office of Rotary Governor.

Ten days after the reluctant and mournful declaration on the radio by Neville Chamberlain that the Second World War had begun, Bernard Shaw wrote cheerfully to his biographer Hesketh Pearson from his home at Ayot St Lawrence in Buckinghamshire, thronging with families streaming out of London to imagined safety: "We are in the thick of this evacuation idiocy. . . . What a comfort to know that if we kill 20 millions or so of one another, we'll none of us be missed!" Pearson comments that this was Shaw "in his totalitarian vein". It was also part of Shaw's habitual provocative posture; and, more interestingly, it was a typical manifestation of that mixture of mischief and an uncanny touch for the raw nerve-end of truth which had always made almost his every sentence an infuriating challenge to our more complacent assumptions about human nature. Yet the great tragic fact of the post-war world, a fact no less stark now than in 1945, has been not that 20 million people could die and not be missed, but that 20 million could be born and not be noticed.

Nor was the fact new in 1945. It is the blind side of history, and history — as the present writer has been at pains to point out — is a series of traffic accidents whose victims fill the chronicles of time; the survivors, maimed or whole, are sometimes labelled heroes, sometimes villains. Those who die fill up their quotas also; the labelling often depends on suborned witnesses and those who made the vehicles involved. The only figures who do not feature in statistics are the pedestrians, the great unmarked percentage.

Rotary marked them. Lord Halifax who, Chamberlain had hoped, would succeed him, but who lost out to the popular all-party demand for Churchill, became Britain's wartime Ambassador to Washington. It was in this post, in 1944, that he said: "The Rotary Movement, which originated in the United States of America, has laid the world under no mean debt . . . you have shown how men of different opinions and different races have been able to come together, comprehend one another's problems, and work them out through better understanding."

And yet there remains upon the Rotary conscience one small white cross on one of the Pacific islands where some of the war's bloodiest, most violent and savage fighting took place. It was made and placed there by a Rotarian in uniform, above the spot where a young US marine was buried, mutilated beyond recognition. The enemy had just been defeated in that one brutal collision, dust and deafening echoes still hung in the stifling acrid air, and when the Rotarian was deciding what to write upon the cross, he glanced numbly at his watch and realised that his fellow-Club members back home were just about to assemble for their weekly lunch. Without hesitation, he wrote upon the cross: HE SERVED BEST, BUT DID HE PROFIT MOST?

The cross abides there still, and so does the question. The Golden Wheel can roll and roll ever still farther on, but one day must come to rest and seek the answer. For us all.

CHAPTER TWENTY-FOUR

The Dam-Busters

Inspire Rotarians, Lord, we ask
To live as we profess.
To dignify the daily task;
And serve in selflessness.

For fellowship which here we share,
We offer thanks to Thee.
We pray that it will be our care
To spread it bounteously.

Flags of many nations, hands across the sea.
We pledge to serve together, the hub of Rotary.
Spokes must keep on turning, serving those in need!

Songs for the Rotary Club

Throughout this book we have had glimpses of Paul Harris through the eyes of those who met him in early days, in middle years and late-middle years when he re-emerged from exile at Comely Bank to reclaim his brainchild, and towards the end of his life. In this concluding chapter, it is time to supply slightly deeper portraits from those who met him on various terms of greater or lesser intimacy throughout the years.

Fred Reinhardt met Paul in 1919, when he first rented office space from him in Chicago's First National Bank Building and later joined him in a law partnership that ended only with Paul's death. "Paul was a good lawyer, a thorough, painstaking, conscientious lawyer who held that 'the practice of law is a trust relationship of the highest possible order'.... As head of our law firm, he conducted a serene and happy office. Never in the 28 years of our association, was a word spoken in anger by anyone to anyone of our office family. Paul set this standard." Reinhardt also recalled two articles on the legal profession Paul had written for various journals. One showed the rapscallion, *How to Get Your Money's Worth, Even Out of a Lawyer*, the other the idealist, *The Evolution of Professional Ethics*. Reinhardt for those twenty-eight years shared a two-sided desk with Paul, and presented it to Headquarters after his partner had died.

A visitor from the Rotary Club of Brighton, England, met the Founder of Rotary with some preconception of awe during the twenties; an awe that remained but soon took on very human shape. "Paul is tall," he wrote, "a willowy man like Lord Balfour, but he has a straight backbone and, with all his length, there is in his figure poise and self-possession . . . his dress is always in quiet good taste, there is nothing flamboyant . . . his voice is subdued, and he talks as if his thoughts were larger than his utterance. . . . He can be as funny as the Cheshire Cat in *Alice in Wonderland* and has an equally enchanting smile." The Brighton visitor gave a memorable vignette of Paul at one of the Conventions: "I can see him sitting in a corner of the Winter Garden . . . listening through six long days of declaration, exhortation and oratory . . . with a faraway look on his countenance, as though pondering what *his* responsibility was for all this talk, grateful that the Movement which he had initiated had developed so remarkably, but doubtful of the wisdom of some of the advances adumbrated; a wistful, thoughtful, humble, and, in some sense, a romantic figure."

Justus J. Johnson knew Harris earlier than most, answering an advertisement Paul put in the *Chicago Tribune* in July 1896, just after Paul had opened an office in Chicago following his celebrated five years of "folly". The ad sought a young man "to read law and tend office while lawyers are in court". Though he later decided on another profession, Johnson never forgot the kindness he experienced from the first day:

> I recall with what patience and clarity Paul Harris would explain weighty words and ideas. Soon I came to look upon him not so much as an employer, but as an older brother to whom I felt free to go for counsel. His humanitarian outlook and love for people made a deep impression on my young mind. . . . In later years, I used to drop in at his office in the First National Bank Building. No matter how busy he was, his cordial greeting and friendly handshake gave assurance I was welcome. Each time, I came away charged with the feeling that I had a true friend, and because of that, I, too, could be a better friend to others.

Glenn C. Mead, the Philadelphia lawyer who succeeded Paul as the Second President of Rotary International in 1912, knew the Founder well, having seen much of him during a critical personal period of his life, when he decided to release the reins of control.

> Paul was a clear and profound thinker . . . it was a joy to meet him and converse with him, no matter what the subject might be. He was well read, well informed, kept himself abreast of the times, and knew what was going on everywhere.
>
> In personal intercourse, Paul seemed always to be at his ease; he never set himself up as an oracle above and beyond his friends and fellow Rotarians — he was just one of us. We not only prized his friendship, but wanted to see him and talk and laugh with him, whenever the opportunity offered. It would be a great oversight not to realize and appreciate what a fund of good humor Paul Harris possessed; and there was never any barb in his fun and joking.

Some seemed disappointed. "He rode no white charger, he carried no flaming sword. He was, rather, a very average young man," complained the historian of his own Club, Rotary Number One, Paul's own creation; "he was good-hearted but prone to procrastinate. However, he had one saving grace — he recognized his own shortcomings." This disconcerting verdict would probably have been endorsed with much hilarity by that very average youth, even after he was only partly hidden from view inside the legend in his own lifetime. After all, the Chicago Club's historian did grant him a second saving grace: "He knew there is no greater fallacy than to think you will surely do at some future time the better things you are capable of doing now but neglect to do; he knew that good intentions long deferred lose their vitality. So, when he caught the gleam, he got going. He called a few of The Boys together."

He did indeed, the first of them being Silvester Schiele, of course, the man who was closest to him in life for forty-eight years, and lies nearest him for ever now in Mount Hope Cemetery, and the man who shared that historic spaghetti supper with him at Madame Galli's restaurant on 23rd February 1905 had first approached the young lawyer, like Johnson, in 1896, Paul's first year in Chicago, to ask him to collect a badly needed $20 debt. Paul obliged (it is interesting to note that he shared this knack of successful debt-collecting with Stuart Morrow, the man who brought Rotary across the Atlantic) and the two bachelors, both in their late twenties, shared an hotel room for a time, but: "Paul was a restless fellow. He'd change rooming houses several times a year just to see all the different sides of the city. Economical, too, he slept in his own office for a time. . . . Madame Galli's saw us often. . . . Stage and opera folk used to habit the place on a Saturday night and often we'd sit and talk with them." As for the morning after: "Sunday was our day to shine. In top hats and Prince Albert coats, with gold-headed canes under our arms — and with no money in our jeans or anywhere else — we'd saunter down the boulevard." He and Paul led the high jinks of the first Rotary Club's early days. "After work on Friday evenings, we'd all meet at a lake pier, 35 or 40 of us, get on a ferryboat and cross to Michigan. There we'd travel out to Paw Paw Lake or to some other resort spot, and for two days we'd swim, play baseball, row boats, fish and eat. Foot racing was one of our prize sports. . . . We just got out and ran, with our celluloid collars and cuffs, peg top pants and button shoes."

Harry Ruggles, the man whom Dr Sigmund Spaeth, the foremost historian of American folk-song and popular music, credits with having invented community singing through his Rotary activities, set this portrait down in 1952.

> When he hung out his shingle as a lawyer in Chicago, back in 1896, he was a handsome chap. Most Rotarians are familiar with this picture as a serious bald-headed, middle-aged man. But you should have seen him when he had a full head of dark hair and a moustache. In those days he could swing as dapper a cane and wear as smart a derby [bowler hat] on Sunday walks along Lake Michigan as any young bachelor in Chicago. . . .
>
> Wherever he went, he would stop and talk to folks. It didn't make any difference who. He always seemed restless to meet more people and to know how they lived.

Then Ruggles amplified, in typically picturesque vein: "Paul had as many sides as a centipede has feet. Speakers will tell you he was a man of noble ideals, a profound thinker, and a leader gifted with imagination. I agree. But as I think back over our many years as friends, I can say truthfully I have known no one to get more fun out of just being human. If there's a secret to Paul's success, it's that he just naturally liked people."

Ruggles confirmed the high jinks, remembering Harris and Schiele calling a Rotarian undertaker to their hotel to take care of a "corpse" that moved; and Paul leading members on a long hike in the country, apparently getting "lost", and then suddenly finding a farm where a huge meal was laid on in readiness for them; and the sober-suited, earnest-looking young attorney suddenly turning somersaults in the air, hanging from the straps of a streetcar. "Till the day he died, there was a lot of the boy in Paul."

Paul revealed his continuing love of the outdoors to a young lady from the *Christian Science Monitor* who was sent to interview him in 1935, the year of Rotary's thirtieth birthday. And he certainly had an up-to-date example at hand, for this was the year he paid his last visit to Wallingford and, on an impulse, to celebrate the occasion, revealed himself (completely) as a sixty-seven-year old rapscallion by taking off his clothes in broad daylight and swimming across the half-mile-wide pond and back, as he had often done as a boy, to Grandmother Harris's dismay and Wallingford's scandal-conscious joy. The lady journalist noted other traits of his which were not infrequently observed and commented upon by those who met him at various times throughout his long life. "The man who received me at the door exhibited the manners and features of a New England aristocrat . . . he struck me as friendly and reserved, you might even say shy. Mr. Harris had been received and honored by kings, presidents and premiers . . . but there wasn't a hint of pretentious pride in his manner. He spoke simply, his spare Yankee face lighting up with a smile now and then."

Two years later, the Reverend Wilfred Float, of the Rotary Club of High Wycombe, Buckinghamshire, entertained Harris on his last visit to the British Isles on his way home from the Nice Convention, and remembered him as

> . . . one of nature's gentlemen. He was shy, especially in the company of ladies, but he had a marvellous facility of being able to make friends easily. He was the same with everyone, and all who met him took an instant liking to this kindly man. There was nothing of the snob about him, and he was never affected by his success in life. He was a very sincere yet a very humble man, although he had no great personality and did not stand out as someone exceptional in a gathering.

In his history of RIBI Roger Levy, who met him several times, emphasises that "everywhere, he impressed those who met him, and heard him, with his simplicity and his sincerity, and his refusal to be seen as a visionary . . . a quiet American who was unforgotten by those who had the privilege to meet him". While Vivian Carter, whom we have met several times in these pages, and who was, in succession, Editor of both *The Rotary Wheel* in Great Britain and *The Rotarian* in the United States, saw him often in the late twenties and thirties, and recounted: "I never met a celebrity less conscious of being one. . . . A fancy of his was to sit in a dark corner and listen, and talk — when drawn out — slowly, deliberately and reservedly on almost any topic raised. . . . No man was fonder of a joke, or fuller of amusing recollections." Carter also recalled

Paul's admitting his "ecstatic joy out of contacts with others".

To a long-time friend, Hugh Galloway (whose photograph of the Founder was one of Paul's favourites), a Past President of RIBI, Paul elaborated this last point: "Of all interests in life, none is so inexhaustible as making and studying friends." He took Galloway on a little tour of his Comely Bank garden, showing him all the trees, each tagged with a label carrying the name of a friend who had planted it there. Another great friend, the first Australian ever to hold that office, Sir Angus Mitchell, also wrote of that garden, but in winter, deep in snow: "As I came down fairly early that morning to their little breakfast room, I saw Paul tramping through the snow to little platforms of trees. On these he was placing nuts and biscuits for the birds and squirrels. This was a regular job for this frail man whose big heart responded to the needs of all living things."

Past RIBI President Verrall Reed came out directly with what he considered to be the central fascination of his seemingly transparent and simple character: "There must have been some driving energy and intense missionary zeal in the make-up of the Founder of a Movement like ours, who not only conceived the idea of the first Club, but became the real pioneer of its organised extension. These qualities of his did not obtrude upon his friends." That kind of comment, expressed so often, is as always sounded with just a slight note of regret that a glowing saint eluded the eye: "He never appeared to seek their admiration, but just their fellowship."

What else, at heart? "We had been lonesome and we had found a cure for lonesomeness," recorded Paul in the last article he wrote for *The Rotarian*, which was published a few weeks after his death.

In February 1943, while the world outside puffed its cheeks and cracked in the howl of war, while Churchill and Roosevelt returned from Casablanca with their vow to pursue "unconditional surrender", while the Germans surrendered in the horror of their own making at Stalingrad and 5,000 tanks collided at Kursk, and while an increasingly alarmed Mussolini dismissed ex-Rotarian Ciano, his son-in-law, from his post as Foreign Minister, Paul entertained at his home six original members of the Chicago Club, including Schiele and Harry Ruggles, who had started Rotary singing. Down in the cellar, in Paul's "Discussion Club room", they began to re-enact one of the early meetings. Schiele, in his role as the first-ever Club President, seized the gavel — and at this point they remembered, as no doubt Paul intended, that then there had been no gavel, no formal rules, just a group of young men sprawled about in hotel bedrooms rented for the day, lying on beds, sitting on chests of drawers.

Jean Harris revealed, many years later: "One thought which Paul and I often discussed in the last years was that, while the world grows more and more complex, we all need to simplify our lives somehow. We need to calm our fevers. We need more reading, more talking in our homes, more simple hospitality." The Harrises often offered that, and often men of six or eight nations sat at their table. The Reverend Andrew Howe, Minister of the Church of Scotland, at Alness, Ross-shire, a nephew by marriage, recalls the later visits to Scotland vividly: "Uncle Paul was a tall sparse figure, rather like what one would imagine Abraham Lincoln to have looked like. He was full of fun, and interested in children."

Rotary was his child. "As Paul travelled," said Ches Perry, the man who had sent Paul on many of those travels, "he not only made his pathways on the face of the earth, but he kept opening new pathways in his brain. . . . He realized that people lacked understanding and goodwill, that people were strangers to one another, and he wanted to do something about it."

He did. In the year of his death, though he did not know it, Paul Harris ranked high on the short list of twenty for the Nobel Prize for Peace.

Just a few days before he died, Paul was chatting with his local pastor and, instead of referring directly to his own evident frailty, he chose to recount the story of John Quincy Adams, sixth President of the United States, when at the age of eighty he was asked how he felt. The great man's reply had been: "John Quincy Adams himself is quite well, I thank you, but the house in which he lives at present is becoming dilapidated. Time and the seasons have nearly destroyed it. Its walls are much shadowed. It trembles with every wind. It is becoming almost uninhabitable now. I think John Quincy Adams will have to move out of it soon, but he himself is quite well, quite well."

Like those of most men at the end of their lives, Paul's thoughts dwelt much on his youth and some time of every day during 1946, with his close friend gone before, deprived of his daily chats with Schiele, Paul wrote a few lines on topics that had often been the subject of those talks.

One summer night of the distant past, three of us, father, brother Cecil, five years old, and I, two years younger, got off the train. . . . All was darkness except as it was broken by the flickering light of a lantern held by a tall man I had never seen before. On the delicate film of my consciousness the scene was etched so deep and clear that it cannot be obliterated or or dimmed while life lasts.

The tall man took my clenched fist in his warm, strong hand which was ever so much larger than my father's, with enormous thumbs which made excellent handles for little boys to hold to when going over rough places and so we walked up the street, father and Cecil following. This tall man was my grandfather. It was a solemn procession and the solemnity was emphasized by the awesome stillness and darkness of the night.

Grandfather, father, Cecil and I turned north at the first corner, crossed the road and grandfather opened a gate and we entered a yard. As we approached the side veranda of a comfortable looking house, a door opened and a dark-eyed elderly lady stepped out into the darkness holding a kerosene lamp above her head and peering out into the night. She was my father's mother and was destined to be mine as well.

These are the most evocative and powerful lines in all Rotary literature. It could have been Oliver himself speaking, or David Copperfield of Pip. They yield nothing to Dickens in imagery and force. In fact, they are the lines of Paul Harris as he starts his last book, retraces his steps for the last time, in memoirs published posthumously, whose title is significantly not *My Early Life* or similar, but *My Road to Rotary.*

From Chapter Two on of the present volume we have seen how Paul's character development led inevitably to his new Club in 1905. *My Road to Rotary* clarified for us for ever, if we still need it clarified, how dominant, indeed obsessive, a part his boyhood played. Of forty-two chapters, the first twenty-eight — well over half — deal with his life as a boy. In Chapter 29 his grandfather dies; in Chapter 30, his grandmother. The boy has gone. The remainder of the book is a superficial rehash of earlier accounts of how he founded his Movement and how it developed. The truth about Harris and the truth about Rotary lie there in those first twenty-eight chapters which could stand alone as a lasting contribution to American literature. The Dickens comparison is evoked even by the name of the heroine who appears fleetingly from his unforgotten days — Nancy, "beautiful in character as well as in person" who "got out of bed one night and made her distracted way down the creek road to the pond" because "there had always been someone she could serve; now there was none". Harris tells us little of what caused this young woman to take her own life, no doubt intentionally so. Nancy's story dies with her. But he tells us a great deal about himself when he gives primacy among the reasons for living to the principle of service. And without the great realisation he gave that principle, he might well have taken that same road in another place, to another pond. His triumph in not doing so is the triumph of the boy, the triumph of Rotary.

At the end of Paul's two long world journeys for Rotary, Ches

Perry urged Paul to take up his pen again — this was in 1935, when he had just completed *Peregrinations*, his account of the second part of those travels. The result was *This Rotarian Age*, which would by its title turn Chesterton's derisive tag to good account and establish a philosophic base for the Movement, with Paul's global impression of his own sprawling brainchild. The organising genius that was Perry allowed himself a glimpse of self-knowledge when he wrote in the Introduction: "If anyone is ever discouraged about being a Rotarian because there is not enough humaneness to the Movement, he will be put at ease by reading this book."

Back in the early twenties Perry had introduced Paul to Big Jim Davidson as "the source of a great river". The description allows us to bring another perspective to bear on their relationship (probably there are many more we shall never know about), apart from the dual portrait of Architect and Builder. Here were two introverted, ungregarious, inarticulate men who, because that river had to reach across mountains and plains to the coast and then open out to the sea, had to remove the log-jam threatened by their own personalities. That river of inspiration had to be made to flow, and to that end, triumphantly achieved, with Paul recalled to the public eye in 1926, the two men turned themselves into dam-busters.

They were both undeniably tough, though Harris might often look otherwise as the years went by. But there was never anything frail-looking about Chesley Perry. Brisk and authoritative, working through every hour to the end (even when he briefly yielded to his doctor's persuasion to "take it easy" for a few days in hospital, he sent long letters to old colleagues, full of advice and firm guidance), the great helmsman of Rotary stood for no more sentimental nonsense from his body than from anything or anybody else.

On 21st February 1960, two days before Rotary's fifty-fifth anniversary, fifty years after he had become the first General Secretary of the Movement and sixteen years after he had become President of Rotary Number One, he wrote letters after lunch and then went out to post them through the sharp wind and snowfall of that Sunday afternoon. His wife Peggy, his secretary for so many years, who had supervised his correspondence all their lives together, knew better than to interfere, warning him only against falling on the mushy pavement along Chicago's beautiful Lake Shore Drive. Ches, well wrapped up, made his way to the nearest post-box through the snow, upright and resolute as ever, reviewing the troops of his years and determined not to fall. He re-entered his apartment, erect and quietly triumphant, mission accomplished. "Well Peggy, you see I didn't fall." And saying it, fell dead. He was eighty-eight and active to the last, and his life had lasted a decade longer than Paul's. But what was done was done; he had no wish to be the subject of a forgotten headstone. His ashes were scattered over Lake Michigan, just offshore from those teeming, exciting, legendary streets where he had spent his entire life in furthering another man's dream.

When he retired — after those two false starts — in 1942, Paul Harris had been the first to pay his tribute: "Ches has built up a great organisation; it is the service station of world-wide Rotary. Such fidelity I have never known. Morn, noon, and night, Sundays and holidays not excepted, he has labored at his desk." Estes Snedecor, the President who brought the International Convention overseas for the first time and presided at the Usher Hall, Edinburgh, endorsed this testimony: "Never have I seen him relax or turn his energy or thought from his one all-consuming purpose — the building of Rotary International. He has been its organizing genius. He has given it breadth, depth, direction, continuity, poise, balance and permanency. He and his organization have withstood the tides of overwhelming ambition upon the part of others, the shifting sands of politics, and the storms of impulsive and short-sighted action."

In the flood of tributes from the Presidents Perry had served, the inevitable corollary to this single-mindedness emerged. Armando de A. Pereira, whose generous spirit had done so much to keep his homeland Brazil, and thus all South America, so strongly in the Movement, and who in one year from the Havana Convention in 1940 had steered uncommitted New World Rotarians into giving their full-hearted support for embattled Britain, gave his view of Perry: "The impression I had of him physically, was good. Few words, but enough to reckon a man of will and command. I was told he was cold, and only thought of work. It seemed so, but the bright look of his eyes told me he had a heart. . . . He is gay and most enjoyable, although some do not so believe, having met him only slightly once or twice."

Walter D. Head, the New Jersey headmaster, President when the first Clubs disappeared under the shock of Hitler's blitzkriegs, remarked ruefully, "It has often been said that it takes a long time to get acquainted with Ches Perry. Maybe that's so, but it is worth it". Russell F. Greinher, President when the First World War had broken out in Europe and the Kaiser's armies had taken the identical route through the Lowlands into France that Hitler's were to take, knew the same man: "I defy any psychiatrist, psychologist, or latter-day scientist to penetrate his brain machinery, tune into his think waves, and tell you how and what he was thinking, until he was ready to reveal it. . . . I have used every method known to the modern Hawkshaw to find out whether he was for or against me, and I here and now confess I have failed."

These men were all describing the perfect civil servant, of course, which was what Perry was. But he was a great deal more than that. From a loose grouping of one new Club, he had single-handedly built the organisation which could administer thousands of them, and it was natural he would resent any free-wheeling attempts to take routes outside it. The structure of Rotary reflected his personality, as its ideals reflected Paul's. Both men were as desperately shy as each other and they combined to build one of the most boisterously extrovert organisations in the world. But they never could have shared that two-sided desk used by Paul and Fred Reinhardt, lest they discovered perchance that Rotary was smaller than both of them.

Now and again the mask would slip, a tiny chink reveal itself in the armour. Arthur H. Sapp, the President who came with Ches Perry to Europe in 1927 to start the first German Club in Hamburg, believed he had discovered one: "With all his zeal for hard work, Ches never lost his sense of humor. Often he had it covered pretty thoroughly, but it would come to the surface at a moment's notice." In this case, the moment was fleeting in the extreme, for Vivian Carter, Editor and Secretary of RIBI, had just written a book entitled *The Meaning of Rotary*, and shortly after was invited to Chicago to take over *The Rotarian*, Perry's very own baby, from its overworked parent; and it was Perry's ice-pick, far more than Capone's guns, which drove him back to London.

Once, the mask slipped completely and without inhibition: Perry spoke his heart and not just his mind, on an occasion when, as far as he knew, no one was listening. He had appeared always as a diehard opponent to any involvement with the Hitler war — it was "not a Rotary War" — But in June 1941, after the Denver Convention, and with the United States six months into the world conflict, the International President Tom Davis dramatically placed a collection of Rotary records, pamphlets and statements into a sealed cairn on Mount Evans, Colorado, for posterity to find, should the hordes of the Rising Sun and the Swastika overwhelm the Bald Eagle, and men of the future wonder what Rotary had stood for. The concluding portion of a statement contributed by Ches Perry (who had nearly retired the year before at Havana) read:

It seemed apparent that if the Master-Slave States conquered the rest of the world, there would no longer be any Rotary Clubs anywhere. But, on the other hand, if the Master-Slave States were defeated by the democratic-industrial-agricultural-capitalistic States, Rotary Clubs would have a great opportunity to encourage the further extension of that system of society and contribute to its betterment and perfection, on the basis of all members of the human race being thoughtful of and helpful to each other, and that this Ideal would so influence all nations in both their domestic and their foreign relations; that wars would cease, and peace and progress and prosperity become the common lot of all men.

It was a noble declaration, one that not even red-hot pincers would have drawn from him, had it not been intended for burial and seal beneath a mound of stone. It proved to posterity that even an apparent block of stone could dream. He described himself ever — especially when he declined that title "General Secretary Emeritus" — as a run-of-the-mill Rotarian; and this was not false modesty, no pose. He believed fiercely that every Rotarian could have the same vision as himself of the destiny of his beloved Movement and could share his selfless lifelong dedication to that destiny. He and Paul Harris had the same vision, which he had accepted unquestioningly from Paul. Every movement has its saint and its zealot, one who must be loved, one who must be obeyed; and both roles must be undertaken by men who are neither one, but accept their roles. In a world where the privileged closed their powerful ranks, in a world where the underprivileged claimed the century and banded together in brotherhood, in that self-divided world, two lonely men, lonely all their lives, had forged a fellowship, reaching across the globe, embracing nations where men of all colours practised all religions, to form a phalanx that held the middle ground and gave to men of business and the professions a means of holding out against barbarism both of the élite and the deprived; to rescue the abused nineteenth-century work ethic and restore it to men of compassion and goodwill who sang and told bad jokes yet who who wished to keep intact the civil value of mankind.

The year before, a testament had also been made by Paul Harris for posterity, together with other Founder Members of Rotary Number One. But for Paul's long-term vision, we must wait until the year AD 2040. In that year a hermectially sealed capsule will be delivered to the Chicago Club by the Chicago Museum of Science and Industry containing a wire-recording with the voices of Paul Harris, Harry Ruggles, Silvester Schiele and other pioneers of the world's first Service Club. We cannot guess what their messages will be, though an eye-witness described how the old men, all lifelong comrades, broke into tears as they spoke to their unseen audience a century hence.

Tom Warren, the British Rotarian who was Vice-President of Rotary International from 1939 to 1942, had endured more than most from the General Secretary during three periods of office while his country stood alone against the Nazi avalanche. Yet he had no hesitation in paying his tribute: "When I assumed the Presidency in 1945, he had vacated the Secretary's chair; but his marked footprints were all around, deep, firm, enduring. He had assembled and trained a devoted staff in his own image; so his inspiration went marching on, with the result we know so well." While some wry and pardonable ambiguity might be detected in that last sentence, there was none in Warren's summing-up: "His passing was unobtrusive, and that was how he lived. He would not have agreed that he was shy and reticent; but he was, and so was often misunderstood. To be reserved and yet to play a leading part in the glamour of world Rotary was amazingly to spread one's accomplishments. This Ches did, and much does Rotary owe him . . . here was the principal architect of our immense organisation."

Thomas Mann, expelled from the Munich Rotary in the dark days when nightmare was engulfing his beloved homeland, maintained that the intellectual basis of Rotary was "the unified ideal of freedom, education, human kindness, tolerance, helpfulness, and sympathy that are the essence of humanity, of civility in its highest form". In the year of Mann's death, five years before his own, Chesley Perry did not offer any intellectual base when speaking at La Salle, Illinois, to a Rotary Business Relations Conference. "The word Rotarian in business", he said, "must become equivalent to the word Sterling on a piece of silver." The cold authoritarian who had heard men of all nations pay tribute to his work, then told the Conference of the tribute he treasured most, paid by an old man whose name he did not know, who had brought some flowers into the lobby of a Rotary Convention hotel in Salt Lake City. The old man thrust the bouquet at the stiff, impassive, immaculately groomed figure before him. "I've been reading in the newspapers about your Convention," he told those eyes of ice, which gave nothing away. "You Rotarians have something so good, so lovely, something the world needs so much, that I wanted to bring to the Convention these flowers from my garden. . . . Will you accept them with my prayers for Rotary's success?"

Perry would. The witnesses to this poignant little scene must have been astounded. The speaker did not say so, but the incident had happened way back in 1919, and this unapproachable, unemotional man had kept those flowers pressed in his memory ever since. How Paul must have smiled when he heard of the incident, if he ever did. But he would not have been surprised.

We shall never really know the truth of the relationship between Paul and Ches any more than we can ever know the real truth about any marriage. And the marriage with Ches was just as important as the marriage with "Bonnie Jean"; one suspects that both were as platonic as each other, though Rotary was the child shared by both these childless men. It was a kind of *ménage à trois* possibly understood by none of them, but if anyone understood it, it would have been Jean, sent by Perry on those sea voyages during which she suffered fearful sickness, she who longed all her life to be free of Chicago and go home to Scotland, where indeed she spent all the time she could while Paul travelled around the British Isles and Europe.

As has been recounted, when London joined in 1912 and Rotary became International, Paul passed control over to Ches and retired to Comely Bank, which Jean named after her home in Edinburgh, though there was far more significance in the address, 10856 Longwood Drive, this being the name of the house where Napoleon had spent his exile on St Helena. As we saw, Perry was forced to end Paul's "exile" when rumours spread through the Rotary world in the 1920s of Harris's death and the rapidly expanding Movement needed the Founder's appearance to hold it together. Ches organised the travels of Paul and Jean but never came with them.

The apartness of these two extraordinary men was complete. Shaw might accuse the Movement of doing nothing else but go to lunch, but the two most important men in World Rotary almost never had lunch together throughout their lives. "No one", wrote Paul at the end of his life, "could by the widest stretch of the imagination say that Ches and I were chums in the usual acceptance of the word." The world where "men were boys again" stopped with the two without whom there would be no Rotary International. They were far less than chums and a great deal more; their intimacy stopped just short of open antagonism.

Of one moment of intimacy we have a record. Ches Perry told of it after Paul Harris died, describing how a few weeks before the event he and the man who was the Founder of Rotary and the founder of Perry sat talking of all they had done together over so many long years. "Bonnie Jean" was in another room "with the ladies".

After a while the two great partners rose and linked arms and made their way slowly across the hallway. Before they entered the other room, however, the tired rapscallion dropped his hand from Perry's arm. "I'll go in under my own steam," he told Perry and faltered ahead with his cane, ready for the sharp glance of the strong, simple Presbyterian soul for whom her husband's incomprehensible love of Robert Burns was quite enough.

We have also two extraordinary cameos. In December 1934 Ches had a room prepared for the Founder's use whenever he should

choose to visit Headquarters. Paul declined to use it, however, whereupon Ches admonished him:

> You should have your own place in the office, and not be hanging around like a poor relation or hovering about like some ghost of the past . . . there is no reason why you shouldn't have your room at the Secretariat. . . . If you are willing to accept the room that has been prepared for you, I see no reason why you should not bring down your tiger skin, dog skin and blanket, and picture of the garden of good will . . . these things are identified with you. . . . Please be reasonable and accept the situation. . . .

Paul, however, had a reason, a very strong-willed Presbyterian reason, and she wanted him kept at Comely Bank. She preferred he remain a "ghost of the past", as she had kept him from 1912 to 1919, once she had brought him through his breakdown.

The second cameo is sited in 1941. Paul has clearly by now won his own private battle at Comely Bank, has accepted the room at Headquarters; he realises that Perry is right and that Rotary needs him there. But beyond that, he dares not go, and Perry writes to Phil Lovejoy, then still Perry's Assistant:

> In a recent communication, Paul said something which led me to believe that his visits during recent years have not brought him as much happiness as he might otherwise have had. I suspect that the situation is that he has come in, said hello to the switchboard operator, gone on into his room and sat there without anybody coming to see him or without having had the gumption to get up and travel around the office to chat with the members of the staff. . . .

Perry proposed that the switchboard girl should alert them all when Paul Harris was in the building, sitting alone in his room, and that they should take it in turn to have a chat with the old boy, though, he added (here we get a glimpse of Perry's humour), "Of course, we do not want to have the whole dozen of us getting jammed in the doorway of his room trying to get in at the same time."

There is still, of course, as there has been for a long time, a room at Headquarters called "The Paul P. Harris Room", maintained as a shrine for visiting Rotarians since his death. It was set up at 35 East Wacker Drive, and it is there today at 1600 Ridge Avenue, Evanston. But in truth, there is little of the sense of the Founder in that room. He isn't there now, and one feels he never was.

The reader will remember how Stuart Morrow, who took Rotary Clubs across the Atlantic to Dublin, delighted Harris and was deplored by Perry, and when Morrow passed through Chicago on his way back to San Francisco, he saw Perry, but Harris's door was closed to him. A few years later the same pattern manifested itself. In 1919, Anton Verkade, impressed by what he saw of Rotary in the United States, visited Paul Harris at Comely Bank and was urged by him to try to start Rotary in the Netherlands. The following year, presumably unaware of Verkade's visit, or deciding to be so, Perry signed a document for another Dutch business man, Jan Van Tijen, who was returning home after living in Texas for many years, authorising *him* to form Dutch Rotary Clubs. Neither Harris nor Perry seemed to appreciate the confusion this might cause, though in fact, when the two distinguished Dutchmen contacted each other, they established Rotary in the Netherlands in harmonious tandem, unlike the respective sponsors in Chicago.

To the end of his long life, Rotary for Ches was a matter of efficient filing and record, of proper returns of membership and per capita dues. In the percipient words of George Means in a memorial article in *The Rotarian*, "its machinery was to his enlightened view a necessary device for the orderly propagation of its ideals". Rotary for Paul, on the other hand, was always as Harry Ruggles recalled it in another *Rotarian* article, with his memories of young men perched on bales of hay "in E.W. Todd's Hay and Grain Store" or "meeting in the bedroom, sitting two deep on beds and tables" after a good supper in various restaurants. In later years Paul recaptured as best he could the informality of those early days when his loneliness fed knowingly on the feasts of fun and fellowship he had artfully brought about, by instituting an informal Discussion Club — for men only — in the basement of Comely Bank. This was his equivalent of a "night out with the boys", and represented Jean's one concession to such an appalling idea. Around that green baize table, the walls of the room packed with framed photographs as were shelves crammed with trophies and medals of all shapes and sizes, had sometimes sat just the survivors of the first Club in 1905, or on other occasions visiting Rotarians from maybe eight nations. Here was truly the one and only "Paul Harris Room" — and Ches Perry never sat there. Nor did Jean.

When the great milestones of the Movement's incredible growth came round, there had to be photographs of Paul and Ches, of course, and there were — three especially. One showed them standing apart on either side of a huge wall atlas at the Secretariat; another depicted them gazing at each other, or not quite at each other, from opposing margins of a huge blow-up of the printed four sections of the Object of Rotary; while a third, taken at Comely Bank, showed them facing each other awkwardly from the edge of their chairs, set each side of a fireplace. Here they were, separated by a world, an ideal and a hearth respectively, and united by them for all time.

This time, Eddie Guest is not enough for us. We must look to another English poet. Turning the pages of old journals which show these haunted, strained pairings of two of surely the strangest, yet most influential, crusaders of this century, trapped in the armour of their business suits, surviving and outpacing all inventions and banal dictators, trapped in Keats's "Silence and slow Time", we can but exclaim fruitlessly, with the poet, "What men or gods are these?"

After Paul died, his widow promptly sold Comely Bank and moved into a downtown hotel. Forsaking the "better elements" of the city from which Paul had so proudly recruited Rotary Number One, she took for several years to the life of an evangelist amongst the drunken, despairing and deprived who sprawled about Skid Row in the reeking tenements and back alleys of Chicago, behind what Kenneth Allsop, in one of many memorable passages in *The Bootleggers*, describes as the "thin rind of beauty" of Lake Shore Drive. After a few blocks, Allsop writes, "you come into the city's turbulent, seamy interior, a jungle of dark canyons and lunging, ugly, squalid streets, which for long sections slide into some of the worst festering slums to be found anywhere, including Glasgow and the Middle East". Including Glasgow — no doubt "Bonny Jean" felt at home, no doubt she had made the same sort of evangelising forays while staying with her clergyman brother during Paul's odysseys around Britain and Europe. But not enough at home. In 1955, Rotary's Golden Jubilee Year, she left Chicago for good and went back to Scotland, to live first with her brother, the Reverend John Youngson Thomson, Minister at Annbank in Ayrshire, within evangelist's reach of Glasgow, and then with her sister Joey who had married the Reverend John Howe, at Dundee, before finally settling to live out her last years in furnished rooms in Edinburgh, where the original Comely Bank Avenue still existed, full of memories of her youth.

The Reverend Andrew Howe, who has followed the calling of both his father and uncle, remembers her stay then, as he remembers the ones before. He had liked his Uncle Paul very much; he was always good with children and especially boys, of course. His Aunt Jean he did not like particularly, but for reasons he found it difficult to identify, though he was kind enough to jot down a few impressions, stressing they were only speculations, about the relationship between Paul, Jean and Rotary. "My Aunt might well have been the dominating factor," he writes, concerning the marriage with Rotary's Founder. "Their backgrounds were different, their convictions must have clashed, at times at least. It is inconceivable that both my Aunt and Uncle would interpret the 'social' and 'socialising' aspects of Rotary in the same way." In emphasising to the writer that he was only speculating, Andrew Howe added: "Could it be, that as Rotary grew more universal and worldly, that personal tensions within the marriage increased? Could it be that Rotary went in a direction which contradicted, or tended to contradict, or annul the simplistic tenets of the Founder's philosophy, and that Aunt Jean — who had a very strong personality, though a gracious manner — encouraged Paul to 'ease out' and leave the Movement to others?"

If so, the tension would have increased, since Paul was by no means inclined to place Rotarians in a strait-jacket of conformity, though, as the Movement spread, he appreciated some form of rules had to be fashioned to contain in a recognisable entity so many different races and nationalities. But always, to him, Rotary was what mattered, the essential ideal — how different men of different mores and cultures chose to interpret it in their own lands, he did not care. Perry did, and that was one tension. Jean Harris did, but even in the home of Rotary itself, and that was another tension.

Today there is one headstone in Chicago, another in Edinburgh, the latter dating from 1963, for Jean outlived them all. Headstones 4,000 miles apart. And even there, Jean made sure Perry didn't have the final say, for two years after Paul's burial she had his coffin dug up and repositioned in the cemetery plot. The home at Comely Bank carries no plaque. All those years, when she was playing host-ess to hundreds of Rotarians from all over the world, was it all a sham? From its huge picture-window Paul had gazed out upon his beloved trees and birds and Friendship Garden constantly. But with binoculars. He should have used them on the lady sitting across the breakfast-table perhaps. Or perhaps he had done so long before, in smiling sorrow but in understanding too. He breakfasted with birds, one visitor said. Certainly with one very strange bird. They had tea also, every day. In the last chapter of *My Road to Rotary*, written during his last days, Paul described "The End of the Journey":

> Jean and I are sitting at our fireside drinking a cup of tea. One who marries a Scottish lady must acquire the habit of sitting at the fireside and drinking black tea. . . . If the tea is good and the fire burns merrily, one enjoys recreation and rest. . . .
>
> Queen of the fireside and the teatable at Comely Bank is my lady Jean and the thought often comes to me that her steadfast devotion to duty was not excelled even by grandmother. I am indeed a fortunate man; of that I am sure, and this is the very place and this is the very hour for reverie,

even though my lady Jean maintains that my reveries far too frequently are preludes to cat-naps and my cat-naps preludes to slumber outright. . . .

"Why, I declare! I believe you have been asleep, Paul. . . ."

Living longest, "Bonnie Jean" had the last shot, of course. In 1950, asked to reminisce about her days with the man whom just the year before she had unceremoniously disturbed in his posthumous slumbers, as she had so often done while he lived, she concluded: "Above all, Paul felt deeply that for the things that are true and real and inmost about any human Movement, we acknowledge the Eternal Power."

As this history has chronicled, she increasingly introduced the Eternal Power from the speaker's platform into Rotary Conventions, while Ches Perry retired and her husband simply tired. It was indeed such publicised utterances as these that awoke echoes of the Great Architect of the Universe and the confusion of Rotary with Masonry, together of course with the Wheel. But it does not ring true. Paul was no unbeliever, yet he never flourished his faith and such a mode of expression was as foreign to his tongue as to his mind. Vivian Carter said of him, "his philosophy was that of a sceptic", and evidence would suggest this to be a shrewd judgment. As Paul said of George Harris: "Even in the midst of his tribulations, father preserved his sense of humor, and not infrequently made use of it not only to provoke laughter but also to gratify his inner craving to get back at a world which had used him so inconsiderately . . . and although he took most naturally to humor, it was of an iconoclastic order."

He had already flung down his challenge, when everyone else was settling for peace and quiet once the Big Bangs, two of them, had done their necessary work — and remembering that the first nuclear chain reaction had first been proved in his own backyard of Chicago, home of big bangs, he had exclaimed, "Is everything all right in Rotary? If so, God pity us."

And the year Jean Harris left Chicago for good, five years later, Ches Perry had shown he shared Paul's challenge to complacency. In that same speech to the La Salle Conference already quoted, he declared:

Rotary has something the world needed. Do we still have it today? Yes. Does the world still need it? Yes. Have we given and are we giving service to the world as we should? I don't think so. What we are doing is all right, but we are doing so little. . . .

What an unhappy, fearful world we have in this middle of the 20th Century! Not because any Rotarian or anyone else who has accepted and practiced the Ideal of Service has ever renounced it, but because so few, comparatively speaking, have never heard of it.

Which is where we return to the article by Professor Walter (*Life Begins at Forty*) Pitkin, referred to near the beginning of the preceding chapter. The comment which the Movement would have done well to ponder closely can now be quoted, divorced from his immediate subject of war wounded and interpreted as if extending over a wider arc. It should still be pondered closely today, whenever Rotarians tend to be complacent about the number of their Clubs alone and affect indifference to the world's misconceptions and ignorance of their Movement:

> There always have been two kinds of handicapped people: those who accept their handicaps, and those who suffer from slight handicaps which they want to make worse because, with such, they can escape responsibilities. . . .
> Dr. Samuel Crowe, the brilliant experimental scientist of John Hopkins Hospital, told me that about seven out of every ten hard-of-hearing patients had lost much of their ability to hear just because they didn't want to hear.

Indifference is a form of defence against something one doesn't want to hear.

Nelson Algren, the famous novelist of the "Windy City", whose best-known work, made into an extremely successful film starring Frank Sinatra, is probably *The Man with the Golden Arm*, has written: "Chicago forever keeps two faces, one for winners and one for losers; one for hustlers and one for squares." And the men who had symbolised these two opposing faces died within two days of one another: Capone on 25th January 1947, and Paul Harris on the 27th. Both their funerals took place during spells of bitterly cold weather, with blizzards blanketing the city, blasting off Lake Michigan; and both funerals were attended by small coteries, though of very different men. But only one of the mourned was the subject of a subsequent memorial service at St Paul's Cathedral in London, on 22nd February, at which the address was given by the Dean, the Very Reverend W.R. Matthews, who chose for his text, as we noted at the beginning of this story, "Unknown, yet well known", words which, the Dean said, were used by St Paul in his Second Epistle to the Corinthians to describe his own position and might, with exaggeration, be also applied to Paul Harris. "Paul Harris", said the Dean, "is a name which would convey nothing to the majority of this country. But what he started — Rotary — is known in almost all the countries of the world."

Or — in the words applied to the Founder of the world's first

Service Club — *unknown, yet well known* all over the world. For
the hymns sung in that mighty cathedral — "Let Saints on Earth in
Concert Sing", "How Sweet the Name of Jesus Sounds" — are not
the tunes and lyrics most associated with Rotary, certainly not in
American communities. One hears rather, at the weekly luncheons,
voices raised to commemorate the unendurable loss of "Sweet
Adeline" which, though the tune is certainly based on an inversion
of the Westminster chimes of Big Ben, was composed by a one-time
member of the Rotary Club of New York, Harry Armstrong, who
wrote the tune in 1896, the year Paul hung out his shingle in
Chicago "to make a life", though it was then called "My Old New
England Home". Had Harris (or anyone else) heard it then, it might
indeed have ended up on the programme of the memorial service,
serving as an anthem to the world young Paul was leaving behind
but whose essence he was to carry all his life, the solid simple values
of Wallingford, Vermont, the values of Rotary. Instead, the "queen
of the echo school of harmonising", as the music historian Sigmund
Spaeth has called the lovely old barber-shop melody, nearly earned
a place in the history of the sort of city politics to which Harris was
strenuously opposed — they had their apogee in Chicago, of course
— when John F. Kennedy's grandfather, John J. "Honey" Fitzgerald,
adapted it as his campaign song in winning two terms as Mayor of
Boston in the early 1900s. But the Adeline of the title was really no
winsome small-town girl in Middle America at all; she was Adelina
Patti, the celebrated opera star, who had been a favourite of Chicago
audiences since she was twelve. Thus she was another enthusiast,
like Caruso, of Madame Galli's spaghetti, one of the "stage and
opera folk" Schiele recalled, and so can be said to have won her
way fairly into Rotary song-books through the years.

Every Rotary Club in the world is like every other Rotary Club in
the world, and no two are the same. To become a Rotarian you
have to be a certain sort of man, but you'll find all sorts of men
have become Rotarians. In the great capitals of the world members
meet and eat once every week in famous hotels or restaurants.
Elsewhere, according to size and locality, they meet in inns and
pubs and hired halls or rented dining-rooms. Most come for the
fellowship and few come for the food. The plaque with the Golden
Wheel can be seen outside hotels and inns and halls in almost every
country in the world, apart from nations under Communist rule,
within whose borders the absence of the Golden Wheel is a decision
of the rulers not of Rotary, for wherever Rotary is wanted, there it
will go, and wherever the sign of the Golden Wheel is shown, there

any Rotarian, of whatever race, creed or country, is welcomed with constant and genuine delight. A Rotarian is never a stranger — to other Rotarians. But neither is he a familiar. And what of non-Rotarians? Therein lies a paradox which troubles many Club members — and they are by no means all — who have accepted internationality as the ultimate goal of the Movement, endorsing Marshall McLuhan's concept of the "global village" with enthusiasm, since it gives them a setting within which their community service can be organised and run on a magnified village basis. Rotarians urge the young to consider themselves as citizens of the world, if not indeed the neighbours of all; and world understanding pre-empts all other Rotary goals at present — though it is not always clear whether this means Rotary's understanding of the world or the world's understanding of Rotary, or whether these are taken to mean the same thing.

Yet citizenship of the world and world understanding are far from being proved a natural sequence. To understand all may be to forgive all but, where neighbours are concerned, it is also to forget nothing. And if man takes root in every other man's garden with pervasive understanding, the trees of self-knowledge, each one masquerading as a transplant from Eden, may all yet perish under honey-fungus. The man who claims to be at home in all nations merely proves to be an insensitive guest; we must accept that any true citizen of the world will always find that, like Eve and Adam, he can never go home again. Throughout this century, but especially in recent decades, many men from many lands have literally tried to open up the Garden of Eden to the paying public and most have merely opened up their veins to the sands where the world began. All hearts may be open to the modern surgeon, but so were they to the Aztec priest. Besides which, if a man ever really becomes a citizen of the world, there is only one way to deport him. Are we up to our old tricks, letting youth try it out first? The casualties of peace are greater than the casualties of war and they lie around unburied. It is the great and enduring glory of Rotary that it is among the few with the courage to look at them, to remember that history is a series of traffic accidents, most of which happen every day outside our own front door. Paul Harris, in his very first writing in Rotary's very first magazine issue, foretasted the glory and foresaw the snare.

Not all Clubs sing. In fact, outside of North America, the various editions of *Songs for the Rotary Club* (from which most of the quotations under the chapter headings of this history have been taken) are sparingly employed. At the enormous Rotary International gatherings, however, all nations sing with a will, though a puzzled

French Rotarian once confessed he had never heard before so many sober men singing in the daytime. Likewise, whereas American Rotarians often impose "fines" (for charity) on any member caught out not addressing his fellows by their first names, British and European Clubs found the practice a highly embarrassing one for a long time — both the use of the names and the fines. Ask a Rotarian of almost any nationality about these customs, and he will say by way of explanation that they are "typically" American ideas, some of which his Club condescends to accept, while others it ignores. In truth, they all began, as with everything Paul Harris was in charge of, as simple expedients: for example, "first names" so that those original lonely men could overcome their inhibitions and get to know each other quicker; and "fines" so that Clubs could have some working capital, since Rotary Number One cost nothing to belong to for three years. As to the latter, Paul Harris finally had to announce whimsically, but firmly, that "owing to the natural reluctance on the part of His Majesty the American Citizen to pay anything in the nature of a fine, we would do well to call the semi-monthly charge of 5 cents (for late or non-attendance) dues instead of fines".

Apologists for Rotary singing have adopted the most extra-ordinary contortions to explain a phenomenon likewise brazenly simple in its origins. Officially, it has been claimed at various times that Club singing was a "social welder", that it was recreational and relaxed strangers, that it was a medium which instilled the spirit of Rotary into one and all, that it established a "cordial" relation-ship and — most absurd of all — that it became "a forerunner of things more cultural in the realm of art and music". Even Paul Harris himself was persuaded that there was authority for the Rotary custom in Plato ("through music the soul learns harmony and rhythm . . . making the soul graceful") and in the Ancient Athenian writer on music, Damon ("Music is valuable not only because it brings refinement of feeling and character, but . . . preserves and restores health"), plus — and one senses "Bonnie Jean's" influence here, countering these pagan references — the psalm singing of the early Christians that baffled Pliny. Harry Ruggles confessed in 1952, with a charming candour that still rings appealingly true to Rotarians of all nations, that he had jumped up and started the first song because "I, for one, had got pretty tired of just chewing the rag."

Not all Clubs have several-course meals at their weekly meetings. The French — again the individualists — often have *apéritif* meet-ings, when members enjoy merely cheese and biscuits with wine on their way home from the office once a week. And the custom of having evening instead of luncheon meetings is spreading rapidly, often because modern firms are more reluctant than before to allow their young executives the necessary time off in the middle of a busy day. A large proportion of new Rotary Clubs are now in fact "Supper Clubs" rather than Luncheon Clubs, which is beginning to make Shaw's gibe look slightly out of date, if only in that one small respect. Yet this is not the startling innovation many older Rotarians think it to be: for the first two years of its life, the Rotary Club of Chicago always met at night, some members catching a meal before they came, others bringing sandwiches.

Not all Rotary Clubs have "Contact Clubs" abroad, with whom they exchange regular visits and co-operate on international projects. Many Clubs are not in contact with Clubs in their neighbouring town, much less their neighbouring country, while others, whose members construe their international duty as met by their dining once a year in a local "ethnic" restaurant, would certainly have had young Paul's sympathy. Nor do such Clubs necessarily achieve much less than those which go enthusiastically overboard and are part of a circle of Contact Clubs embracing five different nations; and they often eat better!

Every Rotary Club in the world is like every other Rotary Club in the world except when you join it. It is then you find Clubs which have only one man from every trade, business or profession; and then one which has three clergymen and five bank managers. Then that you find Clubs with three Foundation scholars, in Africa, Japan and South America; and one whose members have never heard of Foundations since women stopped wearing them. Then that you find some with several volunteers sweating in the tropics for Health, Hunger and Humanity; and one which feels itself besieged by all three outside its suburban door. Then that you hear of a member of the Rotary Club of Stockholm (Classification: King) inviting sixty-five Youth Exchange students to his Palace; of the Rotary Club of Dachau inviting twelve such students to the nearby Concentration Camp Memorial; of the Rotary Club of Buzen in Japan teaching Australian Exchange students the *Chanoyu* tea ceremony; of the Rotary Club of Boardman, Ohio, USA, persuading fifteen Exchange students from Australia, Colombia, Finland, Zimbabwe, Thailand, Sweden, Mexico and the Federal Republic of Germany to sell food at an "International Youth Booth" to raise funds that will combat polio in Malawi; and then of a Club, or even several hundred, which would sooner exchange the Black Death than a student or, worse, a youth. And then that you find one of many thousands of Clubs which have no idea what they are meant to do in furthering world understanding and peace when they can't understand their own jargon-jammed Club Constitution; and one of many thousands which haven't the slightest intention of paying any attention to their District Governor, much less the International President; and one of many thousands of Clubs which have never heard of Paul Harris nor conceived of Chesley Perry. Almost all are familiar with Al Capone because he has been in lots of movies. Paul Harris featured only in a silent film made in 1928 (noted in Chapter Fifteen) and in 1939 — with International President Walter Head and Chesley Perry — on the world's first three-city television hook-up, between Albany, Troy and Schenectady in New York State. Alas, of these productions, neither has been revived on Late-Night TV, that citadel of immortality in the performing arts.

Long gone are the days when members of those early Clubs kept strict accounting in little black books showing exactly how much business they had gained from fellow-members and how much they had given in reciprocity (this posed problems for undertakers and policemen). The accounting habit of reckoning their service values still remains, however; now, certificates are dispensed among Clubs by International Headquarters as witness to and reward of high levels of Foundation giving, numbers of new members and worthwhile projects well carried through. Small wonder that dubious non-Rotarians sometimes scoff that the Good Book of Rotary is ruled for double-entry.

Perhaps because the tremendous story of Rotary, which I hope this book has conveyed, began with a "public convenience", there is a strongly defensive lobby within the Movement who are convinced their aims are not only misunderstood but wilfully underrated. Among themselves, they contrive to wear, when the vexed topic is mentioned, an air of comfortable martyrdom, of injured innocence. But they are far from innocent and little injured — and small use to Rotary they would be if they were. Rotarians are recruited from this world not the next, and if indeed they are misunderstood, it is because, even after seventy-eight years, they misunderstand themselves. Rogues and vagabonds abound in Rotary, and it has a well-filled quota of selfish, self-important, boring men, which so many of us are to those who know and love us. There are also men who are naughty and men who are nice; plus the majority who are both in unequal parts. Mostly undistinguished in worldly terms, and very ordinary people, they are not at all special because they are Rotarians; they are special because they have chosen to belong to Rotary; and Rotary is special because its huge accomplishments were achieved, and are still being achieved, by men in the street for men who need such things as public conveniences. It is the *need* of common men everywhere that makes Rotary important, the still surprising need of a world in surfeit, the astonishing endless short-fall of a civilisation in surplus.

The Golden Wheel is not alone in its awareness of that need, of course, or in experience of letting down buckets to draw up bile. What makes the success of Rotary stand out is its essential lack of solemnity. We live amidst a plethora of aggressive, muscular chari-ties and strident do-gooders, that not only see no discrepancy between their activities and sounding brass and tinkling cymbals but use each with amplifiers. The Rotary Movement, on the other hand, is still charity, in the broadest sense, beneath a jester's cap and bells. The Rotary Club is still reflective of the image of Paul Harris, that of fun and not fanaticism, and one suspects that his own 3-H programme would not have been Health, Hunger and Humanity, though he would have understood and applauded what inspired these aims. Rather, it would have been Humour, Hilarity and Happiness. Even there, Paul was special. Laughter is a world currency and shared with apes, but a smile is every man's secret and his God's. Laugh and the world laughs with you, smile and you smile alone. Which is why Paul was lonely to the end of his days and content to be so. He no doubt fully appreciated the Emerson quotation that hung behind his desk at Headquarters, "He who has a thousand friends has not a friend to spare", keeping the next line to himself: "And he who has one enemy will meet him everywhere".

Apart from the image of the Golden Wheel itself, you will always find it hard to visualise what a Rotary Club is until you join it. After that, you may find it impossible. Rotary's Medicine Man, Stuart Morrow, who made his brother-in-law Bill McConnell the first President of a Rotary Club outside of North America, died in 1942 at the age of eighty-seven, long a pariah from the Movement. But when McConnell himself, long elevated to Elder Statesman of the Movement, had shortly before the Second World War addressed a Rotary Conference at Duluth, Minnesota, where in 1912 the Movement had first announced itself International, he declared: "To clasp the hands and know the thoughts of men in other lands — there lies the way." McConnell was saying for Rotary what H.G. Wells had said in his *Outline of History*, that "human history becomes more and more a race between education and catastrophe". This indeed is what Shaw was saying when he inferred that the Rotary Movement was going nowhere but to lunch and would never go anywhere else. The inference is still resented because it seems so arrantly dismissive; yet who better than Shaw could know that no man is more powerful than a sceptic with a dream and a healthy appetite?

When Paul Harris was not sitting down to compose resounding messages for delivery at Conventions or in the pages of *The Rotarian* on special occasions, he had a simple, uncomplicated notion of what he had set out to do in 1905 and what he hoped others, as many as possible, and in as many nations as possible, had been persuaded to feel, even if most of those followers who had caught his gleam he could never hope to meet, and even if most of them were far removed from the character of country-bred young men rather lost and alone in a big city. "If Rotary has encouraged us", he was once heard to say, "to take a more kindly outlook on life and men; if Rotary has taught us greater tolerance, and the desire to see the best in others; if Rotary has brought us helpful and pleasant contact with others, who are also trying to capture and radiate the joy and beauty of life, then Rotary has brought us all that we can expect."

Paul was not lost in Chicago, in fact. He used the toddlin' town with a skill that was matched only by Al Capone on the other side of the city's face. Each made the town his world in his own image, and it became the world for their two widely different and opposing codes. "Rotary is bigger," admitted Silvester Schiele, many decades after that dinner at Madame Galli's. "Rotary is bigger, but Rotary is not yet better than the man in whose brain it was born. I know, for I've known — and loved — both of them since they were boys."

Bigger, but not yet better. Nor does it need to be. "I am not going to Chicago for the purpose of making money," Paul Harris said, with the clear, unclouded vision of his twenty-eight years. "I am going for the purpose of living a life."

The youngest, or oldest, recruit to Rotary, all these long years later, still needs no other reason.

Selective Bibliography

BOOKS

Allsop, Kenneth. *The Bootleggers.* London: Hutchinson, 1961.

Arnold, Oren. *The Golden Strand: An Informal History of the Rotary Club of Chicago.* Chicago, Ill.: Quadrangle, 1966.

Birkenhead, Lord. *Rudyard Kipling.* London: Weidenfeld & Nicolson, 1978.

Calvocoressi, Peter, and Wint, Guy. *Total War.* Harmondsworth, Middx: Penguin, 1972.

Carter, Vivian. *The Meaning of Rotary.* Introduction by John Galsworthy. London: Percy Lund, Humphries, 1927.

Churchill, Winston S. *The World Crisis.* London: Macmillan, abr. and rev. edn 1942.

——. *The Second World War.* London: Cassell, 6 vols, 1948–54.

Dedmon, Emmett. *Fabulous Chicago.* New York: Random House, 1933.

Diffre, Henri. *Histoire du Rotary en France.* Lyons: BOSC Frères, 1959.

Furnas, J.C. *The Americans.* New York: G.P. Putnam's, 1969.

Gilloon, Philip. *The Golden Wheel.* Jerusalem: Jerusalem Rotary Club, 1979.

Halper, Albert (ed.). *This Is Chicago.* New York: Henry Holt, 1952.

Harris, Paul P. *The Founder of Rotary.* Chicago, Ill.: Rotary International, 1928.

——. *This Rotarian Age.* Chicago, Ill.: Rotary International, 1935.

——. *My Road to Rotary.* Chicago, Ill.: A. Kroch, 1948.

Harrison, Michael. *Rosa* (Rosa Lewis). London: Peter Davies, 1962.

Hart, Sir Basil Liddell. *History of the Second World War.* London: Cassell, 1970.

Herring, Hubert. *A History of South America.* London: Jonathan Cape, 1968.

Hewitt, C.R. *Towards My Neighbour: The Social Influence of the Rotary Club Movement in Great Britain and Ireland.* London: Longmans Green, 1950.

Hungarian Rotarians. *Hungary*. Budapest: Athenaeum, 1931.

Johnson, Paul C. *San Francisco*. London: Ward Lock, 1971.

Kee, Robert. *The Green Flag* (Ireland). London: Weidenfeld & Nicolson, 1972.

Kennedy, Malcolm. *A History of Japan*. London: Weidenfeld & Nicolson, 1963.

Kogan, Herman, and Wendt, Lloyd. *Chicago: A Pictorial History* New York: Dutton, 1958.

Lavender, David. *The American West*. New York: American Heritage, 1965.

Levy, Roger. *Rotary International in Great Britain and Ireland*. Plymouth, Devon: Macdonald & Evans, 1978.

Marden, Charles F. *Rotary and Its Brothers*. Princeton, NJ: Princeton University Press, 1935.

Miller, William. *A New History of the United States*. New York: Dell, 1958.

Page, Thomas. *San Francisco*. Geneva: Editions Minerwa, SA, 1977.

Paine, Albert Bigelow. *The Adventures of Mark Twain*. New York: Grosset & Dunlap, 1944.

Rotary? — A Study of the Chicago Club by the University of Chicago Press. Chicago, Ill.: University of Chicago Press, 1934.

Sheldon, Arthur Frederick. *The Science of Business*, London: Sheldon, 1920.

Shirer, William R. *The Rise and Fall of the Third Reich*. London: Pan, 1964.

Somerville-Large, Peter. *Dublin*. London: Hamish Hamilton, 1979.

Songs for the Rotary Club. Evanston, Ill.: Rotary International, various edns from 1925 to the present.

Spaeth, Sigmund. *A History of Popular Music in America*. New York: Random House, 1948.

Visser, W. *Het Wiel Met de zes Spaken*. Amsterdam: Dutch Rotary Districts, 1973.

Walsh, James P. *The First Rotarian: The Life and Times of Paul Percy Harris, Founder of Rotary*. Shoreham-by-Sea, Sussex: Scan Books, 1979.

Ward, Maisia. *Gilbert Keith Chesterton*. Harmondsworth, Middx: Penguin, 1958.

PERIODICALS

The Rotarian. Issues since 1911.
The Rotary Wheel. Issues since 1915.
Service in Life and Work. Issues 1932–9.

Index

Abyssinia, 319
Acheson, Barclay, Canada, 383
Adams, Jane, 19, 22
Addison, Joseph, 116
Ade, George, *Fables in Slang*, 32
Adenauer, Konrad, 428
Albert, Allen, 1915 RI President,
    123, 136, 237, 293; chairman,
    RI Administration 1935, 295;
    war correspondent, 237; com-
    mends Chicago Report, 293;
    on post-War Rotary, 136-7
Albert, King of the Belgians, 184,
    254
Alcott, Louisa May, 220
Alexander, W.H., 129
Algren, Nelson, *The Man with the
    Golden Arm*, 474
Allsop, Kenneth, *The Bootleggers*,
    315, 471
Almy, P.H.W., 1938 Pres., RIBI,
    298, 322, 340; National Ser-
    vice Committee, 333
Amery, Leopold, 366
Angell, Sir Norman, *The Great Illu-
    sion*, 320
Anglo-American Rotary, 376
Apollo Club, 7
Argentine, *Rotary*: Azul, 301;
    Buenos Aires, 134, 217, 283;
    Formosa, 377, San Juan, 134;
    Santiago del Estero, 305
Armius, 298
Armstrong, Harry, composer, 475

Arnold, John J., Pres., Hamilton
    Club, Bermuda, 214
Asano, 363
Astor, Lady, 114, 334
Ataturk, Mustafa Kemal, 233
Atkins, Ernest, Wandsworth Rotary,
    306, 317, 318-19, 425
Austen, Jane, 110
Australia, 98, 303; *Rotary*, 277-8,
    356; Brisbane, 303; Goulborn,
    303; Newcastle, NSW, 303;
    Sydney, 226, 303; Wollongong,
    303
Austria, Rotary: Baden-bei-Wien,
    324; Graz, 302, 333

Baden-Powell, Lord, 165, 192, 223,
    224, 226, 235
Baird, John Logie, 209
Baldwin, Stanley, 248, 286
Bank of America, 58
"Barbarossa", 380, 390, 391
Barbary Coast, 59
Barnes, Lloyd, Pres., BARC, 204-5
Barrie, James, 222
Bartlett, Vernon, 318
Bateman, Floyd L., Pres., Chicago
    Club, 261
Bear, Montague ("Monty"),
    designer of the Wheel, 49, 50,
    170
Bear Mountain, 18
Beaverbrook, Lord, 323
Belfrage, Kurt, Stockholm Club,

285, 286

Belgium, *Rotary*: Antwerp, 354; Bruges, 354

Benes, Eduard, 335, 405

Benson, Sir Frank, 195

Beresford, Lord Charles, 65

Berkade, Anton, Holland, 257

Berlin, Irving, 110

Bermuda, 186, 213, 379; Hamilton *Rotary*, 214

Berwick, Edward, 61

Besant, Anne, 61

Besant, Frank, 62

Beveridge Plan, and Rotary, 4, 412–13

Bevin, Ernest, on social security, 4, 321, 412–13, 416

Bierce, Ambrose, on boys, 221

Billingham-Grieg, F.L., ed. *London Rotarian*, 388

Bishops College School, Quebec, 358

Black and Tan, 179

Blair-Fish, W.W., ed. *Rotary Wheel*, 365, 390; on centralised control, 449

Blum, Leon, 327

Bolivia, *Rotary*: La Paz, 280

Bond, Carrie Jacobs, composer, 147

"Bonnie Jean", 69, 245, 258, 272, 419, 467–8, 473, 477. *See* Harris, Jean

"boosting", 108, 113, 125

Bottomley, Horatio, 130

Bow, Clara, 211

boy in man, 235–6

Boy Scouts, 235, 300; jamborees, 224, 302; and Rotary, 223–5; war service, 224. *See also* Baden-Powell, Lord; Scout Movement

Boyd, Hugh, Pres., Belfast Rotary, 204

boyhood, 219–21, 223–5, 288–9, 294, 299, 300

Braddon, Sir Henry, Pres., Sydney Rotary, 226

Brazil, 371, 372; *Rotary*, 302, 373, 376; João Pessoa, 305; Santa

Cruz, 376; São Paulo, 373–4

Bread Street Club, 7

Briand, Aristide, 249

British Association of Rotary Clubs, 113, 117, 128, 141, 191, 205; formation, 105, 126; head-quarters, 201; growth, 132, 163, 178, 200

British Isles, 12, 61, 82

Browning, Robert, 55

Bryan, Cornelia (Paul's mother). *See* Harris, Cornelia

Bryan, Henry (Paul's grandfather), 16, 50, 56

Bryan, Reuben, 16

Bullock, Alan, 313

Bunyan, John, 219

Burghers, Robert, Gov., R. District, 73, 322

Burgin, Dr Leslie, 316, 323, 334

Burmah Shell Oil, 230

Burns, Robert, 246, 468

Burton, Pomeroy, 144

business ethics, 142

Busse, Fred, 80

Butler, Samuel, 184

Byrd, Richard Evelyn, 212

Byron, Lord, poet, 196, 345, 369

Cady, Daniel L., 69

Calchen, Bernt, pilot, rotarian, 216

California, 43, 50, 56, 61, 70, 98

Canada, 12, 105, 278; *Rotary*: Calgary, 229; Fort William, 161; Port Arthur, 161; Toronto, 225

Capone, Al, 41, 48, 58, 80, *et seq.*

Capper, Arthur, senator, 249

Carson, Sir Edward, N. Ireland, 95 97

Carter, Mrs. Leslie, 19

Carter, Vivian, ed., *Rotary Wheel*, and *The Rotarian*, 239, 250, 341, 459, 465, 473; sec., BARC, 205

Caruso, Enrico, 32, 39, 60, 80, 475

Catholic Truth Society, 452

Cecil of Chelwood, Viscount, 268

Central and South America, *Rotary*, 305

Cermak, Anton, mayor, Chicago, 272

Chamberlain, Austen, 229

Chamberlain, Houston Stewart, 359

Chamberlain, Joseph, 111

Chamberlain, Neville, 130, 306, 333, 354, 359, 366, 377, 453

Chandler, Raymond, 62

Chelmsford, Lord, Viceroy of India, 174

Cheshire, Leonard, Grp. Capt., V.C., 427

Chesterton, G.K., 79, 192, 452; criticises Rotary, 264–5; *This Rotarian Age*, 110

Chiang Kai-Shek, 211, 299

Chicago, 1, 2, 3, 4, *et seq.*, 474 name, 7; companies, 8, 10, 11; mixed origins, 15; buildings, 8, 10, 35; City Hall, 47, 52; Unity Building, 25, 35, 44, 70, 162; streets, 2, 10, 226; parks, 65, 156–7; Clubs, 9, 34, 40, 65; music, 40, 80; hotels, 53, 54, 78, 80; restaurants, 32, 33; Colosimo's Cafe, 9, 80; Madame Galli's Restaurant, 32, 33, 34, 35, 36, 38, 39, 47, 49, 80, 260, 457–8, 475, 481; social conditions, 9, 12, 41, 43, 58, 80, 88, 89, 180, 201, 471; crime, 40, 70; charities, 147; Great Fire, 10; World Fair, 8, 22, 23, 24, 228; journals, 40, 136; attitudes to Chicago, 7–8, 9, 21, 59. For C. Rotary Club, *see* under United States of America Rotary

Chicago (song), 207

Chicago Booster's Club, 148

Chicago Chamber of Commerce, 78

Chicago Daily News, 381

Chicago Museum of Science and Industry, 466

Chicago Record-Herald, 73

Chicago Times, 264

Chicago Times Herald, 75

Chicago Tribune, 9, 24, 89, 315

Chile Rotary, 282; Santiago, 305

China, 299, 377; *Rotary*: after World War II, 433; Hangchow, 303; Shanghai, 225, 301, 303, 377; Tientsin, 303

Christian Science, 112

Christian Science Monitor, 112, 113, 458

Churchill, Randolph, 23, 94

Churchill, Winston, 75, 88, 101, 114 *et seq.*, 413; Fulton speech, 426; in First World War, 164; *The Gathering Storm*, 369; *A History of the English Speaking Peoples*, 350; *The World Crisis*, 136, 141

Clark, Sheldon, Chicago Rotary, 253

"classification", 43, 45, 63, 64, 72, 73, 100, 113, 227

clubs, 7

Coates, "Herbieto", 169, 225, 372

Cocks, Orrin G., 225

coffee-houses, 7

Cole, Anna Laurie, 26

Collins, Frank, on service, 85

Colosimo, Big Jim, 79, 88

Columbian Exposition, 58

Comely Bank, 185, 199, 216, 241, *passim*; discussion club, 470

community service, 47, 71, 132, 306, 446

community singing, 39, 40, 42, 44, 55, 69, 78, 477

Coolidge, Calvin, Pres., USA, 18, 185, 186

Coombes, Reginald, 174–5, 367, 369

Cos, Henry, 300

Cosgrave, William, Pres., Ireland, 250

Costain, Rev A.J., Colwyn Bay, 320–1

Coudenhove-Kalergi, Count, Vienna, 268

Coward, Noel, 332

Crabtree, John, Pres., RIBI, 275

Crandon, Mrs. Frank, 283

Cuba, 134; *Rotary*: Antilla, 305; Cienfuegos, 225; Havana, 133,

134, 181, 268, 280
Cuno, Wilhelm, German Chancellor,
    212, 257, 300, 319, 450
Czechoslovakia, 5, 299, 335; *Rotary*,
    333

Dana, Richard Henry, Jr., 60
Danzig, *Rotary*, 318
Darrow, Clarence, lawyer, 25, 70,
    210
Dautry, Raoul, Paris, 369
Davidson, James W. (Big Jim), 228,
    229, 277, 302, 357, 435; "boy
    wonder", 218, 235; Eastern
    extension, 217, 228, 229, 230,
    231, 232–4; war correspond-
    ent, 228; Japanese award, 228;
    RI Commissioner, 229
Davidson, Lillian, 218, 228, 229,
    232, 234
Davis, Tom, Pres. RI, 465
Dawson, William, South America,
    281
de Gaulle, Charles, 365, 403, 421
de Valera, Eamon, 118, 179, 274
Deckers, Emile, Antwerp, 352
Delbos, Yvon, France, 328
democracy, 335
Denmark, *Rotary*, 354
Denby, Edwin, Detroit, 185
Depression, the, 270–2, 289, 299,
    313
Detroit, 343
Doherty, James, 315
Dominican Republic, *Rotary*, 420,
    422
Doolittle, James, St Louis, 393
Dormitzer, Else, 407
Dover, Victor, Major, MC, sec.,
    RIBI, 403
Dublin, 94–7, 101, 179
Duluth, 109
Duperrey, Maurice, Pres., RI, 1937,
    311, 327

Eddy, Mary Baker, 112
Eden, Anthony, 314, 328, 333–4
Edinburgh, 126, 188

Edward, V, King, 184, 284, 325
Edward, VII, King, 32, 95
Egypt, 302; Cairo Rotary, 232
El Salvador, *Rotary*: Sonsonate, 302
Ellis, Vivian, 201
Ellsworth, Lincoln, 216
Emerson, Ralph Waldo, 27, 37, 213,
    342, 431, 480
Endowment Fund (renamed, Paul
    Harris Memorial of the Rotary
    Foundation), 438–9
esperanto, 267
Eulalia of Spain, Princess, 48
Europe between the Wars, 248
European Advisory Meeting, 285
European Rotary, 200, 286
Evans, Richard L., Pres. RI, 449
Evanston Secretariat, 437–8

Fascism, 270, 284
Federal Union Movement, 356
Fenian Brotherhood, 28
Ferdinand, Franz, Archduke of
    Austria, 177
Field, Eugene, 33
Field, Marshall, 8
Fields, Gracie, 396–7
Fields, Vina, 11
Fields, W.C., 32
Fiji, *Rotary*, 306
Finland, *Rotary*: Helsinki-Helsing-
    fors, 353, 390–1
First World War, 87–8, 94, 122, 126,
    127, 129, 135, 151, 225, 400;
    Passchendaele, 149; the
    Somme, 151; Armistice, 172,
    193; aftermath, 162–3
    Rotary's services, 130, 143,
    145–6, 163, 165
Fisher, Otto, 328
Fitzgerald, John J. "Honey", 475
Flag of Rotary, 141, 144; over the
    Poles, 212, 216
Float, Rev Wilfred, 371, 459
Florida, 9
Font, Mariano, organised Rotarian
    exiles, 403
Foo Sec, Fong, 329

Ford, Henry, 343, 346; peace ship, 344, 347; *Eternal Jew*, 344
Formosa, *Rotary*, 232
Fort, Paul, French poet, 311
Foundation Scholarships, 442
Founding Four, the, 36, 38
Four Objects of Rotary, 279
Four-Way Test, the, 342
Fourth Object of Rotary: international understanding, 294, 339, 438
France, 252; Allied R. Club, 163, 200, 233; *Rotary*: Avignon, 301; Caen, 404; Le Havre, 366; Moulin, 404; Paris, 202, 252, 451; Poitiers, 404; Strasbourg, 254, 354
Franco, General, 5, 202
Franklin, Benjamin, 154; Junto Club, 7, 71, 106, 155
Frazer, Sir James, *The Golden Bough*, 289
freemasonry, 450
Freud, Sigmund, 124, 415
Fuller, J.E.C., General, 365
fund-raising, 328; through buying honours, 441
Furnas, J.C.; *The Americans*, 40

gallup polls, 327
Gandhi, Mahatma, 174, 190, 306, 360, 411
"gang, the", 235
Garden, Mary, opera singer, 64-5, 80, 82, 292
Gardiner, Abraham Colombo, 360
Gardner, Erle Stanley, 70
General Strike, the, 199, 210
George, Henry, 114
George, Lloyd, 113, 175, 176, 177, 190, 286, 328, 366, 441
George, Prince, Duke of Kent, 318, 414
George V, King, 97, 111, 196, 284, 321
George VI, King, 224, 325
Germany, 177, 179, 273, 284-5, 298, 325, 337; youth, 300-1,

337; *Rotary*, 138, 256-7; and National Socialism, 254, 314-9; clubs disbanded, 326; revival, 425-6, 428-9; R. clubs: Cologne, 256-7, 426; Hamburg, 257; Munich, 180, 318
Giannine, Amadeo Pietro, 59
Gilbert and Sullivan, 24, 123, 169, 198
Golden Wheel, the, 29, 90, 108, 120, 123, 170-1 *et seq.*, 480; design, 50-1, 175-6; Golding's wheel, 133
Graves, Robert, 287
Great Britain, 22, 111, 389; *Rotary*, 114, 116-17, 262, 313-14, 336, 368, 414-15, 447; *R. clubs*: Aberdeen, 225, 239; Birmingham, 103, 129, 250; Brighton, 125-6, 130, 140; Burton-on-Trent, 325; Colwyn Bay, 320; Doncaster, 204, 256; Edinburgh, 79, 103, 105, 113, 128, 129; Glasgow, 44, 105, 107, 113; Hull, 340, 389; Islington, 331; Kingston-upon-Thames, 332; London, 4, 93, 102, 104-5, 129, 131-2, 201, 210, 284; Manchester, 92, 102-3, 105, 114, 129, 136, 317; Newcastle upon Tyne, 140, 149, 354; Plymouth, 389; Portsmouth, 306; Putney, 335; Watford, 342; West Norwood, 389; York, 204
Greece, *Rotary*, 217; Athens, 233
Grehan, T.A., 179
Greinher, Russell F., Pres. RI, 464
Gross, Howard, 146
Group Exchange Teams, 440
Guest, Edgar Albert, 343, 345-6, 377, 408, 471
Gyrator, 375

Halifax, Lord, 453-4
Hampton, Vernon Boyce, Gov., R. Distr., 430

Harding, Warren, Pres. USA, 171,
180, 185, 226; and Rotary,
184, 188
Harris, Cornelia (Paul's mother), 17,
20, 179
Harris, George, (Paul's father), 17,
20, 176, 473
Harris, Howard, (Paul's grandfather),
18, 20, 22, 28, 29, 93
Harris, Jean (Paul's wife), 7, 65-6,
76, 91, 105, 119, 134, 156-7,
171, 212-13, 216, 241, 243,
245, 258, 270, 273, 279, 396,
470; health, 244; religion, 471,
473; travels, 280-1
Harris, Paul Percy, Founder of
Rotary, 4, 10, 25, 34, 38, 51,
66, 90, 161, 244, 251, 460-1;
offices, 6, 12, 67, 78, 81, 83,
90, 106, 109; awards and honours, 276, 261-4, 300, 306,
422-3, 439, 461; memorials,
12, 29, 439, 474; boyhood and
youth, 17, 18, 219, 222, 226,
242, 247, 336, 461-2; "folly",
22, 57, 247, 272; "rapscallion",
17, 54, 156, 158, 219, 250,
254, 273, 399, 456, 468; lawyer, 16, 19, 20, 25, 27, 159,
455; health, 21, 64, 159, 218,
260, 277; appearance and manner, 3, 32, 46, 65, 456, 470;
character, 86, 239-40, 249-50,
305, 457-9, 473; fun and humour, 258, 457, 461, 480; friendship, 27, 36, 37, 76, 330, 399,
456-7, 463, 467-8; travels, 21,
186, 216, 228, 240, 245-59,
360; to Europe, 22, 187,
245-7, 251-4, 257-9, 270,
272, 273-5, 330; to South
Africa, 275; to South America,
279-84, 305; to Far East, 277;
to Australia and New Zealand,
279; inherited characteristics,
17, 21-2, 78, 86; retirement, 6,
12, 106, 109, 120, 156-7;
writings, 435, 456; My Road to

Rotary, 6, 219, 336, 345,
461-2; This Rotarian Age, 265,
373, 463; Peregrinations, 463;
on United Nations, 383; on
War, 339; film: A Visit to the
Home of Paul P. Harris, 241
Harte, Bret, 59-60
Hays, Will, US Postmaster General,
191, 207, 210-11
Head, Walter, Pres., RI, 348, 352,
365, 367, 464
Health Hunger and Humanity Pro-
gramme (3-H), 443, 478, 480
Hearst newspapers, 114
Heering, Peter, Sec., Copenhagen
Club, 405-6
Henderson, Sir James, 203
Herring, Hubert, historian, 374
Hershey, Lewis B., Angola, Indiana
Club, 399
Hines, Rev L.J., 262
Hislop, W.B., historian, 192
history, 115, 476, 480
Hitler, Adolf, 5, 180-1, 183, passim,
423; Hitler Youth, 289
Hoare, Sir Samuel, 333
Holland, Rotary, 257
Hong Kong, Rotary, 231
Hoover, Herbert, Pres., USA, 153,
229, 253
Horniman, A.F., 96
Houston Chronicle, 162
Howe, Rev Andrew, (Harris'
nephew), 461, 471-2
Hull, Cordell, Sec. of State, USA,
378
Hungary, Rotary, 203, 256, 302;
Budapest, 203, 256
Hurst, George, orchestral conductor,
358

Ibero-American Conference, Valpar-
aiso, 305
Illinois Central Railroad, 24
Ilma, Violet, ed. Modern Youth, 342
India, Rotary: Calcutta, 174, 303;
Delhi, 230; Madras, 301;
Poona, 411

Indo-China, 233
Indonesia, *Rotary*, 231
Industrial Revolution, the, 94
innocence, 235–6
Inskip, Sir Thomas, 323
Insull, Samuel, 10–11, 58
Interact Clubs, 445–7
Inter-Allied Outpost of Rotary Clubs of Europe, 417
inter-trading, 132
International Association of Rotary Clubs, 93, 105, 134, 191
International Harvester Company, 8
International Rotary, 139, 150, 266, 369; *See* Rotary International
Iowa, 19
Ireland, 92–7, 126, 178, 179, 250–1; *Rotary*: 16th District, 355; Dublin, 64, 92–3, 96, 99, 103–4, 113, 178, 251, 355, 450
Irish Free State, 196, 207
Irishmen, 61, 63, 116
Italy, 39; *Rotary*, 203, 254, 256, 301, 428; Milan, 256; Venice, 255, 319; Vicenza, 302

Janner, Greville, M.P., 358
Japan, 5, 39, 208, 376–7, 419; *Rotary*, 377, 426–8; Buzen, 478; Osaka, 208; Tokyo, 211, 303, 427; Uwajima, 377
Jefferson, Thomas, 177, 352
Jensen, William, 45–6
Jerome, Jenny, wife of Lord Randolph Churchill, 111
Jerrold, Douglas, 123
Jews, 116, 258, 270, 316, 325, 337, 344, 358, 375, 401, 404, 422
John Paul II, Pope, 453
Johnson, Amy, 217
Johnson, E.A., West Ham, 323
Johnson, Dr Samuel, 41, 126, 192
Johnson, Justus J., 457
Jourdan-Gassin, Charles, Nice, 330
Jury, Henry, 99

Kaiser, the, 163, 171, 177

Kaye, Danny, 441–2
Keats, John, poet, 471
Keenleyside, H.L., Saskatoon, 357
Kellar, Philip R., 145
Kellogg, Frank, Sec. of State, USA, 249
Kellogg-Briand Pact, 249, 252
Kennedy, Capt. E.C., High Wycombe 371
Kennedy, John F., Pres., USA, 129, 377, 437, 475
Kennedy, Joseph P., 377
Kennedy, Patrick, 15–16
King, Henry, 138
Kern, Jerome, 111
Keynes, John Maynard, economist, 182, 270
King, Ernest, Admiral, Lorain, Ohio, 399
Kipling, Rudyard, 7, 30, 47, 60–1, 231, 235, 248, 286
Klumph, Arch C., Pres. RI, 143, 178, 328
Knox, Frank, Sec. of the Navy, USA, 378, 381
Koenig, Theodore, 203
Komatsu, Takashi, Tokyo, 363, 427
Korea, *Rotary*: Seoul, 232
Kroeger, Otto, 321, 325
Kruger, Paul, 356

La Follette, Robert M., Senator, 147
La Rochefoucald, 139
Lane, William, 99
Lansbury, George, 318, 321
Laqueux, Arthur, Pres., RI, 451
Latvia, *Rotary*, 271
Lauder, Sir Harry, 39, 131, 148, 172, 196, 241, 274, 408, 441, 447
Law and Order League, 11
League of Nations, 147, 177, 201, 212, 213
Lebrun, Albert, Pres. of France, 327–8
Lehar, Franz, 40, 203, 266, 286–7
Lenin, Nikolai, 183

Leslie, Anita, *A Story Half Told*, 432

Leverton, Stanley, London Rotary, recruitment plan, 432-3

Levy, Roger, *Rotary International in Great Britain and Ireland*, 131, 192, 312, 368, 415, 417, 448, 459

Lewis, Sinclair, 108, 109, 117, 452

Life magazine, 154

Lincoln, Abraham, 73, 272

Lindbergh, Charles A., 216, 352, 378-9

Lithuania, 451

Little, John, Belfast, 1965 Pres., RIBI, 449

Liverpool, 61

Livingstone, David, 16

Locarno Pact, 201, 284

Loehr, Gustavus, 27, 35-7, 45, 58, 112, 159; salesmanship, 37

Loesch, Frank J., 261

Lombardo, Tony, 315, 437

London, 8, 22-3, 89, 92; *see* Great Britain Rotary

London, Jack, 60

Los Angeles, 63

Loth, Jerzy, Warsaw, RI Director, 323, 349, 352, 353, 405

Lovejoy, Philip C., Gen. Sec., RI, 396, 401, 414-15

Luciano, "Lucky", 370, 394, 422

Luncheon Clubs, 47

Lusitania, the, 123

Lytton, George, Chicago, 253

MacArthur, Douglas, General, Hon. member, Corregidor R., 392, 397, 423; Manila, 401; Tokyo, 427

McCaffrey, Dr Stan, Pres., RI 1981, 126

McConnell, Bill, Pres., BARC, 93, 97-8, 100, 120, 178, 192, 196, 206, 207, 480; Dublin R., 99

McCormack, John, 98

McCormick, Cyrus, 8

McCullough, Crawford, 1921 Pres., RI, 395

MacDonald, Ramsay, 229, 259, 263, 267, 286, 318

Machado, Luis, Havana, 280

McLuhan, Marshall, 476

Macmillan, Harold, 417

Mafia, 171

Malaya, *Rotary*, 217; Ipoh, 301; Penang, 303

Man Nobody Knows, the, 112, 193, 220

Mander, Sir Charles, Pres., RIBI, 267

Manier, Will R., Jr., 384-5

Mann, Thomas, 247, 317, 467; Munich R., 318, 353

Mannerheim, Baron Carl von, Field-Marshall, Finland R., 353, 390-1, 422

Marco Polo, 234

Marshall, Gen. George C., Uniontown, Penn., 419

Masaryk, Jan, 332, 433; on democracy, 335

Masaryk, Thomas, 335

Matsuyama, Shinjiro, mem., London R., 268

Matthews, Very Rev W.R., Dean of St. Paul's, tribute to Harris, 475

Mead, Glenn C., Pres., RI, 155; tribute to Harris, 106, 457

Means, George, Sec., RI, 427, 432, 436-7, 470

Melville, Herman, 110

Menzies, Robert, PM, Australia, 356

Mexico Rotary, 200; Juxtepec, 302; Mexico City, 305

Michigan, Lake, 58, 77, 85, 105, 295

Midwest, 15, 19, 40, 50, 64, 70

Miller, Carl, 340, 341-2

Milne, A.A., 324, 326, 336; on Totalitarianism, 335-6

Milton, John, poet, 177

Minneapolis Morning Tribune, 109

Mitchell, Sir Angus, Pres., RI, 278, 460

Mittelhozer, Walter, Zurich, 253

Moes, Gerry, Ontario, R. Distr. Gov., 357

Moffatt, William, Leeds, 169–70, 226–7
Mohler, Robert, Kansas, 300
Molloy, Frank, 204
Moody, Dwight Lyman, evangelist, 11, 42–3, 78
Moran, Bugs, 226
Morrow, William Stuart, founded R. clubs, 63, 93–106, 112–14, 118, 179, 209, 231; Belfast, 100, 209; Dublin, 64, 99; Birmingham, Liverpool, Edinburgh, 103; lawyer, 99; debt-collecting, 63–4, 457
Morse, R.F., *Brighter Rotary*, 198
Mosley, Sir Oswald, 259
Mountbatten, Admiral Lord Louis, 421
Mukasa, Hiroji, 427; Pres., RI, 363
Mulholland, Frank L., Pres., RI, 1915, 141, 150, 153
"Munich", 332, 359
Munoz, Manuel, 53, 63, 73
Mussolini, Benito, 183, 203, 212, 233, 255, 284, 315, 378, 400, 423, 428
"My job" talks, 93

National Association of Rotary Clubs, 77, 82, 89; in First National Bank Buildings, 81
National Rotarian, the, 65, 82, 85, 99, 104, 114, 160, 222
Nelson, John, 1934 Pres., RI, 273, 295; European visits, 276, 317
New Deal, the, and Rotary, 292
New England, 19–20, 29, 35, 40, 185; *See* under United States of America Rotary
New York Herald, 228
New Zealand Rotary, 303, 356; Auckland, 303; Christchurch, 303
Newton, Charles, 46
Nicholson, Prof. J.H., 322
North Africa: Casablanca, 303
Northcliffe newspapers, 114
Northern Ireland, 15, 101; *Rotary*,

Bangor, 355; Belfast, 92, 103, 105, 113, 178, 225
Norton, Charles Eliot, 110
Nutting, Sir Harold, 179

O'Casy, Sean, poet, 214
Olav, Crown Prince, Norway, 402
Olinger, George, Denver, chairman, Boys Work Committee, 227, 235, 242, 304
Opie, Earle, Chicago, 423
Orwell, George, novelist, 184, 353
Osservatore Romano, 452
Owen, Wilfred, poet, 157

pacifism, 324
Palestine/Israel, *Rotary*: Haifa, 361; Jerusalem, 232, 302, 360; Tel Aviv, 361
Palmer, Potter, 48
Pan-American Conference, Panama, 353
Paraguay, *Rotary*: Asunción, 280
Parker, Dorothy, 186
Pascall, Sydney, Pres., RI, 266–7, 269, 284, 331, 417; RIBI Pres., 208–9
patriotism, 139
Patti, Adelina, 475
Patton, Francis L., Pres., Princeton University, 213
Patton, Gen. George, 428
Paul Harris Fellowships, 439–41, 453
Paul P. Harris Memorial Building, 29
Paul P. Harris Room, at Headquarters, 469
Paul VI, Pope, 452
Peace Conference, 177–8
Pearson, Hesketh, 453
Pentland, R.W., 113, 151
Pereira, Armando de Aruda, 329, 372–4, 376–7, 386, 464
Perry, Chesley (Ches), Gen. Sec., RI, 52, 64, 66, 69, 73, 74 *et seq.*; character, 75, 84, 89, 346, 398–9, 463–5; services, 76, 77, 81, 90, 152, 165, 243, 244,

275, 339, 474; R. extension, 54, 134, 164, 240, 273, 448; World War II, 333, 351, 374; and Harris, 159, 214, 242-3, 281; Chicago, 149; library, 78; Cuba, 75, 370; reports, 266, 367, 397; career close, 90, 354, 364, 394, 399; tribute to, 464

Pershing, John, General, 155, 210

Peru, *Rotary*: Lima, 305

Pettengill, Charles W., Pres., RI, 1964, 448

Philadelphia, 71, 106

Philippines, the, *Rotary*: Manila, 303

Pidgeon, Leslie, Pres, 1917 Int. Ass., 134, 136

Pigman, Herbert A., Gen. Sec., RI, 236, 438

Pilet-Golaz, Marcel, Pres., Switzerland, 353

Pinkham, Jim, 84

Pirelli, Alberto, Pres., Int. Chamber of Commerce, 270

Pitkin, Walter B., *Life Begins at Forty*, 364, 433-4, 474

Plato, 184, 477

Poe, Edgar Allen, 110

Poland, 340; Lodz R., 341; after the War, 433

Popham, Sir Howe, Admiral, 169

Price, Frederick, chairman, 16th R. Distr. Ireland, 355

Princep, Gavrilo, Serbia, 177

prohibition, 180

public conveniences, 68, 71, 78, 102, 479-80

public relations, 73

Puerto Rica, *Rotary*, 225

Pullman, George (sleeping-cars), 8, 10, 58

Quick, Herbert, Los Angeles R., 63; San Francisco, 64

Quisling, Vidkun, Norway, 366-7

Racine, (US city), 14, 17, 26, 41, 93, 240

Racine, Jean Baptiste, author, 26

Raeder, Erich, Grand Admiral, 372

Raffles, Stamford, Kuala Lumpur, 230

Ralston, J. Layton, Halifax, Nova Scotia, 228, 357

Ramsay, A.M., 73-4

Rangoon Rotary, 230

rapscallions, 65, 78, 82, 103, 164, 447

Ratti, Franco, Milan, 451

Reay, Percy, Pres., 1948, RIBI, 415

recruitment, 432-3

Redmond, John, 97

Reed, Verrall, Pres., 1937 RIBI, 330

Reinhardt, Fred, 455, 465

Renard, Louis, Poitiers, 404

Renouf, Clem, Pres., 1978-9 RI, 443

Report on Post war Reconstruction, by London Rotary Clubs, 415-16

Revista Rotaria, Spanish ed. of *The Rotarian*, 304

Rhodes, Cecil, 356

RIBI, 204, 206, 208, 274, 313, 367, 415, 417; and RI, 449; conferences, 198, 217; distr. chairmen, 351; "Manomaly", 448

Richardson, William, 61

Riddle, Rev T.W., Plymouth, 262

Rockefeller, John A., 11, 290

Rogers, Earl, 70

Roman Catholic Church, and Rotary, 265, 450-3

Romberg, Sigmund, New York, 40, 266

Romulo, Carlos P., Vice-Pres., RI, 392-3, 397, 419; Pres., UN Gen. Assembly, 428

Roosevelt, Franklin D., 4, 185, 272, 277, 285, 352, 376, 378; on Rotary, 291, 296

Roosevelt, Theodore, 3, 233, 272

Rota, Samuel Pepys' club, 7

Rotaract Clubs, 445-7

Rotarian, The, 70, 82, 104, 105,

119, *et seq.*, 470; on boys,
224-7, 288; on Scouts, 165,
224; Spanish editions, 273,
304
Rotary, 2, 4, 8, 15, 22, 28, 29, 38,
41, 44, 57, 58, 71, 89, 90, 94,
211, 262; name, 1, 2, 108;
aims and principles, 7, 34, 115,
208-9, 251, 397, 479-80;
recruitment, 269-70; activities,
3, 5, 12, 32, 72, 208; internationalism, 12, 91, 267, 296;
and National Socialism, 285,
298, 314-18, 326; inter-War
period, 309-10; World War II
effects on, 346-8; and youth,
165, 298, 300, 301-6, 444-5;
women in Rotary, 34; poem:
Dedicated to Rotary, 166;
See also Golden Wheel, The,;
International Rotary; Rotary
International
Rotary (formerly, *The Rotary
Wheel*), 130
Rotary?, 1934 Report, 290-7, 375
Rotary bell, 29, 433
Rotary Clubs, 2, 7, 44, 477-9;
membership, 7, 34, 37, 45;
rules, 42, 46; early clubs, 8, 10;
fellowship, 6-7, 40-1; business,
46, 67, 479; "contact clubs"
abroad, 478; *See also* Community Singing; songs
Rotary Foundation Endowment for
World Peace and Understanding, 444, 453
Rotary International, 3, 4, 6, 204-6,
270; constitution and rules, 12,
52, 69, 80, 106, 196, 296, 477;
budget and assets, 438-9;
offices, 103, 160, 245, 283,
449-50; growth, statistics, 6,
57, 104, 163, 172, 186, 236,
272, 294, 306, 310, 396, 432,
434-6; administration, 449;
boards, 6, 73; 244, 374; committees, 225, 292, 296; districts, 163, 208; anniversaries,

6, 210, 312; motto, 90; and
British R., 447; *See also Rotary*; International Rotary
Rotary International Conventions:
first, 68, 225; third, Duluth,
1912, 92, 104, becomes international, 120; code of ethics,
105; fourth, Buffalo, 117;
sixth, San Francisco, 1915,
122; Cincinnati, 1916, 133;
Atlanta, 1917, 135, 139,
142-3, 144, 154; Boys' Work,
223; Kansas City, 1918, 139,
146, 153; 1919, 182; Edinburgh, 1921, 170, 187-96,
224, 447; Los Angeles, 1922,
205-7; territorial units 447-8;
St Louis, 14th, 1923, 184;
Denver, 211; eighteenth, 254,
448; nineteenth, Minneapolis, 252;
Dallas, 255; Chicago, 1930,
259; twenty-second, Veinna,
1931, 267, 268; twenty-fifth,
1934, Detroit, 295, 353;
twenty-seventh, Atlantic City,
1936, 286; boys' work,
299-300; Nice, 1937, 308,
327-30; Cleveland, 1939, 339;
thirty-first, Havana, 1940, 360,
363-70, 372; thirty-second,
Denver, 1941, 376-86; thirty-
third, Toronto, 1942, 395;
thirty-fourth, St Louis, 1943,
419-21, 433; thirty-sixth,
Chicago, 1946, 418; San Francisco, 1977, 441-2; District 73,
meeting at Wiesbaden, 318
Rotary International in Great Britain
and Ireland (RIBI), 204-5;
conferences: 1933, Scarborough, 316; 1934, 318; 1935,
Margate, 319-21; 1939, Brighton, 334
Rotary International Secretariat,
Evanston, 436-7; Zurich
branch, 200
Rotary Movement, foundation, 10
Rotary Number One, 31-55, 69, 74,

81, 88; Two, 56, 68, 70, 106; Six, 73; Seven, 112; Thirty-five, 82; *See also* USA Rotary, Chicago
Rotary Pagoda, The, 173
Rotary Service, British magazine, 390
Rotary Wheel, The, 83, 106, 128-9, 134, 152, 169, 174, 198-9, 250, 257, 275, 297, 317, 322, 331, 341, 351
Ruggles, Harry, 38-40, 42-3, 46, 52, 78, 136, 159, 260; Chicago, 39, 45; community singing, 38-9, 44; on Harris, 458
Rumbold, Sir Horace, 313
Russia, 162, 233, 254, 276, 299, 387; Revolution, 161, 172, 181
Ryan, Thomas, 99

Saigon, 236
St Luke, 41
St Paul, 267
St Paul's Cathedral, 42, 51
Saito, Admiral Viscount, Japan, 232, 277, 285
Sale, Charles ("Chic"), Scarsdale, *The Specialist*, 241
Salvation Army, 10
San Francisco, 53, 56-63, 67, 69, 94, 99, 103; cosmopolitan, 58, 60-1; *Chronicle*, 56, 67-8; 1915 World Fair, 141; *See also* under USA Rotary
Sandhurst, Royal Military College, 23
Sarawak Rotary, 306
Sassoon, Siegfried, 40
Sankey, Ira David, hymn-writer, 42-3, 78
Sapp, Arthur H., Pres., RI, 465
Sayer Smith, E., 102-3
Scandinavia, *Rotary*, 354. *See also* Denmark; Norway
Schiele, Silvester, first Pres., 27, 33-6, 38, 40, 44-5, 51-2, 73, 159, 260, 434, 457, 481

Schipa, Tito, 39
Schneider, Charles, 49
Schneiderhann, Franz, Austria R., 331
Schofield, Herbert, Pres., RIBI, 298, 300, 353
Schweitzer, Dr Albert, 443-4
Scotland, 112, 172, 179, 195
Scout Movement, and Rotary, 136, 165-6; *See* Boy Scouts
Second World War, 106, 269, 336, 356-7, 365-424, 400-1, 421; Europe, 367, 370, 371-2, 379, 386-7, 400, 423; Far East, 362, 387, 391, 393, 400, 421; ending, 423-4; effect on Rotary Clubs, 348, 407, 431; Europe, 382; Britain, 370, 389, 414; France, 369, 404; Belgium, Netherlands, 366-7, 369, 403; Scandinavia, 366, 402; Finland, 369, 408-9; Central Europe, 380; clandestine meetings, 402; Eastern Europe, 381, 391; Palestine, 360; Austria, R., 405; Poland, 348, 349; Sweden, 348; Africa R., 357, 403-4; Far East R., 377, 392-3, 401, 410; Rotary role in War, 351, 352-3, 355-6, 358, 360, 375, 389, 394, 397, 408-9
Selby, Howard, RI director, 268
Selfridge, Gordon, 210
Service Clubs, 3, 6, 47, 78, 87, 231, 244, 299
Service in Life and Work, journal, Brit. R., 270-1, 276, 324-5, 335, 337
Shaw, George Bernard, 5, 12, 22, 52, 61, 66, 94, 95, 96, 111, 123, 168, 292, 350, 389, 453; on Rotary, 5, 199
Sheldon, Arthur Frederick, 52, 68, 75-8, 90, 102, 103, 114, 127, 139, 163, 192, 194-5, 197, 231; salesmanship, 90, 411; *The Science of Business*, 102,

111, 192, 194; on service, 109; on Rotary, 194
Shelley, Percy Bysshe, poet, 297
Sheridan, Richard, playwright, 118
Sirer, William L., *The Third Reich*, 29
Shorey, Hiram, 27, 34–6, 46, 159; recording secretary, 45
Siam, *Rotary*: Bangkok, 231
Sibelius, Jan, composer, 353
Singapore, *Rotary*, 236, 410
Six Objects of Rotary, reduced to Four, 279
Sixth Object, internationalism, 217, 227, 233, 294
Skeel, Ernst, chairman, Constitution Comm., 83, 105, 142
slogans, 271
Smith, Rev Sydney, 31
Smuts, Jan, General, 275, 352, 356
Smythe, Elsa Carlyle, 263
Snedecor, Estes ("Pete"), Pres., RI, 171, 178, 187, 190; tribute to Perry, 464
Society of Social Hygiene, 11
Songs, 39, 110, 475; If you're anxious for to shine, 198; Old Macdonald had a farm, 195; Rubaiyat of A-ro Tarian, 92; Rotary Songs: Eyl! Eyl! Estan aqui, Uruguayan, 169, 171; Fellow Rotarians, you are wanted (Lehar), 286–7; I ain't got seasick yet, 187; I'm a little prairie flower, 154; It's a long way to Reconstruction, 388; Rotary Bruder, auf zur Arbeit, 262
Songs for the Rotary Club, 1, 14, 31, 39, 56, 71, 476; From the North, from the South, 189; Hurrah: It's Rotary today!, 239; Inspire Rotarians, Lord, we ask, 455; O lad of mine, 216; R. Marching Songs (1915) 122; (1918) 138
South African Rotary, 304
South America Rotary, 280, 304–5,
372, 373; *See* under countries
Spaeth, Sigmund, folk-song historian, 458, 475
Spain, 202, 307, 327; *Rotary*, 285, 301, 302; Madrid, 181
Sperry, Elmer Ambrose, 53
Spicer, Ted, London, 386
Spurling, Sir Stanley, Bermuda, R. District 174 Gov., 360
Stafford, Fay, 18, 27, 30
Stalin, Joseph, 284
Stars and Stripes, 144, 170, 178
State of Israel, 273
Stead, William Thomas, journalist, 8, 11, 42, 61, 89, 112, 221, 228; *If Christ Came to Chicago*, 8, 42, 69, 112, 167; *The Truth about Russia*, 12; *The Americanisation of the World*; praise of Harris, 12
Steed, Henry Wickham, journalist, 275–6, 286
Steffe, William, composer, 138
Stephenson, Thomas, Sec., BARC, 113, 125, 129, 135, 141
Stewart, Harry, Gen. Sec., RI, 438
Stimson, Henry, US Sec. of War, 377
Stojadinovic, Milan, Prime Minister, Yugoslavia, 307–8
Stott, Roscoe Gilmore, author, 226
Stowell, Lord, lawyer, 41
Sudan *Rotary*, 308
Sullivan, Louis, 59, 78
Sullivan, Sir Arthur, 138, 198
Sunday, Billy, evangelist, 11, 42, 80, rotarian, 153
Sutter, Johann Augustus, 59
Sutton, Tom, Pres., RI, 450
Swaffer, Hannen, 273, 413
Sweden, *Rotary*, 354; Goteborg, 301; Stockholm, 478
Switzerland, *Rotary*: Basle, 254 Berne, 254; Zurich, 253

Tacoma City, 69
Taiwan (Formosa), *Rotary*, 377
tariff reform, 111
Tausz, Julius, Hungary R., 380

Taylor, Herbert J., Pres., RI and Chicago R., 312; Four-way Test, 309, 311

Te-ching, Yen, Nanking, RI Board of Directors, 377

Teele, Fred Warren, 231; Zurich Secretariat, 200

Terra, Gabriel, Pres., Uruguay, 283

Taylor, A.J.P., 116

Thomas, Theodore, 40

Thomason, Peter, Pres., BARC, 131, 258

Thompson, Big Bill, 136, 140, 146, 157; Mayor, Chicago, 271-2; chairman, 1st Boys Week Comm., 272

Thomson, Rev John Youngson, Jean's brother, 471

Thomsen, T.C., 217, 267; Zurich office, 253

Tickle, Ernest, 167, 168

Tokugawa, Prince Iyesato, rotarian, 261

Tong, Y.C., 173

Toronto, 173, 395

Torrio, Johnny, Chicago, 79

Toynbee Hall, 10, 19

Treadwell, George, Sec., Chicago R., 173; 1934 Report, 290; World War II, 375, 377

Trieste Rotary, 203

Trujillo, Gen. Rafael, Dominica, 420, 422-3

Turkey, 233

Twain, Mark (Samuel L. Clemens), 60, 110, 222; on boyhood, 225; on civilisation, 242; Huckleberry Finn, 219, 220, 222, 224, 241

Tweed, Fred, mem., National Board, 74; East Coast, 73

Ulster, 95, 97, 101; See Northern Ireland

Unbertone, Allesandro, Italy R., 285

UNESCO, and Rotary, 417

United Nations Charter, 417

United Nations San Francisco Conf., RI consultants, 417

United States of America, 12, 14, 15, 16, 48, 50, 56, 98, 99, 113, 240, 345, 351; immigration, 124, 171; relations with Britain, 111

United States, Rotary, 124, 140, 142, 389-90; Second National Convention, 70, 79, 82-7, 105; US Rotary Clubs: Akron, Ohio, 151; Baltimore, 153; Birmingham, Alabama, 140; Blackwell, Oklahoma, 223; Boston, 123; Carthage, Tennessee, 378; Champaign, Illinois, 147; Chattanooga, 147; Chicago (see also Rotary Number One), 23, 29, 31-55, 57, 58-9, 68, 71-3, 81, 140, 179, 222, 226, 231; incorporated, 73; members' classification, 48, 51, 73; official history, 34; rules, 73; merit award, 48, 261; public relations, 73; vocational talks, 45; parade, 148; "fines", 49, 69; first names and nicknames, 49, 69; ladies' night, 45, 48; on crime, 210; commissioned 1934 Report, 294; Cleveland, 145, 280; Dallas, 389; Denver, 146, 198; Des Moines, Iowa, 79; Duluth Women's Club, 119; Evanston, 437; Florida, 153; Franklin, Indiana, 226; Greensboro', North Carolina, 152; Indianapolis, 147; Iowa Falls, 340; Janesville, Wisconsin, 147; Kansas, 141; Leavenworth, 146; Los Angeles, 54, 63, 77, 112, 206; Minneapolis, 85, 108; New York, 73, 112, 266, Huntington, 378; Oakland, 54, 112; Omaha, Nebraska, 79; Racine, 145, 161; San Antonio, 146, 154; San Francisco, 67, 69, 73, 99, 103, 106, 107, 112, 113, 115, 119, 152,

link with Scouts 166; Sand
Springs, Saranac, 390; Selma,
Alabama, 225; Washington,
105
University of Chicago, report on
Rotary 1934, 290–7, 295
Uruguay, *Rotary*, 169; Montevideo,
134, 283
Uyeda, Kukichi, Japan, 329

Van Tijen, Jan, 470
Vargas, Getulio, Pres., Brazil, 372–4,
376, 386
Vatican, 451; *See* Roman Catholic
Church; John Paul II, Pope;
Paul VI, Pope
Verkade, Anton, Netherlands, 470
Vermont, 17, 22, 24, 28, 30, 33, 43,
63, 73, 95, 182, 185, 185
Versailles Conference, 176–7, 179
Victor Emmanuel III, King, Italy,
255
Victoria, Queen, 225
vigilantes, 63, 64; and Rotary, 59–60
Visconti, Guido Carlo, rotarian, 428
vocational service, 45, 291–2, 294,
416, 430
Volkischer Beobachter, 237
Volstead Act of Prohibition, 171
Voltaire, Francois Marie **Arouet**,
205
Von Papen, Count, 425–6

Wallingford, England, 274
Wallingford, Vermont, USA, 16, 17,
18, 20, 26, 40, 54, 213; Paul
P. Harris Memorial Building, 29
Warren, Tom, Pres., RI, 332, 340,
352, 367–8; Pres., RIBI, 338;
democracy broadcast, 385–6;
tribute to Perry, 467
Washington, George, 154
Watson, Carrie, 9
Welfare State, 321
Wells, H.G., 431, 480
Wheeler, Harvey, 103, 113
Whistler, John, 10
White, Albert ("Al"), 45, 46, 159,

260; Pres., Chicago R., 51
White, Charles, Pres., RIBI, 204,
206; provided title Rotary
International, 449
White, William Allen, ed., *Emporia
Gazette*, 242
Whitman, Walt, 110
Wick, Wolfgang, Austria, 449
Wilde, Oscar, 8, 10, 32, 47, 63, 94,
221, 222, 224, 264–5, 292,
321, 445
Wilkes, Lyall, 337
Wilkie, Alex, 128
Wilson, John E., *The Boy Speaks*,
288
Wilson, Woodrow, 122, 126, 136,
142, 143, 145, 147, 165, 178,
180, 185, 213, 419; Peace
Conf., 177–8; Fourteen
Points, 176; and Rotary, 139,
200
Winnipeg, 82, 90, 93, 98, 104
"Wobblies", 11
Wodehouse, P.G., author, 111
Wolf, Max, 46
Wolfe, Thomas, *Look Homeward,
Angel*, 240
Women, 150, 220
Women's Christian Temperance
Union, 11
Wood, Homer, 62–3, 67–8
Wood, Leonard, Major-General, 143
Wordsworth, William, 236, 431
Working Men's Institutes, 10
Wyckoff, George, 223–4

Yeats, W.B., poet, 436
Yerkes, Charles Tyson, 8, 11
Yoshida, Shigeru, PM, Japan, and
Rotary, 428
Young, James, mem., Tokyo R., 401
Young, Tom, Pres., RIBI, 354, 397
Youth, 337–8, 444–7
Yugoslavia, *Rotary*: Pancevo, 302

Zenith City, 108–9